Associated Color:
Zac (white)

rea occupied by
e ancient Maya

Likin (East)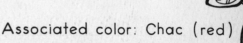

Associated color: Chac (red)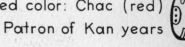
Patron of Kan years

Associated color:
Kan (yellow)

THE ANCIENT MAYA

THE YOUNG CORN-GOD, COPAN, HONDURAS

THE ANCIENT
MAYA

SYLVANUS GRISWOLD MORLEY

ASSOCIATE OF THE CARNEGIE INSTITUTION OF WASHINGTON

STANFORD UNIVERSITY PRESS
STANFORD UNIVERSITY, CALIFORNIA
OXFORD UNIVERSITY PRESS
LONDON: GEOFFREY CUMBERLEGE

Special Representatives
GEOFFREY CUMBERLEGE, OXFORD UNIVERSITY PRESS, LONDON E.C. 4
THE BAKER AND TAYLOR COMPANY, 55 FIFTH AVENUE, NEW YORK 3
HENRY M. SNYDER & COMPANY, 440 FOURTH AVENUE, NEW YORK 16

STANFORD UNIVERSITY PRESS, STANFORD UNIVERSITY, CALIFORNIA

To Frances

PREFACE

THE STORY of the Maya has been "in the writing" for more than sixteen hundred years; in fact, ever since the early part of the fourth century of the Christian Era, when the ancient Maya themselves began to carve their earliest known records on stone monuments.

This purely Maya contribution to their history covers about twelve centuries (A.D. 320–1541), and while very little of historical detail as we understand it has survived, the Maya hieroglyphic inscriptions, nevertheless, furnish us with a more accurate chronological background than that found anywhere else in aboriginal America.

During the century (1550–1650) following the Spanish conquest, a number of native as well as Spanish writers carry on the story for us. Educated Maya who had been taught by the early Catholic missionaries to write their language in the characters of the Spanish alphabet in order to facilitate their instruction in the Catholic faith set down brief summaries of their own ancient history, probably copied directly from their then still surviving historical manuscripts in the Maya hieroglyphic writing.

In addition to the foregoing native sources, several of the early Franciscan Fathers have left admirable accounts of the Maya as they were in the middle-sixteenth century, by far the most important being the contemporary narrative by Fray Diego de Landa, the second Bishop of Yucatan. His *Relación de las cosas de Yucatán*, written in 1566 and extensively quoted in the following pages, is unquestionably our leading authority on the ancient Maya.

During the next two centuries (1650–1840) very little new was added to the Maya story, but in 1839–1841 John Lloyd Stephens, the American traveler, diplomat, and amateur archaeologist, accompanied by Frederick Catherwood, an English artist, visited the Maya area twice and embodied his impressions thereupon in two outstanding works: *Incidents of Travel in Central America, Chiapas, and Yucatan* (1841) and *Incidents of Travel in Yucatan* (1843). Both were illustrated by Catherwood's superb drawings; today, more than a hundred years later, they still remain the most delightful books ever written about the Maya area.

Stephens' writings were chiefly responsible for bringing the great cities of the Maya civilization to the attention of the outside world. Before the publication of his two books, the very existence of these cities was unknown outside of Yucatan and northern Central America, but, after their appearance, knowledge of the Maya, who developed our greatest native American civilization, became general on both sides of the Atlantic. With Stephens also begins the period of the modern exploration of this region.

Since Stephens' time many scientific institutions as well as individual students have been engaged in piecing together different parts of the Maya picture-puzzle. To mention all would expand this preface beyond reasonable limits, but the three most important should be noted: (1) the English archaeologist, Sir Alfred P. Maudslay, the results of whose fifteen years of exploration in the Maya region (1881–1894) were published in the magnificent section on Archaeology of the *Biologia Centrali-Americana*, the first scientific publication about the Maya civilization; (2) the Peabody Museum of Archaeology and Ethnology of Harvard University, which, between 1888 and 1915, sent many expeditions to the Maya area under able leaders who have made many important contributions to our knowledge of the ancient Maya; (3) the Carnegie Institution of Washington, which has been carrying on intensive studies in the Maya field for the past three decades. No fewer than twenty-five annual expeditions under trained archaeologists have been sent to different parts of the Maya area and a vast amount of new material in many fields—archaeology, ethnology, anthropometry, history, linguistics, agriculture, botany, zoology, geography, medicine, and epidemiology—has been obtained.

It will be seen from the foregoing that many different cooks have had a hand in brewing the Maya broth as we have it today, but especially I wish to express here my deep gratitude to my colleagues in the Division of Historical Research of the Carnegie Institution of Washington, without whose untiring and unselfish studies in many phases of the Maya problem, often carried on under most trying, even perilous, conditions, this book could not have been written.

The Maya story as related here may be divided thus:

1. A description of the region where the Maya lived, the several branches into which they were divided, and their physical and psychological characteristics (chapters i and ii, see pp. 3–37).

2. Maya history—the origin of their civilization, its rise, first florescence, and first decline: the Old Empire (A.D. 317–987); its renaissance and final decline: the New Empire (987–1527); and the Spanish Conquest (1527–1697) (chapters iii–vii, see pp. 38–136).

3. Ancient and modern Maya manners and customs—agriculture, government, social organization, life of the common people, religion, deities, hieroglyphic writing, arithmetic, chronology, astronomy, cities, architecture, sculpture, modeling, ceramics, textiles, basketry, matting, painting, lapidary art, mosaics, feather- and metal-work, and flint-chipping (chapters viii to xvi, see pp. 137–440).

4. An appraisal of the Maya civilization and its comparison with other aboriginal American cultures (chapter xvii, pp. 441–55).

Finally, if we are to grasp the real significance of the Maya story, and its essential meaning, we must realize that primarily it was one of the world's most notable experiments in agriculture; in a word, that it was based exclusively upon and conditioned by the cultivation of maize, or Indian corn, than which nothing was of greater importance in ancient Maya life, nor indeed still is even today.

SYLVANUS GRISWOLD MORLEY

HACIENDA CHENKU
MERIDA, YUCATAN, MEXICO
June 7, 1946

ix

TABLE OF CONTENTS

LIST OF TABLES

LIST OF PLATES

(With acknowledgments of sources of photographs)

xiii

xvii

xviii

LIST OF FIGURES

THE ANCIENT MAYA

"If one looks closely he will find that everything [these Indians] did and talked about had to do with maize; in truth, they fell little short of making a god of it. And so much is the delight and gratification they got and still get out of their corn fields, that because of them they forget wife and children and every other pleasure, as if their corn fields were their final goal and ultimate happiness."—CHRONICA DE LA SANTA PROVINCIA DEL SANTISSIMO NOMBRE DE JESUS DE GUATTEMALA, Cap. VII (XVIth century MS).

THE COUNTRY

LOCATION

PROJECTING NORTHWARD into the Gulf of Mexico like a giant thumb, midway between North and South America, lies the Peninsula of Yucatan, where, during the fourth to sixteenth centuries of the Christian Era, there flourished the most brilliant civilization of the New World in pre-Columbian times, namely, that developed by the Maya peoples of southern Mexico and northern Central America. (See endsheets.)

More exactly speaking, the region occupied by the ancient Maya is that comprised today by the states of Yucatan, Campeche, Tabasco, the eastern half of Chiapas, and the territory of Quintana Roo, in the Republic of Mexico; the Department of Peten in Guatemala, and the adjacent highlands to the south, that is to say most of the rest of Guatemala except the Pacific coast-plain; the contiguous western section of the Republic of Honduras, and all of British Honduras, a total of some 125,000 square miles, roughly an area equal in size to the six New England states, New York, New Jersey, and a quarter of Pennsylvania combined, or to the single state of New Mexico.

THREE NATURAL SUBDIVISIONS

As may be seen from the physiographic map of the Maya area in Plate 1, this region divides naturally into three general sections, the second and third merging without a clear-cut line of demarcation: (1) the mountain ranges and intermediate plateaus —the Cordillera of Central America—which swing in a great half-circle to the southwest, south, and southeast; (2) the interior drainage basin of the Department of Peten, Guatemala, with the adjacent exterior valleys, originating in a succession of low hills

3

surrounding the same, which together comprise the southern half of the Yucatan Peninsula, geographically but not politically speaking; and (3) the low, flat, limestone plain which is the northern half of the Peninsula.

In order to understand clearly the story of the ancient Maya, these three natural divisions, with their differing environmental characteristics, should be constantly borne in mind; first because the Maya probably developed their agricultural system, upon which their whole civilization was based, in the Guatemala highlands; second because their highly specialized culture originated in the interior drainage basin and reached its most brilliant esthetic expression in the lush Usumacinta Valley, lying immediately to the west; and third because the Maya renaissance and final decay took place in the third section—the more arid, northern half of the peninsula.

THE HIGHLANDS OF GUATEMALA, WESTERN HONDURAS, AND EASTERN CHIAPAS, MEXICO

The mountain ranges in the south form a great crescent-like support from which the Yucatan Peninsula projects northward (Plate 1). Somewhere in this region, probably in western Guatemala during the third or second millenium before Christ, the Maya developed the agricultural system upon which their whole civilization was later to be based (chapters iii and viii, see pp. 38–49 and 137–58).

This region is a high plateau with mountain ranges of volcanic origin separating the upland valleys (Plate 2, *a*), the highest peaks reaching elevations of more than 13,000 feet—Tajamulco, 13,809 feet; Tacana, 13,330 feet; Agua, 12,306 feet (Plate 2, *b*); Fuego, 12,579 feet; Acatenango, 12,989 feet; Santa Maria, 12,333 feet; and Pacaya, 8,344 feet. The first three are extinct volcanoes, the last four active, all being in Guatemala.

Two principal river systems (Plate 1) drain this region; (1) the Motagua River, rising in the Department of El Quiché, Guatemala, flowing east, northeast, and north, finally reaches the Gulf of Honduras, a southwesterly extension of the Caribbean

Sea, just east of Puerto Barrios; (2) the Usumacinta River, which is composed of three principal affluents—the Pasión, the Salinas or Chixoy, and the Lacantun. The Pasión rises in the Department of Alta Vera Paz and, after flowing generally north and west, is joined by the Salinas; the latter rises in the Department of Huehuetenango and joins the Pasión at the site of the ancient Maya city of Altar de Sacrificios, located on the point of land between the two rivers. The Lacantun drains eastern Chiapas, Mexico, and northern Huehuetenango and El Quiché, Guatemala, and flows eastward into the united Pasión-Salinas, 22 miles below (northwest of) Altar de Sacrificios. Below the junction of the Pasión and the Salinas the river is known as the Usumacinta, one of the largest waterways in Central America. It forms the western boundary of the Department of Peten and reaches the Gulf of Mexico through several different channels—the Palizada, the San Pedro and San Pablo, and the Grijalva rivers being the largest. The Usumacinta River with its tributaries was the principal water highway of the Maya Old Empire (Plate 3, *a*).

The Guatemala highlands, where nearly a million and a half descendants of the ancient Maya still live (chapter ii, see p. 15), are high, extending 4,000 feet and upwards above sea level. The winters are dry and cool, even cold, ice forming in the higher mountains. The summers are less warm than in the Peten and Yucatan lowlands to the north, and the rainy season—May through November—is somewhat shorter than in the Department of Peten. The upland plateaus and valleys are not so heavily forested as the lowlands. There are open grasslands on every side, while a variety of evergreens—fir, pine, spruce, cypress—and some deciduous trees—live oak and *aguacate*—clothe the mountain slopes. True forests disappear at about 10,000 feet, though massive conifers and other trees grow at still higher levels. The land is not cultivated above 10,000 feet, but there are vast, grassy meadows above this elevation, where sheep and goats graze.

There are two large lakes in the highlands, Lake Amatitlan in the Department of Guatemala, and Lake Atitlan in the Department of Solola. The latter, with its waters of deepest sapphire, surrounded by sharply rising mountains of volcanic origin, under skies of purest azure, all bathed in the golden sunlight of the Guatemala highlands, is comparable both in beauty and interest to any of the Italian or Swiss lakes.

Finally, nestling along the inner edge of the right-hand prong of this mountainous crescent in the Department of Izabal is a very large, land-locked lagoon, Lake Izabal, 30 miles long and 12 miles wide, which is connected with the Gulf of Honduras by the *golfete* or little gulf and the Rio Dulce of incomparable beauty (Plate 1). The latter, flowing between steep cliffs of white limestone, festooned with gorgeous draperies of vivid tropical vegetation, enters the Gulf of Honduras at the modern town of Livingston, Guatemala.

Although the fauna of the highlands—the mammalian, bird, and reptilian life—is by no means as abundant as that of the Department of Peten and northern Yucatan, jaguars, pumas, deer, and small mammals are numerous, while the famous quetzal, the national bird of Guatemala, one of the most gorgeous birds in the world, is almost exclusively confined to the highlands of Guatemala and Honduras and the adjacent mountains of Chiapas, though found to a lesser extent as far south as Panama.

Somewhere in this very region, in the upland valleys of western Guatemala, is the place where Indian corn or maize, the great food staple of ancient America, probably originated, perhaps sometime during the third millenium before Christ (chapters iii and viii, see pp. 44, 45, and 140, 141).

THE LOWLANDS OF PETEN AND THE SURROUNDING VALLEYS

The interior drainage basin of central Peten and the surrounding valleys form the second main division of the Maya area. The average elevation of the central Peten savanna, just south of the medial chain of lakes, is about five hundred feet above sea level, though the generally east-and-west-running ranges of hills inclosing the interior drainage basin rise perhaps another five hundred feet. This basin is about sixty miles long east and west, though not more than twenty miles wide at the widest place. At the base of the range of hills forming the northern side of the drainage basin is a chain of thirteen or fourteen lakes, several of which are connected in the rainy season. By far the largest of these is Lake Peten Itza, the ancient name of which was Chaltuna (Plate 4, *b*), located about midway of the basin east and west; this lake is twenty miles long by three miles wide at its widest place.

South of the range of hills on the southern side of the basin lies the great irregularly shaped savanna of central Peten, already mentioned. This is a natural, as opposed to a man-made, savanna (see chapter iv, p. 71), probably always having been open country. Few trees grow on this grassy plain (Plate 4, *a*). The soil is a close, red clay, not suited to the cultivation of maize, which fact, coupled with the almost complete absence of the remains of former human habitations, probably indicates that the savannas were largely unoccupied in ancient times.

The few streams rising in the central savanna find their way south and west into the Pasión River. East of this central Peten savanna, in extreme southeastern Peten and southern British Honduras, rise the jagged Maya Mountains of relatively recent volcanic origin, the highest point of which, Cockscomb Peak, has an elevation of 3,700 feet. The narrow coast-plain east of the Maya Mountains is watered by a number of streams, none of any length, which flow into the Caribbean Sea. The largest, the Sarstoon River, forms part of the present boundary between British Honduras and Guatemala.

In the low ranges to the northwest, north, and northeast of the interior drainage basin, six rivers of medium size have their origin; the first three, the San Pedro Martyr, the Candelaria, and the Mamantel, flowing generally west and north, empty into the Gulf of Mexico on the west side of the Yucatan Peninsula, the first by way of the Usumacinta, the second and third by way of the Laguna de Términos. The remaining three, the Hondo, the New, and the Belize or Old River, flowing generally northeast, empty into the Caribbean Sea on the east side of the peninsula (Plate 1).

The ranges of hills north of the central basin and the valleys between bear generally east and west; the southern slopes of the former are sharp, the northern slopes dropping almost imperceptibly from each crest to the next succeeding water course. Both hills and valleys are completedly covered with a dense tropical forest (Plate 3, *b*), a veritable jungle in which grow mahogany, sapodilla (of which the milk-like sap produces chewing gum and the wood is used for the beams in the interior of Maya temples), rubber, *mamey*, Spanish cedar, *ceiba* or *yaxche* (the holy tree of the ancient Maya, which produces a kind of cotton called kapok), the *copó*, or wild fig (from the bark of which the Maya made their paper, *huun*), breadnut (the fruit of which was eaten in times of drought and the leaves of which serve as fodder), *aguacate*, allspice, cohune-palm, *escoba*-palm, and many others for which there are no equivalent English names, the trees themselves being unknown in northern climates. The forest averages from 125 to 150 feet in height (Plate 5, *a*), but the undergrowth, except in the occasional swamps (Maya *akalche*) which dot the valley floors, remains relatively sparse, owing to the dense shade afforded by the higher trees.

It is precisely in the valleys and on the northern slopes of the ridges—in fact, wherever there was high forest, and not in the open, grassy savannas—that the ancient Maya built their stone cities.

In addition to Indian corn or maize, the great American food staple, other vegetables, fruits, and edible plants were cultivated: black and red beans, two kinds of squash, *chayote*, tomatoes, breadnut, cacao, and a variety of tubers—sweet potato, *jicama*, cassava, and several kinds of yams. Other economic plants raised were chili pepper, vanilla, and allspice for flavoring; and cotton, tobacco, fibers, and gourds for kitchen utensils. The forest itself yielded many useful materials—poles and withes for the framework of the houses, palm-leaf for the thatching of roofs, resin of the *copal* tree (Maya *pom*) for incense in their religious ceremonies, in fact, everything that their mode of life required.

Animal life is much more abundant in this region than in the highlands to the south. The forests of Peten literally teem with

PLATE I
PHYSIOGRAPHIC
OF THE MAYA A

Scale in Miles

Laguna
de Términos

Rio

Rio

Rio Cumpa

Macuspana

Usumacinta

G

F

M

Rio

Rio Salinas

La

Rio Grande
de Chiapas

Laguna
Tepancuapan

U

G

↑ *a*) Cuchumatanes Mountains, **Huehuetenango**, Guatemala.

PLATE 2.—VIEWS OF THE SOUTHERN HIGHLANDS

b) Volcan de Agua, Sacatepequez, Guatemala, with Antigua, the former .
↓ capital in the foreground.

↑ *a*) Usumacinta River near Yaxchilan, Chiapas, Mexico.

b) Rain forest from the Acropolis at Uaxactun, Peten,
Guatemala. →

PLATE 3.—VIEWS
OF THE SOUTHERN
LOWLANDS

↑ *a*) Central savanna, Peten, Guatemala.

PLATE 4.—VIEWS OF THE SOUTHERN LOWLANDS

↓ *b*) Lake Peten Itza and the island town of Flores, Peten, Guatemala.

a) Rain forest from the ground, Peten, Guatemala. →

PLATE 5
VIEWS OF THE SOUTHERN AND
NORTHERN LOWLANDS

b) Low forest and bush of north-
↓ ern Yucatan, Mexico.

jaguar, deer, brocket, peccary, tapir, both the Guatemala howler- and spider-monkeys (the former a medium-sized monkey), and a host of smaller mammals, such as armadillos, vampire bats, agoutis, and other rodents, while birds of brilliant plumage dart through the trees and soar majestically overhead. There are parrots, macaws, toucans, herons, hummingbirds; and many game birds—the famous ocellated turkey, found nowhere else in the world save in the Yucatan Peninsula and more like a pheasant than a turkey; wild turkeys, partridges, quail, curassows, *cojolites*, doves, and roadrunners; vultures, hawks, and eagles, and hosts of smaller feathered folk. There are many snakes, both poisonous and nonpoisonous, the python, the tropical rattler, the justly feared *fer-de-lance*, or *nahuyaca*, the tropical moccasin and other equally deadly pit vipers, the coral snake, and, in the lakes and rivers, crocodiles.

Most abundant of all is the insect life—a plague by night and day—ants of all kinds, termites, hornets, the stingless bee (which makes the delicious wild honey of the Yucatan Peninsula, the principal source of sugar for the ancient Maya), butterflies, gnats, tiny bloodsuckers, fleas, flies of all kinds and sizes, ticks, chiggers, and numberless, nameless other insect pests, and at night, hordes of voracious mosquitoes and innumerable enormous fireflies, a half-dozen of which latter under a glass will give sufficient light to read by.

The climate of Peten is much warmer than that of the southern highlands, and considerably more humid than that of northern Yucatan. The rainy season is much longer, extending from May through January, and showers are not infrequent even in the so-called dry months of February, March, April, and May. The rainfall is high, increasing from about 70 inches in the north to about 150 inches in the south as the Cordillera of Guatemala is approached. Water never freezes, though cold "northers" in the winter frequently drive the temperatures down into the 50's Fahrenheit. The hottest months are April and May, just before the rains break, when the temperatures rise well above 100° F., even in the shade.

This region had everything desired by the ancient Maya, a land truly "flowing with milk and honey." The climate was highly salubrious. Extensive areas, admirably adapted to the Maya system of agriculture, were everywhere available. A rich and varied fauna and flora furnished food, clothing, medicine, and other useful materials in greatest abundance. The local limestone was one of the best building materials in all pre-Columbian America; not only was it easily quarried with tools of stone and wood (the only ones at the disposal of the ancient Maya builders), but it also hardens on exposure to the elements; further, on burning, it easily reduces to lime. Finally, throughout the region there are beds of coarse, limey gravel (*zahcab*, a kind of natural lime cement); in short the three essential elements for a primitive, durable stone-and-mortar masonry architecture were present: easily worked building material, lime, and gravel for making mortar.

These highly favorable environmental factors, coupled with the native genius of the ancient Maya, brought about the beginning of the Maya civilization in what is now the northern central section of the Department of Peten, Guatemala, during the fourth century of the Christian Era (chapter iii, see pp. 42–44).

The earliest stone architecture and sculptured stone monuments are found at the city of Uaxactun (Plate 19), some forty miles north of the eastern end of Lake Peten Itza, the oldest dates in the Maya hieroglyphic writing now known, going back to the first quarter of the fourth century after Christ.

From this northern central section of Peten, as its center of distribution, Maya culture spread during the next two centuries, north, east, south, and west, until it had covered the entire Peninsula of Yucatan and the adjacent valleys and northern slopes of the Cordillera to the south—the Maya Old Empire, which reached its finest flower, its Golden Age, at the cities of Palenque, Piedras Negras, and Yaxchilan in the Usumacinta Valley, just west of the Department of Peten and in the extreme southeast at Copan and Quirigua, during the eighth century of the Christian Era.

The high Peten forest changes into the lower, thicker bush of the northern half of the peninsula, almost imperceptibly. As one goes from south to north, the trees become lower; the giant mahoganies, sapodillas, Spanish cedars, and *ceibas* gradually give place to lower trees and a very much thicker, thornier undergrowth (Plate 5, *b*).

Palmetto grows in abundance along the east coast of the peninsula; and, some distance inland behind the coast, there is a long, finger-like extension of the high, southern rain forest, containing mahogany, Spanish cedar, sapodilla, and other hard woods. This latter stand of high forest extends far into the northeastern corner of Yucatan.

The northern half of the peninsula is low and flat; the humus is very shallow, usually not more than a few inches in depth, as contrasted with the much greater depth of the Peten soil, which is two to three feet deep. Everywhere there are extensive outcroppings of the native limestone (Tertiary and Recent) and very little or no surface water, few lakes and rivers.

A low range, not exceeding 300 feet in height, commences at Champoton on the west coast of the peninsula, parallels the coast as far north as the city of Campeche, runs northeast to the town of Maxcanu and then turning southeastward extends to beyond Tzuccacab in central northern Yucatan (Plate 1). From an airplane this chain of low hills, of uniform height, appears to be an old shoreline. Elsewhere it would be insignificant, but rising as it does from a low, flat plain, itself not more than 20 or 25 feet above sea level, these hills achieve an effect of considerable elevation, far beyond that warranted by their actual height; they are known locally as the *serrania* (Plate 7, *a*).

Only a few lakes and rivers are to be found, the latter being little more than creeks. The largest body of water in the northern half of the peninsula is Lake Bacalar in southeastern Quintana Roo, Mexico, which is 35 miles long but only six or seven wide at the widest place. Several other smaller lakes—Chichankanab and Payegua are located in the central northern peninsula and five still smaller ones at Coba in the northeastern part of the peninsula. There are three small rivers—the Champoton on the west coast, the Lagartos on the north coast, and the Xelha on the east coast, all insignificant, being little more than shallow, narrow arms of the sea.

There are two large bays on the east coast—Ascención and Espíritu Santo—both relatively shallow, especially the latter. As one approaches the Guatemala border in southern Campeche and Quintana Roo, swamps become more and more frequent; these, however, largely dry up in the spring, or dry months. The ranges of east- and west-running hills grow progressively higher toward the south until elevations of 1,000 feet or more are reached in northern Peten.

It will be seen from the foregoing that the northern half of the peninsula is unusually dry; indeed the only surface water, barring the few lakes and small brackish streams near the coast mentioned above, is that afforded by the *cenotes*, or large natural wells; fortunately the latter are fairly numerous, especially in the extreme north. The *cenotes* are natural formations, places where the surface limestone has collapsed, exposing the subterranean water table, which everywhere underlies the northern part of the peninsula. Some of these natural wells are two hundred feet or more in diameter. Their depth varies according to the thickness of the surface strata of limestone where they are located (Plate 7, *b*). Near the north coast this subterranean water table is less than fifteen feet below the ground level, but as one proceeds southward the depth of the *cenotes* below ground level increases to more than one hundred feet.

In a country as devoid of surface water as northern Yucatan, these *cenotes* were the principal factor in determining the location of the ancient centers of population. Where there was a *cenote*, there, inevitably, a settlement grew up. The *cenotes* were the principal source of water supply in former times, even as they are today. Like oases in a desert they were, in short, the most important single factor governing the distribution of the ancient population in northern Yucatan.

It has been pointed out that the physical characteristics of the southern and northern halves of the Yucatan Peninsula merge imperceptibly, without any abrupt break in either the flora or the fauna. The high rain forest in the south gradually gives way to lower trees and impenetrable thickets in the north. Most of the flora, the economic plants, fruits, and trees, characteristic of the southern half of the peninsula, are with but few exceptions also found in the north; and the same is also true of the mammals, birds, and reptiles. Monkeys, however, disappear in the extreme north as well as some of the birds and most of the poisonous snakes.

Maya culture would seem to have reached northern Yucatan first as early as the beginning of the fifth century of the Christian Era, probably by way of the east coast of the peninsula. However, these first bearers of the new and richer manner of living found the region already occupied by groups of Maya-speaking, agricultural people to whom the quickening influence of the Maya civilization had not yet penetrated. The extension of Maya culture to the north by groups from the south continued during the fifth, sixth, seventh, and eighth centuries, not only by way of the east coast but also along the central north-and-south axis of the peninsula and the west coast as well. Throughout this period, however, northern Yucatan remained a provincial, peripheral region of the Old Empire as compared with the older and original centers of the Maya civilization to the south, standing in much the same relation to the latter as did Roman Britain to Rome in the early centuries of the Christian Era.

We shall see later (in chapter v, pp. 83–90) how, under the stimulating influences of the new environment, the Maya recovered from the cultural decline into which they had fallen in the south during the ninth century; and, further, how during the eleventh and twelfth centuries they achieved a true renaissance in their new homes in northern Yucatan, only to fall into a second decay during the thirteenth to fifteenth centuries and to suffer final loss of their political independence at the hands of the Spanish at the end of the seventeenth century.

The whole Maya story was unfolded within the confines of
the Yucatan Peninsula—origin, rise, florescence, decline, renaissance, final decay, and collapse, during a period of about two
thousand years, extending roughly from 300 B.C. to A.D. 1700.
Owing to the almost unequaled isolation of the Maya country
(Plate 1)—surrounded on three sides by vast and, in those days,
completely unknown bodies of water, and on the fourth by the
lofty Cordillera, south of which Maya culture never seems to
have penetrated—the Maya developed their unique civilization
practically without influence from the outside. Its origin, rise, and
first florescence in Old Empire times were exclusively due to the
native genius of the Maya peoples, stimulated and conditioned by
the fertile, happy environment in which they were fortunate
enough to have lived. The decline of the Old Empire appears
to have been brought about by conditions incident to its own
development, the very price, as it were, of the brilliant Maya
cultural advance.

Again in New Empire times, it is true that the Mayan
Renaissance was chiefly due to the conquest of northern Yucatan
by Mexican invaders in the tenth century. Nevertheless the conquerors were relatively so few in number that culturally, at least,
they themselves became so modified by the Maya whom they had
conquered that the resulting cultural blend was far more Mayan
than Mexican.

This whole picture of unique geographic isolation, coupled
with an outstanding indigenous civilization that developed in a
region culturally so highly isolated and practically free from all
alien influences, constitutes perhaps the best laboratory for the
study of an early civilization to be found anywhere in the world.

THE PEOPLE

NUMBER AND DISTRIBUTION OF MAYA-SPEAKING PEOPLES

THE DIFFERENT TRIBES of Maya-speaking Indians scattered over the greater part of Guatemala, the extreme western part of Honduras, all of British Honduras, and the states of Yucatan, Campeche, Chiapas, Tabasco, northern Veracruz, eastern San Luis Potosi, and the territory of Quintana Roo, Mexico, all together number a little less than two million souls, by far the greater part, about 1,400,000 in round numbers, being found in Guatemala.

The Maya linguistic stock has been likened, with some reason, to the Romance languages of the Old World—Italian, French, Spanish, Portuguese, Catalonian, Languedoc, Rumanian, and Romance (Switzerland), which are known to have developed their present-day differences from a common tongue, Latin, roughly within the past two thousand years. This comparison is by no means perfect, however, first, because the period of time involved in developing the different languages of the three principal Maya linguistic families certainly must have been much longer than two thousand years, since the differences between them are far too great to have arisen in only two millennia; and, second, because in the case of the Maya, we have no such clear indication as to what the original Maya language was, no such well-known direct ancestor for it, as we have in the case of the Romance languages, the immediate progenitor of which is Latin.

Nor, indeed, are the special students of the problem in complete agreement, either as to the number of families into which the Maya linguistic stock should be divided, or their present distribution.

However, among those best qualified to judge, there is a con-

15

siderable body of opinion in favor of an original threefold division of the Maya linguistic stock: (1) the proto-Guatemala-Yucatan family in the southern highlands (Guatemala) and in the northern lowlands (the northern half of the Yucatan Peninsula); (2) the proto-Chiapas family in the highlands of Chiapas with northerly lowland extensions in Tabasco, Mexico, and southeasterly lowland extensions across southern Peten, Guatemala, as far as western Honduras; and (3) the Huasteca in the northwestern lowlands of northern Veracruz and the adjacent foothills of eastern San Luis Potosi.

This threefold division of the Maya-speaking peoples and their present distribution is shown in Table I, where the groups of languages composing each family are given, together with the region where each language is spoken and the number of individuals speaking it, based upon the 1940 census figures for the Republics of Mexico, Guatemala, and Honduras, and the Crown Colony of British Honduras. This same information is shown graphically in the linguistic map in Plate 6.

Aside from indicating how many Maya-speaking Indians there are today, as well as their present distribution, this map together with Table I, establishes pretty clearly that the language spoken by the Old Empire Maya was some progenitor of the modern Mayoid group.

Old Empire Maya, I believe, developed linguistically in two directions: (1) to the north, first as a northern extension of Old Empire Maya, and later separating into Itza, Mopan, and other late New Empire dialects, and still later into the northern Maya dialects of today—Yucatec, Icaiche, and Lacandon of the Chiapas lowlands; and (2) to the south as the Chol or Choltí, in the southeast as the Chortí, and in the west as the Tzental and Tzotzil of the Chiapas highlands, and Chontal of the Tabasco lowlands.

The Choltí at the time of the Spanish conquest of Peten (late seventeenth century) occupied a belt extending from Copan in what is now western Honduras, northwestward across the *southern* half of Peten and the *western* side of the Usumacinta Valley, that is northeastern Chiapas, and northward across Tabasco to the Gulf

Linguistic
Stock

Original
Maya
linguistic
stock

II

III

* The figures ab
gures for these state

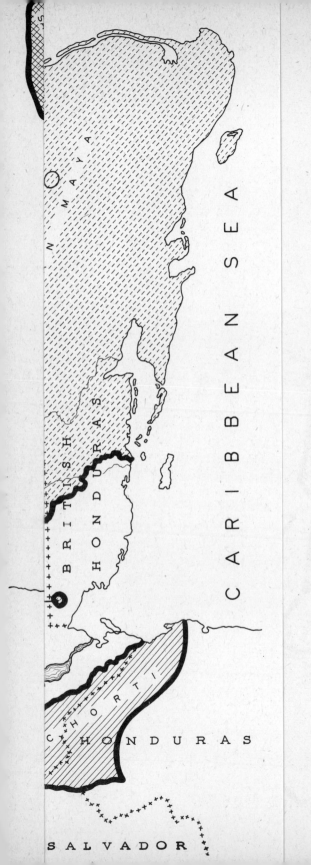

↑ *a*) Sierra or low range of hills, northern Yucatan, Mexico.

PLATE 7.—VIEWS OF THE NORTHERN LOWLANDS

b) *Cenote* or natural cavern with water at bottom, Valladolid, northern
↓ Yucatan, Mexico.

↑ *a*) Woman.   ↑ *b*) Woman, wife of the head-chief.

PLATE 8.—YUCATAN MAYA, TIXCACAL GROUP, QUINTANA ROO, MEXICO

↓ *c*) Youth.   ↓ *d*) Man.

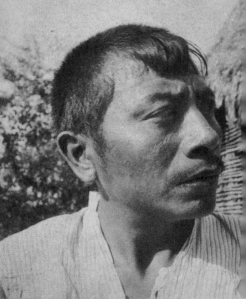

↑　a) Woman.

↑　b) Captain Concepción Cituk, head-chief of the Tixcacal group.

PLATE 9.—YUCATAN MAYA, TIXCACAL GROUP, QUINTANA ROO, MEXICO

↓　c) Young girl.

d) Juan Bautista Poot, minor Tixcacal
↓　chief.

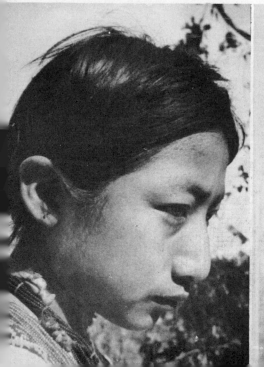

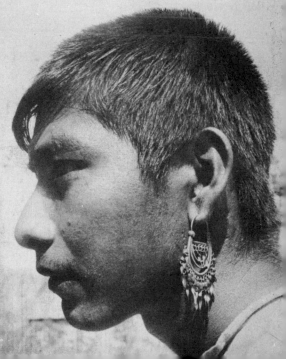

↑ *a*) Young man. ↑ *b*) Family group.

PLATE 10.—YUCATAN MAYA, TIXCACAL GROUP, QUINTANA ROO, MEXICO

↓ *c*) Violinist. ↓ *d*) Drummer.

of Mexico. They were the linguistic connecting link between the
northern half of the peninsula and the southern highlands. At
the southeastern end of this belt, Choltí is transitional between
Yucatec Maya through the Mopan to the Chortí in the extreme
southeast; and at the northwestern end through the Lacandon,
or true Chols (historically different from the modern Yucatec-
speaking Lacandones of the Chiapas lowlands), Choltí is transitional between Yucatec Maya and the Tzeltal-Tzotzil dialects
of the Chiapas highlands.

As early as the late seventeenth century, however, Father
Agustin Cano, in speaking of the Choltí of southern Peten and
the Mopan of eastern central Peten, writes that in talking with
the Mopan people "the Cholti *needed an interpreter.*" Again the
Maya used in a Chontal manuscript of the early seventeenth
century is so different from the immediately contiguous and contemporaneous Yucatec Maya to the northeast that it is evident
that a Chontal Indian of this period talking with a contemporary
Yucatec Maya would have had difficulty in making himself understood, and vice versa. During the seven hundred years which
elapsed between the early tenth century, when the Maya Old
Empire collapsed, and the early seventeenth century—the period
of Father Cano and the Chontal manuscript just mentioned—
divergent linguistic evolution had so changed the northern and
southern dialects spoken by the Old Empire Maya that they had
become mutually unintelligible; indeed they had become separate
languages.

It has been pointed out that the Maya civilization was developed by a people speaking a language of the Mayoid group, i.e.,
of the first linguistic family in Table I. Returning to the second
and third families of the Maya linguistic stock—the proto-
Chiapas–Tabasco and the proto-Huasteca, it will be shown in the
next chapter that the latter had separated from the original mass
of Maya-speaking people, living in the southern half of the
Yucatan Peninsula before some branch of the proto-Guatemala–
Yucatan-family had developed the Maya civilization. Even the
differences between the Quichoid and Mayoid groups within the

same family are such that their very long separation must also be
assumed, a separation certainly going back to before the beginning
of the Christian Era; that is, to considerably before the development of the Maya civilization by some Mayoid people in central
Peten during the first three centuries before and after Christ.

Since we are concerned in this book only with the last, nothing
further will be said about the proto-Huasteca and the proto-
Chiapas–Tabasco tribes, the former inhabiting the northern Veracruz lowlands, and the latter the Tabasco lowlands and adjacent
Chiapas highlands, both families being in Mexico.

NATURE OF THE MAYA LANGUAGE

In Old Empire times (317–987) it is highly probable that
one language was spoken from the southern highlands, northward throughout the entire Yucatan Peninsula, possibly with local
dialectic variations here and there, but fundamentally one fairly
homogeneous tongue.

Says A. M. Tozzer in this connection:

The geographical unity of the Maya speaking peoples is remarkable
when one takes into consideration the colonies of Nahuatl speaking peoples scattered along the Pacific coast of Central America even as far
south as the Isthmus of Panama. The Mayas seem to have been content to
remain very much in one place and it is evident that it was not their
general custom to send out colonies to distant parts of the country. Moreover the wandering of the Mayas among themselves in the comparatively small territory occupied by them is not shown by investigation to
have been great.

Most of the dialects of the Maya seem to have been identified with
certain localities from the time of the earliest Spanish records down to
the present. There does not seem to have been that shifting of population which one might naturally expect. The geographical conditions may
have had something to do with this seeming lack of mingling of the
people of one dialect with those of another. The peninsula of Yucatan
is comparatively isolated from the rest of the Maya territory and the
dialect spoken there is very little changed as far as can be made out from
the earliest times of which we have records. The various mountain
ranges in the south often render communication difficult and a moun-

tain system often separates distinct linguistic differences as regards dialects of the Maya.

During the New Empire (987–1697) considerable modifications took place in the Maya language due to the Mexican (Nahuatl-speaking) invaders of northern Yucatan in the tenth century, though these modifications probably influenced the Maya vocabulary more extensively than its syntax and morphology.

Tozzer in describing the Maya language writes:

Maya is a polysynthetic or incorporating language where a pronominal subject of the verb is always expressed. Maya follows, in general, the same methods of expression as those found in the greater number of American languages. From the point of view of lexicography it is distinct from any of the other languages spoken in Mexico or Central America, ... [and] has no affiliation, as far as can be made out, with any other language of Mexico or Central America. Some authorities claim that the Zapotec is nearer akin to Maya than it is to Nahuatl. Maya [however] is morphologically distinct from the latter.

William Gates, in describing the Maya language, has the following to say:

There are practically no changes of form in its meaningful elements of word development, from the basic neutral roots to their most involved forms of incorporation; the same union of form and value persists from first to last, and the methods of employment are regular and consistent, always recognizable—once the primary classification of the natural major elements has been reached: the natural nouns, adjectives, intransitive and then transitive (effect-producing) words of action, with their needed connecting particles and prepositions. The final language has all the type of "classicity."

Some have claimed that Maya is easier for an English-speaking person to learn than Spanish, which is much more highly declined and conjugated than either Maya or English.

Finally, Alfredo Barrera Vásquez, our greatest modern authority on the Maya language, states that during the four centuries Maya has been in contact with Spanish in Yucatan, it has strongly influenced not only the Spanish vocabulary in use there but also its lexicography, its morphology, phonetics, and syntax, whereas, on the other hand, the Spanish spoken in Yucatan has been able to affect the Maya vocabulary only by the addition of words thereto not previously known among the Maya.

While the foregoing observations refer primarily to the Maya dialect spoken in the northern half of the Yucatan Peninsula, they also apply for the most part to the Maya dialects of the Guatemala and Chiapas highlands—the Quiché, Cakchiquel, Kekchi, Pokomchi, Mam, Pocomam, Tzutuhil, Chortí, Tzental, and Tzotzil.

PHYSICAL CHARACTERISTICS OF THE YUCATAN MAYA

In attempting to draw a picture of what the ancient Maya looked like, to describe their appearance and physical characteristics, we have four lines of evidence upon which to draw: (1) the modern descendants of the ancient Maya, especially in the northern half of the Yucatan Peninsula; (2) representations of the ancient Maya, sculptured on their monuments and painted in their codices, or hieroglyphic manuscripts, and in their frescoes, or on their pottery; (3) a few contemporary descriptions by Spanish writers of the sixteenth century; and (4) a relatively small amount of skeletal material recovered during the course of excavations throughout both the Old and New Empire regions. Of these four sources by far the most important is the first, the modern Maya of Yucatan, many of whom so closely resemble the figures on the monuments and in the paintings that they could have served as models for them (Plates 8, 9, 10, and 11, a and b).

The Maya people compared with ourselves are smaller in stature, broader in the shoulders, thicker-chested, with longer arms and smaller hands and feet. The average height of the men is 5 feet 1 inch and of the women, 4 feet 8 inches. They are one of the broadest-headed peoples in the world. Their cephalic index—the ratio of the breadth of the head to its length—is much higher than our own—85.8 for Maya men and 86.8 for Maya women, as compared with 79 for American men and 80 for American women.

They have better teeth than ourselves; among the modern Maya of Yucatan more than 50 per cent of the individuals are entirely free from dental decay in their permanent teeth until after they are twenty, while among white Americans more than half have dental decay in their permanent teeth before they are nine and more than 90 per cent before they are fourteen. Again, the basal metabolism of the modern Maya is from 5 to 8 per cent higher than that of the average American; and their pulse rate 20 points lower, 52 as compared to our own average pulse rate of 72.

The foregoing data as to height, weight, and head-shape (cephalic index) as given in Table II are for the Yucatan Maya, but figures are also available (except for weights) for some of the other Maya tribes—the Chol, Chontal (Plate 12, *a* and *b*), Tzental, Tzotzil (Plate 13), and Huasteca (Plate 12, *c* and *d*). These will be found in Table II, where for comparative purposes the average heights, weights, and head-shapes of Pueblo and Plains Indians, American Caucasians, and Negroes are also included.

In color the Maya are a warm copper-brown, the women on the whole being slightly darker than the men; this darker pigmentation of the women is seen not only in the color of the skin but also in the color of the eyes, which latter vary from dark brown to black. The hair of both the men and the women is straight, black to dark brown in color, and rather coarse, that of the women being generally lighter than that of the men. The Maya are not a hairy people. The men either have no beards and moustaches at all, or only very meager, sparse ones, while other parts of the body have less hair than in the case of American whites. Indeed, beards and moustaches were held in such little esteem by the Maya in ancient times that Maya mothers burned the faces of their young sons with hot cloths in order to keep their beards from growing, or even plucked out the individual hairs with a small tool something like pincers. Notwithstanding this practice, however, there is plenty of evidence both from the sculptures and the painted pottery of the Old Empire that beards, something like modern goatees, though longer, were worn; it has been suggested that the bearded figures in the Old Empire reliefs were confined to the upper classes, the lower classes only being beardless.

TABLE II

AVERAGE HEIGHTS, CEPHALIC INDICES, AND SOME WEIGHTS FOR MALES AND FEMALES OF CERTAIN MAYA TRIBES, PLAINS AND PUEBLO INDIANS, AMERICAN WHITES, AND NEGROES

Group	Average Height		Average Weight		Average Cephalic Index	
	Male	Female	Male	Female	Male	Female
Yucatan Maya	5 ft. 0.87 in.	4 ft. 8.16 in.	116.3 lbs.	110 lbs.	85.8	86.8
Chontal	5 ft. 2.88 in.	4 ft. 10.32 in.	—		83.2	82.0
Chol	5 ft. 1.32 in.	4 ft. 7.68 in.	—		80.8	80.0
Tzental	5 ft. 1.32 in.	4 ft. 8.64 in.	—		80.8	75.9
Tzotzil	5 ft. 1.32 in.	4 ft. 8.76 in.	—		76.8	76.8
Huasteca	5 ft. 1.80 in.	4 ft. 9.96 in.	—		84.4	86.2
Pueblo Indians	5 ft. 4.68 in.	4 ft. 11.40 in.	126.8 lbs.	123.3 lbs.	82.5	82.5
Plains Indians	5 ft. 7.68 in.	5 ft. 2.40 in.	136.2 lbs.	128.2 lbs.	80.8	80.8
American Caucasians, Amherst and Smith Colleges	5 ft. 8.28 in.	5 ft. 3.84 in.	154.1 lbs.	122.3 lbs.	79.3	80.06
American Negroes, Tuskegee Institute	5 ft. 7.20 in.	5 ft. 2.28 in.	154.1 lbs.	122.8 lbs.	77.38	78.32

Three other physical characteristics of the modern Maya strongly suggest the original northeastern Asiatic origin of the Maya race, as indeed that of all American Indians: (1) the epicanthic eye fold; (2) the Mongolian spot; and (3) the line-patterns in the palms of the hands. The epicanthic fold is an internal fold of the eye which is very characteristic of eastern Asiatics; it is also very common among the modern Maya of Yucatan, being found more often in women than in men (Plate 9, c), and, judging by its frequency in representations of the face in both Old and New Empire sculptures and paintings, it must also have been a prevalent characteristic in ancient times.

The Mongolian spot, as its name implies, is an almost universal physical characteristic of the Mongoloid peoples of eastern Asia. It is an irregular-shaped spot located at the base of the spine, varying in size from a dime to a dinner plate, more often nearer the former than the latter, bluish to purple in color, but fading to a slaty shade as it gradually disappears. It is present at birth in both sexes but disappears in most cases before the tenth year is reached. It is found throughout eastern Asia, and is very common among Maya babies of northern Yucatan today, as presumably it also was in ancient times.

The patterns of certain lines in the palms of the hands of both modern Maya and Chinese so closely resemble each other as to indicate a remarkable degree of racial similarity between the two peoples.

Again the Maya of northern Yucatan occasionally have eyes which are placed somewhat obliquely. This feature, with the epicanthic fold, the Mongolian spot, the black, straight, coarse hair, and the copper-colored skin, verging toward yellow-brown in the lighter Indians, all combine to give many of the Maya a definite east-Asiatic appearance.

Although infant mortality is very high among the Maya, about 70 per cent of all children born alive dying before they reach the age of five, the adult Maya is strong and robust and not given to sickness. If the death rate among Maya children is high, so also is their birth rate correspondingly high, very much higher, in fact, than with us. For example, the average birth rate in the United States for 1935 was 16.9 births per thousand of the entire population, while in Yucatan for the same year three representative, small Indian villages had an average birth rate of 57.4 per thousand, or three and a third times that of the United States for the same year. This exceedingly high birth rate is almost equaled by the high infant mortality—as noted above—and even by a fairly high adult mortality. In a study of the deaths of 605 Indians in northern Yucatan whose corresponding birth dates were also known, 68.8 per cent of the group died before they were 5 years old; 7.9 per cent died between 5 and 15, and the average age at death of the remaining 22.3 per cent was only 38½ years. In another Indian village a census taken in 1933 showed 36 per cent of the population died under 10 years of age, 70 per cent under 25, and 90 per cent before the age of 40.

In spite of the high infant mortality, however, the population of the native villages of Yucatan today presents a relatively youthful appearance due to the above-indicated high adult mortality. Three Indian villages between 1933 and 1937 showed an adult death rate of 26.4, 27.5, and 34.2, respectively, per thousand, as compared with the death rate in the United States of fewer than half that number per thousand for the same year.

Maya girls of today marry at the average age of 16⅔ years and Maya youths at the average age of 21 years, though Bishop Diego de Landa says, "In olden times they married when they were twenty years old; but now they marry at twelve or fourteen." The average Maya girl has her first child when she has been married a little over a year (at the age of 18 years) and she continues bearing for about 18½ years thereafter, her last child being born when she is about 36½ years old. The average Maya woman bears between 7 and 9 children, but succeeds in raising fewer than half of them, the average family consisting of only 3.7 children. These various figures indicate that, in spite of the high rate of infant mortality, the Indian population continues to grow, since Maya women are exceedingly fertile and the race, generally speaking, is healthy.

↑ *a*) Young boy.   ↑ *b*) Young girl.

PLATE 11.—(*a*, *b*) YUCATAN MAYA, CHICHEN ITZA, YUCATAN, MEXICO; AND
(*c*, *d*) QUICHE MAYA, SANTO TOMAS CHICHICASTENANGO, GUATEMALA

↓ *c*) Man.   ↓ *d*) Young man.

↑ *a*) Chontal family.

PLATE 12
CHONTAL MAYA, TABASCO, MEXICO, AND
HUASTECA MAYA, SAN LUIS
POTOSI, MEXICO

↑ *b*) Chontal old married co⋯

c) Huasteca, young wife with baby
↓ carried *hetzmek* or straddled on hip.

↓ *d*) Huasteco, young husband.

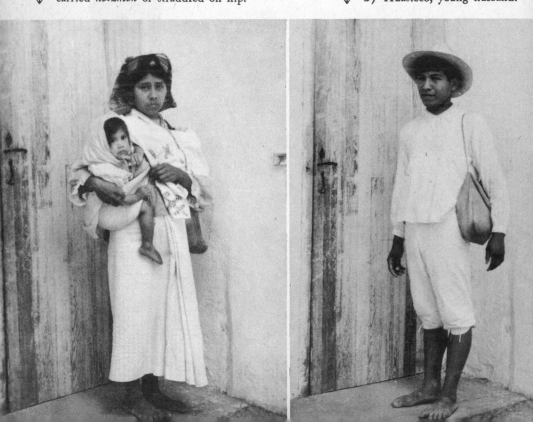

↑ *b*) Young girl, Iztapa.

↓ *d*) Old man, Zinacantan.

↑ *a*) .Youth, Chamula.

PLATE 13. —TZOTZIL MAYA, CHIAPAS,
MEXICO

↓ *c*) Young man, Chamula.

PLATE 14.—DOUBTFULLY DATED, POSSIBLY EARLY MONUMENTS

↑ *a*) **Tuxtla Statuette, San Andres Tuxtla, Veracruz, Mexico.**

↑ *c*) Stela C, Tres Zapotes, Veracruz, Mexico, back view.

Marriage, or at least fairly durable extramarital relationship, is the overwhelming rule in modern Indian villages in Yucatan. In one Indian settlement where a record of the civil status of 70 adult women was kept for eight years, only 4 were found to have remained unmarried, while in the same village there was not one man over 25 who was not either married or a widower living with a woman without benefit of clergy. Marriage, or some equally stable though less legal type of union, is the almost universal rule, and exceptions to it are as rare as the foregoing figures indicate.

Unfortunately no such close studies of other Maya groups have been made as those undertaken by Dr. Morris Steggerda, formerly of the Carnegie Institution of Washington, among the Maya of northern Yucatan; but, judging from general appearance, the highland Maya have a redder and more shiny skin than the Yucatan Maya, and biologically they seem to be of somewhat purer strain; that is they show less non-Maya admixture. However, judged by such basic criteria as stature, color, head-shape, and hair, all Maya-speaking groups would seem to have sprung originally from the same common ancestral stock.

PSYCHOLOGICAL CHARACTERISTICS OF THE YUCATAN MAYA

The Maya of Yucatan are inherently active, energetic, and hard working—all on a diet so low in proteins that an American laborer could not even exist on it. Indeed the average Maya's protein intake from all sources is only one-sixth of a pound per day. Seventy-five to eighty-five per cent of everything he eats is carbohydrates—maize in one form or another, mostly as *tortillas,* an unleavened baked corncake about the size of a pancake, and to a much lesser extent as two beverages called *pozole* and *atole* also both made of corn (pp. 200, 201). The average daily Maya diet contains only 2,565 calories as compared with our own average daily caloric intake of 3,500.

On this diet, which from our point of view is highly unbalanced and protein-deficient, the ancient Maya found energy to build the many pyramids, temples, and palaces which everywhere characterize their great ceremonial centers; on this diet the Maya of the Spanish Colonial Period drew strength to construct the great Catholic churches and monasteries of Yucatan with their massive masonry walls, one at least for every village; and finally on this same monotonous, protein-deficient diet, the Maya of today, working in the hemp (sisal) plantations, raise the fiber from which the binder-twine of the American farmer is made. Thus the Maya would always seem to have been inherently industrious and hard working—not only during the Old and New Empires but also throughout the Spanish Colonial Period and even down to the present day.

As to cleanliness and neatness, the Maya present a curious contradiction. So far as their persons and clothing are concerned they are scrupulously clean, every man, woman, and child bathing at least once a day, and sometimes twice. When the man of the family returns home from work in the cornfield, his wife has a hot bath ready for him. Indeed failure on her part so to do, under Spanish colonial law, gave her husband the right to beat her. As none of the houses outside the few towns has running water, or pumps of any kind, all water has to be carried in earthen water jugs, galvanized iron pails, or reused 5-gallon gasoline tins from the nearest well or *cenote*, where it has to be raised by the old-fashioned bucket-and-rope method, sometimes for as much as a hundred feet. And yet the Maya are always bathing; their devotion to personal cleanliness, which also extends to their clothing, is almost fanatical.

However, when it comes to their thatch-roofed, single-roomed houses, they are far from clean and orderly. Chickens, turkeys, dogs, goats, and pigs roam the house at will, leaving their droppings everywhere. Outside, in the yard, broken dishes, cracked pots, bent pans lie about for years just where they were discarded, all of which lends an air of untidiness and disorder to most Maya homes, inside as well as outside. And yet even in spite of this disorder, the Maya housewife cleans house daily and even sweeps the dirt street in front of her home for good measure.

Some foreigners who have visited Yucatan have thought the
Maya cruel, especially toward animals; but, after long residence
among them, I have reached the conclusion that they are not so
deliberately cruel as they are insensitive to suffering, not only in
others but also in themselves. They are stoical under pain, and
when they see it in others, especially in animals, they are correspondingly indifferent. They will let their dogs slowly starve
to death, and yet they would no more think of killing them outright than it would occur to them that speedy death would be
kinder than the torture of slow starvation. This latter trait, however, may possibly be due to the Christian precept against taking
life. I once asked a servant to drown a litter of kittens, but the
boy replied, "I could not do that, but I will take them out into
the bush, a long way from the hacienda, and leave them there
to die." So long as he had not killed them himself, how they
met their death was no concern of his; if they died in the bush,
as they surely would, it was an act of God—no fault of the boy.

The Maya are fundamentally conservative and unprogressive;
indeed they have even succeeded in preserving their own language
in the face of four centuries of Spanish domination, so that today
the business of the hemp plantations and the affairs of everyday
life in all the smaller towns and villages throughout Yucatan are
conducted in the Maya language and not in Spanish.

Maya dress, especially that of the women has not changed
appreciably in hundreds of years, not since long before the Spanish
Conquest. Their pottery, weaving, and cross-stitch embroidery
have remained much the same throughout Maya history. But
of recent years, under the crushing impact of the machine age
and its time-saving, convenient devices, Maya conservatism has
at last begun to give ground. The automobile and the bicycle
have captured the larger cities and towns, and hand-operated
corn-grinders are everywhere replacing the old stone grinders;
even in the smaller villages motor-driven mills are now in general use for grinding corn. Radios are beginning to appear, sewing
machines and phonographs are common, and even a few electric
lights in the homes of the well-to-do of the smaller towns, most

of which can boast of electric-light plants. Most villages have a
weekly or semiweekly movie, and co-operative movements are
being organized; in short, the Maya are losing their conservatism.

They are a happy, talkative, sociable people much more given
to communal activities than are the Navajo Indians in the southwestern United States, for example. They love to laugh, joke,
and talk; they are good-natured, trusting, unselfish, considerate
of the rights of others, and have a strong sense of justice. They
are courteous and friendly to strangers, thus bearing out Bishop
Landa's estimate of them made nearly four hundred years ago:

> The Yucatecans are very generous and hospitable; since no one may
> enter their houses without being offered food and drink, of what they
> may have had during the day, or in the evening. And if they have none,
> they seek it from a neighbor; and if they come together on the roads,
> all join in sharing, even if little remains for themselves.

The Maya of today show little aptitude for leadership and,
generally speaking, are disinclined to assume administrative
responsibility. This seems strange in view of the high quality of
leadership they surely enjoyed in ancient times, as indicated by
the great ceremonial centers of both the Old and New Empires.
It is probable, however, that, when the Maya civilization was in
its heyday, leadership and administrative functions were confined
exclusively to the nobility and the priesthood; the common folk
were little more than hewers of wood and drawers of water—
essentially a peasant-artisan laboring class, whose industry and
toil, it is true, built the great pyramids, temples, and palaces, but
always under the direction of the civil and religious authorities.
And it was precisely upon these two classes—the nobility and the
priesthood—that the greatest impact of the Spanish Conquest
fell. The Spanish military authorities immediately stripped the
native rulers and nobility of all effective political power, and the
Catholic clergy speedily replaced the native priesthood, so that
soon there were but few Maya leaders left. And yet one finds an
occasional exception among the modern Maya; for example, one
of my closest Maya friends, Don Eustaquio Ceme of Chankom,
is an Indian leader of outstanding ability. Chankom is a little

Indian village of only four or five hundred souls, and were it not for the personal qualities of Don Eustaquio it would be like scores of other similar Indian villages in Yucatan. But the indomitable energy, administrative ability, and civic pride of this one man alone have made Chankom the most progressive community of its size in the whole state of Yucatan; all its municipal improvements —schoolhouse, town hall, stone houses in place of the usual thatched ones, several of them even of two stories, this last a great achievement in the smaller villages—are all due to his leadership and driving force alone. In ancient times he surely would have been an outstanding figure, playing his role on a much larger stage.

Although the modern Maya are generally retiring in nature, shunning rather than seeking civic responsibility, they are pronounced individualists and extremely independent. Children early learn to make their own decisions, and their parents respect their individual rights. In making annual series of anthropometric measurements of groups of Maya children in Yucatan the scientists of the Carnegie Institution invariably found it necessary to seek each child's permission anew, each year, in order to measure him or her as the case might be. Each child was paid the equivalent of ten cents in American money for permitting himself or herself to be measured; but, in spite of their poverty and with idle time to burn, their strong sense of individual independence demanded that they should not grant the request too readily.

The competitive spirit among the modern Maya is not strongly developed. Even as children their games are noncompetitive, and as adults they seem to be singularly without desire to excel. They are content to be small corn-farmers, raising sufficient food for the needs of their families and a little more to trade for such few articles as they cannot themselves produce—cotton-cloth, gunpowder and shot, cheap perfume, soap, and a few personal trinkets—or even less ambitiously they work in the great hemp plantations for little more than subsistence wages. A few of the more able, perhaps descendants of the ancient nobility and priesthood, accumulate a few cattle, horses, pigs, goats, turkeys, and chickens, and even rise to the higher social status of being small store-keepers in their villages, but beyond these humble pursuits the modern Maya do not aspire.

The Maya have a strong respect for law and a keen sense of justice. Among the semi-independent native groups of Quintana Roo—the Santa Cruz Maya for example—there is an unusually high conception of justice. The only punishment among these Indians is the *azote* or bastinado, which is administered with considerable humanity, since in the case of a heavy sentence, say of one hundred lashes, the culprit receives only twenty-five on each of four consecutive mornings. And here is where judicial procedure among the Santa Cruz Maya differs from our own. The sentenced man is not kept in prison between successive lashings; on the contrary he is allowed to be at large, but the responsibility of presenting himself for punishment each morning rests solely upon his own shoulders. No police nor any other villager is sent out to look for him and bring him in to receive his daily punishment. The guilty man of his own accord must present himself to receive his twenty-five daily lashes. And if he fails to do so, if he is not present at the jail at the time appointed for him to be flogged, the whole community regards him as an outlaw, a fugitive from justice, a social outcast, and, further still, any member of the community may kill him at sight without being punished therefor. He is a public enemy and consequently his life is regarded as forfeit to the community.

The Maya are not quarrelsome even when intoxicated, though if they have been wronged they harbor resentment and bide their time for revenge. It will be seen in chapter v how the Cocom, the ruling house of Mayapan, cherished a feud against the Xiu family of Mani for close on to a century, and how Nachi Cocom, the great-grandson of the last Cocom ruler at Mayapan, took wholesale revenge on Ah Dzun Xiu, the Mani ruler of his day, because the latter's great-grandfather had slain Nachi Cocom's great-grandfather ninety-five years before. Disputes among the Maya of today are chiefly due to domestic troubles—infidelity on the part of the husband or wife, and damage to a man's crops by

the livestock of another. Although in rare cases a husband may
kill the paramour of his adulterous wife, more often he either
pardons her and takes her back or allows her to go off with the
other man. Injury to crops by livestock, however, is a more serious matter. The owner of the animals is obliged to pay for the
damage done.

As a people the Maya are unusually honest. Petty thieving
among them is almost unknown, and houses are left unlocked
most of the time. Very rarely does one Indian steal corn from
another, as though some ancient but powerful taboo operated
against such knavery. This is true in spite of the fact that easy
opportunities to steal corn are ever present, since the never-
guarded cornfields more often than not are located several miles
from the nearest village. Says one writer in this connection, "Men
who steal from corn-fields are killed by the guardian-spirits of the
fields and these beliefs are the real locks on the open granaries
in the distant bush."

Nor are the modern Maya given to begging. During the seventeen years the Carnegie Institution carried on archaeological
investigations at Chichen Itza, a free medical clinic was maintained
for Indians of the surrounding region, medicines being distributed
among them without charge. Although the Indians from long
experience came to know that this service was free, invariably
after receiving treatment and medicines at the clinic they offered
to pay for the same, and, when payment was refused, the next time
they visited Chichen Itza they would bring gifts of food, chickens,
eggs, deer meat, and native embroideries. There seemed to be a
deep-felt desire not to accept something for nothing, but rather
to repay an obligation in some way.

All foreigners agree that the modern Maya have a keen sense
of humor, practical jokes being considered by far the most amus-
ing. A boy will strike another an unexpected blow behind the
knee, causing him to fall. During the archaeological excavations
of the Carnegie Institution at Chichen Itza, an absent-minded
wheelbarrow boy would find his barrow quickly overloaded by
the other Indians if he were not on the watch. A well-vouched-

for story is told of a Maya family, who, having assembled for the funeral of one of its members, was plunged into laughter and hilarity when a bat flew into the death-room. The Maya are a cheerful, joking, fun-loving lot, whose friendly, sunny dispositions have been admired by all foreigners who come in contact with them. Maya family ties are very strong, although among adults outward demonstrations of affection, such as kissing and embracing, are rare. Affection between man and wife is shown by each carrying out his or her respective duties in the home. With their children, however, they are much more demonstrative; Maya mothers fondle their babies, talk affectionate baby talk to them, and very rarely punish them physically. Children are trained more by their own desire to conform with established social practices than by disciplinary measures. When physical punishment has to be administered, however, it is the mother and not the father who does it. The older children not only take care of their younger brothers and sisters but also have authority over them. Respect for older members of the family by the younger members is deeply ingrained. The father is the undisputed head of his family and nothing is done without his approval, though respect for the mother is almost equally pronounced. This respect for elders goes straight back to ancient times, for Bishop Landa in writing of the Maya of the sixteenth century says:

The young men respected the elders highly, and took their counsels, and tried to pass as mature themselves. The elders said to the younger ones that since they had seen more, what they said should be believed, so that if the youths heeded their counsels, the elders would credit them more. So much respect was given to the elders that the youths did not mingle with them, except in cases of necessity such as when they were married; and with married men they mingled very little.

I well remember a native marriage which my wife and I attended some years ago that well illustrates this point; indeed, we had been asked to act as godparents of the young Maya couple who were being married. The wedding was held in a long, narrow room with a dirt floor. A plain, deal table at one end, decorated with paper flowers, colored calendars, and colored adver-

tisements of flowers, dresses, carpets, etc., from the catalogues of
American mail-order houses, served as the altar. As part of the
wedding ceremony, the Catholic priest who officiated delivered
an eloquent homily in Maya, exhorting the newly-married pair
to bring up their children in the True Faith, and that whenever
any differences of opinion arose between them and their children,
to remember that the parents were always right. To this advice
two little Maya boys, perhaps eight or ten years old, who squatted
on their haunches down in the front row, whispered to each other,
"That isn't so." Whereupon the priest, who overheard the remark,
stopped the wedding sermon and, walking over to where the boys
squatted on the ground, shook his finger at them and for five
minutes angrily harangued them in Maya, the text, refrain, and
theme song of what he said being "And it's bad little boys just like
you that I am talking about!"

Sex is of only moderate importance in the lives of the Maya.
One writer states that "both men and women are singularly lacking in sex instinct." Bishop Landa remarks upon the extreme
modesty of the Maya women at the time of the Conquest: "The
women were accustomed to turn their shoulders to the men in
passing them, and of turning aside that they might pass; and the
same, when they gave them to drink, until they had finished."

Landa also says that in his day men and women did not eat
together: "The men are not accustomed to eat with the women
but by themselves upon the ground, or at most upon a mat which
takes the place of a table." This curious custom persists even
down to the present day, since Maya women and girls, except in
very rare instances, do not eat with their respective menfolk—
their husbands, fathers, sons, and brothers. The men eat first,
being served by the women, and later the women of the family
eat together by themselves; though whether this custom had its
origin in sex modesty cannot now be determined. Modesty as
such, in small children, is confined exclusively to the little girls,
who have to wear *huipiles* (the Maya woman's dress) from birth,
while their little brothers up to the age of six and even older are
allowed to play about the house and yard stark naked.

Sexual promiscuity among married women, and indeed among unmarried girls, is not uncommon. The former is not regarded with particular disapproval, except by the jealous husband, while the unmarried girl with one or more illegitimate children has no more difficulty in finding a mate than have her more virtuous sisters. Prostitution, however, is uncommon, as it must always be where sexual intercourse is not difficult to obtain. Truth is that the Maya, though not particularly highly sexed, find easy satisfaction of the sex impulse through normal noncommercial relations. Most boys are usually introduced to sex life by older women, or by widows, while young girls have their first sex experience with their youthful lovers. Incest, though very rare, occurs from time to time, usually as between father and daughter.

The modern Maya are not particularly religious and most of the men may be said to be definitely irreligious except for lip service to certain forms of the church. At present Christian worship is carried on almost exclusively by the women, though in ancient times religion was largely an affair of the men. Although practically all children are baptized, and usually with the name of the Catholic saint corresponding to the day of their birth (in four out of five cases), few receive additional instruction in the tenets of the Church because of the present scarcity of priests in the smaller villages, and hence the great majority know very little about the real meaning and significance of Christianity.

The Maya are definitely fatalistic. They have no fear of death at all. What will come, will come. Old people of both sexes have been known to announce that the time had come for them to die and, though not even ill, they have lain down in their hammocks and quietly passed away.

In ancient times, at least judging from the multitude of religious buildings, temples, and monasteries which crowd the great ceremonial centers of both the Old and New Empires, religion must have played a role of supreme importance in the lives of the Maya of that day (chapter xi), but at the present time church congregations are made up almost exclusively of women, with only a scattering of men.

If they are not religious, however, all Maya, both men and women, are intensely superstitious. Countless superstitions, many of them doubtless fragmentary survivals of the ancient Maya religion intermixed with Spanish medieval folklore, dictate many acts of everyday life. A few of these will suffice to illustrate the wide range of these folk beliefs. Many dreams and omens are regarded as sure forerunners of death: If one dreams that he is floating on air, or that he is having a tooth pulled and is suffering intense pain, a member of his immediate family will die; if, in the dream, the suffering is only slight, only a less close relative will die; to dream of red tomatoes signifies a baby will die; to dream about a black bull trying to push its way into your home, or to dream of breaking a water jug indicates that a member of your family will die.

The Maya believe that if a person sees a green snake with red eyes, or an unusually large or unusually small hen's egg, or if he hears the hoot of an owl, misfortune will surely befall him.

Sickness is caused by dwarfs, for whom gourds, filled with food, are placed in the doorway of the house, one for each member of the family, in order to prevent an epidemic. If one gives away embers of burning wood, one's turkeys will die. Eggs set on Fridays will not hatch. This latter belief is suggestive of the bad luck attending Fridays throughout Christian countries, Friday having been the day of the Crucifixion.

There are many weather superstitions. Thin corn-husks indicate a mild winter; thick ones a cold winter. If a swallow flies low, it will rain; if high, it will be clear. Cicadas are honored weather prophets among the Maya. If one variety called *choch* chirps for a long time, it will rain; if another called *chipit-tin* chirps continually, it will be dry. Often the time for the important agricultural activity of burning the cornfield (chapter viii, pp. 144–46) is determined by the chirping of these little insects.

Evil winds take on the form of animals, and individuals struck by them will die. If a match drops on the floor and continues to burn, it is a sign of good luck; if it burns to the end, the person who dropped it will have a long life.

The household broom holds destiny in its humble mission. Sweeping across the foot of a boy indicates he will marry an old woman; across the foot of a girl that she will marry an old man. Sweeping out a house at night will make one poor, and putting a broom behind the door will hasten the departure of a tiresome guest by causing him or her to desire to relieve him- or herself.

The hunter has many difficulties to contend with. If he sells either the head, liver, or stomach of a deer he has killed, he will have bad luck in hunting in the future, and should he dare to sell the paunch, he will never be able to kill another. To bring bad luck to a hunter, one only has to buy meat from him and throw the bones into a *cenote*. The Maya believe there is a king-deer in the bush, with a wasp's nest between his horns called the *zip*; if a hunter should be so unfortunate as to kill this particular deer, he would die immediately.

The following signs indicate that visitors are coming: an oriole singing, a dragonfly coming into the house, a butterfly flying high, a cat washing its face, or a fire hissing.

The Maya, from most ancient times, have lived under the influence of lucky and unlucky days, and the modern Maya continue to follow in their forefathers' footsteps in this respect, with this difference: that the seven days of the Christian week have replaced the 260 days of the ancient *tzolkin* or sacred divinatory year. Now, Tuesdays and Fridays are considered unlucky, Mondays and Saturdays lucky. Marriages are usually celebrated on Mondays; Saturdays are considered lucky days on which to buy lottery tickets.

Again the Maya have always venerated numbers. Nine is, and always has been, especially lucky, perhaps because of its association with the nine steps leading to the ancient Maya heaven, and perhaps because of its having been the number of the Nine Gods of the Maya Underworld, one of the most important groups of deities in the ancient Maya pantheon (chapter xi, pp. 231–33). If a centipede is found on Tuesday it must be cut into nine pieces in order to bring good luck. If a green snake is seen, it will cause one's death within the year, unless it is caught and cut into nine

pieces. Whooping-cough may be cured by hanging gourds of fresh
atole (chapter x, p. 201) in the doorway for nine successive days,
and on the morning of the ninth day the *atole* must be shared with
one's friends. Nine kernels of ground corn applied to granulated
eyelids will cure them; skin troubles may be relieved with a brew
of nine pieces of fish skin, nine pieces of corn cob, and nine small
pebbles; and there are many other lucky practices involving the
use of nine objects, or of performing some specific act nine times,
as in the *hetzmek* ceremony described in chapter xi.

Thirteen is another lucky Maya number, perhaps because of
its important function in the ancient Maya calendar and perhaps
also because it was the number of the Thirteen Gods of the Maya
Upper World (chapter xii, p. 231). The use of thirteen as a lucky
number, however, seems to be confined chiefly to religious ceremonies, as for example when offerings of thirteen loaves of bread,
thirteen bowls of food, and thirteen cakes made of thirteen layers
of bean-paste and tortillas are prepared for a ceremony.

It will be seen from the foregoing that more Maya superstitions have an unpleasant than a pleasant connotation. Many more
things, it would seem, are thought to bring bad luck than good
luck. In spite of their cheery, happy natures the Maya have a
sad and ever-present fatalistic strain, perhaps the heritage of their
pagan past, where death by sacrifice was common and more of
their gods were hostile than friendly.

Concerning the general intelligence of the Maya, opinions
differ. Some white observers believe them to be very bright;
many more including myself classify them as fairly bright; others
as average, and a few only as rather dull; no foreigner, it is to be
noted, ever regards them as downright stupid. They are not in-
ventive, however, but are content to follow the same pattern of
living as did their ancestors. Their memory is considered very
good by foreigners and their powers of observation, especially in
the bush, are excellent, their sharp eyes missing little that happens on either side of the trail. Finally, they are rather imagina-
tive and have a fair sense of beauty, which latter, however, was
probably more highly developed in ancient times than it is today.

THE ORIGIN OF THE MAYA CIVILIZATION

THE THREE PRINCIPAL EPOCHS OF PENINSULAR HISTORY

A SUMMARY of Maya history will be found in Table III, with corresponding dates in both Maya and Christian chronologies and the accompanying ceramic and architectural phases. It will be seen from this table that Maya history may be divided into three general epochs: (1) Pre-Maya, extending from about 3000 B.C. in round numbers to A.D. 317; (2) Maya Old Empire from A.D. 317 to 987; and (3) Maya New Empire from 987 to 1697; further, that each of these epochs may again be divided into three subdivisions: Pre-Maya I, II, and III; Old Empire I, II, and III; and New Empire I, II, and III. (See Table III following p. 40.)

THE MAYA CIVILIZATION DEFINED

We have seen in the first chapter that Maya civilization was based primarily upon agriculture, chiefly as applied to the cultivation of Indian corn, or maize. It was further stated there, and will be more fully explained in the eighth chapter (pp. 137–40), that agriculture in the Americas probably originated in the highlands of western Guatemala but at a date several thousand years before the beginning of the Maya civilization in the lowlands of Peten.

As used throughout this book the term "Maya civilization" is applied exclusively to that ancient American culture which had as its two principal material manifestations a unique hieroglyphic writing and chronology, and, so far as North America is concerned, an also equally unique stone architecture, involving the use of corbeled-stone roof-vaults (pp. 345–47). Wherever these two cultural traits are found together in the Middle American region, that is to say in southern Mexico and northern Central America —and in this region they practically never occur separately—

there the Maya civilization, as defined here, flourished. Conversely wherever neither of these traits is found, even though the language spoken by the local Indians is one or other of the several Maya dialects, such regions are not here considered as having formed parts of the Maya culture area.

THE PROBLEM OF THE HUASTECA INDIANS

We have already seen an example of this latter condition in chapter ii, in the case of the Huasteca Indians of eastern San Luis Potosi and northern Veracruz, Mexico. The Huasteca speak a language definitely of the Maya linguistic family, and physically closely resemble the Maya of Yucatan, yet careful study of the archaeological remains of the Huasteca region has failed to uncover the slightest evidence that they ever knew any form of hieroglyphic writing, or ever made use of corbeled-stone roof-vaulting in their architecture. Linguistically, and probably physically as well, they are and were Maya, but culturally they were something different, the level of their civilization being far below that enjoyed by their distant southeastern relatives of the Yucatan Peninsula.

And yet, in considering the origin of Maya civilization, the Huasteca may not be entirely overlooked, even though their contribution thereto was purely negative. It was shown in chapter ii that the region occupied by the Huasteca is a good three hundred miles northwest of the next nearest Maya-speaking group, namely the Chontal of Tabasco; further, that all other Maya-speaking groups except the Huasteca are contiguous one to another—only the Huasteca lies off by itself, separated from the other linguistically related groups by Totonac- and Nahuatl-speaking peoples in central and southern Veracruz (Plate 6).

This condition, coupled with the fact that the Maya-speaking, Maya-appearing Huasteca never shared with the Maya of the Yucatan Peninsula the latter's unique culture, clearly indicates that the Huasteca became separated from their other Maya cousins sometime *before* the latter had developed the highly distinctive civilization which later came to characterize them.

There are, indeed, some indications that the Veracruz coast plain was originally occupied by peoples who spoke some form of Maya, though now this region is occupied by Tononac- and Nahuatl-speaking peoples. The probable explanation of this condition is that possibly as much as two or three thousand years ago Nahuatl-speaking peoples, formerly living in central Mexico, either moved or were pushed eastward from these positions to the Gulf Coast by pressure of other tribes, who at that time lived to the north and northwest of them, until these emigrants from central Mexico had driven a Nahuatl linguistic wedge between the great mass of the Maya-speaking peoples to the southeast and a single Maya-speaking group—the Huasteca—to the northwest (Plate 6).

If the time element in the foregoing picture is approximately correct, the Maya civilization—or, better, those cultural elements which led up to it—had their beginnings between two and three thousand years ago, roughly sometime during the first millennium before Christ, probably nearer the later than the earlier limit.

THE TRES ZAPOTES AND EL BAUL MONUMENTS AND THE TUXTLA STATUETTE

As to where the Maya civilization had its beginnings there are two different schools of thought: one that believes it originated somewhere on the coast plain of the state of Veracruz, Mexico; and another, to which I subscribe, that holds it originated somewhere near the region where its oldest remains have been discovered, namely near the ancient cities of Tikal and Uaxactun in the northern central part of the Department of Peten, Guatemala.

There are, however, a few scattering dates which, *if accepted, at their face values*, are considerably earlier than either the Leyden Plate or Stela 9 at Uaxactun, which present the two earliest-known certain Maya dates. These doubtful, and indeed disputed, possibly earlier dates are by no means clear, however; they create a situation such as would arise if we were to find a Gothic cathedral dating from 1000 B.C., or a skyscraper with the year

Maya Renaissance			Fine Orange I	
Maya Renaissance	11.10.1.0.0	A.D. 1194	Yucatan Slate II Fine Orange II Plumbate	Period III, corbeled roof-vaulting
New Empire — New Empire II, Mexican Period	11.10.1.0.0 to 11.11.10.0.0	A.D. 1194 to A.D. 1441		
New Empire III, Period of Disintegration	11.11.10.0.0 to 12.4.1.0.0	A.D. 1441 to A.D. 1697	Coarse Red Ware	

1492 carved on its corresponding cornerstone—obvious anachronisms. These few scattering dates are only *apparently* very early, I believe, all of them having *actually* been carved at much later dates than they appear to represent.

There are three of these pseudo-early monuments: Stela C at Tres Zapotes in southern Veracruz, Mexico (Plate 14, *c*); Stela 1 at El Baul in the highlands of Guatemala (Plate 14, *b*); and the Tuxtla Statuette, also from southern Veracruz, Mexico (Plate 14, *a*). The earliest (?) of these three dates is on the monument from Tres Zapotes and is alleged to read 7.16.16.16.18 of the Maya Era, or 21[1] B.C.; next is that on the El Baul monument 7.19.7.8.12, or A.D. 29; and the last is that on the jade figurine from San Andres Tuxtla—8.6.4.2.17 or A.D. 162.

But none of these decipherments it should be warned at the outset is certain, perhaps not even probable. In the case of the Tres Zapotes monument, the first number at the left, 7, which makes it so unbelievably early, is *entirely missing in the original* and has only been *restored* as 7, out of the blue, by those who believe in the maximum antiquity of this carving. The first number actually to appear is the second from the left above, or 16, the supposed katun coefficient of this date, which, however, looks more like 15 in Plate 14, *c*; that is, it appears to be composed of three bars rather than three bars and one dot.

The second possibly earliest date mentioned above is inscribed on a monument (Plate 14, *b*) which is not even Maya in style, being more Mexican in character and obviously having been carved very much later than the *apparently* early date of 7.19.7.8.12 (A.D. 29) inscribed upon it. It is found, moreover, in a region where there are other sculptured monuments which are also much more Mexican than Maya in character, that is the Department of Escuintla, Guatemala. Finally the stylistic characteristics of the Tuxtla Statuette, the third allegedly oldest dated object, are dis-

[1] How Maya dates are to be interpreted will be explained subsequently in chapter xii and how they are to be correlated with the dates of Christian chronology will be described in Appendix I, p. 457. All dates in Christian chronology are A.D., *after* the birth of Christ, unless otherwise stated, though the abbreviation A.D. for Anno Domini will hereinafter be generally omitted.

tinctly non-Mayan; the early Baktun 8 date, which is carved on its front, 8.6.4.2.17 (A.D. 162), is, however, the clearest of these three highly doubtful, allegedly earliest dates (Plate 14, *a*).

Nevertheless the Mexican archaeologists believe that this southern Veracruz region, where the Tres Zapotes monument and the Tuxtla Statuette were found, that of the Olmeca culture, was the original center of distribution of the higher civilizations of all Middle America. Alfonso Caso has recently summarized the Mexican school of thought on this point, with which, however, I disagree, in the following words:

It is very probable that paper is one of those inventions [in the Middle American region] which like writing, seals or markers, the brush, the ritualistic calendar or *tonalpohualli*, the creator gods, the god of rain, etc., must be attributed to a most ancient mother culture, which is found at the bottom of the specialized cultures of central Mexico and northern Central America, and which spread from a place, so it appears, that we must locate in the southern part of Veracruz and in the nearby sections of Tabasco, Oaxaca and Chiapas.

Since, as will be shown later, the earliest dates which are *surely* contemporaneous, that is to say surely executed at the times they severally represent, are more than a century and a half *later* (A.D. 320 on the Leyden Plate and A.D. 328 on Stela 9 at Uaxactun), it is probable that the Tres Zapotes and El Baul monuments and the Tuxtla Statuette are only apparently early, that, in reality, they are anachronistic, carved sometime later than the apparently very early dates inscribed on them.

ORIGIN OF THE MAYA CIVILIZATION IN THE LOWLANDS OF NORTHERN CENTRAL PETEN

Having perhaps disposed of the Veracruz coast plain as the region where the Maya civilization had its beginnings, where next may we look for its place of origin? The answer to this question, under my definition of what the Maya civilization was, is fairly simple and direct, that is—where the earliest examples of the hieroglyphic writing and corbeled-stone roof-vaulting are to be found. If these two *dominant* characteristics of Maya culture are

accepted as our guide, then it will be found that the Maya civilization originated in the lowlands of northern central Peten, Guatemala, either at, or in the immediate vicinity of the great ruined
cities of Tikal and Uaxactun, as already mentioned.

THE OLDEST SURELY DATED OBJECTS IN THE MAYA AREA

The earliest, surely contemporaneous date in the Maya hieroglyphic writing is that engraved on the back of the Leyden Plate,
a small celt-like object of jade, 8½ inches long by 3 inches wide,
found near Puerto Barrios, Guatemala, in 1864; this records the
Maya date 8.14.3.1.12, corresponding to 320 of the Christian
Era (Plate 15, *b*). By contemporaneous date is here meant the
date the Leyden Plate was actually engraved, not an earlier date,
commemorating some past event in Maya history.

Now the captive figure lying on the ground behind the standing, principal figure, a detail found carved on the front of the
Leyden Plate (Plate 15, *a*), so closely resembles the captive
figures on all the monuments at Tikal, where this particular motive
is also portrayed, and, at the same time, it is so entirely different
from all other representations of the captive-figure motive found
elsewhere in the Old Empire that there can be no doubt the Leyden
Plate, although not actually found at Tikal, was surely executed
there. If so, the oldest Maya city now known on the basis of the
dated remains is Tikal in northern central Peten, which, it so
happens, is also the largest of all the ancient Maya ceremonial
centers, in either the Old or the New Empire (chapter xiii, p. 320).

Again, the oldest large stone monument or stela[2] now known
is Stela 9 at Uaxactun, which has carved upon its back (Plate 16, *b*)
the Maya date 8.14.10.13.15 (A.D. 328), only seven and two-
thirds years later than the date of the Leyden Plate, which we have
just seen was probably executed at the near-by city of Tikal, only
11 miles south of Uaxactun. Thus the two earliest contemporaneous Maya dates are found at cities within 11 miles of each other
in northern central Peten; we may therefore conclude that the

---

[2] Stela is the name given by archaeologists to the shaft-like monuments of the
ancient Maya.

Maya civilization was well under way by the beginning of the
fourth century of the Christian Era in this region at the very topo-
graphical center of the Yucatan Peninsula (Plate 1).

MAYA-SPEAKING PEOPLES ON A PRE-MAYA CULTURAL HORIZON IN PETEN

Glancing backward for a moment, it will be remembered that
we have placed Maya-speaking people in the highlands of Guatemala for at least several thousand years before the birth of Christ,
and, further, have credited some Maya-speaking group living in
this same general region with having invented agriculture, as
applied to the cultivation of maize, sometime during the third or
second millenium before Christ (Pre-Maya I, Table III).

Prior to this extremely early period it is probable that the
Yucatan Peninsula, particularly the Peten lowlands, may have
been, indeed probably were, occupied by nomadic peoples, who
lived by hunting and fishing and on the natural products of the
forest—fruits, nuts, roots, and grasses—*long before the knowledge of maize culture reached them from the Guatemala highlands to the south.* If this should be correct, I am certain that these
pre-agricultural nomads of the Peten lowlands must have been
Maya-speaking.

Although the suggestion is purely tentative, since the actual
facts escape verification at this time, it appears probable that
Maya-speaking people from the highlands of Guatemala, carrying the knowledge of maize culture with them, had either themselves pushed northward into all parts of the Yucatan Peninsula
—the Peten lowlands as well as northern Yucatan—or had transmitted the knowledge of corn to that region, a thousand years or
more before the birth of Christ (Pre-Maya II, Table III) and
that a culture based on corn cultivation had flourished there for
still another six or seven hundred years (Pre-Maya III, Table
III) before the beginning of the Maya civilization in northern
central Peten during the early fourth century of the Christian Era.

These speculations as to the people who were living in the
Peten lowlands before the development of the Maya civilization

there, it should be borne in mind, are purely conjectural, though I feel reasonably confident that we may reach two definite conclusions concerning them: (1) the peoples of the two periods immediately preceding the Maya Old Empire (Pre-Maya II and III) were agriculturists, and (2) they spoke some early Maya language.

If we assume that the original inhabitants of the Peten lowlands were Maya-speaking people, who lived by hunting, fishing, and upon the wild products of the forest (Pre-Maya I), to whom later the practice of agriculture was introduced (Pre-Maya II and III) but who continued to live without those higher cultural manifestations which have been defined at the beginning of this chapter as the diagnostic characteristics of the Maya civilization, we are probably not far from correct in the general picture of the human occupation of the Yucatan Peninsula before the beginnings of the Maya civilization early in the fourth century after Christ.

BEGINNINGS OF THE MAYA HIEROGLYPHIC WRITING

We have seen that the earliest Maya dates which may be regarded as surely contemporaneous fall in the first third of the fourth century of the Christian Era (320 and 328), that is to say at the close of the third quarter of Baktun 8 of the Maya Era—8.14.3.1.12 and 8.14.10.13.15, respectively. Both the Leyden Plate and Stela 9 at Uaxactun, however, in addition to presenting the two earliest contemporaneous dates known, have another extremely significant characteristic in common: although the technique of carving in each shows that when they were executed stone carving among the ancient Maya was still in its infancy, was indeed crude, clumsy, and stilted, the calendric data presented by each (the corresponding date in the Maya chronological era), on the other hand, is completely developed; like Minerva it is born fully armed and ready to function. Maya chronology is extremely complicated (pp. 282–89) and yet, when we first encounter examples of it on the Leyden Plate and on Stela 9 at Uaxactun, this elaborate system for counting time is completely developed. There are no simple beginnings, no elementary first

steps which must have preceded the development of the perfected
system. On the contrary, when we first meet it on these two
earliest-known dated objects, it is already complete with all its
intricacies—a flower in full blossom, with no preliminary bud
stage having survived to show how it had developed.

Archaeologists have concluded, from this total absence of
examples showing the earlier stages in the development of the
Maya hieroglyphic writing and chronology, that both originally
must have been recorded on some medium other than stone; that
the first Maya monuments were, in fact, made of some perishable
material like wood, excellent hard varieties of which are to be
found in greatest abundance throughout the Peten forests; and
finally that these earliest wooden monuments, upon which the
beginnings of the Maya hieroglyphic writing and chronology
were carved, have all been destroyed by the moist climate and
heavy rains of the Peten lowlands. With their total destruction, all traces of the earliest stages of Maya writing and chronology have disappeared (Pre-Maya III, Table III).

THE MAYA CHRONOLOGICAL SYSTEM
PROBABLY THE PRODUCT OF A SINGLE MIND

A long time, probably centuries, must have elapsed, while
the early Maya astronomers, by the slow and laborious process
of trial and error, were making and preserving observations on
the sun in order to determine the exact length of the tropical
year (365.24+ days), and probably on the moon as well, in order
to determine the exact length of a single lunation (29.52+ days).
However, once the true lengths of these two periods had been
determined—and the ancient Maya had measured both with
extraordinary accuracy—the development of the Maya calendar
and their superb chronological system could have followed, and
I believe did follow, in a very short time, probably in the span
of a single lifetime, or at most of two or three.

The Maya chronological system is so complex, so delicately
built and balanced, that it is difficult to believe it could have
developed slowly, part here, part there, until it gradually took

final form. On the contrary, it seems more than probable that it was the work of a single mind, possibly working with a few associates, some ancient Maya Hipparchus, who brought the Maya chronological system to perfection in his own lifetime, although the solar and lunar data upon which it was based doubtless had been accumulating for a number of centuries before his time.

MAYA CHRONOLOGY PROBABLY DEVISED DURING FOURTH OR THIRD CENTURY BEFORE CHRIST

There is internal evidence in the Maya chronological system itself that it was first devised, according to one authority, at the end of Baktun 7, that is in 7.0.0.0.0 of the Maya Era (353 B.C.) or, according to others, shortly later, that is in 7.6.0.0.0 (235 B.C.), probably either at Tikal, or at the near-by Uaxactun in northern central Peten.

During the six to seven centuries which elapsed between the invention of Maya chronology on the one hand, and the earliest known contemporaneous stone records (the Leyden Plate at Tikal and Stela 9 at Uaxactun) on the other, the Maya monuments were, in all probability, carved out of wood, and during these same six or seven centuries the Maya priests developed their unique hieroglyphic writing precisely in order to record their, at that time, newly devised chronological system.

With the first stone records at Tikal and Uaxactun in the early part of the fourth century of the Christian Era, the Maya Old Empire may be considered as having formally gotten under way.

MAYA ART, ARCHITECTURE, AND CERAMICS IN AGREE-MENT WITH THE EPIGRAPHY

But it is not only the Maya epigraphy alone which suggests the Tikal-Uaxactun region as the immediate birthplace of the Maya civilization; there are three other outstanding lines of cultural evidence—the art, architecture, and ceramics of these two cities, which also indicate the same thing.

In addition to Stela 9 at Uaxactun there are at least ten other monuments in this city—four actually dated and six others approximately dated by means of their respective stylistic characteristics, all of which date from the last quarter of Baktun 8 of the Maya Era (337–435). The human figures on the fronts of these monuments are poorly proportioned, crudely executed, clumsy, wooden, and lifeless. They are shown usually in modified left profile (Plate 16, *a*), though an occasional figure also appears in modified right profile (Plate 63, *c*); the feet are in tandem position, the toe of the near (left) foot touching the heel of the far (right) foot (Plate 16, *a*). The arms and torso, on the other hand, are portrayed in full front, the head again being in left or right profile, as the case may be. This awkward and physically all-but-impossible posture is typical of the figures on all the earliest-known Maya stone sculptures. It is evident from the technical as well as the esthetic inferiority of these earliest monuments that stone sculpture was only just beginning when they were carved. Later the ancient Maya stone carvers were to soar to previously unimagined heights of sculptural achievement, but in those remote times, toward the end of Baktun 8 of Maya chronology (the fourth century of the Christian Era), they were still groping clumsily, timidly feeling their way in the sculpture of stone, their hands and stone chisels as yet unfamiliar with the new medium, so much more difficult to carve than wood. This very early position of the human figure, found nowhere else in the whole Maya area, except at Uaxactun and Tikal, is truly primitive and surely represents the beginnings of stone sculpture in the Yucatan Peninsula (pp. 362, 363).

The architectural evidence as to the relatively remote antiquity of Uaxactun is equally impressive (chapter xiii). Stylistically considered, the earliest construction yet found in the whole Maya area is the stucco-covered pyramid, E-VII-sub (Plate 17, *b*) which was found completely buried inside the later pyramid, E-VII (Plate 17, *a*) at this city. The style of the stucco masks (Plate 58) which adorn the sides of this buried pyramid is such as to indicate strongly that at the time they were executed the canons of Maya art were just beginning to crystallize. Indeed,

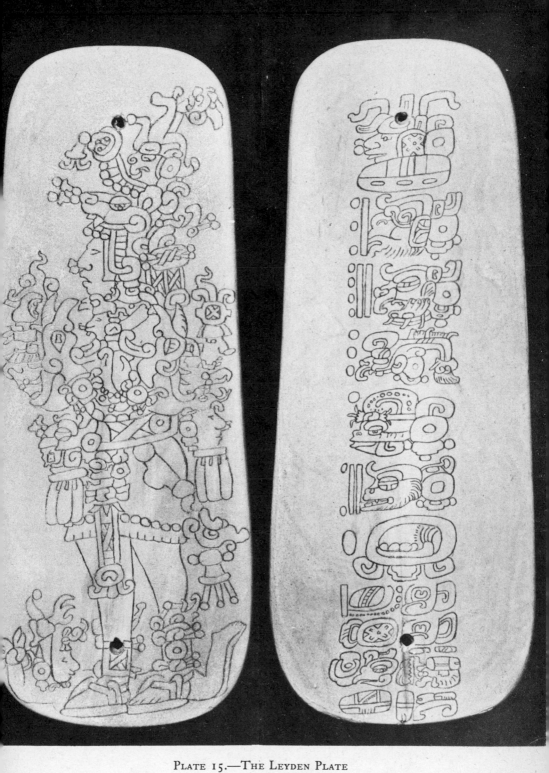

PLATE 15.—THE LEYDEN PLATE

A carved jade pendant, the earliest dated object known from the Maya area.

 a) Front.

↑ *b*) Back.

PLATE 16.—STELA 9, UAXACTUN, PETEN, GUATEMALA

The earliest dated monument known in the Maya area.

↑ *a*) E-VII before excavation.

PLATE 17.—PYRAMIDS E-VII AND E-VII-SUB, UAXACTUN, PETEN, GUATEMALA

↓ *b*) E-VII-sub after excavation, the earliest masonry construction known in the Maya area.

a) Lintel 1,
Oxkintok,
Yucatan,
Mexico.

←

PLATE 18.—SCULPTURES OF THE
OLD EMPIRE

←

b) Stela 11
(back), Yax-
chilan, Chia-
pas, Mexico.

c) Stela 12
(front), Pie-
dras Negras,
Peten, Gua-
temala. →

these masks are so simple and undeveloped as to suggest almost
a pre-Maya origin, as though the esthetic complex, later to be
known as Maya art, was only just coming into being when they
were molded in stucco. Again, the buried pyramid, E-VII-sub,
never had supported a masonry building on its summit, though
four stucco-filled postholes in the lime-plaster flooring on top of
this pyramid indicate that originally it had supported a superstructure of some perishable material, probably of poles and
thatch. The absence of any signs of a masonry superstructure ever
having stood on the summit of this buried pyramid almost certainly indicates that Maya stone buildings with their typical corbeled stone roof-vaulting, had not yet been developed when
E-VII-sub was built.

Finally, although the ceramics of the Maya Old Empire have
not yet been sufficiently studied to permit basic general conclusions on such fundamental points as priority of origin and centers
of distribution of the different types of pottery found therein,
nevertheless, excavations in the refuse heaps and below plaza
floor-levels at Uaxactun have brought to light in the so-called
"black-dirt stratum," which is the lowest level showing human
occupation at this site, the earliest types of pottery and clay figurines yet found anywhere in the Peninsula of Yucatan; types
moreover, especially among the figurines, which strongly resemble
objects from even earlier, non-Maya agricultural horizons in the
highlands of Mexico, Guatemala, and El Salvador (chapter xv).

Thus the four principal lines of archaeological evidence that
are available in the Maya field—the epigraphy, art, architecture,
and ceramics—all indicate that the antecedents of the Maya
civilization had their origin in northern central Peten, in the Tikal-
Uaxactun region, sometime during the three or four centuries
immediately preceding and following the beginning of the Christian Era, that is Pre-Maya III (Table III).

THE OLD EMPIRE

MEANING OF THE TERMS OLD AND NEW EMPIRES

THE TERMS Old Empire and New Empire, it should be made very clear at the outset, once and for all, have no political connotation whatsoever, as used throughout this book; on the contrary, they are employed exclusively in a cultural or esthetic sense, indicating an empire of common thought, common language, common customs, common religion, and common art—a homogeneous people, enjoying a common civilization but, in no sense of the word, political unity.

It will be pointed out in a later chapter (pp. 159–61), where Maya governmental and social organization is described, that there are no known Maya Alexanders, Caesars, Charlemagnes, or Napoleons, but rather the Maya Old Empire would seem to have been composed of a number of city-states, which were ruled, if we may judge by conditions surely known to have prevailed during New Empire times, two to five centuries later, by hereditary dynasties, the members of which filled not only all the highest civil offices of the state but also the highest eccleciastical positions as well.

Without anticipating the more detailed discussion of the governmental organization of the ancient Maya in chapter ix, it may be noted here that the closest analogy to it offered in the Old World would seem to be the city-states of classic Greece—Athens, Sparta, and Corinth, which were united by a common language, religion, and culture, but each of which was politically independent of the others.

In a word, while there is no evidence either for or against the political unity of the various Old Empire cities, there can be no doubt that they all shared a common culture.

In attempting to reconstruct Old Empire history we are confronted at the outset with an all-but-insuperable difficulty—there are no documentary sources relating to this early period, not even vague traditions which might shed a light, however faint, upon the events of this remote epoch of the Maya story. The sixteenth-century Spanish and native historians give much information about later New Empire history, but at best the Spanish sources do not extend back beyond the twelfth century; and the native sources, while they describe a few events which took place as early as the first half of the fifth century (the Early Period of the Old Empire), do so only for the then-provincial northern half of the peninsula, that is Yucatan.

ARCHAEOLOGICAL DATA FOR OLD EMPIRE HISTORY

If we are to trace the rise and development of Old Empire history, it will be found that we shall have to depend upon such archaeological data as have been developed by excavation and upon close study of the Old Empire cities themselves, their epigraphy, art (sculptures and frescoes), architecture, and ceramics. First, and most important of all, is the evidence supplied by the dated monuments, which, by themselves alone, provide a thoroughly reliable chronological framework for Old Empire history. Second, the sculpture and architecture establish stylistic trends; they indicate the boundaries and distribution of archaeologic subprovinces; they outline areas of special influence—in a word, reflect the interplay of those forces which brought about the development, florescence, and decline of the Old Empire. Third and last, the ceramic remains, especially as found in stratified refuse heaps, faithfully register the slightest changes in the most common craft of the mass of the people, namely, pottery making. Because of its universal utility, pottery closely reflects the domestic habits of its makers. Changes due to outside influences are quickly reflected in bowls, vases, pitchers, and plates, while the position of different wares in stratified refuse heaps, which are nothing more than the accumulated debris of living of the common people, show not only the different influences to which these wares have been successively subjected, but also the order in which such influences have made themselves felt. Finally the presence of occasional pottery trade-pieces sometimes permits time relations with other cultures to be established.

If we interpret the archaeological evidence gleaned from a study of the surface remains and from the excavations, in the light of conditions obtaining among the Maya of the New Empire, which are much better known, we shall come as near to a reconstruction of the major trends of Old Empire history as is possible in the present state of knowledge.

THREE PRINCIPAL PERIODS OF THE OLD EMPIRE

The Old Empire for convenience in description may be divided into three principal periods: Early, Middle, and Great. The Early Period may be considered as having begun with the earliest contemporaneous date, 8.14.3.1.12 (A.D. 320), or three years earlier in round numbers of the Maya Era (8.14.0.0.0 (A.D. 317), and as having ended with the close of the first half of Baktun 9, that is, 9.10.0.0.0 (A.D. 633), by which time the last traces of archaism had finally disappeared from Maya sculpture and epigraphy. The foregoing starting point has been arbitrarily selected, as is necessarily the case in dealing with such a complex problem as the beginnings of any culture, but in the case of the Maya civilization, at least, it seems safe to regard its earliest contemporaneous date now known as also that of its formal beginning. The Early Period of the Old Empire is thus regarded here as having extended from A.D. 317 to 633, a little more than three centuries (Old Empire I, Table III). For a number of centuries prior to 317 it is obvious that the ancient Maya had been accumulating cultural experience to the point where they finally were able to carve their first stone monuments. Perhaps as early as the fourth or third century B.C. they had begun to carve monuments out of wood; but this is pure speculation, whereas the Leyden Plate and Stela 9 at Uaxactun are hard archaeologic facts, for which reason 8.14.0.0.0 has been chosen as the date of the formal be-

ginning of the Old Empire, this date being the next katun (or
20-year period) ending *before* the date of the Leyden Plate (only
three years earlier).

The Middle Period began in 9.10.0.0 (A.D. 633) and extended to 9.15.0.0 (A.D. 731), just under a hundred years (Old Empire II, Table III). During this century the Old Empire Maya were consolidating the extensive territorial and cultural gains they had made during the Early Period and were preparing for the tremendous florescence which was to follow during the Great Period.

The Great Period, roughly two and a half centuries in length, began in 9.15.0.0 (A.D. 731) and closed about 10.8.0.0 (A.D. 987). During the first two-thirds of this last period of the Old Empire, the Maya reached esthetic heights never equaled by any other people of pre-Columbian America, and, indeed, never again equaled by the Maya themselves (Old Empire III, Table III); whereas the last third, in complete contrast, was a period of decadence and decline.

While it is true that the foregoing division of the Old Empire into three periods is based primarily upon the stylistic evidence presented by Old Empire sculpture, it will be found, nevertheless, that these same three stylistic-chronologic periods are also clearly reflected in the corresponding ceramic and architectural evidence, as may be seen in Table III.

The two first ceramic periods found in central Peten—Mamom and Chicanel—*precede the beginning* of the Old Empire and the carving of stone monuments; that is, they precede the beginning of the Maya civilization as defined here; and the Mamom ceramic period even precedes the beginning of stone architecture. This latter important cultural advance would seem to have made its first appearance in the Chicanel ceramic period. If we assign, as a minimum, the six or seven centuries from the beginning of the first millenium before Christ down to the fourth or third century before Christ, to the Mamom ceramic period (Pre-Maya II, Table III), and the first three or four centuries before Christ and the first three centuries after Christ, to the Chicanel period

(Pre-Maya III, Table III), we shall probably not be far from correct in terms of our own chronology.

Sculptured stone stelae, Period I of corbeled roof-vaulting, and Tzakol pottery probably all made their appearance together at the commencement of the fourth century of the Christian Era —the beginning of the Maya civilization and the Old Empire as these terms are used here (Old Empire I, Table III).

The Tzakol ceramic period is divided into three subperiods, the first having extended approximately from A.D. 317 to 514; the second from about 514 to 554; and the third from about 554 to 633, or to the close of the Early Period. These three ceramic subperiods coincide with Period I of corbeled roof-vaulting. The Tepeu ceramic phase which followed is also divided into three subperiods, the first having extended from about 633 to 731, that is, coincident with the Middle Period (Old Empire II, Table III); the second from about 731 to 909, coincident with the first two-thirds of the Great Period; and the third subperiod from about 909 to 987, that is, after monumental activity had ceased, down to the final abandonment of the Old Empire region in the tenth century. The Tepeu ceramic period coincides with Period II of corbeled roof-vaulting (Old Empire III, Table III).

The architectural and ceramic correspondence with the sculptural-chronologic periods of the pre–Old Empire and Old Empire will be described more fully in chapters xiv and xv (pp. 358 and 382), but sufficient data have been given here to show that there is real agreement between Maya epigraphy (chronology) and art (sculpture) on the one hand and between Maya architecture and ceramics on the other.

THE EARLY PERIOD—THE RISE AND SPREAD OF THE MAYA
CIVILIZATION (OLD EMPIRE I—8.14.0.0.0 TO
9.10.0.0.0 [317–633])

If the Leyden Plate was carved at Tikal, as I firmly believe, despite the fact that it was actually found some 140 miles to the southeast of that site, near the modern town of Puerto Barrios, Guatemala, then Tikal, on the basis of the dated remains, is the

oldest known center of the Maya civilization. If, on the other
hand, it was executed elsewhere, then Uaxactun with the earliest
known stone monument, Stela 9, becomes the oldest center of
Maya culture.

It matters little whether Tikal or Uaxactun be chosen as the
oldest Maya city now known, since in point of time the Leyden
Plate is only seven and two-thirds years older than Stela 9, and in
distance, Tikal is only eleven miles south of Uaxactun, both sites
being located at the very topographic center of the Yucatan Peninsula. Uaxactun stands at the upper end of a small valley which
heads into the divide on the north side of the interior drainage
basin of central Peten; the small stream meandering down this
valley eventually finds its way into the Hondo River and thence
northeastward into the Caribbean Sea, while Tikal is located
either at the very head of the Holmul Valley, the waters of which
also eventually flow into the Hondo River, or, less probably, it
stands at the northern edge of, and within, the interior drainage
basin (Plate 19).

At this very early date in Maya history—the beginning of the
fourth century of the Christian Era—sculptured stone monuments, corbeled-stone roof-vaulting, and Tzakol pottery as well
had just made their first appearance at Uaxactun. Even if it be
accepted that the Leyden Plate was executed at Tikal in 320, no
monuments surely earlier than 475 have yet been found at this
latter site, although there is one doubtfully dated stela perhaps
assignable to the closing katun or 20-year period of Baktun 8
(416). At Uaxactun, on the other hand, there are no fewer than
six dated monuments, three of which are surely and three probably
referable to Baktun 8. Finally, in addition to these six dated
stelae, there are at least four other monuments at Uaxactun which
on stylistic grounds are probably also referable to Baktun 8. Indeed, of the only five monuments now known which surely date
from Baktun 8, three are found at Uaxactun, and one each at
Uolantun and Balakbal, the former a very small site only twelve
miles south of Uaxactun, the latter a small-to-medium-sized site
only thirty-five miles north of Uaxactun (Plate 19).

As to which is the older, Tikal or Uaxactun, it is difficult to choose between them. Assuming that the Leyden Plate was executed at Tikal, as I believe on the basis of its stylistic characteristics, then Tikal has a date seven and two-thirds years earlier than the earliest known date at Uaxactun. Again Tikal is the largest center of the Maya civilization (chapter xiii, pp. 320–23), while Uaxactun is only a Class 2 center. On the other hand, the earliest dated monument at Uaxactun is nearly a century earlier than the oldest monument even doubtfully dated at Tikal, and, as noted above, Uaxactun has ten monuments dating from Baktun 8, compared to only the one doubtfully dated Baktun 8 monument at Tikal. If the provenance of the earliest dated object now known (the Leyden Plate) and the greater size of Tikal are to be accepted as our guideposts in this matter, then Tikal is the older; if, on the other hand, the earliest dated monument, and not only one but ten of them be accepted as a more reliable indication of greater age, then Uaxactun is the older.

As between the two, I believe that Tikal is probably a little older than Uaxactun, an unsatisfactory conclusion for me since I discovered the latter city. That no certain Baktun 8 monuments have yet been found at Tikal is probably to be explained by the fact that no serious excavations have ever been undertaken there; while Uaxactun, on the other hand, is the most extensively excavated center of the Old Empire. It is entirely possible, indeed probable, that when Tikal has been as largely dug over and as minutely studied as Uaxactun, Baktun 8 monuments will almost certainly also be found there. However, since most of the known earliest monuments are at Uaxactun, it is better for us to start the Maya story there.

Stela 9 at Uaxactun, dedicated in A.D. 328, begins the Maya monumental record (Plate 16). I discovered this monument, still standing on the Acropolis at Group A of this city, on May 5, 1916, but there are strong grounds for believing that originally it had been set up in an outlying section of the city, now known as Group E, and that at some later time, it had been removed to its present position on the Acropolis.

The next two monuments at Uaxactun are twins, both having been erected on the same side of the same plaza (east side of the Main Plaza at Group E, Fig. 33, p. 333), both on precisely the same day—February 3, 357.

With the dedication of Stelae 18 and 19 in 8.16.0.0.0 of the Maya Era, that is at the end of an even katun, or 20-year period (here the end of Katun 16 of Baktun 8), of the Maya chronological era, a practice was inaugurated that was destined to endure for nearly twelve centuries.

The observances of this custom of erecting monuments at the *ends* of successive periods in their chronological era was one of the most fundamental facts of ancient Maya life. At first the ends of even katuns, or approximately 20-year periods (exactly 19.7 years), only were chosen for the celebration of this ceremony; but shortly, as their resources grew and their economic strength increased, the ceremonial centers of the Old Empire were able to erect these stone period-markers more frequently, and the ends of lahuntuns or half-katuns, approximately ten-year periods (exactly 9.8 years), were next chosen, in addition to the katun-endings, for this important ceremony. It should be noted in passing that the ten-year period was the interval commonly selected for the erection of the period-markers throughout Old Empire times.

Toward the end of the Early Period, for the first time in 9.8.15.0.0, that is A.D. 608, at Piedras Negras in western Peten, we find a monument being erected at the end of a hotun or quarter-katun as well, approximately a five-year period (exactly 4.9 years). However, the practice of marking the five-year period-endings by the erection of corresponding monuments proved too costly, too great a strain on the great majority of the Old Empire centers, and only two of them—Piedras Negras and Quirigua—regularly followed this practice, although a few others, notably Copan and Naranjo, occasionally erected their period-markers once every five years. In other words, using the analogy of a grandfather clock, all Old Empire sites, culturally as well as economically able to erect monuments at all were able to strike the hours, that is, to erect monuments at the ends of the successive katuns, and most of them were also able to strike the half-hours as well, that is, to erect monuments at the ends of the intermediate half-katuns or lahuntuns. However, only the two cities above mentioned in the entire Old Empire region were able to, or at least did, strike the quarter-hours regularly, that is, erect monuments every quarter-katun, or hotun, in addition to erecting them on the katun—and lahuntun-endings as well.

We have seen that the earliest monument at Uaxactun, Stela 9, did not follow this practice, having been erected in 8.14.10.13.15 (in other words, on a date that did not coincide with a period-ending), but that Stelae 18 and 19, the two next oldest monuments at this city, both dedicated in 8.16.0.0.0 (less than thirty years later), were the first two monuments to conform to this practice. We may therefore conclude, that in so far as the evidence now available is concerned, this practice of erecting their monuments at the ends of even periods of their era originated at Uaxactun, sometime between 328 and 357.

From the cities of Tikal and Uaxactun in northern central Peten, as its two principal centers of cultural inspiration, the Maya civilization began to expand during the last quarter of Baktun 8 of the Maya era (337–435). At first the new culture spread slowly; indeed only two other small centers, Balakbal and Uolantun, both within 35 miles of Uaxactun, are now known, which have monuments dating from Baktun 8 (Plate 19); but by the beginning of Baktun 9 (435) Maya culture is surely and strongly embarked on its long and brilliant career.

The century embraced by the first quarter of Baktun 9 (435–534) witnessed a tremendous expansion of the sculptured stela–corbeled roof-vaulting–Tzakol pottery complex. In all directions, from northern central Peten as its center of distribution, the rich, new, priest-inspired culture with its amazing chronology, sculpture, architecture, and typical pottery spread to all parts of the Yucatan Peninsula and adjacent highlands to the south, though for the first two decades of this century (435–455) Uaxactun and Tikal, so far as now known, still remain the only two monument-erecting centers.

The custom of erecting sculptured stone monuments had probably spread to Copan on the extreme southeastern frontier of the Maya area, or more than 200 miles south and a little east of the nuclear central region, as early as 465 (Plate 19).

Other cities erecting sculptured stone monuments for the first time during the first quarter of Baktun 9 (435–534) were Cerro de las Mesas (467); Oxkintok and Altar de Sacrificios (475); Tonina (495); Xultun, Piedras Negras, Yaxchilan, Palenque, and Calakmul (514); and Naachtun (524).

A glance at the map of the Maya area in Plate 19 will show that, by the end of the first quarter of Baktun 9, Maya culture had spread to all parts of the Yucatan Peninsula (the only region it ever was to occupy); to the Usumacinta Valley in the west—Altar de Sacrificios, Yaxchilan, Piedras Negras, and Palenque; to the southeastern highlands—Copan; to the southwestern highlands— Tonina; and to central and northern Yucatan—Calakmul and Oxkintok.

About the end of the first quarter of Baktun 9, the early phase of Tzakol pottery changes to the middle phase, perhaps owing to the tremendous spread of Maya culture and the consequent reaction of new influences on the then current ceramic wares of central Peten, Early Tzakol (Table III).

The occupation of the entire Yucatan Peninsula and adjacent highlands to the southeast and southwest by Maya culture in early Baktun 9 is to be interpreted as indicating that the environmental factors of the nuclear region no longer presented any real difficulties to the already strongly entrenched and advancing Maya. During this century they pushed into all parts of the Maya homeland, founding new cities and enlarging the older ones. The extensive phase of Old Empire history was concluded, the intensive phase about to begin.

Ten new cities appear in the monument-erecting group during the second quarter of Baktun 9 (534–633)—Tulum (564), Pusilha (573), Ichpaatun (593), Yaxha (close of the sixth century), Uxul (613), Naranjo (615), Tzibanche (619), Coba (623), Chinkultic (628), and El Encanto (first half of seventh century).

A glance at the map in Plate 19 will show that five of these new centers were established in the central nuclear region—El Encanto, Yaxha, Naranjo, Pusilha, and Uxul; one in the southwestern highlands—Chinkultic; and four in northeastern Yucatan—Tzibanche, Ichpaatun, Tulum, and Coba, the last destined to become in later times one of the greatest centers of the New Empire.

The end of the first half of Baktun 9 (9.10.0.0.0 or A.D. 633) coincided with the end of the Early Period of the Old Empire. At, or about the same time, the Tzakol ceramic phase and Period I of corbeled roof-vaulting both also seem to have come to an end (Table III).

By the end of the Early Period the large cities had all been erecting carved stone period-markers, the oldest of them for more than three centuries, and this custom was still spreading. It was indeed, one of the most fundamental and persistently followed practices of Maya culture. At the beginning, when the first stone monuments were erected, as already explained, no regular interval seems to have determined the dates of their respective dedications; but very early, as early as the beginning of the last quarter of Baktun 8, the dates chosen for this important, recurrent ceremonial would seem to have been the closing days of the successive katuns, or twenty-year periods. Later, we have seen that as the cities of the Old Empire waxed in power and wealth a shorter interval was adopted, so that they could erect their monuments more frequently, that is, on the half-katun endings as well. And still later, toward the close of the Early Period, at Piedras Negras in 9.8.15.0.0 (608), for the first time a monument was also erected on a hotun—or a quarter-katun ending. This last practice did not have many adherents, however, only two cities, Piedras Negras and Quirigua, having followed it consistently.

Why only two sites marked every passing hotun-ending, while all the others did not, remains an unsolved mystery. Possibly lack of enough economic strength to erect a sculptured stone monument as often as once every five years, or perhaps lack of necessary cultural leadership to do so may explain this fact; or again insufficient interest among the people as a whole to celebrate this

festival so frequently may be the correct answer; the truth is that
we do not know.

This practice of erecting monuments at the ends of even periods of their era, it cannot be overemphasized, was one of the most important facts of ancient Maya life. It must have influenced and absorbed the activities of a considerable part of the population of every Maya center where monuments were erected, and, finally, it must not only have determined the time for some of their most important festivals and ceremonials but also must have profoundly affected their religion as well. It is, in fine, the most fundamental phase of Old Empire ceremonial life of which we have archaeological evidence, and the persistence with which it prevailed, practically unchanged for more than eleven centuries, is ample proof that it was one of the most deep-rooted customs of their own times.

By the end of the Early Period all parts of the Maya area had been brought under the stimulating influence of the Maya civilization; even the far-flung regions in the distant north and southwest had already begun to feel the quickening impulse of the higher priestly culture. The Maya world was now completely delimited; there remained only its more intensive occupation.

THE MIDDLE PERIOD—THE CONSOLIDATION AND DEVELOPMENT
OF PREVIOUS CULTURAL GAINS (OLD EMPIRE II—
9.10.0.0.0 TO 9.15.0.0.0 [633–731])

The Middle Period is relatively short, just under a hundred years. It was a century given over to consolidating the tremendous territorial gains made in the Early Period, while in sculpture the idiosyncracies of the Peten limestone were finally mastered, paving the way for the great sculptural masterpieces of the next century. In architecture, Period II of corbeled roof-vaulting replaced Period I, and continued to the end of the Old Empire and slightly beyond. In ceramics, a new phase had been introduced, early Tepeu (Table III). It was a century of preparation, of cultural intensification, of ripening experience for the Golden Age which was to follow.

During the Middle Period, at least fourteen new ceremonial centers seem to have been established; El Tortuguero (645), Jaina (652), El Amparo (665), Etzna (669), Tila (685), Quirigua, Tzendales, Lacanha, and Quexil (692), El Palmar (711), Itsimte and Xamantun (721), La Florida and Oxpemul (731).

We see in Plate 19 that all parts of the Old Empire region are still growing: Itsimte, El Palmar, Xamantun, and Oxpemul in the central nuclear region; Tzendales, Lacanha, La Florida, and El Tortuguero in the Usumacinta Valley, Quirigua in the southeast; El Amparo, Quexil, and Tila in the southwest highlands, and Jaina and Etzna in the northwestern part of the peninsula (state of Campeche, Mexico). Of the fourteen centers founded during the Middle Period, only two, Quirigua and Etzna, were destined to become cities of outstanding importance, the former because of its complete series of superlatively fine sculptured monuments, and the latter because of its striking and extensive architectural remains.

With the close of the Middle Period in 731, the early Tepeu ceramic phase also came to an end. The Old Empire Maya now stood at the threshold of the Great Period; they were ripe for an extraordinary cultural florescence. Stone sculpture already had four centuries of experience behind it; its subject matter was developed, its traditions and technique fixed. The stage was set for outstanding esthetic achievement, the curtain about to rise on the most brilliant act of the ancient Maya drama.

THE GREAT PERIOD—THE GOLDEN AGE, DECLINE AND FALL OF THE OLD EMPIRE
(OLD EMPIRE III—9.15.0.0.0 TO 10.8.0.0.0 [731–987])

During the first three katuns of the Great Period (731–790) the Old Empire continued to expand in every direction, not only in the central nuclear region but also in the peripheral outlands. Although only two new large centers, Seibal and Nakum, both in Peten (Plate 19), reached the point of erecting monuments during this closing phase of the Old Empire, there are eight additional medium-sized and smaller centers, also in Peten or in the

immediately adjoining region to the east—Tayasal-Flores, Polol,
La Milpa, Ixlu, Ixkun, Tzimin Kax, Ucanal, and Benque Viejo
—and at least twelve other small sites, six in the Usumacinta
Valley immediately to the west—La Amelia, El Cayo, El Caribe,
La Mar, Cancuen, and Aguas Calientes; two in the southeastern
highlands—Santa Elena Poco Uinic (Chiapas) and Quen Santo
(Guatemala); one in the southeast—Los Higos (Honduras); and
three in the far north—Santa Rosa Xtampak, Holactun (Campeche) and Chichen Itza (Yucatan, Plate 19), all of which managed to erect one or more monuments for the first time during
the Great Period.

The Maya at the end of Katun 18 (790) were now at their
esthetic apogee. Palenque in the Usumacinta Valley, as much as
a century and a half earlier, at the beginning of the Middle
Period, had begun to produce masterpieces of low relief sculpture
in its temple tablets, a highly specialized medium of esthetic expression found only at this city and at one or two near-by centers,
a medium which reached its most notable example in the tablet
of the Temple of the Cross at Palenque (Plate 32, b), thirty
years later in 692. The latest known example of the low-relief
tablet is the surpassingly beautiful all-hieroglyphic slab of stone
found at the foot of the tower in the Tower Court of the Palace
group, also at Palenque, which was dedicated in 783. Yaxchilan,
also in the Usumacinta Valley, began producing beautiful reliefs
as early as 692 but did not reach her sculptural zenith until 726
in the very fine Lintels 24 (Plate 71, b), 25 (Plate 71, a), and 26
in Structure 23; and, thirty-five years later, in 761, magnificent
stelae were still being erected at this city.

Piedras Negras, also in the Usumacinta Valley, first reached
its plane of highest esthetic production at the very beginning of
the Great Period, in 731, and continued at this high level, producing the greatest masterpieces of Old Empire sculpture down
to 795, a period of sixty-five years, but reaching its peak of sculptural brilliance in 761 in the peerless Lintel, or Wall Panel, 3
from Structure 0-13, the finest sculpture ever produced in ancient
America (Plate 69, a).

Maya sculpture reached its zenith at these three great ceremonial centers of the Usumacinta Valley between 692 and 795,
approximately a century of superlative sculptural achievement,
first at Palenque; next, about a generation later, at Yaxchilan;
last, and still another generation later, at Piedras Negras, where
sculptural art reached an all-time high, not only among the Maya,
but also in all aboriginal America (chapter xiv, p. 368).

At the end of Katun 18 (790), the Old Empire also reached
its widest extension, no fewer than nineteen different cities having
erected period-markers to commemorate this one katun-ending
alone: twelve, Tikal, Naranjo, La Honradez, Ixkun, Tayasal,
Polol, Cancuen, Seibal, Aguas Calientes, Uxul, Calakmul, and
Xamantun in Peten; Piedras Negras in the Usumacinta Valley
immediately west; Copan and Quirigua in the southeast; Tonina,
Santa Elena Poco Uinic and Chinkultic in the southwestern Chiapas highlands; and Etzna in the northern half of the Yucatan
Peninsula. Reference to the diagram in Figure 1 shows graphically this all-time high of monumental activity in 9.18.0.0.0
(790), and further the sharp decline in the practice of erecting
period-markers after Katun 18.

At the end of Katun 19 (810), twelve different cities erected
corresponding period-markers. They were Uaxactun, Naranjo,
Tzimin Kax, La Amelia, Calakmul, and Xamantun in the central
area; Piedras Negras in the Usumacinta Valley to the west;
Quirigua to the southeast; and four other places in the Chiapas
highlands: Chinkultic, Chiapa (the latter yielding the Stone of
Chiapa), and two sculptures of unknown origin, a stela and an altar
now in the National Museum of Mexico. But by the end of the
next katun, that is 10.0.0.0.0 (830), the number of sites which
were able to erect corresponding period-markers had dropped
from twelve to three: Uaxactun and Oxpemul in the central area;
and Tila in the Chiapas highlands.

There was a gain of two sites at the next katun-ending in
10.1.0.0.0 (or 849), five centers having erected period-markers
on this date, all in the central Peten area: Tayasal-Flores, Nakum,
Benque Viejo, Ucanal, and Seibal. But this was the swan-song

MA

Name

Tikal............
Uaxactun.....
Balakbal......
Uolantun......
Copan .....
Cerro de las N
Altar de Sacr
Oxkintok......
Tonina.........
Xultun ......
Yaxchilan....
Piedras Negr
Naachtun.....
Tulum..........
Pusilha ....
Ichpaatun....
La Esperanz
El Encanto...
Naranjo.......
Uxul........
Tzibanche...
Calakmul.....
Coba..........
Chinkultic....
Palenque ...
El Tortuguer
Jaina.........
Etzna.........
Stela, Nationa
Tila ....
Tzendales...
Quexil.........
Morales.......
Quirigua.......
El Palmar...
La Honradez
Xamantun....
Itzimte.........
Oxpemul.....
La Florida..
Seibal.........
Santa Rosa
Polol.........
Holactun......
Nakum.....
La Amelia....
El Cayo......
Ixkun.........
El Caribe....
Los Higos...
Stela, Nation
La Mar.........
Aguas Calier
Cancuen......
Santa Elena
Tayasal-Flor
Ucanal........
Tzimin Kax...
Stone of Chi
Ucanal.....
Ixlu.............
Comitan......
Quen Santo..
Chichen Itz

of Old Empire monumental activity. The next lahuntun-ending
(half-katun), 859, was commemorated by the erection of monuments at two cities only—Xultun and Ixlu, both in central Peten; the next katun-ending, 867, was celebrated by the erection of monuments at three cities—Tikal, Tayasal-Flores, and Seibal, again all in Peten; the next lahuntun-ending, 879, was commemorated by four sites—Ixlu and Xamantun in the central region; Quen Santo in the western Guatemala highlands; and Chichen Itza in northeastern Yucatan.

It is a curious coincidence of ancient Maya history, although only purely accidental and without significance, that the last lahuntun-ending, that of 879, should have been commemorated at two such widely separated points as Chichen Itza in the far northeastern corner of Yucatan and at Quen Santo in the equally distant southwestern highlands of western Guatemala, at least 400 miles apart in an air line (Plate 19).

The last katun of the Old Empire to be commemorated by the dedication of a corresponding monument was 10.3.0.0.0 (889). Only three cities were able to erect monuments on this date—Uaxactun, Xultun, and Xamantun, all in the central area. The next katun-ending, 10.4.0.0.0 (909) is found engraved on a jade gorget, or small plaque, from Tzibanche in southern Quintana Roo, Mexico. This is the latest certain Long Count date to be found anywhere in the Old Empire and, indeed, anywhere in the Yucatan Peninsula.

It is hardly to be presumed that the cities of the Old Empire were abandoned immediately after each had erected its last known monument; and, in fact, there is some evidence to indicate that the late Tepeu ceramic phase extended beyond the cessation of monumental activity. Undoubtedly many people lingered on at various Old Empire cities after the latter had ceased to erect monuments; but I do not believe that the sites long retained their importance as ceremonial centers, or as cultural foci sufficiently strong to carry on the splendid traditions of the past six centuries in art, architecture, ceramics, and religion. Those who stayed behind after the leaders had left suffered further cultural decline.

The old pattern of living, which had depended upon elaborate social and governmental organization, was gone. The last remnants of the Old Empire Maya, living under simpler, less-managed conditions, gradually dwindled in numbers until they too moved elsewhere, joining those who had gone before. That this final exodus from the Old Empire was long delayed after the cessation of monumental activity, taking the latter as representative of the whole complex of high culture, seems unlikely; probably not more than a century at most. Certain it is, that when Cortes crossed Peten from northwest to southeast in 1524–1525, six and a third centuries after the erection of the last monument in this region, all the Old Empire cities were entirely abandoned; and when the first Spaniards saw Yaxchilan and Tikal in 1696, one hundred and seventy-one years still later, both these large cities were found to be completely overgrown with a dense tropical forest.

The periods of time during which the different centers of the Old Empire were occupied, or, more accurately speaking, the periods of time between the earliest and latest known dated monuments at each, are shown in Figure 2. The names of the centers appear in the column at the left. The vertical lines represent the hotun- or 5-tun-endings during the Old Empire; above each line is given the corresponding date in Maya and in Christian chronology. Every *other* line is heavier, indicating the lahuntun-, or 10-tun-endings, and every fourth line, corresponding to the katun-, or 20-tun-endings is still heavier. The thick, solid, horizontal lines indicate the length of time between the earliest and the latest known dates at each site listed. Finally, the beginning or end of any solid horizontal line, shown as broken, indicates that at such sites there are monuments which, on stylistic grounds, though actual dates are lacking, are either earlier or later than the earliest or latest *surely* dated monuments at such sites, as the case may be.

It should be pointed out that in the foregoing summary of Old Empire history mention has been made only of those centers which have datable hieroglyphic inscriptions. If we were

to include the countless smaller settlements, each with its plaza
and three or more associated stone buildings, now in ruins, but
which have no hieroglyphic monuments, the number of Old
Empire centers would be endlessly multiplied. Wherever one
travels in the Department of Peten, Guatemala, the ruined remains of these small ceremonial centers are to be found on every
side, attesting to the former density of population of the Old
Empire region (chapter xiii, pp. 315, 316). Since at present there
is no way of dating these many smaller centers, most of them
nameless and little more than small groups of mounds scattered
through the Peten forests, they cannot be brought into this picture of the Maya Old Empire.

CAUSES OF THE DECLINE AND FALL OF THE OLD EMPIRE

A number of different causes have been suggested by various
authorities as responsible for the decline and fall of the Maya
Old Empire—earthquakes, climatic changes so violent as to ne-
cessitate the abandonment of the region, recurrent epidemics of
malaria and yellow fever, foreign conquest, civil war, intellectual
and esthetic exhaustion following a period of forced productivity
in art, architecture, and sculpture accompanied by corresponding
social decay, political decline, and governmental disorganization,
and finally economic collapse due to the failure of the Maya
agricultural system to meet the ever-growing needs of the increasing population. Let us examine each of these suggestions more
closely before attempting to decide between them.

The first cause, earthquake activity, seems to be the least
likely of all. It rests primarily upon two principal factors—(1)
the present ruined condition of the Old Empire cities, the fallen
temples and palaces and the overthrown, shattered monuments,
and (2) the prevalence of severe earthquakes in the highlands of
Guatemala, immediately south of Peten. Against this suggestion,
however, the following objections may be raised. Although the
Guatemala and Chiapas highlands are frequently, and sometimes
violently, shaken by earthquakes, the Peten lowlands, owing to
their distance from the principal earthquake belt in the highlands

where the heaviest tremors occur and also to the loose character of the Peten soil—humus about a yard in depth—do not experience the heavy shocks of the highlands; when felt at all, earthquakes there are much less severe than in the highlands. Again, all the destruction seen in the Old Empire cities, the disintegrated temples, the dismembered palaces, and the overturned monuments, may easily be accounted for by the rank vegetation, the irresistible tropical growth which in the end levels all before it. Finally, no region, either in the Old World or the New, has ever been generally and permanently abandoned because of earthquake activity. Individual cities, it is true, have been permanently abandoned on account of earthquake and accompanying volcanic activity—witness Pompeii and Herculaneum for example—but whole countries, never; and since the present exuberant vegetation alone is more than sufficient to have brought about the observed destruction of the buildings and the overturning of the monuments, the earthquake hypothesis may be rejected.

The idea that climatic changes brought about the destruction and abandonment of the Old Empire cities is based upon the assumption that the Peten lowlands had a much lower annual rainfall during Old Empire times than they have today, owing to a supposed southward shift of general climatic zones in the Western Hemisphere. This *assumed* decreased rainfall in Peten is further supposed to have brought about better living conditions there, involving less sickness and a less luxuriant vegetation, the latter correspondingly easier for the Maya farmer to manage. Later, toward the end of the Old Empire, the general climatic zones are supposed to have shifted again, this time in the opposite direction (northward), bringing back an increased rainfall to the Peten lowlands; the dry seasons are assumed to have become so short that the bush could no longer be effectively burned, and agriculture, as practiced by the ancient Maya (chapter viii, pp. 152, 153), had to be given up. Diseases became more prevalent as the climate became increasingly worse, until finally the Maya were obliged to abandon the region entirely, seeking new homes elsewhere.

The data upon which this hypothesis is based are derived from evidence concerning past rainfall in central and northern California, as established by the varying thicknesses of the tree-rings in the great redwoods of the latter region. While these tree-rings doubtless present an accurate record of rainfall in the northern half of California for a long period of time, it is highly doubtful that changes in the rainfall of California were accompanied by corresponding changes in the rainfall of a region as distant from California as the southern half of the Yucatan Peninsula, a good twenty-five hundred miles to the southeast. To say nothing of other discrepancies involved in accepting this explanation, twenty-five hundred miles is too great a distance for climatic changes in one region to have affected materially the climate of another region, and this hypothesis may also be rejected.

According to the supporters of the malaria and yellow fever hypothesis, constantly recurring epidemics of these two diseases are supposed to have either so debilitated or so decimated the Old Empire Maya that they were forced to abandon their cities in the supposedly unhealthy Peten lowlands, and to seek more healthful surroundings elsewhere. This explanation must be eliminated at the outset, however, for the simple reason that neither malaria nor yellow fever was prevalent in the Americas before the coming of the white man. This is certainly true of malaria, and probably also true of yellow fever as well. Malaria is known to have been an Old World disease—the marsh fever of Roman times associated with the Pontine marshes—while yellow fever, despite the contentions of some authorities to the contrary, almost surely had a west African origin. The earliest account of yellow fever in the New World, sufficiently accurate to permit its diagnosis as such from the description of the disease, is the epidemic of 1648 in Yucatan. This took place long after the introduction of the first Negro slaves from the west coast of Africa into northern Yucatan, and they probably brought yellow fever with them when they came over from Africa, where the disease is indigenous.

Concerning foreign conquest and civil war as possible causes which may have brought about the fall of the Maya Old Empire and the subsequent abandonment of the region where it flourished, it should be pointed out that any archaeological indications of such hypothetical conquests and wars have not as yet been found. Old Empire sculpture is conspicuously lacking in the representation of warlike scenes, battles, strife, and violence. True, bound captives are occasionally portrayed, but the groups in which they appear are susceptible of religious, even astronomical interpretation, and warfare as such is almost certainly not implicated. Nor do the architecture and ceramics of the Old Empire show that foreign, non-Maya forms had ever been extensively introduced, so that abandonment due to foreign conquest appears to be ruled out. It is not improbable that civil wars may have swept the Old Empire from time to time, coalitions of city-states pitted one against another. Similar internecine strife embroiled the city-states of the New Empire more than once as we shall see in the next chapter; but that such civil wars finally caused the complete abandonment of the Old Empire region, I find it hard to believe, and consequently I also reject the "end by wars" hypothesis.

Again it has been suggested that the tendency toward flamboyancy in Maya art, that is, extravagancy and over-elaboration of design, which became more and more pronounced as the Great Period neared its end, must indicate a corresponding physical, moral, and political decadence among the late Old Empire Maya, sufficient in itself to have brought about the downfall and abandonment of their cities. Even granting that this admitted decadence became the dominant characteristic of Maya art toward the close of the Great Period, it does not necessarily follow that it was due to intellectual and esthetic exhaustion alone. As will be shown in the next section of this chapter, the deterioration of art was but a symptom of a more general decadence, involving all phases of Maya culture, which was a general characteristic of late Old Empire times.

In summing up this question it seems necessary, in order to explain the final collapse of the Old Empire during the ninth century of the Christian Era, to look for a far more immediately

coercive, physical cause. Indeed it seems certain that the principal
force which brought about the extinction of the Old Empire and
the evacuation of the southern lowlands was of much greater
urgency than any of the causes previously suggested—nothing
less, in fact, than the complete failure of their agricultural system
to provide for the ever-increasing food needs of the growing
population.

FAILURE OF THE MAYA AGRICULTURAL SYSTEM

The Maya system of agriculture will be fully considered in
chapter viii (pp. 137–58), and its description will not be anticipated here other than to point out that if it is followed uninter-
ruptedly over a long period of time in any one region, it finally
ceases to yield sufficient crops to support the resident population.
When the Maya civilization first developed in the lowlands of
northern Peten during the centuries immediately preceding the
birth of Christ, this region was densely forested. However, the
repeated clearing and burning of ever-increasing areas of forest to
serve as corn lands gradually converted the original forests into
man-made grasslands, artificial savannas. When this process was
complete, or nearly so, when the primeval forests had been largely
felled and replaced in time by these artificially produced grasslands, then agriculture as practiced by the ancient Maya came to an
end, since they had no implements whatsoever for turning the soil
—no hoes, picks, harrows, spades, shovels, or plows.

The agricultural-collapse hypothesis, first advanced by plant
biologists of the United States Department of Agriculture, is by no
means proved, but I believe that it far better explains the observed
archaeological facts than any of the others suggested. It best explains the progressive cessation of dated monuments in the different Old Empire centers, which events, we have seen, occurred not
all at once but scattered over a period of about a century. The
replacing of the original forests by man-made savannas, thus
marking the end of cultivation so far as Maya agricultural
methods were concerned, must have come about very gradually,
reaching a really acute stage at different cities and eventually

causing their respective abandonments at different times (Fig. 2), depending in each case upon such variable factors as relative sizes of the population in question, respective periods of occupation, and general fertility of the surrounding areas.

The point at which complete abandonment and emigration elsewhere finally came to be generally recognized as the only remaining solution for their desperate economic plight must have been reached, in the very nature of the case, at different times in different cities, giving rise to different closing dates at each, the extremes, as we have seen, covering about a century. This explanation better conforms with the known archaeological facts than any of the other hypotheses suggested.

Other adverse factors following in the wake of the decreasing food supply, such as accompanying social unrest, governmental disorganization, even religious disbelief, doubtless all played their respective parts in the collapse of the Old Empire structure; but it appears highly probable that economic failure—the law of diminishing returns, another way of saying the high cost of living —was chiefly responsible for the final disintegration of the Maya Old Empire.

PERIPHERAL OCCUPATION OF NORTHERN YUCATAN, 455–909

Before proceeding to a description of the New Empire, it is first necessary to present what is known of the introduction of Maya culture into northern Yucatan *from Old Empire centers*, during Old Empire times, particularly since this Mayanization of northern Yucatan is exclusively an Old Empire cultural manifestation, entirely *preceding* the New Empire history of the northern half of the peninsula.

Although documentary evidence in the form of native Maya chronicles now becomes available for the first time to help us in the reconstruction of ancient Maya history, before examining these documentary sources let us summarize the *archaeological* evidence bearing upon the colonization of the northern half of the peninsula by Old Empire Maya, as indicated by the dated buildings and monuments.

A total of twenty-one surely dated monuments and buildings at ten sites are now known in northern and central Yucatan, in Campeche, and in Quintana Roo, Mexico; these will be found listed in Table IV.

A glance at this table will show that there are two principal groups of dated cities represented here: one, a chain of five sites in the east coast region, from south to north—Tzibanche, Ichpaatun, Tulum, Coba, and Chichen Itza (Plate 19); and the other, a chain of five sites in the west coast region, from south to north—Santa Rosa Xtampak, Etzna, Holactun, Oxkintok, and the Island of Jaina.

The dates in Table IV indicate that these ten sites were contemporaneous with the last four and a quarter centuries of the Old Empire—475–909; that is to say that they were all provincial settlements of the Old Empire, far removed from the great centers of cultural inspiration in the south, analogous to the Roman towns in Britain during the first and second centuries of the Christian Era.

It will also be noted from Table IV that the earliest certain date we have in the northern half of the peninsula is inscribed on the hieroglyphic door lintel at Oxkintok in the northwestern corner (Plates 19 and 18, a), 9.2.0.0.0 of the Maya Era, or 475.

Most unfortunately for an accurate chronological background, one based upon exactly dated contemporaneous monuments, the magnificent Maya Long Count, the so-called Initial Series (chapter xii, pp. 285–88), did not long survive transplanting in any of the peripheral areas after the collapse of Old Empire culture in the central nuclear region. In the north, during New Empire times, however, an abbreviated form of the Long Count was used in its place—what we may perhaps call the Short Count—but this is neither so accurate nor so well understood as the older Initial Series method of dating. For this reason New Empire history lacks the solid chronological framework offered by the surely dated monuments of the Old Empire.

Take, for example, a common form of abbreviation used in writing dates in our own Christian chronology, which leads to

TABLE IV

SURELY DATED MONUMENTS AND BUILDINGS IN YUCATAN, NORTHERN CAMPECHE, AND QUINTANA ROO, MEXICO

City	Location in the Northern Half of the Peninsula	Class (See p. 318)	Name of Monument	Date	
				Maya Era	Christian Era
Oxkintok	West coast region	3	Lintel 1	9. 2. 0. 0. 0	A.D. 475
Tulum	East coast region	3	Stela 1	9. 6.10. 0. 0	A.D. 564
Ichpaatun	East coast region	4	Stela 1	9. 8. 0. 0. 0	A.D. 593
Tzibanche	East coast region	3	Wooden door lintel	9. 9. 5. 0. 0	A.D. 618
Coba	East coast region	2	Stelae 4 and 6	9. 9.10. 0. 0	A.D. 623
Coba	East coast region	2	Stela 3	9.10. 0. 0. 0	A.D. 633
Coba	East coast region	2	Stela 2	9.10.10. 0. 0	A.D. 642
Coba	East coast region	2	Stela 21	9.11. 0. 0. 0	A.D. 652
Island of Jaina	West coast region	4	Stela 1	9.11. 0. 0. 0	A.D. 652
Coba	East coast region	2	Stela 5	9.11.10. 0. 0	A.D. 662
Etzna	West coast region	2	Stela 18	9.12. 0. 0. 0	A.D. 672
Coba	East coast region	2	Stela 1	9.12.10. 5.12	A.D. 682
Coba	East coast region	2	Stela 20	9.12.12. 0. 5	A.D. 684
Etzna	West coast region	2	Stela 19	9.13. 0. 0. 0	A.D. 692
Etzna	West coast region	2	Stela 2	9.15. 0. 0. 0	A.D. 731
Coba	East coast region	2	Stela 16	9.15. 1. 2. 8	A.D. 732
Coba	West coast region	2	Stela 5	9.15.19. 0. 0	A.D. 750
Santa Rosa Xtampak	West coast region	2	Stela 7	9.15.19.17.14	A.D. 751
Santa Rosa Xtampak	West coast region	3	Temple of the Initial Series	9.16.13. 0. 0	A.D. 764
Holactun	West coast region	2	Hieroglyphic Stairway	9.17.12. ?. ?	A.D. 782
Etzna	East coast region	1	Temple of the Initial Series	10. 2.10. 0. 0	A.D. 879
Chichen Itza	East coast region	3	Jade gorget	10. 4. 0. 0. 0	A.D. 909
Tzibanche					

much confusion between the English and our own American usage.
The complete way of writing July 4 of the current year is "Thursday, July 4, Anno Domini 1946"; however, most people write this same date much more simply as 7/4/46, suppressing altogether three non-essential parts: (1) the corresponding weekday, Thursday, (2) the Anno Domini, indicating the Year of Our Lord, and (3) the nineteen hundred of the nineteen hundred and forty-six complete years that have elapsed since the birth of Christ to this date, adding instead only 46 to indicate the number of the current year of the current century. It may be argued in defense of this abbreviated way of writing July 4 of the current year that it is sufficiently accurate for all practical purposes, but, strictly speaking, even this is not true. The English also use an almost identical form of abbreviation in writing dates, but with this important difference. Whereas in America, we put the month first (the number 7 in the foregoing date indicating July), followed by the day (4 in this case), the English reverse these two positions, putting the day before the month, thus 4/7/46, which we would read as April 7, 1946, but which they read as July 4, 1946. This gives rise to confusion between American and English usage in writing such abbreviated dates.

This analogy is not without application to the difference between the Maya Long and Short Counts. The Short Count, we shall see in chapter xii (pp. 291–95), while it is based upon the Long Count, and indeed stems directly from it, is much more abbreviated, requiring only two or three hieroglyphs to record any given date as compared with the ten hieroglyphs necessary to express the position of any single day in the Long Count. Moreover, as in the case of our own abbreviated method of writing dates, the Short Count is less accurate and more confusing than the Long Count, which makes New Empire chronology correspondingly less dependable, as it is also less well understood, than that of the Old Empire.

Returning to the ten surely dated cities now known in the northern half of the peninsula, these, it will be remembered, divide geographically into two groups: an eastern group in the general east coast region, and a western group in the general west coast region (Table IV).

The entry of Maya culture into northern Yucatan from the southern half of the peninsula during the fifth and sixth centuries of the Christian Era was presumably accomplished in successive waves along two main lines of migration, probably first along the east coast, though the earliest date is in the west (Lintel 1 at Oxkintok, 475, Plate 18, *a*), and a little later along the west coast, based upon an analysis of the archaeological evidence; this is further corroborated by an ancient Maya tradition, preserved by Father Lizana in his *Historia de Yucatán:*

The early fathers who first emplanted the Faith of Christ in Yucatan knew that the people here [the Maya] came, some from the west and some from the east, and thus in their ancient language they call the east in another way than today. Today they call the east Likin which is the same as where the sun rises, as with us. And the west they call Chikin which is the same as the setting or end of the sun or where it hides itself, as with us. And anciently they called the east, Cenial and the west Nohenial,[1] cenial which is to say the small descent, and nohenial the great descent. And the reason they say this is because from the part of the east there came down to this land [of Yucatan] few people, and that of the west, many and with this word they understand few or many, the east and the west; and the few people from one part and the many from the other.

It is evident from this quotation that the Maya themselves believed some of them had come from the east (really the southeast), but that more had come from the west (really the southwest), thus agreeing closely with the evidence of the dated monuments in the northern half of the peninsula. This being the case, let us next compare the foregoing traditionary and chronologic evidence with the architectural and documentary evidence.

Lying directly north of the central nuclear region of the Old Empire, that is directly north of Peten and its northern cultural

---

[1] Father Lizana erred slightly in spelling these two Maya words; the former should be written *dzemal* and the latter *nohemal*. *Dze* means "small" or "little," and *emal* means "descent"—"the little descent"; *noh* signifies "great" and *emal*, "descent"—"the great descent."

extensions in southern Campeche and Quintana Roo, Mexico, is
an architectural subprovince known as the Chenes, a region in
southern and central Campeche, so named because of the many
large natural wells there, *chen* in Maya, meaning "well."

The architecture of the Chenes region (chapter xiii, p. 353)
is somewhat different from that of the Old Empire. The latter
depends very little upon dressed and carved stone elements in
façade decoration, stucco, often very elaborately modeled, being
generally used instead of cut stone. In Chenes architecture, on
the other hand, carved stone elements are extensively employed
in the exterior decoration of buildings; occasionally the entire
façade is elaborately sculptured. This characteristic somewhat
sharply differentiates Chenes architecture from that of the Old
Empire.

Another architectural subprovince of northern Yucatan is that
known as the Puuc, so-called because it is the characteristic architecture of the many New Empire cities which lie in the hilly
region of northern central Yucatan, known in Maya as the *puuc*,
to the west and north of the Chenes region. Puuc architecture
will be described more fully in chapter xiii (pp. 353, 356), but
its principal characteristics may be summarized here as having less
elaborately sculptured façades than those of the Chenes region,
a stronger tendency to geometric forms, a more general use of
sculptured façade elements, which were carved *before* being built
into the façades, and the very general use of plain, low, round
columns, either monolithic or built up of drums, with plain, square
capitals.

Finally, at least one other architectural subprovince of the
New Empire must be mentioned—that centering around the Itza
capital of Chichen Itza in northeastern Yucatan, where a very
strong architectural influence from the highlands of central
Mexico (Tula in the state of Hidalgo) made itself felt; this is
characterized by feathered serpent columns, sloping façade bases,
and other elements typical of the architecture of the central Mexican plateau.

The line of cultural penetration into northern Yucatan along the east coast region followed Old Empire architectural traditions pretty closely. Much of the masonry at Coba, the largest Old Empire center in northeastern Yucatan in this colonization period, is characteristically Old Empire in type; and the architectural-sculptural-chronologic evidence from the northeastern corner of the peninsula is such as to indicate its close cultural connections with the central nuclear region of the Old Empire. This close affinity between the architecture and the sculpture of the Old Empire is seen to a lesser degree at Yaxuna, a medium-sized site some sixty miles west of Coba and only twelve miles south-southwest of Chichen Itza.

It is precisely at this point—the colonization of the east coast region—where the documentary sources (the *u kahlay katunob* or chronicles from certain native Maya manuscripts called the Books of Chilam Balam) begin their several accounts of ancient Maya history. These native chronicles will be fully described in chapter xii (pp. 301–3), but that description may be anticipated here to the extent of saying that only five of them are known: one from the Book of Chilam Balam of Mani; three from the Book of Chilam Balam of Chumayel; and one from the Book of Chilam Balam of Tizimin.

Of these five chronicles, the second and third from the Book of Chilam Balam of Chumayel are less useful than the other three. The third chronicle from the Chumayel manuscript is little more than an alternating sequence of Katuns 4 Ahau and 8 Ahau, a kind of litany, which makes no pretense at historical continuity. It simply presents a series of events that happened in these two katuns or twenty-year periods with no mention of any events which occurred in the other eleven intervening katuns of the Short Count. The second chronicle from the Chumayel manuscript differs considerably from the other three chronicles, not only in its chronology but also in the nature of the events it describes. The remaining three, however, all make mention of the *Dzemal* or "Little Descent" and are in substantial agreement concerning it.

The Mani manuscript has the following entry concerning the Little Descent:

Then took place the discovery of the province of Ziyancaan, or Bakhalal; Katun 4 Ahau, Katun 2 Ahau, Katun 13 Ahau, [specific 20-year
periods] three score years they ruled Ziyancaan when they descended
here; in these years that they ruled Bakhalal it occurred then that Chichen
Itza was discovered. 60 years.

The first chronicle from the Book of Chilam Balam of Chumayel is much more brief:

In Katun 6 Ahau took place the discovery of Chichen Itza.

The Katun 6 Ahau mentioned in the last quotation above is
probably 9.1.0.0.0 6 Ahau 13 Yaxkin of the Long Count, or the
twenty-year period running from 435 to 455 (Table V). The
province of Ziyancaan Bakhalal is the present southeastern corner
of Quintana Roo, Mexico, the region surrounding Lake Bacalar.
The Mani chronicle states that the province of Bakhalal was discovered in 435–455, and that during the next three katuns while
the Maya were at Bakhalal, that is between 455 and 514, Chichen
Itza was discovered; further, since the first chronicle from the
Chumayel manuscript states that Chichen Itza was discovered between 455 and 514, it is evident that these two sources are in
substantial agreement as to the date of the discovery of the site
of this city.

The Tizimin chronicle says about this event:

"Katun 8 Ahau; it occurred that Chichen Itza was learned
about; the discovery of the province of Ziyancaan took place."

This chronicle states that Chichen Itza was first heard of, and
the Province of Ziyancaan discovered in 416–435, again in close
agreement with the other two chronicles, concerning the date of
this earliest important event of New Empire history.

These several entries, taken into consideration with (1) the
chain of dated sites in the east coast region, (2) the fact that Coba
is connected with Yaxuna, only 60 miles west of it, by a stone
causeway, Yaxuna itself being only twelve miles south-southwest
of Chichen Itza, and (3) the presence of a surely deciphered
Initial Series date of 10.2.9.1.9 (878) at Chichen Itza itself, all

together afford broad archaeological substantiation of the Lizana tradition. So much for the *Dzemal*, or Little Descent, where "from the part of the east there came down to this land [i.e., entered the northern half of the peninsula] few people." These several events covering the introduction of Maya culture into the northern half of the peninsula will be found in Table V, which presents a summary of the leading events of both Old and New Empire history and of the Spanish Conquest.

Let us next examine the archaeological background in the west coast region for the *Nohemal* or Great Descent. It seems probable, from a study of the three architectural subprovinces of the northern peninsula previously defined, that Chenes architecture is older than Puuc architecture, which, in turn, is earlier than the last or Mexican architectural phase at Chichen Itza.

We have just seen, moreover, that the earliest stone architecture in the east coast region (Coba and Yaxuna) is generally Old Empire in style. The same is also true of the west coast region, where the earliest type of stone architecture is to be found at Oxkintok, which also has the earliest dated inscription (475) now known in the northern half of the peninsula. The movement which carried Maya culture for the first time to the northwestern corner of Yucatan in the latter part of the fifth century may well be called the first wave of the Great Descent—those "many" who, Lizana says, came from the west.

The region where the Chenes type of architecture flourished is immediately contiguous to that part of the Old Empire area, where the latest dated monuments in the Old Empire have been found, namely at Uaxactun, Xultun, and Xamantun, only 25 to 75 miles south of the southern edge of the Chenes country (Plate 19).

It seems not improbable, indeed, that the Chenes region may have been colonized by Old Empire Maya pushing northward from Uaxactun, Xultun, La Honradez, Xamantun, Oxpemul, Calakmul, and other Old Empire sites in the northern central Peten area after the cessation of monumental activity in the south, perhaps between 889 and 987. This may be considered as the

second wave of the western current which carried Maya culture to northwestern Yucatan; and with this second wave the colonization of the New Empire (from, and as far as, the Old Empire is concerned) came to an end.

By this time, the middle of the tenth century, I believe the Old Empire cities had been very largely, if not indeed entirely, abandoned. The colonization of the New Empire (from the Old Empire) was over, and Maya culture had been introduced into the northern half of the peninsula along two principal lines of penetration: (1) the less numerous and probably slightly earlier migration, the Lesser Descent (416–623) along the east coastal region and stemming from Old Empire cities in northeastern Peten; and (2) the more numerous migration, itself composed of several different waves, of which the two first were a penetration from the southwest as early as 475, and a second penetration, somewhat farther east and some two to five centuries later (652–987), but also along the general west coast region, both of these migrations stemming directly from Old Empire centers in northern central Peten and possibly from the Usumacinta Valley as well.

The former is quite clearly Father Lizana's Lesser Descent from the East, the latter, equally clearly, his Great Descent from the West. This brings us to the end of the colonization of the northern half of the peninsula during Old Empire times (416–987), which was effected from its northerly centers.

One other outstanding peripheral event of Old Empire times in northern Yucatan should be mentioned before closing this résumé of Old Empire history—namely the abandonment of Chichen Itza by the Itza in 692.

The Maya chronicles do not tell us why the city was abandoned, merely stating the simple fact that after having had their homes there for ten score years (since 495) they left Chichen Itza in a Katun 8 Ahau (9.13.0.0.0 or 692) and moved southwestward across Yucatan, establishing themselves anew on the southwestern coast in the region south of the modern town of Campeche. Or as the chronicles tersely record this event: "Then they went to establish their homes at Chakanputún. There the Itza had their homes, holy men."

This occupation of the southwest coast region by Old Empire Maya, around 692, is amply substantiated by the archaeological evidence. We have seen in Table IV that there are several cities in this region which date from this general period—652 to 751. This is also precisely the same region as that to which the Itza are said to have removed from Chichen Itza in 692.

The settlement of this region by Old Empire Maya, some from Chichen Itza and possibly others from Old Empire centers to the south, in the latter half of the seventh century and the first half of the eighth century brings to a close the introduction of Maya culture into northern Yucatan from the Old Empire. In the tenth century a new caste takes possession of the stage and another epoch, the New Empire, begins.

THE NEW EMPIRE

THREE PRINCIPAL PERIODS OF THE NEW EMPIRE

THE TWO MAIN divisions of ancient Maya history, the Old and New Empires, are not only chronological, but in part at least, geographical as well. Chronologically, the Old Empire, as its name signifies, is everywhere earlier than the New Empire. Geographically, on the other hand, although the Old Empire covered all sections of the Yucatan Peninsula, north as well as south, the New Empire is confined exclusively to the northern half of the peninsula except for a very late (middle of the fifteenth century) reoccupation of the region around Lake Peten Itza by the Itza. Thus while the Old Empire extended over the whole peninsula, the New Empire covered only its northern half. It is important to remember, however, that the Old Empire occupation of the northern half of the peninsula was only *peripheral* in character, a provincial extension to the north, the center of Old Empire cultural inspiration always remaining in the south.

The New Empire may be divided into three periods: the Puuc Period, or Maya Renaissance, the so-called League of Mayapan, from 987 to 1194 (New Empire I in Table III); the Mexican Period, or the Ascendency of Mayapan from 1194 to 1441 (New Empire II in Table III); and the Period of Disintegration from 1441 to 1697 (New Empire III in Table III).

THE MAYA RENAISSANCE AND THE LEAGUE OF MAYAPAN
(NEW EMPIRE I—10.8.0.0.0 TO 10.18.10.0.0 [987–1194])

As stated before, the colonization of northern Yucatan was but a provincial expression of Old Empire culture, a faint reflection of the higher order flourishing at the same time in the heart of the Old Empire to the south. But, with the coming of new blood from the southwest in the tenth century, new leaders, who introduced a new religion, new customs, new architecture, new life, and who formed a new political confederation, the League of Mayapan, the northern Yucatan Maya rose to new cultural heights; they lost their erstwhile provinciality and became in themselves a new source of cultural inspiration, especially in the field of architecture.

The Puuc Period, or the League of Mayapan, may be regarded as the true Maya Renaissance. During the two centuries following the inauguration of the League (approximately 997–1194) under the new leadership from the southwest, the Maya experienced a veritable cultural rebirth and regeneration, a second period of cultural brilliance (New Empire I, Table III).

Old Empire cultural infiltration from the southeast, Lizana's Little Descent, was now well over, but the Great Descent from the southwest was to continue perhaps for several centuries more. In a Katun 8 Ahau of the Short Count, probably 10.6.0.0.0 8 Ahau 8 Yax of the Long Count (928–948), a group of Maya-speaking people began moving slowly northeastward across the peninsula. Part of these at least were Itza, though others, under a leader named Kukulcan, certainly were of central Mexican (highlands) origin, but they had been living in what is now southwestern Campeche, the region around Chakanputun (the modern Champoton) for some two to two and a half centuries. After forty years of wandering, during which the native chronicles picturesquely record that this Itza-Mexican group was "under the trees, under the boughs, under the vines, to their sorrow," they reached Chichen Itza, where they established their capital in a Katun 4 Ahau, 968–987 (Table V).

Chichen Itza, we have seen, had already been previously occupied by Old Empire Maya from the southeast, the original Itza, who reached there via Coba and Yaxuna, some four and a half centuries earlier. We are left in the dark, however, as to whether the Itza-Mexican reoccupation of Chichen Itza was peaceful or whether it was effected by conquest.

Bishop Landa in his famous *Relación de las cosas de Yuca-*

tán, written as early as 1566, and our principal Spanish source for late (New Empire) Maya history, would seem to infer, in the following quotation, that this occupation was peaceful:

Chichen Itza is a very fine site, ten leagues from Izamal and eleven from Valladolid. It is said that it was ruled by three lords who were brothers who came into that country from the west, who were very devout, and so they built very beautiful temples and they lived very chastely without wives, and one of them died or went away, upon which the others acted unjustly and indecently and for this they were put to death. . . . . It is believed among the Indians that with the Itzas who occupied Chichen Itza there reigned a great lord, named Kukulcan, and that the principal building, which is called Kukulcan, shows this to be true. They say that he arrived from the west; but they differ among themselves as to whether he arrived before or after the Itzas or with them. They say that he was favorably disposed, and had no wife or children, and that after his return he was regarded in Mexico as one of their gods and called Quetzalcouatl; and they also considered him a god in Yucatan on account of his being a just statesman; and this is seen in the order which he imposed on Yucatan after the death of the lords, in order to calm the dissensions which their deaths had caused in the country.

This Kukulcan established another city after arranging with the native lords of the country that he and they should live there and that all their affairs and business should be brought there; and for this purpose they chose a very good situation, eight leagues further in the interior than Merida is now, and fifteen or sixteen leagues from the sea. They surrounded it with a very broad stone wall, laid dry, of about an eighth of a league, leaving in it only two narrow gates. The wall was not very high and in the midst of this enclosure they built their temples, and the largest, which is like that of Chichen Itza, they called Kukulcan, and they built another building of a round form, with four doors, entirely different from all the others in that land, as well as a great number of others round about joined together. In this enclosure they built houses for the lords only, dividing all the land among them, giving towns to each one, according to the antiquity of his lineage and his personal value. And Kukulcan gave a name to this city—not his own as the Ah Itzas had done in Chichen Itza, which means the well of the Ah Itzas, but he called it Mayapan, which means "the standard of the Maya," because they called the language of the country *Maya,* and the Indians (say) *"Ichpa"* which means "within the enclosure." This Kukulcan lived with the lords in that city for several years; and leaving them in great peace and friendship, he returned by the same way to Mexico, and on the way he stopped at Champoton, and, in memory of him and of his departure, he erected a fine building in the sea like that of Chichen Itza, a long stone's throw from the shore. And thus Kukulcan left a perpetual remembrance in Yucatan.

All the sources, both native and Spanish, agree that these newcomers, at least Kukulcan and his immediate followers from the southwest, were of Mexican origin. Indeed, both the Landa account just quoted, and the opening entry of the Mani chronicle, quoted below, clearly indicate this:

This is the account of the katuns. They left the region of their homes: Nonoual. The Tutul Xiu were there to the west of Zuyua. The land from whence they came [was] Tulapan Chiconautlan. It is said that they travelled four katuns [until] they arrived here in the company of Holon Chan Tepeuh and his subjects. When they left [this] region it is said that it was [Katun] 8 Ahau, [Katun] 6 Ahau, [Katun] 4 Ahau, [Katun] 2 Ahau.

Four score years and one year. Because one tun [of Katun] 13 Ahau [had passed] then when they arrived here to [this] region. Four score years and one year all together [lasted] their journey [since] they left their lands and came here to [this] region, this Chacnouitan. These are the years: 81 years. [Katun] 8 Ahau, [Katun] 6 Ahau, [Katun 4 Ahau], [Katun] 2 Ahau, the leader Tutal Xiu arrived at Chacnouitan. One year there lacked of five score years, they were in this Chacnouitan. These are the total years altogether: 99 years.

The chronicle from the Tizimin Manuscript has the following account of this same event:

[Katun] 8 Ahau, [Katun] 6 Ahau, [Katun] 4 Ahau, [Katun] 2 Ahau. Four score years and one year, in the first tun of [Katun] 13 Ahau. [Katun] 8 Ahau, [Katun] 6 Ahau, [Katun 4 Ahau], [Katun] 2 Ahau, the leader Tutul Xiu arrived in Chacnabiton; it was one year less than five score years.

According to both these passages, the Xiu departure from the land of Nonoual in the country of Tulapan to the west of Zuyua took place in a Katun 8 Ahau of the Short Count, which

I believe had the following Long Count position: 10.6.0.0.0 8 Ahau 8 Yax (948). Three of the four place-names in this quotation are of central Mexican (Nahuatl) origin and indicate that the "land of Nonoual in the country to the west of Zuyua," from which they had originally come, lay somewhere to the southwest of the northern half of the Yucatan Peninsula, while the fourth place-name, the land of Chacnouitan, may well have been the southwestern corner of the Peninsula of Yucatan itself, the ancient Chakanputun (modern Champoton). In any event it would seem from the wording of the chronicles that the land of Chacnouitan was surely somewhere in the southern or southwestern part of the *northern* half of the peninsula.

According to the passage from Landa already quoted, after leaving Chichen Itza, presumably during a Katun 4 Ahau (968–987), Kukulcan founded another city in northwestern Yucatan, which he called Mayapan. He set over the city as its ruling house a family named Cocom, and before finally leaving the peninsula he erected at Champoton on the west coast a fine building in memory of himself and of his departure from the land.

Finally, according to the Mani and Tizimin chronicles, Uxmal was founded in a Katun 2 Ahau, sometime between 987 and 1007, by a leader named Ah Zuitok Tutul Xiu, who, with his people, presumably also came from the southwest (Table V). Antonio de Herrera, the official historian of the Crown of Spain, writing in 1598, states explicitly that the Tutul Xiu, at least, came from the south. Although Herrera says "south," it is clear from his statement that the direction he really means is "southwest":

While the Cocoms were living in this good order, great companies of people entered from the south, from the slopes of the sierras of Lacandon, who, they were sure, were from Chiapas; and they wandered forty years through the abandoned places of Yucatan and finally they reached the *sierras* which lie almost opposite the city of Mayapan, ten leagues from it, where they settled and built very fine edifices. And at the end of some years, those of Mayapan, being pleased with their manner of living, sent to invite them to build dwellings for the lords in the site of the city. The Tutul-xius, for thus the foreigners were called, in view of this civility, went to the city and built.

All three of these migrations, those of Kukulcan and his followers, both Itza and Mexican, the Cocom, and the Xiu, were the final waves of Lizana's Great Descent.

We see at the end of the tenth century the play of new forces in the northern Yucatan scene. Chichen Itza, an Old Empire peripheral center, passed into the hands of a new dynasty, which had come from Chakanputun on the southwest coast of Yucatan.

Mayapan, destined to become the political center of northern Yucatan in the Mexican Period, was founded from Chichen Itza by a prince named Kukulcan, of Mexican origin. Finally, Uxmal was founded about the same time by a leader whom the chronicles call Ah Zuitok Tutul Xiu, whose appellative Xiu is almost certainly of Mexican origin, and who, other sixteenth-century Spanish sources definitely state, was a native of Mexico.

Who then were these newcomers that took over the administration of one and founded the two other leading city-states of northern Yucatan at the end of the tenth century, forming a confederacy known as the League of Mayapan?

Evidence both documentary and archaeological is not wanting to indicate that at least the leaders, nobles, and priests may well have been, perhaps originally were, of Mexican origin, though if so they and their ancestors had lived in the peninsula long enough —from two to two and a half centuries in the region of Chakanputun—to have acquired the Maya language before they occupied Chichen Itza and founded Mayapan and Uxmal.

All the Spanish authorities agree that but one language, Maya, was spoken throughout the peninsula, though the strong Mexican flavor of the culture brought by these later groups from the southwest, as well as the specific statements that their leaders were of Mexican origin, makes it probable that originally some of their ancestors at least had come from central Mexico, perhaps even from Tula, the ancient Toltec capital. Even though this should be true, however, it is important to note that they had lived in the southwestern part of the peninsula long enough to have become completely Mayanized in speech and perhaps even in culture before taking over the political direction of northern Yucatan.

So far as Chichen Itza and Mayapan are concerned, probably the two first centers in the north to be established by the Maya-Mexican newcomers, the archaeological evidence of a strong Mexican influence is overwhelming. This has been repeatedly reported at Chichen Itza, the greater part of which dates from the New Empire rather than the pure Maya (Old Empire) period, and it has also been found to hold true at Mayapan, though to a much lesser degree.

Concerning the beginning of the Puuc Period of New Empire history, it seems safe to conclude that during the last half of the tenth century several groups of closely related peoples, probably of Mexican origin so far as their leadership was concerned, though all spoke Maya, entered the peninsula from the south-west and proceeded to assume the political direction of northern Yucatan, establishing Maya-Mexican dynasties at the capitals of the three leading city-states: the followers of Kukulcan at Chichen Itza, the Cocom at Mayapan, and the Xiu or Tutul Xiu at Uxmal.

In this same Katun 2 Ahau (987–1007) the League of Mayapan was organized. Perhaps as intruders forming only a relatively small minority, and thus feeling the need of mutual protection in their new homes, the leaders of these three cities formed a confederacy called the League of Mayapan, under which they ruled the country jointly.

There seems to have followed an era of general prosperity under the league, since two of its members, Chichen Itza and Uxmal, during this period grew to be the greatest cities of the New Empire, the only Class 1 sites in the northern half of the peninsula according to my grouping of the Maya cities, based on their relative sizes (chapter xiii, p. 318).

Architecture reached new levels of attainment at both these cities. At Chichen Itza the imposing pyramid temples with their barbaric feathered-serpent columns in honor of Kukulcan—the founder of the new dynasty, and later perhaps deified as the Feathered Serpent, patron deity of the city (Plates 40, *b*, and 44, *a*)—the vast colonnaded halls, and the Caracol or astronomical observatory, a high, round tower (Plate 42, *a*), are especially typical of this period. Uxmal, on the other hand, became as typically Maya Renaissance (Puuc) in its architecture. Indeed the Maya Renaissance reached its most magnificent expression at Uxmal in the Palace of the Governors—probably the finest edifice ever constructed in ancient America (Plates 25, *a*, and 38, *b*)—and in the scarcely less spectacular Monjas Quadrangle (Plates 46 and 47). The Xiu capital was the greatest Maya center of the New Empire, as Chichen Itza was its greatest Maya-Mexican center.

Other sites, the very names of which are now unknown, multiplied on every side; and, under the peaceful conditions which prevailed during the eleventh and twelfth centuries, northern Yucatan enjoyed a prosperity literally never equaled before or since.

This period, as already noted, may well be called the Maya Renaissance. Art and architecture flourished anew, the latter indeed as never before. This was the last distinguished phase of Maya culture. After its end in the tenth tun, or year of a Katun 8 Ahau, that is in 1194, brought about by a disastrous civil war between Chichen Itza and Mayapan to be described in the next section (New Empire II, Table III), the Maya never again regained their cultural pre-eminence in any field. And while it took the Maya political machine in northern Yucatan another two and a half centuries to "run down," and still another two and a half centuries before it finally collapsed at the end of the seventeenth century in central Peten, a cultural decline set in from this time forward, from which the Maya never again recovered.

THE MEXICAN PERIOD. THE ASCENDENCY OF MAYAPAN, AND MAYA DECLINE (NEW EMPIRE II—10.18.10.0.0 TO 11.12.0.0.0 [1194–1441])

The cause of the war between Chichen Itza and Mayapan remains obscure. Although a Helen of Troy motive has been injected into this event, based upon two very obscure passages in the Books of Chilam Balam of Mani and Tizimin, telling how the bride of a certain Ah Ulil, the ruler of Izamal, had been kidnaped by Chac Xib Chac, the ruler of Chichen Itza, the real issue would appear to have been long-standing political and economic jealousies between the east as represented by Chichen Itza and the west as represented by Mayapan.

At this time the Cocom leader at Mayapan was named Hunac Ceel, or, as he is less frequently designated, Ah Nacxit Kukulcan, the latter possibly more in the nature of a title in memory of the founder of the dynasty than a name, just as the given name Caesar eventually became a title. In the ensuing war against Chichen Itza, Hunac Ceel summoned to his aid mercenary troops from Mexican garrisons kept at Xicalanco, the region lying just west of the Laguna de Términos (eastern Tabasco, Mexico). The Mexican origin of these mercenary troops is further confirmed by the fact that all seven of the warriors who are mentioned as Hunac Ceel's commanders in this war—Ah Zinteyut Chan, Tzuntecum (Mexican Tzontecomatl), Taxcal (Taxcatl), Pantemit (Pantemitl), Xuchueuet (Xochihuehuetl), Ytzcuat (Itzcoatl), and Kakaltecat (Cacaltecatl)—surely have Mexican names.

Bishop Landa, without mentioning the names of these Mexican chiefs specifically, states that the Cocoms had Mexican allies:

The Governor Cocom began to covet riches and for this reason he arranged with the troops of the garrison, which the kings of Mexico kept at Tabasco and Xicalango, to hand over the city to them. And thus he brought the Mexican people into Mayapan, and oppressed the poor and made many slaves, and the lords would have put him to death but for the fear which they had of the Mexicans. And the lord of the Tutul Xius never consented to this. And the Yucatecans, finding themselves in this situation learned from the Mexicans the use of arms, and they soon became masters of the bow and arrow, the lance and the axe, their shields and strong cuirasses made of quilted cotton, as well as the other instruments of war, so that finally they neither admired the Mexicans nor feared them; on the contrary they took little account of them; and in this situation they lived several years.

The war which brought about the disruption of the League of Mayapan in 1194 seems to have been confined principally to Mayapan and Chichen Itza, though other smaller states were doubtless involved; but there is no mention of the third member of the confederacy, the Xiu of Uxmal, as having taken any part in it. Landa hints at the non-participation of the Xiu in this war when he says, "the Lord of the Tutul Xiu never consented to this," that is to Cocom's enslavement of the Maya after the fall of Chichen Itza.

The war, however, had one definite and immediate political repercussion—Mayapan became the leading city-state in northern Yucatan for the next two and a half centuries.

Although both the native and the Spanish historians are largely silent as to the events of this long period, the Mani, Tizimin, and Chumayel chronicles indicate attempted reprisals by the Itza in the two katuns immediately following the fall of Chichen Itza, 1194–1234; but apparently these were unsuccessful. The Cocom obliged the other Maya lords, probably including the dethroned ruler of Chichen Itza and his principal nobles, to reside at the walled city of Mayapan, and to administer the affairs of their respective cities, towns, and villages through deputies. Thus the persons of the Maya lords themselves became hostages for their own good behavior, and thus the tyranny of the Cocom increased, their growing despotism strengthened and reinforced by the presence of their Mexican allies, garrisoned in the walled Cocom capital.

Bishop Landa graphically describes the dramatic ending of these tyrannies:

Among the successors of the Cocom dynasty was another one, very haughty and an imitator of Cocom, who made another alliance with the Tabascans, placing more Mexicans within the city, and began to act the tyrant and to enslave the common people. The chiefs then attached themselves to the party of Tutul-xiu, a patriotic man like his ancestors, and they plotted to kill Cocom. This they did, killing at the same time all of his sons save one who was absent; they sacked his dwelling and possessed themselves of all his property, his stores of cacao and other fruits, saying that thus they repaid themselves what had been stolen from them.

Thus in the very first year of Katun 8 Ahau, 1441, goaded beyond further endurance by Cocom tyranny, the Maya chieftains, uniting under the leadership of Ah Xupan Xiu, the then Xiu ruler, who was living at Mayapan along with all the other Maya lords, attacked Mayapan, sacked the city, and slew its ruler and all his sons except one who was absent on a trading expedition to Ulua at the time. After this successful culmination of the war, the victors withdrew to their respective provinces, towns, and villages, and all centralized government in Yucatan came to an end.

In another passage Landa inferentially fixes the date of the foundation of Mayapan as having taken place about 941, which is in remarkable agreement with the native chronicles as to the time of this same event:

. . . . after having been established in this city [Mayapan] for more than five hundred years, they abandoned and left it desolate, each going to his own country.

According to the chronicles, Mayapan was founded sometime during Katuns 6 Ahau and 4 Ahau (948–987), and further, since five centuries prior to 1441 takes us back to 941, it will be seen that Landa and the native chronicles are in general agreement as to the foundation date of this, the last great Maya capital, during the Mexican Period.

With the fall of Mayapan, all centralized authority in the northern half of the peninsula collapsed, and complete political disorganization followed. All the great centers were abandoned, never again to be reoccupied; Yucatan fell apart into a score of petty provinces, which, urged on by ancient feuds and jealousies, waged incessant warfare, one against another. These conflicts, added to the divers calamities during the century following the fall of Mayapan (1441–1541), the first part of the Period of Disintegration, to be described in the next section, reduced the country to political chaos, and paved the way for its final conquest by the Spaniards in 1527–1546. The Maya, as cultural leaders, were finished; and, with the fall of Mayapan, the Mexican Period of the New Empire came to an end and the disintegration of Maya culture was all but complete (New Empire II, Table III).

Bishop Landa, in describing the various calamities that afflicted Yucatan during the century between the fall of Mayapan in 1441 and the final conquest of the country by the Spaniards in 1527–1546, incidentally definitely fixes the former event as having taken place in the year 1441 of the Christian Era. Four of the five native chronicles (all, in fact, except the always differing third chronicle from the Book of Chilam Balam of Chumayel) as well as the two leading early Spanish authorities— Cogolludo, writing in 1656, and Villagutierre Soto Mayor in 1700—clearly fix the same event as having taken place in a Katun 8 Ahau of the Maya Era, 1441–1461, or in other words, during the very first year of this particular Katun 8 Ahau, which extended from 1441 to 1461.

Taking the year of his writing, 1566, as his point of departure for working backward, Landa says:

> Since the last plague, more than fifty years have now passed, the mortality of the wars was twenty years prior, the pestilence of the swelling was sixteen years before the wars, and the hurricane other sixteen years before that, and twenty-two or twenty-three years after the destruction of the city of Mayapan. Thus according to this count it has been 125 years since its overthrow, within which the people of this country have passed through the calamities described.

This fixes the date of the plague as having fallen in 1516 or possibly in 1515, the date of the mortality due to the wars as in 1496, the date of the pestilence as in 1480, the date of the hurricane as in 1464, and the date of the destruction of Mayapan as in 1441. The chronicle from the Book of Chilam Balam of Tizimin and the first and second chronicles from the Chilam Balam of Chumayel record that there was a pestilence in Katun 4 Ahau (that is, in 1480–1500), which pestilence, according to Landa happened at the very beginning of this katun, in 1480. Again, the first chronicle from the Book of Chilam Balam of Chumayel describes an epidemic of smallpox as having taken place in Katun

2 Ahau (1500–1520). This is doubtless Landa's pestilence "with
great pustules that rotted the body," which occurred according to
his reckoning in 1515 or 1516. Small though these two items of
confirmation may be, they indicate, nevertheless, the high degree
of reliability of the native chronicles, our principal documentary
sources for the reconstruction of New Empire history.

After the fall of Mayapan, as previously noted, all the larger
cities were abandoned. The Itza left Chichen Itza, retiring far
to the south, to the shores of Lake Peten Itza in what is now the
Department of Peten, Guatemala, and establishing their new
capital, Ta Itza, or Tayasal, in the same Katun 8 Ahau, on a
promontory at the western end of the lake. The Chels, a prominent noble family of Mayapan, after the fall of the city, established their principal settlement at Tecoh. The single surviving
son of the slain Cocom ruler, gathering together the remnants
of his people about him, established his rule at Tibolon, near
Sotuta. Even the victors, the Tutul Xiu, did not return to Uxmal,
but founded a new capital, which they called Mani, meaning in
Maya "it is passed."

The last important event in the pre-Conquest history of Yucatan was the ill-fated pilgrimage of the Xiu ruler and his court
to offer human sacrifice in the Well of Sacrifice at Chichen Itza in
1536. As will be shown in the next chapter, not a Spaniard remained in Yucatan in 1536. After the two previous unsuccessful
attempts to subjugate the Maya in 1527–1528 and again in 1531–
1535, the Spaniards had withdrawn a second time from the peninsula leaving it completely free of foreign invaders.

Ah Dzun Xiu, also known as Napot Xiu, at this time the ruler
of the Tutul Xiu at their new capital of Mani, thought the moment auspicious for undertaking a pilgrimage to the Well of
Sacrifice at Chichen Itza to appease by human sacrifice the Maya
gods, who, for so many years, had been so evilly disposed, afflict-
ing the land with calamity after calamity, and especially during
the last few years with devastating droughts. He applied to Nachi
Cocom, the ruler of Sotuta, through whose province the pilgrims
were obliged to pass in going from Mani to Chichen Itza, for a

safe conduct. The Xiu ruler doubtless feared reprisals on the part of Nachi Cocom, on account of the leading part his (Ah Dzun's) own great-grandfather, Ah Xupan Xiu, had played in the slaying of Nachi Cocom's great-grandfather, the last ruler of Mayapan. Because of this fear, the Xiu ruler took the precaution of first securing a promise of safe passage for himself and his people across the Cocom province.

Nachi Cocom, however, had not forgotten the death of his great-grandfather nearly a century before, for which he held Xiu treachery responsible, and he therefore welcomed the Xiu request as offering a long-awaited opportunity for wholesale revenge. The request for a safe-conduct was promptly granted, and presently a pilgrimage headed by Ah Dzun Xiu himself, Ah Ziyah Xiu, his son and heir-apparent, and forty other leading men of the Xiu nation set out from Mani for Chichen Itza via the province of Sotuta. Nachi Cocom with a large delegation of his people met them at Otzmal, five miles southeast of the Cocom capital.

The Xiu pilgrims were royally entertained for four days, but at a banquet on the evening of the fourth day the Cocom fell upon their guests and killed them all, to a man. This act of treachery split the warring Maya anew, pitting the two most powerful houses in the northern peninsula, the Cocom of Sotuta and the Xiu of Mani, against each other to the bitter end. The Xiu, even before 1536, had offered their submission to the Spaniards, in the second phase of the conquest (1531–1535), as we shall see in the next chapter, but the Cocom, on the other hand, had conspicuously refrained from so doing. This doubtless added further fuel to ancient Cocom hatred of the Xiu and was an additional motive for the Otzmal massacre, which all but wiped out the Xiu ruling family.

This massacre, coming so shortly before the third and final phase of the Spanish Conquest, sealed the fate of the New Empire Maya. Reviving old hatreds as it did, it effectually prevented a united stand against the Spaniards when they returned to Yucatan in 1540 in their last and successful attempt to subdue the country. Exhausted by civil war, betrayed by a number of their own leading native houses, notably the Xiu, Chels, and Peches, who from the first had been friendly to the white invaders, decimated by different calamities—famines, hurricanes, and pestilences—each of which in turn had ravaged Yucatan during the previous century, the New Empire Maya were in no condition to resist the better-armed Spaniards and finally succumbed to their superior might (New Empire III, Table III).

THE SPANISH CONQUEST OF YUCATAN

THE FIRST ENDURING MAYA CONTACT WITH THE WHITE MAN IN 1511

THE SPANISH CONQUEST now lay immediately ahead. Four or five years before the great plague of 1515 or 1516, that is in 1511, the first white men reached Yucatan. In the latter year, a Spanish official named Valdivia set out from Darien in a caravel for the island of Santo Domingo to report to the Admiral (Diego Colon, son of Cristobal Colon, known to us as Columbus), and to the governor of that island, concerning the quarrels in Darien between Diego de Nicuesa and Vasco Nuñez de Balboa, the discoverer of the Pacific Ocean; Valdivia took with him twenty thousand ducats of the royal treasure. Near Jamaica the caravel foundered on some shoals called Las Viboras and sank. Valdivia and some eighteen sailors escaped in a small boat without sails and without food of any kind. The Yucatan Current, which flows strongly here, carried the survivors westward for fourteen days, during which time seven men died from hunger, thirst, and exposure; the remaining twelve were cast upon the east coast of Yucatan, probably somewhere in the Province of Ekab in the northeastern corner of the peninsula. But even on land further misfortunes were in store for them. They were seized by an unfriendly Maya lord, who immediately sacrificed Valdivia and four companions to his idols and gave their bodies to his people for a feast. Geronimo de Aguilar, Gonzalo de Guerrero, and five others were spared for the moment as being too thin for this cannibalistic orgy. Says Aguilar, in describing their situation, "I together with six others remained in a coop, in order that for another festival that was approaching, being fatter, we might solemnize their banquet with our flesh."

Not relishing this anticipated fate, Aguilar and his companions managed to escape and fled through the northern Yucatan forest to the country of another lord, an enemy of the first chieftain who had sacrificed Valdivia and the others. This second lord, more merciful than the first, only enslaved the Spaniards, but soon all of them died except two, Aguilar and Guerrero. The former was serving still a third Maya chieftain, named Taxmar, when Cortes finally reached Yucatan eight years later, in 1519. Gonzalo de Guerrero in the meantime had drifted farther south and finally entered the service of Nachan Can, Lord of Chetumal, whose daughter he married and by whom he had children. He rose to a powerful position in that province. When Cortes' messengers offered to take Guerrero back to the Spaniards in 1519, he declined, electing to spend the remainder of his life with his Maya family. Aguilar slyly suggests that Guerrero was ashamed to rejoin his countrymen "because he has his nostrils, lips, and ears pierced and his face painted, and his hands tattooed . . . . and on account of the vice he had committed with the woman and his love for his children."

This was the first enduring contact between the Maya and members of the white race, and it is not improbable that the pestilence of 1515 or 1516, the *mayacimil*, or "easy death" which was characterized by great pustules that "rotted their bodies with a great stench so that the limbs fell to pieces in four or five days" may well have been the dreaded smallpox, perhaps introduced among the Maya by some member of the ill-fated survivors of the Valdivia expedition four or five years earlier or, perhaps even more probably, transmitted overland from Darien to northern Yucatan by Indian traders, who are known to have plied their calling back and forth across the intervening region.

THE FRANCISCO HERNANDEZ DE CORDOBA EXPEDITION, 1517

Early in 1517, Francisco Hernandez de Córdoba sailed westward from Santiago de Cuba with three ships in search of slaves. It is not clear just where he first sighted the Yucatan mainland; some believe it was off Cape Catoche, the northeastern point of the peninsula; others believe that he first landed at the Isla de Mujeres, a short distance below that cape. The Isla de Mujeres was so named because of the statues of Maya goddesses found in the temple there, which were being worshiped as idols. According to the latter view—that Isla de Mujeres was his first landfall—Córdoba, after leaving this island, turned northwest to Cape Catoche and thence, skirting along the north coast of the peninsula and rounding its northwestern point, sailed southward as far as the Bay of Campeche, where he landed on Saint Lazarus Day, February 23, 1517. At Campeche the Spaniards found a temple of stone and on its summit an idol "with two ferocious animals which were eating its sides, and a long, thick serpent of stone swallowing a lion; and these animals were covered with the blood of sacrifices." Here they heard of a large town near by called Champoton, a little farther south along the same coast, whither they next proceeded. The Lord of Champoton, one Ah Moch Couoh, received the Spaniards with open hostility, and a hot fight followed. In spite of the noise, smoke, and flame of gun-fire, which the Maya heard and saw for the first time in this battle, the Indians fought bravely, inflicting heavy losses both in killed and wounded on the infinitely better armed Spaniards; they even succeeded in capturing two of the latter alive and carrying them off to be sacrificed. Córdoba himself received no fewer than thirty-three wounds and "sadly returned to Cuba" to report the new land as very good and rich, because of the few gold trinkets he had found at Isla de Mujeres, Ekab, and Campeche; he died of his wounds shortly after his return.

THE JUAN DE GRIJALVA EXPEDITION IN 1518

Diego de Velasquez, then governor of Cuba, was greatly excited by these discoveries, especially by the reports of gold, and fitted out another expedition consisting of four ships and two hundred men under command of his own nephew, Juan de Grijalva. Francisco de Montejo, the future conqueror of Yucatan, was also a member of this second expedition, which left Cuba early in April 1518.

Grijalva took with him as pilot, one Anton de Alaminos, who had piloted the Córdoba expedition; the first landing was made at the Island of Cozumel off the east coast, where, according to the chronicler of the expedition, the Maya fled at sight of the Spaniards. Grijalva continued southward along the east coast, passing three large towns, one of which is described as follows:

We followed the shore day and night, and the next day toward sunset we perceived a city or town so large, that Seville would not have seemed more considerable nor better; one saw there a very large tower; on the shore was a great throng of Indians, who bore two standards which they raised and lowered to signal us to approach them; the commander [Grijalva] did not wish it. The same day we came to a beach near which was the highest tower we had seen. . . . We discovered a wide entrance lined with wooden piles set up by fishermen.

The largest of the several sites seen by Grijalva along the east coast of the peninsula, was probably the ancient town of Zama (perhaps the modern archaeological site of Tulum), and the "highest tower" was almost certainly the Castillo of Tulum. The large bay, mentioned above, was Ascension Bay, which was so named because the flotilla discovered it on Ascension Thursday, 1518.

This was the southernmost point reached on the east coast and from here Grijalva sailed north again, touching at Cozumel a second time on the trip back. The flotilla next sailed round Cape Catoche and the northern end of the peninsula to Campeche on the west coast. Continuing southward from Campeche, Grijalva discovered the Laguna de Términos, named the San Pablo and San Pedro River, and entered the Rio Tabasco. In this region, or in that lying immediately to the west, which was next visited, considerable treasure was obtained, including the first pieces of Aztec turquoise-mosaic work the Spaniards had seen. Following the coast northward, Grijalva first heard of the Aztec nation, presumably at some place on the Veracruz coast, and finally reached as far north as the Panuco River. On the return voyage to Cuba, the armada put in at Champoton to avenge the defeat of

Córdoba, the year before; here the Maya again attacked the Spaniards fiercely, killing one and wounding fifty others among whom was Grijalva "who received two arrow wounds and had a tooth and a half broken!" Because of the savagery of the Indians here, the place was named Puerto de Mala Pelea, meaning "Port of the Bad Fight." From Champoton, Grijalva sailed to Campeche, where, after another skirmish with the Maya, he finally returned to Havana, having been gone for five months.

THE HERNANDO CORTES EXPEDITION IN 1519

The voyage of Grijalva caused tremendous excitement in Cuba, more so even than the discoveries of Córdoba. Yucatan was thought to be a land of gold and plenty, where fortune smiled, awaiting only the brave and adventurous to seize its riches. A third expedition was quickly fitted out, consisting of eleven ships, five hundred-men and some horses, the latter at that time almost worth their weight in gold in the New World. Hernando Cortes, the future conqueror of Mexico, was put in command of the armada, and with him went a number of other captains: Francisco de Montejo, the future conqueror of Yucatan, Pedro de Alvarado, the future conqueror of Guatemala, Diego de Ordaz, Gonzalo de Sandoval, Cristobal de Olid, and Bernal Diaz del Castillo, all of whom were destined to win imperishable fame in the conquest of Mexico.

The armada first anchored off the Island of Cozumel, where Cortes spent some days. Idols in the temples were destroyed, and a cross was erected in one of them. While here, Cortes learned of the presence of "bearded men" on the mainland. These, by the description the Indians gave of them, seemed to be white men and Cortes sent messengers to summon them. In this manner Geronimo de Aguilar, already mentioned, was rescued, and later served Cortes well as interpreter throughout the conquest period.

Leaving Cozumel, the armada sailed around the north coast of the peninsula, touching at Campeche, but continuing on to the Tabasco River, which was renamed Grijalva in honor of its discoverer the year before. In Tabasco, Cortes was given a beautiful young Indian girl named Malinal (for one of the twenty days of the Aztec calendar), afterward christened Marina, who was destined to play a vital role in the conquest of Mexico.

Whether Chontal Maya or some Nahuatl dialect was the native language of this girl is uncertain. Her father, who was a *cacique* or chief, seems to have died when she was still young and she was given by her mother to people in Xicalanco, who later gave her to others in Tabasco, who in turn, finally gave her to Cortes. Marina spoke both Maya and Nathuatl, and since Geronimo de Aguilar spoke Maya and Spanish, between the two they supplied Cortes with a means of communicating in Nahuatl with the Aztecs; and together they played roles of incalculable importance in the conquest of Mexico, especially in its early stages, when there were literally no other interpreters available. See chapter ix (pp. 178, 179) for further details about this beautiful Mexican girl.

The conquest of the Aztec nation, the heroic defense and fall of Tenochtitlan, is another story, but Cortes, the conqueror of Mexico, reappears in the Maya drama (chapter vii, pp. 117–22).

THE CONQUEST OF YUCATAN BY FRANCISCO DE MONTEJO

The conquest of Yucatan lasted, on and off, for nineteen years (1527–1546), and may be divided into three active phases, separated by two intermediate quiescent periods:

First phase (1527–1528). Conquest of Yucatan attempted from the east

First interregnum (1528–1531)

Second phase (1531–1535). Conquest of Yucatan attempted from the west

Second interregnum (1535–1540)

Third phase (1540–1546). Conquest of Yucatan completed from the west

Francisco de Montejo, the Adelantado of Yucatan, was a member of both the Grijalva and the Cortes expeditions in 1518 and 1519, respectively. He did not take part in the conquest of Mexico, however, having been sent back from Veracruz to Spain in 1519 by Cortes in charge of the Royal Fifth—the King's share of the booty, gold, and other treasures—which had been collected from the Indians up to this point. At the same time Montejo was to plead Cortes' cause at the Spanish Court, because certain irregularities in connection with Cortes' departure from Cuba had brought him into open rupture with Diego de Velasquez, the Governor of Cuba, who had originally placed him in charge of the expedition.

During the seven years Montejo was at Court attending to Cortes' tangled affairs, he applied to the King of Spain on his own behalf for permission to conquer Yucatan at his (Montejo's) own cost. In a royal decree, dated December 8, 1526, Montejo was finally granted the hereditary title of Adelantado, a title sometimes conferred upon adventurous gentlemen who were willing to risk life and fortune in an attempt to expand the possessions of the Spanish Crown, and he was further authorized to raise an army for the conquest and colonization of Yucatan.

FIRST PHASE: CONQUEST ATTEMPTED FROM THE EAST (1527–1538)

The Montejo armada, consisting of three ships and some three hundred to four hundred men (authorities differ as to the exact number) set sail from Spain about the middle of 1527 under Montejo with Alonso d'Avila as second in command; a stop was made at Santo Domingo to pick up supplies and horses, and one ship was left behind to bring additional supplies later. The two other ships made the island of Cozumel toward the end of September, where Ah Naum Pat, the Lord of Cozumel, received them peaceably; after a brief stop, the two ships sailed for the mainland, where Montejo took possession of the land in the name of God and the King of Castille, somewhere near the flourishing town of Xelha in the Province of Ekab, which Montejo rechristened after his own birthplace in Spain, Salamanca de Xelha, the first of no fewer than seven settlements established in Yucatan that were to be named Salamanca.

Considerable discontent having developed among the soldiers,

Montejo, taking a leaf out of Cortes' book, resorted to a trick
practiced by the conqueror of Mexico eight years before at Veracruz—he set fire to his two ships, literally burning his bridges
behind him. Leaving forty men at Xelha under command of
d'Avila, and another twenty at the near-by town of Pole, Montejo
set out with 125 men on a tour of the towns and villages in the
northeastern corner of the peninsula. None of the towns visited
on this tour survives today, and indeed, even the location of most
of them is unknown: Xamanha, Mochis, and Belma; the last, the
largest town in the Province of Ekab, is perhaps to be identified
with the modern settlement of El Meco on the east coast opposite Isla de Mujeres. Here the chiefs of the surrounding towns
were called together to swear allegiance to the Spanish Crown.

From Belma, the little army proceeded to the town of Conil in
the Province of Ekab, a settlement which is said to have been
composed of 5,000 houses; here the Spaniards rested for two
months. They left Conil in the spring of 1528 for the capital
of the Province of Chauaca, a town named Chikin Chel, but sometimes also called Chauaca. Here the first serious encounter with
the Indians took place. The Maya, abandoning the town in the
night, attacked vigorously the next morning, but were defeated.

From Chauaca the army moved to Ake, some ten miles north
of the modern town of Tizimin, where the greatest battle thus
far fought with the Indians took place, in which more than twelve
hundred Maya were killed. In this action

the Indians appeared with all the arms which they use in the wars: quivers
of arrows, poles with their tips hardened by fire, lances with points of sharp
flints, two-handed swords of very strong woods inset with obsidian blades,
whistles, and beating the shells of great turtles with deer horns, trumpets
of large conch-shells of the sea; naked except for the shameful parts
which were covered with a cloth, [their bodies] daubed with earth of
divers colors, so they appeared as most ferocious devils; their noses and ears
pierced with nose- and ear-plugs of bone and stones of varied colors.

As a result of this battle, all the neighboring Maya chiefs surrendered, at least for a time.

From Ake the little army, always dwindling in numbers because of the repeated attacks, moved to Sisia and Loche, and from the latter returned to Salamanca de Xelha by an inland route, passing through the Provinces of the Tazes and the Cupules, two northeastern Maya tribes.

On returning to Xelha, Montejo found his first settlement in desperate straits. Of the forty Spaniards he had left there, only twelve remained, while all twenty of those he had stationed at the near-by town of Pole had been massacred. Finally, of the 125 Spaniards who had accompanied him during his journey into the interior, only sixty returned. The entire force now must have numbered fewer than one hundred men.

The third vessel of the little flotilla finally having arrived from Santo Domingo, Montejo decided to continue exploration of the coast to the south. D'Avila was sent overland, and Montejo in the ship recently arrived from Santo Domingo sailed southward. He discovered a settlement called Chetumal on a good bay and learned that Gonzalo de Guerrero, a Valdivia survivor, was in the vicinity. Although Montejo sent messengers to persuade him to rejoin his countrymen, Guerrero refused a second time, as he had refused Cortes nine years before. The Adelantado and d'Avila failed to meet in the Province of Chetumal as the Maya purposely kept them apart by false reports as to their respective whereabouts. D'Avila, after waiting some time for his chief to rejoin him, finally made his way back to Xelha and moved the Spanish settlement from this location to the site of the near-by town of Xamanha, which was rechristened Salamanca de Xamanha, the second settlement named after Montejo's birthplace in Spain.

Montejo, after waiting in vain for d'Avila to appear at Chetumal, continued southward by water to the Ulua River in Honduras, at which point he turned back, rejoining his lieutenant at Xamanha. Finally, late in 1528, leaving d'Avila at Xamanha as Lieutenant Governor, Montejo sailed around the northern coast of the peninsula and returned to New Spain (Mexico), which brought to an end the first and unsuccessful attempt to conquer Yucatan from the east.

Montejo, having in the meantime secured his own appointment as *Alcalde Mayor* of Tabasco, left Mexico City for that province in 1529, taking with him his son, also named Francisco de Montejo; with their combined efforts they succeeded in pacifying the province and founded the third town of Salamanca at Xicalanco near the north coast of Tabasco.

At this juncture d'Avila was brought back from the east coast of Yucatan and sent to reduce the Province of Acalan south and east of the Laguna de Términos, where he established the fourth Spanish settlement of Salamanca at Itzamkanac, the capital of the province. Montejo did not long enjoy his new position in Tabasco, however; the deposed former Spanish governor, having succeeded in regaining power there, threw Montejo into prison. Later the Adelantado was allowed to rejoin his son at Salamanca de Xicalanco, and finally, both father and son moved over to Champoton in southwestern Yucatan, whither d'Avila had already preceded them, at which point the opening of the second phase of the conquest of Yucatan begins.

SECOND PHASE: CONQUEST ATTEMPTED FROM THE WEST (1531–1535)

From Champoton the Adelantado moved to Campeche, where the fifth town of Salamanca was established. From this point as a base of operations, the second attempt to reduce Yucatan was launched with from 400 to 500 soldiers. D'Avila was sent to the Province of Chauaca in the east. On his way thither he passed through the Province of Mani, where the Xiu gave him a friendly reception; finally he reached the Province of Chetumal in the far southeast, where he founded a *Villa Real*, or Royal Town. The natives here were of different caliber from those in the west, as the Spaniards had found to their cost during the first attempt to subdue Yucatan from the east in 1527–1528, and they resisted so stubbornly that d'Avila found himself obliged to abandon the newly founded Royal Town and to embark in canoes for Honduras. He got as far southeast as Trujillo, in the latter province, before returning to Salamanca de Campeche in 1533 after an absence of two years.

After the departure of d'Avila for the east in 1531, the Montejos, father and son, had to withstand a strong attack at Campeche in which the elder Montejo nearly lost his life, having been dragged from his horse by the fanatical Maya, intent on sacrificing him; indeed, he was saved only by the prompt intervention of one of his faithful soldiers. The Spaniards, however, won the battle, which resulted in the surrender of the Province of Ah Canul, north of Campeche.

Montejo next sent his son with the title of Lieutenant Governor to conquer the northern provinces, instructing him to divide the services of the Indians encountered among his followers; the Adelantado himself remained behind at the newly founded town of Salamanca de Campeche. The younger Montejo first went to the Province of the Cupules, to the site of the former Itza capital at Chichen Itza, which by this time was completely abandoned and overgrown with trees. He was received somewhat reluctantly by the Cupul ruler, Naabon Cupul, who lodged Montejo in his own house. The latter, finding the numerous population at least submissive, if not enthusiastically friendly, founded the first *Ciudad Real* or Royal City at Chichen Itza, and divided the towns and villages of the region among his soldiers, each Spaniard being allotted the services of between two and three thousand Indians.

The Cupules soon became dissatisfied under Spanish rule, quickly tiring of paying tribute, of forced labor, and of various other oppressions of the white strangers. After six months of the foreign yoke, Naabon Cupul, incited by the Maya priests, tried to kill Montejo, but in the attempt lost his own life. The death of their ruler increased the hatred of the Cupules for the Spaniards, to whom they finally refused to pay tribute and to render forced service; about the middle of 1533, together with the Indians of the neighboring provinces of Ekab, Sotuta, and Cochuah, they blockaded the small Spanish garrison at Chichen Itza; for-

tunately for the invaders, however, the Xiu, Chel, and Pech
tribes in the western peninsula remained faithful.

The younger Montejo, seeing that the whole countryside was
roused against him, determined to abandon the newly founded
Royal City, which could hardly have been more than a small military camp in spite of its imposing name, and to rejoin his father
in the west. To accomplish this maneuver, according to an early
chronicler, he resorted to the following ruse.

. . . . finally one night they abandoned the town, leaving a dog attached
to the clapper of a bell, and a little bread placed at one side so that he could
not reach it; and the same day they wearied the Indians with skirmishes,
so that they should not follow them. The dog rang the bell in his efforts
to reach the bread, which greatly astonished the Indians, who thought the
Spaniards wished to attack them; later when they learned how they had
been tricked they resolved to look for the Spaniards in all directions, as
they did not know which road they had taken. And those who had taken
the same road overtook the Spaniards, shouting loudly as at people who
were running away, because of which six horsemen awaited them in an
open place and speared many. One of the Indians seized a horse by the
leg and felled it as though it were a sheep.

The younger Montejo finally reached Dzilam in the Province
of the Chels where the young Chel lord, Namux Chel, who was
already a Christian, received him with friendship. Later in the
spring of 1534 the younger Montejo rejoined his father at Dzibikal in the Province of Chakan near T'ho (the present Merida),
affairs at Dzilam having gone from bad to worse.

Returning to the Adelantado, whom we left at Campeche in
1531, we find that by 1533 he had advanced as far inland as the
Province of Mani and visited the Xiu ruler there, presumably
Ah Dzun Xiu, who, as we have seen in the preceding chapter, lost
his life three years later in 1536 at Otzmal. The Xiu throughout
the conquest repeatedly showed their friendship for the Spaniards, and it was largely owing to their timely aid on more than
one occasion that Spanish authority was finally established permanently in the peninsula. As just noted, the Montejos, father and

son, met at Dzibikal in the spring of 1534, and shortly afterward the Adelantado founded the second Royal City at Dzilam, where the Spaniards are said to have "suffered many privations and dangers."

When the Adelantado determined to return to Campeche, the friendly Namux Chel, the young Lord of Dzilam, offered to conduct him thither in person, accompanied by two of his first cousins. The two cousins were taken in chains, perhaps as hostages, though Namux Chel was provided with a horse for the long overland journey, which was calculated to be forty-eight leagues or about 125 miles. Montejo left his son at Dzilam to carry on the work of conquest and pacification as best he might. The Adelantado was well received by the Indians around Campeche, where he was presently joined by d'Avila as previously noted, and, not long afterwards also by his son, who found his position at Dzilam so difficult as to be no longer tenable.

Just at this juncture the conquest of Yucatan received a further serious setback. News of the conquest of Peru and the gold and riches to be had there reached the disheartened followers of Montejo at Campeche; tales, we may be sure, that lost nothing in the retelling. Already the Spaniards had been fighting through the thick bush of northern Yucatan, a hot, parched and unfriendly country, for seven years, having found no more gold than would fill a few helmets, and no mines of any sort. Moreover, they had begun to realize that no matter how hard they might fight there would be no rich rewards in spoils and booty such as the soldiers of Cortes had reaped thirteen years earlier in the highlands of central Mexico, and such as the companions of Pizarro were now gaining in Peru. In the face of the latter golden lure, the Adelantado could no longer hold together his already depleted forces. The little army gradually dwindled until it became necessary, at least temporarily, to abandon the conquest of Yucatan a second time. Finally, late in 1534 or early in 1535, the Adelantado withdrew from Campeche to Veracruz with his son, his nephew, also named Francisco de Montejo, and the remnant of his badly depleted army.

Ever since he had first visited Honduras in 1528, the Adelantado had been petitioning the Spanish King for the governorship of that province, which, combined with the *Adelantazgo* of Yucatan, already his by royal grant, and certain administrative rights in Tabasco and Chiapas, which he claimed, would have given him a tremendous jurisdiction—all of what is now southern Mexico and northern Central America. In answer to his several petitions, Montejo was finally named Governor and Captain General of the province of Honduras-Hibüeras in 1535, although notice of this appointment did not reach him until after he had left Yucatan for Mexico City, and he did not actually go to Honduras the second time until 1537.

The Honduras episode was unsuccessful from the outset. When he reached the province a revolt among the Indians broke out; hardly had this been subdued, when Montejo found himself far more seriously involved with another Adelantado, also an old companion-at-arms, Pedro de Alvarado, who had been named Governor and Captain General of Guatemala by royal appointment. But the latter also claimed jurisdictional rights over Honduras as well as Guatemala, and in August 1539 Montejo was obliged to give up his interests in Honduras-Hibüeras to Alvarado in return for the latter's rights to the governorship of Chiapas; after this, Montejo returned to Tabasco, where his son was acting as Lieutenant Governor and Captain General during his father's absence.

As early as 1535 a Franciscan named Fray Jacobo de Testera had gone to Champoton to subdue Yucatan, if possible, by peaceful means; indeed, the Crown had promised him that all Spanish soldiers would be excluded from the country until he had first made an attempt to subjugate it by preaching. He was having some success at this when Captain Lorenzo de Godoy suddenly appeared at Champoton with Spanish soldiers sent by Montejo the Younger to reduce the region. Trouble between Testera and Godoy broke out immediately and the former, disgusted with the military intrusion, returned to Mexico.

Affairs at Champoton under Godoy went from bad to worse. The Couohs of the surrounding region were becoming more and more warlike until, in 1537, Montejo the Younger was obliged to send his cousin from Tabasco to take charge of the situation at Champoton; here the latter founded the sixth settlement of Salamanca—Salamanca de Champoton. The new Spanish leader at Champoton was more politic than Godoy had been and managed to persuade the Indians to be less hostile; but want and misery continued and this last Spanish toe hold in Yucatan became more and more precarious.

THIRD PHASE: CONQUEST COMPLETED FROM THE WEST BY FRANCISCO DE MONTEJO THE YOUNGER (1540–1546)

The Adelantado was now about 67 years old and had been trying to reduce Yucatan for thirteen years but with only negligible results. He was weary, disillusioned, impoverished, and resolved to entrust the active prosecution of the conquest to his son, who was to be aided by the latter's cousin of the same name, Francisco de Montejo.

In 1540 the Adelantado drew up a formal document turning over the conquest of Yucatan to his son and giving him elaborate instructions as to the course he was to adopt toward the Indians, the division of land among his soldier-colonists, and even the place where he was to locate the Spanish capital of the as yet unconquered province. Early in 1541 Montejo the Younger left Tabasco by water for Champoton, where his cousin had already been stationed, as we have seen, for more than two years, during which time the warlike Couohs of other days had become very friendly. Shortly after his arrival at Champoton, Montejo moved his headquarters to Campeche, which had been previously founded as a Spanish city on October 4, 1540, by his cousin; this was the first permanent Spanish *cabildo* or town government to be set up in the northern Maya area. The army again now numbered between 300 and 400 soldier-colonists under the command of Montejo, the son, with his cousin as second in charge.

Early in 1541 Montejo summoned all the Maya lords to
Campeche to render submission to the Spanish Crown. The Xiu
ruler and a number of neighboring caciques obeyed the summons,
but the ever-hostile Province of Ah Canul refused. Montejo
then dispatched his cousin to subdue the Ah Canules, while he
remained behind at Campeche to await the arrival of new recruits.
His cousin set out from Tenabo in Campeche and met the Ah
Canules in the Province of Chakan, near T'ho (the modern
Merida), defeating them. In the late summer of 1541, Montejo
the Younger on his way from Campeche to T'ho, met more of the
Xiu chieftains at Tuchicaan, a village on the road between Campeche and T'ho, and received their submission. Finally, in the
early fall of 1541, Montejo the Younger reached the site of T'ho,
whither his cousin had preceded him, and on the following 6th of
January O.S. (1542), the Day of the Holy Kings, he founded
what later became "The Very Noble and Very Loyal City of
Merida," setting up the second Spanish *cabildo* in the northern
Maya area.

On January 23, seventeen days after the foundation of
Merida, the Spanish sentries stationed at the base of the large
Maya pyramid where Montejo's little army was encamped
sighted a great multitude of Indians escorting a young Maya
lord, seated in a palanquin. From the deference shown him it
was obvious that he was a personage of high degree. At first the
Spaniards were terrified, fearing an immediate attack in force,
but to their great relief the Indian lord, on descending from his
palanquin, made signs that he came in peace, bringing with him
large supplies of corn, vegetables, and fowl, of which the Spaniards, who were all but starving, were in dire need.

Through an interpreter, this Indian indicated that he was the
Lord Tutul Xiu, supreme ruler of the large Province of Mani,
that he greatly admired the bravery of the white men, and that he
wanted to know them and see some of their religious ceremonies.
Montejo, delighted at the happy turn of events, ordered the
chaplain of the army to celebrate "a solemn Adoration of the
Holy Cross" in which all the Spanish soldiers took part. The Xiu

ruler was deeply impressed, even imitating the movements of the Spaniards in the ceremony, and said that he wished to become a Christian himself. He stayed at the Spanish camp for two months, during which time he was instructed in the Catholic faith, and before he left, he was baptized Melchor, probably because in very truth he was "a king bearing gifts."

The results of this visit were far-reaching, no less than the peaceful reduction of the whole western half of the northern peninsula. Ever since the fall of Mayapan a century earlier, the Xiu Province of Mani had been the most powerful political unit in northern Yucatan and its peaceful submission to the Spaniards was followed by that of other western provinces, including those of the powerful Peches and Cheles. Before leaving T'ho, the newly baptized Melchor promised to send ambassadors to the other Maya lords, urging them, even though they were not his vassals, to give obedience to Montejo, a promise that was faithfully carried out, and thus the pacification of the west was finally accomplished without further fighting. However, the east still remained unconquered.

In the spring of 1542, after the submission of the western provinces, Montejo the Younger sent his cousin to the Province of Chauaca. All the eastern lords received him peacefully (for the time being) except the Cochua chieftains. On May 28, before moving against the latter, Montejo, the nephew, founded the town of Valladolid at the site of the principal town in the Province of Chauaca, which was then said to number from six hundred to a thousand inhabitants. After a brief though bitterly contested campaign against the Cochua lords, Montejo defeated them.

Next the Cupules, incited by their priests, revolted at the town of Zaci and were in turn subdued. Montejo finally reached the east coast at Pole in the Province of Ekab and tried to cross the channel separating the mainland from the island of Cozumel, but was prevented from so doing by stormy weather. In the attempt, however, nine Spaniards were drowned and a tenth was killed by the Maya. Exaggerated reports of these losses encouraged both the Cupules and the Cochuas to revolt again.

Owing to the unhealthfulness of the site chosen for the first settlement of Valladolid, Montejo on March 14, 1544, moved the new settlement to the Indian town of Zaci, already mentioned, and here the modern city of Valladolid has remained to the present day. The Indian town of Zaci was the governmental and religious center for forty villages within a day's journey of it, and of as many more within a radius of forty to fifty miles.

Landa describes the unrest among the eastern Maya as follows:

The Indians received with sorrow the yoke of slavery, but the Spaniards had the towns of the country well divided into *repartimientos* [individual holdings].

The eastern provinces, Cupul, Cochua, Sotuta, and Chetumal, and to a lesser degree that of the Tazes, still managed to retain their independence, and it was obvious that further military action against them would be necessary.

But the conquest of Yucatan at long last was drawing to a close; only one more bloody revolt in the east was to occur before final Spanish victory. This revolt involved a conspiracy of practically all the eastern provinces, and the night of November 8, 1546, was chosen for the uprising, perhaps because that date fell on the auspicious Maya day "1 Imix," the first day of the Maya sacred, or ritualistic, year of 260 days.

Through information from friendly Indians, Merida and Campeche in the west had previous word of the impending revolt, but in the east, the surprise was complete. Says a contemporary Spanish writer:

Late in the year of '46 the natives of all these provinces, of the Cupules, Tazes, and Chikin Cheles rose and rebelled against His Majesty, making a great massacre of the Spanish *encomenderos* [those among whom the Indians had been divided] of whom they killed eighteen Spaniards who were in their towns, where they sacrificed them . . . . and besides more than four hundred Indian free-men who served the Spaniards as servants, without leaving anything alive, if it was a thing that savoured of the Spanish, including the herds and other things, until help came from the city of Merida in the same year and the natives became peaceful again, the culprits being punished.

When the revolt began both the younger Montejos, son and nephew, were in Campeche, awaiting the arrival of the Adelantado from Chiapas. The latter reached Merida in December, but the *cabildo* had already dispatched Captain Francisco Tamayo Pacheco with soldiers to Valladolid to quell the uprising. The Adelantado raised additional troops in his plantations at Champoton and Campeche and sent them to Valladolid in command of his nephew. The latter, after losing twenty Spaniards and several hundred of the contingent of friendly Indians, finally defeated the coalition of the eastern Maya chieftains in a single engagement and shortly afterward conquered the extreme southern province of Uaymil-Chetumal, where the seventh and last town of Salamanca was founded by Melchor Tamayo Pacheco, a brother of Francisco. This last uprising for a time seriously challenged Spanish authority in Yucatan; but with these victories, which came at the very end of 1546, the third and last phase of the conquest of Yucatan was brought to a successful conclusion.

THE SPANISH CONQUEST OF PETEN

THE HERNANDO CORTÉS EXPEDITION TO HONDURAS-HIBÜERAS. 1524–1525

THE CONQUEROR of Mexico was the first white man to enter the region occupied by the Maya Old Empire, when in 1524–1525 he traversed the Department of Peten, Guatemala, from its northwest to its southeast corners, on his historic march from Mexico to the Province of Honduras-Hibüeras.

Three years after the conquest of Mexico in 1521, Cortés sent one of his captains, Cristobal de Olid, to Honduras to subdue that distant region. Olid, finding himself so far from his leader, seized the opportunity to rebel against the latter's authority and to set himself up independently. News of this defection having reached Mexico, Cortés set out from Tenochtitlan (now Mexico City) on October 12, 1525, thirty-three years to the very day after Columbus had discovered the New World, to march overland to Honduras to subdue his disloyal captain.

This heroic anabasis, from Espíritu Santo in the Province of Coatzacoalcos of the Vice-royalty of Nueva España (now Puerto Mexico in the State of Veracruz, Mexico) through Nito, an undetermined site probably located on the southeast bank of the Rio Dulce (now in the Department of Izabal, Guatemala) to Trujillo in the Province of Honduras, now the republic of the same name, took about six months, from October 1524 to April 1525. This formidable undertaking constitutes one of the greatest sustained efforts in military history. Because of the all-but-impassable character of the intervening terrain—swamps, marshes, lagoons, many deep rivers, especially in Tabasco, trackless forests and precipitous mountain ranges—across the very heart of the Maya Old Empire, in the hot, humid Atlantic coast-plain of

117

Middle America, the attendant hardships and privations were almost beyond mortal endurance and the army was always just one step ahead of actual starvation.

Cortes was accompanied by about 140 Spanish soldiers, of whom 93 were mounted, and by more than 3,000 Indians from Mexico, with some 150 horses, a herd of pigs, artillery, munitions, and supplies; and—because he dared not leave them behind—also by Quauhtemoc, Cohuanacox, and Tetlepanquetzal, the deposed rulers of Tenochtitlan, Texcoco, and Tlacopan, respectively. To transport such a large body of men across this then unknown wilderness, a journey of more than five hundred miles, even today with the best modern camp equipment available—portable kitchens, collapsible shelters, mosquito-bars, condensed foods, adequate medical supplies, and the like—would tax severely the strength and endurance of a well-organized modern army; but when it is remembered that this expedition was undertaken in the early years of the sixteenth century, when the New World had been discovered less than four decades earlier and Mexico conquered less than four years before, Cortes' outstanding qualities of leadership, his courage, daring, judgment, diplomacy, and, above all, his tenacity of purpose, are magnified to well-nigh unbelievable proportions. Indeed, his march across the Maya area in 1524 and 1525 remains one of the outstanding achievements in human history.

Cortes entered the Maya area in what is now central Tabasco, Mexico, and crossed the Usumacinta River, probably just below the modern town of Tenosique. Pushing generally eastward through swamps and jungles, he reached the Province of Acalan, ruled by a Chontal-Maya lord named Paxbolon Acha, toward the close of February 1525. Somewhere near the western frontier of this province in, or perhaps more likely very near, the northwestern corner of Peten, occurred what was probably the blackest deed of Cortes' brilliant career—the summary execution of the last Aztec emperor, Quauhtemoc, and of his fellow ruler, Tetlepanquetzal, the Lord of Tlacopan.

Although, when these princes had surrendered at Tenochtitlan four years before, Cortes had solemnly promised them their lives, here in the distant wilds of Acalan, this promise was broken, though, it must be admitted, under considerable provocation. The two eyewitnesses of this tragedy who have left accounts of it are Cortes himself and one of his captains, Bernal Diaz del Castillo; both are in agreement that there was a conspiracy among the Aztec lords to fall upon the Spaniards in the swamps, morasses, and trackless jungles, which they had reached, and there to slay them all. That this was no idle fear is further confirmed by a recently discovered nearly contemporary document, forgotten for more than three centuries in the dusty files of a government archive at Seville, Spain, the famous Archives of the Indies. This document, dated in 1612, is no less than a petition of the Chontal ruler of that day, one Pablo Paxbolon, a grandson of the Paxbolon Acha who was Lord of the Province of Acalan when Cortes passed through that region early in 1525. This petition is an application to the Crown of Spain for a pension for himself, because of his grandfather's services to the Crown, nearly a century earlier.

The petitioner relates how Quauhtemoc approached his grandfather and urged the latter to join the conspiracy against the Spaniards, pointing out how Cortes was abusing the Chontal and robbing them. Paxbolon Acha, however, was wary of these counsels (according to the prejudiced testimony of his grandson it must be remembered) and, seeing for himself that Cortes was not robbing his subjects, but, on the contrary, was paying for all the food he was getting from them, he finally betrayed the conspiracy to the Spanish leader.

The danger was obviously very great. The Spaniards were probably outnumbered fifty to one by the Indians, counting both the Aztecs and the Chontal Maya of Acalan, and immediate action was imperative. Cortes arrested the two leaders forthwith and hanged them without delay. Pablo Paxbolon, however, in his account of the affair says the two Aztec lords were beheaded. An interesting Aztec hieroglyphic manuscript, the Mapa de Tepechpan, dating from the middle sixteenth century, seems to indicate that both accounts may be correct. This manuscript portrays Quauhtemoc's *headless* body *hanging by his feet* (Fig. 3). Above appears the body of the dead Aztec ruler swathed in bandages—the Aztec symbol denoting death; his name-glyph, an eagle, is attached to his head, and below appears his headless body hanging by its feet from a tree.

Cortes, with 600 Chontal Indians as carriers, left Itzamkanac, the capital of the Province of Acalan, on March 5, 1525, and, proceeding generally southeastward, reached the shores of Lake Peten Itza and the Province of the Itza eight days later. Here Canek, the Itza ruler, having crossed from Tayasal, the Itza capital, in six canoes with thirty of his warriors, met Cortes on the northern shore of the lake. Cortes had the Catholic priests with the expedition celebrate Mass, which so impressed Canek that he promised to destroy his idols and replace them with the worship of the Cross. He invited Cortes to visit Tayasal, which invitation the latter accepted, though strongly against the wishes of his men, who feared treachery. He took with him twenty Spanish soldiers, while the rest of the army proceeded around the western end of the lake to wait for him on the southern shore.

Before rejoining the army, Cortes asked Canek to care for a favorite horse which had gone lame until such a time as he should either return or send for it. This animal, or rather an idol made to look like it, under the name of Tzimin Chac, "The Thunder Horse," will be discussed in a later section of this chapter.

After crossing the savannas southeast of Lake Peten Itza, the army entered a terrible terrain, the rugged, broken country on the western flanks of the Maya Mountains (Plate 1). Here they encountered a pass so tortuous and rugged that, although it was only twenty miles in length, it took the tired army twelve days to traverse it. During this time more than two-thirds of the horses were lost, either through falling down precipitous slopes, or because they had to be killed on account of broken legs.

Emerging from this pass of punishment, they reached a large river greatly swollen by torrential rains, which had never ceased falling all the time the army was crawling through the pass. Turning upstream to look for a better fording place, they encoun-

tered a series of "terrifying and impetuous rapids." Today these
same rapids at the southwestern corner of the present British
Honduras, on the border of Guatemala, are ironically known as
"Gracias a Dios." It took the army two days to find its way over
these rapids, more horses being lost in the crossing. Beyond
lay the village of Tenciz, which the badly crippled little
force reached on April 15, the Saturday before Easter
in 1525. Here the weary Spaniards rested two days.

After leaving Tenciz, the army became lost in a
wilderness of hills, the modern Santa Cruz Mountains,
north of Lake Izabal (Plate 1). The Indian guides
deserted here, and had it not been for the lucky capture
of an Indian boy, who finally led them from the cul-de-
sac in which they found themselves, all would
have surely perished of hunger at the moment
when the march was practically over.

Just beyond this point, for the first time,
Cortes heard definite news of the Spaniards
he was seeking; and, to the unbounded delight of every soul in the exhausted army, it
was learned that Nito, the objective of their
incredible wanderings, which I believe was
located on the southeastern bank of the Rio
Dulce, at last lay only two days' journey
ahead.

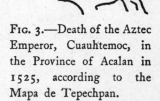

FIG. 3.—Death of the Aztec
Emperor, Cuauhtemoc, in
the Province of Acalan in
1525, according to the
Mapa de Tepechpan.

The final lap of this heroic odyssey took
the completely exhausted Spaniards three days instead of two
before they finally emerged on the northwestern bank of the Rio
Dulce opposite Nito; here Cortes was met by one Diego Nieto
representing the authorities of the little settlement. Cortes with
ten or twelve companions crossed immediately to the other side
of the river and the rest of the army straggled in during the next
five or six days, thus ending one of the greatest adventures in
human history.

On his march diagonally across the Maya area, Cortes visited
the site of only one important Maya center, namely Tayasal,

though he must have passed within a few miles of several others, notably Palenque, Laguna Perdida, Itsimte, Polol, Motul de San José, Ixkun, and Pusilha, and indeed ended his journey at Nito, not far northeast of Quirigua (Plate 19).

THE PERIOD FOLLOWING THE EXPEDITION OF CORTES— 1525–1696

With the conquest of Yucatan completed (1546), there remained only one independent Maya group—the powerful Itza nation, centering around the western end of Lake Peten Itza in northern Peten, Guatemala—which was able to continue to resist the Spaniards and to maintain its political independence for yet another century and three quarters.

Tayasal, the Itza capital, was a long distance either from Merida in northern Yucatan (300 miles) or from St. James of the Gentlemen of Guatemala, the Spanish capital in the southern highlands (180 miles), and for nearly a century after Cortes had visited Tayasal in 1525 neither Yucatan nor Guatemala made any attempts to reduce the remote and extremely hostile Province of the Itza.

Between 1550 and 1556 several Franciscan missionaries had made evangelizing expeditions from Campeche into the near-by Province of Acalan, south and east of the Laguna de Términos, and had finally persuaded the Chontal Maya of that region to move nearer to Campeche, where they could be more easily instructed in the Catholic faith. The capital of Acalan was moved from Itzamkanac, several days' journey into the interior, to Tixchel at the eastern end of the Laguna de Términos in 1557, but the warlike Itza, farther to the southeast, were left severely alone, undisturbed in their independence.

In 1618 two Franciscans, Fathers Bartolome de Fuensalida and Juan de Orbita, having secured permission from the governor of Yucatan and the Provincial of their Order in that province to attempt to Christianize the Itza peaceably, set out from Merida for Tayasal. They left Merida in the spring of 1618, traveling by way of Lake Bacalar in the southeast, and were accompanied by the *alcalde* (mayor) of Bacalar and a number of Indian converts, sacristans, and choristers. With the delays incident to travel in those remote parts, combined with a wholesome fear of the Itza on the part of their Indian guides, the fathers did not succeed in reaching Tayasal until nearly six months later, when Canek, the Itza ruler, received them with friendliness.

They remained at Tayasal for some days, attempting to Christianize the Itza, but Canek, though greatly interested in the Mass, baptism, and other services held by the missionaries, steadfastly refused to renounce his own religion, protesting that the time had not yet arrived when, according to their ancient prophecies, it was foretold that the Itza were to accept a new faith.

While going about the town the fathers were shown a large idol in the form of a horse called Tzimin Chac or the "Thunder Horse." It will be remembered that Cortes had left a lame horse in the hands of the Canek of that day (1525), promising either to return for it himself or to send for it. After Cortes' departure, the Itza treated the horse as a god, offering it fowl, meats, and garlands of flowers, on which diet the horse died. The Itza, terrified at the death of a god on their hands, made a stone idol in likeness of the horse, which they worshiped in order to prove they were not responsible for its death. When Father Orbita saw this image, he became so infuriated at the idolatrous abomination that, in an excess of holy zeal, he seized a stone and smashed the image into bits. The Itza, equally outraged at such a sacrilege, tried to kill the missionaries on the spot, but Father Fuensalida, nothing daunted by their fury, seized the occasion to preach a sermon of such eloquence that the tumult subsided and the missionaries' lives were spared. Although the fathers remained at Tayasal for some days longer, they saw that they were making no progress in Christianizing the Itza and finally took friendly farewell of Canek, who seems to have borne them no ill will for destroying his idol. Father Fuensalida reached Merida on December 8, 1618; Father Orbita, however, remained at Tipu, a small settlement on the southeastern frontier near Lake Bacalar.

The fathers set out from Tipu for Tayasal a second time in

September of the following year, accompanied by some Tipu Indians as guides and servants; they reached the Itza capital at the beginning of October and remained there for eighteen days. Although Canek was at first friendly, the Tipu Indians, having become suspicious of the Itza, finally deserted in a body; later, however, three of them came back to serve the fathers. Truth is that the Itza priests were becoming increasingly jealous of the growing influence of the Catholic missionaries and finally persuaded Canek's wife to urge her husband to expel them. One morning the fathers' house was surrounded by a number of armed Indians; the fathers themselves were hustled down to the lake shore and into a canoe with their Tipu servants and told never to return, as the Itza wanted no more of their religion. Father Orbita, who seems to have been the more violent of the two priests —he it was who had destroyed the idol of the Thunder Horse the year before—made some resistance, but a young Itza warrior seized the collar of his habit and twisted it so violently that Orbita fell to the ground senseless. The little party of five were shoved off in a canoe without food or drink, the Itza confidently hoping all would die of hunger on the long trip back to Tipu.

The Tipu Indians, however, had managed to secrete a little food about their clothing, upon which the five managed to subsist until they reached Tipu. The fathers rested here for a few days, but, seeing that the time was not opportune for continuing their attempts to convert the Itza, they left Tipu and returned to Merida, where they arrived before the end of the year.

Three years later, in 1622, the governor of Yucatan authorized Captain Francisco de Mirones to conduct a military expedition against the Itza and, if possible, to conquer them, and on March 30 of that year Mirones with 20 Spaniards and 140 Indians left Hopelchen in Campeche for the Itza country. A Franciscan missionary, Father Diego Delgado, joined the army six days later. The force marched to a place called Sacalum, where Mirones' treatment of the Indians was such that Father Delgado, in disgust, decided to leave the soldiers and go on ahead without them. He left the camp secretly and proceeded to Tayasal by

way of Tipu, taking with him eighty converted Tipu Indians as
well as a number of choristers and sacristans from Hecelchakan.

Father Delgado and his Indians were escorted from the
northern shore of the lake to Tayasal by the Itza with a great
show of friendship, but on reaching the town all were seized and
sacrificed to the Itza idols, the Franciscan priest being reserved
until the last. He continued preaching to the end, however, until
his breast was slit open and his heart offered to the Itza gods.
As many as a hundred persons lost their lives in this massacre,
which took place in July 1623.

News of the death of Father Delgado and his Indians reached
Merida slowly, but as soon as the authorities at the capital heard
of it they sent word to Captain Mirones at Sacalum to be on his
guard. On February 2, 1624, the Spaniards at Sacalum were all
in the village church, without arms, listening to the army chaplain celebrate the Mass, when suddenly the Indians fell upon
them and slaughtered all; afterwards the Indians fled to the
forests. A few days later a relief party with reinforcements arrived at Sacalum only to find the bodies of their slain companions
cast into a hole.

These two massacres, in which nearly two hundred and
fifty persons lost their lives, about one-third of whom were Spaniards, put a sudden stop to all attempts either to Christianize or to
conquer the Itza; and when about twelve years later, in 1636, the
faithful Tipu Indians began to apostatize, returning to their former idolatry, the last link of friendly Indian contact between
northern Yucatan on the one hand and the Province of the Itza
on the other, was severed.

And thus affairs remained for nearly three-quarters of a century. The Spanish continued to consolidate their positions in
Yucatan and in Guatemala, but the territory lying between,
dominated chiefly by the Itza, now Peten, Guatemala, remained
unconquered and un-Christianized, a continual irritation to both
the military and ecclesiastical authorities of the two provinces.

In June 1695, Martin de Ursua, then governor of Yucatan,
as an essential preliminary to the conquest of the Itza, sent a

contingent of Spanish soldiers and Indians to the village of Cauich, near the modern town of Bolonchen-Cauich in northern Campeche, to begin building a road through the forests to the shores of Lake Peten Itza. Toward the end of the month, the road builders had reached a village called Nohthub in southern Campeche, where three Franciscans headed by Father Andres de Avendaño, and ten Indian singers, sacristans, and servants joined them. The priests, as usual, soon became disgusted with the way the Spanish captain, Paredes, treated the Indians, and they returned to Merida, where they arrived in mid-September.

At the end of the rainy season, on December 15, 1695, Father Avendaño again left Merida for the Province of the Itza accompanied by two other Franciscans, four Indian singers from Yucatan, and three Indian guides. Instead of going around by way of Tipu, involving a considerable detour to the east, as the other missionaries had previously done, Father Avendaño followed the new road from Bolonchen-Cauich as far south as it had been built and then pushed on through the forests with his Indian guides to Lake Peten Itza.

They reached the lake at its western extremity on January 13, 1696, and were given a boisterous reception by the Chakan Itza living at the western end, who forthwith stole all the presents they were bringing to Canek—everything they had, in fact, except the clothes on their backs. The next day Canek met them at the village of the Chakan Itza, having crossed from Tayasal with an escort of eighty canoes. When the party reached the Itza capital, the fathers were taken to a house where they thought they saw the leg-bone of a horse suspended in a box, presumably from the horse that Cortes had left at Tayasal one hundred and seventy-one years before.

The fathers remained at Tayasal for three and a half days, during which time they baptized more than three hundred Indian children. Father Avendaño urged Canek and his councillors to surrender to the Crown of Spain and accept Christianity. The Itza council took this proposal under consideration, saying they would reply later; but their final decision was as before that, though near at hand, the time had not yet arrived when their ancient prophecies had foretold that they should give up the worship of their old gods; and, further, that if Governor Ursua would send the fathers back in another four months the Itza would become vassals of the Spanish King and embrace Christianity.

Canek, learning of a plot among the Chakan Itza, who had not approved the council's decision, to waylay the fathers on their return trip and kill them, persuaded Avendaño to change his plans and to return to Merida by the longer and more circuitous, though safer, route through Tipu and Lake Bacalar. On the night of January 17, 1696, the three fathers with their four faithful Indians from Yucatan, after taking an affectionate farewell of Canek and his family, embarked in a canoe for the village of Alain at the eastern end of the lake.

From this point on, bad luck and increasing hardships beset the fathers. The promised guides to Tipu were not forthcoming and after waiting for two days at Alain, during which a plot to kill them was frustrated by Avendaño, the fathers set out on January 20 on the long, dangerous return journey to northern Yucatan. At the end of ten days they became completely lost in the trackless forests of northeastern Peten. At first they traveled east-northeast from the eastern end of the lake, going in the general direction of Tipu. At the end of five days the little party came to a large stream, probably the Holmul River, which they followed down for another five days, becoming hopelessly lost.

At this point they determined to strike back west, hoping thus to be able to reach the general north-south road, which Ursua was having built from Bolonchen-Cauich in Campeche to the shores of the lake. In this general direction they pushed on for fifteen days more, living, or rather nearly dying, on a meager diet of wild honey, green *mamey*, which they cooked, and palm nuts. On the fourth day of this exhausting trek (February 2), Avendaño became so weak that the two other Franciscans, taking one of the four Indians as a guide, pushed on in hope of locating some frontier settlement and bringing back help and supplies to their exhausted leader.

After six days of terrible hardships, Father Avendaño came upon the ruins of an ancient city, which he describes as follows:

> With so few comforts and so many hardships my strength was failing rapidly, which brought home to me the truth of the adage that the Biscayans, my countrymen, have, namely, that "the belly supports, or carries the legs, and not the legs, the belly."
>
> Among these high mountains which we passed there are a number of ancient buildings; among them I recognized some as living places, and although they were very high and my strength very little, I climbed them, but with difficulty. They are in the form of a convent with small cloisters and many rooms for living, all roofed, surrounded by a terrace and whitened with lime inside, which latter abounds in these parts, because all the hills are of limestone; and these said buildings are of such form that they did not appear like those of this province [Yucatan] which latter are entirely of dressed stone put together without mortar, especially as to their arches, but these [in Peten] are of stone masonry plastered over with lime.

A glance at the map in Plate 19 will show that following Father Avendaño's course east-northeast from the eastern end of Lake Peten Itza for ten days, and thence northwest for another six days, the only archaeological site answering the foregoing description he could possibly have reached is Tikal, and he was therefore the first European to see this greatest of all ancient Maya cities.

By a curious quirk of historical timing, a month later almost to the very day, a Spanish expedition under the *Maestro de Campo* Jacobo de Alcayaga, coming down the Lacantun and Usumacinta rivers, discovered the site of another large ancient city, which from its description could only have been Yaxchilan:

> In another landing that some soldiers made, they came upon a site, which, because of its many stone foundations and most ancient ruined buildings, had the appearance of having been a very old settlement; this site was about a league in circumference.

Thus Tikal and Yaxchilan, the largest, and one of the largest cities, respectively, of the Old Empire were seen for the first time by European eyes within a month of each other.

Father Avendaño, after leaving Tikal with his two remaining
Indians (one having died after the two parties separated), traveled
westward and northward for another three days until Avendaño's
failing strength gave out altogether. Seeing that he was holding
the Indians back, he ordered them to leave him propped up against
a tree with a lighted fire and a gourd of water, and to push on for
help. That night a squirrel playing with a sapodilla, a tropical
fruit common in the Peten forests, miraculously pushed the fruit
within reach of Avendaño's staff. The father writes that he was
too weak to move, but by means of his staff he drew the sapodilla
to him and ate it—which saved his life.

The next morning his faithful Indians returned with ten carriers. After leaving Avendaño the day before, they had finally
come out on a broad trail which led them to the stopping-place
of Chuntuqui on the new road from Bolonchen-Cauich to Lake
Peten Itza. Here they found some Indian carriers and took them
back to rescue the father. Avendaño says at first sight he mistook
his rescuers for angels. The Indians carried him in a hammock
to Chuntuqui, where they arrived on February 19, having been
lost in the forests of northern central Peten for thirty-one days.
At Chuntuqui he found the two other Franciscans and the Indian
that had accompanied them, who had left him eighteen days
before in search of help. After resting at Chuntuqui for a few
days, Avendaño and his companions continued on their way to
Merida, where they reported on their mission.

THE CONQUEST OF THE ITZA, 1696–1697

We have seen in the preceding section that the Governor of
Yucatan had commenced building a road from Bolonchen-Cauich
in Campeche to Lake Peten Itza on June 12, 1695. Although
the road had been opened for another fifty miles beyond Chuntuqui by September of that year, heavy rains prevented supplies
being brought forward, so that the road gangs were obliged to
return to Zucthok, north of the present boundary between Mexico
and Guatemala, until the rainy season was over.

As the result of an embassy from Canek, which reached

Merida at the end of December 1695, Ursua became convinced that the Itza were at last ready to submit to Spanish rule. Acting on this assumption he ordered Captain Paredes, who was still at work on the road, to proceed to Tayasal and take possession of the Province of the Itza. Paredes, finding himself unable to comply with the order in person, sent in his place Captain Pedro de Zubiaur with sixty Spanish soldiers, some Indian warriors and servants, and Father San Buenaventura as chaplain, to take possession of the province.

By this time the road had advanced to within some twenty miles of the lake, and Zubiaur's command, pushing through this last section of the forest, reached the lake shore on January 18, 1696. From Ursua's instructions, Zubiaur had confidently expected a peaceful reception by the Itza, but to his astonishment he was met by just the reverse. As the Spaniards approached the lake, they saw a great flotilla of canoes filled with heavily armed Indians advancing rapidly toward them. Leaping ashore, the Itza attacked vigorously, seizing some of the friendly Indians from Yucatan and hurrying them into the canoes as prisoners. Father San Buenaventura, a lay Franciscan brother, and a Spanish soldier were also made prisoners, and a fourth Spaniard was killed in the fight; all this happened before the Spaniards could even as much as draw a sword. The Itza numbered about two thousand.

Battle thus having been forced upon them, the Spaniards defended themselves bravely, but, seeing themselves so greatly outnumbered, Zubiaur withdrew to the main camp of Captain Paredes. A second and larger Spanish force was dispatched to the lake a day or so later, and, having met with a similar hostile reception, it discontinued all further immediate attempts to press the attack.

The news of the hostile reception of Father Avendaño, as well as that of Zubiaur's defeat, reached Ursua at the same time, and it became evident that the Itza were to be reduced only by military force. One hundred extra soldiers, shipwrights, and carpenters were needed to build a pirogue and a galley to navigate the lake and thus dominate not only Tayasal but also the other Itza villages on the lake shore. These were at once recruited in Merida and sent to Paredes with instructions to press forward as speedily as possible the work of opening the road the remaining twenty miles.

Ursua at this time became engaged in a law suit with a political rival, and, although he won the suit, before so doing he had already ordered Captain Paredes to retire to Campeche to await his coming with larger forces the next year.

The close of 1696 and the beginning of 1697 were spent in reassembling the army at Campeche. This army consisted of 235 Spanish soldiers, 120 Indian muleteers and road workers from the villages of Sotuta, Yaxcaba, Tixcacal, and Peto, and an unspecified number of Indian carriers from Mani. The infantry, artillery, and supply trains with food, small arms, ammunition, and marine equipment to make the boats were sent on ahead under Paredes with orders to Zubiaur to proceed to within five miles of the lake with the ship carpenters and calkers, and there to cut and trim sufficient timber for a galley, ninety feet long, and for a pirogue, and to await there the arrival of the rest of the army. Ursua followed shortly with the cavalry, his personal suite, the Royal Standard, its guard, and the rest of the supplies. He left Campeche on January 24, 1697.

On March 1, the timbers for the galley and the pirogue being ready, the whole army with the artillery, supply train, and lumber for the boats moved forward to the shore of the lake, where a fortified camp was built, not only to insure the safety of the little army and its supplies but also to permit work on the galley and pirogue to go forward without interruption by the Itza.

For the next twelve days the Itza made hostile demonstrations against the Spanish camp. Flotillas of canoes maneuvered in front of the camp daily; and companies of painted warriors surrounded it on the land side, beating their war drums and sounding their reeds to demoralize the Spaniards, threatening them all the while with death and sacrifice.

On March 10, a great number of canoes were seen approaching the Spanish camp from the direction of Tayasal, the first canoe carrying a white flag. It was an embassy from Canek consisting of the Itza high priest and other chiefs, who came to offer peace. Ursua received them in a friendly manner and through them invited Canek to visit the Spanish camp the third day hence (March 12). The embassy was then dismissed after distributing among its members a number of gifts—axes, cutlasses, glass objects, earrings, silk ribbons, and other trinkets, and the camp settled down to await the arrival of the Itza ruler the next day but one.

But to no avail. The morning of March 12 dawned, but the Itza ruler did not appear; instead a great flotilla of canoes, the most numerous that had yet come against them, was sighted moving swiftly across the lake toward the camp, while on shore numerous companies of shouting, prancing warriors threatened to attack momentarily. However, as night fell, both canoes and land forces withdrew.

At this serious juncture, Ursua called a council of war of all his officers and laid before them in detail what had happened up to that date, requesting each in turn to give his opinion as to what he believed should be done in the present crisis. All were of one opinion, that further efforts to reduce the Itza by peaceable means were useless, that the only remaining course was to conquer them by force of arms. This decision having been unanimously reached, a decree ordering the attack on Tayasal the following morning was read to the army the same afternoon, to the accompaniment of rolling drums.

The next morning, March 13, before dawn, when the army had confessed and received communion, and Mass had been celebrated, breakfast was eaten and the soldiers selected for the attack embarked on the galley. Ursua took with him 108 Spanish soldiers, five servants, the Vicar-general of the army, the latter's assistant, and a nephew of Canek, who had shown himself friendly to the Spanish cause from the first. He left behind, as a garrison in the fort, 127 Spaniards and all the Indian bowmen, road workers, and servants.

The galley, driven by the Indian oarsmen, swept toward Tayasal at dawn. The order of the preceding day was read again aboard ship; the Vicar-general adjured all who had sinned to ask

forgiveness and, this having been done, he granted a general
absolution. ·

Presently those on the galley saw a number of canoes putting
out from the shore in two flanking squadrons, the occupants
shouting and threatening with their weapons, but Ursua, paying
no attention to them, ordered the oarsmen to row with all speed
possible toward the town itself, which was now clear to everybody
in the early morning light.

The number of canoes grew so rapidly that presently, as the
galley neared the shore, they formed a crescent around it, completely cutting it off from the lake. The Spaniards were now
close enough to see not only the fortifications that had been built
against them—the breastworks of stone and earth on the shore,
on the slopes of the hills covered with houses and up to the heights
crowned by pyramids and temples—but also the multitude already
under arms waiting to defend them. At Tayasal, as well as on
the smaller islands, every available place was black with the Itza,
prepared to defend their homes with their lives.

Having come within bowshot of the galley, and having seen
that the Spaniards paid no attention to their warlike demonstrations
but continued a course straight for the shore, the Itza on land as
well as those in the canoes began to discharge a hail of arrows
at the galley. In spite of this galling attack, Ursua still held
back, shouting in a loud voice above the tumult, "No one fire,
for God is on our side and there is no cause for fear."

The Itza pressed closer, the arrows fell more thickly, and
still in the face of the growing impatience of his officers and men,
Ursua held fire, shouting that no one was to discharge a shot
either from the artillery or arquebuses, or even from a stone-
thrower, under pain of death. The Itza, mistaking this restraint
for cowardice, mocked the Spaniards as not only already vanquished but killed and eaten, as was the Indians' barbarous practice.

Finally the Spanish general made one last appeal; the galley
was slowed down and through an interpreter he told the Itza to
stop their shouting and to calm themselves, that the Spaniards

came in peace and friendship, not in war, and that unless the Itza laid down their arms they, and they alone, would be responsible for the slaughter which would surely follow.

Although the Itza heard Ursua's plea, since the interpreter repeated it several times in a loud voice, they again mistook his forbearance for weakness, and jeering at the Spaniards, let fly more and more arrows.

The Spaniards were so closely crowded together on the deck of the galley that it was a miracle all were not killed outright. Notwithstanding the congestion, only two were wounded—Sergeant Juan Gonzalez with an arrow wound in his arm, and a soldier named Bartolome Duran.

The latter, infuriated and beside himself with pain, forgot Ursua's repeated orders not to begin fighting and discharged his arquebus at the Itza, whereupon others immediately followed his example until firing from the galley became general. So eager for the fray were the Spaniards that, not waiting for the galley even to ground, they leaped into the water, which came to their knees, Ursua with them, firing their arquebuses, the noise of which was deafening. Even here the Spanish general showed his mercy, for he prevented his men from discharging either the artillery, or the stone-throwers, only the smaller arms being used in the fight. Had the artillery been brought into action, the slaughter would have been frightful, as the enemy were so numerous and their canoes so closely packed together that they crowded up to the very muzzles of the cannons.

Having gained the shore, the Spaniards continued firing with such effect that soon the Itza, terrified with the din of the arquebuses, were in full flight, not only from their fortified positions in the town but also from the rest of the Tayasal peninsula. From the ruler down to his lowliest subject, everyone who could took to the lake, swimming frantically for the opposite shore. The stretch of water which separates Tayasal from the mainland is so long and deep and the water itself was by this time so thick with people that swimming was well-nigh impossible and many perished in their mad flight.

Sword and shield in hand, Ursua and the victorious Spaniards pressed up the hill, while the galley with the twenty soldiers who had remained aboard to guard it, was rowed back and forth, the men shooting from its deck. The plight of the Itza in the canoes was thus as bad as that of those in the town, and they too sought to escape by hurling themselves into the lake and swimming for the mainland, so that soon the entire population of Tayasal was in the water and the peninsula was completely deserted.

The battle was over by half-past eight in the morning, so rapid had been the journey across the lake, the advance, the fight, and victory; and Ursua, reaching the highest point of the hill, crowned by a large temple, planted the Royal Standard on its summit, while the Spanish colors were broken out at the same time from other heights. From the highest temple, Ursua with his principal captains and the two Catholic priests gave thanks to God, not only for their victory but also for having preserved them from any loss of life, the two soldiers mentioned being the only ones who were even wounded during the entire conflict. On every side there were congratulations because of the happy outcome of the battle, and Ursua thanked his officers and men for their bravery, their constancy and faith, which alone had made possible the whole epic undertaking.

The amenities being thus concluded, and seeing themselves masters of the town and, because of the great fear that had overtaken the Itza, of the whole lake and the different settlements around its shores as well, where no further resistance was anticipated, Ursua formally renamed Tayasal "Nuestra Señora de los Remedios y San Pablo de los Itzaes," because a picture of that saint had been found miraculously floating on the water near the galley that morning before the little expedition set sail from the camp.

After dividing his force into companies to guard different parts of the town, Ursua, the Vicar-general, and his assistant made a tour of the twenty-one temples, breaking the innumerable idols found in them as well as in the dwellings of the Itza; poor indeed was the household that did not contain at least two or three of these baked clay images of their gods. So vast was the number of their idols that the destruction and burning of them alone took the entire Spanish force from shortly after the battle about eight-thirty or nine in the morning to half past five in the afternoon, when the trumpeter's call of "retreat" summoned the soldiers to their first meal since early morning.

As the final act of the day, Ursua with the two priests selected the principal temple, where human sacrifice had so recently been offered to the Itza deities, to be the sanctuary of the Christian God, as if thus to emphasize more signally, the triumph of the True Faith over that of the Demon.

And thus between dawn and nine in the morning of a single day the power of the Itza was crushed, and the last independent Maya political entity was brought under the domination of the Spanish Crown, though the formal act of possession for and in the name of the Spanish King was deferred until the next day, March 14, 1697.

AGRICULTURE

THE ORIGIN OF AGRICULTURE IN THE NEW WORLD

ALL OF OUR plant biologists agree that high civilization in the New World was first developed in connection with the cultivation of maize, or Indian corn (*Zea Mays* L.), the staff of life of the American Indian in pre-Columbian times, indeed just as it still is today for the great mass of our fellow Americans living to the south of us; but as to where corn originated in the Americas there is no such unanimity of opinion. One school of thought believes that agriculture developed in South America, in the highlands of Peru, while another holds that it developed in northern Middle America, more specifically in the highlands of western Guatemala. Since both schools accept maize as the first cultivated plant in the New World, determination of the place where maize originated also answers the larger question as to where in the New World agriculture had its origin.

These two schools of thought base their opposing arguments each upon a different fact, one pointing to Peru as the place of origin, the other to northern Middle America; one believes that where the greatest number of maize varieties is to be found, there this cereal must have first developed; the other holds that no matter how humble, maize must have had some native ancestor or relative from which it could have developed. If we accept the greatest number of maize varieties as the determining factor indicating place of origin, then we must look to the Peruvian highlands as the region where Indian corn was first developed, since Peru has more varieties of maize than any other region in the Americas. On the other hand, if we accept the nearest, indeed, the only known relatives of maize as the controlling factor indicating its place of origin, then we must look to western Guatemala where are found the only two grasses that will cross with maize: the native grass known as *teosinte*, both a perennial and an annual species, and Tripsacum of which there are several species in Guatemala.

Those who accept Peru as the place of origin are obliged to ignore completely these two close relatives of maize. As one eminent plant biologist shrewdly puts it:

> They [the protagonists of the Peruvian origin hypothesis] prune the *teosinte* trunk from the maize family tree and eliminate Tripsacum, the only other known relative, from the roots. This leaves maize unencumbered by living relatives and permits originating it in South America from some pre-maize form *as yet unknown*.
>
> The elimination of *teosinte* is achieved by designating the two known species as bastards formed by a rare cross between maize and Tripsacum. This cross, which has been made by Mangelsdorf [the chief supporter of the Peruvian origin hypothesis] and others, cannot have happened often because it must be made using maize as the female parent, and then only by opening the husks and shaving off the silks. The [resulting] cross itself is sterile but produces an occasional perfect pollen grain. One of these latter is presumed to have fertilized another corn kernel and from the second fertilization or back-cross, the wild species we now know as *teosinte* are supposed to have been derived.

Having thus eliminated *teosinte*, a widespread wild species in western Guatemala, from the ancestry of maize by assuming that it is the result of a cross between a previously domesticated plant (maize itself) and another wild grass—Tripsacum—the proponents of this hypothesis are free to move the geographic origin of maize anywhere in the New World; and since the ancient Peruvians are known (1) to have developed more varieties of Indian corn than any other people in the Western Hemisphere; and (2) to have been agriculturists of exceptional ability, probably the most highly skilled farmers in the New World in pre-Columbian times, it is only necessary to assume further that the ancient Peruvians had discovered a pre-maize plant, and to leave it to their generally admitted agricultural skill to develop maize from this *entirely hypothetical* pre-maize ancestor. This hypothetical pre-

maize ancestor is supposed to have been a wild grass, very re-
motely resembling our present-day pod corn, but without ears
and bearing its seeds in the tassel, in short, a perfect-flowered
wild grass.

There are many technical genetic objections to this explanation of the origin of maize, which oversimplifies what is an exceedingly complicated biological problem; but in addition to the
strong contrary biological indications, this hypothesis has two
other objections, even more weighty, neither of which up to the
present time has been satisfactorily overcome: (1) no such grass
as this supposed pre-maize ancestor of Indian corn is assumed to
have been has as yet been found anywhere in South America; and
(2) under this hypothesis the assumed pre-maize ancestor is a
more primitive grass even than the already known *teosinte* and
Tripsacum. In short, this *assumed* South American pre-maize
ancestor, which, it must be remembered, has yet to be found, is
antecedent not only to Indian corn but also to both *teosinte* and
Tripsacum. And if assumptions are carried back as far as this,
there is no conflict with the opinion of any botanist, since all agree
that the original progenitor of *the whole maize tribe* was a perfect-
flowered grass. Indeed even the proponents of a South American
origin of maize appear to be weakening in their position since
Mangelsdorf and his colleague, Cameron, have recently published a report suggesting Guatemala as a secondary center for
the origin of maize varieties, in which they state:

Even a cursory study of this collection [from thirty-eight localities in
western Guatemala] demonstrates at once the great diversity of maize in
western Guatemala. Here, in an area less than half the size of the state of
Iowa, are found probably more distinct types of corn than occur in the
entire United States.

And elsewhere Mangelsdorf states that, although he has not
found popcorn in any of the samples he has seen from Middle
America, he believes it must occur there since "the other types,
flour, flint and dent all seem to be abundant." In short, it is a
region where Indian corn reached maximum diversification.

The northern Middle American region, on the other hand, has two native grasses which are more primitive than maize, though not so primitive as the hypothetical South American grass, postulated under the Peruvian-origin hypothesis. The fact that there are two certain maize relatives known to be native of the highlands of western Guatemala has led me to conclude, though the question is far from settled, that the highlands of northern Middle America have a better claim to having been the region where Indian corn originated than have the highlands of Peru.

Under the Middle American place-of-origin hypothesis, it is assumed that sometime in the fairly remote past *teosinte* crossed, perhaps accidentally, with another wild grass and thus produced Indian corn.

In conclusion it may be pointed out that there are three theories as to the origin of maize, none of which has been sufficiently substantiated to exclude the other two: (1) development from *teosinte* by the orthodox biological methods of variation, mutation, and selection; (2) hybridization of *teosinte* and some unknown member of the grass family; and (3) development from some extinct, or at least as yet unknown, pre-maize plant. The first two theories restrict the place of origin to somewhere in western Guatemala, the third has no geographic restrictions, not even excluding an Old World origin. The choice between North and South America as a place of origin for maize depends largely upon individual preferences, since we have no experience, no criteria of judgment, to help us in deciding which of two contingencies is the more likely to have taken place, that is whether the assumed pre-maize became extinct, or whether the intermediate mutational stages from *teosinte* to maize have completely disappeared, leaving only the beginning and the end of the series. I regard the latter as the more probable explanation of the two, as it is the common method by which our present species both of plants and animals were derived from their ancestral forms, and I believe further that maize, and consequently agriculture in the New World, originated in western Guatemala. On this theory, the real explanation as to why the ancient Peruvians had domesticated more plants than the ancient Maya is not because the former originated agriculture but rather because the nature of their area and the rigors of their climate forced them to utilize every possible plant.

MAYA MAIZE AGRICULTURE

The modern Maya method of raising maize is the same as it has been for the past three thousand years or more—a simple process of felling the forest, of burning the dried trees and bush, of planting, and of changing the location of the cornfields every few years. This is practically the only system of agriculture practiced in the American wet tropics even today, and indeed is the only method available to a primitive people living in a heavily wooded, rocky, shallow-soiled country like that of the northern Yucatan Peninsula where a plow cannot be used, and where draft animals are not obtainable.

This system is commonly known as *milpa* agriculture, from *milpa*, the Aztec word for "cornfield." It was so named because the Spaniards first came in contact with this method of raising Indian corn in Mexico, and, since the sixteenth century, the use of this Aztec word to denote a cornfield has gradually spread to all other parts of Mexico and Central America. The Yucatan Maya word for cornfield is *col*, and all the Maya languages have similar words for it. Indeed, making the cornfield is the most important single activity of Maya men today, as it was in ancient times.

Nor, so far as we now can judge, has *milpa* agriculture changed materially since Old Empire times, and even before. In those remote days the chief, perhaps the only, agricultural tools available were the fire-hardened, pointed planting stick (Maya *xul*), the stone axe (Maya *bat*), and the fiber bag for carrying the seed corn (Maya *chim*). The most important modern additions to the foregoing ancient agricultural implements are the steel machete, or cutlass, which is a heavy, single-bladed knife, about two feet long, the steel axe, which has replaced the old stone axe, and the iron point into which a wooden handle is fitted, used now instead of the former fire-hardened planting stick. Indeed, no other system of agriculture is feasible, especially in northern Yucatan where (1) the soil is very shallow, usually not more than a few inches deep, though occasionally pockets from 6 inches to 2 feet in depth occur, and (2) where outcroppings of the native limestone are so numerous that any agricultural implement suitable for turning the soil, such as the plow, harrow, pick, hoe, spade, or shovel, would be useless. Experts from the United States Department of Agriculture who have studied the Maya method of cultivating corn declare that it is the only agricultural system practicable for tilling the rocky, shallow soil of northern Yucatan. Modern farming implements and machinery in the northern Maya area would be as superfluous as a fifth wheel.

Because maize forms such a preponderant part of the modern Maya dietary—from 75 to 85 per cent of everything a Maya eats is Indian corn in one form or another—it is necessary to understand clearly Maya *milpa* agriculture and its several steps, which have changed but little since ancient times.

Maya *milpa* agriculture has been divided into eleven different steps, or stages, as follows: (1) locating the field; (2) felling the forest and bush; (3) burning the dried bush; (4) fencing the field; (5) planting the field; (6) weeding the field; (7) bending the cornstalks; (8) harvesting the corn; (9) storing the corn; (10) shelling the corn; (11) hauling the corn to the village.

1. *Locating the field.*—The selection of a plot of ground for the new cornfield is a most important step. The *milpero*, or corn farmer, working alone, spends at least one day carefully looking for the proper kind of soil, which he determines by the height and thickness of the forest and bush growing on it: the higher the trees, the thicker the bush, the richer the soil. Another desirable factor is proximity to water. Yucatan is a parched land with very little surface water, and the Maya corn farmer tries to locate his *milpa* as near water, either in *cenotes* or shallow water holes, as possible. The distance of the cornfield from the village where the corn farmer lives varies within certain limits. In a survey of five villages in northern Yucatan 162 cornfields were found to vary from 2⅛ to 15⅓ miles from the nearest

village. The average distance in northern Yucatan today between house and cornfield is 3½ miles, but an extreme case is reported from the highlands of Guatemala where the Indians of a certain village have to go as far as 50 miles in order to find suitable forest lands in which to make their cornfields. People who have exhausted neighboring stands of forest growth go farther and farther afield until they find proper forest or bush conditions for their *milpas*, sometimes as much as two days' journey from their home villages, having to carry their crops on their own backs.

When the field has been selected, the farmer divides it into *mecates*, or squares measuring 65⅗ feet (20 meters) on each side, making piles of loose stones as markers at the four corners of each *mecate*. In measuring his land, the Maya farmer uses a rope which is invariably a little longer than the regulation 20 meters; indeed in northern Yucatan these measuring ropes actually average 21.5 meters, or 70 feet instead of 65⅗ feet, in length. The Maya say the *mecates* have to be measured a little larger "because of what the birds take."

2. *Felling the forest and bush.*—Today the bush is felled with a steel axe or machete. When the trees are very large, now rarely the case in northern Yucatan, they are ringed and allowed to die. The *milpero* begins to fell the bush soon after sunrise and continues until early afternoon. Usually two *mecates* are cut a day, or about one-fifth of an acre. As cornfields in Yucatan average about 100 *mecates* in size (10 to 12 acres) it takes 50 days to cut the average cornfield. High bush is usually cut in August at the height of the rainy season. The trees are full of moisture at this time and are easier to fell. The low trees, vines, and bushes are cut first, and later the higher trees. The fallen trees and bushes are sometimes dragged into piles to facilitate burning. Fields that have already had one year's corn crop grown upon them are not bushed until a few weeks before burning— only long enough to hold the weeds in check.

In ancient times this step in *milpa*-making must have taken a much longer time and must have been much more laborious than today. Stone axes had to be used, not only to ring the larger trees, but also to batter down the smaller ones, a time-consuming process. Clearing Maya cornfields has been enormously facilitated by the introduction of the steel axe and machete.

3. *Burning the dried bush.*—The felled bush is burned in March or April, that is not until after the blazing suns of February and March (Maya *yaxkin*) have thoroughly dried it. The cornfield is fired on a day when the wind is blowing strongly in order to secure a good "burn." A torch made from a branch of the *catzim tree*, the end of which has been frayed, is used, and fires are started at a number of places on the side from which the wind is blowing. The gods of the winds are summoned by constant whistling to help in the burning, for nothing is more fatal to a good "burn" than to have the wind suddenly die down before the bush is entirely consumed. The flames have to be whipped by a good, strong breeze in order to insure complete combustion of the dried trees and bush.

There is evidence, both archaeological and documentary, indicating that the day upon which the cornfields were to be burned was chosen by the priests with considerable care. At the Old Empire city of Copan, for example, there are two monuments—Stelae 10 and 12—standing on opposite ranges of hills that enclose the western and eastern sides of the Copan Valley at this point. These two monuments are 4⅛ miles apart in an airline, the true bearing of Stela 10 as observed from Stela 12 being N. 81° 09′ W. Both are roughly about the same level above the Copan River, 600 and 900 feet, respectively (Fig. 4). As observed from Stela 12, the sun sets directly behind Stela 10 on April 12 and again on September 7. It has been suggested that April 12, falling as it does just about the time the cornfields are burned in the Copan region, was the official date chosen by the priests to begin burning the *milpas* around the city, and that the purpose of erecting these two monuments in these two positions on these two particular hilltops east and west of the city was to have them define a certain line of sight in order to determine the date upon which the Copan cornfields should be burned. We may imagine the Copan astronomer-priests gathering around Stela 12 on the *east* side of the valley in the late afternoon of April 12 of each

year to observe the sun set behind Stela 10 on the west side of the valley. Previous experience had shown them that on that evening the sun would set behind Stela 10 as observed from Stela 12. When the sun sank out of sight directly behind Stela 10 on the evening of April 12, runners were then sent throughout the valley and surrounding hills that same night to advise the Indians that on the next day the gods had decreed their cornfields should be

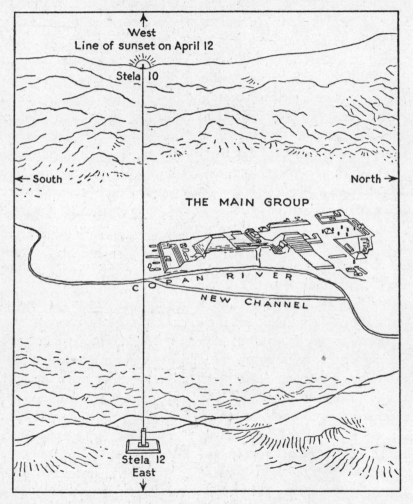

Fɪɢ. 4.—The sundial composed of Stelae 10 and 12, Copan, Honduras.

burned. Stelae 10 and 12 are both painted a dark red on all four sides, and are known locally today as the "Piedras Pintadas," or Painted Stones.

Nor is evidence lacking in the documentary sources to indicate that also in New Empire times the day for burning the cornfields was of ceremonial importance, since it was selected by the priests. In the Codex Perez (post-Conquest) the days of a sacred year are given which deal especially with the ritual of burning the cornfields. In it, such expressions are used as: "On this day 'The burner' [Maya *ah toc*] takes the fire; on this day 'The burner' applies the fire," etc., apparently describing the ceremonial procedure to be followed in burning the cornfields.

Curiously enough, cornfield fires do not start forest fires in the Yucatan Peninsula. The forest and bush, even in the dry season, are too green to burn. The flames sweeping against the standing trees kill those on the edges of the *milpas*, it is true, but the fire does not penetrate very far into the living green, and gradually dies out. In Mexico today, there are laws which require fire lanes to be cleared around the edges of the fields to prevent *milpa* fires from spreading to adjacent forests; but, practically speaking, the individual Maya in his cornfield, remote from the nearest town or village, pays little attention to these fire-preventive regulations. In spite of his disregard of them, however, forest fires are virtually unknown in Yucatan.

4. *Fencing the field.*—This fourth operation in *milpa*-making was not necessary in ancient times, since the Maya formerly had no domesticated animals, no horses or cattle, which today make fencing especially necessary when the cornfields are near a town or village. These fences are very temporary affairs made of brush, hastily thrown together, and last only two or three years; however, since the cornfields themselves are practically never planted for more than two years in succession, these temporary fences last as long as the fields they enclose are in use.

5. *Planting the field.*—Planting is one of the most important operations in making the *milpa*. It is begun immediately after the first rains, which all good Maya devoutly believe will fall on

the Day of the Holy Cross (May 3). As a matter of fact, in
Yucatan at least, it usually does rain on that day. Although planting may be undertaken as late as the middle of June, but in no
case until after the first rains, sowing the *milpa* is usually completed before the end of May. It takes two days to shell sufficient
corn to plant a 10- to 12-acre cornfield (100 *mecates*) and the actual planting of such a tract requires 12 days. The Maya use about
9½ pounds of seed corn per acre, while the practice in the United
States is to use only about 8 pounds per acre. The corn is planted
in holes made with the iron-pointed planting stick already mentioned (Fig. 5); the holes are 4 to 5 inches deep and are roughly
laid out in lines, at least, as nearly as the usually rough character
of the terrain will permit. From three to six kernels of corn are
dropped into each hole, the holes being about four feet apart; and
an average of from two to three stalks of corn grow on
each hill. In the usual 10- to 12-acre *milpa* there are
about 5,000 hills of corn. When the grains of corn are
dropped into the hole, bean and squash seeds are occasionally planted at the same time in the same hole; the
hole is then closed by a brush of the foot.

Bishop Landa described this same process nearly four
centuries ago as follows:

> They plant in many places, so that if one fails the others will
> suffice. In cultivating the land they do nothing more than clear
> the brush, and burn it in order to sow it afterward, and from the
> middle of January to April they work it and then when the
> rains come they plant it, which they do by carrying a small sack
> on the shoulders, and with a pointed stick, they make a hole in
> the ground, dropping in it five or six grains, covering them with
> the same stick. And when it rains, it is marvelous how it grows.

Fig. 5.—Plant-
ing corn with
the planting
stick. Page 36,
Codex Tro-
Cortesianus.

Thus there would seem to have been little change in the
Maya method of planting corn from ancient times down to today.

6. *Weeding the field.*—The number of times a cornfield is
weeded during the growing season (May to September inclusive)
varies considerably. A new *milpa*, made in high bush, needs to

be weeded only once, when the corn is about 2 feet high and the weeds the same height or even higher. A second-year *milpa,* however, has to be weeded more frequently—twice or even three times before the corn matures. When one realizes that it actually takes more time to weed a *mecate* of low bush than to fell a *mecate* of high bush, one wonders why the modern Maya ever tries to plant the same field for two years in succession.

A second-year *milpa* has far more weeds and vines in it than the high bush. This is due principally to the modern method of weeding with a machete. In ancient times, weeds were pulled out by the roots and the consequent scattering of seeds was held to a minimum; today, however, weeds are cut with a sweep of the machete and the seeds are scattered in every direction. This difference, slight as it may appear, is nevertheless of very great importance in its influence upon the length of time any given cornfield may be successively cultivated. When weeds were pulled out by their roots, as was done in ancient days, weed competition was eliminated sufficiently to permit the cultivation of the *milpas* for two, three, four, or sometimes even five successive years before they had to be abandoned. Today, in Yucatan, due not to soil exhaustion but to weed competition resulting from the use of the machete, the yield from a second-year *milpa* is from 10 to 20 per cent less than that of the first year.

That soil exhaustion is not the chief factor responsible for this decrease in the yield of Maya cornfields today has been demonstrated in the Carnegie Institution's experimental *milpa* at Chichen Itza. After the harvest, each successive year, specimens of soil have been taken from this cornfield; and, over a period of ten years, the annual analyses of these specimens have shown no appreciable decrease in the amount of necessary nitrogenous salts, nor a sufficient amount of deterioration in the chemical composition of the soil to account for the diminishing yearly yield. Therefore it seems probable that increasing weed competition and not decreasing soil fertility is chiefly responsible for the diminishing yield from Maya *milpas* today. In conclusion, I believe that the difference between ancient and modern methods of weeding is

probably chiefly responsible for the fact that today Maya cornfields are planted for only two consecutive seasons, whereas formerly they were probably used for four or five or even more consecutive years before they were abandoned.

7. *Bending the cornstalks.*—When the corn is ripe, the stalks
are bent over. This practice is general throughout Middle
America and is done *after* the ears have matured in September
or October. This practice, it may be pointed out, has no counterpart in American corn farming. The Maya have one kind of corn
which matures in two and a half months, another which ripens in
four months, and still another which ripens in six months. Corn
grows very tall in Yucatan, the average stalk being 12 to 13 feet
high. The stalks are bent just below the ears, until the latter point
toward the ground; in this bent-over position the corn is left to
harden. The Maya say the purpose of bending the stalks is to
keep rain from entering the ears, which causes them to mold;
also in this position the birds have less chance of tearing off the
husks and getting at the corn.

8. *Harvesting the corn.*—About a month after bending over
the stalks, say in November, the Maya corn farmer begins to
gather in his crop; harvesting is at its height in January and
February and continues through March into April, the corn being
harvested as needed. Husking is done with a pin made of wood,
bone, or deerhorn; only the outside of the husk is removed
in this preliminary operation. A man can harvest an acre in about
three days, and the average yield is about 17 or 18 bushels of
shelled corn per acre, or about 35 bushels on the ear.

9. *Storing the corn.*—Storing practices vary. In northeastern
Yucatan, raised rectangular cribs are built at the cornfields, the
corn being stored on the ears, without shelling, the outer husks
only having been previously removed in the preceding step. The
crib is made of saplings and the roof of thatch, both materials
being found in abundance in the near-by forest. The ears are
stored vertically as close together as possible. The final husking,
that is removal of the inner husk, is usually done just before planting the new crop in May. In northern central Yucatan the ears

are shelled at the *milpa*, and the corn is hauled to the village, where it is stored in a circular bin lined with palm leaves, which occupies one end of the room and extends from floor to ceiling.

10. *Shelling the corn.*—The corn may be shelled in several ways: (1) by hand; sometimes the whole family will be seated on the floor of the shelter house at the cornfield, busily engaged in shelling the ears; (2) by putting the ears in a hammock which holds from ten to fifteen baskets of ears; the hammock is beaten vigorously with a club, the kernels falling through the meshes of the hammock to the ground; and (3) by putting the ears in a pole rack surrounded by thatch to keep the grains from scattering, and then beating the ears with long poles, the kernels falling through to the ground as in the second method. Shelling is usually done at night, because the chaff is thought to cause less itching at night than in the daytime. The corn is finally stored in hemp bags, each containing 2 *cargas* or 190 pounds per bag.

11. *Hauling the corn to the village.*—Corn is hauled from the *milpa* to the village, either on the backs of men or horses, or, where there are automobile highways, by trucks. A man can carry one *carga* (95 lbs.) and a horse two. As highways increase in number, and motor trucks today are venturing over what formerly would have been considered rough, impassable country roads, horse- and man-transport are slowly disappearing.

THE YIELD OF CORN

The foregoing eleven steps, or stages, are those followed today in raising corn in Yucatan and, with the possible exception of fencing the *milpa* (No. 4) and hauling the corn to the village (No. 11) on the backs of draft animals or by motor trucks, they are the same as those followed by the ancient Maya. Corn culture has remained virtually unchanged for at least three thousand years.

The average size of *milpas* in the Chichen Itza area of northeastern Yucatan is about ten to twelve acres. This estimate is based upon a survey of 638 *milpas*, which were planted over a period of five years in three villages near Chichen Itza. However, since the measure of the Maya farmer—the *mecate* rope—is always slightly oversized, the average corrective factor which has to be applied to a Maya's own estimate of the size of his cornfield is actually 1⅙ *mecates* for every *mecate* measured on the ground. The average *milpa* in the Chichen Itza area, allowing for this correction, is therefore more nearly twelve than ten acres.

In northern Yucatan the same cornfield is not planted for more than two years in succession. The third year a new *milpa* site is selected, and the old *milpa* is allowed to lie fallow for 10 years until sufficient bush and woody growth have come back to warrant its being felled again. Thus, if the average cornfield is 12 acres in size and each field is in corn for only two years and then has to lie fallow for another ten years, it will take 72 acres of land to maintain the average family permanently. That is, to support a village of 500 people (100 families) 7,200 acres, or about 11.2 square miles, are necessary.

In the highlands of Guatemala, in forested regions with only occasional fertile valleys, as many as from 100 to 200 acres are required to support the average Indian family, and in partially denuded, or impoverished areas, 500 or even 1,000 acres may be necessary to sustain the average family permanently.

The general practice in Yucatan is to replant five or six acres of first-year cornfield and to fell another five or six acres of forest to put into new *milpa*, bringing the total area up to ten or twelve acres of *milpa* each year. *Milpas* are rarely planted a third consecutive year. Experience has shown that the yield of a third-year *milpa* is less than half that of a new *milpa*; and also that by the third year the brush fences are so decayed and broken down that they offer little protection against incursions of cattle.

Surprisingly, there seems to be little, if any, relationship between the size of a family and the size of its corresponding corn patch. For example, in a test survey made with this point particularly in mind, the average *milpa* for families of two persons was found to be 6.7 acres in 1934, 10.6 acres in 1935, and 14.7 acres in 1936. However, the average *milpa* for families of seven persons in the same village was 10.4 acres in 1934, but only 10.1 acres in 1935, and 11.3 acres in 1936.

The average yield for a first-year *milpa* in the Chichen Itza area is nearly 1⅔ *cargas* per *mecate*, or about 25 bushels of corn per acre. Although the Maya say the second year's crop amounts only to half the first year's crop, reliable figures show that the second year's crop is, at worst, only about 20 per cent less than the first year's yield.

A *milpa*, if continuously planted year after year, however, will produce less and less corn. An experimental *milpa* near Chichen Itza which was planted for eight consecutive years (1933–1940) showed the following results. During the first four years (1933–1936) this cornfield was weeded with a machete—that is, the weeds were cut down with sweeps of this long-bladed knife in the modern way; but during the last four years (1937–1940) it was weeded in the ancient way—that is, the weeds were pulled out by their roots. The yield per acre from this experimental *milpa*, year by year, was as follows:

Year	Pounds	Bushels
1933	708.4	13
1934	609.4	11
1935	358.6	6
1936	149.6	3
1937	748.0	13
1938	330.0	6
1939	459.8	8
1940	5.5	0.1

For the first four years the annual yield of corn rapidly decreased under the modern method of weeding, that is cutting rather than pulling up the weeds by their roots. The fifth year the experimental *milpa* was weeded the ancient way, by completely pulling up the weeds, removing even their roots. Under this more thorough method of weeding, the yield slightly exceeded even the first year's crop, but lost more than half the next year (the sixth year). It gained again in the seventh year, dropping to almost nothing for the eighth year because of a three-year plague of locusts which began in Yucatan in 1940.

The figures above indicate that the ancient method of weed-

ing, while it may not have produced more corn in any one year
than the modern method, certainly prolonged the life of the
average cornfield from two years to perhaps seven or even eight
years before it finally had to be abandoned. If the ancient Maya
milpa was cultivated continuously for four times as long as the
modern Maya *milpa* (that is, for eight years as compared to two
years) then less land would have been necessary to maintain the
average family permanently, probably only about half as much
land as the modern average Maya family of five requires, or
36 instead of 72 acres.

If Maya cornfields in ancient times continued in production
for longer periods than they do today (as I strongly believe)
this obviously must have had a corresponding effect on the length
of time the cities, towns, and villages around which they were
located were occupied; in fact it almost certainly made it possible
to occupy the ceremonial centers longer than would be practicable today, because of the present-day necessity of changing
milpa locations every third year. Thus formerly the cities, towns,
and villages enjoyed longer periods of occupation because available bush- and forest-lands in their immediate vicinities were
being converted into man-made savannas less rapidly than today,
and thus agriculture, as understood by the Maya, was practicable
in the immediate vicinities of their ceremonial centers for considerably longer periods of time.

But grass, the undefeatable enemy of *milpa* agriculture,
eventually crowded out the bush, so that woody growth no longer
returned to those cornfields which were lying fallow, but instead
grass grew up. At last, when grass had finally replaced former
stands of forest and high bush in the vicinities of the centers of
population, great and small, then Maya *milpa* agriculture was at
an end. And this is precisely what happened to the experimental
milpa of the Carnegie Institution near Chichen Itza in the closing
three or four years it was planted: grass everywhere invaded this
acre-and-a-half tract of land so that it became more and more
covered with a thick grassy mat, through which even weeds, to
say nothing of cornstalks, could not push their way.

Returning to the yield per *mecate* (one-tenth of an acre), in general the Maya of the Chichen Itza area expect from one to one and a half *cargas* of shelled corn per *mecate*, or from 1.7 to 2.5 bushels per *mecate*, or from 17 to 25 bushels per acre. However 2 bushels per *mecate* or 20 bushels per acre is a fair average yield for the Chichen Itza area. But Chichen Itza is one of the best corn-producing regions in the northern peninsula, and the yield described above is considerably better than that of most other localities. A more accurate average for the northern peninsula as a whole would probably be not more than one *carga* per *mecate*, or ten *cargas* per acre, or 17 bushels per acre.

Based upon a survey of a number of villages in northern Yucatan, it may be estimated that the corn-growing regions in the northern peninsula produce from 10 to 12 *cargas* per person, or from 17 to 20 bushels per individual per year, including both children and adults.

The agricultural survey of Yucatan undertaken by Dr. Morris Steggerda, formerly of the Carnegie Institution of Washington, has developed another fact of outstanding historical significance. The Maya corn farmer, in performing the eleven steps previously outlined—assuming that his cornfield is the average size for northern Yucatan, 100 *mecates* or 10 acres (12 acres allowing for the overlength of the average *mecate* measuring rope)—will have worked only 190 days out of the year, leaving 175 days for activities other than the mere production of maize, his principal food. But even this does not tell the whole story, for during the 190 days spent on the average 10- to 12-acre *milpa* the Maya farmer raises well over *twice* as much corn as he and his family actually consume.

The average Maya family is composed of five persons. This figure is based upon a survey of 265 households, distributed among four Indian villages in northern Yucatan. The average daily consumption of corn per individual was found to be 1.31 pounds, and for the average family of five, 6.55 pounds daily.

The modern Maya, unlike his ancestors, has a few animals: pigs, goats, dogs, cats, chickens, turkeys, sometimes a horse, and more rarely a cow. He feeds his miscellaneous livestock and chickens another 3.25 pounds a day, making the average daily corn consumption of himself, his family, and his livestock 9.8 pounds, or a total of 64 bushels per year. But we have seen that the average 10- to 12-acre cornfield produces 168 bushels of shelled corn per year, and since the average consumption per family is only 64 bushels a year even including the livestock, there is an average family surplus of 104 bushels per year. It is this surplus of corn which, turned into cash, buys the few outside necessities and little luxuries which the Maya family itself cannot produce: gunpowder and shot for hunting, cotton cloth for the *huipiles* of the women-folk, cotton shirts and pantaloons or overalls for the men and boys, colored thread for embroidery, perfumes, and face-powder, ribbons for the women's hair, perhaps kerosene, if there is an oil lamp in the household, *aguardiente* for the men, jewelry for the women, an occasional horse, cow, or pig, and money for the herb doctors in case of sickness. Their wants are simple and the corn surplus is usually sufficient to provide the means to satisfy them all.

However, if the Maya farmer and his wife are content to do without most of these store-bought extras—and many families do get along without them—and if they keep only a few pigs and chickens, no horses and cows, he can produce enough corn for his family and limited livestock in only 76 work days; and if he has no livestock at all (as his Old and New Empire ancestors did not have) he can raise enough corn for himself and his family in only 48 days. In short, he has between 293 and 317 days out of every year—nine and a half to ten and a half months—for nonfood-producing activities.

Here is the surplus time—roughly nine to ten months—during which, in both the Old and New Empire periods, the pyramids, temples, palaces, colonnades, ball courts, dance platforms, courts, plazas, and causeways were built; during which in the Spanish Colonial Period, the massive churches, great monasteries, and other public buildings were erected; and during which today the extensive hemp fields of northwestern Yucatan are cultivated, bushed, and cut. With so much free time on his hands, the Maya Indian for the last two thousand years has been successively exploited, first by his own native rulers and priests; next by his Spanish conquerors, again both civil and religious; and more recently by private owners in the hemp fields of Yucatan.

OTHER CULTIVATED AND WILD, EDIBLE, AND USEFUL PLANTS

After maize, the second most important food crop of the Maya is beans (*buul*). These, as already noted, are often planted in the same holes as the corn and grow up around the cornstalks. There are two varieties, the small black bean and the red bean, the former being the overwhelming favorite. Beans in addition to being planted with the corn are raised in separate patches by themselves; in ancient times beans must have contributed a large part of the protein intake of every Maya, as they still do today.

Numerous varieties of both squash and pumpkin are grown, sometimes in the backyards, but as often as not in the *milpas* among the corn. Sweet potatoes, tomatoes, and cassava also are raised. Other common food plants of the Maya are: *chayote*, a herbaceous vine bearing a tender fruit not unlike summer squash; *chaya*, the leaves of which are boiled and served as a vegetable; *jicama*, which is a root that looks like a turnip, is sweet, and is eaten raw; and many fruits—the *mamey*, a large sweet, red-meated fruit that grows wild throughout the Yucatan Peninsula; the *avocado*, a rich and important item in the Maya dietary; the sapodilla—a tree, the delicious fruit of which is a universal favorite, the milk of which makes chewing-gum, and the timber of which was used by the ancient Maya in their temples as door-lintels; the papaya; also several species of annonas, the cashews, oranges, bananas, plantains, granadilla, *guava, ciricote, nanze,* and many others.

Another tree which grows everywhere in the Yucatan Peninsula is the breadnut (Maya *ox, Brosimum alicastrum*). It is particularly common in the high forests near the ruins of ancient settlements, as is also the sapodilla. This greater frequency of both the breadnut and sapodilla in the vicinity of former centers of Maya population strongly suggests that both the Old and New Empires Maya planted these two trees in the vicinity of their settlements, just as their modern descendants still do today. The leaves of the breadnut are the chief fodder of mules and horses in the Yucatan Peninsula. The outer covering of the fruit is sweet and edible and the seeds, when boiled, are also eaten as a vegetable, or are dried and ground into flour. This tree must have been an important source of food in ancient times.

Among plants raised for seasoning and flavoring are chili-pepper, vanilla, allspice, *oregano, apazote* (chenopodium), *culantro* (coriander), and other herbs, roots, and leaves.

A considerable number of plants are raised for their fibers. Although today the Maya buy machine-made cotton textiles, this is only a very recent development. Formerly cotton was extensively planted, since Maya clothing was almost entirely made of handwoven cotton textiles (pp. 405–9). Another important fiber is *henequen*, hemp, or *sisal*, as it is variously called. Today this constitutes almost the only exportable product of Yucatan, and is literally the economic lifeline of the entire northern half of the peninsula. The fiber of the *bayal* palm is widely used in making baskets and the young leaves of the *guano* palm in making hats and mats.

Maya colors are for the most part of vegetable origin. The arnatto tree, known locally as *achiote*, is raised for its fruit, which yields a rich orange-red color and is extensively used in flavoring chicken, other meats, and rice. Logwood is common in the *akalches*, or swamps, of the middle part of the peninsula and, until the appearance of aniline dyes, was exported in tremendous quantities. The *mora* tree yields the fustic wood of commerce, which gives green, and also the yellow-brown color used in khaki.

The Yucatan forests afforded in greatest abundance all the materials required in the construction of the thatched houses of the common people: sapodilla and other woods for the house timbers, posts, etc.; mahogany and Spanish cedar for the doors, windows, and frames; *guano* and corozo palms for thatching as well as a coarse, wild perennial grass called *ac* from the savannas, also used in thatching. From the forests comes a quantity of vines and lianas which are used in tying together the wooden framework of the house—the beams, posts, poles, and saplings—as nails are never used in making the Maya thatched house even today. Mahogany and Spanish cedar are also used for making the dugout canoes which ply the numerous rivers in the south.

Other useful nonedible plants and trees are gourds for water bottles and food containers, tobacco, rubber, the copal and gumbo-limbo trees, the resin of the last two being used as incense; and fat pine for torches, the soapberry tree, the fruits of which give a soapy pulp that lathers, and the lignum vitae and *maha* trees, the wood of the former being used for making the containers in which the universal drink, chocolate, is made, and the wood of the latter furnishing the swizzle sticks with which it is mixed.

The Yucatan Peninsula furnished everything the ancient Maya manner of living required, and indeed in the greatest abundance —building stone, lime, and gravel for their religious and governmental buildings, timber and thatch for the houses of the common people, an exceedingly rich and varied flora, which supplied every kind of non-flesh food, seasonings, kitchen utensils, medicines, fibers for textiles and basketry. The forest also supplied game of all kinds; the jaguar and deer were especially hunted, their pelts being made into cloaks and sandals for the rulers and priests; finally there were many birds of beautiful plumage.

But amidst all this abundance, nature's richest gift to man was maize—the Maya staff of life—without which they never could have developed their highly distinctive culture, the most brilliant aboriginal civilization of the New World. And if we bear constantly in mind the fact that from three-fourths to five-sixths of everything the average Maya eats, even today, is corn in one form or another, and that their culture was based directly upon, and derives straight from, agriculture as applied to the cultivation of corn, we shall have learned the most basic fact about the Maya civilization.

····

GOVERNMENT AND SOCIAL ORGANIZATION

DOCUMENTARY SOURCES FOR OLD EMPIRE HISTORY LACKING

WE HAVE NO DIRECT evidence as to the type of governmental and social organization prevalent in the Old Empire, since no contemporary evidence bearing upon these points has survived. Nor, indeed, has any account thereof been identified in the inscriptions; and contemporary manuscripts are, of course, completely lacking. What little we may say about the governmental and social organization of the Old Empire depends entirely upon (1) the indirect evidence furnished by what is known of the governmental and social organization in the New Empire, happily a very considerable amount of information, and (2) the direct evidence supplied by the sculptures, vase-paintings, and frescoes of the Old Empire. If we may draw analogies from the above-mentioned material, especially from what is known of New Empire governmental and social organization, and project it backward into Old Empire times, we may perhaps partially restore the unknown latter from the known former. Moreover, since Maya culture in all its essential elements is known to have been continuous, the governmental and social organization of both Old and New Empire will be treated together, though most of the material on these subjects presented in this chapter, it should be remembered, has been drawn from New Empire sources and primarily concerns the New Empire.

POLITICAL AND SOCIAL ORGANIZATION OF THE OLD AND
NEW EMPIRES

As stated elsewhere in this study (chapter iv, p. 50), the city-states of both the Old and New Empires were distinctly *not* empires in any political sense of the word. There was no Pharaoh, no Caesar, no emperor who ruled over all the land at any one time, though there can be no doubt that the whole Yucatan Peninsula was held together by a common culture, a common language, and a common religion. Perhaps the closest analogies in the Old World to the government of both the Maya Old and New Empires are afforded by the city-states of Greece—Sparta, Athens, and Corinth—from the sixth to the second centuries before Christ; or again by the city-states of Italy—Venice, Genoa, and Florence —during the thirteenth to sixteenth centuries; or again by the cities of the Hanseatic League in Germany—Lübeck, Hamburg, and Bremen—also during the thirteenth to sixteenth centuries. The city-states of Greece and Italy and the cities of the Hanseatic League in Germany were in each case united by a common civilization; in each case their people spoke a common language; and finally, in each case, they had a common religion. Culturally they were homogeneous, politically they were independent.

Projecting backward the conditions known to have existed in the New Empire, we are justified in assuming that the Maya Old Empire was divided into a number of independent city-states, perhaps loosely held together in some sort of a confederation, such as is known to have existed in the New Empire during the eleventh and twelfth centuries. Where there was such close continuity in culture, language, and religion, there must have been a corresponding continuity in political institutions; to suppose otherwise is illogical.

Relying upon archaeological evidence, such as minor differences in the sculpture, architecture, and ceramic wares of the different parts of the Old Empire region, which indicate a corresponding number of archaeological subprovinces, we may perhaps go even farther and hazard the guess that each of these archaeological subprovinces originally corresponded roughly to a politically independent city-state. In the late New Empire, we have seen, there were three such principal political entities— Chichen Itza, Uxmal, and Mayapan; but in the Old Empire, it would seem, there may perhaps have been at least four: (1) central and northern Peten, Guatemala; southern Campeche, Mexico, and

British Honduras (the heart of the Old Empire region), the
largest city and probable capital of which was Tikal; (2) the Usumacinta Valley, the capital of which may have been either Palenque, Piedras Negras, or Yaxchilan, or perhaps all three in turn; (3) the southeastern subprovince with Copan as its capital; (4) the southwestern subprovince, possibly with Tonina as its principal governmental center.

THE TERRITORIAL RULER

At the head of the state stood the *halach uinic* (Maya for "True Man"), or territorial ruler. This position was hereditary in a single family in each city-state, descending from father to oldest son. Bishop Landa, in describing conditions in late New Empire times, twice states definitely that the lords were succeeded by their oldest sons:

If the lord died, although his oldest son succeeded him, the other children were always very much respected and assisted and regarded as lords themselves; . . . . if, when the lord died, there were no sons [old enough] to reign, and he [the deceased lord] had brothers, the oldest of the brothers, or the best qualified, reigned, and they taught the heir their customs and feasts against the time he should become a man; and these brothers [paternal uncles of the heir], although the heir was [ready] to reign, commanded all their lives; and if he [the deceased lord] had no brothers, the priests and principal people elected a man proper for the position.

This clearly indicates descent from father to oldest son with provision for regencies by paternal uncles, if there were any, when the heir was a minor. The native chronicles of the sixteenth century also leave little room for doubt that the *halach uinic* was the supreme ruler of each state, and that at the time of the Spanish Conquest, at least, this office customarily descended from father to oldest son. The *halach uinic* was also called *ahau*, a word the sixteenth-century Maya manuscript-dictionaries define as "king, emperor, monarch, prince, or great lord." This was also the title used by the Maya of the Colonial Period in referring to the King of Spain. The powers enjoyed by the *halach uinic* were very broad. He probably formulated both foreign and domestic policies of the state, with the aid and advice of a state council composed of the leading chiefs, priests, and special councillors (*ah cuch cabob*). He appointed the town and village chiefs (*batabob*), who stood in some sort of feudal relation to him, and the most important of whom were almost certainly his close blood relatives.

During the New Empire one of the most important duties of the *halach uinic* was the examination of candidates for the chieftainships of the various towns and villages. This took place at the beginning of each katun and was in effect a kind of civil service examination for the purpose of weeding out from the ranks of the legitimate aspirants to these offices the upstarts, pretenders, and those who applied for the positions under false pretenses. Many of the questions and answers are trivial and some contain references to post-Spanish objects, such as the horse; nevertheless these questionnaires which have been called "interrogations of the Chiefs" prove conclusively that: (1) the practice of examining prospective candidates for chieftainship in order to determine their eligibility and fitness therefor was firmly established; (2) proof of legitimacy in this matter was considered to be the possession of certain esoteric knowledge, supposed to have been handed down from father to son in those families which were regarded as eligible to chieftainship; and (3) this esoteric knowledge was called the "language of Zuyua."

The name Zuyua, we have seen (p. 86), is the place where the Xiu family is said to have originated—"to the west of Zuyua." This name is inseparably connected with the Mexican penetration of Yucatan in the tenth century, and its use to describe the esoteric language of the chiefs' questionnaires strongly indicates that only members of families in which this Mexican chieftainship lore had been handed down were eligible to such offices. Whether such noble families actually must be of Mexican descent is not certain, but the long-standing and firmly established Nahua affiliations of the ruling families is beyond question

(p. 88); and it is not improbable that, theoretically at least,
families which were eligible for chieftainship appointments were
thought to have had a Mexican origin like the ruling houses.

In addition to the fact that the *halach uinic* was the highest
administrative and executive officer of the state, it is not improbable that he was, at the same time, the highest ecclesiastical
authority as well. It has even been suggested that the form of
government in the city-states of the Old Empire may well have
been that of a theocracy, the highest civil and religious powers
being combined in the person of one individual, the *halach uinic*
—a sort of hereditary papacy, if such were possible.

Judging from the sculptures of the Old Empire, the insignia of
the *halach uinic* varied, depending upon which of his several
functions—civil, religious, or military—is represented. As administrative head of state he carried in his right hand the Manikin
Scepter, and in his left a round shield. The Manikin Scepter consists of a small anthropomorphic figure with a long curling nose
like the masks on monument pedestals. One of the legs terminates in the head of a serpent (Fig. 6, *a*, *b*, and *c*), the scepter being
held by the serpent-headed leg. The Manikin Scepter is probably
also found on a fresco in the Temple of the Warriors at Chichen
Itza. Here the seated figure of a *halach uinic* holds in his right
hand by its serpent-headed leg what is probably a New Empire
version of this same type of scepter (Fig. 6, *c*), and in his left hand
he grasps the usual round shield. In the Old Empire reliefs the
halach uinic also holds a round shield in his left hand, as pointed
out above; on the front of the shield is a representation of the
head of the sun-god (Fig. 6, *g*).

These two emblems—scepter and shield—constitute the insignia of the *halach uinic*, as the highest officer of state in his administrative capacity. As head of the religious hierarchy, the
halach uinic holds the Double-Headed Ceremonial Bar (Fig. 6,
h). This is usually carried horizontally across the breast, though
occasionally it is held diagonally, one end resting on the shoulder (see Plate 67, *b*). The ends of this emblem terminate in
heads which are sometimes serpentine, sometimes human. In

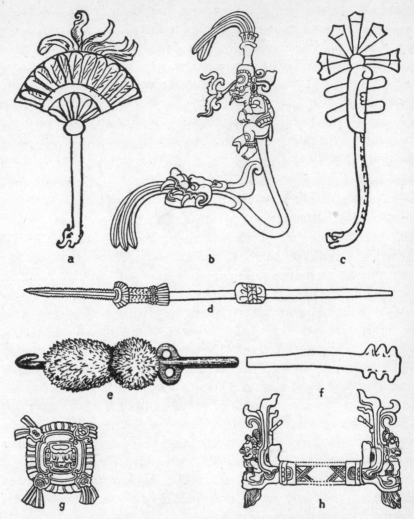

Fig. 6.—Ceremonial insignia, and weapons of the Old and New Empires: (*a*) Probably a late New Empire example of the Manikin Scepter, from the Xiu genealogical tree; (*b*) the Manikin Scepter during the Old Empire, from Zoö-morph P at Quirigua; (*c*) probably a New Empire example of the Manikin Scepter, from a fresco in the Temple of the Warriors at Chichen Itza; (*d*) a spear, symbol of military rank during both the Old and New Empires; (*e*) a throwing-stick, symbol of military rank during both the Old and New Empires; (*f*) a war club, symbol of military rank during both the Old and New Empires; (*g*) a small, round ceremonial shield used during the Old Empire; (*h*) a double-headed ceremonial bar, symbol of highest religious rank during the Old Empire.

one case—on the back of Stela 11 at Yaxchilan (Plate 18, *b*)—a *halach uinic* is shown impersonating a deity with a mask of the god's head held in front of his face. Finally, as the highest military officer of the state, he carries a weapon of some sort, usually a spear (Fig. 6, *d*), occasionally a throwing-stick, *hulche* (Fig. 6, *e*), or a club (Fig. 6, *f*), but never the bow and arrow, which were unknown in Old Empire times and do not appear in Maya history until the Mexican Period of the New Empire. In late New Empire times the position of *halach uinic* is described as follows:

[He was] *cacique* and governor of the town . . . . ; he, it was, who served thus in the said town, and he was its father, Lord and *halach uinic*, which in our language is "great Lord," with whom they had to take counsel, and act according to his opinion. [And again] The lords were absolute and what they ordered was carried out without fail.

RULING HOUSES OF THE LATE NEW EMPIRE

At the time of the Spanish Conquest, the five leading families of the peninsula were: (1) the Xiu, or Tutul Xiu with their capital at Mani, though formerly at Uxmal; (2) the Cocom with their capital at Sotuta, though formerly at Mayapan; (3) the Canek with their capital at Tayasal at the western end of Lake Peten Itza in central Peten, Guatemala, though formerly at Chichen Itza in the northeastern corner of the peninsula; (4) the Chel descended from a former priest of Mayapan, with their capital at Tecoh; and (5) the Pech with their capital at Motul.

Easily the foremost of these was the Xiu, perhaps because this family had taken the leading part in the successful revolt against Mayapan in 1441, as a result of which Cocom, the *halach uinic* of Mayapan, was slain and his capital destroyed.

In the Peabody Museum of Archaeology and Ethnology at Harvard University there is preserved a leather portfolio of family papers, the proofs of nobility of the Xiu family, which were accumulated during the Spanish Colonial Period. There are 145 individual documents in this collection, written either in Maya or Spanish, on hand-made European paper, the three earliest—a map, a land treaty, and a genealogical tree—being the most interesting. All three of these date from 1557, only fifteen years after the Spanish Conquest.

The Map (Plate 20) shows the Province of the Xiu with its capital, Mani, at the center. The symbol for each town and village is a Catholic church with a tower surmounted by a cross, or in the cases of the smaller villages, with crosses only. The symbol used for Uxmal, the former Xiu capital, which was entirely abandoned by the middle fifteenth century (that is, before this map was made) is the somewhat crude representation of a Maya temple.

The land treaty (Plate 21) which accompanies the map and bears the same date (1557) has the distinction of being the earliest known document to be written in the Maya language, but *with the characters of Spanish script*. It describes the boundaries between the Xiu state and the adjoining provinces.

The genealogical tree (Plate 22) is perhaps the most interesting of the three. At the bottom sits Hun Uitzil Chac Tutul Xiu, the founder of Uxmal (chapter v, p. 87). The foundation of this city, according to the fragmentary hieroglyph to the left of the fan held in this first Xiu's left hand, took place in a Katun 2 Ahau (987-1007, Table V). The handle of this fan, it will be seen (Fig. 6, *a*), also terminates in the head of a serpent, and the fan itself is probably a late New Empire form of the Manikin Scepter of the Old Empire. Compare Fig. 6, *a*, *b*, and *c*. At Hun Uitzil Chac's right kneels his wife Yx . . . . of Ticul; she points with pride to their joint achievement—the spreading Xiu family tree. It is to be noted, however, that the tree rises from *his* loins and not from hers, a graphic insistence upon patrilinear descent. Between Hun Uitzil Chac and his first descendants that appear on the tree, two brothers—Ah Dzun and Ah Uitz Xiu—there is a gap of 18 generations, covering a little more than four centuries. The former of these two brothers was the grandfather of another Ah Dzun, also called Napot Xiu, who, we have seen in chapter v (pp. 95–97), lost his life at Otzmal in 1536 through Cocom treachery.

The object of the tree was obviously to prove conclusively to the Spanish Crown the descent of the Conquest-period Xiu from

the former royal house of Uxmal. For this reason the founder
of Uxmal, Hun Uitzil Chac, appears as the progenitor of the
family. The intervening 18 generations were suppressed, perhaps because they were unnecessary to the purpose of the picture,
or perhaps because of family pride. Because from 1194 to 1441
the Xiu were vassals of the Cocom family, they were compelled to
live at Mayapan, the Cocom capital, along with all the other
Maya lords; this continued until 1441, when they rebelled, as
related on pages 92 and 93, under Ah Xupan Xiu, the then Xiu
halach uinic. This latter Xiu was the father of the two brothers,
Ah Dzun and Ah Uitz, the first names on the tree above the
figure of Hun Uitzil Chac, the founder of the family.

The papers in the ancient leather portfolio at the Peabody
Museum at Harvard carry the Xiu story down to the time of the
Mexican Independence in 1821; and finally from living members
of the family it has been possible to continue their history down
to the present day. Indeed the present head of the family, don
Nemesio Xiu, who lives at Ticul in northern Yucatan (Plate 23,
a and *b*), belongs to the thirty-eighth generation beginning with
Hun Uitzil Chac, the founder of Uxmal. My wife and I had the
pleasure of standing as godparents at the marriage of don
Nemesio's oldest son, Dionisio, in 1940 (Plate 23, *c* and *d*).
Dionisio's infant daughter Genoveva, and son, Gerardo, the latter
born on April 23, 1943, are descendants in the fortieth generation
counting from the founder of the family.

How far the Xiu have fallen during the past thousand years,
since those distant days when they ruled over one of the greatest
city-states of northern Yucatan, is strikingly reflected in the residences of the heads of the family during that period. Plate 25, *a*,
is a photograph of the Palace of the Governor at Uxmal, the
official residence of the Xiu when they were *halach uinicil*, or independent native Maya rulers. Plate 25, *b*, shows their residence
in the early Colonial Period, when the Xiu had been created
Spanish *hidalgos*, or nobles, by royal patent; this is the house of
Francisco de Montejo Xiu at Mani, that Ah Kukum Xiu who,
before baptism, so greatly aided Francisco de Montejo the

Younger in the conquest of Yucatan (pp. 113, 114). Finally Plate 25, *c,* is a picture of the simple thatched home of don Nemesio Xiu on the outskirts of Ticul; the present head of the family is a humble Mexican corn farmer, in no way to be distinguished, either socially or economically, from thousands of other Maya corn farmers throughout Yucatan—from native rulers to Spanish nobles to small Mexican corn farmers in the last thousand years.

Ancient Maya society seems to have been divided into four general classes: the nobility (Maya *almehenob*); the priesthood (Maya *ahkinob*); the common people (Maya *ah chembal uinicob*); and the slaves (Maya *ppencatob*).

The Nobility.—Below the *halach uinic* stood the *batabs* or lesser chiefs. They were the local magistrates and executives, who administered the affairs of the towns and villages which were dependent upon the territorial capital ruled directly by the *halach uinic*. In the New Empire and probably in the Old Empire as well, although appointed by the *halach uinic,* they were members of a hereditary nobility called *almehenob,* meaning in Maya "those who have fathers and mothers"; even well down into Spanish colonial times the hereditary nobles were called *caciques* or natural lords, by the Spaniards. They exercised both executive and judicial authority in their respective communities, and, although in times of war all served under one supreme military chief, called the *nacom,* who held office for three years, each *batab* personally commanded his own soldiers. He administered the affairs of the town or village in his charge, presided over the local council, and saw to it that the houses were kept in repair and that the people cut and burned their fields at the times indicated by the priests. In his capacity as judge he sentenced criminals and decided civil suits. If the latter were of unusual importance he consulted the *halach uinic* before passing judgment. Although no tribute was paid directly to the *batab,* being rendered only to the *halach uinic,* the *batabs* were supported, nevertheless, by what the people grew and made. One of the *batab's* principal duties was to see that his town or village paid its appointed tribute promptly to the *halach uinic.*

PLATE 20.—ANCIENT MAP OF THE PROVINCE OF MANI, YUCATAN, MEXICO

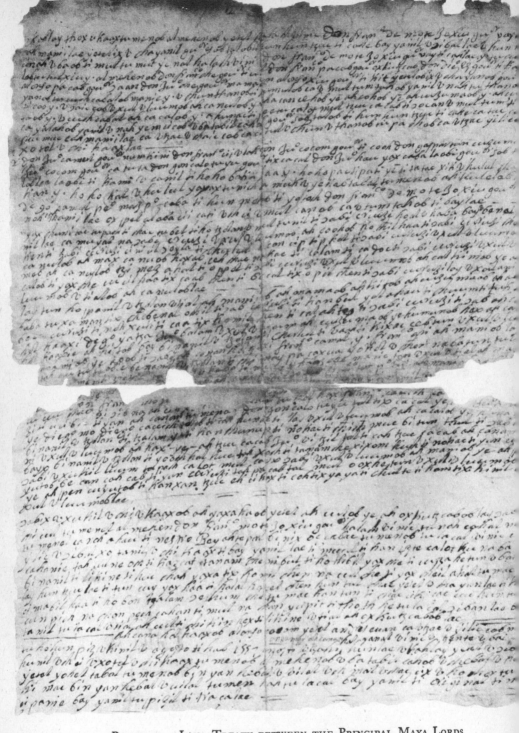

PLATE 21.—LAND TREATY BETWEEN THE PRINCIPAL MAYA LORDS
OF NORTHERN YUCATAN IN 1557

Perhaps the oldest known example of the Maya language written in
Spanish script.

Plate 22.—Genealogical Tree of the Xiu Family of Mani, the
Former Ruling House of the City-State of Uxmal

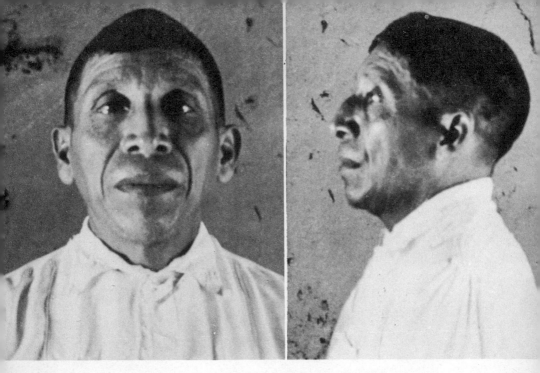

↑ *a*) Don Nemesio Xiu, front.   ↑ *b*) Don Nemesio Xiu, profile.

PLATE 23.—THE PRESENT HEAD OF THE XIU FAMILY AND HIS OLDEST
SON, TICUL, YUCATAN, MEXICO

↓ *c*) Don Dionisio Xiu, front.   ↓ *d*) Don Dionisio Xiu, profile.

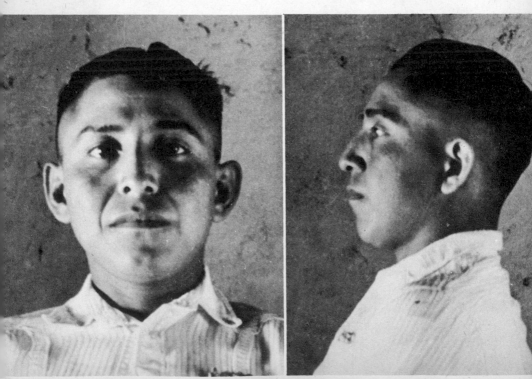

There were two kinds of war captains: one hereditary, presumably the *batab*, the other, of much greater importance, who was elected for a period of three years. The latter, as already mentioned, was given the title of *nacom*.

This one, called the *nacom*, could not, during these three years, have relations with any woman, even his own wife, nor eat red meat. They held him in great veneration and gave him fish and iguanas, which are like lizards, to eat. In this time [his tenure of office] he did not get drunk, and he kept separate in his house the utensils and other objects which he used, and no women served him and he had but little communication with the people. At the end of these three years [of office all was] as before. These two captains [the *nacom* and *batab*] discussed the affairs of war and put them in order . . . .

[And again] They bore him [the *nacom*] in great pomp, perfuming him as if he were an idol, to the temple where they seated him and burned incense to him as to an idol.

It would seem from the foregoing that the elected *nacom* formulated the strategy of war as a kind of chief of staff, while the *batabs*, the hereditary chiefs, led their respective contingents into battle; that is, they were the field commanders.

Next below the *batab* were the town councillors, or elders, the *ah cuch cabob*, two or three in number; each had a vote in the town government and without their assent nothing could be done. Finally each stood at the head of a subdivision of the town, or village, a sort of ward. They are likened by the Spanish writers of the sixteenth century to the *regidores* in Spanish town governments, and may perhaps be compared to our own aldermen.

The *ah kulelob*, or deputies, accompanied the *batab* wherever he went and were his assistants, mouthpieces, and messengers, who carried out his orders; there were usually two or three of them and they may perhaps be compared very roughly to our special-assignment policemen.

The duties of the *ah holpopob*, meaning in Maya "those at the head of the mat," are not so clear. They are said to have assisted the lords in the government of their towns, and through them the townspeople approached the lords. They were the advisers of their lords on matters of foreign policy and concerning embassies from other states. They are also said to have been masters of the *popolna* or house where the men met to discuss public affairs and to learn the dances for the town festivals. Finally, the *ah holpop* was the chief singer and chanter in charge of the dances and musical instruments in each town.

The lowest grade of officials were the *tupiles*, or town constables, the ordinary policemen, who stood at the bottom of the law-enforcement structure.

Some of the secondary figures in Old Empire sculptures, frescoes, and vase-paintings, it is not unreasonable to suppose, are representations of some of these officials, which, if they were not known under these same New Empire titles, doubtless had others that denoted similar, if not indeed identical, offices. Again, it is to be remembered, we are trying to interpret Old Empire conditions in the reflected light of known New Empire institutions.

The ruling houses and nobility of the New Empire took great pride in preserving their family histories, genealogical trees, and the records of their descent, a case in point being the Xiu, the former ruling house of Uxmal described in the previous section. Although evidence on this particular point is wholly lacking for the Old Empire, in view of the close connection and cultural continuity between these two principal epochs of ancient Maya history, it seems highly probable that the rulers and lords of the earlier period must also have been equally meticulous in preserving their family histories, or, in fact, that the rulers could not have been chosen from any other class than a hereditary nobility.

The Priesthood.—The Maya priesthood must have been of equal if not even of greater importance than the lords and lesser chiefs; indeed, Bishop Landa describing conditions in the late New Empire says that both classes were hereditary and were derived from the nobility:

They taught the sons of the other priests and the second sons of the lords who [were] brought them from their infancy, if they saw that they had an inclination for this profession; . . . . and his [the high-priest's] sons or his nearest relatives succeeded him in office.

And Herrera, another early Spanish historian, writes:

For the matters concerning the worship of their gods they had one who was the high-priest, whose sons succeeded him in the priesthood.

Indeed, there is little doubt that all the highest offices, both civil and religious, were hereditary, being filled from the members of one family in each state, or from their immediate connections by marriage.

Landa says that the high priest in late New Empire times was called *Ahaucan* Mai. This, however, seems to be more than a simple title, rather a combination of the title *ahaucan* and the family name, Mai, common in Yucatan, even today. The high priest may well have been called simply the *ahaucan* since this word in Maya means "the Lord Serpent" and, in combining the surname Mai with it, Landa was doubtless referring to a specific family named Mai in which the office seems to have been hereditary at Mayapan. Landa says further that

He was very much respected by the lords and had no *repartamiento* of Indians [no Indians specially set aside for his personal service], but besides the offerings, the lords made him presents and all the priests of the town brought contributions to him . . . . . In him was the key of their learning and it was to these matters that they [the high priests] mostly dedicated themselves; and they gave advice to the lords and replied to their questions. They seldom dealt with matters pertaining to the sacrifices except at the time of the principal feasts, or very important matters of business. They provided priests for the towns when they were needed, examining them in the sciences and ceremonies and committed to them the duties of their office, and set good example to people and provided them with books and sent them forth. And they employed themselves in the duties of the temples and in teaching their sciences as well as writing books about them. . . . .

The sciences which they taught were the computation of the years, months and days, the festivals and ceremonies, the administration of the sacraments, the fateful days and seasons, their methods of divination and their prophecies, events and the cures for diseases and their antiquities [history] and how to read and write with their letters and characters [hieroglyphics] with which they wrote, and [to make] drawings which illustrate the meaning of the writings.

The great temple establishments in the ceremonial centers of the Old and New Empires, with their manifold activities of ritual, sacrifice, divination, astronomical observations, chronological calculations, hieroglyphic writings, religious instruction, management of the monasteries, where the many priests lived, was almost as big business for those days as directing the ship of state. The high priests of the different states must have been not only extremely able administrators, but also outstanding scholars, astronomers, and mathematicians, and all this in addition to their purely religious duties. They were also councillors of state, advising the *halach uinic* on political matters. Being of the ruling house themselves, their interest in the state was as great as that of the *halach uinic;* indeed it may not be too far fetched to liken them to the great princes of the Church in Europe during the Middle Ages, who were prelates, statesmen, administrators, and warriors, all in one.

Another class of priests were the *chilanes* or diviners, the mouthpieces of the gods, whose duty it was to give the replies of the gods to the people—in effect, oracles. The *chilanes* were held in such high respect that the people carried them on their shoulders when they appeared in public.

Another priest was the *nacom,* (not to be confused with the war chief of the same title), who was elected for life, and, according to Landa, was held in little esteem, since he was the functionary who actually slit open the breasts of the sacrificial victims and plucked out their hearts:

At this time came the executioner, the *nacom,* with a knife of stone, and with much skill and cruelty struck him [the sacrificial victim] with the knife between the ribs of his left side under the nipple, and at once plunged his hand in there [the opening in the breast] and seized the heart like a raging tiger, tearing it out alive, and having placed it on a plate, he gave it to the priest, who went quickly and anointed the face of the idols with that fresh blood.

The little esteem shown the *nacom* for his leading role in human sacrifice recalls the odium with which the embalmers were regarded in ancient Egypt. Those who actually opened the bodies after death for the purpose of withdrawing the entrails, prior to embalming, were stoned from the house by relatives of the deceased.

The *nacom* was assisted in the ceremony of human sacrifice by four aides called *chacs*, respectable old men chosen anew on each occasion.

The *chacs* seized the poor man whom they were going to sacrifice and with great haste, placed him on his back upon that stone and all four held him by the legs and arms so that they divided him in the middle.

Other duties of the *chacs* were to assist at the puberty ceremony, to kindle the new fire in the month of Pop at the beginning of the Maya New Year, and to fast and anoint the new idols with blood drawn from their own ears in the month of Mol, which was dedicated to making new idols. The four *chacs* also assisted at a ceremony in the month of Tzec to bring about an abundance of honey.

Ahkin was, and still is today, the general name for "priest" in Maya, even being applied to priests of the Catholic Church. The word means literally in Maya "he of the sun." Some of the *ahkines* had specialized duties, for example as prophets of the thirteen Maya ages, or thirteen differently numbered katuns (p. 292). "These ages are thirteen in number; each age has its separate idol and its priest with a separate prophecy of its events." Again, at a sanctuary on the island of Cozumel, another *ahkin* acted as the oracle, and at the Sacred *Cenote*, or Well of Sacrifice at Chichen Itza, an *ahkin* served in the same capacity. It was also an *ahkin* who received the hearts of the sacrificial victims from the hands of the *nacom* and offered them to the idols of the Maya gods.

The modern Maya of northern Yucatan, when they practice the few ancient ceremonies which have survived among them, such as the *cha-chac*, or rain-bringing ceremony, employ the service of an *ahmen* or medicine-man—in Maya, literally "he who understands." The *ahmen* is also the prophet and, at the same time, the inflicter as well as the healer of diseases.

The priesthood was an influential class, probably the most powerful single group in the state, more so even than the nobility. Their knowledge of the movements of the heavenly bodies (the sun, the moon, Venus, and possibly Mars), their ability to predict both lunar and solar eclipses, their penetration into every phase of the life of the common people, made them feared and respected and gave them a hold on the superstitions of the masses equaled by that of no other class. That we hear of no class struggle between the Maya nobility and priesthood such as that which occurred in ancient Egypt during the Twentieth and Twenty-first Dynasties is probably to be explained by the fact that among the ancient Maya the highest members of each group were probably more or less closely related.

The Common People.—The great mass of the people in both the Old and New Empires were the humble corn farmers, whose sweat and toil supported not only themselves but also their supreme ruler (the *halach uinic*), their local lords (the *batabob*), and the priesthood (*ahkinob*). In addition to this no inconsiderable task, they were the actual builders of the great ceremonial centers, the lofty pyramid-temples, the vast colonnades, the palaces, monasteries, ball courts, dance platforms, terraces, and raised stone highways (Maya *sacbeob*) which connected the principal cities. They likewise quarried, dressed, and sculptured the enormous quantities of stone and building blocks employed in these great constructions. They, with their stone axes, felled the thousands of trees which served for the fuel of the kilns where the local limestone was burned to make lime for the mortar; and with the same axes and stone-chisels they felled, fashioned, and carved the hardwood door-lintels and roof-beams of sapodilla, the only wood that has been found in connection with Maya stone architecture. They were the masons, who dressed the building blocks, the stoneworkers who sculptured the stelae and carved the different elements in the elaborate stone-mosaic façades. And these same common folk were even the beasts of burden who carried the stone from the quarries to the building sites, who climbed the pole scaffoldings, tied together

with wild vines and lianas from the forest, carrying the heavy
carved stone elements to their places, *on their own heads*.

Other obligations of the lower class were to pay tribute to the *halach uinic*, to give presents to their local lords, and to make offerings to the gods through the priests. This tribute, these presents and offerings, in the aggregate, must have bulked large. They consisted of all kinds of produce of the field—maize, beans, tobacco, cotton—a kind of woven cotton cloth called *pati* (Spanish *manta*), domesticated fowls, salt from the salt beds along the coast, dried fish from the sea, all kinds of game—deer, peccary, *jaleb* (Aztec *tepiscuintli*), and birds—cacao, *pom* (copal) for incense, honey and wax from the forests, and finally strings of green-stone beads (jade), red-stone beads (coral), and shells. Their lands were held as community property and tilled in common. Bishop Landa says:

The common people at their own expense made the houses of the lords . . . . . Beyond the house, all the people did their sowing for the lord, cared for his fields and harvested what was necessary for him and his household; and when there was hunting or fishing, or when it was time to get their salt, they always gave the lord his share, since these things they always did as a community. . . . . They also joined together for hunting in companies of fifty, more or less, and they roast the flesh of the deer on grills, so that it shall not be wasted [spoil] and having reached the town, they make presents to their lord and distribute [them] as among friends. And they do the same in their fishing.

The common people lived on the outskirts of the towns and villages; indeed, position in the social scale depended on the distance a man's house was from the central plaza of the city, town, or village where he lived (pp. 312, 313).

It was this social class, by far the largest in the state, these lowly corn farmers, hewers of wood and drawers of water, these simple artisans, masons, stonecutters, carpenters, lime-burners, these carriers of burdens of every sort, who, directed by the nobility but inspired by the priesthood, raised the great cities of stone that abound throughout the Yucatan Peninsula from the foothills of the cordillera in the far south to the shores of the Yucatan Channel in the far north—a prodigious human achievement.

We do not know what generic term was used to describe the common people in ancient times, though the sixteenth-century Maya dictionaries composed by Spanish priests give *ah chembal uinicob, memba uinicob*, and *yalba uinicob* as meaning "the common people, the plebeians"; these terms in Maya mean literally "the inferior or lower men." At the time of the Spanish Conquest, and indeed even today in northern Yucatan, the common people, particularly the Maya Indians, are called *mazehualob*, a word borrowed from the Nahua peoples of central Mexico, which means the lower classes as compared with the nobility. As used at present in northern Yucatan, however, this term carries a distinct connotation of social inferiority and depreciation.

Slaves.—At the bottom of the social scale were the slaves, called *ppentacob* in Maya. Slavery seems to have been practiced in both the Old and New Empires, despite Bishop Landa's explicit statement that it was not introduced until late New Empire times by one of the later Cocom rulers of Mayapan. This is difficult to believe, however, in view of the frequent representations of the so-called "captive figures" on the Old Empire monuments. Sometimes these captives are bound by ropes, their hands being tied behind their backs, as, for example, on Stela 12 at Piedras Negras (Plate 18, *c*) or on Altar VIII at Tikal (Plate 51, *b*). These "captive figures" are, almost certainly, representations of enslaved prisoners of war, though they may well stand for the people of a whole town or village collectively rather than represent any specific individual. Sometimes their faces are different from those of the principal figures, a difference which may indicate that the lords belonged to a special hereditary class.

In New Empire times, when we have direct, documentary evidence of the existence of slavery, the condition in each case would seem to have arisen in one of five different ways: (1) by having been born a slave; (2) by having been made a slave in punishment for stealing; (3) by having been made a prisoner of war; (4) by having become an orphan; and (5) by having been

acquired by purchase, or trade. Although children born into slavery were uncommon, the condition existed, but in such cases provision was made by law and custom for the possible redemption of such slave children. If a person were caught stealing, he was bound over to the person he had robbed, remaining the latter's slave for life, or until he was able to repay the value of the articles stolen. Prisoners of war were always enslaved. Those of high degree were sacrificed immediately, but those of lower rank became the property of the soldier who had captured them. Slaves of this kind, that is, prisoners of war, are represented in a mural painting from the Temple of the Warriors at Chichen Itza, where they are portrayed as naked, their bodies being painted with black and white stripes, curiously enough, not unlike the striped clothing worn by the inmates of our own prisons (Plate 24).

Orphans were acquired for sacrifice either by purchase or even by kidnaping; some people made a special business of kidnaping children for this purpose. If purchased, the price of a small boy varied from five to ten stone beads. In one case we read of two fathoms of thick beads having been paid for each of two boys, who were to be sacrificed. Orphans who had been brought up by rich lords were frequently sacrificed, especially when they were the children of slave women, or when their fathers were already dead. Finally, slaves were acquired by purchase or in trade. Landa, in enumerating the vices of the Maya mentions

idolatries and repudiation of their wives and orgies of public drunkenness and buying and selling slaves. . . . . The occupation to which they are most inclined was trade, carrying cloth and salt and slaves to the lands of Tabasco and Ulua [the present Ulua Valley in Honduras], exchanging all of it for cacao and stone-beads which were their money; and with this they were accustomed to buy slaves or other beads because they were fine and good, which their chiefs wore as jewels at their feasts.

One early authority writing of Nicaragua says that "a slave costs one hundred almonds [cacao-beans], more or less, according to his condition and the agreement between the buyer and seller." If this is true, either the value of cacao-beans must have been ex-

tremely high in ancient times or the price of slaves correspondingly low.

The most famous slave in all Maya history was the beautiful
Mexican girl, Marina, already mentioned in chapter vi (pp. 102,
103), who became the mistress of Cortes and assisted more than
any other one person in the conquest of Mexico. She was born of
noble Mexican parents at Paynala in the Province of Coatzacoalcos. Her father had died when she was but a little girl, and her
mother remarried and had a son by her second husband. The
mother and stepfather, desiring that Marina's half-brother should
succeed them in their honors, instead of the girl, who was the
rightful heir, gave her secretly by night to some Indians from
Xicalanco, spreading the report at the time that she had died.
The Xicalanco Indians later sold her to some Indians in Tabasco,
who in turn gave her to Cortes among a group of twenty slave
girls when the future conqueror of Mexico landed in Tabasco
in the early spring of 1519.

Marina, whose Nahuatl name was Malinal (the name of one
of the Aztec days), which the Spaniards corrupted into Malinche,
was born of Nahuatl-speaking parents, that being the language of
the Province of Coatzacoalcos. Later, as a child and young girl in
Xicalanco and Tabasco, she had learned to speak Maya, probably
the Chontal dialect (Plate 6). Geronimo de Aguilar, a Spaniard,
who, as we have seen in chapter vi (pp. 98, 99), was a prisoner and
slave of the Maya in eastern Yucatan from 1511 to 1519, there
learned to speak Maya. Bernal Diaz del Castillo, one of Cortes'
companions-at-arms, writes of Marina and Aguilar as follows:

> Doña Marina knew the language of Coatzacoalcos, which is that
> common to Mexico, and she knew the language of Tabasco, as did also
> Geronimo de Aguilar, who spoke the language of Yucatan and Tabasco,
> which is one and the same. So that these two could understand each other
> clearly, and Aguilar translated into Castilian for Cortes.

By means of this noble-born, Mexican-Maya slave-girl and this
Spanish prisoner, Cortes carried on all his conversations with
Moctezuma and his Aztec subjects during the early stages of the

Conquest, indeed until after Marina herself had mastered Spanish
and the services of Aguilar could be dispensed with.

Marina bore Cortes a natural son, don Martin Cortes. She accompanied the conqueror of Mexico on his epic march across Peten to the Province of Honduras-Hibüeras in 1524–1525 (chapter vii, pp. 117–22), during which Cortes gave her in marriage to a Castilian *hidalgo* named don Juan de Jaramillo. After the Conquest the Spanish Crown granted her several estates in and around the former Aztec capital, and there she lived in the enjoyment of wealth, probably to a ripe old age, since mention is made of a grandchild during her lifetime.

TRACES OF FORMER CLAN ORGANIZATION

Although by the time of the Spanish Conquest almost all traces of clan organization among the ancient Maya had disappeared, nevertheless, there are suggestions that originally some such a system had been prevalent. For example, Bishop Landa says:

They always called their sons and daughters by the name of the father and the mother, that of the father as the proper name, and that of the mother as the appellative name as follows. The son of Chel [patronymic] and Chan [matronymic] is called Na Chan Chel, which means the son of such and such people [using the mother's family name, here Chan, as a middle name]. And this is the reason [why] the Indians say that those bearing the same name are all of one family, and that they are treated as such. And on this account when one comes to a place which is not known to him and he is in need, he at once makes use of his name, and if there are any of the same name there, they receive him at once and treat him with the greatest kindness. And thus no woman or man was ever married to another of the same name, for that was in their opinion a great infamy.

This is direct reference to the prevalence of an exogamous surname marriage taboo, probably based originally upon a fundamental clan system of social organization, that is, a number of persons claiming descent from a common ancestor.

This ancient Maya taboo against marriages between persons having the same family names has survived down to the present day among the Tzental and Lacandon Maya. In a number of

Tzental villages in the highlands of Chiapas, Mexico, marriage between persons having the same Indian family name is either forbidden outright, or at least, strongly discouraged, as if of too close blood relationship. This taboo operates so strongly in some villages that it extends even to Tzental families who have lost their Indian surnames and have adopted Spanish surnames. If the latter are the same, and such cases occasionally arise, marriages between such persons are forbidden.

Among the few surviving Lacandon Maya of the Chiapas lowlands occupying the dense forests on the southwest side of the Usumacinta Valley, now reduced to something like two hundred souls, children included, everyone was found to belong to one clan or another, the clan to which an individual belonged being inherited from his father, as are Maya surnames among both the Yucatan and Tzental Maya. These clan names among the Lacandon—and some eighteen of them have been enumerated—are all derived from animals or birds, such as the spider-monkey, the howler-monkey, the wild boar, the peccary, the deer, the jaguar, the tapir, the gibnut, the swallow, the pheasant, the partridge, the parrot, the macaw, etc., all of which suggest a former totemic significance. Although not common, marriages between persons of the same surname, and hence clan-name, among the modern Lacandon do occur, and if exogamy ever existed among them it has disappeared before the stern necessity of finding mates of any surname and clan at all, when the total number of the entire group has dwindled almost to the vanishing point.

Superimposed on the clan organization of the Lacandon, there is evidence of still larger social groups composed of several clans each, which are not so clearly understood. It has been suggested that the latter may be the remains of a former more elaborate social organization composed of groups of families, at least originally supposed to have had a common ancestor.

Returning to the Maya of the late New Empire, however, except for the surname exogamy taboo mentioned by Bishop Landa, all traces of clan organization, whether originally totemic or not, seem to have disappeared before the time of the Spanish Conquest.

LIFE OF THE COMMON PEOPLE

BIRTH, NAMES, AND THE *HETZMEK* CEREMONY

FROM THE CRADLE to the grave, the life of the common people was dominated by their religious beliefs as interpreted by the priesthood; indeed the ceremonial pattern of every man's or woman's life was predetermined for him, or her, as the case might be, according to the day of the *tzolkin*, or sacred year of 260 days, upon which he or she happened to have been born. Among the Cakchiquel of the highlands of Guatemala there was the belief that the day of one's birth even controlled one's temperament and destiny. This accidental fact in itself determined in advance for the ancient Maya the gods who were friendly to him, as well as those who were hostile; those upon whose help he could rely because he had been born on a day when their influence was friendly, and those whom he must placate all his life because he had been born on a day when their influence was hostile. Finally, among some Maya tribes—the Cakchiquel, for example—the given name of every Cakchiquel was fixed automatically for him, since his name had to be that of the day upon which he was born, as for example Hunimox (Maya Hun Imix), etc. This practice, however, if ever present among the Maya of northern Yucatan, had disappeared long before the time of the Spanish Conquest.

The ancient Maya loved their children deeply, just as their descendants do today. Children were greatly desired and the women even "asked them of the idols with gifts and prayers." In order to induce pregnancy, recourse was had to the priests, who prayed in behalf of the woman and placed under her bed an image of the goddess Ixchel, "the goddess of making children," that is, of pregnancy and childbirth.

As soon as the child was born, it was washed, and four or five days later the headboards, which were to flatten artificially the little one's forehead, were bound to its head. Depressed foreheads were considered a mark of beauty among the ancient Maya, and this deformation was achieved, four or five days after birth, by binding the heads of the babies between a pair of flat boards, one at the back of the head, the other against the forehead. These boards were left in place for several days, and, after they were removed, the head remained flattened for the rest of the child's life. This head-flattening was as much of a convention among the ancient Maya as the practice of binding the feet of the women formerly was among the Chinese. All Maya representations of the human head in profile show that this practice must have been all but universal, certainly among the upper class.

Another mark of distinction was to be cross-eyed, and mothers deliberately tried to bring about this condition by hanging little balls of resin to the hairs falling between their children's eyes. These pellets of resin dangling between the eyes made the children look at them and thus tended to cross their eyes. The ears, lips, and septum of the nose were pierced to hold gold, copper, jade, wood, shell, bone, and stone ornaments.

A ceremony performed among the modern Maya of Yucatan which undoubtedly is a survival from ancient times is that of the *hetzmek*, or carrying the baby astride the hip for the first time. It is fully as important as the baptismal and puberty ceremonies to be described later. Maya babies and young children are carried astride the left hip. The child is held in place by the left arm of the person carrying it (Plates 10, *b*, and 12, *c*). This is done for the first time in the case of a baby girl when she is three months old, and in the case of a baby boy when he is four months old; this difference in time for this ceremony as between boys and girls is said to be because the Maya hearth (*koben*), symbolic of woman's activities in the home, has three stones; and the cornfield, symbolic of man's activities in the field, has four corners.

Usually there are two godparents for this ceremony—a husband and wife; though if there be but one, it is a man for a boy and a woman for a girl. Nine different objects, symbolic of what the child will use in later life, are placed on a table: in the case of a boy—a book, a machete, an axe, a hammer, a gun, a planting stick, and other articles that he will need, and in the case of a girl—a needle, thread, pins, gourd, a *xamach* or iron griddle for baking *tortillas*, and the like, again articles useful to the activities of her sex. The father hands the baby to the godfather, who sets the child astride his left hip and, approaching the table, selects one of the nine objects and puts it in the child's hand; he then walks around the table, admonishing the child as to its use. "Here you have a book. Take it so that you may learn to read and write." The god-father makes nine circuits of the table, each time selecting one of the nine objects and putting it into the child's hand, instructing him at the same time as to the object's use. He keeps track of his circuits around the table by means of nine grains of corn placed among the other objects, removing a grain each time he makes a round. He then turns the child over to the godmother, who re-peats the operation. She keeps count of her circuits of the table by means of nine calabash seeds previously placed there, eating a seed after each circuit. The child is then given back to the god-father, who returns it to the father saying, "We have made the *hetzmek* for your child." The parents kneel before the god-parents in sign of gratitude and an assistant distributes food, rum, boiled fowls, and *tortillas* to those present.

In ancient times, while the child was still very young, it was carried to a priest, who forecast its horoscope, even to the pro-fession it was to follow in later life; finally the priest gave the child the name it was to bear during childhood, in a kind of bap-tismal rite.

The ancient Maya had three, and sometimes even four differ-ent names: (1) his *paal kaba* or given name, equivalent to our John, William, Mary, or Helen, for example; (2) his father's family name, equivalent to our Smith or Jones, the Maya word for which is unknown; (3) his *naal kaba* or father's and mother's family names combined, something like our hyphenated appella-tives—Smith-Williams; and (4) his *coco kaba* or nickname, like our "Shorty" or "Fatty." A more detailed description of ancient Maya personal names will be found in Appendix II.

Until about the age of three or four years, the children were brought up by their mothers, occasionally being kept at the breast until the end of that period. When a boy was about four or five, a small white bead was fastened to the hair on the top of his head, and when a little girl reached the same age a string was tied around her waist from which was hung a red shell as a symbol of her virginity. To remove either of these, especially the shell from the girl, before the puberty ceremony (erroneously called baptism by Landa) was thought to be highly dishonorable.

The ceremony, described below by Landa as a Maya baptismal rite would seem, in view of its character, to have been rather more in the nature of a puberty ceremony. First Landa infers that it took place when the children were about twelve, that is, at the age of puberty; second, he states definitely that girls were considered to be of marriageable age immediately after this ceremony, but not before; and third, still another sixteenth-century manuscript says that "boys were baptised when they were between fourteen and fifteen years old [that is, after they had adolesced]." There were two earlier ceremonies in the child's life: (1) the giving of the *paal* name when a baby was but five days old, and (2) the *hetzmek*, or carrying-astride-the-hip ceremony, when a child was three or four months old. Either of these, and especially the first, is more similar to baptism than is the ceremony described by Landa below, which almost certainly is a puberty rite; the first, we have seen, involved the giving of the child's first name, and the second the presence of godparents.

PUBERTY

According to Bishop Landa, the day the puberty ceremony was to be held was carefully selected, pains being taken to ascertain in advance that it would not be an unlucky day. A principal man of the town was chosen as sponsor, whose duty it was to assist the priest during the ceremony and to give the corresponding feast, as well as four honorable old men to serve as *chacs* or assistants to the priest and sponsor in conducting the ceremony.

For three days prior to the occasion, the fathers of the children for whom the rite was being held, as well as the other officials, fasted and abstained from intercourse with their wives. On the appointed day all assembled in the court of the sponsor's house, which had been newly swept out and strewn with fresh leaves for the occasion, the boys in one row, the girls in another. An old man was assigned to act as godfather for the former, and an old woman as godmother for the latter. When this was done the priest purified the dwelling and expelled the evil spirit. This was accomplished in the following way: the four *chacs* seated themselves on stools at the four corners of the court and held a cord which ran from one to another, forming an enclosure inside of which stood the children whose puberty was being solemnized, their fathers, and the officiating priest; the priest was seated on a stool before which there was a brazier with platters of *pom* incense and ground maize. Next the boys and girls, in order, approached the priest, who gave each a little maize and incense, which they threw into the brazier. When each had done this, the brazier, the cord which the *chacs* had held, and a little wine were given to an assistant, who was told to carry them outside the town and leave them; he was also admonished neither to drink the wine on the way out nor to look behind him on the way back. This, it was thought, if faithfully carried out, would expel the evil spirit from their midst.

After the evil spirit had been expelled the court was swept out again, fresh leaves were strewn about, and mats were spread on the floor. The priest now changed his vestments to a handsome jacket and a miter-like headdress of red and other colored feathers, taking in his hand an aspergillum for sprinkling holy water about. This latter consisted of a finely worked short stick with tails of the rattlesnake hanging from it. The *chacs* approached the children and placed on their heads pieces of white cloth, which their respective mothers had brought for this purpose. A few of the older children were asked if they had committed any sin or obscene act, and if they had, and confessed it, they were separated from the others, though Landa does not tell us whether they were refused permission to participate further in the rite or not. This concluded, the priest ordered everyone to be seated and to preserve absolute silence, whereupon he began to bless the children, scattering holy water over them with the aspergillum. After having pronounced a benediction, he sat down and the sponsor of the ceremony, with a bone given him by the priest, tapped each child nine times on the forehead, moistening the forehead, the different parts of the face, and the spaces between the fingers and toes with holy water, but saying nothing. This holy water was compounded of cacao beans and certain flowers dissolved in virgin water (rainwater) found in rock hollows in the forest.

After this anointing, the priest removed the white cloths from the children's heads, whereupon each child gave the *chacs* some beautiful feathers and cacao beans which he or she had brought as gifts. The priest next proceeded to cut the white beads from the boys' heads. The attendants carried flowers and pipes upon which they smoked from time to time, giving each child a whiff of the former and a puff of the latter. Next, gifts of food, brought by the children's mothers, were distributed to the children, a little for each one, and then a wine offering was made as a gift from the children to the gods. This wine had to be drunk at one draught by a specially appointed official, who, it was thought, would commit a sin if he so much as paused for breath while drinking it.

The young girls were then dismissed, each mother removing from her own daughter the red shell which the latter had worn as a symbol of her purity. After the removal of this shell the girl was considered to have reached a marriageable age. The boys were dismissed next. When all the children had withdrawn from the court, their parents distributed among the spectators and the officials pieces of cotton cloth which they had brought as gifts. The ceremony closed with feasting and heavy drinking. The sponsor of the ceremony, in addition to his three days of preliminary fasting, had to fast for nine days after the occasion as well, a provision that was strictly obeyed. This ceremony was called "the descent of the gods," and it will be seen from its very nature, as well as from the ages of the children participating in it, that it is much more likely to have been a puberty ceremony than a baptismal rite, which Landa mistakenly calls it.

Formerly children of both sexes were allowed to go stark naked until about four or five, after which the boys were made to wear breech-clouts and the girls skirts. Today the same holds true for boys, but little girls are put into *huipiles* from birth.

Hair on the face was not admired, and the mothers tried to discourage its growth by scalding the faces of their young sons with hot cloths.

As the boys grew older they began to live in a house set apart for the young unmarried men of the community. They came together here for their diversions—ball games, throwing and catching of sticks, dice played with beans, and other pastimes; usually all slept together in this house until marriage. They painted themselves black until they were married, but were not supposed to tattoo themselves before that event. The youths were constantly with their fathers and at an early age accompanied them to the family cornfield, working by their sides. Says Landa: "In all other things they always accompanied their fathers, and thus they became as great idolators as they, and served them very well in their labors."

After the puberty ceremony, as just noted, the girls were considered ready for marriage. Their mothers taught them to be modest. Whenever they met a man anywhere, they turned their backs to him, stepping to one side to allow him to pass; when giving a man a drink of water they dropped their eyes. If the young girls were caught looking at a man, their mothers rubbed chili pepper into their eyes as a punishment, and if they were found to be unchaste, they were soundly whipped and chili pepper was rubbed into their private parts. Mothers taught their daughters how to make *tortillas*, which occupation consumed a great part of every woman's time; indeed, making *tortillas*, washing clothes, and bearing children were the three principal activities of a Maya woman's life in former times just as they still are today. In addition, the women were the housekeepers, cooks, weavers, and spinners. They raised fowl and went to market to buy and sell the articles which they produced, and, when need arose, they carried burdens alongside their menfolk and assisted them in sowing and cultivating.

MARRIAGE

Bishop Landa says that formerly the Maya married when they were twenty years old but that in his time they married when they were twelve or fourteen. In the eighteenth and early nineteenth centuries Maya boys of Yucatan married at about seventeen or eighteen and girls at about fourteen and fifteen. Today in the Indian villages of the northern peninsula the average age of the boys at marriage is twenty-one years, and that of the girls nearly seventeen.

The fathers took great care to find suitable wives for their sons, preferably girls of the same social class and of the same village. Certain relationship taboos, as previously mentioned, existed. It was considered very wicked for one to marry a girl who had the same surname as oneself, or for a widower to marry either the widow of his own brother, or his stepmother, or the sister of his deceased wife, or his maternal aunt, though first-cousin marriages were not forbidden.

It was thought to be mean-spirited if a man sought a mate for himself, or for his children personally, instead of employing the services of a professional matchmaker (*ah atanzahob*). This custom has survived in rural districts in northern Yucatan down to the present time. The matchmaker having been selected, the ceremony was discussed and the amount of the dowry which was to be paid for the girl's hand was agreed upon. This usually consisted of dresses and other articles of little value, for which the boy's father paid the girl's father, while the boy's mother at the same time made ready clothing for her son and daughter-in-law to be. Today, in northern Yucatan, the groom or his family defrays all expenses of the wedding, even including the bride's trousseau; this is true of all classes of society from the most aristocratic *hacendado* (plantation owner) down to the humblest Indian laborer in the hemp fields.

When the day appointed for the ceremony arrived, the relatives and guests assembled at the house of the bride's father. As soon as the priest entered the house, the fathers of the couple presented the young people to him. The priest then made a speech setting forth the details of the marriage agreement, the amount of the dowry, etc., after which he perfumed the house, blessed the bridal pair with prayers, and all the company sat down to a feast which concluded the ceremony. From this time forward the young couple were allowed to live together, and the son-in-law stayed in the house of his wife's parents, working for the latter for a period of six or seven years. His mother-in-law saw to it that her daughter gave the young husband food and drink as a token of their recognition of the marriage, but if the young man failed to work for his father-in-law for the appointed time, the latter kicked him out of the house, giving his daughter to some other man, over which "great scandals arose."

Sometimes marriages were arranged between families when the boy and girl were still very young, and after they had come of age the arrangement was faithfully carried out. Widows and widowers remarried without ceremony—no feast and other formalities; the man simply went to the house of the woman of his choice, and, if she accepted him, she gave him something to eat as a sign thereof. Custom decreed that widowers and widows should remain single for at least a year after the death of their previous mates, during which time they were supposed to abstain from sexual intercourse; those who failed to conform with this practice were held to have but little restraint, and it was thought some calamity would befall them because of it.

Although the Maya, generally speaking, were monogamous, divorce was easy; indeed it consisted in little more than simple repudiation. It was of common occurrence as an early Spanish witness indicates:

They did not have marital relations with more than one woman [at a time], but they left her for trifling reasons, and married another, and there were men who married ten and twelve times; and the women had the same liberty to leave their husbands and take another, but the first time they got married it was by a priest.

190   And on this account they repudiate more easily, since they marry without love and ignorant of married life and of the duties of married
people.

This is probably true more often than not, even of the present-
day Maya, who marry without love in the modern American
sense. Today it seems rather a matter of routine. The boy has
adolesced; he wants a home and children of his own, and therefore either his parents, some old friend of the family, or in the
remoter villages the *ah atanzah,* or professional matchmaker,
arranges for his marriage with a suitable girl, not necessarily con-
sulting either the boy's or the girl's feelings about his or her prospective mate. Romantic, passionate love in the modern American
way, certainly in the lush Hollywood manner, is largely lacking
among the modern Maya of Yucatan.

I well recall an incident out of my own experience at Chichen
Itza, which clearly illustrates this point. My wife and I agreed
to arrange a marriage for our chauffeur, a young Maya boy of
nineteen; the most suitable girl we could find seemed to be the
daughter of the head man of a neighboring village, then a girl
of about fifteen. The boy indicated that this choice was ac-
ceptable to him, and I opened formal negotiations for the girl's
hand by letter. At first, as custom decreed, the proposal was rejected on the grounds that the girl was "too young to leave her
mother"; but the matter was pressed further in formal correspondence setting forth the good qualities of the boy and urging
favorable consideration of his suit. Finally the youth was allowed
to visit the girl's house and see her, though always in company
with some member of her family. Every week end for a couple
of months he went to her home, carrying gifts—sugar, honey,
wheat bread, wine, perfume, chocolate, soap, and occasionally
a tin of California fruit. We always thought it was the California tinned fruit, a great luxury in Yucatan, that finally won the
father's consent. Toward the end of this probationary period,
the boy took his mother, stepfather, and sister to visit his prospective in-laws, until finally a day was set for the wedding.

As matters thus approached a satisfactory conclusion, we became
concerned lest the match might not turn out happily for our godson. Up to this time we had had no indication from anyone
throughout the entire period of the courtship that the girl even
so much as liked the boy. Somewhat apprehensive on this score, I
asked the girl's father one day if he thought his daughter would
love our godson. To which, without an instant's hesitation, he
promptly replied: "Of course she will. She's a good girl;
she will love whom I tell her to!" And strange to say the girl
did precisely that. Indeed this marriage has turned out more
happily than any other among the Maya with which I am acquainted.

DRESS

The principal garment of the men was the breechclout called
ex in Maya. It was a band of cotton cloth, five fingers broad (the
width of the hand), and long enough to be wound around the
waist several times and passed between the legs so as to cover
the private parts, one end hanging down between the legs in
front, the other between the buttocks behind. These breechclouts
were woven on hand looms by the women, the two ends being
more or less elaborately embroidered with feathers:

They wore the *mastil* [probably a corruption of *maxtli*, the Aztec
word for the same garment] between their legs, which was a large strip
of woven *manta*, which, tying it on the abdomen and giving it a turn
below, covered their private parts, the two long points having on them
much plumage hanging before and behind.

The *ex* is represented everywhere on the sculptures, frescoes, and
painted vases of both the Old and New Empires, from the gorgeously decorated breechclouts worn by the rulers, priests, and
nobles, richly embellished with plumes, jade beads, and colored
shells (Fig. 7, *a, b, c, d, e, f*), down to the simple, unadorned,
workaday loin cloths of the lower classes.

In addition to the *ex*, the men sometimes wore a large square
cotton cloth called the *pati*, knotted around the shoulders, which
was more or less elaborately decorated according to the station of

FIG. 7.—Examples of Maya breechclouts, or *ex* (*a*, *b*, *c*, *d*, *e*, *f*) from the monuments of the Old Empire.

the wearer. This also served the poor as a covering for their beds ▬
at night.

Sandals made of the dry, untanned hide of the deer and
tied with hemp cords completed the costume of the common people. On the Old Empire monuments, the sandals are shown as
exceedingly elaborate, having richly adorned, high projecting
backs and ornate, conical-shaped knots over the insteps (Fig. 8,
a, b, c, d, e, f). One very important difference between representations of ancient Maya sandals, in both the Old and New Empires
(Fig. 8, *g, h, i, j*), and those now in use, however, is to be noted.
In ancient times the sandals were bound to the feet by two thongs,
or cords, one passing between the first and second toes, the other
between the third and fourth toes (Fig. 8, *k*); today, on the other
hand, from the highlands of Guatemala to the northernmost tip

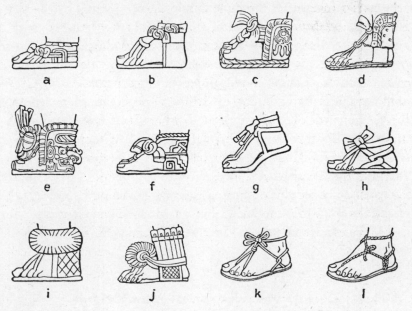

FIG. 8.—Maya sandals, or *xanab*: (*a, b, c, d, e, f*) examples of sandals from the
Old Empire monuments; (*g, h, i, j*) examples of sandals from the New Empire
monuments; (*k*) ancient method of fastening sandals with two cords, one passing
between the first and second toes, the other between the third and fourth toes;
(*l*) modern method of fastening sandals with a single cord passing between the
first toe and the second toe.

of Yucatan, only the first of these thongs, the one passing between the first and second toes, has survived (Fig. 8, *l*).

The men wore their hair long with a bare spot burned on the top of the head like a large tonsure. The long hair was braided and wound around the head like a coronet except for a long queue which was allowed to fall behind. The boys, as already noted, painted their faces and bodies black until they were married; after marriage faces and bodies were painted red. Black was also used when they fasted. This body painting was done, it was said, "for the sake of elegance." Warriors painted themselves black and red: "In order to show ferocity, and, to appear more fierce and valiant [they] painted their eyes and noses and the whole face, body and arms with black and red." Prisoners were painted in black and white stripes, and the priests were painted blue. In preparation for one of the most important ceremonies of the year, which was celebrated in the month of Mol, they painted with a blue pigment everything from the utensils of the priests down to the spindles with which the women wove; even the wooden columns of the houses were painted blue (p. 249). Two priests holding the arms and legs of a sacrificial victim, depicted in a fresco from the Temple of the Warriors at Chichen Itza, and the victim himself are all three painted blue from head to feet (Plate 28, *f*). Many of the balls of *pom* incense, which were found in the Well of Sacrifice at Chichen Itza were also painted a bright turquoise blue. Indeed, blue was the color associated with sacrifice among the late New Empire Maya just as it was among the Mexicans, from whom they possibly may have derived this association.

Paint was also used in tattooing:

Those who do the work, first painted the part which they wish with color, and afterwards they delicately cut in the paintings, and so with blood and coloring-matter the marks remained on the body. This work is done a little at a time on account of the extreme pain, and afterwards also they were quite sick with it, since the designs festered and matter formed. In spite of all this they made fun of those who were not tattooed.

The Maya are said to have been great lovers of perfume and to
have used flowers, resins, and sweet-smelling herbs in its preparation.

Several accounts of the principal garment worn by the Maya
women have come down to us, but none is clear. Landa says:

The women of the coast and of the Provinces of Bacalar and of
Campeche are more modest in their dress, for, besides the covering which
they wore from the waist down [a kind of skirt], they covered their
breasts, tying a folded *manta* [*pati*] underneath their armpits. All the
others did not wear more than one garment like a long and wide sack,
opened on both sides, and drawn in as far as the hips, where they fastened
it together, with the same width as before.

Herrera writes: "They wore a dress like a sack, long and wide,
open on both sides and sewn as far as the hips." A third early
writer states: "The Maya women wore their kind of petticoats,
which is like a sack open at both sides, and these, tied at the waist,
covered their private parts." In addition a cotton kerchief was
worn over the head, "open like a short cowl, which also served
to cover their breasts."

Although none of these descriptions by itself is complete,
together they give a fair idea of the costume of the Maya women
of Yucatan at the present time (Plate 26). This dress was formerly called *kub*, a word now entirely forgotten; today this garment is known as the *huipil*, an Aztec word. It is a white, loose-
fitting, single-piece, cotton dress, of the same width from top to
bottom, sewn at the sides, with holes for the arms and a square-
cut opening for the head. The armholes and neck opening, as
well as the bottom of the garment, are beautifully embroidered
in cross-stitch (*xocbil chui*, Maya for "threads that are counted"),
the designs being flowers, birds, insects, and animals in bright
colors. This garment, with its unusual cross-stitch embroidery,
is almost certainly a survival from ancient times. The one shown
in Plate 26, *d*, is from Merida in northern Yucatan, and the one
in Plate 26, *c*, from Tixcacal, Quintana Roo.

Underneath is worn a very full, long petticoat (Maya *pic*),
which hangs below the *kub* or *huipil*. This is sometimes em-

broidered around the bottom, but, if so, always in white. A Maya woman or girl literally never leaves her house for any reason, either to go to market or to church, or to visit her nearest neighbor, without her *rebozo* (Maya *booch*), a scarf of colored cotton, though occasionally of silk, which she wears either draped gracefully around her neck or thrown over her head. Unless she is inside her own house, she would actually feel undressed without it. This may be a survival of the cotton kerchief worn over the head, mentioned above. Today slippers of European style are universally worn by the women, but formerly they as well as the men probably used sandals for festive occasions, going barefoot the rest of the time.

Women and girls wore their hair very long and took great care of it. The hair was done up in various ways—parted in the middle, sometimes braided, the style for married women differing from that of the young girls. Little girls had their hair dressed in two or four hornlike projections, which are said to have been very becoming. The women, like their husbands, anointed themselves with a sweet-smelling red ointment, to which those who could afford it added a fragrant, sticky resin, the odor of which lasted for many days. They tattooed themselves from the waists up, except for their breasts, the designs used being more delicate and beautiful than those tattooed on the men.

A large book could be written about the dress and paraphernalia of the rulers, nobility, and priesthood, based upon the wealth of pertinent material in the sculptures, frescoes, and vase-paintings of both the Old and New Empires (Plates 24, 63–69, 71, 72, and 87–90). The official regalia and robes of the *halach uinic*, the festive and war apparel and accouterments of the nobility, and the insignia and vestments of the priesthood must have been of barbaric splendor, and yet these articles of dress, elaborately decorated as they appear to have been, may be reduced basically to the same few garments of the common man—the breechclout, *ex*, the *pati* or cape, the sandals, and, in addition, a headdress.

The breechclouts of the upper classes portrayed in the sculptures are in many cases of great intricacy. The ends, falling in

front and behind, are richly worked with feathers, and the part
passing around the waist is heavily incrusted with jade beads, jade
ornaments representing human heads, shell pendants, etc. Sometimes, as at Palenque, short trousers coming to just above the
knee were worn. The simple square cotton *pati* of the common
man becomes a magnificent cape, sometimes of handsomely embroidered cotton stuff; or again a strikingly marked jaguar skin,
draped around or even fashioned to fit the shoulders, the tail
hanging down behind; or yet again of brilliantly colored feathers,
the longer plumes shimmering and swirling in every passing
breeze. The gorgeous, iridescent, blue-green tail feathers of
the quetzal, sometimes three feet long, seem to have been reserved
for the ruler alone. The quetzal is indeed a regal bird, whose
habitat is closely restricted to the highlands of Guatemala and
immediately adjoining parts of southern Mexico and Honduras,
and to a lesser extent as far south as Panama. It is the national bird
of the Republic of Guatemala, as is the eagle for us. The sandals,
as already noted, became increasingly elaborate as the wearer rose
in the social scale, until those of the *halach uinic,* as represented
on the monuments of the Old Empire, are extremely ornate—
high, richly embroidered projections, or cuffs behind, and richly
ornamented knots falling over the insteps in front (Fig. 8, *a, b,
c, d, e, f*).

It was in the headdresses, however, that the greatest magnificence was displayed. The framework of these was probably
of wicker or wood, carved to represent the heads of the jaguar, serpent, or bird, or even the heads of some of the Maya gods. These
frames were covered with jaguar skin, feather mosaic, and carved
jades and were surmounted by lofty panaches of plumes, a riot
of barbaric color, falling down over the shoulders (Plate 53, *f*).
Sometimes the panache took the form of a stiffly feathered crest.
Always, however, it was the most striking part of the costume,
and indicated the rank and social class of the wearer.

Costume accessories consisted of collars, necklaces, wristlets,
anklets, and knee-bands; these were made of feathers, jade beads,
shells, jaguar teeth and claws, crocodile teeth and, in New Empire

times when metal appears for the first time, also of gold and copper. Other kinds of costume jewelry were nose ornaments, earrings, and lip plugs of jade, stone, obsidian, shell, wood, and bone. Ornaments of the lower classes were confined largely to simple nose plugs, lip plugs, and earrings of bone, wood, shell, and stone.

THE ROUND OF DAILY LIFE

The Maya household in ancient times, doubtless just as it still does today, rose very early. The women were up first—between three and four in the morning—to prepare the family breakfast, which consisted of *tortillas*, beans, and for the poorer people, *atole*. The business, first of preparing the corn for the *tortillas*, and then of making them, was, and still is, one of the most important activities of a Maya woman's life—next to bearing and raising her children.

This number one household duty of Maya women may be divided into five steps as described below:

1. The dried, shelled corn is first put into an *olla* (Maya *cum*), or cooking pot with sufficient water and lime to soften the kernels. The mixture is then brought nearly to the boiling point and kept at this temperature until the hull is softened, being stirred occasionally. The *olla* is then set aside and allowed to stand until the following morning. The softened, hulled corn is called *kuum* in Maya.

2. Sometime after breakfast the next morning, the *kuum* is washed until it is perfectly clean and free of hulls.

3. The *kuum* is then ground. In ancient times this was done by hand with stone grinders; the understone was called *caa*, and the grinder proper called *kab*. Today hand-operated metal mills have generally replaced the old stone grinders, and even power-driven mills are the rule in the larger villages. The ground corn is called *zacan* in Maya; when ground it is covered with a cloth and allowed to stand until later in the morning.

4. About an hour before the main meal of the day, now usually eaten in the early afternoon, a small, low round table,

about fifteen inches high, called the *banqueta*,[1] is washed. This table always stands near the *koben* or typical Maya three-stone hearth. Next a round griddle (Maya *xamach*), now made of iron, but formerly of baked clay, is also wiped clean, placed on the three-stone hearth, and allowed to heat. Next a section of plantain leaf (Maya *u lee haas*), roughly six inches square, is heated on the *xamach* until it becomes soft and pliant; this is then placed on the *banqueta* with a pinch of ashes underneath to make it turn easily on the low table, after which preliminary preparations the Maya woman is ready to make her *tortillas* (Maya *uah*).

5. She pinches off a lump of freshly ground *zacan* (it must be fresh, as it sours quickly) about the size of a hen's egg and places it on the piece of plantain leaf previously prepared. Both hands are used in making the *tortilla*, which is about the size and shape of an American pancake; the left hand forms the edge of the *tortilla* while the right flattens the lump of *zacan* and, at the same time, gives it a rotary motion on the *banqueta*. Rapidly a perfectly round and very thin, flat cake takes form under her skillful fingers. The almost continuous pats the women give the *tortillas* in making them produces a highly typical sound, heard throughout all Maya villages in Yucatan just about midday. When shaped, the *tortilla* is laid on the heated *xamach* to bake, first on one side and then on the other. It is next placed on the hot fagots of wood below the *xamach* until it puffs out, when the woman picks it up by the edge and gives it a smart blow on the *banqueta*, which flattens it out again. Finally the *tortilla* is placed in a gourd (Maya *lec*) to keep it hot, where it is joined by literally scores of others, since the average Maya man usually eats no less than twenty at one meal, and he demands that they be piping hot.

A sixteenth-century account of the eating habits of the ancient Maya has the following to say:

As to the meals which they ate in the time of their antiquity, they eat the same today. This is corn boiled in water and crushed. When made

---

[1] The Maya name for this low table has not been preserved.

into dough, they dissolve it in water for a drink [*pozole*], and this is what they ordinarily drink and eat. An hour before sunset it was their custom to make certain *tortillas* of the said dough. On these they supped, dipping them into certain dishes of crushed peppers, diluted with a little water and salt. Alternately with this they ate certain boiled beans of the land, which are black. They call them *buul,* and the Spanish, *frijoles.* This was the only time they ate during the day, for at other times they drank the dissolved dough mentioned above.

From the foregoing the principal difference between ancient and modern Maya eating habits would appear to be in the hour of the main meal of the day; formerly, judging from the account above, it was in the late afternoon "an hour before sunset," while now the main meal is usually eaten at noon, or early afternoon.

Maya men and women even today do not eat together. The men of the family, father and sons, eat first, squatting around the *banqueta,* served by the mother and daughters; afterward, when the men have gone about their work, the women and girls sit around the *banqueta* and have their meal. The *tortillas* eaten at breakfast are those left over from the day before, but toasted crisp for the morning's meal, the fresh *tortillas* not being ready until the main meal of the day, after the men return from work.

The men leave for the cornfields between four and five o'clock in the morning, after which the women turn to their principal task of the forenoon—preparing the *zacan* for the *tortillas,* and making and baking the latter. Any spare time they may have after this is devoted to washing and other household duties—cooking, sewing, weaving, embroidering, etc.

For refreshment until his return to the house in the early or even middle afternoon, the man working in the cornfields takes with him in the morning a lump of *pozole* as large as an apple, wrapped in a piece of plantain leaf. *Pozole* is very much like *zacan,* only it is allowed to boil longer until it hardens into a thick mass, which holds together more easily, and sours less rapidly. About ten, the man knocks off work for a few minutes to mix a lump of *pozole* in a cup made from half a gourd (Maya *luch*) filled with water. The resulting drink looks like milk and is extremely nourishing, sustaining the laborer for the rest of the morning; though if he works until two or three in the afternoon, he may drink *pozole* two or even three times; and perhaps he will have brought along some toasted *tortillas* as well.

The men return from the fields in the early afternoon, after which they eat the main meal of the day—fresh, hot *tortillas*, beans, eggs, a little meat if such is available, deer, beef, pork, or chicken, perhaps a few vegetables and chocolate, if the family can afford it. After this meal, though in some households before, the man takes his daily bath of warm water, which his wife is expected to have ready for him. He bathes in a wooden tub, usually hollowed from a piece of Spanish cedar; the ticks are removed from his body, usually by his wife, and clean clothes are laid out for him. The Maya, as already noted, are personally one of the cleanest peoples in the world, and after a long, half-day of heavy work in the fields, the man expects, and gets, his warm bath. Indeed, during the Colonial Period the law gave him the right to beat his wife if she did not have his warm bath ready for him when he returned from work, and this Spanish law was doubtless based upon an earlier Maya practice.

Bathed and dressed, the men sit around talking until the evening meal, which is light—*tortillas*, beans, and chocolate or *atole*. The latter is a hot drink made by mixing *zacan* in cold water, the mixture being brought to a boil; it is sometimes sweetened with honey (now more often with sugar), or left unsweetened.

The family retires early against the early hour of rising the next day, probably by eight o'clock, and certainly before nine unless some special business, such as a religious ceremony or rite, a council, feast, or dance is afoot—or perhaps just talking in the moonlight, which they like to do. Formerly everybody slept, as they still do today, in one room, and probably in beds or on low platforms of poles. Landa says in this connection:

And then they build a wall in the middle dividing the house lengthwise, and in this wall they leave several doors into the half which they call the back of the house, where they have their beds, and the other half they whitened very nicely with lime [this outer room would seem to have been a sort of porch open at the front and sides] . . . . and they have beds made of small rods [saplings] and on the top a mat on which they sleep, covering themselves with their *mantas* [*patis*] of cotton. In summer they usually sleep in the whitened part of the house [that is, the porch], on one of those mats, especially the men.

A seventeenth-century writer speaks of a bed in a house in the lowlands, southwest of the Usumacinta River, made of a crude wooden framework sufficiently large to hold four persons together, with "small beds for children," while an eighteenth-century writer reports of the Yucatan Maya, "His bed is the floor, or a framework of boards, supported by four sticks."

Today every Indian in Yucatan, and most of the *mestizos* (mixed-bloods, Indian and white) sleep in hammocks. Whether the hammock was introduced into Yucatan by the Spaniards or whether it was of native origin is not definitely known, though it seems almost certain that, had they been in general use in Yucatan, Landa could not have failed to have mentioned them, whereas he states explicitly, as quoted above, that they "had beds made of small rods."

It has been shown in the chapter on agriculture (p. 155) that the food needs of the average Maya family today can be supplied in less than two months of full work days—days of eight work hours each, not half-time only. In ancient times, when there were no steel machetes or axes, it doubtless took much longer not only to fell the bush and plant a first-year cornfield, but also to keep it free of weeds. On the other hand, it was also shown (p. 153) that, whereas now a cornfield can be planted for only two successive years, there are good grounds for believing that formerly the same cornfield could be, and was, planted for seven or eight successive seasons. In any event it is evident that the ancient Maya had a great deal of spare time, certainly more than half the year, when he was not engaged in raising food for his family's needs.

That this leisure time of the common people was highly organized by the nobility and priesthood is abundantly proved by

the colossal programs of public works which all cities and towns
both of the Old and New Empires were able to carry out. These
vast constructions of stone and mortar depended upon a highly
organized and ably directed society. Some, perhaps most, of the
spare time of the common people went into quarrying the vast
quantities of stone required in these great building projects and
into transporting them from the quarries to the building sites;
into felling wood for the thousands of limekilns; into gathering gravel for the endless quantities of mortar; into carving the
worked-stone elements; into dressing the plain building-blocks, in
sculpturing the monuments; in building the enormous foundation
platforms, sometimes covering many acres of ground; and finally
in constructing the pyramids, temples, and palaces themselves.
And all this, in addition to supporting the ruler, the nobility, and
the priesthood in economic idleness. In view of all that they did,
and, driven as they were by the demands of a highly exigent
ruling class, priesthood, and religion, the common people could
have had but few idle hours, little time which they could really
call their own.

SICKNESS, DEATH, BURIAL, AND THE LIFE HEREAFTER

When a man was ill he summoned a priest, a medicine-man,
or a sorcerer—Landa lumps all three together in disgust at their
heathen rites and hocus-pocus. This curer of ills, by a combination of prayers, special ceremonies, bleeding of the afflicted parts,
and the administration of native herbs, either cured or killed his
patients, his reputation as a healer depending upon which of the
two predominated. Yucatan is blessed with many medicinal herbs
and plants, and an extensive pharmacopoeia was at the disposition
of these native sorcerer-doctors. Several seventeenth-century
Maya manuscripts, listing many ills from which the Indians suffered, together with their corresponding cures, have come down
to us, and some of their remedies have undoubted merit. It is true
that many smack of medieval European superstition mixed with
pagan Maya magic, as for example, the following remedy for
toothache:

You take the bill of a woodpecker and bleed the gums a little with it; if a man thirteen times; if a woman, nine times. [The gum] shall be slightly pierced by the bill of the woodpecker. Thus also a piece of a tree struck by lightning is to be grated with a fish-skin and wrapped in cotton-wool. Then you apply it to the tooth. He will recover by this means.

Possibly this bleeding of the gums might alleviate some kinds of toothache, but the "thirteen times in the case of a man" and the "nine times in the case of a woman" are surely ritualistic survivals, thirteen and nine being the two most sacred numbers among the ancient Maya, the former corresponding to the number of Gods of the Upper World and the latter to the number of Gods of the Lower World (pp. 231, 232). Again the "tree struck by lightning" is pure superstition.

On the other hand, some of the native plants undoubtedly possess definite medicinal properties, as for example the *kanlol* (*Tecoma stans*), a flowering shrub with a yellow trumpet-like blossom, which grows everywhere in northern Yucatan. Two to ten drops of a fluid extract made from this, taken hourly, is a strong diuretic and probably a mild heart stimulant as well.

Landa says:

There were also surgeons, or better said, sorcerers, who cured with herbs and many superstitious rites . . . . The sorcerers and physicians performed their cures by bleedings of the parts, which gave pain to the sick man; . . . . [the Maya] believed that death, sicknesses and afflictions came to them for their wrong doing and their sin; they had a custom of confessing themselves, when they were already sick.

According to the same authority, the Maya had great fear of death, and when it intervened their grief was excessive:

This people had a great and excessive fear of death and they showed this in that all the services, which they made to their gods, were for no other end, nor for any other purpose than that they [the gods] should give them health, life and sustenance. But when, in time, they came to die, it was indeed a thing to see the sorrow and the cries which they made for their dead, and the great grief it caused them. During the day they wept for them in silence; and at night with loud and very sad cries, so that it was pitiful to hear them. And they passed many days in deep sorrow. They made abstinences and fasts for the dead, especially the husband or wife; and they said that the devil had taken him [or her] away since they thought that all evils came to them from him [the devil], and especially death.

As soon as death occurred, the body was wrapped in a shroud and the mouth filled with ground maize (Maya *koyem*) and one or more jade beads "which they use for money, so that they should not be without something to eat in the other life." The common people were buried under the floors of their houses or behind them. Usually the thatch and sapling houses of the poor were abandoned after a death because of their great fear of it, unless there happened to be a number of people in the family. In addition, idols, presumably figurines of clay, wood, or stone, as well as objects indicating the profession or trade of the deceased, were thrown into the grave; in the case of a priest, some of his books, his hieroglyphic codices (p. 295); if a sorcerer, some of the magic stones he used in his incantations; if a hunter, his bow and arrows; if a fisherman, his hooks, nets, and harpoons.

In the remoter villages of Yucatan there still survives the memory of a strange burial custom, which is said to have been of common occurrence long ago, despite the fact that no early Spanish or native source makes any mention of it. It is called the *bool keban* or *antah bool zipil*, "help in paying for sin," and is in effect a symbolic sharing of the dead man's sins by his surviving relatives and friends. This ceremonial cleansing is said to have been effected by the following extraordinary practice. The deceased was laid out in a long wooden bathtub, and the body was then washed with *atole*, the hot drink made of ground corn described in a preceding section of this chapter. This act was a symbolic washing away of the sins of the deceased. The *atole* was then distributed among members of the family and friends, each of whom drank a portion (Plate 27, *c*), thus assuming a part of the sins of the deceased and aiding his soul's entry into Paradise. Since not one early source mentions this custom, however, I strongly doubt its antiquity, certainly its general prevalence at any time.

The burial customs of the ruling classes were naturally more elaborate. Landa says that the bodies of the nobles and persons of high esteem were burned, their ashes being placed in great urns, and temples built above them, which statement archaeological investigations in the Maya area amply confirm. Excavations in the pyramid supporting the High Priest's Grave at Chichen Itza, in a similar pyramid at Mayapan, in the substructures of Temples A-I and A-XVIII at Uaxactun, in the pyramid of the Temple of the Cross at Palenque, in the substructure of Building B (Group II) at Holmul, not to mention others, have established the fact that burials were made in these several pyramids and substructures, *under the floors* of the buildings they supported.

Graves of important personages have also been found in small, stone-lined, burial vaults with typical corbel-arched roofs, built just under plaza floor levels at Chichen Itza, Palenque, Uaxactun, and Copan. Most of these pyramid and plaza subfloor burials were accompanied by more or less elaborate mortuary furniture, in some cases exquisitely painted pottery vessels, carved jade beads and pendants, ornately chipped objects of flint and obsidian, and in the case of the High Priest's Grave at Chichen Itza, even baroque pearls were found.

In northern Yucatan, another burial custom among the nobility, according to Landa, was to enclose the ashes of the dead in hollow statues either of pottery or of wood. In the case of a wooden statue it was made to look like the dead man. The back of the statue's head was left hollow and here the ashes from a part of the cremated body were placed, the opening being sealed with skin stripped from the back of the head of the deceased; the rest of the body was buried. These statues and crematory urns of the dead were preserved with great veneration among the family idols.

Among the Cocom, the ruling house of Mayapan, a special burial custom obtained. The bodies of the dead Cocom lords were boiled until the fleshy parts could be completely removed from the bones. The back half of the head was then sawed off,

leaving the front half, the bony foundation of the face, intact.
Then, where the fleshy parts of the face had been, a new face
was built up with a kind of resin, so that it looked like the face
of the man whose skull it was. These restored faces were kept,
together with the wooden effigies previously mentioned, in the
oratories of their houses with the family idols, being held in great
veneration and respect, and on feast days offerings of food were
made to them so that the Cocom lords might lack for nothing in
that other land whither they had gone.

Again archaeology partially confirms Landa's statement here,
since in dredging the Well of Sacrifice at Chichen Itza (pp. 432–
36) a skull was recovered which has the crown cut away; the eye
sockets were filled with wooden plugs, and there were the remains of painted plaster on the front, evidently with the idea of
reproducing a likeness of the face of the deceased. Finally there
has recently been found in the Department of El Quiché, Guatemala, the front part of a human skull covered with a thick coat
(1 inch) of lime-plaster, which was modeled to represent a human
face.

RELIGION AND DEITIES

RISE AND DEVELOPMENT

DURING THE three, four, or perhaps even five thousand years since the Maya exchanged their nomadic life for a sedentary one based upon agriculture as applied to the cultivation of Indian corn, their religion had undergone corresponding changes. At first, though of those remote days not a shadow of a tradition has survived to help us in our speculations, the Maya religion was probably a simple nature worship, personification of the natural forces which influenced and in large measure shaped their lives: the sun, the moon, the rain, the lightning, winds, mountains, plains, forests, rivers, and rapids. These forces surrounded them, and their interplay formed the background against which the Maya lived their nomadic lives.

Such a simple, natural religion required little formal organization; no priesthood or esoteric lore to interpret it; no set ritual or elaborate ceremonials to practice it; not even specialized places of worship, such as temples, to house it. Each family head could have been, and doubtless was at the same time, the family priest, and the family temple was little more than a humble, temporary hut set apart but close to the equally temporary dwellings of the family—much the same condition, for example, as still exists among the Lacandon Maya in the forests of the Usumacinta Valley in eastern Chiapas, Mexico (Pre-Maya I, Table III, facing p. 40).

Later agriculture was introduced, bringing in its train fixed dwellings and more leisure time, and religion became more organized, the gods themselves more specialized. A priesthood whose business it was to interpret the will of the gods to the mass of the people grew up; the need for more formal sanctuaries—temples—arose; religion became a business of the few for the many. Fixed homes made possible more permanent ceremonial centers and encouraged the erection of more ambitious sanctuaries and the development of a more elaborate ritual.

During the many centuries—perhaps over a millenium—which elapsed between the introduction of agriculture and the invention of the Maya calendar, chronology, and hieroglyphic writing, probably either in 7.0.0.0.0 or 7.6.0.0.0 of the Maya Era, 353 or 235 B.C. (see chapter iii, p. 47), the Maya religion doubtless remained much the same, changing very slowly—the beginnings of individualized gods, a budding priesthood, a richer ritual, and more elaborate sanctuaries, though still not of masonry. This second period (Pre-Maya II, Table III) was probably contemporaneous with the Mamom ceramic phase at Uaxactun.

However, with the introduction of the calendar, chronology, and hieroglyphic writing, all three of priestly invention, Maya religion underwent important modifications, again in the direction of greater complexity and formalization. A religious philosophy, devised by a professional priesthood and built around the increasing importance of astronomical manifestations and the development of the calendar, chronology, and associated deities, gradually took shape. This last change, while it almost certainly began as early as the third century before Christ (Pre-Maya III, Table III), first becomes archaeologically apparent to us with the earliest appearance of sculptured stone monuments at Uaxactun about 8.14.0.0.0 (A.D. 317), which latter in turn probably coincided with the introduction of corbeled roof-vaulting and the beginnings of Tzakol pottery, also found first at Uaxactun (Old Empire I, Table III). There is every probability that such highly specialized cultural traits as the Maya hieroglyphic writing and calendar, Maya stone architecture with its distinctive corbeled roof-vaults, and Tzakol pottery each could have had but a single place of origin; and further, since we find the earliest occurrence of all three at one and the same site, namely Uaxactun, the conclusion is unavoidable that not only one but all three originated either at Uaxactun itself or very near by, perhaps even more likely at the great ceremonial center of Tikal, the largest city of the Maya culture, less than twelve miles distant from Uaxactun (chapter iii, p. 43).

Something fundamentally important, what we may perhaps designate as no less than the birth of the Maya civilization, took place in northern central Peten, sometime during the three or four centuries immediately preceding and following the beginning of the Christian Era. Was this quickening of the cultural pulse due to some outside influence, or was it of autochthonous origin? Perhaps we shall never surely know. But the fact that these innovations first appear in the very center of the vast region which later became the Maya Old Empire—in other words that they were a central, not a peripheral manifestation—strongly suggests that they originated where the earliest occurrences of them have been found, that is at either Uaxactun or Tikal.

Perhaps the native genius of the ruling house of this incipient city-state achieved the cultural miracle; I certainly prefer this explanation of the origin of the Maya civilization, rather than assume that it was derived from some other region entirely outside the Maya area, in support of which hypothesis no adequate archaeological evidence has as yet been advanced.

As early as the fourth century after Christ, Maya culture was firmly established in northern central Peten, where we have seen it had also probably originated; Maya religion had become a highly developed cult based upon a complete fusion of a more primitive personification of nature with a more sophisticated philosophy, built around a deification of the heavenly bodies, a worship of time in its various manifestations never equaled anywhere in the world before or, for that matter, since. This religion, while shared by the common people, was highly esoteric in nature, being interpreted and served by a closely organized priesthood composed of astronomers, mathematicians, prophets, ritualists, and, as it grew more and more complex, by skilled administrators, even statesmen (p. 172).

Judging from the generally peaceful tenor of Old Empire sculptures, the almost complete absence of representations of human sacrifice (only two examples are known, both from Piedras

Negras, Plate 28, *a* and *b*), the dignified and lofty calm of the figures, Maya religion throughout the Old Empire period must have been an august, stately faith, not debased as it was in later times by wholesale human sacrifice, which we shall see was an importation from Mexico in New Empire times. Just as the Old Empire was the Golden Age of Maya culture, so was it also the noblest period of Maya religion, before the latter's beliefs and practices had degenerated into bloody orgies.

There are no archaeological reasons for believing that the Maya religion suffered any fundamental changes during the Old Empire, but in the New Empire, during the Puuc and Mexican periods (New Empire I and II, Table III, see chapter v, facing p. 38), sweeping changes of a debased nature were introduced.

A number of different sixteenth-century Spanish writers definitely affirm that the Mexicans introduced idolatry, which statement probably was meant to include human sacrifice as well:

The old men of these provinces [Yucatan] say that anciently, near to eight hundred years ago, idolatry was not practiced, and afterwards when the Mexicans entered it and took possession of it, a captain, who was called Quetzalquat [Quetzalcoatl] in the Mexican language, which is to say in ours, plumage of the serpent. . . . . introduced idolatry into this land and the use of idols for gods, which he had made of wood, of clay and of stone. And he made them [the Maya] worship these idols and they offered many things of the hunt, of merchandise and above all the blood of their nostrils and ears, and the hearts of those whom they sacrificed in his services. . . . .

They say that the first inhabitants of Chichenyza [Chichen Itza] were not idolators, until a Mexican captain Ku Kalcan [Kukulcan] entered into these parts, who taught idolatry, and the necessity, so they say, to teach and practice it.

Finally Herrera, the official Historian of the Indies for the Crown of Spain, leaves no doubt about this point, stating bluntly that "the number of people sacrificed was great. And this custom was introduced into Yucatan by the Mexicans."

Moreover, the archaeological evidence, such as it is, supports the interpretation that idolatry, as meant in the quotations above, very definitely included the practice of human sacrifice. At Chichen Itza, for example, the greatest Mexican-Maya metropolis of the New Empire, probably the whole cult of the Well of Sacrifice, where so many human victims were offered (pp. 239–41), dates from the Puuc and Mexican periods. Indeed, of the eight representations of human sacrifice now known anywhere in the Maya area, four occur at Chichen Itza: two in frescoes in the Temple of the Jaguars (Plate 28, *e*), one in a fresco in the Temple of the Warriors (Plate 28, *f*), and the fourth on a gold disk from the Well of Sacrifice. Two others are from the hieroglyphic manuscripts: the Codex Dresdensis (Plate 28, *c*) and the Codex Tro-Cortesianus (Plate 28, *d*), both also dating from the New Empire. And the other two, as previously noted, are found on Old Empire monuments: Stela 11 (Plate 28, *a*) and Stela 14 (Plate 28, *b*), both at Piedras Negras. In view of the foregoing direct evidence, documentary as well as archaeological, there can be no doubt that the sanguinary character of the Maya religion as found by the Spaniards in the early sixteenth century, and noted by virtually all the early writers, was due chiefly to Mexican influence and was first introduced into Yucatan by the Mexican invaders in the tenth century.

The Maya religion suffered its final change—or better, extinction—when the Spaniards forcibly substituted the Christian religion for the old pagan beliefs and practices in the middle of the sixteenth century. But, curiously enough, the very few survivals of the ancient faith that have remained are not those of the priestly class, the esoteric cult of the astronomical gods and the involved philosophy behind them, but rather those of the simple gods of nature—the Chacs, or rain-gods of fertility; the *alux* or little folk of the cornfields like elves, who, though they may be mischievous, are on the whole well-disposed toward mankind; the *xtabai*, or evil sirens, who, by day are the *yaxche* trees of the forest but at night become beautiful young maidens who lure men to destruction. The homely everyday beliefs of the common people about nature have outlived and outlasted the more formalized gods of priestly invention.

Nor should this be a matter of surprise; the more sophisticated gods, who were the creatures of the professional priesthood, indeed, who, generally speaking, lived only through the latter, were forgotten as soon as the priests who had brought them into being and served them had passed away. And it was precisely upon the old pagan priesthood that the full weight of the Spanish Conquest fell most crushingly. The Christian god was a jealous god and his ministers quickly saw to it that the native priests either gave up their old beliefs or were exterminated; and with them went the old esoteric religion, learning, and philosophy, while the simple nature faith and mythology of the common people, much more generally shared, has, in part at least, survived down to the present day.

These survivals, as we now find them, it must be admitted are a motley mixture of Catholic saints and pagan deities. In Yucatan, the Archangel Gabriel and other Christian saints become the Pauahtuns of ancient Maya mythology, the guardians of the four cardinal points; the Archangel Michael leads the Chacs, the former rain-gods. In British Honduras, it is St. Vincent who is the patron of rain and St. Joseph the guiding spirit of the corn-fields. As I have observed elsewhere:

Here and there, however, fragments of the old religion lingered in the minds of the common people, gradually becoming confused, it is true, as time went on, with elements taken from their conquerors. Certainly today Maya folklore is the result of a now unconscious fusion of two groups of ideas; the Maya's aboriginal animals, spirits and even gods, now live in friendly and natural relations with the animals, spirits and saints of his conquerors; the latter have, indeed, become the blood brothers of the former.

COSMOGONY AND CHARACTER

The creator of the world, according to ancient Maya belief was a god named Hunab, or Hunab Ku, who was the father of Itzamna, the Maya Zeus: "They worshipped a single god who was named Hunab and Zamana, which [Hunab] is to say one only God." Indeed Hunab Ku means precisely that in Maya: *hun*, "one," *ab*, "the state of being" and *ku*, "god." This creator-god however, was so far above ordinary mortals, so remote from everyday affairs, that he seems to have figured but very little in the everyday life of the common people. According to the Popol Vuh, or sacred book of the Quiche Maya of the highlands of Guatemala, the creator fashioned mankind out of corn.

The Maya also believed that there had been several worlds previous to the present one and that each had been destroyed by a deluge. Landa records this tradition but fails to state the number of worlds previously thus destroyed:

Among the multitude of gods which this people adored, they worshipped four, each of whom was called Bacab. They said they were four brothers whom God [Hunab Ku], when he created the world, placed at the four points of it, to hold up the sky, so that it should not fall. They also said of these Bacabs, that they escaped when the world was destroyed by the deluge. They gave to each one of them other names and [thus] designated by them the part of the world where God placed him [each one] to bear up the heavens.

In confirmation of this tradition, the end of the world by a deluge is graphically depicted on the last page of the Codex Dresdensis (Fig. 9). Across the sky stretches a serpent-like creature with symbols of constellations presented on its side and signs for solar and lunar eclipses hanging from its belly. From its widely opened jaws, as well as from the two eclipse signs, pours a flood of water, falling straight earthward. Below the heavenly serpent, the Old Woman Goddess with long talon-like fingernails and toenails (see next section), patroness of death and destruction, a writhing serpent on her head, and crossbones decorations on her skirt, holds an inverted bowl from which also gushes a destroying flood. Finally at the bottom stands Ek Chuah, the black God of War (see p. 228), the Moan bird of evil omen on his head; he holds in his right hand two javelins and in his left a long staff, all three pointing downward. The whole picture vividly symbolizes the destruction of the world and mankind by water, in agreement with the tradition reported by Landa.

The modern Maya of northern Yucatan believe there have

been three worlds previous to this one. The first world was inhabited by dwarfs—the *saiyam uinicob*, or "adjuster men," who are thought to have built the great ruined cities. This work was done in darkness, for the sun had not yet been created. As soon as the sun rose for the first time, the dwarfs were turned to stone, and their images are still to be seen in the ruined cities today; perhaps the so-called Atlantean figures found at Chichen Itza (Plate 73, *d*) are representations of them. The first world was terminated by a universal deluge *haiyococab*, or "water over the earth." The second world was inhabited by people called the *dzolob*, or "offenders"; this was terminated by the second flood. The third world was populated by the Maya themselves, the common people or *mazehualob* (chapter ix, p. 176); this world was terminated by the third flood, called the *hunyecil* or *bulkabal*, which means "the immerging." This last deluge was followed by the present, or fourth world, peopled by a mixture of all the previous inhabitants of the peninsula, and this too will eventually be destroyed by a fourth flood.

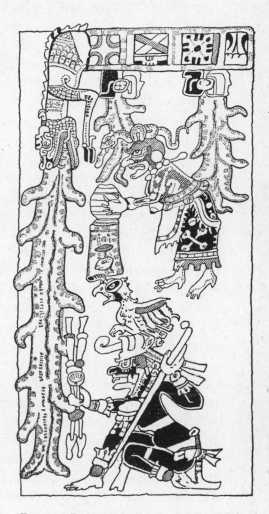

Fig. 9.—Destruction of the world by water. Page 74, Codex Dresdensis.

The Maya religion had a strong dualistic tendency, the eternal struggle between the powers of good and evil over the destiny of man. The benevolent gods, bringing thunder, lightning, and rain, fructify the corn and insure plenty; the malevolent ones, whose attributes are death and destruction, cause drought, hurricanes, and war, which ruin the corn, bringing in their train famine and misery. This contest is graphically depicted in the codices, where Chac, the rain-god, is shown caring for a young tree, while behind him follows Ah Puch, the death-god, who breaks the tree in two (Fig. 10). Here is good balanced against evil in the everlasting struggle for the soul of man, a contrast found in many religions, even in some far older than Christianity.

The Maya conceived the world as having thirteen heavens, arranged in layers, the lowest being the earth itself. Over each presided one of the thirteen Gods of the Upper World or *Oxlahuntiku*—meaning in Maya, *oxlahun*, "thirteen," *ti*, "of," and *ku*, "god" (here "gods") and by association "heaven." In addition to the thirteen upper worlds there were nine underworlds, also arranged in layers, over each one of which presided its own special god, one of the *Bolontiku* or Nine Gods of the Lower World, meaning in Maya, *bolon*, "nine," *ti*, "of," and *ku*, "god." The ninth and lowest underworld was Mitnal, ruled by Ah Puch, the Lord of Death, described in greater detail in the following section.

To the ancient Maya the principal object of religion and worship was to procure for themselves life, health, and sustenance —an end which Landa in a passage previously quoted (pp. 204–5) eloquently expresses. A number of other early authorities also echo the same thought: "They worship idols . . . . in order to petition [the gods] for health and good seasons"; or again in the following prayer: "All powerful god, these sacrifices we make to thee and we offer thee these hearts so that thou mayest give us life and temporal goods"; again sacrifices were made "in order to buy food from the gods so that they [the people] might have much to eat."

The gods were invoked and placated by a number of different offices. Practically all important ceremonies began with fasts and abstinences, some of the former lasting for as long as three years. They were scrupulously observed, moreover, and to break one's

↑ *a*) Palace of the Governor, Uxmal, Yucatan, Mexico; the Xiu as independent Maya rulers.

↑ *b*) House of Francisco de Montejo Xiu, Mani, Yucatan, Mexico; the Xiu as Spanish hidalgos or nobles.

↑ *c*) House of don Nemesio Xiu, Ticul, Yucatan, Mexico; the Xiu as Mexican corn-farmers.

PLATE 25.—RESIDENCES OF THE HEADS OF THE XIU FAMILY UNDER THREE NATIONS: THE NATIVE MAYA, SPAIN, AND MEXICO

↑ *a*) Huipil from San Pedro Sacatepequez, Guatemala.

↑ *b*) Huipil from Comalapa, Guatemala.

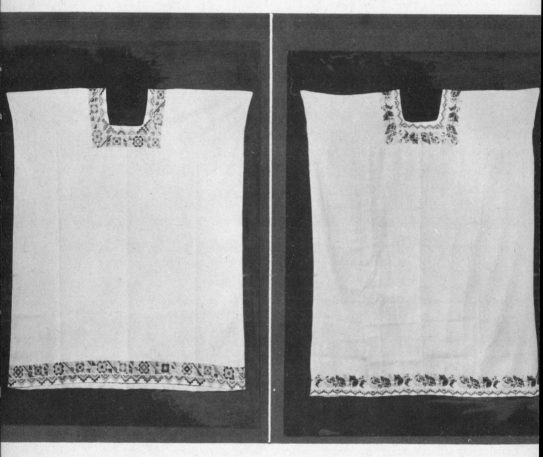

↑ *c*) Huipil from Tixcacal, Quintana
Roo, Mexico.

↑ *d*) Huipil from Merida, Yucatan,
Mexico.

PLATE 26.—HUIPILES, OR DRESSES OF MAYA WOMEN FROM THE HIGHLANDS
OF GUATEMALA (*a* AND *b*) AND FROM QUINTANA ROO AND
YUCATAN, MEXICO (*c* AND *d*)

fast was considered a very great sin. These preparatory purifications which also included sexual continence, were mandatory upon the priests and upon those who assisted directly in the ceremonies, but were only voluntary for others. In addition to fasting and continence, their abstinences included giving up flesh-foods and the use of salt and chili pepper as seasoning, of which they were inordinately fond.

Sacrifices were an important part of Maya worship; they ranged all the way from simple offerings of food, *tortillas*, beans, honey, incense, tobacco, etc., the first fruits of the fields, all kinds of animals, birds, and fish, living as well as dead, raw and cooked, to all kinds of ornaments and other valuables—jade and shell beads, pendants, feathers, jaguar skins, etc.—and, in New Empire times, to the general practice of human sacrifice—men, women, and children. The offerings varied according to the urgency of the occasion.

Fig. 10.—The rain-god nourishes a tree; the death-god uproots it. Page 60, Codex Tro-Cortesianus.

If the sacrifice was to cure a sickness, to avert some minor trouble, to insure success in hunting, fishing, or some trading expedition, offerings of food, or ornaments only might be made; but in times of great common need, such as droughts, hurricanes, or the dreaded plagues of locusts, which periodically visit Yucatan, human victims were sacrificed, especially in order to bring general rains.

Prayers formed an essential element in Maya ritual and the aid of the gods was sought in every sort of activity—in divination, prophecy, and horoscopes, in puberty and marriage rites, in every kind of general ceremony, to deliver them from trouble as well as to oppress the devil who caused it, to bring about pregnancy in the case of a childless woman, to expel the evil spirits before beginning all ceremonies, to avert drought and plagues of locusts which resulted in famine, disease, thefts, and discord, dynastic and hierarchical changes which led to wars, and for success in every sort of undertaking—agriculture, hunting, fishing, trading, making of idols, and battle.

Blood-letting and scarification played a leading part in religious observance. Although Landa says only the men indulged in these blood-letting practices, the Codex Tro-Cortesianus shows both a man and a woman in the act of drawing blood from their ears with a flint or obsidian knife (Fig. 11). Blood was drawn from the ears (especially the lobes), the nose, the forehead, the cheeks, the lower lips, the elbows, arms, thighs and legs, and the private parts. The blood thus obtained, as well as that of sacrificial victims, human as well as animal, was liberally sprinkled over their idols.

They make sacrifices of their own blood, sometimes cutting the edges [of their ears] in pieces, and thus they left them as a sign [of their devotion]. Other times they pierced their cheeks, other times the lower lips; again they scarify parts of the body; or again they perforate their tongues in a slanting direction from side to side, passing pieces of straw through the holes, with horrible suffering; and yet again they slit the superfluous part [the foreskin] of the virile member, leaving it like their ears, which deceived the general historian of the Indies [Oviedo] into saying that they practiced circumcision. . . . . The women do not practice these blood-lettings although they were very devout; furthermore, of all things that they have, whether it be birds of the sky, animals of the earth, or fish of the sea, they always anointed the face of the demon [their idols] with the blood of these.

The perforation and cutting instruments used in these blood-letting rites were the bony snout of the swordfish, the barb of the sting-ray, fishspines, thorns of the gourd tree, and knives and blades made of flint, obsidian, bone, and shell.

The burning of incense formed an indispensable part of every religious ceremony. Their incense was made principally of copal (*pom*), a resin extracted from the copal tree (*Protium copal*) found very commonly throughout the Yucatan Peninsula, and less frequently of rubber, chicle, and another resin called *puk ak* in Maya. There were special plantations where the incense trees were grown; incense was highly prized and carried as an article of trade far and wide. The incense was made into small cakes, decorated with cross-hatching on top, and painted a bright turquoise blue. Scores of such incense cakes were recovered in the dredging of the Well of Sacrifice at Chichen Itza (see a later section of this chapter, p. 239). The *chacs,* or priest's assistants, prepared a large number of small balls of fresh incense, laying them out on small boards made expressly for the purpose, just as the Lacandon Maya of Chiapas still do today. The incense was then taken and burned in specially shaped pottery vessels with the head or whole figure of some deity modeled in high relief on the outside of the vessel.

Pom burns with a heavy, black smoke and a fragrant, aromatic odor. Sometimes, failing to have the hearts of large animals at hand, burnt offerings of which were occasionally made,

FIG. 11.—Blood-letting rite. Page 95, Codex Tro-Cortesianus.

Landa says imitation hearts were molded out of *pom* incense: "And if they were not able to have large animals like tigers [jaguars], lions [pumas], or crocodiles, they fashioned hearts out of their incense." Landa's statement here has been corroborated by the discovery in the center of one of the cakes of incense dredged from the Well of Sacrifice at Chichen Itza of a human-shaped heart made out of some vegetable substance, probably ground corn. Finally, faint memories of the ancient faith and its holy places still linger among modern Maya in remote regions. Thus, for example, the Lacandon still burn *pom* incense in typical Maya incense burners (Plate 81, *d*), in the principal temple (Structure 33) at the ruins of Yaxchilan, while the semi-independent Maya of eastern Yucatan still offer the same incense in the sanctuary of the Castillo, or principal temple at the ruins of Tulum on the east coast of the peninsula.

Another religious observance was dancing, of which there were many kinds, varying with the different ceremonies of which they formed an essential part; but social, secular dancing such as we have today, was entirely unknown. Each sex had its own particular dances, and only rarely did men and women dance together. In one of their war dances more than eight hundred dancers took part:

There is another dance [*holcan okot*] in which eight hundred Indians, more or less, dance with small banners, taking long war-steps to the beat [of a drum], among them there is not one who is out of step.

In another dance, great skill was shown in catching reeds with a little stick:

One is a game of reeds, and thus they call it *colomche*, which means that. In order to play it, they form a large circle of dancers, whom the music accompanies, and two of them enter the circle in time to the music, one with a handful of reeds with which he dances holding himself upright; the other dancer crouches, both of them always inside the circle. And he with the reeds throws them with all his strength at the other, who with great skill, catches them, by means of a small stick. Having finished throwing, they return in time to their places in the circle, and others go out to do the same thing.

Dancing was very popular; says another sixteenth-century writer in this connection:

There were many other dances of which there would be more than one thousand kinds, and they considered this as an extremely important thing and so great a number of people assemble to see it that more than fifteen thousand Indians would gather, and they came from more than thirty leagues [75 miles] to see it, because, as I say, they considered it an extremely important affair.

Dancing among the Maya, as previously noted, and indeed among all American Indian tribes, was a religious rite rather than a secular diversion as with us.

Examples of dancing figures are rare in the Maya reliefs, but the two dancing figures on the altars of Zoömorphs O and P at the Old Empire city of Quirigua are of outstanding merit, especially that on the former (Plate 27, *b*). Here a masked dancer of heroic size—seven and a half feet high—is poised with greatest ease on the pointed toe of his left foot, like a modern toe dancer. The left arm is raised above the head, the left hand grasping a small shield; the right hand holds a small bag, resting naturally against the right hip. The whole figure, in every line, expresses grace, elegance, and flowing movement.

The Maya believed in the immortality of the soul and a life hereafter which the soul enjoyed when it left its earthly body. The future was divided, according to Landa, although there is some suspicion of Catholic influence in his statement, into a good life and a bad one, into a place of rest and a place of suffering.

Suicides by hanging, warriors killed in battle, people who were sacrificed, women who died in childbirth, and the priests when they died went directly to the Maya Paradise:

They also said and held it as absolutely certain that those who hanged themselves went to this heaven of theirs; and thus there were many who on slight occasions of sorrows, troubles or sicknesses, hanged themselves in order to escape these things and to go and rest in their heaven, where they said that the Godess of the Gallows, whom they call Ixtab, came to fetch them.

Other causes for suicide were grief, fear of torture, even a desire to throw blame upon one's husband or wife for mistreatment.

The Maya Paradise is described as a place of delights, where there was no pain or suffering, but on the contrary an abundance of good foods and sweet drinks, where grew the *yaxche,* or sacred tree of the Maya (the *ceiba*), under the branches and grateful shade of which they could rest and forever cease from labor. The penalty exacted from those whose lives had been evil was that they had to descend into a lower region called *Mitnal*—the Maya Hell. There devils tormented them with hunger, cold, weariness, and grief. Hunhau, the Lord of Death, an abbreviation of the day Hunahau, or 1 Ahau, was also regarded as the prince of all the devils, and presided over this bottommost Hell. And they believed further that neither their Paradise nor Hell would ever end, since the soul itself could not die but must go on forever.

Discounting Hunab Ku, the creator, who does not appear to have played an important part in the life of the common people, perhaps being regarded by them more as a distant, priestly abstraction than as a personal creator, there stood at the head of the Maya Pantheon the great Itzamna, son of Hunab Ku. In the codices, Itzamna is represented as an old man with toothless jaws, sunken cheeks, Roman nose, and occasionally bearded (Plate 29, *a*). He has two name-glyphs—the first, which may be a somewhat conventionalized representation of his own head, and the second, which contains as its main element the day-sign Ahau. This day-sign we have already seen (chapter ix, p. 161), meant "king, emperor, monarch, prince or great lord"; thus the second of Itzamna's two name-glyphs declares his position as head of the Maya Pantheon. He was patron of the day Ahau, the last and most important of the twenty Maya days (pp. 266–67).

Unfortunately, Old Empire representations of few if any of the Maya deities have survived. As already observed, I believe that most of the figures presented in the sculptures, frescoes, and vase-paintings of the Old Empire are those of men—rulers, priests, acolytes, warriors, and prisoners. The pictures of Maya gods shown here are taken from one or other of the three known Maya hieroglyphic manuscripts which date from the New Empire (p. 295). Although direct evidence is thus lacking for the Old Empire period, it seems highly probable, in view of the close cultural continuity of the Old and New Empires, that the Maya Pantheon remained largely the same for both periods, except for two important and outstanding exceptions: (1) the introduction of a new deity named Kukulcan from Mexico into Yucatan in the tenth century; and (2) the increasing importance of the rain-god, Chac, in Yucatan as compared with Peten, which latter

---

[1] The German scholar, Paul Schellhas, has classified the deities represented in the three Maya codices, giving each a letter designation. In his classification, Itzamna is God D.

region has a much higher rainfall than Yucatan, where it was not
so necessary to call upon the rain-god as frequently as in the much
drier climate of northern Yucatan.

Itzamna was Lord of the Heavens, and also Lord of Day and of Night. In these two latter capacities, he is intimately associated with Kinich Ahau, the sun-god, "Lord of the Eye of the Sun" (God G), who was especially worshipped at Izamal in northern Yucatan, and with Ixchel, the moon-goddess (Goddess I). Indeed Kinich Ahau may simply be only a special manifestation of Itzamna in the latter's capacity as Lord of the Day, that is, the sun. Itzamna, the inventor of writing and books (the codices), is said to have been the first priest to have named the different places in Yucatan, and to have divided the lands there. These activities by their very nature indicate that the cult of Itzamna did not originate in Yucatan, which is the region of the New Empire, but was brought thither from somewhere else; and since we know that both the priesthood and hieroglyphic writing first developed in the Old Empire, it is obvious that he must have been a deity who was transplanted from the Old Empire to the New. As the first priest and inventor of the hieroglyphic writing, and, by extension, of the calendar and chronology as well, he is clearly a god that went back to the beginnings of Maya history and probably always stood at the head of the Maya Pantheon.

During the important ceremonies in connection with the Maya New Year, Itzamna was especially invoked to avert calamities. In the month of Uo, at a ceremony in his honor in his manifestation as the sun-god, the most learned of the priests present consulted the sacred books to ascertain from them the auguries for the coming year. Again in the month of Zip, together with his wife Ixchel, he was invoked as the god of medicine. And again in the month of Mac he was worshiped by the old men in a ceremony with the Chacs, or rain-gods. Itzamna was a benevolent deity, always the friend of man. He is never connected with destruction, devastation, or disaster, and never appears in the codices associated with the symbols of death.

Chac, the God of Rain, is represented in the codices with a long, proboscis-like nose and two curling fangs projecting downward from his mouth, one forward, the other backward; his headdress is usually a knotted band (Plate 29, *b*), and his name-glyph has an eye which, in the Codex Tro-Cortesianus, is definitely T-shaped ⊤⊤. This latter element, it has been suggested, represents tears streaming from the eye, which in turn may symbolize pouring rain and hence fertility. This same sign is also the glyph for the day, Ik, of which the rain-god was probably the patron deity, as Itzamna was of the day Ahau.

Chac was a universal deity of first importance. Indeed, if we were to judge only by the number of his representations in the codices, he would have to be regarded as more important even than Itzamna. Pictures of Chac occur 218 times in the three known Maya codices, as compared with 103 occurrences of Itzamna, while the latter is not found at all in the Codex Peresianus. Chac was a rain-god primarily, and by association, god of the wind, thunder, and lightning, and hence by extension, of fertility and agriculture in a broad sense; that is the idea of growth and germination, and by still further extension, even of the cornfields.

The rain-god was regarded not only as a single god but also at the same time as four gods—a different Chac for each one of the four cardinal points, each cardinal point having its own special associated color (see endsheets): Chac Xib Chac, the Red Man—Chac of the East; Sac Xib Chac, the White Man—Chac of the North; Ek Xib Chac, the Black Man—Chac of the West; and Kan Xib Chac, the Yellow Man—Chac of the South. This conception is analogous to our own belief concerning the Holy Trinity, or three Gods in one: God the Father, God the Son, and God the Holy Ghost. The rain-god was thus regarded as four gods in one.

In the month of Chen or in that of Yax a great festival was held in honor of the Chacs which was called the *ocna*, meaning "enter the house." The four gods known as the Bacabs, who were closely associated with the four Chacs and also with the four

↑ *a*) Stela 1, La Amelia, Peten, Guatemala.

↑ *b*) Dancing figure, Altar of Zoömorph O. Quirigua, Izabal, Guatemala.

PLATE 27.—SCULPTURES OF THE OLD EMPIRE AND A RELIEF
BY A MODERN MAYA SCULPTOR

c) Ceremony of the symbolic sharing of sin. Sculptured tablet by Miguel
↓ Tzab, Merida, Yucatan, Mexico.

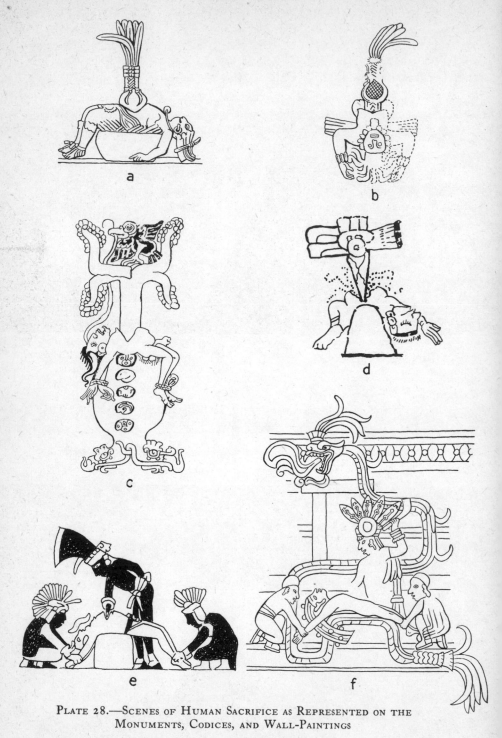

PLATE 28.—SCENES OF HUMAN SACRIFICE AS REPRESENTED ON THE
MONUMENTS, CODICES, AND WALL-PAINTINGS

(a) Stela 11, Piedras Negras, Peten, Guatemala; (b) Stela 14, Piedras Negras;
(c) Codex Dresdensis; (d) Codex Tro-Cortesianus; (e) Temple of the Jaguars,
Chichen Itza, Yucatan, Mexico; (f) Temple of the Warriors, Chichen Itza.

cardinal points, were consulted in advance to indicate a propitious day for the ceremony which was devoted to the renovation of the Temple of the Chacs. During this ceremony, held once a year, the clay idols and pottery incense burners were renewed, and, if necessary, the temple itself was rebuilt. A tablet in hieroglyphic writing commemorating the event was set into the temple wall.

Just as Itzamna was associated with the sun-god, so Chac seems to have been associated with the wind-god, who will be described later; indeed the wind-god may again be only a special manifestation of the rain-god, and may have had no separate existence.

The rain-god (or gods) was a benevolent deity like Itzamna, always the friend of man, associated with creation and life, and never his enemy; never is he allied with the powers of death and destruction. For the ordinary Maya corn farmer whose paramount interest in life was his cornfield, that is to say for the vast majority of the people, Chac was the all-important deity, and his friendly intervention was sought by the average Maya more frequently than that of all the other gods combined. The mask-panels with long curling noses found throughout the Maya area, but especially in New Empire architecture, are probably nothing more nor less than representations of the head of this god (Plate 60, *a* and *b*).

THE GOD OF CORN (GOD E)

The third deity in point of frequency of representation in the codices appropriately is the corn-god or the god of agriculture, who occurs 98 times in the three manuscripts. He is always represented as a youth (frontispiece) and sometimes with an ear of corn as his headdress (Plate 29, *c*). Occasionally this ear is shown sprouting from the glyph for the day Kan, which itself is the symbol for corn in the codices. Kan was also the day of which this god was the patron. Of all the gods represented in the codices this youthful deity shows the greatest amount of head-deformation. Notice his markedly retreating forehead. His name-glyph is his own head, which merges at the top into a highly conventionalized ear of corn, surmounted by leaves.

This god was the patron of husbandry and is shown in the codices engaged in a variety of agricultural pursuits. He, or a priest impersonating him, is occasionally depicted in Old Empire sculpture—for example on the front of Stela 40 at Piedras Negras (Plate 54, c)—with an ear of corn as his headdress, scattering grains of the cereal on the head of the Earth Mother; or again on the back of Stela H at Copan. He is always shown as a young god. Like the corn he typifies, he has many enemies and his destinies were controlled by other gods, those of rain, wind, drought, famine, and death. In one place he is shown under the protection of the rain-god and in another in mortal combat with a death-god.

Although his specific name as the God of Corn is unknown, in later New Empire times his identity seems to have been merged with that of a more general agricultural deity known as Yum Kaax, "Lord of the Forests," and at least some of his fertility functions were probably taken over by the more powerful Chac. He would seem to have been essentially, as his pictures indicate, a corn-god, representing the spirit, not only of the growing grain, but also of the mature cereal. Like Itzamna and Chac he was a benevolent deity, a god of life, prosperity, abundance, and fruitfulness, and is never, except as engaged in mortal combat, associated with the symbols of death.

AH PUCH, THE GOD OF DEATH (GOD A)

The fourth god in point of frequency of representation in the codices, in keeping with the excessive fear of death among the ancient Maya, is the God of Death (God A), who occurs 88 times in the three manuscripts. He is represented with all the paraphernalia of death (Plate 29, d); he has a skull for a head, bare ribs, and spiny vertebral projections; or, if his body is clothed with flesh, the latter is bloated and marked with black circles, suggesting discoloration of the body due to decomposition. Neverfailing dress accessories of the death-god are his sleigh-bell ornaments. These appear sometimes fastened in his hair or to

bands around his forearms and legs, but more often they are
attached to a stiff ruff-like collar (Plate 29, *d*). These bells in all
sizes, made of copper (occasionally even of gold), were found in
considerable quantities during the dredging of the Well of Sacrifice at Chichen Itza, presumably where they had been thrown,
together with the sacrificial victims (see p. 240 below). See Plate
94, *b*, and Figure 55, *d*, *e*, and *f*.

Like Itzamna, whose antithesis he is, Ah Puch has two name-
glyphs and is the only other deity thus distinguished. The first
represents the head of a corpse with its eyes closed in death, and
the second is the head of the god himself with truncated nose,
fleshless jaws, and a flint sacrificial knife as a prefix. A frequent
sign associated with the God of Death is not unlike our own per-
centage sign ⅍. The God of Death was patron deity of the
day Cimi, which means "death" in Maya.

In the case of Ah Puch, as in that of Itzamna and of Chac,
we are dealing with a deity of first importance as attested by the
frequency of his representations in the codices. As the chief
demon, Hunhau, he presided over the ninth and lowest of the
nine Maya underworlds, or Hells. Even today as Yum Cimil,
the Lord of Death, the modern Maya believe he prowls around
houses of the sick, looking for prospective prey.

Ah Puch is distinctly a malevolent deity, the first we have encountered. He, or his name-glyph, is frequently associated with
the God of War and Human Sacrifice, to be described presently,
and his constant companions are the dog, the Moan bird, and the
owl, all three of which were considered to be creatures of evil
omen and death.

XAMAN EK, GOD OF THE NORTH STAR (GOD C)

The fifth most common deity in the codices is Xaman Ek, the
North Star god, who occurs 61 times in the three manuscripts. He
is always portrayed (Plate 29, *h*) with the same snub-nosed face
and peculiar black head-markings. He has only one name-glyph,
his own head, which has been likened to the head of a monkey.
This same head, with a different prefix to that found in his own

name-glyph, is also the hieroglyph for the cardinal point North (see endsheets), thus tending to confirm his identification as God of the North Star; moreover, the nature of the occurrences of his name-glyph in the manuscripts is such as to indicate that he must have been the personification of some heavenly body of first astronomic importance. Since his head is the hieroglyph for the cardinal point, North, there can be little doubt that he was indeed God of the North Star.

In one place Xaman Ek is spoken of as "the guide of the merchants," as well he may have been, since the North Star is the only apparently fixed star in the latitudes of Peten and Yucatan that does not radically change its position throughout the year. Merchants are also said to have offered *pom* incense to him at altars along roadsides. He was a benevolent deity and is found in association with the rain-god and was probably patron of the day Chuen.

EK CHUAH, THE BLACK WAR CAPTAIN (GOD M)

Ek Chuah is the sixth most commonly represented deity in the codices, occurring 40 times. He has a large, drooping underlip and is usually shown painted black—the color of war—in the Codex Tro-Cortesianus, or partly black in the Codex Dresdensis (Plate 29, *f*). In the former his mouth is always encircled with a red-brown border, emphasizing his thick lips. His name-glyph is an eye rimmed with black. This god seems to have had a two-fold and somewhat contradictory character; as God of War he was malevolent, but as God of Traveling Merchants he was friendly. In the former capacity he appears with a lance in hand, occasionally engaged in combat, even vanquished by another war-god, more especially a god of death in war and of the killing of war prisoners. In his malevolent character, we have seen him with Ixchel, armed with javelins and lance, taking part in the destruction of the world by water (Fig. 9, p. 215). As a friendly god, he appears carrying a bundle of merchandise on his back like an itinerant merchant, and in one place he is shown with the head of Xaman Ek, the North Star, whom we have seen is said to have been the "guide of the merchants." Finally, Ek Chuah was the patron of cacao, and those who owned cacao plantations held a ceremony in his honor in the month of Muan. In one aspect he seems to have been hostile to man, in another, friendly—a two-faced deity like the Roman Janus.

THE GOD OF WAR, OF HUMAN SACRIFICE, AND VIOLENT DEATH (GOD F)

This deity occurs 33 times in the codices, the seventh in frequency, and always in connection with death. His most constant characteristic is a black line partly encircling his eye and extending down over his cheek (Plate 29, g). His own head, with the number 11 in front of it, is his name-glyph. He may be the patron of the Maya day, Manik, the sign for which is the grasping hand, perhaps symbolical of his capturing prisoners of war or of taking whatever he wants. He is sometimes shown in company with Ah Puch, the God of Death, at scenes of human sacrifice. He is also a war-god in his own right and is shown burning houses with a torch in one hand while he demolishes them with a spear in the other. The custom of sacrificing noble prisoners of war has already been mentioned, and thus the concept of a war-god, a god of death by violence and by human sacrifice, all seem to be combined in this deity.

THE GOD OF THE WIND, POSSIBLY KUKULCAN (GOD K)

The suggested association of the famous Maya-Mexican culture hero, Kukulcan (the well-known Quetzalcoatl of Mexican mythology), with the Maya God of the Wind is not surely established. The wind-god is rarely portrayed in the codices, there being less than a dozen representations of him altogether and not one in the Codex Tro-Cortesianus, a late New Empire manuscript. Moreover, in view of the predominant position held by Kukulcan in late New Empire times, it seems strange indeed that, if the wind-god were Kukulcan, many more representations of him should not have been found in the codices, all three of which date from the New Empire.

The association of the wind-god with Chac, the rain-god, on the other hand is very close. We see Chac offering the head of the wind-god, in connection with a katun-ending ceremony in the Codex Peresianus (Fig. 16). Indeed the identification of the wind-god as Kukulcan rests almost entirely upon an identical association in Aztec mythology of Quetzalcoatl with Ehecatl, the wind-god, who sweeps the path of the rain-god. Since the Maya wind- and rain-gods are also closely associated, and since both the Maya wind-god and Quetzalcoatl-Ehecatl, the Aztec wind-god, both have large, foliated proboscises, there may well be some connection between the Maya wind-god and Kukulcan. This connection, however, is only suggested, not definitely established, and Chac himself, the principal Maya rain-god, has been identified as Kukulcan by several authorities. Some believe the connection between the wind-god and the rain-god—a natural association in itself—is so close as to indicate that the former is only a special manifestation of the latter and thus should not be regarded as a separate deity. His name-glyph (Plate 29, e) is frequently found in connection with that of Chac. He was patron of the day Muluc and was a benevolent deity.

IXCHEL, GODDESS OF FLOODS, PREGNANCY, WEAVING, AND PERHAPS OF THE MOON (GODDESS I)

Ixchel was an important personage in the Maya Pantheon, though apparently more often unfriendly than not. We have already seen her as an angry old woman emptying the vials of her wrath upon the earth in a scene depicting the destruction of the world by flood (Fig. 9); again in Plate 29, i, she is a personification of water as the destroyer, of floods and cloudbursts, and as such was certainly a malevolent goddess.

But Ixchel seems to have had another, friendlier side. She was probably the Maya Juno, the consort of Itzamna, Lord of the Heavens, and since her husband occasionally appears as the sun-god, she would seem to have been the moon-goddess, the patroness of pregnancy, and inventress of weaving. She is usually portrayed in the codices as an old and hostile water-goddess, surrounded by symbols of death and destruction, a writhing serpent on her head, crossbones embroidered on her skirt, and with fingernails and toenails like the talons of a beast of prey—indeed, some have called her the old tiger-clawed goddess.

IXTAB, GODDESS OF SUICIDE

Mention has been made of the fact that the ancient Maya believed suicides went directly to Paradise. There was a special deity who was regarded as the particular patroness of those who had taken their lives by hanging themselves—Ixtab, Goddess of Suicide. She is shown in the Codex Dresdensis (Plate 29, *j*) hanging from the sky by a halter which is looped around her neck; her eyes are closed in death, and a black circle, representing discoloration due to decomposition, appears on her cheek.

PATRON GOD SERIES

THE THIRTEEN GODS OF THE UPPER WORLD AND THE NINE GODS OF THE LOWER WORLD

As already mentioned in connection with the rain-god, the ancient Maya conceived of some of their deities not only as a single entity but at the same time as composite or multiple in character, like our own conception of the Holy Trinity—three gods in one. Chac, we have seen, was considered as a single god and at the same time as four gods. Similarly the *Oxlahuntiku*, or Thirteen Gods of the Upper World, although regarded collectively as a single deity, were considered to be thirteen separate and individual gods; and the *Bolontiku*, or Nine Gods of the Lower World, were likewise regarded in the same dual capacity. Thus the *Oxlahuntiku* were one god and thirteen gods at the same time, and the *Bolontiku* one god and nine gods at the same time.

In certain myths preserved in the Book of Chilam Balam of Chumayel, this same unity, both of the *Oxlahuntiku* and of the *Bolontiku*, and at the same time their composite character as well, is clearly set forth, while in the stone inscriptions of the Old Empire this dual conception of the *Bolontiku* is repeatedly emphasized. For example, each one of the nine *Bolontiku* was, in turn, the patron of a day of the Maya calendar; it was believed that these nine gods followed each other in endless succession throughout time, just as do the seven days of our own week. Thus, if God *x* were patron of the 1st day, he would again also be patron of the 10th day, the 19th day, the 28th day, etc., *ad infinitum;* and similarly, if God *y* were patron of the 2d day, he would again be patron of the 11th, the 20th, the 29th day, etc. While we do not know what the nine *Bolontiku* looked like, no

Fig. 12.—Name-glyphs of the Nine Gods of the Lower World.

representations of them having as yet been identified in the codices, their name-glyphs, that is the nine different signs or hieroglyphs which represent them, have been identified (Fig. 12). An analogous case would be: if we knew that the letters G e o r g e   W a s h i n g t o n spelled the name of the first President of the United States, but we did not know either how to pronounce this name or what the man George Washington really looked like.

Against the south wall of the left chamber of Temple 40 at Yaxchilan there had formerly been a row of nine seated anthropomorphic figures made of stucco, each about two feet high, which may have represented these nine gods. Unfortunately all of them have been destroyed except for their feet, which are preserved only to the level of their respective knees (Plate 30, *b*). Since there are nine pairs of these feet, it is probable that the corresponding seated figures to which they belonged originally had represented the Nine Gods of the Lower World.

Along the eastern base of the square tower of the Palace at Palenque there were found the badly destroyed remains of nine similar figures, also in stucco, which probably had represented these same nine gods. Unfortunately all details by which they might have been identified, both in the series at Yaxchilan as well as in that at Palenque, have disappeared.

In the case of the *Oxlahuntiku*, we do not even know their corresponding thirteen name-glyphs, although together with the *Bolontiku*, they must have constituted one of the most important groups of the Maya Pantheon. However, it would seem to be only a matter of time before the name-glyphs of the *Oxlahuntiku* will also be identified in the inscriptions of the Old Empire. It has been suggested that the 13 head-variant numerals (see chapter xii, p. 280) are in reality the heads of the thirteen *Oxlahuntiku*.

THE THIRTEEN GODS OF THE KATUNS

There were thirteen different katuns, or 20-year periods, each having its own, special patron. Although the names and name-glyphs of this group of thirteen deities are unknown, they seem to be shown in the fragmentary manuscript known as the Codex Peresianus (p. 299), one side of which presents nothing but a succession of katuns with their corresponding patron deities, some of whom may be recognized, as for example the rain-god and the wind-god in the representation of Katun 7 Ahau (Fig. 16).

Another series of patron deities, the names of which we do not know, are the nineteen patrons of the nineteen months, or divisions, of the Maya year, though here again, as in the case of the *Bolontiku*, we do know most of their corresponding nineteen name-glyphs (Fig. 13). Some of these are the signs of heavenly bodies, others the heads of animals or birds, and still others forms of unknown meaning. Astronomical month-patrons are: the sun, patron of the month Yaxkin, and the moon, patron of the month Chen (Fig. 13, second row); the planet Venus, patron of the

Pop Jaguar	Uo God of Number 7 (?)	Zip	Zotz Bat
Tzec	Xul	Yaxkin Sun	Mol	Chen Moon
Yax Venus	Zac Toad	Ceh New Fire Symbol	Mac	Kankin
Muan	Pax	Kayab	Cumhu	Uayeb North Star (?)

FIG. 13.—Name-glyphs of the patron-gods of the nineteen Maya months.

month Yax (third row). Animal or bird month-patrons are: the jaguar for the month Pop, and the bat for the month Zotz (Fig. 13, top row), the toad for the month of Zac (third row). Others are: the sign for the new fire ceremonial, patron of the month Ceh, and the sign for the day Ik, patron of the month Mac (Fig. 13, third row). Although the name-glyphs of these nineteen month-patrons are almost all recognizable, their corresponding names are unknown, as well as what these nineteen month-patrons really looked like.

GODS OF THE TWENTY DAYS

Still another series of patron deities was that of the twenty gods which presided over the twenty different Maya day-names (p. 267). We have already seen that Itzamna was the patron of the days called Ahau;[2] Chac of the Ik days; the corn-god of the Kan days; Ah Puch of the Cimi days; Xaman Ek of the Chuen days; the God of War and Human Sacrifice of the Manik days; the wind-god of the Muluc days; and the remaining thirteen days doubtless had their own special patron deities as well, which have not been surely identified as yet.

GODS OF THE FOURTEEN NUMERALS O AND 1-13

Another and most important series of gods were the patrons of the fourteen head-variant numerals—zero and one to thirteen inclusive. Indeed these head-variant numerals are nothing more nor less than the heads of these fourteen deities, one each of which was associated with one of these fourteen numbers (see chapter xii, p. 279). The most obvious of these associations is that between Ah Puch, the God of Death, whose head is the fleshless skull, and the head-variant numeral for 10, which is nothing more nor less than the fleshless skull itself (Plate 30, *a*). The sun-god was the patron of the number 4, and Chac, the God of Rain, patron of the number 13. The heads of the numbers 1-13 inclusive, as already suggested, may be those of the thirteen *Oxlahuntiku*.[3]

---

[2] Each of the 20 Maya day-names is preceded by one of the numbers from 1 to 13 inclusive (see chapter xii) so that there are 13 days Ahau, 13 days Ik, etc.

[3] These number-gods are also depicted as the numerical coefficients in the exceedingly rare full-figure glyphs, found only in seven inscriptions in the Maya hieroglyphic writing: (1) Lintel 48, Yaxchilan; (2) Stela D, Copan; (3) Temple 26, Copan; (4, 5) Stela D, east and west sides, Quirigua (Plate 72, *b*); (6) Zoömorph B, Quirigua; and (7) Altar of Zoömorph O, Quirigua (Plate 27, *b*).

GENERAL NATURE

There were many rites and ceremonies for all sorts of needs, individual as well as group, from the *hetzmek* observance in behalf of the baby of a humble woodcutter to general feasts in order to alleviate widespread famine brought about by long-continued drought, but a similarity of pattern runs through all of them: (1) preliminary fasting and abstinences including a temporary taboo on sexual relations for the officiating priest and principals, symbolic of spiritual purification; (2) selection in advance by priestly divination of an auspicious day to celebrate the rite; and at the ceremony itself, (3) first an expulsion of the evil spirit from the midst of the worshipers; (4) incensing of the idols; (5) prayers; (6) and—most important of all—the sacrifice, if possible, of some living thing, a deer, dog, fowl, or fish, and on more important occasions a human victim or victims. In all sacrifices of living things, whether animal, fowl, fish, or man, the blood of the victim was smeared on the face of the idol of the god in whose honor the ceremony was being held. The priests themselves were smeared with blood, their hair being foul, clotted, gory mops. Most of the ceremonies closed with feasting, drinking, and general drunkenness; this last, according to the early Catholic fathers, was the inevitable conclusion of every Maya ceremony.

HUMAN SACRIFICE

Human sacrifice was performed in several ways; the most common, and perhaps the most ancient since it was practiced in Old Empire times (Plate 28, *a* and *b*), was by removing the heart. The intended victim, after being stripped, painted blue (the sacrificial color), and having a special peaked headdress set on his head, was led to the place of sacrifice, sometimes the temple courtyard, sometimes on the summit of the pyramid supporting the temple. The evil spirits were first expelled and the altar, usually a stone that was convex on top in order to curve the victim's breast upward, was also smeared with the sacred blue paint.

The four *chacs*, also painted blue, next grasped the victim, one *chac* to each arm and leg, and together stretched him on his back over the altar. The *nacom* now advanced with the sacrificial flint knife in his hand and plunged it into the victim's ribs just below the left breast. Thrusting his hand into the opening, he pulled out the still throbbing heart and, placing it on a plate, handed it to the *chilan*, or officiating priest; whereupon the latter swiftly smeared the face of the idol of the god to whom the sacrifice was being made with blood. If the victim had been sacrificed on the summit of a pyramid, the *chacs* threw the corpse to the court below, where priests of lower rank skinned the still warm body, except the hands and feet. The *chilan*, having removed his sacrificial vestments, arrayed himself in the still-dripping, bloody skin of the victim and solemnly danced with the spectators. Sometimes the bodies of victims were buried in the temple courtyards, and sometimes, particularly if the sacrificial victim had been a valiant and brave soldier, his body was divided and eaten by the nobles and other spectators at the ceremony. The hands and feet were reserved for the *chilan*, and if the victim was a prisoner of war, his captor wore certain of his bones as a decoration and mark of prowess. Women and children were as frequently sacrificed as men.

Archaeological corroboration of this ceremony is found in the wall-paintings at Chichen Itza, not once but several times (Plate 28, *e* and *f*). One such scene (Plate 28, *f*) portrays a human sacrifice to Kukulcan, the Feathered Serpent, patron deity of this city. A lower coil of the serpent-god's body itself forms the sacrificial altar, the upper coils and the head rising behind the altar in front of the doorway of his temple. Two *chacs*, instead of four, are shown, probably because of difficulties in handling the perspective involved in drawing one figure directly behind another. The *chilan* stands between the altar and the serpent-god with his hand upraised holding the sacrificial knife ready to slit the victim's breast. Several of these knives have been recovered from the Well of Sacrifice at Chichen Itza. One has a blade of finely chipped flint and a handle of wood, carved in the likeness of two intertwined serpents, their bodies overlaid with gold (Fig. 14).

In other representations of human sacrifice (Plate 28, *a–d*) the victim's breast is shown as already opened, and rising out of it there seems to be a portrayal of the dead man's soul, conceived, in one case at least, as a tree ascending toward the heavens with

FIG. 14.—Sacrificial knife from the Well of Sacrifice, Chichen Itza, Yucatan, Mexico.

a bird perched on its branches (Plate 28, *c*), in confirmation of the tradition preserved by Landa that the soul of those sacrificed went directly upward to the Maya Paradise.

Another form of human sacrifice was by bow and arrow:

If he [the victim] was to be sacrificed by arrows they stripped him naked and anointed his body with a blue color, and put a pointed cap on his head. When they had reached the victim, all of them, armed with bows and arrows, made a solemn dance with him around the stake, and while dancing they put him up on it and bound him to it, all of them keeping on dancing and looking at him. The foul priest in vestments went up and wounded the victim with an arrow in the parts of shame, whether it were a man or woman, and drew blood and came down and anointed the face of the idol with it. And making a certain sign to the dancers, as they passed rapidly before him [the prisoner] still dancing, they began one after another to shoot at his heart, which had been marked beforehand with a white sign. And in this manner they made his whole chest one point like a hedgehog of arrows.

This latter sacrifice is depicted in an incised drawing from the walls of Temple II at Tikal (Fig. 15), probably scratched there by some passing Indian long after the city had been abandoned; this same ceremony is also shown in the Mexican codices; indeed it was probably a direct importation from central Mexico in late New Empire times.

An unusual ceremony of human sacrifice was practiced in the
Well of Sacrifice at Chichen Itza. Victims of both sexes in times
of dire national necessity, such as famines, epidemics, and especially in case of unduly prolonged droughts, were hurled into
this great irregularly-shaped pocket in the limestone. The Well of
Sacrifice at Chichen Itza (Plate 42, *b*) is roughly oval; it varies
in width from 150 to 190 feet and is 65 feet in depth from the
level of the surrounding country to the surface of the water, which
in turn is another 65 or 70 feet deep to the bottom of this great
natural hole in the Yucatan limestone; the sides are either vertical or undercut. Pilgrimages were made from great distances to
attend these sacrifices and all kinds of valuables were hurled into
the well with the living victims, both men and virgins, to appease
the angered rain-deities. It is connected with the Castillo, or

FIG. 15.—*Graffitti* from Temple II at Tikal, Peten, Guatemala, showing arrow-
shooting ceremony.

principal temple dedicated to Kukulcan, by a stone causeway 1,000
feet long, 20 feet wide, and varying in height from 3 to 15 feet
above the general ground-level, depending upon surface inequalities. Says Landa:

Into this well they have had, and then [middle-sixteenth century] had,
the custom of throwing men alive, as a sacrifice to the gods in times of
drought, and they believed they did not die though they never saw them
again. They also threw into it many other things, like precious stones
and things that they prized. And so if this country had had gold, it would
be this well that would have the greater part of it, so great was the devotion which the Indians showed for it.

This prediction, made by Landa nearly four centuries ago, has received startling confirmation from archaeology in modern times. In 1905–1908 the Peabody Museum of Archaeology and Ethnology of Harvard University carried on extensive dredging operations in the Well of Sacrifice at Chichen Itza, bringing to the surface from its dark and forbidding waters a veritable treasure of sacrificial offerings. These articles include gold and copper repoussee plates, masks, cups, saucers, bells, pendants, bracelets, earrings, finger-rings, and buttons of gold. Many copper sacrificial bells of the sleigh-bell type of different sizes were found (emblems of the God of Death), small ceremonial axes, etc.; great numbers of plain, highly polished jade beads as well as carved jade beads, pendants, and plaques; objects of wood—the sacrificial knife, already mentioned—and several throwing sticks (Maya *hulche*, Aztec *atlatl*). There were fragments of cotton textiles, some showing unusual weaves; ornaments made from carved bone and shell; about fifty human crania of men and women, human long bones, some of the latter being carved, perhaps to be used as trophies of war. And most numerous of all were the cakes of *pom* incense, usually found resting on the bottoms of crude pottery vessels and painted a bright turquoise blue.

Study of the gold and copper objects found in the Well of Sacrifice indicate that they were brought to Chichen Itza from points as far distant as Colombia and Panama to the south and from as far north as the state of Oaxaca and the Valley of Mexico. See chapter xvi (pp. 432–36) for a more detailed description of some of these objects.

In addition to its use as a place where offerings and human sacrifices were made to bring rain, there was also present a prognosticative element in these ceremonies at the Well of Sacrifice. The victims, especially girl-slaves, their hands and feet unbound, were thrown into the well by their masters at daybreak, and if, by chance, any survived the plunge, a rope was lowered at midday to haul them out and they were asked by the lords what manner of year, whether good or bad, the gods had in store for them. If a girl did not survive the ordeal, that is, did not re-

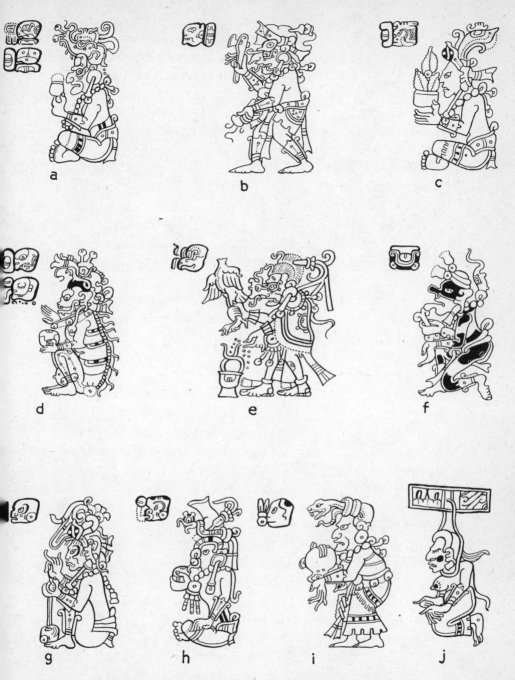

PLATE 29.—PRINCIPAL DEITIES OF THE MAYA PANTHEON AS
REPRESENTED IN THE CODICES

(a) Itzamna, head of the Maya Pantheon (God D); (b) Chac, the rain-god
(God B); (c) Yum Kax, the corn-god (God E); (d) Ah Puch, the death-
god (God A); (e) the wind-god, perhaps Kukulcan (God K); (f) the war-god
(God M); (g) the god of sudden death and of human sacrifice (God F); (h)
Xaman Ek, the North Star-god (God C); (i, Ixchel, wife of Itzamna and the
goddess of childbirth and weaving (Goddess I); (j) Ixtab, the goddess of suicide.

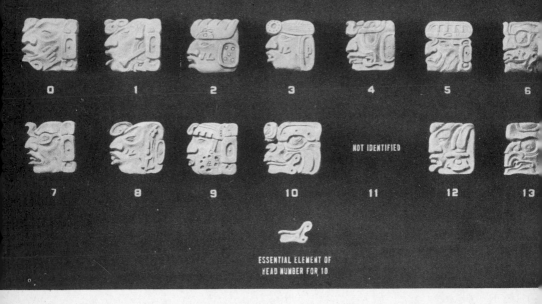

↑ *a*) Head-variant numerals, the Maya "Arabic notation."

PLATE 30.—MAYA HEAD-VARIANT NUMERALS AND REMAINS OF STATUETTES
OF THE NINE GODS OF THE LOWER WORLD

b) Stucco statuettes of the Nine Gods of the Lower World, in Temple 40,
↓ Yaxchilan, Chiapas, Mexico.

appear at midday when the ropes were lowered into the well, "all that lord's people [that is, the master of the girl and his retainers] as well as the lord himself threw large stones into the water and with great hue and cry took flight from there."

THE THIRTEEN KATUN-ENDINGS

A ceremony of first importance and one of great antiquity as well, since it goes back to the beginnings of the Old Empire, was the erection of the katun-stone or monument at the end of each katun or 7,200-day period. Each one of the thirteen differently named katuns had its own special patron deity and its own peculiar rites. It has been shown earlier (chapter iv, p. 57) that, although this ceremony started as a *katun*-ending rite at Uaxactun in 8.16.0.0.0 (357), as the Old Empire developed and grew more powerful it soon came to be generally celebrated twice each katun: once at the halfway point, and once at the end. The first of these two celebrations, the one at the intermediate *lahuntun* or 3,600-day period-ending, was ceremonially of lesser significance, but the second, the one at the katun-ending, was of great importance. In a few cities of the Old Empire, notably Quirigua and Piedras Negras, the quarter katun-endings as well, i.e., the *hotun* or 1,800-day period-endings, were thus commemorated. In late New Empire times, however, when we have a number of contemporary references to this ceremony, it was being celebrated only on the katun-endings, as it had been at the very beginning.

One of the most constant features of this ceremony, and one that persisted for nearly twelve centuries (357–1519), was the erection of a monument inscribed with hieroglyphics, which gave the date of the monument in Maya chronology and additional astronomical, chronological, and ritualistic data; usually also there is a figure panel showing a ruler or priest, either with or without accompanying assistants and prisoners. These monuments were erected for nearly twelve hundred years, and their unveiling and dedication at the ends of the successive katuns and half-katuns of Maya history was one of the most important ceremonies of ancient Maya life.

In late New Empire times the ceremony was celebrated, according to Bishop Landa, as follows: Take, for example, the Katun 7 Ahau, which ran from 1323 to 1342, possibly represented on page 6 of the Codex Peresianus illustrated on this page (Fig. 16). During the first half of this 20-year period (1323–1332), the idol of Katun 7 Ahau ruled alone in the temple, though he had already been a guest there for the ten years previous to his actual rule (from 1313 to 1323). During the second half (1332–1342) of his own Katun 7 Ahau (1323–1342), the idol of the following katun, 5 Ahau, who was to rule from 1342 to 1362, was placed in the same temple as a guest and was shown respect as the successor-to-be to the idol of Katun 7 Ahau. In 1342, when the rule of 7 Ahau had finished, his idol was removed from the temple and the idol of 5 Ahau was left there to rule alone for ten years more (that is, from 1342 until 1352), when the idol of Katun 3 Ahau, who was to succeed the idol of 5 Ahau in 1362, was placed in the temple as guest for ten years (1352–1362), until the idol of 3 Ahau should rule alone, beginning in 1362. Thus the idol of each katun would seem to have enjoyed worship for thirty years—the first decade when he was only the guest of his predecessor, before his own rule of 20 years began, perhaps to acquire the powers of his predecessor; the second decade when he ruled alone (the first half of the katun of which he was the actual patron); and the third decade (the second half of his own katun) when he shared the rule with his successor. The foregoing description sounds more complicated than the practice itself really was.

FIG. 16.—Ceremony celebrating the end of the 20-year period, called Katun 7 Ahau, perhaps A.D. 1323–1342. Page 6, Codex Peresianus.

Landa has the following account of this ceremony:

Whoever put in order this computation of katuns, if it was the devil, he did it, as he usually does, ordaining it for his own glory, or, if it were a man, he must have been a good idolator, for with these katuns of theirs, he increased all the principal trickeries, divinations and delusions with which these people, besides their miseries, were entirely deluded, and this was the science to which they gave the most credit, and that which they valued most, and not all the priests knew how to describe it. The order which they used in counting their affairs, and in making their divinations, by means of this computation, was that they had in the temple two idols dedicated to two of these characters [the idols of Katuns 7 Ahau and 5 Ahau in the example given above]. They worshipped and offered homage and sacrifices to the first [7 Ahau] . . . . as a remedy for the calamities of his twenty years [1323–1342]. But for the ten years [1332–1342], which remained of the twenty [1323-1342] of the first idol [7 Ahau], they did not do anything for him more than to burn incense to him and to show him respect. When the twenty years [1323-1342] of the first idol [7 Ahau] had passed, he began to be succeeded by the destinies of the second [5 Ahau] and [they began] to offer him [5 Ahau] sacrifices, and having taken away that first idol [7 Ahau], they put another [5 Ahau] in its place, in order to worship that for ten more years [by himself, 1342–1352].

Each differently named katun of the thirteen possible ones (see pp. 291–95) had its own patron deity, its own special ceremonies and observances, and its own particular prophecies. It will be shown in the last chapter how powerfully the prophecies for the fateful Katun 8 Ahau affected the destinies of the Itza, the last politically independent Maya group. Perhaps no ceremony in the Maya religion was as important as that held in connection with these katun-endings, and it is certainly the oldest one of which we have record.

NEW YEAR CEREMONIES

Another most important group of ceremonies centered around the commencement of the Maya New Year. It will be shown in chapter xii (p. 272) that at the time of the Spanish Conquest the Maya year-bearers, that is to say those days upon which a New

Year could begin, only four in number, were the days named Kan, Muluc, Ix, and Cauac, each being associated with one of the cardinal points: Kan years with the East, Muluc years with the North, Ix years with the West, and Cauac years with the South (see end-sheets). Each kind of year had ceremonies peculiar to it and to no other. These New Year ceremonies began in the closing five days of the preceding year—the Uayeb—or unlucky days, when everyone stayed at home lest some misfortune should befall him. The celebrations corresponding to the four kinds of Maya New Years—the Kan, Muluc, Ix, and Cauac years—although differing in details, all follow the same general pattern.

Kan years.—The New Year ceremonies for Kan years began during the five closing days, the Uayeb, of the preceding year, that is the Uayeb days of a Cauac year. A hollow pottery idol of a god called Kan[4] U Uayeb was set up temporarily on a pile of stones at the south entrance to the town, or village, because south was the cardinal point of the dying Cauac year. A lord was chosen at whose house all the feasts connected with the current New Year's ceremony were to be held, and here an idol, Bolon Dzacab ("Nine Generations") who was to be patron of the new Kan year was erected. Bolon Dzacab was an agricultural god who has been identified with the God of the Winds (God K), described in an earlier section. Next the whole community went to the south entrance where the idol of Kan U Uayeb had previously been set up, and there the priest incensed it with a mixture made of ground corn and *pom*; and cutting off the head of a turkey, he offered the fowl to the idol. The idol, amidst rejoicing and dancing, was then carried to the house of the lord who was the donor of the feast, where the idol of Bolon Dzacab had already been installed. Here the idol of Kan U Uayeb was placed in front of that of Bolon Dzacab and many gifts of food, drink, flesh, and fowl were offered to the two idols; afterward these offerings were distributed among those present, the officiating priest being given a haunch of venison.

[4] The first syllable *kan* in the name of this god is another Maya word *kan* meaning "yellow," the color associated with the dying Cauac year, and not the first day, Kan, of the Kan years.

The devout drew blood from their ears and smeared the idols with it, offering heart-shaped loaves of corn meal and squash seeds to the idol of Kan U Uayeb.

The idols of these two gods were kept at the lord's house for the five days of Uayeb. Failure to incense them regularly during this period, it was believed, would surely be followed by certain special sicknesses which afflicted mankind during Kan years. As soon as the five Uayeb days had passed, the idol of Bolon Dzacab, patron of the new Kan year, was taken to the temple, and that of Kan U Uayeb was set up at the east gate, east being the cardinal point and red the color associated with Kan years (see endsheets). Here the idol of Kan U Uayeb stood until the end of the Kan year over which it presided. Kan years were considered good ones "because the Bacab Hobnil who ruled with the sign Kan, they said, had never sinned as had his brothers [especially the two who presided over the Ix and Cauac years], and it was on this account that no calamity came to them in it [a Kan year]."

Later in the year if, in spite of their previous devotions, calamities and misfortunes began to happen, the priests ordered another idol to be made and erected to the god Itzamna Kauil. This was placed in the temple, three balls of rubber were burned before it, and a dog or, if possible, a man was sacrificed to it. This sacrifice was effected by hurling the dog or man from the summit of the pyramid onto a pile of stones heaped up in the court below for this express purpose. The heart was then removed and was offered to the new idol, on a plate covered with another plate, together with gifts of food. This second ceremony closed with a dance given by the old women of the community, dressed in special garments peculiar to the occasion. Landa says this ceremony was the only one celebrated in a temple at which women could be present.

Muluc years.—In Muluc years, which followed Kan years, an idol called Chac U Uayeb was taken to the east entrance where the idol of Kan U Uayeb had been left the year before. The same ceremonies were repeated, only in Muluc years the idol, set up in the house of the lord chosen to give the feast, was called Kinich Ahau, the sun-god. The same dances were performed, offerings of food and incense were made, and when the five unlucky days were over the idol of Chac U Uayeb was carried to the north entrance and there set up on one of the two piles of stone. Muluc years were thought to be good years because they believed the Bacab who presided over them "was the best and greatest of the Bacab gods."

If the Muluc years turned out badly, however, the priests had another god up their sleeves, called Yax Cocay Mut, "the green firefly pheasant," of whom an image was made and worshiped. The special evils that were prone to happen in Muluc years were a scarcity of water and an abundance of sprouts in the corn. The old women had to perform a special dance on high stilts (Fig. 17) and to offer dogs made of pottery with food placed on their backs.

Ix years.—In Ix years the idol Sac U Uayeb was erected at the north entrance of the town and a statue of Itzamna, the patron of the current Ix year, was set up in the house of the lord selected to give the feast. The same series of rites were performed and at the end of the year the idol of Itzamna was carried to the temple and that of Sac U Uayeb to one of the two piles of stone at the west gate. Ix years were considered unfavorable; people were especially prone to fainting fits, swoons, and troubles of the eyes; there were supposed to be, in Ix years, great scarcity of water, hot suns, drought, famine, thefts, discords, changes of rulers, wars, and, most dreaded of all, plagues of locusts. If any of these calamities occurred, the priests ordered an idol made to Kinich Ahau Itzamna and again the old women executed a special dance.

Fig. 17.— Woman on stilts. Page 36, Codex Tro- Cortesianus.

Cauac years.—In Cauac years an idol called Ek U Uayeb was made and carried to the west entrance of the town, and another of Uac Mitun Ahau was made and placed in the house of the lord who was giving the New Year's feast that year, and the same ceremonies followed in other years were repeated. Uac Mitun Ahau may be translated "Lord of the Sixth Hell" or Lower World. When the usual ceremonies had been performed the idol of Uac Mitun Ahau was carried from the house of the lord giving the feast to the temple, and the idol of Ek U Uayeb was carried to the south entrance of the town, where it was installed for the coming year.

Cauac years were considered to be the most dangerous of all; they were years when heavy mortality was to be expected; hot crop-destroying suns, flocks of birds, and swarms of ants to devour the young seeds. But again the priests came forward with their never-failing remedy. This time the people had to make idols of four gods—Chic Chac Chob, Ek Balam Chac, Ah Canuol Cab, and Ah Buluc Balam—which were installed in the temple and, after further ceremonies, incensing, burning a huge fire of fagots, dancing on the cooling embers in bare feet, and a general drunkenness followed as before.

The following New Year, a Kan year again, the ceremonies appropriate to Kan years began all over again in the five Uayeb days of the outgoing Cauac year, and thus the round of New Year's ceremonies continued to follow each other without interruption, year after year.

Throughout the year other feasts and ceremonies were celebrated to appease or propitiate this god or that; to obtain rain or good harvests, to insure success in hunting, fishing, trading, war, and other activities; most of these have long since been forgotten and lack of space permits mention of only a few of the most important.

CELEBRATIONS OF THE VARIOUS MONTHS

The month of Pop.—On the Maya New Year's Day, the first day of the month of Pop, which fell on July 16 of our Old Style calendar in the year 1556, or on July 26 of that year in our present corrected, or Gregorian, calendar, a universal and very solemn renovation ceremony was held in which all kinds of articles in daily use were renewed—pottery vessels, wooden stools, fibermats, clothes, and the cloths in which their idols were wrapped. The houses were swept clean and old utensils were thrown out upon the town refuse pile never to be even so much as touched again. The four *chacs* who were to serve the priest for the ensuing year were chosen and the priest himself prepared the balls of incense for the New Year ceremony.

The month of Uo.—During the second month, Uo, the priests, physicians, sorcerers, hunters, and fishermen celebrated festivals to their respective special patron gods. A priest consulted the sacred books to ascertain the auguries for the coming year and, after feasting and drinking, the festivities closed with a dance in honor of the month, which seems to have been devoted largely to certain vocational festivals. The special ceremonies of the physicians, sorcerers, hunters, and fishermen were continued into the following month of Zip.

The months of Zotz and Tzec.—During the fourth month, Zotz, the owners of bee-hives began to make preparation for their feast, which was held in the following month, Tzec. Their divine intercessors were the four Bacabs, and of these four brothers, Hobnil, the Bacab who was patron of the Kan years, was their special friend. Incense was burned and pictures of honey were painted on the incense boards. The object of this feast was to increase the yield of honey, and the owners of hives all contributed an abundance of honey to it, from which a wine was brewed with the bark of the *balche* tree; heavy drinking of this beverage concluded the ceremony.

The month of Xul.—On the sixteenth day of the sixth month, Xul, which began on November 17 (Gregorian), there was celebrated one of the most important festivals of the Maya year, namely that in honor of the great god Kukulcan. Formerly this ceremony was observed all over Yucatan, but after the fall of Mayapan in 1441 it was held only at the Xiu capital of Mani, though other provinces sent rich gifts, among which were certain magnificent banners of featherwork used in the rite.

A great multitude from surrounding towns and villages assembled at Mani on the day of the feast, having prepared for it in advance by preliminary fastings and abstinences. At evening a great procession of lords, priests, common folk, and clowns, which latter were a special feature of the celebration, set out from the house of the lord who was giving the feast and proceeded in an orderly array to the Temple of Kukulcan, which had previously been adorned for the occasion. Upon arriving at the temple, the preliminary exorcisms and prayers were made; the feather banners were broken out from the summit of the temple-pyramid, and all the participants spread out their personal idols of wood and clay on leaves in the court in front of the temple. A new fire was kindled, incense was burned throughout the court, and offerings were made of food cooked without salt or chili pepper, and of a beverage composed of ground beans and squash seeds mixed.

The lords and all those who had fasted remained at the temple without returning to their homes for the remaining five days and nights of the month, incensing and making offerings to their idols, praying, and performing sacred dances. During these five days the clowns passed among the houses of the well-to-do, playing their comedies and farces and collecting gifts, which at the end of the feast were divided among the lords, priests, and dancers. The banners and idols were then gathered together and taken to the house of the donor lord, from whence each participant departed for his own home. It was believed Kukulcan himself descended from heaven on the last day of the feast to receive the devotion and offerings of the worshipers. This feast was called *chic kaban*, which among other things may mean "clown-named."

The months of Yaxkin and Mol.—During the seventh month, Yaxkin, preparations were made for another general ceremony in honor of all the gods, a sort of Maya All Saints Day, which was celebrated in the eighth month, Mol, on a day fixed by the priests. It was called, according to Landa, *olob-zab-kamyax*, probably a corruption of the Maya phrase *yolob u dzab kamyax* meaning "they wish to administer the receiving of the blue color [ceremony]." After all had assembled in the temple and the usual preliminaries of exorcism and incensing had been carried out, the principal object of the ceremony, which was to anoint everything with the sacred blue ointment, was begun. All sorts of utensils, from the priest's sacred books to the grinding stones of the women, even the doorposts of the houses, were smeared with this blue ointment. The boys and girls of the town were assembled, and the joints of the backs of their hands were struck nine times to make them skillful in the pursuits of their fathers and mothers. An old woman called the *ixmol* or "conductress," dressed in a feather robe, did this for the girls and a priest did it for the boys. The ceremony concluded with a drunken feast.

The bee-keepers also celebrated a second festival in the month of Mol in order that the gods should provide flowers for the bees.

Still a third ceremony, and one of very great importance, held in Mol, or in some other month if the priests found the omens of Mol were not propitious therefor, was called "making gods," and, as its name signifies, was for the purpose of making their wooden idols. The sculptors who carved these idols were fearful of their own art, since it was believed to be very dangerous to make representations of the deities, and they consented to do it only with great reluctance, fearing some member of their families would die or a fainting sickness might fall upon them. As soon as the sculptor who was to make the idols had been selected, the priest, the four *chacs*, and the sculptor all began to fast, while the man for whom the idols were to be made built a thatched hut in the forest, fenced it, cut the wood from which the idols were to be carved, and carried the pieces to the hut, and finally installed a large, covered pottery urn so that the idols could be decently kept under cover while they were being made.

The wood used for making the idols was always the same—Spanish cedar, the most easily carved of all the native woods, being soft and without grain. The Maya word for Spanish cedar is *kuche*, which itself means "god tree," perhaps because the idols of the gods were made from it. Incense was taken to the hut to offer to four gods, called *Acantuns*, one each presiding over one of the four cardinal points, as well as instruments for scarification and drawing blood from the ears, and tools for carving the wood.

When all these had been provided, the priest, the four *chacs*, and the sculptor were shut up in the hut and went to work, first cutting their ears and smearing the images of the four *Acantuns* with their blood, incensing, and praying. This was kept up until the idols were finished, while the man for whom they were being made carried food to the hut for those working there. Absolute continence was required of all, and no outsider was allowed even to approach the hut.

The month of Chen.—In the next month, Chen, when the idols were finished, the man for whom they had been made paid the priest, *chacs,* and sculptor with gifts of game, birds, and beads, and reverentially removed the idols from the hut to a previously prepared arbor in his own yard. Here the priest and sculptor first cleaned themselves of the soot with which they had been anointed while the idols were being fashioned, and the former blessed the idols with great solemnity and fervent prayers. Finally, the evil spirits having been exorcized and incense burned, the idols were wrapped in cloth, placed in a small basket, and turned over to the owner, who received them with great devotion and reverence. The ceremony, as usual, closed with feasting and drinking.

The month of Yax.—A renovation ceremony, already described in connection with the rain-god, Chac (p. 225), was celebrated in the month of Yax, on which occasion the clay idols and incense burners were renewed, probably with ceremonies not dissimilar to those just mentioned in connection with the making of wooden idols.

The month of Zac.—During the eleventh month, Zac, the hunters again celebrated a festival like the one they had held in the month of Zip, the purpose of which was to make amends to the gods for any blood they might have shed in the chase. Any bloodshed, except in sacrifice, was believed to be an abomination for which atonement had to be made.

The months of Ceh and Mac.—There is no special ceremony described as having taken place in the twelfth month Ceh, but in the next month, Mac, the old men celebrated a feast in honor of the four Chacs and Itzamna, called the Tupp Kak, or "the killing of the fire." A great hunt was organized in which as many animals and birds as possible were caught. On the day of the ceremony these were brought to the courtyard of the temple, where a great pile of dry fagots had been piled up, and, after the usual exorcisms and incensing, the animals and birds were sacrificed and their hearts thrown into the fire. When the hearts were consumed the *chacs* extinguished the fire with jars of water, after which the ceremony proper began. For this feast only the lord who gave it was obliged to fast. All assembled in the court of the temple, where a stone altar had been built with a stairway on one side; this was very clean and decorated with green branches. The priest burned incense in order to expel the evil spirit, and when the altar had been thus ceremonially purified, mud from a well was smeared on the bottom step and the sacred blue ointment on the other steps. Incense was burned again, and the Chacs and Itzamna were invoked with prayers and offerings; eating and drinking closed this ceremony as all others. The Tupp Kak was celebrated in order to obtain a year of good rains; the month Mac fell in the latter part of March and early April, not long before the beginning of the rainy season early in May, and it was thought that the service described above and the accompanying invocations would assure plentiful rains for the corn.

The months of Kankin and Muan.—No special ceremony is reported for the fourteenth month, Kankin, but in the following month, Muan, a festival in honor of Chac Ek Chuah (God of Cacao) and Hobnil (Bacab of the Kan years) was celebrated by owners of cacao plantations. A dog with cacao-colored spots was sacrificed on one of the cacao plantations, incense was burned, blue iguanas, blue bird-feathers, and game were offered to the idols of these gods, and the long pods of the cacao beans were given to each official who had participated in the rite. When the offerings and prayers were over, the ceremony closed with the usual feasting and drinking, but this time with no drunkenness, since Bishop Landa says "there were three drinks of wine for each one and no more."

The month of Pax.—In the month of Pax, there was a ceremony called *Pacum Chac*, meaning perhaps, "the recompensing of Chac" in honor of a god called Cit Chac Coh, "Father Red Puma," who, judging from the nature of the ceremony, was a patron of warriors. This was a general ceremony, the lords and priests of the smaller towns and villages going to the larger centers, where the celebration was held in the Temple of Cit Chac

Coh. For five days preceding the festival, prayers, gifts, and incense were offered at the temple; sometime before the fifth day,
all repaired to the house of the war captain, the elected *nacom*,
and with great pomp, incensing him the while as though he were
a god, they bore him in a palanquin to the Temple of Cit Chac
Coh, where he was seated and incensed further. The remainder
of the five days were spent in feasting, in drinking, and in dancing
the *holcan okot*, or dance of the warriors. The preliminary five
days having passed, the ceremony proper began, and since it was
a rite to secure victory over their enemies in war it was celebrated
with great solemnity (see Table VI, pp. 254–55).

The ceremony opened with the same ordeal by fire as practiced
in the month of Mac, which was followed by prayers, offerings,
and incensing. While this was going on, the lords carried the
nacom on their shoulders in his palanquin around the temple, incensing him as they went. This finished, a dog was sacrificed, its
heart being placed on a covered platter and offered to the idol of
Cit Chac Coh. The *chacs* opened a large jar of wine, which closed
the festival. The *nacom* was escorted back to his home by the other
celebrants, where the lords, priests, and leading people, everybody
in fact except the *nacom* himself, got ceremonially and royally
drunk. The next day, everyone having recovered from the preceding night's orgy, the *nacom* distributed among the participants
in the feast great quantities of incense and eloquently urged them
to observe all the festivals of the coming year with diligence and
fidelity in order that the year should be prosperous, after which
each returned to his own town or village.

The closing months of Kayab, Cumhu, and Uayeb.—As will
be seen from the foregoing description a fairly strenuous program
of religious ceremonies had been going on for the previous sixteen
Maya months and all felt the need for some relaxation before the
exacting rites of the New Year began. These lighter festivities,
held during the last three months, Kayab, Cumhu, and Uayeb,
were called the *sabacil than* and were celebrated as follows:

They sought in the town, among those who were the richest for some
one who would be willing to give this festival, and advised him of the

TABLE VI

List of Ceremonies, Their Objectives, and Corresponding Patron Gods and Sacred Dances Celebrated During the Year, According to Bishop Landa

Month	Patron of Month	Name of Ceremony	Patron God or Gods	Object of Ceremony	Group or Groups Participating in Ceremony	Name of Dance
Pop	Jaguar	....	All gods	New Years rites and renewal of all utensils	General	....
Uo	God of Number 7	Pocam	Kinich Ahau Itzamna	Ascertain prognostications for the year	Priests, physicians, sorcerers, hunters, fishermen	Okot uil
			Ixchel, Itzamna, Cit Bolon Tun, Ahau Chamahes	To these gods of medicine for their help	Physicians, sorcerers	Chan tuniah
Zip	A serpent-god		Acanum, Suhui Dzipitabai	To these gods of the hunt for successful hunting	Hunters	....
			Ah Kak Nexoy, Ah Pua, Ah Cit Dzamal Cum	To these gods of fishing for successful fishing	Fishermen	Chohom
Zotz	Bat	No special ceremonies reported; devoted to preparation for those of the following month				
Tzec	God of the Day Caban (?)	....	Four Bacabs, but especially Hobnil, Bacab of Kan years	To the god of bees for an abundance of honey	Owners of bee hives	....
Xul	Unknown	Chic Kaban	Kukulcan	Blessing of the idols	General	Sacred dances
Yaxkin	Sun	No special ceremonies reported; devoted to preparation for those of the following month				

Month	God	Ceremony	Gods	Purpose	Participants	
Mol	An old god (?)	Olob zab kamyax	All gods	Anointing all utensils with sacred blue ointment	General	
				For flowers for the bees	Owners of bee hives	
			Four Acantuns	Making new idols of the gods	Individual having new idols made for him	
Chen	Moon	Idol-making ceremonies continued				
Yax	Venus	Oc Na	Chacs	Renovation of Temple of Chac	General	
Zac	God of the Uinal, or 20-day time period		Acanum, Suhui Dzipitabai	To appease gods of hunt for having shed blood in the chase	Hunters	
Ceh	New Fire	No special ceremony reported				
Mac	A young god (?)	Tupp Kak	Chacs, Itzamna	To secure rains for the corn and a good year	Old men	
Kankin	Unknown	No special ceremony reported				
Muan	A young god (?)		Ek Chuah, Chac, Hobnil	Successful year for the cacao plants	Owners of cacao plantations	
Pax	A god with a Roman nose	Pacum Chac	Cit Chac Coh	To obtain victory in war	Warriors	Holcan okot
Kayab						
Cumhu	A young god (?)					
Uayeb	unknown	Zabacil Than		For pleasure and diversion	General	Dances
	Unknown		U Uayeb Kan (yellow) U Uayeb, Chac (red) U Uayeb, Sac (white) U Uayeb, Ek (black) U Uayeb	Preparation for the New Years ceremonies, one each for the four kinds of years: Kan, Muluc, Ix, and Cauac	General	

day, in order that these three months that remained before the New Year should have more diversion. And what they did was to assemble in the house of him who gave the festival, and there they performed the ceremonies of driving out the evil spirit, and burned copal [*pom*] and made offerings with rejoicings and dances, and they made wine-skins of themselves, and this was the inevitable conclusion. And so great was the excess which there was in the festivals during these three months that it was a great pity to see them, for some went about covered with scratches, others, bruised, others with their eyes enflamed from much drunkenness, and all the while with such a passion for wine that they were lost because of it.

It must be remembered, in judging Landa's constant complaints about the drunkenness with which he says most Maya ceremonies concluded, that every observance of the ancient religion was anathema to him. Everything about the old pagan faith was nothing more than the work of the Devil himself and as such was to be damned outright by crook and candle. The old bishop was as bigoted as the Maya priests he condemns, and his observations about the drunken orgies with which he says these ceremonies always concluded should probably be taken with a grain of salt. For a résumé of the ceremonies and dances of the Maya year see Table VI.

GROWTH OF THE PANTHEON

The Maya had a large number of gods, though the most powerful and the most frequently invoked were those described in a previous section of this chapter. Probably not more than a dozen deities enjoyed most of the worship, the aid of the others being sought only on special occasions or as specific need for their help arose.

We have seen that originally the Maya religion was relatively simple, a direct personification of the forces of nature, which immediately influenced the lives of the common people—the sun, moon, rain, wind, thunder, lightning, floods, etc. (Pre-Maya I); further, that with the introduction of corn culture, the pantheon was enlarged to admit agricultural and fertility deities whose appeasement and continued good-will now became necessary for the first time (Pre-Maya II). Still later, when the Maya civilization began to take shape with the invention of the calendar, chronology, and hieroglyphic writing, during the fourth or third century before Christ, a further expansion of the pantheon became necessary to make room for the new group of astronomic and calendric deities, whose functions were more specialized than those of the older, simpler, and more general nature gods. The newer gods required the services of a professional priesthood to worship them and to interpret their wishes to the mass of the people. And so matters continued for more than six centuries (Pre-Maya III), the Maya religion growing more and more esoteric, the Maya gods more and more specialized, the Maya priesthood more and more highly organized, and Maya worship, ritual, rite, and ceremony more and more complex, but, it is to be noted, without the excessive practice of human sacrifice and without the general use of idols, whether of stone, wood, or clay (Old Empire I, II, and III).

All authorities are agreed that both mass human sacrifice and idolatry were introduced into Yucatan by the Maya-Mexican invaders under Kukulcan during the tenth century of the Christian Era. It has been pointed out that, while human sacrifice was practiced in Old Empire times, it was only in moderation, and that it was not until the Puuc and Mexican periods of the New Empire that hecatombs of human victims were offered to the gods after the fashion then prevailing in central Mexico (New Empires I and II).

Similarly the Old Empire Maya were not, generally speaking, worshipers of images in a literal sense, all authorities again agreeing that idolatry as such was also a Maya-Mexican importation into Yucatan; in which latter period the number of idols is said to have been enormous. Landa states: "They had a very great number of idols and of temples which were magnificent in their own fashion, and besides the community temples, the lords, priests and leading men also had oratories and idols in their houses, where they made their prayers and offerings in private." And again, "They had such a great quantity of idols, that those of their gods were not enough, for there was not an animal or insect of which they did not make a statue." Another seventeenth-century Spanish priest in writing of Tayasal on Lake Peten Itza, the last independent Maya stronghold, says: "They have many other public idols, as there are nearly as many as there are priests' houses and the streets of the district." Another writer in 1562 mentions "that there must have been more than 100,000," which number, the royal *alcalde mayor* of Merida, writing three years later, raises to "almost a million of them." Even discounting such obvious exaggeration as these last two statements, all the early writers agree that there were very great numbers of idols, practically everyone —lords and priests, rich and poor alike—each having his own private collection of them, many of them having to be renewed each year.

Among this multitude of gods many were the creation, one might almost say the private racket, of the professional priesthood. The common man, the simple corn farmer, whose toil and sweat alone made possible the whole complicated governmental, social, and religious structure, turned most frequently to Chac, the rain-god, since by Chac's propitiation and appeasement, by Chac's good will, he lived and by Chac's wrath he was undone.

HIEROGLYPHIC WRITING, ARITHMETIC, AND ASTRONOMY [1]

H. G. WELLS in his *Outline of History* says that the invention of a graphic system is the true measure of civilization, while Edward Gibbon, in his *Decline and Fall of the Roman Empire*, states that the use of letters is the principal characteristic which distinguishes a civilized people from a herd of savages. According to such standards, the Maya were the most civilized people of the New World in pre-Columbian times, since they and they alone developed an original system of writing.

THE DEVELOPMENT OF WRITING

The world over, writing seems to have passed through three definite stages of development:

I.—*Pictorial or representative writing*, wherein a picture of the idea to be conveyed is actually portrayed. Thus a deer hunt is represented by the picture of a deer and a man throwing a spear at it. Nothing is left to the imagination. The picture tells the whole story. This has been called pictographic writing.

II.—*Ideographic writing*, wherein the characters or signs stand for ideas rather than represent pictures of such ideas. In ideographic writing the characters employed have usually lost all resemblance to the pictures of the ideas for which they stand, being little more than conventionalized symbols. Thus among the Indians of the Northwest Coast the idea of a whale is represented by its spout. In Chinese writing, the ideograph for "trouble" is the conventionalized symbol for a woman, repeated twice, standing under a gate, and the ideograph for "war," the symbols for three

---

[1] This chapter, in shorter form, was originally published in my *Guide Book to the Ruins of Quirigua* (Carnegie Institution of Washington, Supplementary Publication No. 16, Washington, D.C., 1935).

259

women standing under the same gate. Chinese, without any attempt at wise-cracking, is perhaps the best example of ideographic writing extant today.

III.—*Phonetic writing,* wherein the characters have lost all semblance to, or even mental association with, the objects they originally portrayed and denote only sounds. The signs no longer stand for pictures, or even ideas. They are completely divorced from any attempt at realistic representation. Instead, they stand for sounds only, and as used in combinations denote only combinations of sounds. Phonetic writing may be further divided into (1) syllabic writing and (2) alphabetic writing. In the former the characters represent syllables, that is compound rather than simple sounds, while in the latter each of the characters or letters stands for a single sound. The Egyptian hieroglyphic writing is an example of the former; modern alphabets are examples of the latter.

The Maya hieroglyphic writing belongs to Class II above. Its characters represent ideas rather than pictures (Class I) or sounds (Class III).

MAYA WRITING ONE OF THE EARLIEST EXAMPLES OF A GRAPHIC SYSTEM

Maya writing represents one of the earliest stages in the development of graphic systems extant today. Perhaps the most important fact about the Maya hieroglyphic writing for the modern student of graphic systems is that, barring the purely pictorial efforts of Class I, like the palaeolithic paintings in the Cave of Alta Mira, Spain, or the pictographs scratched on cliffs in Arizona and New Mexico, for example, it may well represent the earliest stage of a formal graphic system that has come down to us.

This does not mean that the Maya hieroglyphic writing is the oldest graphic system extant today. Far from it. The earliest Egyptian and Sumerian inscriptions go back to the fourth millennium before Christ, whereas the earliest Maya text does not reach back even so far as the beginning of the Christian Era. What may be fairly claimed for the ancient Maya writing, however, is this:

although devised several thousand years *later* than either the
Egyptian hieroglyphic or the Sumerian cuneiform writing, it represents a far *earlier* stage in the development of writing than
either.

When we first glimpse the Egyptian hieroglyphics, they had
already advanced to a semiphonetic stage. In addition to the many
ideographs present, perhaps as many as half of the characters are
phonetic, mostly syllabic, but in a few cases already definitely
alphabetic. A similar condition obtains in the earliest cuneiform
clay tablets where phonetic elements are also numerous.

The Maya system, however, although devised several thous-
and years later than either the Egyptian or the Sumerian, actually
represents an earlier stage in the development of writing than
either—namely, a graphic system which is almost entirely ideographic (Class II) but just on the verge of developing phoentic
characters (Class III).

MAYA "ROSETTA STONE"

The Maya "Rosetta Stone," if we may borrow the analogy
from Egyptology, may perhaps be said to be the *Relación de las
cosas de Yucatan*, written about 1566 by Bishop Diego de
Landa, already extensively quoted in this book.

At the time of the Spanish Conquest of Yucatan, the Maya
hieroglyphic writing was still in use. The Maya civilization toward the end of the New Empire had passed into a decline, a loss
of cultural impetus, a definite slowing down of the whole social
mechanism. However, knowledge and use of the hieroglyphic
writing among the priesthood and ruling class continued down to
the time of the Spanish Conquest and even later.

Landa, in his *Relación*, gives a brief description of the Maya
calendar, drawings of the signs for the different days and months,
and some general information, much of which is irrelevant, though
little is actually misleading. He tells us that his chief source of
information about the calendar was one Nachi Cocom (pp. 95, 96),
who had been a native prince before the Conquest period and who
was well versed in reading the hieroglyphic writing.

The worthy bishop, though he says he regards the whole matter as "the work of the devil," nevertheless gives sufficient data with which as an entering wedge it has been possible to work slowly toward an approximate understanding of the meaning of the Maya inscriptions. Indeed, it is now possible to read about one-third of the hieroglyphs, sufficient to permit comprehension of the general tenor of these ancient stone records.

STORY TOLD BY THE MAYA INSCRIPTIONS

The Maya inscriptions treat primarily of chronology, astronomy—perhaps one might better say astrology—and religious matters. They are in no sense records of personal glorification and self-laudation like the inscriptions of Egypt, Assyria, and Babylonia. They tell no story of kingly conquests, recount no deeds of imperial achievement; they neither praise nor exalt, glorify nor aggrandize, indeed they are so utterly impersonal, so completely nonindividualistic, that it is even probable that the name-glyphs of specific men and women were never recorded upon the Maya monuments.

If not of such familiar matters as wars, conquests, public works, accessions and deaths of rulers, of what then do the Maya inscriptions treat? What is the burden of their story?

First and most important of all was the dedicatory date of each monument, the date in Maya chronology when it was formally put into public service, the so-called Initial Series, usually recorded at the beginning of each inscription. This date was inscribed with such meticulous care that the great majority of dated Old Empire monuments are so accurately fixed in Maya chronology that their dates cannot recur, that is to say, cannot repeat themselves, until after a lapse of 374,440 years, virtual eternity so far as human records are concerned.

We have seen in the preceding chapter that each one of the nineteen divisions of the 365-day calendar year had its own particular deity. The name-glyph of the patron god in whose month the corresponding Initial Series date fell is recorded in the first

hieroglyph of each text in the great majority of Old Empire inscriptions (Fig. 13, p. 234).

Another group of very important deities, also noted in the
previous chapter, was the Bolontiku, or Nine Gods of the Lower
World. The name-glyphs of these nine gods are also recorded on
most Old Empire monuments immediately following the record
of the days over which they respectively and successively presided
(Fig. 12, p. 232).

The priests, very early in the use of the Maya calendar, undoubtedly perceived that having a calendar year of fixed length,
365 days, and no elastic month like our own month of February
with which to take up the extra quarter-day, amounting to very
nearly one whole day every four years, their calendar year had begun to gain upon the true year at a fairly brisk pace, amounting to
as much as fifteen days in the lifetime of a man who lived to be
sixty years of age.

If this discrepancy had continued uncorrected for any length
of time, the stations in the farmers' year—the very *raison d'être*
of their elaborate calendar—would very quickly have become dis-
placed. The time for burning the forest and bush for their cornfields (chapter viii, pp. 144–46), for example, instead of falling
toward the end of the dry season in March or April, as it did at the
beginning, would, according to their 365-day calendar, have crept
backward through the months—February, January, December,
November, October, September, and presently their calendar
would have been telling them to burn at the height of the rainy
season when burning was obviously impossible.

The priests doubtless foresaw this difficulty, insuperable in
any calendar which consists of a changeless 365-day year as did
that of the ancient Maya, and solved it once for all, simply and
effectively.

They must have reasoned something like this: "Let us permit
our calendar year to gain on the true year as fast as it will. Our
calendar year has always consisted of 365 days and we cannot, indeed must not, change our wonderful system of measuring time.
What we can and will do, however, is this: We will allow our

calendar to continue to function without change, but when we erect a monument, we will engrave upon it, in addition to the current official calendar date of its dedication, the *calendar-correction* for that particular date. In this way, no matter what month our calendar may happen to register, for we realize *that all our months move forward through all the seasons, all the way around the year*, we will always know, whenever we erect a monument, the true position of its corresponding date in the true year."

As a matter of fact, this is precisely what the Maya priests did throughout the Old Empire in a kind of corrective, secondary count which has been called the "Secondary Series" by modern students. As monument after monument was erected in the different cities on the successive hotun-, lahuntun-, or katun-endings, as the case might be, almost without exception the corresponding calendar-correction necessary to bring the recorded year position, that is, the recorded month-day, into harmony with the true year-position on any given day was clearly set forth; this correction naturally increased as time went on, the error accumulating at the rate of one day every four years. See a later section of this chapter.

Thus the priests kept the calendar year in harmony with the farmers' year, and the endless round of agricultural duties—felling, burning, planting, and harvesting—went forward smoothly, each coming around to its immemorially appointed season, no matter where the official calendar happened to place it at any given moment.

This awesome knowledge of the movements of the heavenly bodies, this ability to predict eclipses, the appearances and disappearances of Venus from the eastern and western skies as Morning and Evening Star, respectively, must have been a source of tremendous power to the Maya priesthood. It proved to the largely ignorant masses, in a peculiarly convincing way, that their priests held close and intimate communion with some of their greatest deities—the Sun, the Moon, Venus, et cetera—and were correspondingly to be obeyed. The seemingly uncanny familiarity of the priests with the greatest celestial facts of daily life undoubtedly contributed heavily to the respect in which they were held by the common people, some priests, especially the prophets, being so highly venerated, as we have seen in chapter ix (p. 172), that whenever they appeared in public they were carried in litters on the shoulders of bearers (Plate 88, *b*).

But, beyond the foregoing matter, what else do the Maya inscriptions tell? What is the burden of the remaining roughly two-thirds of the undeciphered hieroglyphs?

We cannot answer this question surely as yet, but, judging from the third of the glyphs the meanings of which have been thus far determined, we are perhaps justified in guessing that the undeciphered remainder probably refer to ceremonial matters, offerings, lucky and unlucky days, and to malevolent and benevolent deities connected with the ritualistic year and the special observances with which they were to be severally propitiated.

Certain it is that we shall eventually find hieroglyphs for a group of special moon-gods—the patrons of the six different months of the eclipse period. We may find special hieroglyphs for Venus in her different phases. Some of the unknown signs undoubtedly represent deities; others, the special kinds of offerings with which they were to be propitiated; still others, the special rites with which they were to be severally worshiped, that is to say more and more of ritual, of liturgy, of astrology, and of religion, and less and less of history in the Old World sense of personal or nationalistic records.

MAYA CALENDAR

Since arithmetic and the calendar play such an important part in the Maya inscriptions, a brief description of Maya arithmetic and the Maya calendar is necessary to their better understanding.

TZOLKIN OR SACRED YEAR OF 260 DAYS

In all probability the only part of their highly elaborate calendar and chronology with which the common folk, the corn farmers, the hewers of wood and drawers of water, were familiar was the sacred year of 260 days, the *tzolkin* or "count of days." This time-

Fig. 18.—Glyphs for the twenty Maya days: (*a*) Imix; (*b*) Ik; (*c*) Akbal; (*d*) Kan; (*e*) Chicchan; (*f*) Cimi; (*g*) Manik; (*h*) Lamat; (*i*) Muluc; (*j*) Oc; (*k*) Chuen; (*l*) Eb; (*m*) Ben; (*n*) Ix; (*o*) Men; (*p*) Cib; (*q*) Caban; (*r*) Eznab; (*s*) Cauac; (*t*) Ahau.

period was the most fundamental fact of their religion, since it determined for everybody the very pattern of his or her ceremonial life. The ancient Maya, man or woman, as explained previously (chapter x, p. 181), regarded his or her birthday not as the position in the tropical year, that is the month-day, upon which he was born, as we do, but the day of the *tzolkin*, or 260-day sacred year upon which he was born. The god of the particular day of this 260-day period upon which a man was born was his patron saint, his guardian deity, his celestial godfather, so to speak. Doubtless the god of the month in which he was born was also closer to him than the other eighteen month-gods, but his own particular *tzolkin* god was his strongest protector, his closest ally among the Heavenly Ones. Indeed, we have seen that among the Cakchiquels of the highlands of Guatemala a man took his given name from the day of the *tzolkin* upon which he happened to have been born, as Oxlahuh Tzii (Maya 13 Oc) for example.

The 260 days of the sacred year were formed by prefixing the numbers 1 to 13 inclusive to the twenty Maya day-glyphs, the names of which are given below, beginning with Ik, one of the Old Empire year bearers, and their corresponding hieroglyphs in Figure 18.

Ik	Manik	Eb	Caban
Akbal	Lamat	Ben	Eznab
Kan	Muluc	Ix	Cauac
Chicchan	Oc	Men	Ahau
Cimi	Chuen	Cib	Imix

The Maya calendar, however, had no day named Ik, Akbal, or Kan alone, that is no day-name without an accompanying number, but, instead, each one of the twenty day-names in the list above, as already noted, had a number from 1 to 13 inclusive prefixed to it, thus—1 Ik, 2 Akbal, 3 Kan, and so on. Not until every one of these thirteen numbers had been attached in turn to every one of the twenty day-names given above was a *tzolkin* complete.

If we commence with the number 1, for example, and prefix it to the first name in the list, Ik, viz. 1 Ik, and proceed without

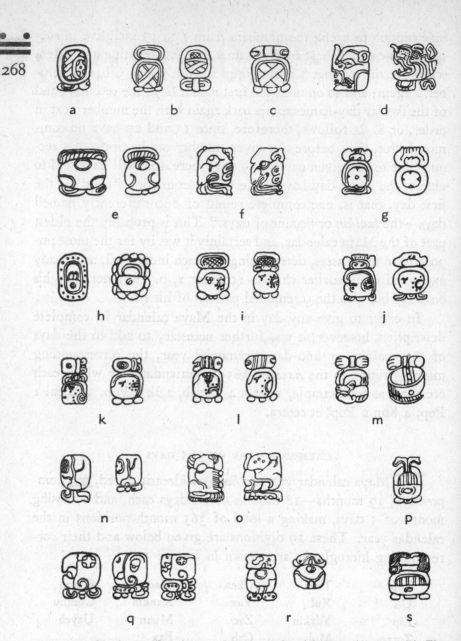

FIG. 19.—Glyphs for the nineteen Maya months: (a) Pop; (b) Uo; (c) Zip; (d) Zotz; (e) Tzec; (f) Xul; (g) Yaxkin; (h) Mol; (i) Chen; (j) Yax; (k) Zac; (l) Ceh; (m) Mac; (n) Kankin; (o) Muan; (p) Pax; (q) Kayab; (r) Cumhu; (s) Uayeb.

interruption to prefix the numbers from 1 to 13 inclusive in succession to each of these twenty names, the fourteenth name, Men, will have the number 1 again; the fifteenth name, Cib, the number 2 again; and so on until the first name, Ik in the second round of the twenty day-names comes back again with the number next in order, or 8. It follows, therefore, since 13 and 20 have no common factor, that, before any given number can be prefixed a second time to any given name, 259 days thereafter will have had to elapse, the 261st day having the same designation "1 Ik" as the first day, that is, one complete round of 260 differently named days—the *tzolkin* or "count of days." This is probably the oldest part of the Maya calendar, and certainly it was by far the most important to the masses, determining for each individual, as already explained in an earlier chapter (chapter x, p. 181) not only his birthday but also the ceremonial pattern of his life.

In order to give any day in the Maya calendar its complete description, however, it was further necessary to add to the days of the *tzolkin,* or 260-day ceremonial year, the corresponding month-position in the *haab* or 365-day calendar year which each occupied, as for example, 1 Imix 4 Uayeb, 2 Ik 0 Pop, 3 Akbal 1 Pop, 4 Kan 2 Pop, et cetera.

CALENDAR YEAR OF 365 DAYS

The Maya calendar year, or *haab,* as already noted, was composed of 19 months—18 months of 20 days each, and 1 closing month of 5 days, making a total of 365 month-positions in the calendar year. These 19 divisions are given below and their corresponding hieroglyphs are shown in Figure 19.

Pop	Tzec	Chen	Mac	Kayab
Uo	Xul	Yax	Kankin	Cumhu
Zip	Yaxkin	Zac	Muan	Uayeb
Zotz	Mol	Ceh	Pax	

In order to show clearly how the 260 days of the *tzolkin* were combined with the 365 positions of the *haab* or calendar year, let us represent them graphically as two cogwheels (Fig. 20), the smaller wheel, *A*, having 260 cogs, each named for one of the 260 days of the *tzolkin*, and the larger wheel, *B*, having 365 cogs, each intercog space being named for one of the 365 positions of the *haab* or calendar year.

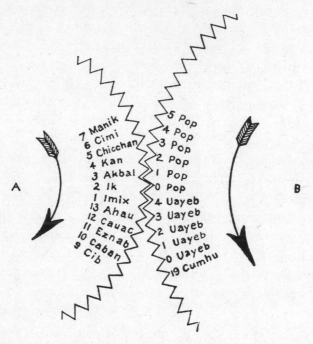

FIG. 20.—Diagram showing the enmeshing of the 365-day calendar year (B) with the 260-day sacred year (A).

Before we can enmesh these two wheels we must know two further facts about the Maya calendar. First, the Maya New Year's Day, or the first day of their first month, was written 0 (zero) Pop, Pop being the first month of the year (see above); and the first position in that month was written 0 rather than 1, as we would write it. This follows from the fact that the Maya regarded time as a series of elapsed periods, and a month position 1 Pop indicated to them the second day of Pop rather than the first day. This latter method is the way we number the hours of the day. For example, when we say one o'clock, in reality the

first hour after noon is gone and we are about to start the second
hour. So it was with the ancient Maya when they wrote 1 Pop;
the first day, 0 Pop, had already passed and the second day
(written 1 Pop) was about to commence. It follows from the
foregoing that although the Maya months were each 20 days in
length, except the last which had but 5 days, their month-positions
were numbered from 0 to 19 inclusive, and in the case of the last
month from 0 to 4 inclusive, and *not* as we would have numbered
them from 1 to 20 inclusive and 1 to 5 inclusive in the case of the
last month. This makes the first day of the Maya year 0 Pop, and
not 1 Pop as we would write it.

The second fact we must know before combining the *tzolkin*
with the *haab* is that only 52 of the 260 differently named days
of the former could ever occupy the first position of the *haab*,
or indeed, the first position of any one of its 19 divisions. These
52 days are those in which the names Ik, Manik, Eb, and Caban
appear (at the tops of the four columns on page 267), and since
each one of these names had the number 1 to 13 inclusive prefixed
to it in turn, it results that only 52, or 4 x 13, of the 260 different
days of the *tzolkin* could begin the Maya calendar year or any one
of its 19 divisions. These 52 possible Maya New Year's Days, or
year-bearers as they have been called, fell, during the Old
Empire, upon the following days:

1 Ik	1 Manik	1 Eb	1 Caban	1 Ik
2 Manik	2 Eb	2 Caban	2 Ik	2 Manik
3 Eb	3 Caban	3 Ik	3 Manik	etc, etc.
4 Caban	4 Ik	4 Manik	4 Eb	
5 Ik	5 Manik	5 Eb	5 Caban	
6 Manik	6 Eb	6 Caban	6 Ik	
7 Eb	7 Caban	7 Ik	7 Manik	
8 Caban	8 Ik	8 Manik	8 Eb	
9 Ik	9 Manik	9 Eb	9 Caban	
10 Manik	10 Eb	10 Caban	10 Ik	
11 Eb	11 Caban	11 Ik	11 Manik	
12 Caban	12 Ik	12 Manik	12 Eb	
13 Ik	13 Manik	13 Eb	13 Caban	

It should be observed, however, that at the time of the Spanish Conquest, the days with which the Maya New Year began had shifted forward two positions, and that instead of beginning with days named Ik, Manik, Eb, or Caban, they began with days named Kan, Muluc, Ix, or Cauac (p. 267).

CALENDAR ROUND

We are now in position to bring together, or enmesh, the two wheels in Figure 20, A representing the *tzolkin* and B the *haab* or calendar year. Let us do this in such a way that the cog of Wheel A, named after the day "2 Ik" of the *tzolkin*, will fit into the intercog-space on Wheel B corresponding to the Maya New Year's Day or position "0 Pop," giving the complete designation of this particular day as "2 Ik 0 Pop."

Now let us revolve both wheels, A to the right like the hands of a clock, and B to the left, counterclockwise. Our problem is to find out how many complete revolutions each wheel will have to make before the cog named "2 Ik" on Wheel A will return to the intercog-space named "0 Pop" on Wheel B.

This problem is an old arithmetical friend of grammar school days—the least common multiple. We must first ascertain the least common multiple of 260 and 365, during which process we shall also have ascertained how many complete revolutions the two wheels in Figure 20 will have to make before any one of the 260 different cogs of Wheel A will return to the same intercog-space of Wheel B from which it started, in a complete number of revolutions of each wheel.

Both 260 and 365 are divisible by 5, the first giving a quotient of 52, the second one of 73, but there is no further common factor, so the least common multiple of 260 and 365 is 5×52×73 =18,980; therefore our first wheel, A, will make 73 complete revolutions, while the second wheel, B, will make 52 complete revolutions before cog "2 Ik" of Wheel A will return to intercog-space "0 Pop" of Wheel B in a complete number of revolutions of each.

Translating this problem of arithmetic back into terms of the

Maya calendar, we may say that before any given day of the
tzolkin could return to any given position of the *haab,* 73 *tzolkins*
or 52 *haab,* or 18,980 days would have had to have elapsed. This
is true since $73 \times 260 = 52 \times 365 = 18,980$ days.

In other words, once every 52 *haab* or calendar years of 365
days each, any given day, for example, "2 Ik," coincided with
the first position of the year, "o Pop," and this combination, or
any other combination possible, recurred thereafter at intervals
of 52 years each, throughout time. Thus any Maya who lived
more than 52 years began to see New Year's Days of exactly the
same name or, in fact, any other given days repeat themselves.

We do not know the ancient Maya name, or even the hieroglyph for this period of $52 \times 365 = 18,980$ days, important as
it must have been, but modern students of the Maya calendar
have called it the Calendar Round, because in this period of time
the 260 days of the *tzolkin* will have occupied all of the 365
positions in the *haab* possible for them to occupy before the
sequence will have begun to repeat itself, that is, one complete
round of the 18,980 possible dates or 1 Calendar Round.

Not one of the peoples of Middle America who probably
borrowed their respective calendars from the Maya, such as the
Aztecs, the Mixtec, and the Zapotec for example, ever devised
or made use of any time period higher than this 18,980-day
period (52 years of 365 days). The Aztecs, for example, conceived time as an endless succession of these 52×365 day-periods
to which they gave the name *xiuhmolpilli,* meaning in their language "year bundle," that is to say, the complete round of the
years.

The Aztec had two special glyphs for this period, arising
directly from their beliefs concerning it. The first was a knot
(Fig. 21, *a*) indicating thereby that the bundle of 52 years had
been tied up, finished, or completed at the end of this period, and
the second was the fire-drill and stick for kindling the Sacred
Fire (Fig. 21, *b*). The Aztec believed that the world would come
to an end only at the close of one of these 52-year periods; and
on the last night of the *xiuhmolpilli,* we are told, the population

of Tenochtitlan (Mexico City) withdrew to the hills surrounding the city to await the coming of dawn. When the sun rose on that morning, there was general rejoicing, the Sacred Fire was rekindled, the houses were cleaned and set in order and the business of life was resumed as usual. The gods had given mankind another 52-year lease of life.

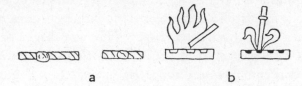

a   b

FIG. 21.—Aztec glyphs for the *xiuhmolpilli* or 52-year period: (*a*) two examples of the knot; (*b*) two examples of the stick and drill for kindling the sacred fire.

Neither the Maya name nor the corresponding glyph for this highly important time period is known, although it was almost certainly a Maya conception originally, being the basis of their calendar system.

The Maya, like the Aztec, also conceived time as an endless succession of these 18,980 different possible combinations of the 260 days (the *tzolkin*) and the 365 different positions of the calendar year (*haab*); but at a very early date, probably as early as the fourth century before the beginning of the Christian Era, they perceived that even the first few multiples only of this period —37,960, 56,940, 75,920, 94,900, 113,880, etc.—would involve them immediately in complex numbers, which became increasingly difficult to handle as time went on.

MAYA ARITHMETIC

In order to escape such rapidly mounting calendric chaos, the ancient Maya priests devised a simple numerical system which even today, more than two thousand years later, stands as one of the most brilliant achievements of the human mind.

Some time during the fourth or third centuries before Christ, the Maya priests *for the first time in the history of the human race devised a system of numeration by position, involving the conception and use of the mathematical quantity of zero*, a tremendous abstract intellectual accomplishment.

Formerly it was believed, and not so many years ago either, that positional mathematics and the conception of zero which it involves had been developed but once in human history, namely, by the Hindus who devised the decimal notation with its accompanying numerical symbols about the eighth century of the Christian Era. From India this decimal numerical system passed to Arabia, hence the term Arabic numerals, and was carried from Arabia by the Arabs into Egypt. From northern Africa the Moors introduced it into Spain, and it did not come into general use among our own ancestors of western Europe until the fifteenth century—about seven hundred years after its invention in southern central Asia.

We now know, however, that the ancient Maya had developed their own system of positional mathematics, based upon 20 as its unit of progression instead of 10, that is, vigesimal instead of decimal, at least a thousand years earlier than its invention in the Old World by the Hindus and nearly two thousand years before positional mathematics came into general use among our own ancestors of western Europe.

But for a single break in the third order of units to make the third order approximate the length of the solar year as nearly as possible, the Maya vigesimal system is almost as simple as our own decimal system.

The unit of the Maya calendar was the day or *kin*. The second order of units, consisting of 20 *kins*, was called the *uinal*. In a perfect vigesimal system of numeration, the third term should be 400, that is, 20 × 20 × 1, but at this point, *in counting time only*, the Maya introduced a single variation, in order to make the period of their third order agree in length with their calendar year as nearly as possible. The third order of the Maya vigesimal system, the *tun*, therefore, was composed of 18 (instead of 20) *uinals*, or 360 (instead of 400) *kins*; 360 days or *kins* being a much closer approximation to the length of the 365-day calendar year than 400 days.

Above the third order, however, the unit of progression used to form all the higher numbers is uniformly 20, as will be seen below, where the names and numerical values of the nine known different orders of time periods are given:

20 *kins*	= 1 *uinal* or 20 days
18 *uinals*	= 1 *tun* or 360 days
20 *tuns*	= 1 *katun* or 7,200 days
20 *katuns*	= 1 *baktun** or 144,000 days
20 *baktuns*	= 1 *pictun* or 2,880,000 days
20 *pictuns*	= 1 *calabtun* or 57,600,000 days
20 *calabtuns*	= 1 *kinchiltun* or 1,152,000,000 days
20 *kinchiltuns*	= 1 *alautun* or 23,040,000,000 days

* The period of the fifth order, the *baktun*, was originally called the "cycle" by modern investigators. The ancient name for this period, however, was probably *baktun* as given above.

The break in the third order of units mentioned above, 360 instead of 400, the latter of which is the correct value of the third term in a strictly vigesimal system, however, was used only *in counting time;* in counting everything else the Maya followed the vigesimal progression consistently—1, 20, 400 (instead of 360), 8,000 (instead of 7,200), 160,000 (instead of 144,000), 3,200,000 (instead of 2,880,000), and so on.

TWO FORMS FOR EACH MAYA GLYPH

Practically speaking every Maya hieroglyph occurs in two forms in the inscriptions—(1) what has been called the normal or regular form and (2) a head-variant, the latter being the head of a deity, man, animal, bird, serpent, or even some mythological creature who lived only in the minds of his creators; and very, very rarely (only seven examples known), there is a third form where the glyph is the full figure of a deity, man, animal, bird, or serpent.

The glyphs for the foregoing nine time periods are given in Figure 22, normal forms at the left, head-variants at the right. In the cases of the last three periods, corresponding head-variants have not been identified as yet.

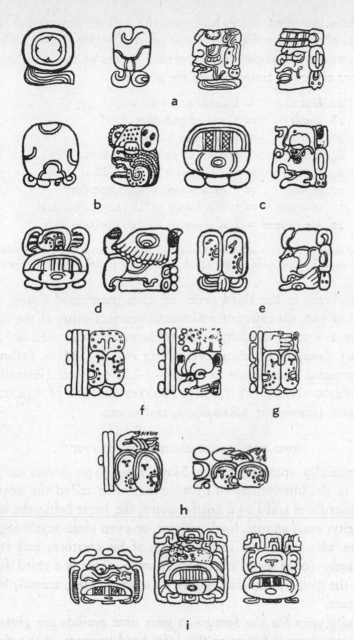

Fig. 22.—Glyphs for the nine known Maya time-periods: (*a*) *kin*; (*b*) *uinal*; (*c*) *tun*; (*d*) *katun*; (*e*) *baktun*; (*f*) *pictun*; (*g*) *calabtun*; (*h*) *kinchiltun*; (*i*) *alautun* or Initial Series introducing-glyph.

Like ourselves, the ancient Maya made use of two different notations in writing their numbers: (1) bar-and-dot numerals which may be compared to our own Roman notation, and (2) head-variant numerals, which may be likened to our Arabic notation.

In the first notation, the dot • has a numerical value of I and the bar —— a numerical value of V, and by varying combinations of these two symbols, the numbers from I to XIX inclusive were written as shown in Figure 23. The numbers *above* XIX, however, involved the use of their positional mathematical system, already mentioned, and will be described later.

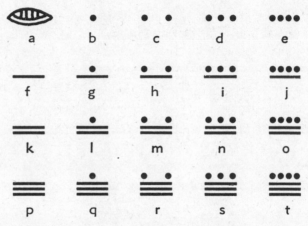

FIG. 23.—Glyphs for the numbers o and I to XIX inclusive, in bar-and-dot notation, the Maya "Roman Notation": (*a*) zero; (*b*) I; (*c*) II; (*d*) III; (*e*) IV; (*f*) V; (*g*) VI; (*h*) VII; (*i*) VIII; (*j*) IX; (*k*) X; (*l*) XI; (*m*) XII; (*n*) XIII; (*o*) XIV; (*p*) XV; (*q*) XVI; (*r*) XVII; (*s*) XVIII; (*t*) XIX.

It is readily apparent from Figure 23 that the Maya bar-and-dot notation was superior to Roman notation in two respects. To write the numbers from I to XIX inclusive in Roman notation, it is necessary to employ three symbols—the letters I, V, and X— and two arithmetical processes—addition and subtraction: VI is V plus I, but IV is V minus I.

On the other hand, in Maya bar-and-dot notation, in order to write the numbers from I to XIX inclusive, it is necessary to employ only two symbols—the dot and the bar—and only one arithmetical process, namely addition. In other words, Maya bar-and-dot notation used not only one symbol less to write the numbers from I to XIX inclusive than Roman notation requires, but also one arithmetical process less.

The second notation employed by the ancient Maya in writing their numbers made use of different types of human heads to represent the numbers from 1 to 13, inclusive, and zero. The Maya head-notation is comparable to our own Arabic notation, wherein there are ten different symbols representing zero and the first nine numbers—0, 1, 2, 3, 4, 5, 6, 7, 8, and 9. These fourteen Maya head-variant numerals are nothing more nor less than the heads of the patron deities of the first fourteen numbers described in the preceding chapter.

It will be remembered that in forming the days of the *tzolkin*, 13 numbers from 1 to 13 inclusive were prefixed to the glyphs for the twenty days in succession. There is evidence that the ancient Maya regarded the first thirteen numbers and zero as *the primary numbers*, since each one of them has a special head to represent it, that is each of those numbers has its own patron deity (Plate 30, *a*).[2]

The head-variant for 10 is the death's head, or skull, and in forming the head-variants for the numbers from 14 to 19 inclusive, the fleshless lower jaw of the death's head (Plate 30, *a*) was the part used to represent the value of 10 in these composite heads for these six higher numbers. Thus if the fleshless lower jaw is applied to the lower part of the head for 6, which is characterized by a pair of crossed sticks in the large eye socket, the resulting head will be that for 16; that is, 10 + 6 (see Plate 30, *a*, where, to the head for 6, a fleshless lower jaw has been attached). Or again, if this same fleshless lower jaw is applied to the lower part of the head for 9, which is characterized by a circle of dots on the lower cheek (Plate 30, *a*), the resulting head will be that for 19; or 10 + 9; further, by applying the fleshless lower jaw to the

[2] The head-variant for the number 11 has not yet been surely identified.

heads for 4, 5, 7, and 8 (Plate 30, *a*), the heads for 14, 15, 17, and 18, respectively, are also obtained.

It is not improbable that the 13 heads representing the 13 numbers from 1 to 13 inclusive are those of the *Oxlahuntiku* or Thirteen Gods of the Upper World as opposed to the *Bolontiku* or Nine Gods of the Lower World, and that each one of the former was associated with one of these thirteen numbers, being its especial patron.

MAYA VIGESIMAL SYSTEM OF MATHEMATICS

In order to write the numbers *above* the first order of units, (those above 19), the ancient Maya made use of their positional system of numeration. In our own decimal system, the positions to the *left* of the decimal point *increase by tens from right to left* —units, tens, hundreds, thousands, etc. In the Maya positional system, however, the values of the positions *increase by twenties from bottom to top, with the single exception of the third position which, in counting time alone, is only 18 instead of 20 times the second*, an irregularity already mentioned.

To illustrate this, let us see how the Maya would have written various numbers of days above 20, selected at random. Take for example, the number 20 itself. This is 1 complete unit of the second order and no units of the first order, and thus involves two symbols, a symbol for zero in the first or lowest position to show that no units of the first order are involved in the number, and one unit of the second order.

One of the commonest symbols for zero in the Maya hiero- glyphic writing was the conventionalized shell (the lower or first symbol in Fig. 24, *a*), and by placing a shell ⬭ in the first or lowest position to denote 0 units of the first order and a dot • in the second position to denote 1 unit of the second order, the number 20 was written (Fig. 24, *a*).

The number 37 was written as shown in Figure 24, *b*, that is, 17 units of the first order and 1 unit of the second order; the number 300 as shown in Figure 24, *c*, that is, 0 units of the first order and 15 units of the second order. The number 360, the

third order of units, was written as shown in Figure 24, *d*, that is,
0 units of the first order, 0 units of the second order, and 1 unit
of the third order of days.

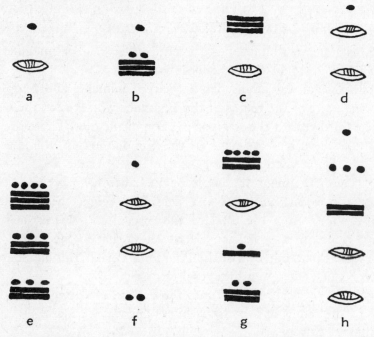

<small>Fig. 24.—Examples of Maya numbers above XIX in bar-and-dot notation: (*a*)
20; (*b*) 37; (*c*) 300; (*d*) 360; (*e*) 7,113; (*f*) 7,202; (*g*) 100,932; (*h*)
169,200.</small>

The number 7,113 was written as shown in Figure 24, *e*, that
is, 13 units of the first order, 13 units of the second order, and 19
units of the third order. The number 7,202, involving four orders
of time units, is shown in Figure 24, *f*, or 2 units of the first order,
0 units of the second order, 0 units of the third order, and 1 unit
of the fourth order. The number 100,932 is shown in Figure
24, *g*, or 12 units of the first order, 6 units of the second order,
0 units of the third order, and 14 units of the fourth order.
Finally the number 169,200, involving five orders of time units,
is shown in Figure 24, *h*, or 0 units of the first order, 0 units of
the second order, 10 units of the third order, 3 units of the fourth
order, and 1 unit of the fifth order.

STARTING POINT OF THE SYSTEM

In addition to this masterpiece of mathematical achievement, the ancient Maya seem to have been the first people anywhere in the world to have perceived the necessity for having a fixed base, or starting point, some definite event, either real or imaginary, from which to count their chronological era.

The ancient Egyptians dated their monuments and temples from the years of the reigns of the Pharaohs who erected them— "In the third year of the reign of the Son of the Sun, Thutmose"; "In the fifth year of the reign of the Son of the Sun, Rameses," etc. But this method of dating was relatively crude and inaccurate. If no monument or temple happened to have been erected during the closing years of any particular reign, these closing years dropped from the total of the record, and this error was always cumulative, never compensative, so that in the course of the several thousand years of the Pharaonic Period, this one source of error alone amounted to several centuries.

Even until fairly recent times the custom of dating from the years of the reigns of successive sovereigns was a general practice throughout Europe.

Most peoples, however, sooner or later have realized the necessity of having a fixed starting point from which all their chronological records could be counted; but the indications are that the ancient Maya were the first of all peoples to reach this important and, chronologically speaking, basic concept.

The specific events, selected by different peoples of the world at different times for the starting points of their respective chronologies, may be classified into two general groups: (1) those starting from specific historical events, and (2) those starting from obviously hypothetical, that is to say assumed, events.

The most familiar chronology of the first group is our own Christian Era, the starting point of which is the birth of Christ, our years being reckoned as B.C. (Before Christ) or A.D. (Anno Domini—"In the Year of Our Lord"), according as they precede or follow this event.

The Greeks reckoned time by four-year periods called Olym-
piads from the earliest Olympic Festival of which the winner's
name was known, namely, from the games held in 776 B.C., the
winner of which was a certain Coroebus. The Romans took as
their starting point the supposed foundation of Rome by Romulus
and Remus in 753 B.C., counting their years from this event.

The Babylonian chronological epoch was called the "Era of
Nabonassar," and dated from the beginning of that king's reign
in 747 B.C. The death of Alexander the Great in 325 B.C. ushered
in the "Era of Alexander." With the occupation of Babylon in
311 B.C. by Seleucus Nicator began the so-called "Era of the
Seleucidae." The conquest of Spain by Augustus Caesar in 38 B.C.
marked the beginning of a chronology which endured for more
than fourteen centuries in the Iberian Peninsula. The Moham-
medans selected as the starting point of their chronology the
Flight of the Prophet Mohammed from Mecca in A.D. 622, events
being described in Mohammedan chronology as having occurred
so many years after the Hegira or Flight. Indeed, this last chronology has persisted in Turkey down to within the past two decades, having finally been abolished by Kemal Pasha.

It will be noted that every one of the foregoing chronological
systems has for its starting point some actual historical event, the
occurrence, if not the date, of which is indubitable. There are,
however, other chronologies, those belonging to the second group
mentioned above, that begin with an event the very nature of
which renders the date of its starting point necessarily hypothetical. Here should be included those chronologies which reckon
time from a supposititious date of the creation of the world.

For example, the "Era of Constantinople," the chronological
system used in the Greek Church, commences with the Creation,
which is reckoned as having taken place in 5509 B.C. The Jews
consider the same event as having taken place in 3761 B.C. and
begin their era at that time. Perhaps the most familiar example of
a chronology belonging to this second group is that of the old
family Bible, which fixes the creation of man, that is the birth of
Adam, as having occurred in 4004 B.C. Archbishop Usher is re-

sponsible for this chronology, having naïvely fixed the date of Adam's birth by adding the years of the generations beginning with Adam and ending with Joseph, the father of Christ as given in the Bible (the Book of Genesis and the Gospel according to St. Matthew), reaching a total of 4,004 years.

While we do not know the nature of the event with which the ancient Maya began their chronology, it is practically certain that it was hypothetical rather than historical.

This is true because the zero date of the Maya chronological era, "4 Ahau 8 Cumhu," precedes their earliest contemporary records—the Leyden Plate and Stela 9 at Uaxactun (chapter iii, p. 43) by 3,433 years and 3,440 years respectively. In other words for more than 3,400 years after the beginning of their time count —that is, during the first 8 *baktuns* and nearly through the ninth *baktun*—there is not a single contemporary date; of the Maya Era the first record occurs in 8.14.3.1.12. This can mean only one thing, namely, that the starting point of Maya chronology was selected as such a very long time (probably nearly 3,000 years) *after* it was actually current time; and further, that this long blank period, devoid of contemporaneous records of any kind, probably is to be interpreted simply as a priestly approximation of past time as a whole, rather than regarded as a chronological era that had been in use for more than three thousand years before its first records appear.

It was suggested on page 47 that the actual inauguration of the Maya calendar probably took place in 7.0.0.0.0, or 7.6.0.0.0 of the Maya Era—either 2,760 or 2,878 years after its zero date. In view of this fact and in view of the absence of all contemporary records dating from the first three thousand four hundred years of the Maya Era, we are forced to conclude that the astronomer-priests who devised Maya chronology selected for its starting point a date 7 *baktuns* (2,760 years) earlier than the date of its actual inauguration. Therefore it seems much more likely that Maya chronology began with some hypothetical event, rather than with an actual historical occurrence. Possibly it may have commenced with a supposititious event like the creation of the world, from which the chronologies used in the Greek and Jewish Churches, as well as in the old family Bible, are reckoned. Perhaps it may even have been counted from the supposed date of the birth of their gods, in which indefinite and remote past we must leave this question as yet undetermined.

THE INITIAL SERIES, OR LONG COUNT

The Initial Series method of dating was first so named by A. P. Maudslay, the English archaeologist and explorer. When it occurs, this time count is usually found at the beginning of the inscription; hence the name "Initial Series," which Maudslay gave to it.

Ernst Förstemann, the German archaeologist, first worked out the details of the Initial Series count as they are presented in the codices, in 1887. J. T. Goodman, the American archaeologist, though better known as the man who gave Mark Twain his first literary job as cub reporter on the *Virginia City Enterprise* of Virginia City, Nevada, first deciphered this time count in the inscriptions on the monuments in 1890, basing his work on Maudslay's magnificent reproductions of Maya sculptures. Goodman's discoveries, made quite without knowledge of Förstemann's slightly earlier investigations, are in perfect agreement with the latter's findings and prove beyond all possibility of doubt that the ancient Maya Initial Series time count is now as clearly understood as our own Gregorian calendar.

A brief description of a typical Initial Series follows: At the beginning stands a large glyph, usually four times as large as the other glyphs in the inscription, which has been called the introducing-glyph because it "introduces" the Initial Series time count (Fig. 25). The only part of this large initial glyph which varies in the different inscriptions (except for minor differences in style) is the central element, of which there are nineteen different forms, one for each of the nineteen divisions or months of the Maya calendar year, already described (Fig. 13, p. 234). These variable central elements, in all probability, as suggested in the preceding chapter, are the name-glyphs of the deities who presided

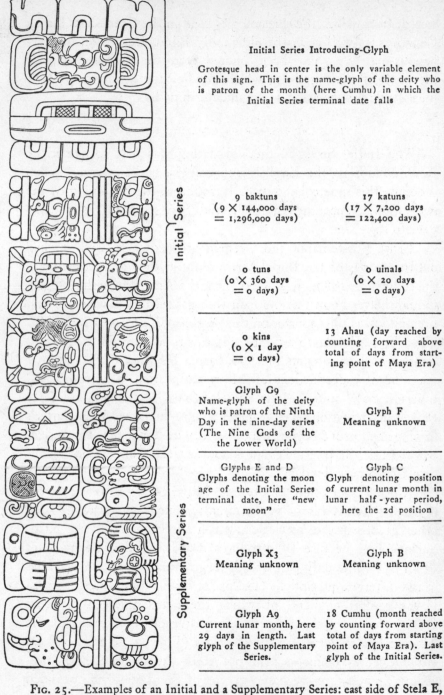

Initial Series (label along left side of glyph column)

Supplementary Series (label along left side of glyph column)

Initial Series Introducing-Glyph

Grotesque head in center is the only variable element of this sign. This is the name-glyph of the deity who is patron of the month (here Cumhu) in which the Initial Series terminal date falls

9 baktuns (9 × 144,000 days = 1,296,000 days)	17 katuns (17 × 7,200 days = 122,400 days)
0 tuns (0 × 360 days = 0 days)	0 uinals (0 × 20 days = 0 days)
0 kins (0 × 1 day = 0 days)	13 Ahau (day reached by counting forward above total of days from starting point of Maya Era)
Glyph G9 Name-glyph of the deity who is patron of the Ninth Day in the nine-day series (The Nine Gods of the the Lower World)	Glyph F Meaning unknown
Glyphs E and D Glyphs denoting the moon age of the Initial Series terminal date, here "new moon"	Glyph C Glyph denoting position of current lunar month in lunar half-year period, here the 2d position
Glyph X3 Meaning unknown	Glyph B Meaning unknown
Glyph A9 Current lunar month, here 29 days in length. Last glyph of the Supplementary Series.	18 Cumhu (month reached by counting forward above total of days from starting point of Maya Era). Last glyph of the Initial Series.

FIG. 25.—Examples of an Initial and a Supplementary Series: east side of Stela E, Quirigua, Department of Izabal, Guatemala.

over the nineteen divisions or months of the year. The form recorded in any given introducing-glyph is probably that of the name-glyph of the specific deity who was patron of the month in which the corresponding Initial Series terminal date fell, here the god of the month, Cumhu (Fig. 13).

Maya inscriptions are to be read from left to right and top to bottom in pairs of columns so that the two columns of smaller glyphs immediately below the large introducing-glyph in Figure 25 are to be read from left to right and top to bottom.

The first five glyphs in these two columns, following this order of reading, are the number of baktuns, katuns, tuns, uinals, and kins involved in writing this particular date, that is, the periods of 144,000, 7,200, 360, 20, and 1 days, respectively, that have elapsed from the starting point of Maya chronology—the date 4 Ahau 8 Cumhu, described above but not actually recorded— down to the date reached by this particular Initial Series number.

Although the unit of the Maya Initial Series is the day, while that of our own Christian chronology is the year, the two systems are not unlike in their respective methods of record. For example, when we write the date Monday, December 31, A.D. 1945, we mean that 1 period of one thousand years, 9 periods of one hundred years, 4 periods of ten years and 5 periods of one year have elapsed since the birth of Christ, the starting point of our own chronology, called "Anno Domini," (abbreviated to A.D.) meaning "In the Year of Our Lord," to reach a day Monday, which was the 31st day of the month of December.

Similarly, when the ancient Maya wrote the Initial Series 9.17.0.0.0 13 Ahau 18 Cumhu, shown in Figure 25, they meant that 9 periods of 144,000 days (9 baktuns), 17 periods of 7,200 days (17 katuns), 0 periods of 360 days (0 tuns), 0 periods of 20 days (0 uinals) and 0 periods of 1 day (0 kins) had elapsed since the starting point of their chronology, 4 Ahau 8 Cumhu (unexpressed, but assumed), until the day "13 Ahau" which occupied the month-position "18 Cumhu," was reached.

The day of this terminal date—here "13 Ahau"—is usually found (nine out of ten times) in the sixth position after the in-

troducing-glyph, or immediately following the fifth and last time
period (the kins) of the Initial Series number (Fig. 25).

In almost all cases, the glyph immediately following the day
of the Initial Series terminal date, the one in the seventh position
after the large introducing-glyph (Fig. 25), is called Glyph G,
and has already been described in the preceding chapter. It has
nine forms, one corresponding to each of the *Bolontiku*, or "Nine
Gods of the Lower World," referring in each inscription to that
particular one of these nine gods who was the patron of the specific
day of the Maya Chronological Era, reached by the accompanying Initial Series number. In the Initial Series here described, the
day-patron was the sun-god, patron of the Ninth Day (Fig. 25).
See also Figure 12 (p. 232). And following this last glyph is
another of unknown meaning, Glyph F, the last sign of the Initial
Series, except for the corresponding month part which follows
immediately after the last glyph of the Supplementary Series.

THE SUPPLEMENTARY SERIES, OR MOON COUNT

Between Glyph F and the corresponding month part (the position of the day in the calendar year), here "18 Cumhu," of the
Initial Series, there usually stands a group of six glyphs which
have been called the Supplementary Series, since they supplement
the meaning of the Initial Series. They give information (1)
about the moon on the date recorded by the accompanying Initial
Series, that is the age of the moon, probably counted from new
moon; (2) the length of the particular lunar month in which the
Initial Series date fell, that is, whether it was composed of 29 or
30 days, here 29 days; (3) the number of the particular lunation
in the lunar half-year period, here 2; and a few other as yet
undetermined points. Finally, following the last glyph of the
Supplementary Series is the month-glyph of the Initial Series
terminal date, in the text illustrated here, "18 Cumhu" (Fig. 25).

And thus by means of their simple, yet highly efficient,
vigesimal numerical system, as expressed in their amazingly accurate Initial Series or Long Count, the ancient Maya were able
to fix any given date in their chronology with such a high degree

of precision that it could not recur, fulfilling all the prescribed conditions, until after a lapse of 374,440 years—a truly colossal achievement for any chronological system, whether ancient or modern.

THE SECONDARY SERIES, OR CALENDAR-CORRECTION FORMULAE

A third count in the Maya inscriptions is the so-called Secondary Series, which would seem to have been in the nature of calendar-correction formulae, somewhat like our own bissextile, or leap-year corrections. The ancient Maya, as already noted, had a calendar year composed of only 365 days, and it is evident that from the very beginning of its use their calendar year soon began to gain upon the true tropical year; the seasons and various stations of the agricultural year rapidly fell behind their corresponding positions as indicated by the Maya calendar. Further, since the ancient Maya had no elastic month like our own month of February, which usually has 28 days, though every fourth year (generally speaking) it has an extra day added to it so as to take care of the accumulated error of nearly one day in four years, some other method had to be devised for keeping the calendar year of 365 days from running *ahead* of the true year of nearly 365¼ days. In order to effect this correction in their calendar, the Maya seem to have devised the Secondary Series.

To express any single day in the Maya Chronological Era by means of the Initial Series method of dating, ten different glyphs were necessary, as we have just seen. Although this method of dating was of almost unbelievable accuracy, it was, nevertheless, quite cumbersome, requiring no fewer than ten different signs to express a single day. Moreover, its repetition for every additional date in an inscription was superfluous, since, if in any inscription one date was fixed in their chronological era by means of the record of its corresponding Initial Series, other dates could be calculated therefrom by either addition or subtraction. Such secondary dates, derived from the Initial Series date either by subtraction therefrom if earlier than the Initial Series date,

290

or by addition thereto if later, have been called Secondary Series, because they are secondary to the Initial Series.

The Secondary Series as calendar-correction formulae seem to have worked somewhat as follows. Let us take, for example, the date 9.16.0.0.0 2 Ahau 13 Tzec of the Maya Era (751, May 9). Counting from July 16 (July 26 Gregorian)—that is, from the Maya New Year's Day, o Pop—the month-position 13 Tzec above actually fell on October 27 (Gregorian) in 751, or nearly six months after the Maya calendar said it would fall—171 days *later* to be exact. The priests knew this perfectly well, and in order to correct this error devised the following calendar-correction formula—8 uinals and 11 kins, which was the Maya way of expressing 171 days, or 8 periods of 20 days, or 160 days + 11 periods of 1 day, or 11 days. This period (8.11) was then counted *forward* from 9.16.0.0.0 2 Ahau 13 Tzec to reach a new date 9.16.0.8.11 4 Chuen 4 Kankin (751, October 27), which was the position 13 Tzec originally occupied in the tropical year but which calendar gains by 9.16.0.0.0 actually had brought around 171 days earlier, so that, by this particular katun-ending of Maya chronology, the position in the year originally represented by 13 Tzec, or October 27, now fell on May 9, or on the month-position 7 Muan of the Maya year. It is certain that the common people knew nothing about, indeed could not have understood, these abstract priestly calculations; what the priests told them was something much more simple, perhaps like this, "Our calendar says that on the katun-ending 9.16.0.0.0 2 Ahau 13 Tzec of our era, the rainy season should be almost over (*13 Tzec =* October 27), but in reality the rains are just beginning (May 9), therefore, before we can celebrate the festival appropriate to 13 Tzec, or to the end of the rains on October 27, we must let 171 days more go by from May 9 until 9.16.0.8.11 4 Chuen 4 Kankin (751, October 27), when the end of the rains will have returned again (October 27). This we must do in order to have the festival which our gods originally fixed for 13 Tzec still fall at the end of the rainy season, as it originally did."

Thus the Secondary Series were used as calendar-correction

formulae for bringing the calendar year of 365 days into harmony
with the tropical year of very nearly 365¼ days (365.24 pretty
closely expresses the fractional day), which is the identical purpose of our own bissextile correction.

THE U KAHLAY KATUNOB, OR SHORT COUNT

As early as the beginning of the Great Period of the Old
Empire (731) the extremely accurate Initial Series dating was
beginning to pass out of current use, being replaced by a more
abbreviated system, which modern students have called "Period-
Ending dating." In this method of dating only some specific
time-period and the date upon which it ended are stated, as for
example in the Initial Series 9.16.0.0.0 2 Ahau 13 Tzec just mentioned, this long record requiring ten glyphs to express it is
reduced to only three glyphs: (1) Katun 16 ending on (Fig.
26, *a*); (2) the day 2 Ahau (Fig. 26, *b*); and (3) the month-
position 13 Tzec (Fig. 26, *c*). While not so accurate as an Initial
Series, which, as we have seen, was exact to a day within a period
of 374,400 years, nevertheless a period-ending date, giving the
katun number (16 in the example above) and both the day and
month-position of the terminal date (2 Ahau 13 Tzec here),
was exact to a day within a period of nearly 19,000 years.

a   b   c

FIG. 26.—Period-ending date: Katun 16 ending on 2 Ahau 13 Tzec, corresponding to the Initial Series 9.16.0.0.0 2 Ahau 13 Tzec. (*a*) end of Katun 16;
(*b*) 2 Ahau; (*c*) 13 Tzec.

However, by late New Empire times, the Maya chronological
system suffered even further abbreviation, and this time so sharply
that accuracy within a period of only 256 years could be achieved.
This new system, also based on the old Long Count, was called in
New Empire times the *u kahlay katunob*, or "Count of the

Katuns," what Maya students have called the "Short Count," in contradistinction to the Initial Series, or "Long Count."

Going back to our previous example, the Initial Series, 9.16.0.0.0 2 *Ahau* 13 Tzec, which coincides with an even katun-ending of the Long Count, the day upon which this particular katun ended was "2 Ahau," and, in the *u kahlay katunob* method of dating, everything else was eliminated except this ending-day; that is to say all the specific time periods, the 9 baktuns, the 16 katuns, the 0 tuns, the 0 uinals, and the 0 kins, and the month-part of the terminal date, or 13 Tzec, were suppressed. This particular katun was known simply as Katun 2 Ahau, that is simply as a katun which ended on a day 2 Ahau.

This method of dating had the merit of requiring only one glyph to express it—any given day Ahau *plus the understanding* that this day ended some katun of the Long Count. To be sure, such abbreviated katun-ending dates were accurate only to within a period of 256¼ years, which is to say that any given katun-ending, as for example Katun 2 Ahau, recurred at intervals of every 256¼ years. Thus if a Katun 2 Ahau ended in 751, another Katun 2 Ahau would end in 1007, another in 1263, etc. This is true because there were only thirteen differently named katuns in this method of dating, that is, the thirteen different days Ahau—1 Ahau, 2 Ahau, 3 Ahau, etc.—and since each katun was 19.71 years long, a katun of any given name, as for example, 2 Ahau, could return after a lapse of 13 katuns or 13 × 19.71 years =256¼ years.

It should be pointed out that the katuns of the *u kahlay katunob* were named after their *last* days in each case, and that their successive last days did *not* follow each other in an ordinary ascending numerical sequence, as for example: Katun 1 Ahau, Katun 2 Ahau, Katun 3 Ahau, etc., but in an entirely different order in which the number of the day Ahau with which each successive katun ended and after which it was named was *two less* than that of the *last* day of the preceding katun, viz., Katun 13 Ahau, Katun 11 Ahau, Katun 9 Ahau, Katun 7 Ahau, etc. (See column, "The Short Count," in Table V, facing p. 79.) This round of the thirteen differently named katuns was represented graphically by the ancient Maya as a wheel, the periphery of which was divided into thirteen divisions, one for each of the 13 differently numbered or differently named katuns.

Bishop Landa not only describes but also illustrates one of these katun-wheels (see Fig. 27):

Not only did the Indians have a count for the year and months, as has been said and previously set out, but they also had a certain method of counting time and their affairs by their ages, which they counted by twenty-year periods, counting thirteen twenties, with one of the twenty signs of

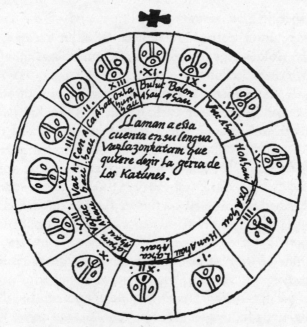

Fig. 27.—Katun-wheel. After Bishop Landa.

their months, which they call Ahau, not in order, but going backward as appears in the following circular design. In their language they call these [periods] katuns, with these they make a calculation of their ages that is marvelous; thus it was easy for the old man of whom I spoke in the first chapter [of Landa's original manuscript] to recall events that had taken place three hundred years before. Had I not known of these calculations, I should not have believed it possible to recall thus after such a period.

The direction of movement in the wheel illustrated by Landa (Fig. 27) is from right to left, counterclockwise, in order that the katuns shall pass the cross at the top, above the section marked Buluc Ahau (11 Ahau), in the proper sequence—the days Ahau decreasing by two each as already noted, namely, Katun Buluc Ahau (11 Ahau), Katun Bolon Ahau (9 Ahau), Katun Uuc Ahau (7 Ahau), Katun Ho Ahau (5 Ahau), etc. The words in the center of Landa's wheel read

They call this count in their language *uazlazon katam* [more properly *uazaklom katun*] which means the round or return of the epochs [katuns].

The specific katun from which this round of the katuns was originally counted seems to have been a Katun 8 Ahau, perhaps because the Golden Age of the Maya, Baktun 9, was counted from a katun which ended on the day 8 Ahau, viz. 9.0.0.0.0 *8 Ahau* 13 Ceh. In any event the doubling over, or repetition, of the sequence began again after each Katun 8 Ahau had completed itself, and these Katuns 8 Ahau were therefore called the *uudz katunob*, or the katuns which are doubled back. By referring to Table V (facing p. 80) it will be seen that the katun with which Baktun 9 closed—9.0.0.0.0 8 Ahau 13 Ceh (435)—ended with the day 8 Ahau, and it will be shown further in the last chapter of this book what a fateful influence these Katuns 8 Ahau, the *uudz katunob*, exerted upon the course of Maya history.

Each one of the thirteen katuns of the *u kahlay katunob* had its own patron deity (see p. 241), its own prophecies peculiar to it, which are set forth at considerable length in the Books of Chilam Balam, and its own special ceremonies. A series of eleven katuns, part of an *u kahlay katunob*, are presented on pages 1–11 inclusive of the Codex Peresianus, beginning with a Katun 4 Ahau (perhaps 1224–1244) on page 1 and closing with a Katun 10 Ahau (perhaps 1421–1441) on page 11; one of the intermediate katuns, a Katun 7 Ahau (perhaps 1323–1342) on page 6 of this Codex, has been reproduced in part in Figure 16 on page 242 of this book.

The *u kahlay katunob*, or Short Count, was, in effect, a his-

torical synopsis presented in a succession of katuns or twenty-year
periods (more exactly 19.71 years), and so long as the sequences
remained unbroken, that is with no gaps or repetitions, it was
accurate enough for all ordinary purposes, and, at the time of the
Spanish Conquest, this record—the *u kahlay katunob*—stretched
back through sixty-two katuns, to the beginning of Baktun 9
(435), a matter of eleven centuries.

THE THREE KNOWN MAYA HIEROGLYPHIC MANUSCRIPTS

Only three original pre-Columbian Maya codices or hieroglyphic manuscripts have survived the early fanaticism of the
Spanish priesthood and the inevitable vicissitudes of time and
weather. In central Mexico, including all the native manuscripts
known, both pre-Conquest and those of native origin dating from
the last three-quarters of the sixteenth century, upwards of four
hundred have come down to us, perhaps as many as fifty being of
pre-Columbian origin. But of the Maya native books which
treated of history, chronology, astronomy, the different aspects
of religion—ritual, divination, prophecy, and medicine, a treasure-
house of Maya literature that would have cleared up many a
mystery, particularly in the field of history, had they survived
—only three have come down to us: the Codex Dresdensis, the
Codex Tro-Cortesianus, and the Codex Peresianus.

Landa in speaking of the Maya codices says:

These people also made use of certain characters or letters, with which
they wrote in their books their ancient affairs and their sciences, and with
these and drawings and with certain signs in these drawings, they understood their affairs and made others understand them and taught them. We
found a great number of books in these characters, and, as they contained
nothing in which there was not to be seen superstition and lies of the devil,
we burned them all, which they regretted to an amazing degree and caused
them affliction.

The Maya codices were made of the bark of a tree called
in Maya *copo* (*Ficus cotonifolia*), pounded into a pulp and held
together with some sort of a natural gum as a bonding substance.
They were made in long strips and folded like a screen. The

Codices Tro-Cortesianus and Peresianus are almost exactly the same size, the individual leaves being about 9¼ inches high and 5 inches wide; the Codex Dresdensis is a little smaller, its leaves being about 8 inches high by 3½ inches wide. A coating, or wash, of fine white lime was applied to both sides of this mangled-bark paper strip, which was folded like a screen, and on the smooth glossy finish thus obtained columns of glyphs and pictures of gods and ceremonies were painted in many colors: dark red, light red, blue, yellow, brown, green, and an intense, almost lustrous, black. The pages are divided into two, three, and sometimes four horizontal sections by red lines, and the order of reading was across the pages from left to right, always in the same horizontal section until the particular matter being treated, perhaps to be likened to a chapter, was finished. These so-called "chapters" sometimes extend across as many as eight or more consecutive pages or folds. The codices were bound between decorated boards to protect the rather fragile bark-paper, and when they were completely opened out they were quite long. The Codex Tro-Cortesianus, for example, is 23½ feet long and has 56 leaves, or 112 pages, not a single page being blank; the Codex Dresdensis is 11¾ feet long and has 39 leaves, or 78 pages, 4 of the pages being blank; the Codex Peresianus, which is only a fragment in its present condition, is 4¾ feet long and has 11 leaves or 22 pages, with none blank.

Some of the Aztec, Mixtec, and Zapotec codices from central Mexico were made of deerskin, which was smoked in order to preserve it, and others even of cotton stuffs, but if these materials were ever used by the ancient Maya in making their hieroglyphic manuscripts no examples of them have come down to us, nor does Landa make any mention of them.

Unfortunately not one of the three known Maya codices treats of history as such, though we have seen in the preceding section (p. 294) that one side of the Codex Peresianus probably deals with the patron gods and ceremonies corresponding to eleven consecutive katuns—Katun 4 Ahau to Katun 10 Ahau inclusive, perhaps 1224–1441. A situation roughly comparable to that confronting us in regard to the three surviving Maya codices would be the following. If we could imagine that there existed only one hundred books in all the United States, each devoted to a single subject, such as history, astronomy, geology, botany, zoology, medicine, mathematics, physics, economics, religion, ritual, horoscopy, literature, and so on, and further, if all these books were destroyed by fire, three only being saved—the treatise on astronomy, the manual on ritual, and the textbook on horoscopy—all the others being destroyed, including the only book on history in the entire collection, we would have a situation analogous to what has *survived* of ancient Maya literature in the three known Maya codices. The Codex Dresdensis, although it includes many horoscopes and some ritualistic material, is essentially a treatise on astronomy. The Codex Tro-Cortesianus, although it includes some ritualistic matter, is primarily a textbook of horoscopes to assist the priests in making their divinations. The fragmentary Codex Peresianus, while it gives some horoscopes, is basically ritualistic, one side being completely given over to a katun sequence and its corresponding patron deities and ceremonies. But of history as we know it not a single event is described, although the Spanish and native writers of the sixteenth century all are in unanimous agreement that the Maya recorded their history in their hieroglyphic manuscripts, but most unfortunately not one of the three surviving codices is of a historical nature.

Not one of these three codices, it should be noted, moreover, was found in the New World, that is to say, under archaeological conditions in the Maya area. Indeed the climate of the Yucatan Peninsula is so moist, the rainfall so excessive, mildew so destructive, that it is highly doubtful whether a codex could have survived even if it had been buried in a tomb or a temple.

The Codex Dresdensis was found in Vienna, Austria, in 1739; it was given to the Librarian of the then Royal Library at Dresden, who was passing through Vienna *en route* to Rome on a collecting trip; its earlier history is unknown. Since this manuscript was obtained in Vienna, and since Austria and Spain had a

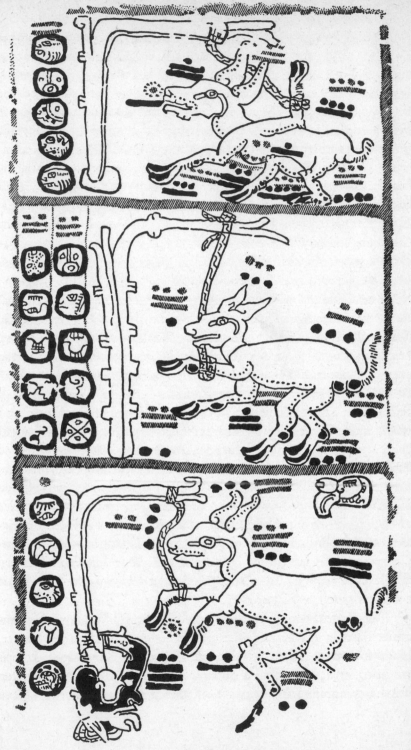

Fig. 28.—Design showing the snaring of a deer. Page 45, Codex Tro-Cortesianus.

common sovereign at the time of the Spanish Conquest of Yucatan
in 1527–1546, the Emperor Charles V, it is highly possible that
some Spanish priest or soldier, perhaps even Montejo himself,
sent this codex back to Spain. The sender may have acquired the
codex, considered it a good souvenir of the new land, and sent it
home—something like our own custom of sending back souvenir
postcards to relatives and friends during a visit to foreign countries. From Spain it possibly followed the Emperor to Austria,
where Charles V spent so much of his time and where so much
of the Moctezuma treasure and contemporary copies of the letters
from Cortes to Charles V have been discovered. The Codex
Dresdensis is now in the State Library at Dresden, Germany. A
sample page, showing the destruction of the world by water, has
been shown in Figure 9 (see chapter xi, p. 215).

The Codex Tro-Cortesianus, divided into two unequal sections, was discovered during the sixties of the last century in
Spain. Although each section was found in a different place,
students have been able to prove that both pieces are parts of the
same manuscript. The larger section was owned by a Señor Juan
de Tro y Ortolano, of Madrid; the smaller section belonged to a
Señor Jose Ignacio Miró, who acquired it in Extremadura, and
called it the Codex Cortesianus, believing that it had been brought
there by Cortes. Since Francisco de Montejo, the conqueror of
Yucatan, as well as many of his men, came from Extremadura,
it is much more likely that Montejo himself or one of his soldiers
brought the whole codex—the two sections being in one piece
at that time—from Yucatan to his home in the Province of Extremadura. Both sections rejoined and called the Codex Tro-
Cortesianus are now in the Museum of Archaeology and History
at Madrid; page 45 from this manuscript showing the snaring of
a deer is given in Figure 28.

The Codex Peresianus was found in the Bibliothèque Nationale at Paris in 1860 in a basket of old papers in a chimney corner,
black with dust, its very existence apparently forgotten. It was
wrapped in a piece of torn paper with the word "Perez" written
on the wrapping, and because of this it was named the Codex

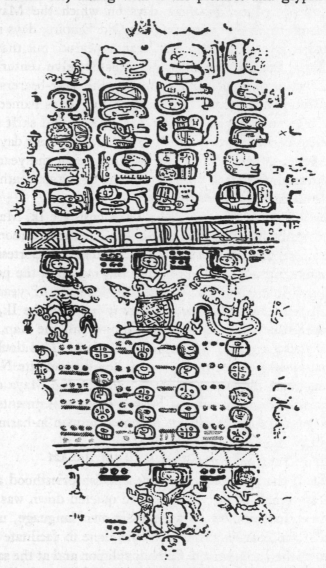

■·■
■■■
300
Peresianus. This manuscript is only a small part of the original codex, and moreover is in much worse condition than either of the other two; the plaster coating around the margins of the pages has all fallen off, taking with it the pictures and glyphs except

FIG. 29.—Three signs of the Maya zodiac (middle section): the scorpion, the turtle, and the rattlesnake. Page 24, Codex Peresianus.

those painted in the middle parts of the pages (Fig. 29). The
Codex Peresianus still remains where it was found, in the Bibliothèque Nationale at Paris.

It has been pointed out in a preceding section (p. 272) that
the Maya year-bearers—those days on which the Maya New
Years could begin—were, during the Old Empire, days in which
the names Ik, Manik, Eb, and Caban appeared, but that by the
time of the Spanish Conquest more than twelve centuries later
two shifts forward had taken place in the year-bearers: first a
shift forward of one day to the set of four days named Akbal,
Lamat, Ben, and Eznab; and, still later, a second shift forward
in the year-bearers, again of one day to the set of four days named
Kan, Muluc, Ix, and Cauac, the last four being the year-bearers
which were in use during the early decades of the sixteenth century
at the time of the Spanish Conquest.

The year-bearers in the Codex Dresdensis are Ik, Manik, Eb,
and Caban, following the usage of the Old Empire monuments.
There are no sure months-signs in the Codex Tro-Cortesianus, so
this manuscript presents no evidence bearing upon the point, but
the Codex Peresianus has the intermediate set of year-bearers
Akbal, Lamat, Ben, and Eznab, midway between the Ik, Manik,
Eb, and Caban series of the Old Empire and the Kan, Muluc,
Ix, and Cauac series of the late New Empire. This double shift
forward in the year-bearers between the Old and late New Empire was doubtless due to the inexactness of the Maya calendric
formulae and the necessity of making these adjustments so that
the calendar and the tropical year should remain in harmony.

THE BOOKS OF CHILAM BALAM

One of the first concerns of the Spanish priesthood after the
noise and tumult of the Conquest had quieted down was to teach
the Maya Indians how to write their own language, using the
letters of the Spanish script. This was done to facilitate the conversion of the natives to the Catholic religion and at the same time
to wean them away from their old pagan faith and all that per-
tained to it. Surprisingly few letters, only two as a matter of fact,

had to be added to the letters of the Spanish alphabet in order to render accurately sounds present in Maya that were wanting in Spanish. The Portuguese *x* was used to represent the *sh* sound in Maya, which is extremely common in that language, as for example—Uxmal, pronounced Ushmal and Yaxchilan, pronounced Yashchilan, and an inverted *c* (ɔ) now written *dz* to render the sound *dz* or *tz*, also very common in Maya, as for example "Ah ɔun," now written "Ah Dzun."

While the natives were supposed to use this new writing exclusively for purposes of the new (Christian) religion, they managed to record in it a considerable amount of old pagan matters, such as prophecies, myths, prayers, chiefs' questionnaires, rituals, astronomical data, incantations, songs, current events, such as hangings, the building of a hospital, an epidemic of smallpox, the arrival of a judge, and, most important of all, chronological synopses of their own ancient history—the *u kahlay katunob* previously mentioned. And so during the century following the Spanish Conquest a number of these native manuscripts, written on European paper in the Maya language but with the characters of the Spanish script, began to appear all over northern Yucatan. They have been called the "Books of Chilam Balam." *Chilan* or *Chilam* was the name of a class of priests, who were soothsayers, prophets, and oracles, and *Balam*, which means "jaguar," also signifies something mysterious or hidden; the whole phrase may perhaps be freely translated "The book of the soothsayer of hidden things."

Originally there must have been many of these native manuscript notebooks, wherein all sorts of scraps of the ancient learning were set down by natives of the upper class who had survived the Conquest; unfortunately only a few of these books have come down to us. They were distinguished one from another by the addition of the name of the town where each was written—The Book of Chilam Balam of Mani, composed at the village of Mani, The Book of Chilam Balam of Tizimin, written at the village of Tizimin, and so on. Fragments of some ten or twelve are known, though by far the most important are the Books of Chilam Balam of Mani, Tizimin, Chumayel, Kaua, Ixil, Tusik, and the Codex

Perez, the last containing rescripts from several others, the originals of which are now lost.

Historically, the most significant sections of the Books of Chilam Balam are the *u kahlay katunob*, or native chronicles— summaries of the *katuns*, setting forth very briefly the leading events of Maya history. There are five of these native chronicles preserved in the Books of Chilam Balam—one in the Mani Manuscript, one in the Tizimin Manuscript, and three in the Chumayel Manuscript. Of these, the Mani, the Tizimin, and the first Chumayel *u kahlay katunob* give the most accurate summaries of New Empire history, for which, as a matter of fact, they are our principal sources. Indeed, there is little doubt that the *u kahlay katunob* of the Books of Chilam Balam are literal translations of Maya historical codices, the originals of which are now lost or destroyed. A combined synopsis of the *u kahlay katunob* is given in Table V (facing p. 80).

THE "POPOL VUH" AND THE ANNALS OF THE CAKCHIQUELS

In the highlands of Guatemala, chiefly among the Quiche and Cakchiquel Maya, a similar body of native literature developed. It was written in the Quiche and Cakchiquel, rather than in the Maya language, using the letters of the Spanish script.

It was found necessary, however, to add five special new characters to the Spanish alphabet in order to express correctly sounds present in Quiche but wanting in Spanish; and these were called "the characters of Father de la Parra," after the Franciscan friar who devised them in the middle sixteenth century.

Although this method of writing the native language was originally developed in northern Yucatan to facilitate the conversion of the Indians to the Catholic faith, educated Quiche in the south quickly seized upon the de la Parra alphabet, using it to preserve fragments of their own ancient literature.

The Popol Vuh, or "Book of the Quiche" is easily the most outstanding work of this nature in the southern Maya field. It preserves fragments of the cosmogony, religion, mythology, migration traditions, and history of the Quiche, who were by far the most powerful Maya people of the southern highlands. The elegance of the language and the literary style of the Popol Vuh, the lofty philosophy it expresses, coupled with the rich and varied life it reveals, emphasizes the magnitude of the loss we have suffered in the almost complete annihilation of Quiche learning brought about through the Spanish Conquest.

The Annals of the Cakchiquels, as its name signifies, treats more of the history of the Cakchiquel people and less of their cosmogony, mythology, and religion than the Popol Vuh. It covers a longer stretch of time than the Popol Vuh of the Quiche, and describes events both of the Spanish Conquest and the post-Conquest period. It treats fully of the genealogy of the Xahila, the ruling family of the Cakchiquel nation.

There are several other native post-Conquest manuscripts of similar nature emanating from the Guatemala highlands, all of them written in the Quiche language.

ASTRONOMICAL KNOWLEDGE

THE SOLAR YEAR

Eminent astronomical authorities have said that the ancient Maya possessed a more accurate knowledge of astronomy than did the ancient Egyptians down to the Ptolemaic Period of Egyptian History (325 B.C.–30 B.C.). For example, the so-called astronomical texts found on occasional coffin-lids of burials during the Eleventh Dynasty (2200–2000 B.C.) show far less knowledge of the movements of the sun and moon than that possessed by the Old Empire Maya.

The Maya, we have seen, had a fixed calendar year, only 365 days in length, with which to measure an astronomical phenomenon—the exact time required for the earth to make one complete revolution around the sun—which, according to modern science, requires 365.2422 days to complete. The ancient Maya priests, however, fully realized the discrepancy between their calendar year and the true tropical year and by means of the Secondary Series, as already explained, took care of the accumulated error at any given time in their chronological era. Indeed the

caliland-correction formulae worked out by the ancient Maya
astronomer-priests at Copan, back in the sixth or seventh century
of the Christian Era, were slightly more accurate than our own
Gregorian leap-year correction, which was not introduced until
nearly a thousand years later, in 1582 by Pope Gregory XIII, as
the following tabulation will show:

Length of the year according to modern astronomy .... 365.2422 days
Length of our old, uncorrected Julian year.......... 365.2500 days
Length of our present, corrected, Gregorian year ...... 365.2425 days
Length of the year according to ancient Maya astronomy 365.2420 days

Pope Gregory's correction is 3/10,000 of a day too *long*, while
the ancient Maya correction was only 2/10,000 of a day too *short*.

THE MOON

The Maya had also made notable advances in measuring the
exact length of a lunation, or one complete revolution of the moon
around the earth. According to the perfected observation of modern astronomers with instruments of precision, this period is composed of 29.53059+ days. How then, since Maya arthmetic had
no fractions, did the ancient Maya priests measure such a complex
and refractory fraction as $\frac{53,059}{100,000}+$ of a day? The result was accomplished much as we keep our own calendar year in harmony
with the true year by our leap-year correction. First we have three
years of 365 days each, followed by a fourth, or leap year, which
last is 366 days in length. This method of leap-year interpolation
is continued until an even century in our Christian Era is reached
as for example 1900, which was *not* a leap year, the rule *thus far*
being that even centuries are *not* leap years. This method of leap-
year correction is continued until a century is reached that is divisible by 400, as for example the years 1200, 1600, and 2000,
all of which were or will be leap years, or years of 366 days in
length. This method of interpolation is continued until a century
is reached that is divisible by 8,000, as, for example the year
8,000 or 16,000, when leap year will again be omitted. Our
process is one of a slight *over*correction every four years, com-

pensated for by a slight *under*correction once every century, compensated for by another slight *over*correction every four centuries, compensated for by another slight *under*correction every eight thousand years; in short a series of over- and undercorrections—checks and balances—which keep the calendar pretty closely in harmony with the natural phenomenon.

So it was with the ancient Maya. At first, since they had no fractional days, perhaps they tried out a revolution of the moon as being composed of 30 days, since one lunation is nearer 30 than 29 days, but soon they saw that the actual new moons were falling *short* of 30 days. Next, they allowed 29 days for a lunation, only to discover, even more quickly, that the moons were *exceeding* 29 days in length. When this happened, some old astronomer-priest must have exclaimed, "I have it! It is neither one nor the other; neither 29 days, nor 30 days that our mother, the moon goddess, needs to make her journey around us, but exactly between the two; so let us first make a lunation of 29 days and the next of 30 days, the next of 29 days, the next of 30 days, and so on indefinitely; in this way we will measure exactly the number of the days of her journey about us."

But even this correction failed them, though more slowly. Every two lunations of this kind gave them an average lunation of 29.5 days, whereas the exact figure is 29.53059+ days; or in other words, this kind of a lunar calendar was gaining on the actual phenomenon itself at the rate of $\frac{53,059}{100,000}+$ of a day every lunation, an error which reached one whole day in about $33\frac{1}{3}$ lunations, or one day in every $2\frac{2}{3}$ years. This must have discouraged the old astronomer-priests, and yet they saw they were on the right track. Finally, a lunar calendar that was amazingly accurate for a primitive people was developed by the age-old process of trial and error, by means of which all human experience is gained.

On pages 51–58 of the Codex Dresdensis, 405 consecutive lunations (about $32\frac{3}{4}$ years) are presented, the lunations being arranged in 69 separate groups. These groups are usually composed of six lunations each, but occasionally they have only five.

Of the 60 six-lunation groups out of the total of 69 groups re-corded, each totals, sometimes 178 days and sometimes 177 days, depending upon whether an extra 30-day month has been inter-polated or not, giving $30 + 29 + 30 + 29 + 30 + 30 = 178$ days, or $30 + 29 + 30 + 29 + 30 + 29 = 177$ days. Each of the re-maining 9 five-lunation groups on the other hand, always totals 148 days, or $30 + 29 + 30 + 29 + 30 = 148$. These pages of the Codex Dresdensis are nothing more nor less than a solar eclipse table, since the closing days of *every one* of these 69 lunar groups are days upon which, under certain conditions, a solar eclipse would be visible somewhere on the earth. Furthermore, the extra 30-day lunar months are so skillfully interpolated that nowhere throughout these 405 successive lunations—nearly a third of a century—does the discrepancy between the calendar measuring these successive new moons and the actual new moons themselves amount to as much as one day—surely a magnificent achievement for a primitive people working without instruments of precision.

ASTRONOMICAL OBSERVATORIES

It may well be asked at this point how then did the ancient Maya achieve such a high degree of astronomical accuracy, if they had no telescopes, no astrolabes, or other instruments upon which modern astronomers depend? The answer is simply this. If the lines of sight, that is, of observation, are sufficiently long, accuracy to within less than a day's error may be achieved in fixing the synodical revolution, or the apparent revolution, as opposed to the sidereal or true revolution, of many of the heavenly bodies. Maya temples are lofty. The five great pyramid-temples at Tikal, for example, vary from 70 to 150 feet in height, sufficiently high to obtain clear lines of sight from their summits over the top of the forest to distant points on the horizon. A pair of crossed sticks was set up inside a darkened chamber of the temple on top of the pyramid, and from this as a fixed point of observation, the place where the sun, moon, or the planet Venus for example, rose or set, was noted with reference to some natural feature on the horizon, such as a notch between two hills, or the top of a hill. When the heavenly body under observation rose or set, as the case might be, behind this same point on the horizon a second time, it had made one complete synodical revolution. The Pueblo Indians of Arizona and New Mexico still mark the positions of sunrise and sunset on the horizon, as observed from their villages, at the solstices when the sun is moving most slowly, saying that the sun "rests" for a few days in the "Sun houses" at these points, before beginning his journey back.

Such an astronomical line of sight has already been mentioned at Copan for determining when the cleared cornfields should be burned (p. 144); and in the next chapter, astronomical observatories at other Maya cities will be described. Unfortunately, the

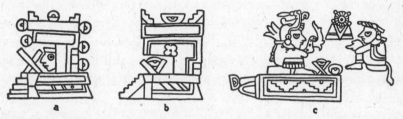

FIG. 30.—Representations of astronomical observatories in the Mexican codices: (*a*) from the Codex Nuttall; (*b*) from the Codex Selden; (*c*) from the Codex Bodleian.

three known Maya codices have no representations of such observatories, but pictures of them are occasionally found in the Mexican codices. In Figure 30, *a*, is shown such an observatory from the Codex Nuttall. In the doorway of a temple is a pair of crossed sticks, and, looking out of the doorway, through the crossed sticks, there is the head of a man. Again in Figure 30, *b*, from the Codex Selden, simply an eye in the notch made by a pair of crossed sticks in the temple doorway appears. In still a third Mexican codex, the Bodleian, the eye between two crossed sticks, a star descending into a notch, as well as two observers, are shown (Fig. 30, *c*). With such simple instruments as these, the ancient Maya probably measured the movements of the heavenly bodies, predicted eclipses and the heliacal risings and settings of the Morning and Evening Star.

Venus was one of the most important stars observed by the ancient Maya astronomers. There seem to have been at least two names for it: *Noh ek*, "the great star"; and *xux ek*, "the wasp star." Landa mentions Venus as the Morning Star but gives no specific name for it: "They used the Pleiades and Gemini as guides by night, so as to know the hour of the Morning Star."

Pages 24 and 46–50 of the Codex Dresdensis set forth a remarkable Venus calendar which was good, in the aggregate, for 384 years.

The planet Venus makes one synodical revolution—that is, it returns to the same position in the heavens as observed from the earth, according to modern astronomical observations made with instruments of precision—in almost exactly 583.920 days. The individual revolutions thus run in series of five—approximately 580, 587, 583, 583, and 587 days each, but any consecutive five revolutions average very close to 583.920 days each. The Maya, dealing as they did only with whole numbers, called this period 584 days, but they knew that this value was a little too high—in fact, that the actual average was *less* than 583.935 days. As just noted the true length of the average period is 583.920 days.

Venus in her synodical revolution divides into four periods as follows: (1) after inferior conjunction she is Morning Star for about eight months, roughly 240 days; (2) she then disappears for three months during superior conjunction, roughly 90 days; (3) she reappears as Evening Star for another eight months, roughly 240 days; (4) she disappears again for 14 days during inferior conjunction; after which she reappears again as Morning Star, completing the cycle. The Maya astronomer-priests arbitrarily assigned slightly different values to these four phases of Venus, although the total number of days in one synodical revolution always remained the same, 584 days. According to Maya astronomy, Venus was Morning Star for 236 days (4 days less than above); invisible during superior conjunction for 90 days (the same as above); Evening Star for 250 days (10 days more than above); and invisible during inferior conjunction for 8 days

(6 days less than above) making a total of 584 days. It has been suggested that the lengths of these four Venus phases were arbitrarily fixed as given above so as to agree with completed lunations. If so, Venus was Morning Star for 8 moons; invisible after her phase as Morning Star for 3 moons; she was Evening Star for 8½ moons, and invisible thereafter for only 8 days, or what was left of the 584 days after 19½ moons (576 days) had been subtracted therefrom.

But ascribing 584 days to one synodical revolution of Venus was a little too long, we have seen, since the exact figure is only 583.92 days. The ancient Maya priests were perfectly aware of this error of 8/100 of a day every 584 days and, further, knew how to correct it. One of their most important ceremonial periods was a purely artificial time unit composed of 5 synodical revolutions of Venus, or $5 \times 584 = 2,920$ days. They also had discovered that this period was exactly equal to 8 of their calendar years: $8 \times 365 = 2,920$ days, a coincidence which was of the highest ceremonial significance to them. It exactly combined 8 of their 365-day solar years with 5 of their 584-day Venus years and, moreover, supplied a convenient period for correcting the Venus calendar, which, as we have seen was falling behind the apparent Venus year at the rate of 8/100 of a day every synodical revolution of the planet or 2/5 of a day every 8 calendar years ($5 \times \frac{8}{100} = \frac{40}{100} = \frac{2}{5}$ of a day).

As presented in the Codex Dresdensis, the Venus calendar is in reality three distinct calendars, each composed of 65 synodical revolutions of the planet, or each Venus calendar is equal to 104 calendar years; no two of them, however, are either contemporaneous or continuous; that is to say there is a gap between the first and second, and another gap between the second and third. The corrections were inserted at intervals, when the calendar Venus-year of 584 days overran the synodical Venus-year either by 4 days or 8 days. Starting with the first of these three Venus calendars, at the end of the 57th Venus-solar period, $57 \times 2,920 = 166,440$ days, the accumulated error had reached 8 days, and, by dropping *back* 8 days from the date of the end of the 57th Venus-solar period of the first calendar, the *zero date* of the second calendar is reached, and a shift was then made to the second calendar. Similarly at the end of the 61st Venus-solar period of the second calendar, an error of 4 days had accumulated, and, dropping *back* these 4 days from this point in the second calendar, the *zero date* of the third calendar is reached, and so on. By use of this table the Venus-solar-period was kept in harmony with the actual appearances and disappearances of that planet for a long time— 384 years—before the accumulated error began to render the table no longer usable.

OTHER STARS AND CONSTELLATIONS

The Pleiades were called *tzab*, the Maya word for the rattles of a rattlesnake, perhaps because of the fancied resemblance of this constellation to the rattler's tail rattles. Gemini was called *ac*, "the tortoise," because of some imaginary resemblance of that constellation to a tortoise.

It has been suggested that the ancient Maya may have had their own zodiac, which was composed of thirteen, instead of twelve houses as is our own; and further, that the Maya zodiac may be represented on pages 23 and 24 of the Codex Peresianus. If so, and it appears as not improbable, the first three signs, or houses of the Maya zodiac would seem to have been—Scorpion, Tortoise, and Rattle, or Rattlesnake, since these are the first three figures shown as hanging from a constellation band in the middle section of page 24 (Fig. 29, p. 300).

The North Star was also of great importance. Its apparent immovability in the nightly skies, the orderly and majestic procession of the other constellations around it, the Great Dipper on one side, Cassiopeia on the other, made it a beacon of unique integrity and dependability among the many moving constellations and planets, the true friend and guide of the traveling merchant.

CITIES AND ARCHITECTURE

NATURE OF THE MAYA CITIES AND POPULATION

SOME OBJECTION has been made to calling the ancient Maya ceremonial and governmental centers cities and towns, on the ground that they were not concentrations of populations in relatively limited areas like our modern urban centers; but Landa's account of a New Empire settlement is so clear that there can be little doubt that he is describing a town, even in the modern sense of the word. Two important differences, however, must be admitted: First, Maya centers of population were not so concentrated, not so densely packed into congested blocks as are our modern cities and towns. On the contrary, they were scattered over extensive, more lightly inhabited suburbs, fringing out into continuous small farms—a suburban, as contrasted to a closely concentrated, urban type of occupation. Second, the assemblages of public buildings, temples, sanctuaries, palaces, pyramids, monasteries, ball courts, observatories, dance platforms, etc., were not usually disposed along streets and avenues as in our own modern cities and towns; instead the buildings were erected around the sides of courts and plazas which were the religious precincts, governmental and trading sections of the city (Plates 33, 34, 39, and 49).

Says Landa in describing an ancient Maya town:

Before the Spaniards had conquered that country [Yucatan] the natives lived together in towns in a very civilized fashion. They kept the land well cleared and free from weeds, and planted very good trees. Their dwelling-place was as follows—in the middle of the town were their temples with beautiful plazas, and all around the temples stood the houses of the lords and priests and then [those of] the most important people. Thus came the houses of the richest, and of those who were held in the

↑ *a*) Tikal, Peten, Guatemala.

↑ *b*) Copan, Honduras.

↑ *c*) Quirigua, Izabal, Guatemala.

PLATE 31.—PAINTINGS OF CITIES OF THE OLD EMPIRE BY CARLOS VIERRA
IN THE SAN DIEGO MUSEUM, SAN DIEGO, CALIFORNIA

↑ *a*) Wooden lintel, Temple IV, Tikal, Peten, Guatemala.

PLATE 32.—SCULPTURES OF THE OLD EMPIRE

↓ *b*) Sanctuary tablet, Temple of the Cross, Palenque, Chiapas, Mexico.

highest estimation nearest to these, and at the outskirts of the town were
the houses of the lowest class.

Archaeological studies of the Carnegie Institution of Washington at the Old Empire center of Uaxactun, in an attempt to reach an estimate of the former population of that city, confirmed this civic-and-religious-center, small-farm-suburban type of settlement—the public and religious buildings arranged around courts and plazas in the center like public squares, the dwellings of the nobles and principal persons surrounding them, and the house sites and small farms of the common people extending outward for miles in every direction.

This attempt to estimate the former population of Uaxactun was carried out in the following manner: a large cross was laid out on the ground with its center at the main group of ruins—the ceremonial center of the city—each arm being 400 yards wide and 1 mile in length from the central point to its extremity. Each arm was then divided into 68 squares, 100 yards to a side, each square containing 10,000 square yards, which made a total of 272 squares for the four arms of the cross, or 2,720,000 square yards. It was thought that these 272 squares, arranged as indicated, would constitute a fair sample of the land in the immediate vicinity of the ceremonial and governmental center. The arms of this cross were laid out to run due north-south and east-west. The squares in each arm were then searched by four men walking abreast, each man being responsible for one tier of squares running along the longitudinal axis of each arm. Each square was examined carefully for any traces of artificial construction, especially for vestiges of house sites, which, in the case of those of the common people, would appear only as low platform-mounds not more than a foot or two in height above the general ground level; the houses themselves, having been built of thatch and sapling, would have disappeared within a decade after the city was abandoned.

The survey showed that of the 2,720,000 square yards examined, 1,180,000 square yards, or 43 per cent, of the area were taken up by logwood swamps or other low, marshy, uninhabitable areas, leaving 1,540,000 square yards, or 57 per cent available for human occupation. Discarding the former 43 per cent as always having been useless land, it was found that, of the remaining habitable area, 400,000 square yards (14.7 per cent) were occupied by the ceremonial and governmental precincts of Groups A and E, the largest two of the eight groups or plaza-complexes at Uaxactun. This left a remainder of 1,140,000 square yards (114 squares), or about 42.3 per cent of the total area examined (272 squares), on which people could live, after the part devoted to public and religious buildings, courts, and plazas had been deducted (40 squares). These last 114 squares were found to contain 52 house-mounds and 50 water reservoirs (*chultuns*), though no specific association between the location of the former and the latter could be ascertained.

In utilizing these figures, if we assume that all the house-mounds found were occupied at the same time and, further, that the average family consisted of five persons, there would have been the extremely dense population of 1,083.35 individuals (men, women, and children) per square mile of habitable land. Even if we assume that only one out of every four house-mounds was occupied at the same time, the number of persons per square mile would have been 271, approximately the same density of population as that of the state of New York and about half that of the state of Rhode Island.

Of course it is now impossible to say just how large an area was served by the religious and governmental center at Uaxactun, but if we arbitrarily fix an average limit of 10 miles from the center for the area occupied by the dependent agricultural population there would have been a population of about 50,000 people in round numbers. This population figure is based upon an average density of 271 people per square mile, including the agricultural inhabitants who were accustomed to assemble at Uaxactun for important religious ceremonies, for trading, and for its communal building program. Furthermore, of this number, some 15,000, or two out of seven, may be considered as having been able-bodied laborers, men and youths, a portion of whose time

(p. 155) could be commandeered by the city for its public works, such as quarrying, burning limekilns, transporting building materials, construction, and maintenance—the last a tremendous task in a region where vegetation grows so rapidly.

Uaxactun, as we shall see presently, was a city of the second class. Thus if a center of secondary rank could boast a population of 50,000—a figure based only upon an assumed 25 per cent simultaneous occupation of all the house-mounds within the 20-mile circle centering at Uaxactun and consequently perhaps 50 or even 75 per cent too low—the first-class cities may very easily have had dependent agricultural populations of 200,000 souls or more. Such cities as the Old Empire metropolises of Tikal and Copan, and those of Chichen Itza and Uxmal during the New Empire, perhaps numbered as many as 60,000 able-bodied men capable of serving the state.

The total population of the Yucatan Peninsula in late Old Empire times (eighth century), when the geographical extension of the Maya civilization was at its maximum (Katun 18), must have been far greater than that of today, perhaps even three or four times as great.

In describing only the heart of the Old Empire region, an area 50 miles on a side, centering around Tikal and Uaxactun, I have pointed out elsewhere that

evidence multiplies that this section of the Old Empire was one of the most densely populated areas of its size in the world during the first six centuries [now extended to eight] of the Christian Era, and the occupation of the land between the different larger centers like Tikal, Uaxactun, Xultun, Nakum, Naranjo, etc., must have been practically continuous.

Another archaeologist writes:

If we select a seed population of 8,000, a peak of 8,000,000 is found after ten doublings. This is not excessive for 1200 years of undisturbed social evolution, and indeed it seems that the strongly urban conditions of the sixth century demand an even greater number.

Extending the population figures obtained from the house-mound survey at Uaxactun to the whole peninsula, we may estimate the total area of the Yucatan Peninsula as 100,000 square miles in round numbers, about half of which may, perhaps, be regarded as having been habitable. Allowing from 271 to 1,083 persons per square mile, depending upon whether it be assumed that only one-quarter of the house-mounds or all of them had been occupied at the same time, we reach estimates ranging from a minimum of 13,300,000 to a maximum of 53,300,000. While our controlling data are not secure enough to permit much reliance being placed upon these figures, the northward expansion of the Maya at the peak of the Old Empire may well have involved a maximum population for the entire peninsula of somewhere in the neighborhood of the smaller figure, perhaps as many as seven times the total of all Maya-speaking groups in this same region today, certainly four or five times as many, would be a conservative estimate.

CLASSIFICATION OF THE CENTERS OF POPULATION

The basic factors in any attempt to classify the cities, towns, and villages of the Maya civilization, according to their supposed degrees of relative importance, would seem to be: (1) their respective areas; (2) the number and extent of the architectural remains they respectively contained; and (3) the number and excellence of their sculptured monuments. Even such obvious standards of comparison as these, however, are open to serious objections, leading as they do to conflicting results. For example, some sites are outstanding because of the size, number, and decoration of their respective buildings but they have few, if any, sculptured monuments; others present the opposite condition— relatively insignificant architectural remains, coupled with numerous and notable sculptured monuments. Still another factor causing uncertainty is that we do not know what sites were specially distinguished by the excellence of their ceramic wares, by their skill in jade carving, by the superiority of their feather-work, and by the fineness of their weaving. These crafts were all highly esteemed by the ancient Maya and undoubtedly contributed greatly to the relative importance of any given site.

However, it seems best, in attempting to make a classification of
the Maya sites according to their supposed degrees of relative
importance, to judge them objectively by the obvious standards
first mentioned; that is, by their respective sizes, the extent of
their architectural remains, and the number and excellence of
their sculptured monuments, quite regardless of any additional
importance they may or may not have had as centers of pottery,
textile, or lapidary production, or manufacture of other articles
of trade.

A classification into four groups has been made in Table VII,
which is shown graphically in Plate 19 where the first-, second-,
third-, and fourth-class centers are each represented by different
symbols.

Before describing some of the more important of these centers, at greater length, a further word of explanation about Table
VII is necessary. All sites except twelve listed in this table and
shown in Plate 19 have this one point in common: regardless of
their respective sizes, all have one or more hieroglyphic inscriptions. The twelve exceptions are Holmul, in the Old Empire
region, and Mani, T'ho, Izamal, Sotuta, El Tabasqueño, Chun-
chintok, Hochob, Ppustunich, Civiltuk, Acanceh, and Dzibilchaltun in the New Empire region. Indeed, if all the sites in Classes
3 and 4 were included in Table VII, the sites in these two classes
alone would be so numerous that they could not be shown on such
a small-scale map.

Although there are only four Class 1 sites listed in Table VII
(Tikal and Copan in the Old Empire and Chichen Itza and Uxmal
in the New Empire) there are two others—Calakmul in the
central Peten region and Coba in northeastern Yucatan—which
possibly should be included in Class 1 rather than at the head of
Class 2. Calakmul should possibly be included because it has more
monuments (103) than any other city of the Maya civilization,
and Coba, because of its very extensive architectural remains, as
well as its numerous sculptured stelae (24). Both sites, however,
have been assigned to Class 2; in the case of Calakmul, because
in spite of its mass production of monuments the individual sculp-

TABLE VII

CLASSIFICATION OF THE CENTERS OF THE MAYA CIVILIZATION ACCORDING TO THEIR SUPPOSED DEGREES OF RELATIVE IMPORTANCE IN ANCIENT TIMES

Class 1	Class 2	Class 3	Class 4	
Tikal	Calakmul	Balakbal	Uolantun	Bonampak
Copan	Coba	Xmakabatun	Kaxuinic	El Amparo
Chichen	Uaxactun	Chochkitam	El Encanto	Quexil
Itza	Xultun	Ucanal	Ixkun	Jonuta
Uxmal	La Honradez	Tzimin Kax	Yaltitud	Tila
	Nakum	Seibal	Benque Viejo	Comitan
	Naranjo	Altar de	Chunhuitz	Tenam
	Yaxchilan	Sacrificios	Cancuen	Quen Santo
	Piedras	Itsimte	Aguas Calientes	Ichpaatun
	Negras	Polol	El Caribe	Santa Rita
	Naachtun	Tayasal	La Amelia	Corosal
	Quirigua	Yaxha	Laguna Perdida	Dzilam
	El Palmar	Lubaantun	Motul de San	Jaina
	Rio Bec	Pusilha	José	Ichmul
	Palenque	Tzibanche	Ixlu	Tabi I
	Tonina	Uxul	San Clemente	Dzibilnocac
	Kabah	Becan	La Florida	Cave of Loltun
	Sayil	Oxpemul	Rio Amarillo	Ikil
	Etzna	Xamantun	Los Higos	Pechal
	Santa Rosa	Alta Mira	Oxlahuntun	Pasión del
	Xtampak	Comalcalco	Tzendales	Cristo
		Chuctiepa	Lacanha	El Tabasqueño
		Chinkultic	El Cayo	Chunchintok
		Tulum	La Mar	Hochob
		Labna	Chinikiha	Ppustunich
		Mayapan	El Tortuguero	Civiltuk
		Oxkintok	Santo Ton	Acanceh
		Keuic	Santa Elena	Dzibilchaltun
		Holactun	Poco Uinic	Chama
		Xculoc		
		Huntichmul I		
		Nohpat		
		Tzocchen		
		La Milpa		
		Holmul		
		Yaxuna		
		Mani		
		T'ho		
		Izamal		
		Sotuta		
4 sites	**19 sites**	**39 sites**	**54 sites**	

tured stelae are for the most part of little esthetic merit, and in the case of Coba, although there are many buildings, few if any of them are of architectural distinction. Moreover, Coba's twenty-four sculptured stelae are also all mediocre in character, certainly not to be compared with the monuments at Copan for example.

Of the nineteen centers listed in Class 2, twelve are in the heart of the Old Empire; one (Tonina) is in the southwestern highlands, the largest city in that region; one (Rio Bec) is in the Chenes area of central Campeche; and five are in northern Yucatan. If centers in northern Yucatan and Campeche which at the present time are not definitely known to have hieroglyphic inscriptions were included in Table VII, the total of the Class 2 sites would doubtless be considerably increased.

The chief difficulty encountered in making the classification shown in Table VII was to distinguish between small Class 2 and large Class 3 sites; indeed the question may well be raised whether it would not be better to group all Class 2 and Class 3 sites together, and have only three classes. The principal objection to such a procedure, however, is that it involves grouping together in the same class sites of such widely differing importance as Yaxchilan, Piedras Negras, and Palenque on the one hand (the sculptures of which are unquestionably the finest in the Maya area), and Chochkitam, Becan, and Tzocchen for example on the other hand. These last three are of far less importance than the first three. Rather than include such important cities as the first three in the same group with such relatively unimportant ones at the last three it seems much better to hold to my original fourfold classification.

Of the thirty-nine sites in Class 3 nothing further need be said, but concerning the fifty-four Class 4 sites, one important point should be borne in mind: in assigning sites to this class, neither the area covered by them nor the size and number of their respective architectural remains have been taken into consideration; assignments to this class have been made exclusively upon the fact of their having hieroglyphic inscriptions, but not more than four or five each.

DESCRIPTIONS OF THE MORE IMPORTANT MAYA CITIES

Unfortunately the ancient names of the vast majority of cities, towns, and villages of the Maya civilization have been lost with the passing centuries. This is one hundred per cent true of the Old Empire, with the possible exception of Copan. Although the site now known by this name was called Copan as early as the sixteenth century when the Spaniards first reached the Copan region, the site itself had long since been abandoned and was in ruins at that time and there are grave doubts as to whether this was its original name. As for the names of all other known centers of the Old Empire, probably not one antedates the close of the eighteenth century, and many of them have been named by modern archaeologists during the last fifty years.

In the New Empire the situation is only slightly better. We know the original names of about half a dozen sites from the Books of Chilam Balam—Chichen Itza, Chakanputun, Uxmal, Mayapan, Izamal, Coba, and T'ho (the modern Merida)—but the ancient names of innumerable others have long since been forgotten, lost in the mists of time.

Tikal, the Largest City of the Maya Civilization

The largest center of the Maya civilization, either of the Old or New Empire, and probably the oldest as well (see p. 43), was Tikal in northern central Peten at the head of the Holmul Valley (Plate 31, *a*). The civic and ceremonial heart of the city—the temple and governmental precincts—covers about one square mile, but beyond this in every direction there are smaller courts and plazas, surrounded by ruined stone buildings, which extend outward with decreasing frequency for two or three miles. Tikal may be divided into eight groups, A–H, of which the most important is Group A (Plate 33). This group is built on an artificially leveled tongue of land between two ravines, and is connected by a graded stone causeway with Group G to the southeast, and by a much longer causeway crossing the north ravine with Groups E and H to the north; Groups D and H are connected directly by a third causeway.

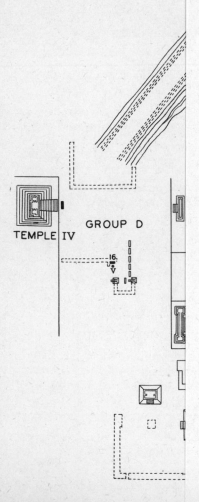

SCALE
0

PLATE 33.—MAP OF THE
PETEN,

TEMPLE IV

GROUP D

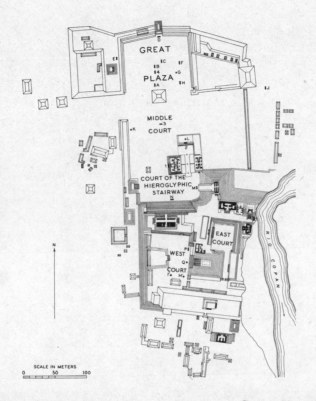

GREAT

PLAZA

MIDDLE
COURT

COURT OF THE
HIEROGLYPHIC
STAIRWAY

EAST
COURT

WEST

COURT

RIO COPAN

N

SCALE IN METERS
0   50   100

PLATE 34.—MAP OF THE CENTRAL SECTION OF COPAN, HONDURAS

↑　*a*) Jaguar Stairway, East Court, the Acropolis.

PLATE 35.—VIEWS OF COPAN, HONDURAS

b) South jaguar figure from the
↓ Jaguar Stairway.

c) Hieroglyphic Stairway, Temple
↓ 26.

↑ *a*) Milpa before burning, showing the felled trees and bush.   ↑ *b*) Milpa burning.

PLATE 36.—MISCELLANEOUS VIEWS

↓ *c*) Section of the Acropolis at Copan, Honduras, exposed by the Copan River.

↑ *a*) Copan, Honduras.

PLATE 37.—AIR VIEWS OF OLD EMPIRE CITIES

↓ *b*) Coba, Quintana Roo, Mexico.

↑ *a*) Chichen Itza, Yucatan, Mexico.

PLATE 38.—AIR VIEWS OF NEW EMPIRE CITIES

↓ *b*) Uxmal, Yucatan, Mexico.

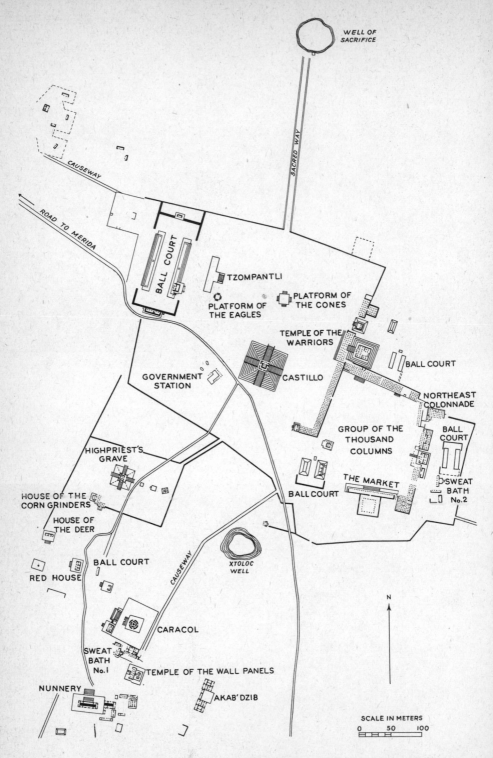

WELL OF
SACRIFICE

SACRED WAY

CAUSEWAY

ROAD TO MERIDA

BALL COURT

TZOMPANTLI

PLATFORM OF
THE EAGLES

PLATFORM OF
THE CONES

TEMPLE OF THE
WARRIORS

BALL COURT

GOVERNMENT
STATION

CASTILLO

NORTHEAST
COLONNADE

HIGHPRIEST'S
GRAVE

GROUP OF THE
THOUSAND
COLUMNS

BALL
COURT

HOUSE OF THE
CORN GRINDERS

THE MARKET

SWEAT
BATH
No. 2

HOUSE OF
THE DEER

BALL COURT

BALL COURT

RED HOUSE

CAUSEWAY

XTOLOC
WELL

N

CARACOL

SWEAT
BATH
No. 1

TEMPLE OF THE WALL PANELS

NUNNERY

AKAB' DZIB

SCALE IN METERS

0   50   100

PLATE 39.—MAP OF THE CENTRAL SECTION OF CHICHEN ITZA,
YUCATAN, MEXICO

↑ *a*) Temple of the Warriors, general view showing Northwest Colonnade in foreground.

PLATE 40.—VIEWS OF CHICHEN ITZA, YUCATAN, MEXICO

↓ *b*) Temple of the Warriors, close up showing feathered-serpent columns.

↑ *a*) Big ball court.

PLATE 41.—VIEWS OF CHICHEN ITZA, YUCATAN, MEXICO

↓ *b*) Temple of the Jaguars surmounting south end of east wall of big ball court.

The most outstanding architectural characteristic of Tikal, aside from its size, are its five great pyramid-temples, the highest constructions in the Maya area (Plate 31, *a*). From the ground level at their respective bases to the tops of their lofty roof-combs, or ornamental walls which rise above their roofs, the temples measure in height as follows: Temple I, 155 feet; Temple II,.143 feet; Temple III, 178 feet; Temple IV, 229 feet (the highest structure in the Maya area (see Plates 52, *b*, and 70, *b*); and Temple V, 188 feet.

These enormous constructions are further noteworthy in that they have the finest wood-carvings in the Maya area. The twelve doorways, five exterior and seven interior, in these five temples were originally spanned by lintels of sapodilla wood, eight of them having been carved with magnificent representations of religious ceremonies. Most of these have been either destroyed or removed to foreign museums, the finest having been taken to the Museum of Archaeology at Basle, Switzerland (Plate 32, *a*). Figure 31 shows part of another one of these lintels—the figure of a *halach uinic* seated on his throne; rising behind him is the superb figure of a rampant jaguar, probably the divine patron of his family.

While the architecture of Tikal is imposing, even grandiose, stone sculpture at this great city languished except during the Early Period (317–633). Of the 83 stelae known at Tikal, only 20 are sculptured; the remaining 63 are plain. It has been suggested that these latter were originally covered with plaster and painted with figures and hieroglyphs instead of being carved, which may very well have been the case, although evidence either for or against this suggestion is now lacking. Of the twenty sculp-, tured stelae at Tikal, all but five, or 75 per cent, date from the Early Period.

The famous Leyden Plate found near Puerto Barrios, Guatemala, was a jadeite pendant (Plate 15) bearing the earliest contemporaneous date in the Maya hieroglyphic writing, 8.14.3.1.12 (320). My wife has recently shown that it was engraved at Tikal. This fact, coupled with that of the large number (fifteen) of

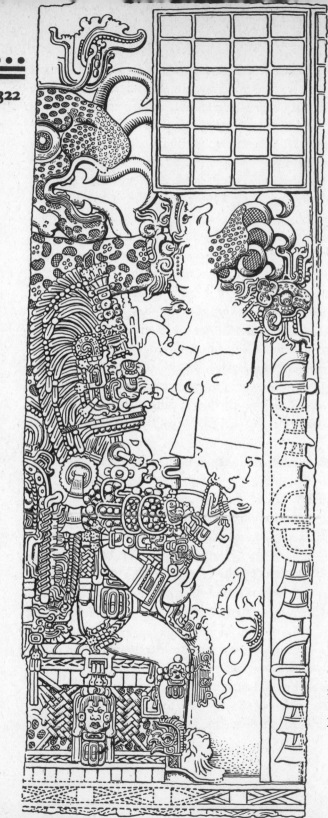

Fig. 31.—Part of a wooden door-lintel from Temple IV, Tikal, Peten, Guatemala. Now in the British Museum, London.

Early Period stelae found at this site and the additional fact that its size was considerably greater than that of near-by Uaxactun, indicates that Tikal, with very little doubt, was the oldest known center of Maya civilization. Uaxactun, fewer than twelve air miles from Tikal, has the next oldest date in Maya chronology.

COPAN, THE ALEXANDRIA OF THE MAYA WORLD

The second largest metropolis in the southern half of the peninsula was Copan, the scientific center of the Old Empire. This city consists of a main group and some sixteen dependent, outlying subgroups, one as much as seven miles distant from the ceremonial center. The main group, or Main Structure as it has been called (Plates 31, *b*, 34, and 37, *a*), covers about seventy-five acres and is composed of the Acropolis and five adjoining plazas. The Acropolis is an architectural complex of pyramids, terraces, and temples, which by reason of constant additions has grown into one great masonry mass covering twelve acres of ground and rising 125 feet at its highest point. It supports, among many other buildings, the three finest temples in the city: Temple 26 dedicated in 756 in connection with the completion of the Hieroglyphic Stairway; Temple 11 also erected in 756 in memory of an important astronomical discovery made at Copan (the determination of the exact length of the intervals between eclipses); and Temple 22 dedicated in 771 to the planet Venus, the last being the most spectacular building in the city.

There are no fewer than five courts or plazas at the Main Structure: (1) the Main Plaza, (2) the Middle Court, (3) the Court of the Hieroglyphic Stairway, and on the Acropolis, (4) the Eastern Court, (5) the Western Court. The Main Plaza, a large stadium 250 feet square and surrounded on three sides by tiers of stone seats, has a sacrificial pyramid occupying the center of the fourth or open side; there are nine magnificently sculptured monuments standing in this one court alone, and a number of elaborately carved altars.

The Court of the Hieroglyphic Stairway is some 310 feet long by 125 feet wide, at one end of which, just behind Stela M and its altar, rises the superb Hieroglyphic Stairway, 33 feet wide and composed of 62 steps. The faces of these steps are sculptured with some 1,500 to 2,000 individual glyphs, the longest inscription in the city, and also the longest in the Maya hieroglyphic writing (Plate 35, *a*). At the middle point of every twelfth step there is a seated, heroic-sized, gorgeously dressed, anthropomorphic statue. This monumental sculptured stairway, one of the most spectacular constructions in the whole Maya area, leads to Temple 26.

Both the Eastern and Western Courts on the Acropolis proper have floor levels considerably above the general ground level. The former has the beautiful Jaguar Stairway (Plate 35, *c*) on its western side, which is flanked by heroic-sized figures of rampant jaguars, the bodies of which were originally incrusted with disks of highly polished black obsidian to simulate the spots of a jaguar (Plate 35, *b*). The West Court has a very fine Reviewing Stand, Stela P, the latest monument of the Early Period (Plate 67, *d*), and several handsome altars.

One of the most interesting archaeological features at Copan is the cross-section of the Acropolis exposed by the Copan River (Plate 36, *c*). Some time since the city was abandoned in the early ninth century the Copan River has changed its course and, flowing over against the eastern base of the Acropolis, has cut away a great portion of it, exposing a vertical face 118 feet high at the highest point and nearly 1,000 feet long at the base—the largest archaeological cross-section in the world, wherein a number of earlier plaza floor-levels and buried drains can be clearly distinguished.

The Carnegie Institution of Washington has been carrying on excavations and repairs at Copan in co-operation with the government of Honduras since 1935. The course of the Copan River has been changed to its original channel so that the Acropolis is no longer threatened with destruction (Plate 37, *a*); more than a dozen fallen and broken monuments have been repaired and re-erected (Plate 68), much enhancing the appearance of this group of ruins. Temples 11, 21*a*, 22, 26, and the Ball Court (Structures 9 and 10) have been excavated and repaired; and several tunnels have been driven through the Acropolis in order to find whether it contained earlier buried constructions.

One of the most significant discoveries at Copan was the finding of two small fragments of gold, the feet of a hollow figurine, in the foundations of Stela H dedicated in 782. These are the only two pieces of gold, or indeed of any metal, ever recovered from an Old Empire city (Fig. 55, c, p. 432).

Sculpture reached spectacular heights at Copan; indeed, it was only surpassed in this art by the three great cities of the Usumacinta Valley—Palenque, Piedras Negras, and Yaxchilan—to be described later. Further, there is evidence to indicate that Copan was perhaps the greatest center of learning in the Old Empire, especially in the field of astronomy. The formulas of the Copan astronomer-priests for the determination of the true length of the solar year and of the eclipse periods were more accurate than those of any other Old Empire city; in short, because of her outstanding attainments in astronomy, Copan may be called the Alexandria of the Maya World.

CHICHEN ITZA, THE MECCA OF THE NEW EMPIRE

The greatest New Empire metropolis, and sacred city as well, was Chichen Itza in northeastern Yucatan, which was founded by Maya (Itza) emigrants from the Old Empire early in the sixth century. The city did not, however, reach its zenith until the eleventh, twelfth, and thirteenth centuries under Mexican rulers who had established themselves there in the tenth century (Plate 45, b). The civic and religious precincts cover an area of approximately two square miles, nearly two miles long by nearly a mile wide. While extending over a greater area than Tikal, the various groups at Chichen Itza are less numerous, smaller, and more scattered (Plates 38, a, 39, and 45, b).

The architecture, as might be expected from its history, shows two distinct styles: (1) a Maya period, the buildings of which date from the sixth to tenth centuries, pure Maya in style; and (2) a Maya-Mexican period, the buildings of which date from the eleventh to fourteenth centuries and show many architectural features imported from central Mexico (see last section of this chapter).

Perhaps the most striking architectural features at Chichen Itza are the pyramid-temples with feathered-serpent columns. Seven of these are known, of which the Castillo, or principal Temple of Kukulcan, is the largest and possibly the oldest (Plate 44, *a*), and the Temple of the Warriors is perhaps the most spectacular (Plate 40, *a*). One, the Temple of the Chac Mool, is buried in the pyramid supporting the later Temple of the Warriors. These serpent-column temples, dedicated to Kukulcan, the Feathered Serpent, who was the patron deity of Chichen Itza, were an importation from central Mexico introduced by Kukulcan himself during the tenth century (Plates 40, *b*, and 41, *b*).

There are no fewer than seven ball courts known at Chichen Itza: six that were still in use when the city was last occupied and a seventh, earlier one, completely buried under a later terrace behind the Monjas. These ball courts vary greatly in size; the largest, which is in the northern part of the city, is 545 feet long by 225 feet wide on the outside; the inside, that is, the actual field of play, is 480 feet long by 120 feet wide (Plate 41, *a*); the smallest court behind the Red House is only 65 feet long and 20 feet wide. A game something like basketball was played in these courts. Instead of baskets at the two ends of the court, however, there were two stone rings, one let into each of the long facing walls at their middle points. The balls used in the game were made of solid rubber, and the description of them given by the early Spanish historians constitutes the first European notice of rubber that we have. The object of the game was to drive the ball through one or the other of the two rings, whose openings were perpendicular to the ground. The winning stroke was further complicated by the fact that the ball could not be thrown by the hand, but had to be struck by the elbow, wrist, or hip. Leather pads were fastened to these parts of the body in order to make the ball rebound more easily. The winning stroke, we are told, was made so rarely that, by an ancient rule of the game, the player making it had forfeited to him all the clothing and jewelry of

the spectators. When the ball was thus driven through the ring,
however, all the spectators took to their heels to avoid paying the
forfeit, and the friends of the lucky player ran after them to
exact it. The winning stroke in the very nature of the case must
have been made very rarely, perhaps more by accident than by
design, like a hole-in-one at golf.

Another distinctive feature at Chichen Itza is the great
colonnades, sometimes 400 feet long (Plates 40, *a*, and 61, *b*).
Thrones have been found in these, and it has been suggested
they were used as council halls. These colonnades completely
surround the Court of the Thousand Columns, a great open plaza
containing four and a half acres, which may well have been the
market place of the ancient city; indeed, there are so many colonnades in this part of Chichen Itza that this section has been called
the Group of the Thousand Columns.

One of the most important structures at Chichen Itza is a
round tower or astronomical observatory (Plate 42, *a*). This
tower, called the Caracol, is 41 feet high and surmounts double
rectangular terraces, themselves combined 31 feet high. The tower
proper has a central core of masonry in which there is a spiral stairway, winding up to a small observation chamber near the top of the
tower. Such a stairway in Spanish is called *caracol* because of its
fancied resemblance to the convolutions of a snail-shell or *caracol*.
The presence of this winding stairway thus gave rise to the
name by which this building is now known. Square openings
through the thick walls of this chamber (Fig. 32) lead to the outside, fixing certain astronomically important lines of sight. For
example, one line of sight through the west wall cuts the setting
sun in half on March 21 and again on September 21, at the vernal
and autumnal equinoxes, respectively. Other lines coincide with
moonsets on these two important natural stations of the year. The
observation room near the top is still partially preserved.

Chichen Itza is probably better known than any other city
of the Maya civilization because of the extensive excavations and
restorations carried on there by the Ministry of Public Education
of the Mexican government and by the Carnegie Institution of

Washington during the past two decades. A number of buildings of different types have been excavated and repaired, wall-paintings and sculptures have been uncovered, and many archaeological specimens brought to light. The two most spectacular discoveries have been a magnificent turquoise mosaic plaque (Plate 43, *a*) and the Red Jaguar throne, a life-sized statue of a jaguar, painted a brilliant mandarin red and studded with seventy-three disks of apple-green jade in imitation of the actual markings of the jaguar

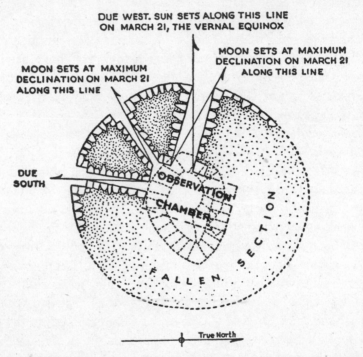

FIG. 32.—Plan of the Caracol, Chichen Itza, Yucatan, Mexico, showing its use as an astronomical observatory.

(Plate 73, *c*). The mosaic plaque, found in a stone urn with a stone lid, was excavated from beneath the floor of the sanctuary of the Temple of the Chac Mool—a temple found buried under the Temple of the Warriors. The Red Jaguar throne was discovered in the sanctuary of the temple buried beneath the Castillo (Plate 44, *a*) and, like the mummy of Tutankhamen, was left where it

↑ *a*) *Caracol* or astronomical observatory.

PLATE 42.—VIEWS OF CHICHEN ITZA, YUCATAN, MEXICO

↓ *b*) The Sacred *Cenote* or Well of Sacrifice.

a) Turquoise mosaic disk found in the Temple of the Chac Mool buried inside the pyramid supporting the Temple of the Warriors. →

PLATE 43.—TURQUOISE MOSAIC DISK

b) Covered round box of limestone in which the disk was found. →

↑ *a*) The Castillo or principal temple.

PLATE 44.—VIEWS OF CHICHEN ITZA, YUCATAN, MEXICO

↓ *b*) Dance platform in front of the Castillo.

↑ *a*) Painting (Old Empire), Palenque, Chiapas, Mexico.

↑ *b*) Painting (New Empire), Chichen Itza, Yucatan, Mexico.

↑ *c*) Painting (New Empire), Uxmal, Yucatan, Mexico.

PLATE 45.—PAINTINGS OF CITIES OF THE OLD AND NEW EMPIRES BY CARLOS VIERRA IN THE SAN DIEGO MUSEUM, SAN DIEGO, CALIFORNIA

was found. It is the most outstanding archaeological object ever discovered in the New World.

In the northern part of the city, there are two great natural wells or *cenotes*, which doubtless contributed very greatly to the importance of this site in ancient times. They are: the Xtoloc Cenote which was formerly the water supply of Chichen Itza, with two masonry stairways winding down its precipitous sides, and the great Well of Sacrifice (Plate 42, *b*), already described in a previous chapter (p. 239). Chichen Itza during the Mexican Period of the New Empire was the most sacred city in Yucatan. Pilgrimages were made thither from all parts of Central America, southern and central Mexico; and sacrifices of every sort—gold, jade, pottery, incense, etc., even living human victims—were hurled into the sinister depths of this well. Chichen Itza was, in truth, during late New Empire times the Mecca of the Maya world.

UXMAL, THE NEO-CLASSIC MAYA METROPOLIS OF THE NEW EMPIRE

Uxmal (Plates 38, *b*, and 45, *c*) was founded by the Xiu, one of the Maya-Mexican tribes which invaded Yucatan at the end of the tenth century (chapter v, p. 87). The city is located in a great, cup-like valley just behind the range of hills that sweep up from the southwest and southeast, coming to a point just south of the modern town of Maxcanu. Says Landa concerning the foundation of this city:

And they say that these tribes [the Xiu or Tutul Xiu] wandered around in the uninhabited parts of Yucatan for forty years without there being any water in that time except that which came from the rain, and that at the end of that time they reached the mountains which lie almost opposite the city of Mayapan and ten leagues from it. And there, they began to settle and to construct very good buildings in many places; and the people of Mayapan became very good friends with them and were glad to see that they cultivated the land as the natives do; and in this way those of Tutul Xiu subjected themselves to the laws of Mayapan and thus they intermarried and as the lord Xiu of the Tutul Xiu was such, he came to be very much esteemed by everybody.

The most beautiful Puuc buildings in all Yucatan (see last section of this chapter), what we may properly call the true Maya architectural renaissance, the neo-classic period of Maya architecture, are to be found at Uxmal (Plates 25, a, 46–48, and 51, a, c, and d). And curiously enough, the Mexican influence so strongly noticed at Chichen Itza is almost non-existent at the Xiu capital. There are no serpent-column temples at Uxmal, though there are six at Chichen Itza; no colonnades at Uxmal, though there are more than a dozen at Chichen Itza; there is only one small ball court at Uxmal, while there are six at Chichen Itza, in addition to a seventh buried under a later construction. Not a single building at Uxmal has the sloping base (see last section of this chapter), so common at Chichen Itza. Architectural conventions and ideas from central Mexico seem to have been little followed at Uxmal. On the contrary the Puuc, or neo-Classic Maya, here reached its finest expression.

The cutting and fitting of the individual elements of the elaborate stone-mosaic façades at Uxmal reached a perfection never equaled elsewhere in the Maya area. The edges of these intricately shaped elements are sharply cut, their surfaces smoothly dressed, and the elements themselves exactly fitted one to another in the exceedingly intricate patterns of the mosaics. The individual elements of these great mosaic façades are enormous, single stones frequently measuring a yard in length and weighing up to several hundred pounds. Although to our thinking the term mosaic refers to something small, even minute in scale, as used in Maya architecture it refers to these great façades, the individual elements of which are each cut to fit with other elements of the giant mosaic designs. The Governor's Palace, probably the administrative center of the Xiu state, surmounts a triple terrace 50 feet high and covering five acres of ground; the palace itself is 320 feet long, 40 feet wide, 26 feet high, and contains twenty-four chambers. The elaborate and rich mosaics decorating its four façades are composed of some twenty thousand specially cut and fitted stone elements. The Governor's Palace at Uxmal is, in my opinion, the most magnificent, the most spectacular single building ever erected in the Americas in pre-Columbian times (Plate 25, *a*).

Scarcely less beautiful, and probably even more imposing because of its greater mass, is the justly renowned Nunnery Quadrangle and adjacent House of the Magician (Plates 46–48). The former is composed of four different buildings with magnificently sculptured façades, arranged around the four sides of a majestic court some 250 feet long by 200 feet wide.

This court is entered through a central arcade in the building on its south side (Plate 46, *b*). The structure on the north or opposite side surmounts a considerably higher terrace, some eighteen feet above the level of the court, and is reached by a broad stairway 90½ feet wide; architecturally it is the most important unit of the quadrangle, though the two flanking units, the so-called East (Plate 47, *a*) and West (Plate 47, *b*) Ranges are scarcely less imposing.

This quadrangle probably served as a place of residence for the priests, who officiated in the near-by, and unfortunately, misnamed "House of the Magician" (Plate 48), which was the highest construction at Uxmal and the principal temple of the city.

In addition to the Puuc, or neo-classic Maya architectural influences found at Uxmal, a Chenes strain is noted there (see p. 353). This is especially apparent in the west façade of the principal temple, the so-called House of the Magician, which is Chenes in general character (Plate 48). Puuc architecture, however, predominates at Uxmal.

Although Chichen Itza covers considerably more ground than Uxmal, the architectural effect of the Xiu capital is much more imposing because its six largest groups are all concentrated in a relatively small area, with the result that their architectural effect is more immediate, more imposing, and more monumental; while at Chichen Itza, as previously pointed out, the larger groups are more scattered. The largest groups at Uxmal (Plate 49) are: (1) the Governor's Palace (Plate 25, *a*); House of the Turtles; Ball Court and Great Pyramid (Plate 51, *a*); (2) the Nunnery Quadrangle (Plates 46 and 47), and House of the Magician (Plate 48); (3) the South Group; (4) the Cemetery Group; (5) the Northwest Group; and (6) the House of the Old Woman, and associated structures. The greater concentration of buildings at Uxmal, together with the extreme beauty of the stone carving there, makes this site the best example of Maya neo-classic (Puuc) architecture in all Yucatan.

UAXACTUN, THE ANCIENT

While lack of space prevents extended description of all the Class 2 cities, a few words may be said about the more important ones.

Uaxactun is especially noteworthy to the archaeologist for five reasons:

1. It has the oldest monument yet discovered in the Maya area (Plate 16)—Stela 9 dating from 8.14.10.13.15 of the Maya Era (A.D. 328). In addition it has ten of the only other thirteen known stelae dating from Baktun 8, toward the end of which four-century period the Maya began to erect stone monuments (chapter iii, pp. 47, 48).

2. The Carnegie Institution of Washington carried on intensive archaeological studies at this site for twelve years (1926–1937), during which time invaluable scientific data and archaeological material of all kinds, including the finest examples of polychrome pottery ever found in the Maya area, were collected. Just as more is known about Chichen Itza than any other city of the New Empire, owing to the excavations by the Carnegie Institution, so, for the same reason, more is also now known about Uaxactun than any other city of the Old Empire.

3. Owing to the foregoing extensive excavations, the types of stone architecture and the ceramic periods represented at Uaxactun are better known than at any other Old Empire center; and, more important still, direct associations between specific architectural types and ceramic phases, together with their corresponding approximate dates in Maya chronology, have been so surely worked out for Uaxactun that they are now serving as standards of comparison elsewhere in the Old Empire.

4. The first astronomical observatory in the Old Empire was found at Uaxactun, and its type defined, which, in turn, led to the discovery of between twelve and eighteen similar observatories at as many other Old Empire sites. These Old Empire observatories would seem to have had for their primary purpose the fixing of the positions of the equinoxes and solstices in the year, in the following manner. A pyramid was built on the west side of a court, facing due east (Fig. 33). Opposite, on the east side of the

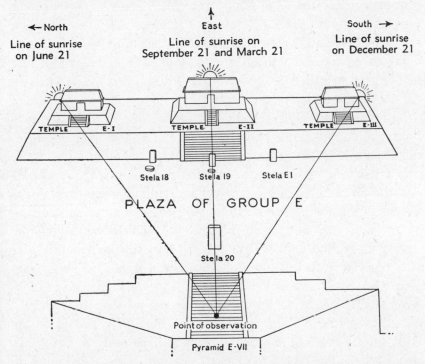

FIG. 33.—Diagram of the astronomical observatory at Group E, Uaxactun, Peten, Guatemala, for determining the dates of the solstices and equinoxes.

same court, three temples were erected on a terrace, their façades all running north and south and so arranged as to establish the following lines of sight when observed from points on the central axis of the stairway ascending the east side of the pyramid on the opposite or west side of the court. As observed from points on this axis the sun, on its way north, was seen to rise directly behind the middle point of the middle temple (E-II in Fig. 33) on March 21, the date of the vernal equinox; to rise behind the left or north front corner of the north temple (E-I in Fig. 33) on June 21, the date of the summer solstice; behind the middle point of the middle temple again on its way back south on September 21, the autumnal equinox; and behind the right or south front corner of the south temple (E-III in Fig. 33) on December 21, the winter solstice. This assemblage of buildings was a practical instrument for determining the four natural stations of the year: the longest and shortest days (June 21 and December 21, respectively), and the two intermediate positions when day and night are of equal length (March 21 and September 21). These buildings constituted an observatory which even the lowliest in the city could understand.

5. The finest Old Empire wall-painting ever brought to light was found in Structure B-XIII at Uaxactun. This represents some religious ceremonial (Plate 50). There is the figure of a woman, seated on a dais in a flat-roofed building, and outside the building twenty-five other individuals, some men, some women, are standing about. Below this scene is a horizontal band of 72 day-signs (not shown in Plate 50), which begins with the day 12 Imix, and ends with the day 5 Eb; this is evidently part of a *tzolkin* or Sacred Year of 260 days (p. 265). This fresco is painted in red, orange, yellow, gray, and black on a white background. It was in an admirable state of preservation when it was discovered; it probably dates from the Early Period of the Old Empire and is the oldest known wall-painting in the Maya area, perhaps going back to the sixth century of the Christian Era.

PALENQUE, YAXCHILAN, AND PIEDRAS NEGRAS

The three largest cities of the Usumacinta Valley—Palenque (Plate 45, a), Yaxchilan, and Piedras Negras—were also those where sculpture reached its esthetic peak, the culmination of Maya genius in this particular field of art, which was equaled nowhere else in ancient America. This amazing development in sculpture started at Palenque as early as the beginning of the

Middle Period, 9.10.10.0.0 (642), probably owing in part to the fact that the Palenque sculptors were fortunate in having a very superior grade of limestone, so hard and fine-grained as almost to have the quality of lithographic stone. Also, the stucco-work at Palenque is equaled nowhere else in the Maya area (Plate 77). The low-relief tablets of limestone are characterized by a delicacy of line and flowing beauty of composition coupled with a brilliance of technique that compares not unfavorably with the best low-relief sculptures of ancient Egypt. Although excellent low reliefs were produced at Palenque for nearly a century and a half from 9.10.10.0.0 to 9.17.13.0.0 (642–783), the peak of esthetic achievement was reached in 9.13.0.0.0 (692), when three different temples with their exquisite low-relief wall tablets were dedicated, the tablet in the Temple of the Cross perhaps being the finest (Plate 32, *b*).

With the exception of Copan, which was first described in 1576 by Diego García de Palacio, *Oidor* of the *Audiencia Real* of Guatemala, Palenque has been known longer than any other city of the Old Empire.

Palenque seems to have been discovered about the middle of the eighteenth century, and such is the distinction of its low-relief sanctuary tablets, the exquisite quality of its molded stucco decorations, and the refinement of its architecture that it is justly considered one of the most beautiful of all the ancient Maya cities.

The Palace Group is one of the most outstanding constructions in the Maya area. Its individual ranges of rooms, handsomely arranged around several courts, its high, square tower of four stories, and its many subterranean chambers and passages make it practically unique; the graceful proportions of the city's several pyramid-temples—the Temples of the Cross, Foliated Cross, Sun, Inscriptions, Count, and Beau-Relief—give Palenque a note of architectural elegance hardly equaled by any other center of the Maya civilization.

Yaxchilan, the second of these three cities, reached its highest level of artistic production in sculpture about a generation later, when Palenque was at its apex, about 9.13.0.0.0 (692). This level of maximum achievement was maintained for another generation, or until 9.14.15.0.0 (726), during which thirty-five years, four outstanding temples were erected at Yaxchilan— Structures 44, 21, 42, and 23. These buildings were richly embellished with twelve sculptured-stone lintels, three in each building. Two of the three in Structure 23 (Plate 71) are the finest sculptures of their kind in the Maya area.

Piedras Negras (Plate 52, *a*) was the last of the three great Usumacinta Valley centers to reach a similar plane of sculptural brilliance, again just about the time Yaxchilan was at its apex, that is completing the three superlative door-lintels in Structure 23 in 9.14.15.0.0 (726), just mentioned. The period of maximum brilliancy at Piedras Negras culminated in 9.16.10.0.0 (761), a generation later, in the magnificent Wall Panel No. 3, from Temple O-13 (Plate 69, *a*), made of a warm ivory-colored limestone of finest texture. Nowhere in the whole field of ancient American sculpture is there to be found a work of such surpassing beauty, such exquisite balance and harmony of design, such preeminent technical perfection. It is the finest flower of Maya art, the apex of sculptural attainment in the ancient New World.

One other point about Piedras Negras deserves special mention. The practice of erecting period-markers at the ends of the successive *hotuns*, or 1,800-day periods of the Maya Era, was more consistently followed here than at any other Maya city. For more than two centuries, from 9.8.15.0.0 to 9.19.0.0.0 (608 to 810), there is not a single one of these 22 consecutive hotun-endings which was not celebrated by the erection of a corresponding sculptured monument, and not one of these monuments is now missing —a tremendous and sustained sculptural *tour de force*.

CALAKMUL, NARANJO, AND NAKUM

These three cities, large centers of mass production in sculpture and architecture, all in the central Peten region, are interesting more because of their size than for the distinction of their respective buildings and monuments. Calakmul, as we have

↑ *a*) The so-called Nunnery Quadrangle, looking north.

PLATE 46.—VIEWS OF UXMAL, YUCATAN, MEXICO

b) South wing of the Nunnery Quadrangle, looking south; Palace of the
↓ Governor in the middle background.

↑ *a*) East wing of the Nunnery Quadrangle.

PLATE 47.—VIEWS OF UXMAL, YUCATAN, MEXICO

↓ *b*) West wing of the Nunnery Quadrangle.

PLATE 48.—HOUSE OF THE MAGICIAN, UXMAL, YUCATAN, MEXICO

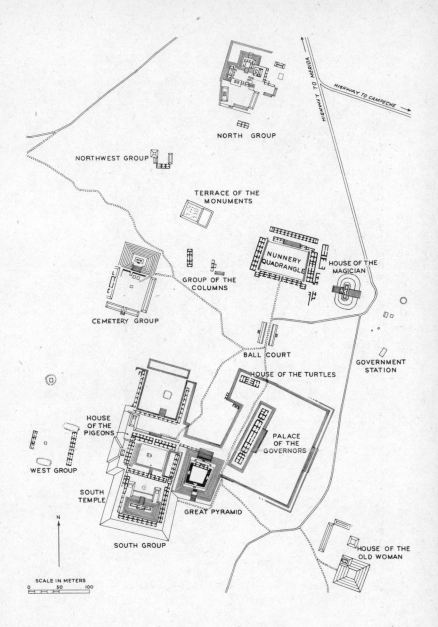

PLATE 49.—MAP OF THE CENTRAL SECTION OF UXMAL, YUCATAN, MEXICO

PLATE 50.—DRAWING OF A WALL-PAINTING IN

PLATE 51.—VIEWS OF UXMAL, YUCATAN, MEXICO, AND ALTAR FROM TIKAL

(*a*) Part of north face of temple near summit of the Great Pyramid, at Uxmal;
(*b*) Altar VIII from Tikal, Peten, Guatemala; (*c*) Stone mask step in front of
doorway leading to sealed chamber in building near summit of the Great Pyramid
at Uxmal; (*d*) Detail of masks on corner of the same building.

↑　*a*)　General view of Piedras Negras, Peten, Guatemala.

PLATE 52.—RESTORATIONS OF OLD EMPIRE CITIES

↓　*b*)　Model of Temples II, III, and IV, at Tikal, Peten, Guatemala.

↑ a

↑ b

↑ c

↑ d

(a) Sculptured rock out-cropping, Calakmul, Campeche, Mexico; (b) exterior of Maya thatch and sapling house, Tizimin, Yucatan, Mexico; (c) interior, showing three - stone oven at left and *banqueta* at extreme right; (d) beehives in thatched shelter, Piste, Yucatan, Mexico, found in all Maya villages; (e) interior of chamber in Palace of the Five Stories, Tikal, Peten, Guatemala; (f) Stela 10 (front), Seibal, Peten, Guatemala.

e
←

f
→

PLATE 53.—MISCELLANEOUS VIEWS OF NORTHERN YUCATAN (b, c, d) AND OF THE OLD EMPIRE (a, e, f)

← *a*) Stela 12 (T-26), Tonina, Chiapas, Mexico.

← *b*) Stela E, Quirigua, Izabal, Guatemala, largest shaft of stone ever quarried by the ancient Maya.

c) Stela 40, Piedras Negras, Peten, Guatemala, showing the corn-god sowing corn. →

PLATE 54
SCULPTURES OF THE
OLD EMPIRE

have already seen, has more stelae, 103 (73 sculptured, 30 plain) than any other city in the Maya area. Not content with marking the passing period-endings with the erection of a single monument at the end of each katun and half-katun, occasionally several monuments were set up at one time; thus, in 9.15.0.0.0 (731) no fewer than seven different stelae were erected to commemorate this particular katun-ending. However, even at the height of the Great Period, the Calakmul monuments were not of especial esthetic merit, no sculptures of outstanding distinction having been produced there. The emphasis would rather seem to have been placed more on mass production, on quantity rather than on quality. The architecture at Calakmul, while extensive, is also not particularly distinguished, emphasis again having been placed on the size and number of the buildings rather than on their individual excellence.

A most interesting feature at Calakmul is a sculptured outcropping of the native limestone, an irregularly shaped ledge measuring 21 feet long by 17 feet wide and perhaps 10 or 12 inches high in the center. Seven captive figures with their hands bound behind their backs are carved on the top of this outcropping, the largest figure measuring 9 feet high (Plate 53, a).

Naranjo is another city characterized by extensive architectural remains and 47 stelae (36 sculptured, 11 plain), but again neither buildings nor monuments are specially noteworthy. Naranjo was considerably smaller than Calakmul, the latter of which is the largest Class 2 site known.

Nakum was a very large and important center. Its architectural remains are extensive, much more so than those of Naranjo but less so than those of Calakmul. It has fewer monuments, however—only 15 stelae (3 sculptured and 12 plain) compared either with Calakmul or Naranjo. There is some basis for believing that Nakum was founded only shortly before the end of the Old Empire, which might well account for the scarcity of monuments there. The only three dated stelae at Nakum are all late (771, 810, and 849, respectively); in fact, no Early or Middle Period dated monuments have been found in this city.

Quirigua (Plate 31, *c*), though one of the smallest cities of the second class, is one of the most striking because of its splendid series of monuments, composed of 12 sculptured stelae, 4 sculptured zoömorphs or great boulder-like mythological animals, and one temple. This series of 17 *hotun*-markers covers a period of about 65 years from 9.15.15.0.0 to 9.19.0.0.0 (A.D. 746–810), one *hotun*-ending, 9.17.5.0.0 (775), even being marked by the erection of two stelae. The ancient Quirigua sculptors with their stone chisels were held in restraint in the carving of their monuments because of the hardness of the native sandstone at Quirigua, a sedimentary rock containing many coarse quartz crystals. Elsewhere, but not at Quirigua, a certain flamboyancy of design and execution crept in, especially toward the close of the Great Period. Here the hardness of the local stone held the sculptors to simpler designs, which give the Quirigua monuments a greater dignity and nobility than those of most other Maya cities, and render them correspondingly more attractive to the modern eye.

The largest block of stone ever quarried by the ancient Maya was found at Quirigua—that from which Stela E, dedicated in 9.17.0.0.0 (771), was fashioned. This giant shaft of sandstone measures 35 feet long, 5 feet wide, 4 feet 2 inches in thickness, and weighs 65 tons (Plate 54, *b*).

The largest center in the southwest highlands was Tonina, a provincial city, and, so far as its monuments are concerned, the least typical of all Maya Old Empire sites. The Tonina stelae, of which the 16 (15 sculptured and 1 plain) now known, are all very low compared with the stelae of other Maya cities; the latter average between 8 and 10 feet in height, while none of the Tonina stelae is more than 7 feet high, most of them being under 6 feet. They differ from all other Maya stelae also in another very important respect: they are carved in the complete round, like statuary (Plate 54, *a*), a characteristic shared by no other stelae in the Maya area. Except for their relatively diminutive size, the Tonina stelae closely resemble the figures on the fronts and backs of the Quirigua and Copan stelae (Plates 54, *b*, and 68, respectively).

Coba was the earliest important Old Empire city in north-eastern Yucatan, 9.9.10.0.0 (623); it seems to have been founded about one hundred and fify years later than Oxkintok, dated 9.2.0.0.0 (475), in northwestern Yucatan, the latter having the oldest surely dated sculpture (the Hieroglyphic Lintel, Plate 18, *a*) in the northern peninsula. Coba is also the next to largest Class 2 center known. It is beautifully located amidst five small lakes, a very rare physiographic feature in the all-but-waterless plain of northern Yucatan. The largest, Lake Coba, from which the site takes its name, is just under a mile in length and half a mile in width (Plate 37, *b*).

The city is chiefly notable for the following four character-istics:

1. Its highly favored location around the shores of the five lakes just mentioned.

2. Its exceedingly long period of occupation, probably longer than that of any other Maya city, either of the Old Empire, or the New, going back to 9.9.10.0.0 (623) and coming down to late New Empire times, say the fourteenth or fifteenth centuries—a matter of seven or eight hundred years.

3. The presence of more Old Empire stelae—32 (23 sculptured and 9 plain)—than at any other two cities in northern Yuca-tan combined.

4. The *sacbeoob*, or raised, artificial roads, of which there are at least sixteen known, a veritable network of stone causeways connecting the central section of the site with its outlying groups.

The word *sacbe* (*sacbeoob*, plural) means in Maya "artificial road"—*sac*, "something artificial, made by hand," and *be*, "road." These roads are built of the local limestone and vary in height from two to eight feet above the ground level, depending upon surface inequalities of the terrain (Plate 55, *a*). They usually run straight as an arrow; their sides are built of roughly dressed stone and their tops covered with a limy gravel, a natural lime-cement called *sahcab*, which hardens under wetting and pressure. The roads are about 15 feet wide and vary in length from less than a mile to 62.3 miles. The longest causeway (Plate 19) runs generally westward from Coba to Yaxuna and is straight except for the following very slight deviations: during the first 20 miles west from Coba there are five minor changes of direction, probably introduced to allow the road to pass through small intervening settlements; the causeway is straight throughout its middle third, 21.3 miles long, and straight for the last stretch of 21 miles, the bearing of this last section being almost the same as that of the second section. Two of these causeways, which intersect each other just south of the narrow isthmus between the two largest lakes at Coba, appear clearly as two straight lines across the face of the forest in the airplane picture of the Coba region shown in Plate 37, *b*.

Perhaps the most interesting discovery in connection with the Coba-Yaxuna highway was the finding of an ancient Maya road-roller just west of the small site of Ekal where the causeway changes direction for the last time, and goes west. This large cylinder of limestone, now broken in two pieces (Plate 55, *b*), measures 13 feet long, 2 feet 4 inches in diameter, and weighs 5 tons. There is room for fifteen men to have pushed this at one time and when rolled back and forth along the highway on top of the lime-gravel finish, it must have packed the latter into a hard-surface layer.

Several important deductions may be made from this causeway: First, it was built from east to west, that is, from Coba to Yaxuna; and, further, when it was constructed—probably not later than the Middle Period of the Old Empire—Coba was the largest city in northeastern Yucatan. This becomes apparent when it is noted that of the seven changes in direction of the highway the first six are made within 20 miles of Coba in order to pass through smaller settlements dependent on it, whereas the western terminus Yaxuna, at that early date in the Maya occupation of Yucatan, was still a small place in the then-remote wilderness. Again, had Chichen Itza then been the metropolis that it later became this highway would have connected Coba with Chichen Itza and not Coba with Yaxuna. A fine highway from New York to Gary, Indiana, instead of being carried on the few remaining miles into Chicago would be a modern analogy. Obviously when this highway was built, Chichen Itza had not yet been established as a center of Maya culture. Indeed, I strongly believe that Old Empire culture was first introduced into northeastern Yucatan along the east-coast region and via Coba, and that it was first carried to Chichen Itza by Old Empire Maya from Yaxuna about 9.4.0.0.0 (514), as already described (chapter iv, pp. 76–80).

KABAH, A CITY OF THE PUUC, OR YUCATAN HILL COUNTRY

The region behind or south of the two converging ranges of low hills that come together just northwest of Uxmal (Plate 1) is called the Puuc (Maya hilly country). During the eleventh and twelfth centuries, this section of Yucatan supported the densest population in the entire northern half of the Peninsula, a population which was gathered around many ceremonial centers, the most important of which was Uxmal, already described, and the second largest, Kabah, located only nine miles southeast of Uxmal and connected therewith by a stone causeway. Kabah was doubtless a dependent city of the Xiu state, since it was so near the Xiu capital and, moreover, is connected with it by the causeway just mentioned. The most interesting structure at Kabah is the so-called Palace of the Masks (Plate 56, a), which is 151 feet long and contains ten handsome chambers arranged in two tiers of five each; the chambers of each pair are built one directly behind the other, with a single outside doorway for each pair. The exteriors of most Maya buildings, as will be explained in the next section, are usually devoid of sculptural decoration below the medial molding, while the often exceedingly rich and intricate mosaics are principally concentrated in the upper half of the façades. The Palace of the Masks, however, is different in this respect. It stands on a low platform, the face of which is decorated with a single row of mask panels; above this is a rich lower molding, surmounted by the lower half of the façade composed of three rows of mask panels running entirely across the front of the building. The medial molding of this building is perhaps the most ornate of any in Yucatan; above it, in the upper half of the façade, there are again three rows of mask panels, the top-most row being surmounted by a third and terminal molding. The effect of this lavishly sculptured façade is overwhelming, and the building itself is one of the handsomest examples of Puuc architecture that has come down to us.

Another unique feature at Kabah is the stone arch shown in Plate 56, *b*. It stands disconnected from any other building at the beginning of the stone causeway leading to Uxmal, the arch having a span of fifteen feet. What was it?—a triumphal arch commemorating some long-forgotten Maya victory? Or, perhaps more likely, was it a formal gateway dedicated to some deity of the Maya pantheon? Who knows? All who could have told are gone, and these questions, like so many others, remain unanswered.

ARCHITECTURE

ORIGIN

Maya stone architecture is as distinctive as Greek, Roman, or Gothic. It has its own canons, its own structural practices, its local variations, but fundamentally it is one, and has but a single point of origin—namely northern central Peten, probably at the city of Tikal or Uaxactun.

It has been suggested that the thatched hut of modern Yucatan, with its sharply pitched roof of two slopes, which has remained unchanged since Old Empire times, was the prototype of the Maya corbel-arched stone buildings. This theory is not improbable. The thatched hut of the common people, just the same two thousand years ago as it still is today, was rectangular with rounded ends; it is about 22 to 24 feet in length by 12 to 14 feet in width. The side walls and rounded ends are made of saplings daubed with mud, or of undressed stone, not more than 7 feet in height; resting on them, a framework of poles, rising another 12 or 15 feet, supports the sharply pitched two-slope roof of thatch (Plate 57, *a*).

Representations of these homes of the common people occur both in wall-paintings and façade decorations of the New Empire (Plates 57, *b*, and 90, and Fig. 54, p. 424). The actual foundations of such a house, even to the prints of the saplings which formed the rounded ends and straight side walls, have been found in one of the earliest levels of the palace (Structure A-V.) at Uaxactun. The sharply sloping interiors of these thatch-roofed houses somewhat resemble the steep slopes of the corbel-vaulted, stone-roofed buildings, and this resemblance is further enhanced by the wooden cross-poles found in the chambers of Maya stone buildings (Plate 53, *e*), which look like the cross-poles of Maya thatched huts. The sharply sloping roofs of the latter were doubtless for the purpose of shedding water rapidly, so that it would not penetrate the thatch, but the resemblance between the thatched huts and the stone buildings, particularly as viewed from the inside of each, is so close as to suggest forcibly that the interior slopes of the thatched roofs originally gave rise to the idea of the stone-corbel roof-vaults.

All materials for stone masonry were everywhere close at hand, and in the greatest abundance: an easily worked building-material, the local limestone, which, on burning, yielded lime; and many gravel deposits, the gravel of which was used in mortar in place of sand. It was inevitable, given the high intelligence and native genius of the ancient Maya, coupled with their strong religious fervor, that they should develop a great religious architecture of their own, which is just what they did. Beyond the immediate needs of their domestic economy—corn-planting, pottery-making, and weaving—no other activity consumed so much of their remaining time and energy as did their architecture.

THE OLDEST EXAMPLE OF MAYA ARCHITECTURE

We saw in Table III (facing p. 40) that there were presumably no stone buildings in the first and second periods at Uaxactun, Pre-Maya I and II; but since the people had to live in something, and had to have shelters for even their simple gods, they undoubtedly had houses of thatch, which have since entirely disappeared. In the third period—Pre-Maya III—however, low stone walls one or two courses high begin to appear. It is doubtful that stone buildings proper were erected at the beginning of this period; the low stone walls found in association with early Chicanel pottery were simply retaining or facing walls of low platforms, which supported superstructures of perishable materials only, such as saplings and thatch. Toward the close of Pre-Maya III, however, we find our first large stone construction. Strictly speaking it was still not a building but a pyramid for supporting a superstructure of saplings and thatch.

The earliest example of Maya stone architecture that has survived is the stucco-covered under-pyramid, E-VII-sub, at Uaxactun (Plate 17, b), and the reason for its remarkable state of preservation is simple: Very shortly after it was finished, perhaps sometime during the second century of the Christian Era, it was completely covered by a rough-rubble, masonry pyramid, E-VII (Plate 17, a). The sides of this later construction also had originally been decorated with great stucco masks like the earlier E-VII-sub (Plate 58). The top of this later, stucco-covered pyramid was so small that it obviously could never have supported a stone building; there was not enough space for one on its summit. Furthermore, when the rubble-hearting of the later E-VII which had completely encased and preserved E-VII-sub was removed, it was found that this earlier pyramid also had never supported a stone superstructure, because in the lime-plaster flooring of the summit of E-VII-sub four filled-in postholes forming a rectangle were found; these undoubtedly had originally held the corner posts of a thatch-and-sapling superstructure.

This stucco-covered pyramid, ascended by four stairways, one on each side, and decorated with sixteen heroic-sized stucco masks each eight feet square (Plate 58), is a marvel of early Maya architecture. It was never painted, and its lime-stucco finish when first uncovered glistened like silver in the sunlight. Its style is so early as to be proto-Maya, rather than pure Maya

a) Side of causeway at highest point.

PLATE 55.—STONE CAUSEWAY CONNECTING THE CITIES OF COBA, QUINTANA
ROO, AND YAXUNA, YUCATAN, MEXICO

b) Stone road-roller, found broken on top of the causeway.

↑ *a*) Palace of the Masks, the principal building.

PLATE 56.—VIEWS OF KABAH, YUCATAN, MEXICO

↓ *b*) The arch.

↑ *a*) Maya thatch and sapling house, Hacienda Tanlum, Yucatan, Mexico.

PLATE 57.—MAYA THATCH AND SAPLING HOUSE

b) Reproduction of house in stone as an element of façade decoration,
↓ South wing of the Nunnery Quadrangle, Uxmal, Yucatan, Mexico.

↑ *a*) Human type.

PLATE 58.—STUCCO MASKS, PYRAMID E-VII-SUB, UAXACTUN, PETEN, GUATEMALA

↓ *b*) Serpentine type.

in character. However, though built of masonry, it is only a substructure, and clearly antedates the first stone buildings proper.
It is in fact, barring the low walls of the early Chicanel ceramic
period just mentioned, the oldest Maya stone construction that
has come down to us and probably dates from the second century
of the Christian Era.

CORBELED-STONE ROOF-VAULTING

With the introduction of the stone-stela complex and Tzakol
pottery at Uaxactun about 8.14.0.0.0 (317), we meet the earliest
example of corbeled-stone roof-vaulting in the Maya area. This
is found in one of the lowest levels of the palace at Uaxactun,
however, and is not used in the roof-vault of a chamber but only
in that of a tomb. Probably as early as 8.17.0.0.0 (376), however, the first corbeled vaults were being used to roof chambers.
The earliest examples of roof-vaults are very crude, composed of
rough, unshaped, flat stones, laid in a thick bed of mortar and
small stone; the under slopes of the corbeled arches, or soffits,
are also covered with a thick coat of plaster, and present very
uneven surfaces (Fig. 34, *d* and *g*).

About a hundred years after its introduction at Uaxactun,
during the fourth century, the use of corbeled roof-vaults began
to spread in all directions. It reached the extreme southeast at
Copan, possibly as early as 9.0.0.0.0 (435); northwestern Yucatan at Oxkintok, surely as early as 9.2.0.0.0 (475); northeastern
Yucatan at Tulum, perhaps as early as 9.6.10.0.0 (564); and the
Usumacinta Valley by 9.10.0.0.0 (633), or possibly even earlier.

Before the end of the Old Empire, in 10.8.0.0.0 (987), the
corbeled roof-vault had penetrated to every part of the Maya
area and, curiously enough, it was restricted to the Maya area.
It is not found today in any of the immediately adjacent regions;
its westernmost occurrence is at Comalcalco in the state of Tabasco,
Mexico, and its southeasternmost occurrences at Papalguapa and
Asunción Mita in southeastern Guatemala. The corbeled roof-
vault does not occur at all in the highlands of Guatemala except in
the roofing of a few scattered tombs. Its scarcity probably is due

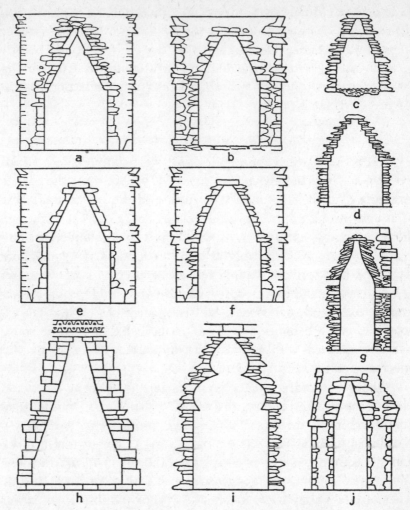

FIG. 34.—Cross-sections of Maya corbeled vaults: (*a*) Monjas Annex, Chichen
Itza; (*b*) section of ordinary arch with flat capstones and undressed sides,
characteristic of the Old Empire; (*c*) viaduct, Palenque; (*d*) Temple E-X,
Uaxactun; (*e*) section of ordinary arch with flat capstones and dressed sides,
characteristic of the New Empire; (*f*) section of ordinary arch with flat capstones,
dressed sides, and curved soffit slopes; (*g*) Palace (Structure A-V), Uaxactun;
(*h*) arcade through Governor's Palace, Uxmal; (*i*) Trifoil arch, Palace, Palenque; (*j*) second story, Monjas, Chichen Itza.

to the intense earthquake activity of this latter region. Finally,
the only section of either the Old or New Empire where corbeled-
stone roof-vaulting has not been found is in the Pasión Valley.
This valley is wide and the ranges of hills bounding it stand well
back from the river, which explains a relative scarcity of building
stone along or near the riverbank. Most of the six or seven
known sites, none so large as Class 2, are located near the riverbank, away from the hills. Moreover, not one of these sites has
been excavated, and it is probable that corbeled-stone roof-vaults
will eventually be found at one or more of them.

FLAT, LIME-CONCRETE AND BEAM ROOFS

In addition to the corbeled roof-vaults described above, there
is another type of roofing found in Maya architecture—namely
flat, lime-concrete and beam roofs. Although these latter would
logically seem to have preceded the more complicated corbeled
roofs, they have not been commonly found, perhaps because
when fallen they are difficult to identify.

They have been discovered in the Old Empire at Piedras
Negras, Uaxactun, and Tzimin Kax; in the New Empire at
Chichen Itza; and at relatively late sites along the east coast of
Yucatan, notably at Tulum and Chac Mool. These lime-concrete
roofs were constructed on top of crossbeams, the interbeam spaces
first being filled with temporary wattlework of saplings. On this
wattlework and on the beams, a lime-concrete roofing was then
built up to the thickness of a foot or more; when the latter had set
firmly the wattlework was removed leaving individual small arches
between the beams. This method of roofing is still practiced commonly in Yucatan today. In actual excavation, the residue of such
roofs is hard to identify as such, since they disintegrate into little
more than small stones and a powdery lime. However, in practically all cases where vault-stones are not found in excavating
masonry buildings, it is safe to assume that such structures had
formerly been roofed with these flat, lime-concrete and beam
roofs; and they were probably far more common than the meager
evidence we now have of them suggests.

Practically all Maya buildings were built on substructures which vary in height, depending upon the use of the buildings they support; they vary from low terraces 2 to 6 feet high in the case of palaces, monasteries, and domiciliary buildings, to as much as 150 feet high in the case of the highest pyramid-temples (Temple IV at Tikal). These substructures are ascended by broad, steep stairways on one or more sides. The buildings proper are usually set back on the summits of their respective substructures, leaving a wide space between their fronts and the stairways giving access to them. At the back and sides, however, they are built close to the edges of the substructure.

Maya façades are usually divided into two main horizontal bands or zones by a medial molding running entirely around the building about halfway up the height of the exterior wall. Another similar molding runs around the top of the building (Plates 46, *b*, and 47). Roofs are made of hard lime-concrete and are flat, usually a little higher in the center than around the edges, though never by more than a foot; they slope toward the sides to facilitate the immediate drainage of the heavy rainfall. At Copan, Chichen Itza, and Uxmal, there are sometimes projecting gargoyle-like roof drains to carry off the water from the roofs.

On top of the roof, parallel with the front of the building and usually directly over the central axis, a high wall running the entire length is frequently found. These roof walls are sometimes as high again as the building itself, and are nonstructural in nature, their only purpose being decorative.

These nonstructural walls on the tops of Maya buildings have been called roof-combs; they have no counterpart in our own architecture, unless it be in the false fronts of wooden buildings in our early western boom towns.

Ground plans vary greatly according to the purpose which the building served (Fig. 35). Temples (Fig. 35, *b*) usually have fewer rooms than palaces; indeed, the usual type of temple has but two chambers, one directly behind the other, entered by one or three exterior doorways in the front wall. The inner chamber

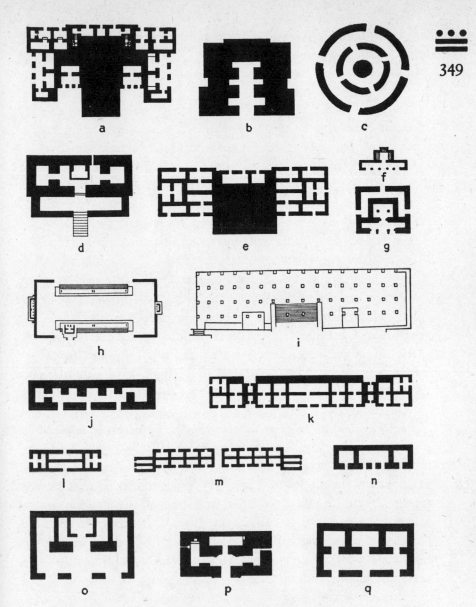

Fig. 35.—Maya ground plans: (a) Palace, Santa Rosa Xtampak; (b) Temple IV, Tikal; (c) Caracol or astronomical observatory, Chichen Itza; (d) Temple E-II, Uaxactun; (e) Akabtzib, Chichen Itza; (f) Vapor bath No. 2, Chichen Itza; (g) Castillo or principal Temple of Kukulcan, Chichen Itza; (h) ball court, Chichen Itza; (i) Northwest Colonnade, Chichen Itza; (j) Structure 33, Yaxchilan; (k) Governor's Palace, Uxmal; (l) House of the Turtles, Uxmal; (m) House of the Pigeons, Uxmal; (n) Structure 21, Yaxchilan; (o) Temple of the Sun, Palenque; (p) Temple 22, Copan; (q) Red House, Chichen Itza.

was the sanctuary proper, while the outer chamber was used for less sacred ceremonies (Fig. 35, *q*). In the palace type of building, which is usually long, there are generally two ranges of chambers, one directly behind the other. These may have doorways in the front wall, in which case the inner chambers are entered through doorways in the back walls of the chambers directly in front of them; or again the back range of chambers may be entered directly through doorways in the back wall of the building (Fig. 35, *e* and *m*). In this latter case doorways are rarely found in the long central wall separating the two ranges, and almost never are they found in the transverse partition walls. These last observations apply especially to the "palaces" of the New Empire; however, at Piedras Negras (Old Empire) doorways in both the medial and transverse walls are not infrequent.

There are no windows as such, though occasionally small rectangular openings pierce the upper half of the façade for ventilating the otherwise airless chambers. A number of ground plans are shown in Figure 35; they exhibit considerable variety, but most of them may be traced back directly to a few simple forms, of which the two most common are the temple type and the palace type.

Another point worthy of mention in connection with Maya architecture is that no matter how skillfully their individual building blocks may have been cut and dressed (and in the case of mosaic elements, carved as well), all walls, both exterior and interior, were originally covered with lime-plaster, which hid all joints. Again, and especially in the case of buildings in Yucatan, no attempt was made to break joints. This is proved by the fact that the blocks appearing in Yucatan façades are not truly functional in character, being only in the nature of a veneer; this veneer frequently peels off, leaving the walls standing. The walls are, in fact, monolithic, being made of solid lime-concrete.

In the smaller towns and villages of northern Yucatan, limekilns are still made as they were in ancient times, and the local limestone is still burned to make lime just as it probably has been done for the last two thousand years. A place in the forest is se-

lected and completely cleared. Fagots of wood about two feet long
are next cut and laid in a circle varying from ten to twenty feet in
diameter depending upon the size of the kiln to be built. These
fagots are laid with their lengths parallel to the radii of the circle,
a hole about a foot in diameter being left in the center. This
neatly laid pile of wood is built to a height of about four feet
(Plate 76, *a*). On top of it, beginning about a foot back from its
outer edge, are piled broken pieces of limestone about the size of
one's fist. These are heaped to a height of another two feet.

When this is finished the kiln is fired by dropping leaves and
rotten wood into the bottom of the hole at the center and igniting
them. The fire thus works from the bottom up and from the
inside of the kiln outward. Two precautions, the Maya believe,
are vital to a successful burn: first there must be no wind at all,
so that the kiln will burn evenly on all sides at the same time, the
flames working straight upward through the piled fagots and stone
fragments; and second no women must be allowed even to approach the spot, and should one as much as touch the kiln the
burn will be a failure. It takes thirty-six hours for a kiln to
burn completely, and when a good burn has been achieved the
limestone fragments are completely reduced to a pile of powdered
lime (Plate 76, *b*).

Some archaeologists consider that the labor involved in cutting the wood for Maya lime-kilns and door-lintels with only
stone axes was greater even than that involved in quarrying the
enormous quantities of stone used in their buildings.

As is to be expected, not only pronounced temporal differences
but also marked regional variations developed in Maya architecture during the twelve hundred odd years that these ancient
people were erecting stone buildings. These variations are clearly
reflected in different types of assemblage, and in details of construction as well as in styles of decoration. However, considering the long span of time covered by their building activity, the
large area where it flourished, and the many diverse local influences which affected its development, Maya architecture is,
on the whole, singularly homogeneous.

An attempt has been made in Table VIII to classify Maya buildings and other constructions objectively, that is, according to their probable uses as temples, palaces, etc. Such a classification is by no means rigid as there are bound to be borderline cases which will fall equally well into one or the other of two groups; but in general, the characteristics and, in many cases, the functions of the buildings are so obvious that the classification given in Table VIII will be found to be fairly exhaustive.

DECORATION OF BUILDINGS

In the early part of the Old Empire the buildings do not appear to have been heavily decorated, certainly not with carved-stone elements. Façades, as a rule, were vertical with medial and top moldings; these latter were made of projecting courses of rough stones and in all cases were brought to a finish with coats of plaster (Plate 59, a and b). Some Old Empire buildings, at Copan, Palenque, and Tikal for example, have sloping façades above the level of the medial molding, which are much like our own mansard roofs of the 'seventies and 'eighties. Later the upper zones of the façade, that is, the area between the medial and top moldings, began to be somewhat sparingly decorated, mostly with stucco at first. This type of façade decoration reached its highest development in the Old Empire at Palenque during the Middle Period when both the upper and lower zones of the façade were richly embellished with elaborate designs, even including hieroglyphic inscriptions. These designs were molded in very hard lime-stucco, built upon, and held in place by rough stones projecting from the façade.

There does not seem to have been much carved-stone decoration in the upper half of the façade during the Old Empire except at Copan and Quirigua, certainly nothing comparable to that found in New Empire buildings. Occasionally sculpture was employed in exterior decoration—in wall panels (Piedras Negras), or on ramps flanking stairways (Palenque, Copan, Quirigua), and on the risers of steps (in rare cases on the treads).

↑ *a*) The Labyrinth (Structure 19), Yaxchilan, Chiapas, Mexico.

PLATE 59.—OLD EMPIRE FAÇADES

↓ *b*) Temple of the Five Stories (Structure 10), Tiḳal, Peten, Guatemala.

↑ *a*) Corner mask panel from the House of the Magician, Uxmal, Yucatan, Mexico.

↑ *b*) Mask panel at top of west stairway, House of the Magician, Uxmal, Yucatan, Mexico.

PLATE 60.—NEW EMPIRE FAÇADES, PUUC PERIOD

↓ *c*) The Church, Nunnery group, Chichen Itza, Yucatan, Mexico.

a) Tzompantli, or Place of the Skulls, Chichen Itza, Yucatan, Mexico.

PLATE 61.—NEW EMPIRE FAÇADES, MEXICAN PERIOD

b) Colonnade, interior of the Market, Chichen Itza, Yucatan, Mexico.

↑ *a*) "Quarry stumps" on base of Stela J, Quirigua, Izabal, Guatemala.

PLATE 62.—QUARRYING OPERATIONS, OLD EMPIRE

↓ *b*) Two partially quarried shafts, Calakmul, Campeche, Mexico.

These steps are sometimes found to be carved with hieroglyphic inscriptions (Copan, Quirigua, Palenque, Yaxchilan, Naranjo, Seibal, La Amelia, Etzna). The use of sculpture as a means of decoration in the interiors of Old Empire buildings is also not common. It occurs on sanctuary tablets at Palenque already described and illustrated (Plate 32, *b*), on the jambs of and flanking interior doorways at Copan, and on the risers of interior steps and wall decorations at Quirigua, but it is still unusual.

As we come down to the New Empire, however, we find the practice of using sculpture as decoration changed. In the Chenes region just north of the Old Empire, in central Campeche and western Quintana Roo, Mexico, façades are elaborately decorated, not only above, but also below the medial molding. These Chenes façades are indeed the most ornate and complicated in the Maya area. The Puuc area, lying in the low hilly country of northern central Yucatan, north and northwest of the Chenes region, is the most fertile and densely populated section of the New Empire. In this area, which is the home of the neo-classic Maya architecture, sculpture is largely confined to the upper zones of façades (Plates 25, *a*, 46, *b*, and 47), though an occasional sculptured lower zone is also found (Plate 56, *a*). The designs are largely geometric: small, engaged half-columns, frets, latticework patterns, and mask panels (Plate 60), though occasionally human, animal, bird, and serpent figures are tenoned into the upper halves of the façades.

In the Puuc region the individual elements of these vast, sculptural mosaics in heroic size are better-shaped, -dressed, -carved, and -fitted than they are anywhere else, either in the New Empire or the Old. Here architecture reached heights never attained before, and never, so far as the Maya are concerned, equaled again. Sculpture, so exquisitely developed during the Old Empire, principally in the decoration of stelae and altars, languished as an independent art in New Empire times. It became subordinate to architecture, and, indeed, was almost exclusively restricted to façade embellishment, with the result that separate, independent pieces of sculpture largely disappeared.

TABLE VIII

Classification of Maya Buildings and Other Constructions According to Their Probable Uses

Kind of Building, or Construction	Examples		Corresponding Plates in This Book	
	Old Empire	New Empire	Old Empire	New Empire
Pyramid-temples	Temples I, II, III, IV, V, Tikal; Temple 26, Copan	Castillo, Chichen Itza; House of the Magician, Uxmal	II, III, and IV, Plate 52, a; IV, only, Plates 70, b, 32, a	Plates 44, a, 48
Small temples	Structures 20, 21, 33, 42, 44, Yaxchilan	Red House, Chichen Itza; House of the Old Woman, Uxmal		
Palaces	Palace, Palenque; Palace (Structure A-V), Uaxactun	Monjas, Chichen Itza; Governor's Palace, Uxmal		Plate 25, a
Astronomical observatories	Structures E-I, E-II, E-III, E-VII, Uaxactun; Structures II, III, IV, VIII, Naachtun	Caracol, Chichen Itza; Round Tower, Mayapan	E-VII, only, Plate 17, a, b	Plate 42, a
Ball courts	Structures 9 and 10, Copan; Structure 14, Yaxchilan	Ball court, Chichen Itza; Ball court, Uxmal		Plate 41, a, b
Colonnades	Structure J-2, Piedras Negras; Structure 74, Yaxchilan	Northwest Colonnade, Chichen Itza; Colonnade, Ake		Plate 40, a
Dance platforms	Structures 66, 78, 79, 80, 82, Tikal	Dance platform in front of Castillo, Chichen Itza; Structure 8, Tulum		Plate 44, b
Peristyle courts	Not yet found	Market-place and Structure 2-D-6, Chichen Itza		
Vapor baths	Structure P-7, Piedras Negras	Structures 3-E-3 and 3-C-17, Chichen Itza		

Arches, or gateways....Not yet found	Arch, Kabah; Portal, Labna	Plate 56, b
Shrines ....Not yet found	Small structure at edge of Well of Sacrifice (Structure 1-D-1), Chichen Itza; Structure 7, Tulum	
Skull platforms ......Not yet found	Place of the Skulls, Chichen Itza; Platforms in Cemetery, Uxmal	Plate 61, a Plate 73, f
Monumental stairways..Jaguar Stairway, Copan; Hieroglyphic Stairway (Structure 5), Yaxchilan	Not yet found	Plate 35, b and c
Reviewing stands .....North side, West Court, Copan	Not yet found	
Square stadiums for public spectacles ..... Great Plaza, Copan; Ceremonial Plaza, Quirigua	Not yet found	
City walls ....Becan*	Mayapan; Tulum	
Causeways ....Coba-Yaxuna; Coba-Kukicaan	Uxmal-Kabah; Izamal-Kantunil	Plate 55, a
Foundation platforms..Terrace of Group A, Tikal; Terrace of Group A, Uaxactun	North terrace, Chichen Itza; Terrace of the Governor's Palace, Uxmal	Plate 38, b
Bridges and aqueducts..Pusilha; Becan; Palenque	Not yet found	

* A moat also has been found around this site, which may possibly be early New Empire rather than late Old Empire.

Sculpture suffered because of this limitation. While architecture in the New Empire reached new levels of beauty and dignity, sculpture declined, never again approaching the magnificent productions of the Old Empire. Such New Empire sculptures as there are, for the most part, are heavy, awkward, and in some cases, even crude (Plates 73 and 74). Gone are the skill and cunning of the Old Empire chisels, gone the grandeur and dignity of the earlier religion which inspired the Praxiteles' of the Old Empire to the execution of their masterpieces.

A still later architectural phase is the mixed Maya-Mexican architecture which reached its highest expression at Chichen Itza. The ubiquitous feathered serpent, Kukulcan, the Mexican Quetzalcoatl, dominates the scene. The chief temples are erected in his honor. His likeness sprawls over columns and balustrades. His buildings are characterized by battered (sloping) bases, their roofs ornamented with striking stone frets. The closest analogy offered by modern architecture are the grills, or low iron fences, which run around the edges of old-fashioned, mansard roofs. Some structures are definitely of Mexican origin, such as the Tzompantli, or Place of the Skulls, where the skulls of sacrificial victims were preserved, impaled on wooden stakes. The Tzompantli at Chichen Itza is an open platform about 185 feet long, 40 feet wide, and 6 feet high, the sides of which are decorated with sculptured representations of skulls fixed upon stakes, four skulls to a stake (Plate 61, a). Buildings at Chichen Itza, as well as substructures, are decorated with human, animal, bird, and serpent motifs, less and less use being made of the purely geometric elements common in the decoration of Puuc architecture. Heroic-sized reclining human statues, the so-called Chac Mool figures stand at the portals of the temples (Plate 73, a) for the purpose of receiving offerings from the faithful. Finally, this Maya-Mexican architecture is characterized by the frequent use of great colonnades, which probably served as assembly halls or council chambers. Sometimes these are as long as two or three hundred feet and contain four and five ranges of corbeled arches supported by sapodilla beams running from column to column.

Against their back walls are sculptured thrones, flanked by benches with sloping backs for reclining (Plates 40, *a* and 61, *b*). Architecture has become less massive, but more open, less heavy, but more graceful.

It is strange that, with all their great knowledge of masonry, the ancient Maya failed to develop the principle of the true or keystone arch, only having achieved the corbeled or so-called false arch. This is doubly strange in view of the fact that they must have occasionally seen examples of naturally formed true arches when their stone buildings began to collapse.

Not infrequently, when wooden door-lintels in Maya buildings decay and give way, only a small part of the masonry above them falls, only enough to permit a natural arch to form over the opening, the wall and roof above often remaining intact. Indeed, in a structure at Nakum, such an accidental but nevertheless true arch was thus formed and was plastered over so as to give it the appearance of a keystone arch.

And yet with this example, and others like it, constantly before them the ancient Maya never seem to have recognized and deliberately utilized the principle of the true arch in their buildings.

SCULPTURE AND MODELING

MATERIALS AND TOOLS

LIMESTONE was the principal stone used by the ancient Maya for sculpturing because it was by far the most plentiful, being found practically everywhere in the Yucatan Peninsula. A few cities like Quirigua, Pusilha, and Tonina employed sandstone, the native rock in their respective localities, and the city of Copan used andesite, a volcanic tuff. However, these are the rare exceptions; limestone was almost universally the material utilized by ancient Maya sculptors.

Wood, stucco, and clay were also employed in Maya sculpture and modeling, although much less commonly than stone. By the fourth century of the Christian Era stone had replaced wood as a medium for sculpture except in the case of carved sapodilla doorlintels (Plate 32, *a*) and chamber-beams (Plate 53, *e*). As we have seen, some idols were carved from Spanish cedar in the New Empire, but unfortunately none of them survived. Idols were also modeled from clay, particularly in the form of incense burners, and stucco found extensive use in architectural decoration. The lapidary art, particularly as applied to jade carving and engraving, will be described in chapter xvi (pp. 425–30).

It is probably true that wood sculpture preceded stone sculpture among the Maya, as would appear to be the natural order, but no evidence survives. This, however, is readily understandable in view of the heavy rainfall and excessive humidity of the Old Empire climate. If the earliest monuments were of wood, they would long since have rotted away in a region where the oldest trees, in spite of their great size, are less than two hundred years old.

The earliest Maya stelae were probably made of wood as

already mentioned in chapter iii (p. 46). We get our first
glimpses of Maya chronology as recorded in the hieroglyphic
writing on the stone stelae of the early fourth century, where it is
already a fully formed, perfected, and intricate device for measuring time. No simple beginnings have been found, no faltering
first steps, no preliminary trials and errors. When we first encounter it, Maya chronology is already complete as it stands, which
might indicate that the earlier stages of this development were
recorded on wood or some other perishable medium.

The tools of the Maya sculptors were of stone exclusively,
although wooden mallets were quite probably used at one time.
The principal tools were chisels and hammerstones. The former
(Fig. 36) vary in length from two to six inches and have one cutting edge, the opposite end being rounded to receive blows from a
hammerstone or wooden mallet; the hammerstones are roughly
spherical in shape and vary from two to three inches in diameter.
Both types of tools are made from hard basic rocks such as basalt
and diorite.

FIG. 36.—Maya stone chisels.

The native limestone is relatively soft as it occurs in the
ground, but becomes much harder after exposure. It was quarried with comparative facility, and it was also easily carved while
still fresh from the quarries. In the previously mentioned cities
of Quirigua, Tonina, and Pusilha the sculptors' medium was
sandstone, which has the same quality of relative softness as the

local Peten and Yucatan limestones, being rather soft while still in the ground and hardening noticeably on exposure to weather. On the other hand, the andesite used in Copan is of about the same hardness before being quarried as afterward, and it is so fine-grained, even-textured, and free of cleavage planes that it is admirably adapted to being carved with chisels of basalt or diorite.

Copan andesite, however, has one serious drawback—it contains nodules of flint which are so hard that the basalt and diorite chisels of the Copan sculptors could not have worked them.

When such nodules were encountered they were either removed altogether, making a depression in the face of the monument, or they were left protruding. Sometimes examples of both practices occur on the same monument, as for example, on Stela D, and sometimes, when the inclusion was too difficult to remove entirely, the projecting part was battered off.

FIG. 37.—Initial Series introducing glyph on Stela 2, Copan, Honduras.

In the case of the human head in the center of the Initial Series introducing-glyph on Stela 2 (Fig. 37), clever manipulations by Copan sculptors incorporated a stubborn nodule into the design itself. The human, animal, bird, and reptilian heads so often represented in Maya inscriptions almost invariably are shown facing the observer's *left*, but this particular profile faces to the *right*. However, by reversing the direction in which the head faced, this flinty inclusion, fortunately round, fell in exactly the right position to serve as the earplug.

Maya sculpture was doubtless finished by abrasion, that is by rubbing down and wearing off minute surface inequalities. After this it was invariably painted, usually a dark red. This red pigment was probably made from an oxide of iron that was to be had in quantities from anthills which abound in the forest. Other colors were used, however, blue being the next most common. The pigments were ground and probably mixed with copal, for the paint used still adheres to the stone in many places with the tenacity of a good varnish; indeed varnish made from the resin of the copal tree, found everywhere, is the best commercial varnish known today. Although the colors have for the most part worn off the monuments because of exposure to the elements, traces of the original paint can still be found occasionally where the relief is high and undercut.

In quarrying the shafts of stone from which the stelae were to be made, advantage was taken of natural cleavage planes in the local rock. This is best seen in the case of some of the Quirigua stelae, the cross-sections of which are trapezoidal in shape,

FIG. 38.—Quarry at Mitla, Oaxaca, Mexico. After Holmes.

no single corner being a right angle. The following method was employed in quarrying at the Old Empire center of Calakmul as shown in Plate 62, *b*; here two blocks of stone lying side by side appear in process of being quarried. In this case the blocks seem to have been freed from the surrounding limestone by digging down along their sides and ends with stone chisels and mauls, preparatory to prying them loose from the bedrock with long hardwood poles. Several of the Quirigua stelae still show these so-called "quarry stumps" on their plain undressed butts (Plate 62, *a*).

The late William Henry Holmes, former Head Curator of Anthropology at the United States National Museum, has sketched an ancient quarry site near the ruins of Mitla in the State of Oaxaca, Mexico (Fig. 38), which shows blocks of stone in various stages of being freed from the native rock deposit according to the process described above.

The French artist, Jean Charlot, has very kindly made for this book four original drawings illustrating the four principal steps in making a Maya stela as he conceives the process to have been: (1) quarrying the shaft, (2) transporting it, (3) erecting it, and (4) sculpturing it.

The first step has been described above (Plate 64, *a*), and the second is shown in Plate 64, *b*. The forests of Peten abound in hardwood trees of all kinds and sizes, sections of which would have served admirably for rollers, and wild *agaves* as well as other fiber-yielding plants for making ropes and cables are equally common. The third step, that of erecting the shaft, which was done *before it was sculptured*, is shown in Plate 65, *a*. A three-sided square or rectangular socket to fit the butt of the shaft was made, sometimes of masonry but more often of tightly packed stones and clay. Then, by means of a ramp of earth or logs and an "A" type of frame built out of stout beams the shaft was probably pulled upright and the fourth side of the socket was filled in afterward. It is important to note that the shafts were brought from the quarries in an unfinished state, only roughly blocked out; then they were set up and later carved, scaffolds of poles being built so that the sculptors could reach the upper parts of the shaft (Plate 65, *b*). The designs are so intricate and the relief so delicate that sculpturing could have been done only *after* the shaft had been erected in the position it was to occupy finally.

STONE SCULPTURE

The earliest stone sculptures in the Maya area, not counting the Leyden Plate, which is of semiprecious jade, are the earliest group of monuments at Uaxactun in northern central Peten and date from the fourth century of the Christian Era (chapter iv, p. 56). The human figures on these earliest monuments are always shown in the same position—head, legs, and feet in profile, either left or right; torso and arms in full front; and feet in tandem. This is the first position of the human figure in Maya art. It is found on the Leyden Plate, the earliest dated object known (320; see Plate 15, *a*), and on Stela 9 at Uaxactun, the earliest known large stone monument (328; see Plate 16). This earliest position of the human figure in Maya art, moreover, is found exclusively at Uaxactun and seems to have passed out of use even there before the close of Baktun 8 (435).

The next position is a little easier and more natural. The toes of the *near* or *back* foot are advanced slightly, overlapping the heel of the *far* or *front* foot, so that the position of the feet is no longer tandem. This position is seen on Stela 2 at Tikal and again on Stela 5 at Uaxactun (see Plate 63) with the rest of the body remaining unchanged. This second position also appears first at Uaxactun before the close of Baktun 8 (435). The profile presentation of the human figure spread from Tikal and Uaxactun to other cities; it persisted throughout Maya history with little change and is by far the most common position of the human figure in Maya art.

To Uaxactun or possibly to Tikal also belongs credit for having sculptured the human figure in *full front view* for the first time, for the earliest certain example of this is on Stela 26 at Uaxactun, dedicated in 9.0.10.0.0 (445). This very early monument was discovered beneath the floor of Shrine II in one of the earliest levels of the palace (Structure A-V). The figure on its front would almost appear to have been intentionally rubbed off (Plate 63, *b*). The carving even when new was in low relief, but notwithstanding this and in spite of the practical certainty that an attempt had been made to efface the carving in ancient times, it is still possible to distinguish the outline of the lower half of the face (the curve under the chin) and the arms and feet, which were placed at an angle of 180 degrees. Possibly an even earlier example of the human head, arms, and torso in front view is to be found on Stela 4 at Tikal (Plate 63, *a*), which may have been dedicated as early as the close of Baktun 8.

The full front view of the human figure is restricted to the following eight cities: Tonina, where it is the invariable rule (Plate 54, *a*); Copan and Quirigua, where it is the general rule

(Plates 54, *b*, and 68, *b*) but where there are two known exceptions at each site; Piedras Negras, where it occurs on about half of the stelae; and Palenque, Yaxchilan, Naachtun, and Seibal, where it occurs but once at each. This particular stance reached its greatest perfection at Copan and Quirigua, while the full front view of the human figure seated cross-legged is best expressed at Piedras Negras.

The fronts of the four Piedras Negras monuments, shown in Plate 66, constitute one of the best series for the study of the same subject—the human figure seated cross-legged in a niche—to be found anywhere in the annals of ancient sculpture. The earliest of these four monuments, Stela 25, was dedicated in 9.8.15.0.0 (608). The seated human figure sculptured on the front of this monument is heavy, wooden, and lifeless (Plate 66, *a*), and the niche is so shallow that there is not enough depth to permit treatment of the figure in high relief. Eighty years later on Stela 6, dedicated in 9.12.15.0.0 (687), this same composition was attempted a second time (Plate 66, *b*). Considerable advance in sculpture, however, had been made during the intervening years, and the niche is deeper, permitting the figure to be treated more successfully. The face, judged by itself, is unusually well done but, taken into consideration with the rest of the body, is still out of proportion, being much too large. However, by the time this composition was attempted the third time on Stela 11, dedicated 43 years later in 9.15.0.0.0 (731), notable improvement had been made (Plate 66, *c*). The niche has become so deep that the anatomical proportions of the seated figure can and do approach those of life; details are beautifully executed and the drapery above the niche is gracefully and naturally held back by four cords. This design was sculptured for the last time at Piedras Negras on Stela 14, dedicated 30 years later in 9.16.10.0.0 (761). This monument is perhaps the finest stela at Piedras Negras (Plate 66, *d*). The niche is by this time sufficiently deep to present the seated figure practically in the half-round; its anatomical proportions are correct, details are exquisitely carved, and the drapery above the niche is even more realistically handled

than on Stela 11. Finally, this monument presents a masterly
combination of high and low relief; the seated figure is in high
round carving, while the surrounding decorations, the standing
figure at the lower left, and the sacrificial victim at the lower
right are in low, flat relief. These four monuments with their
identical subjects were executed over a period of 153 years, and
they constitute one of the best series illustrating progress in sculpture to be found anywhere in the ancient world.

The front presentation of the standing human figure was brilliantly achieved both at Copan and Quirigua, although the figures
at the latter are probably more to our modern taste than those at
the former because they are more restrained. This restraint was
doubtless due to the greater intractability of the Quirigua sandstone as compared with the Copan andesite, so far as stone chisels
are concerned. However, in ancient times the Maya themselves
probably much preferred the Copan stelae with their superabund-
ant, almost flamboyant decoration, the carving occasionally being
in the full round.

Returning to Early Period sculptures once more, it should be
pointed out that during most of this period the human figures
portrayed are heavy, wooden, and anatomically out of proportion.
Take for example the profile figure appearing on the Early Period
Stela 27 at Yaxchilan (Plate 67, a), dedicated in 9.4.0.0.0
(514). Nothing could be more awkward and lifeless, and indeed
when it was discovered in 1931 by a Carnegie Institution Expedition, it was called the Wooden Soldier of Yaxchilan. By the end
of the Early Period, however, notable advances had been made
toward a more naturalistic presentation. This is well exemplified
in Stela 25 at Naranjo, where a standing figure is shown in left
profile (Plate 67, b). This monument was dedicated in 9.9.2.0.4
(615), by which time the proportions of the body were becoming
more natural and, except for the forced position of the feet, which
are still at a stiff angle of 180° with each other, the figure is
lifelike and the position easy.

Compared with the stiffness, almost rigidity, of the earliest
representation of the human figure in full front view, the same

presentation at the close of the Early Period on Stela P at Copan, dedicated in 9.9.10.0.0 (623), shows great improvement, though the figure still falls far short of natural proportions and posture (Plate 67, *d*).

Coming down to the Middle Period (633–731), the last vestiges of archaism disappeared during this century, though in some less inspired provincial centers the sculptors were still doing very mediocre work. Take for example Stela 21 at Naachtun (Plate 67, *c*), dedicated about the middle of the period (687), which is incredibly dumpy and misshapen for such a late date. This awkwardness can better be explained by provincial ineptitude rather than by true primitive crudeness; indeed, some cities, even at the height of the Great Period, never outgrew their provinciality.

The contrast between this last monument and Stela A at Copan (Plate 68, *b*), dedicated in 9.15.0.0.0 (731), less than half a century later, is arresting. Compare the crudity and grossness of the former with the beauty and elegance of the latter or with the already described very fine Stela 11 at Piedras Negras (Plate 66, *c*), dedicated on the same day as Stela A at Copan. Such stylistic differences between monuments erected so close together in point of time may best be explained by what I have called provincial lag, the contemporary esthetic backwardness of smaller centers as compared to the creative brilliance of some of the larger cities—Copan, Quirigua, Palenque, Yaxchilan, and Piedras Negras. It has been said that what Paris wears today New York will wear next month, and the vast hinterland of the Middle and Far West will wear next year when mass production has at last begun to grind out the styles in quantity. This principle of provincial lag of course operates universally and always has. The farther away from centers of esthetic inspiration peripheral settlements are located the longer it takes the latter to catch up with the "big cities" in clothes and customs as well as in architecture and art.

Thus, in evaluating the artistic achievements of any Maya center, its relative importance must be taken into consideration as well as its distance from the nearest center of high esthetic inspiration. Returning to the two monuments last mentioned, Stela 21 at Naachtun and Stela A at Copan, the considerable stylistic differences observed between them are not to be explained only by the slight difference of fifty years in their ages nor by the fact that the former is a Class 2 site and the latter a Class 1 center. The truth is that the whole northern central Peten region, where the Maya civilization originated and where its largest center, Tikal, is located, never reached the supreme heights in stone sculpture attained either by the three great cities of the Usumacinta Valley—Palenque, Yaxchilan, and Piedras Negras in the west or by Copan and Quirigua in the southeast. Naachtun is only about seventy-eight miles in an air line from Piedras Negras, the nearest of the three largest Usumacinta cities just mentioned, and 200 miles from Quirigua. Artistically it was never anything else but backward.

The first century and a half (731–889) of the Great Period of the Old Empire (731–987) witnessed the most brilliant development of New World sculpture in pre-Columbian times. This period was in many ways the Golden Age of the Maya civilization, and this cultural flowering is perhaps exemplified in sculpture better than in any other field of art. By the beginning of the Great Period, stone-carving no longer presented any real difficulties to the Old Empire sculptors. By this time four centuries of sculptural achievement lay behind them and any technical difficulties arising from stone as a medium of sculptural expression had long since been mastered; creative instinct was free to follow wherever inspiration led, to express itself without restraint within the framework of its own traditions and experience.

Among the wealth of sculptures at hand which date from the Great Period, it is difficult to select those which are most typical. One of the most beautiful monuments at Piedras Negras, Stela 14, has already been illustrated (Plate 66, d). Another almost equally striking monument, Stela 12 (Plate 18, c), dedicated in 9.18.5.0.0 (795), shows profile presentation of the human figure exclusively. This remarkable composition, in addition to the figure of a *halach uinic* seated on his throne with scepter in hand and flanked by two standing lords and a third lord seated below him, has eight prisoners squatting at the bottom of the sculptured panel with their arms bound behind their backs with ropes. The several levels in this composition perhaps represent an attempt to show perpective.

The most beautiful sculpture ever produced by the American Indian is the superlative Wall Panel No. 3 from Structure O-13 at Piedras Negras, already mentioned in an earlier chapter (Plate 69, *a*). This masterpiece of ancient American art was executed at Piedras Negras in 9.16.10.0.0 (761) and is a perfect combination of high and low relief. In a number of places on the panel arms and legs are sculptured in the full round, standing completely free of the background and attached thereto only at the ends. The composition represents a *halach uinic* seated on a magnificent throne, the back of which is a mask panel; he is flanked on each side by three standing figures. The middle figure on the right has almost entirely disappeared, though both feet may still be distinguished; judging from its height, it would appear to have been that of a youth. On the ground before the throne seven figures are seated cross-legged, four on the left and three on the right, facing an altar. The figure on the extreme right is the only one of the fourteen figures in the entire composition that has its face still preserved. Miss M. L. Baker has made a restoration of this wall panel (Plate 69, *b*) for the Museum of the University of Pennsylvania at Philadelphia, where the original was on exhibition, though it has now been returned to the National Museum of Archaeology and History at Guatemala City.

A University of Pennsylvania expedition discovered a throne at Piedras Negras that was built against the back wall of the long principal chamber of Palace J-6 (Fig. 39) which was almost identical with the throne represented in the above-mentioned wall panel, the principal difference between these two thrones being that the two front supports of the throne shown on the wall panel are undecorated (Plate 69, *a*), while those of the actual throne

← *a*) Stela 4, Tikal, Peten, Guatemala, perhaps the first representation of the human figure in full front view in the Maya area.

b) Stela 26, Uaxactun, Peten, Guatemala, first representation of the human figure in full front view at this city. →

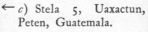

← *c*) Stela 5, Uaxactun, Peten, Guatemala.

d) Stela 2, Tikal, Peten, Guatemala. →

PLATE 63
MONUMENTS OF THE EARLY
PERIOD OF THE OLD
EMPIRE

↑ *a*) First step. Quarrying the shaft.

PLATE 64

FOUR STEPS IN THE MAKING OF A MAYA MONUMENT AFTER TH

↓ *b*) Second step. Transporting the shaft.

a) Third step. Erecting the shaft.

PLATE 65

Fourth step. Sculpturing the shaft.
→

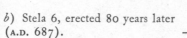
← *a*) Stela 25, erected in A.D. 608.

b) Stela 6, erected 80 years later (A.D. 687). →

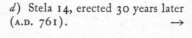
← *c*) Stela 11, erected 43 years later (A.D. 731).

d) Stela 14, erected 30 years later (A.D. 761). →

PLATE 66.—FOUR SCULPTURES AT PIEDRAS NEGRAS, PETEN, GUATEMALA, WITH IDENTICAL DESIGNS, EXECUTED OVER A PERIOD OF 153 YEARS

← a) Stela 27, Yaxchilan, Chiapas, Mexico, erected in A.D. 514.

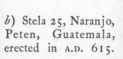

b) Stela 25, Naranjo, Peten, Guatemala, erected in A.D. 615. →

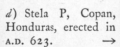

c) Stela 21, Naachtun, Peten, Guatemala, erected in A.D. 687. ←

d) Stela P, Copan, Honduras, erected in A.D. 623. →

PLATE 67
SCULPTURES OF THE
EARLY AND MIDDLE
PERIODS OF THE OLD
EMPIRE

a) Stela H, Copan, Honduras, erected in A.D. 782.

b) Stela A, Copan, Honduras, erected in A.D. 731.

PLATE 68.—SCULPTURES OF THE GREAT PERIOD OF THE OLD EMPIRE

↑ *a*) Wall Panel, as found; the finest sculpture ever produced in ancient America.

PLATE 69.—WALL PANEL No. 3, TEMPLE O-13, PIEDRAS NEGRAS, PETEN, GUATEMALA

↓ *b*) Pen-and-ink restoration by M. Louise Baker.

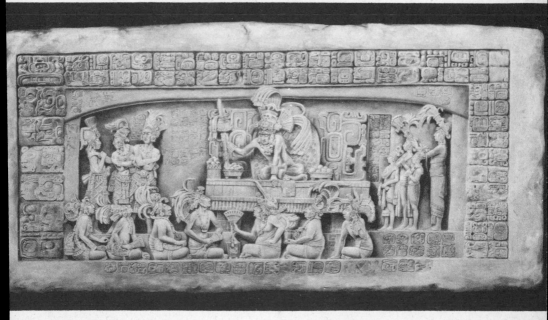

are covered with hieroglyphic inscriptions on three sides (Plate 70, *a*). The latter was dedicated in 9.17.15.0.0 (785), 25 years later than the wall panel, and measures 4 feet 7 inches high including the mask-panel back. The seat is 2 feet 7½ inches above the floor level and 3 feet deep from front to back; the throne itself is 6 feet 1 inch wide. It was so located in the principal hall of this palace that it could be seen from any point in the large court below and in front.

At Yaxchilan sculpture reached its highest point in the three superb lintels of Structure. 23 — Lintels 24, 25, and 26, the first two of which are now in the British Museum. Lintel 24 (Plate 71, *b*) is the most outstanding example of sculptural art at Yaxchilan in harmony of composition, balance of design, brilliance of execution, appreciation of anatomical proportions, and refinement of detail. Both Yaxchilan and Palenque reached their sculptural peaks shortly before the beginning of the Great Period, as already noted. Structure 23 (one of

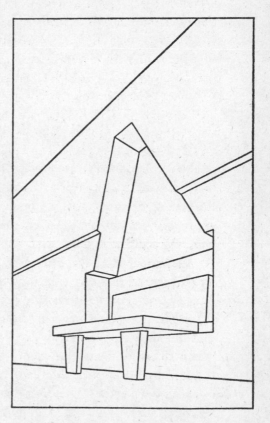

Fig. 39.—Location of throne in Palace J-6, Piedras Negras, Peten, Guatemala.

the doorways of which Lintel 24 originally spanned) was dedicated in 9.14.15.0.0 (726). The finest monuments at Yaxchilan—Stelae 1, 4, 3, 7—fall little short of the lintels in Structure 23, though one and perhaps all of them date from the 35 years immediately following the execution of this lintel, at a time when the esthetic crest at Yaxchilan was already receding.

There is a tremendous amount of Great Period sculpture at Copan, more in fact than at any other city of the Old Empire. Many magnificent monuments were sculptured there during the Great Period: Stelae A (Plate 68, *b*), B, D, M, N, C, H (Plate 68, *a*), F, and 4, and Altars Q, R, S, and T. There were also spectacular buildings and other constructions: Temples 11, 22, and 26, the Jaguar Stairway (Plate 35, *a*), and the Reviewing Stand, the last two in the Eastern and Western Courts, respectively. All were erected and carved during the half-century between 731 and 782. The longest hieroglyphic inscription in the Maya area—the Hieroglyphic Stairway of Structure 26 (Plate 35, *c*)— was dedicated in 9.16.5.0.0 (756). The exquisite head and torso of the corn-god illustrated in the frontispiece was also carved during this same half-century. Lack of space prevents mention of all the best sculptural work at Copan, but it should be noted that this great southern metropolis produced a greater number of outstanding sculptures than any other center of the Maya civilization.

Quirigua, although only a medium-sized site of Class 2, has 22 sculptured monuments, some of them among the finest in the Maya area. Two have already been described—Stela E, the largest single stone ever quarried by the ancient Maya (Plate 54, *b*), and the altar of Zoömorph O (Plate 27, *b*). A third monument which deserves particular mention is Zoömorph P (Plate 72, *c*), thought by some to be the finest piece of sculpture ever produced in ancient America. This massive boulder-like piece of sandstone measures 9 feet 8 inches long, by 11 feet 6 inches wide, by 7 feet 3 inches high and is completely covered, top and all four sides, with an intricate sculptured design; it was dedicated in 9.18.5.0.0 (795). Perhaps the finest glyphs ever carved on stone by the ancient Maya are to be found at Quirigua, especially those on Stela F (Plate 72, *a*), dedicated in 9.16.10.0.0 (761), and the very rare full-figure glyphs on Stela D (Plate 72, *b*), dedicated five years later in 9.16.15.0.0 (766).

By the end of Baktun 9 (830), however, the crest had been

passed and sculpture throughout the Old Empire was headed downhill. There followed a cultural recession, so far as sculpture is concerned, from which the ancient Maya never recovered.

Examples of late Old Empire sculpture clearly reflect this cultural decline. Stela 10 at Xultun (Fig. 40), dedicated in 10.3.0.0.0 (889), is one of three monuments erected on this katun-ending, the last surely dated sculptures from the Old Empire. The loss in both esthetic inspiration and technical skill is evident, and flamboyancy clutters the composition. The figures are poorly proportioned and wooden-like, while the mass of costume detail obscures the design.

It was noted in the preceding chapter that, during the New Empire, sculpture as an independent art had almost ceased to exist, that is, it was confined almost exclusively to the embellishment of architecture. Indeed, except in the largest centers, independent sculptures are almost nonexistent. At Chichen Itza no stelae at all have been found, but there are a number of pieces of independent statuary which fall into one or another of the four following categories: (1) the so-called Chac Mool figures, (2) jaguar thrones, (3) standard-bearers, and (4) Atlantean figures. The first are reclining human figures (Plate 73, a) with heads turned either to the right or left. They vary in size from larger than life to somewhat smaller. At least a dozen have been discovered at this city, and two of them still retain inset pieces of polished bone to represent the whites of the eyes, the fingernails and toenails. All are very similar, each holding a stone plate clasped by the two hands and resting on the abdomen. The usual location of these reclining figures is just in front of the temple doorways; this, together with the stone plates held in their respective hands, suggests that their function might have been to receive offerings from the faithful on these plates before the worshipers passed inside the temple.

The jaguar thrones are life-sized representations of jaguars with heads also turned either to the right or left and with a flat back to serve as the seat. Sculptured representations of these jaguar thrones are found at Tikal, Piedras Negras, Palenque,

Fig. 40.—Front view of Stela 10, Xultun, Peten, Guatemala.

and Xultun, but striking examples of the actual thrones have been found at Uxmal and Chichen Itza (Plate 73, *c*). Painted representations in frescoes also occur in the Temple of the Warriors at Chichen Itza.

The standard-bearers constitute the third group of statues mentioned above; their purpose was to support staffs from the tops of which hung feather banners. The usual type is a truncated cone about a foot high and a foot in diameter at the base with a hole in the top for inserting the butt of the staff. Sometimes these standard-bearers take the shape of small human statues about three feet high (Plate 73, *b*) with the forearms extended horizontally in front of the figure, the hands forming a hole through which the staff passed, and the butt resting between the feet. Another standard-bearer recently found at Chichen Itza shows a figure kneeling on its left knee and grasping the staff in its right hand (Plate 73, *e*).

The fourth group, the Atlantean figures, are anthropomorphic statuettes standing about two to two and a half feet high with arms raised above their heads. They were used to support daises or altars in the sanctuaries of the temples (Plate 73, *d*).

At Uxmal there are sixteen sculptured stelae, but even the best of them, Stela 7 (Fig. 41) is overly ornate, flamboyant, and decadent as compared with the great sculptural masterpieces of the Old Empire. At this city there was found a very lovely human head (life size) emerging from the jaws of a highly conventionalized serpent head (Plate 74, *c* and *d*) with tattooing on its right cheek. The head can hardly be called an independent piece of sculpture, however, since it is attached to the façade of a range of chambers built across the western base of the pyramid supporting the House of the Magician and really formed only an element of the architectural decoration. This head is now in the National Museum of Anthropology and History at Mexico City.

Sculpture as an independent art became increasingly less important as the New Empire neared its end, but as an adjunct to architecture it reached a dignity and beauty equaled nowhere else in ancient America.

Fig. 41.—Front view of Stela 7, Uxmal, Yucatan, Mexico.

From the few examples that have survived, wood carving would seem to have reached its most perfect expression at Tikal in the superlatively fine door-lintels of the five great pyramid-temples at that city which are described in the preceding chapter. In the very nature of the case such a perishable material as wood could hardly have survived the dampness and humidity of the Old Empire climate, except in very sheltered positions; and indeed the only objects of wood recovered either from the Old or New Empire are from places which are protected from the weather, such as door-lintels or beams inside of chambers.

Just as Palenque was the city where the finest stuccowork in the Maya area was done, so Tikal was the city where the most beautiful wood carving was executed. Beyond all question the finest wood carvings ever produced by the ancient Maya are the wooden lintels at Tikal.

A photograph of the most complete one of these has already been illustrated in Plate 32, *a*, and a drawing of part of another is shown in Figure 31 (p. 322). The sculptured wooden lintels at Tikal are each composed of from four to ten beams of sapodilla with an over-all length of from 7 to 17½ feet depending on the width of the doorway to be spanned. The design on the lintel in Plate 32, *a*, shows an elaborately decorated serpent, its body arching in the middle to form a central niche; the head is to the left, and issuing from its widely opened mouth there are the head, arms, and torso of a god; the serpent's tail is at the right, terminating in two lovely curls. An exquisitely executed hieroglyphic inscription fills the upper left and right corners of this composition, and across the top between the glyph panels stretches a great bird with spreading wings, the *kukul* (Aztec *quetzal*) or Sacred Bird of the Maya. In the centrally placed niche formed by the upward curl of the serpent's body is the figure of a *halach uinic*, his head in left profile, body in full front view, the left hand grasping a spear, and the right a small round shield. This richly clad ruler is seated on a throne rising from a platform that can be reached by a stairway of five steps across the front; the feet rest lightly on the toes and the legs spread naturally. This lintel originally spanned one of the doorways of Temple IV, which was dedicated in 9.16.0.0.0 (751) when Maya sculpture was at its zenith; this lintel is the finest complete wood carving in the Maya area. Another far less beautiful example of a carved sapodilla-wood lintel from the Old Empire was found over an interior doorway of Temple VII at Tzibanche, west of the southern end of Lake Bacalar (Plate 19). This presents an inscription of eight hieroglyphs but no figures and is on the whole rather poorly executed; it probably dates from the late Early Period, perhaps from 9.9.5.0.0 (618).

Occasionally the wooden poles spanning chambers from one side of the vault to the other have been treated with a carved decoration somewhat resembling an old-fashioned apothecary's mortar. An example of one of these at Tikal was found in a fourth-story rear chamber of the Palace of the Five Stories (Plate 53, e).

In the New Empire, carved wooden lintels have been found at both Chichen Itza and Uxmal. The best preserved lintel at Chichen Itza spans the inner doorway of the Temple of the Jaguars on top of the west wall of the large ball court (Fig. 42). Each of the two beams composing this lintel has the same design carved upon it: the sun disk, with a human figure inside it and outside it another human figure which is enveloped in the coils of a feathered rattlesnake; both figures are facing a centrally placed altar. Although the design is pleasing and the carving well executed, it falls far short of the carved wooden lintels at Tikal. The sapodilla lintels in the Castillo at Chichen Itza were also carved originally, but in most cases the low relief has been hacked off with machetes.

A charming account of travels in the Maya area (see Bibliography, p. 497) has been left by John Lloyd Stevens, the American traveler, diplomat, and amateur archaeologist who visited Uxmal in 1840 and again in 1841. He found a sapodilla beam in the outer south chamber of the Governor's Palace at Uxmal, which he took with him to the United States when he left Yuca-

a) Lintel 25, from Structure 23. →

b) Lintel 24 from Structure 23, the finest sculptured stone door-lintel in ↓ the Maya area.

PLATE 71.—SCULPTURED LINTELS, YAXCHILAN, CHIAPAS, MEXICO

← *a*) Stela F, Quirigua, Izabal, Guatemala; the hieroglyphics on this monument are probably the finest ever carved by the ancient Maya.

b) Stela D, Quirigua, Izabal, Guatemala. →

PLATE 72. — SCULPTURES OF THE GREAT PERIOD OF THE OLD EMPIRE

c) Zoömorph P, Quirigua, Izabal, Guatemala. ↓

PLATE 73.—SCULPTURES OF THE NEW EMPIRE (*a–e*) AT CHICHEN
ITZA, AND (*f*) AT UXMAL, YUCATAN

(*a*) Chac Mool; (*b*) support for a banner in the form of an anthropomorphic figure; (*c*) Red
Jaguar Throne; (*d*) Atlantean figure altar support; (*e*) support for a banner in the form of
an anthropomorphic figure; (*f*) altar in the so-called cemetery.

PLATE 74.—SCULPTURES OF THE NEW EMPIRE AT CHICHEN ITZA AND AT UXMAL

(a) Seated figure (front), Northwest Colonnade, Chichen Itza, Yucatan, Mexico; (b) same figure (profile); (c) head (front view) emerging from the mouth of a serpent, passageway beneath stairway on the west side of the House of the Magician, at Uxmal, Yucatan, Mexico; (d) same head (profile).

tan. It was subsequently destroyed by a fire in New York in 1842, an irreparable loss, first because Stephens says it was the only beam in the entire metropolis that was carved and second because the destroyed inscription might well have dated this structure, the most beautiful ever erected in pre-Columbian America.

Other smaller objects of carved wood were taken from the Well of Sacrifice at Chichen Itza, the most notable of which is the handle of a wooden sacrificial knife, carved in the likeness of two intertwined rattlesnakes (Fig. 14). A beautiful chipped-flint blade was hafted to this and its handle is covered with a thin sheet of gold.

STUCCO MODELING

Stucco seems to have been generally used in the exterior decoration of Old Empire buildings, as noted in the preceding chapter, but to a lesser extent in the treatment of New Empire façades. Palenque was the city where stuccowork reached its highest development, and the tablets in various parts of the palace and the now largely destroyed panel against the back wall in the sanctuary of the Temple of the Beau Relief are the finest examples of this plastic art in the entire Maya area. Take for example two panels from the west façade of House D of the Palace (Plate 77, a and b). Note the beautiful molding of the figures and their graceful postures; the masterly modeling of the feet and arms in the left panel and the right-hand figure in the right panel; the rich yet restrained treatment of costume details—sandals, jade-bead skirt, feather headdresses, belts, earrings, necklaces, bracelets, anklets, and elaborate garters; the handsome throne in the left panel; and the decorative bases and borders in both panels. Nothing finer in stucco was ever produced in ancient America than that at Palenque, and its supremacy in this field is unchallenged.

Even provincial centers within the Palenque sphere of influence showed this mastery of the stucco technique, though to a lesser degree. Comalcalco, about one hundred miles northwest of Palenque, is a case in point. Some years ago a tomb was found at this site. Entrance had originally been gained through a doorway in the west wall, which was blocked up when found. On the remaining three walls there were representations of standing human figures in stucco, three to a side, each figure measuring about 4 feet high; two, as restored, are shown in Plate 78, *a* and *b*, and the same two, as found, in Plate 78, *c*. Although much cruder than the stucco figures from the Palace at Palenque, nevertheless these Comalcalco figures are not without considerable merit. It was a true eye which saw them and a sure hand which modeled them.

Examples of stuccowork in the New Empire are not so common. Some heroic-sized human heads have been found at Izamal in northern Yucatan and at Nocuchich in the Chenes country of central Campeche. The best examples of stuccowork in the New Empire, however, are at Acanceh in northern central Yucatan. Here in the upper half of a façade above the medial molding are the remains of a handsome stucco panel, composed of animals, birds, and serpents, among which the bat, squirrel, serpent, and a bird may be clearly recognized (Plate 79). When this was uncovered some forty years ago, the frieze still retained many traces of its original coloring, a bright turquoise blue predominating. While excellent, this frieze is again far inferior to the superb stuccowork at Palenque.

CLAY MODELING

Although modeling in clay might equally well have been described in the next chapter on ceramics, it seems best to consider some of the modeled pottery heads and figures here.

The practice of making modeled clay heads goes back to a very early period in ancient Middle American art. Such heads have been found in considerable quantities in the prehistoric cemetery underneath the lava flow at San Angel and Tlalpan just outside Mexico City, probably dating from the first millenium before Christ. Similar heads have been found in the very lowest levels of Group E at Uaxactun in the so-called "black earth" stratum, the earliest layer showing human occupation at this city (Plate 80, *a* and *b*). These Uaxactun heads are exceedingly crude;

the eyes consist of little more than round holes punched in
almond-shaped depressions; the eyebrows, if indicated at all,
appear as shallow lines; the nose, mouth, and lips are modeled
without skill. Found with these very early heads of modeled
clay, which go back at least to the first or second century before
Christ, are typically crude and grossly shaped female torsos (Plate
80, *c* and *d*).

Very few examples of such heads and female torsos have been
found which may be ascribed to the Middle Period of the Old
Empire, but a number of very fine modeled clay figurines have
been recovered that surely date from the Great Period. Some of
these were obviously modeled by hand directly and then baked, but
many others were made from molds of baked clay; some of these
ancient molds have been found. Unquestionably the finest of the
latter is a one-piece mold of the front of a seated female figure
about 8 inches high; a modern plaster of Paris cast made from
this original mold is shown in Plate 81, *c*. This mold was found in
a mound not far from the west bank of the Chixoy or Salinas River
in the extreme eastern part of the state of Chiapas, Mexico, and the
exquisite seated statuette made from it recalls the best stuccowork
at Palenque, the same softness of line, the same flowing roundness
of the molded clay, the same brilliant mastery of the medium.
This mold is now in the Peabody Museum, Harvard University.

Another Old Empire center where figurines and heads of
baked clay reached a high degree of perfection was Jonuta on
the right bank of the lower Usumacinta River. Excellent clay
figurines were made at still a third Old Empire center, although
a provincial one; this was the Island of Jaina (Plate 82), located
off the west coast of the northern peninsula. It will be noticed
from the map (Plate 19) that the four sites last mentioned are
all in the western half of the Maya area, the first three being in
the Usumacinta Valley. While modeled clay heads and figurines
are found everywhere in the region covered by the Maya civilization and far beyond for that matter, and although they occur
throughout Maya history from earliest Old Empire times down to
the closing days of the New Empire, they reached their highest

perfection during the eighth and ninth centuries of the Christian Era in the Usumacinta Valley, where the finest techniques of modeling in plastic materials such as stucco and clay had been developed.

The art of modeling and molding, like the sister-art of sculpture, deteriorated in quality during the New Empire, though some charming figurines were still being made (Plate 82). Idols, pipes, incense burners, and other objects of baked clay, showing a modeled or molded technique, are numerous, especially incense burners (Plate 85, *b*); but all are inferior in execution to the clay modeling of the Usumacinta Valley during the last half of the Middle and the first half of the Great Period. One of the finest examples from the New Empire is the pottery pipe found during the excavation of the North Colonnade at Chichen Itza (Plate 81, *a*). The total length of this pipe is 20½ inches, the stem proper, from tip to center of bowl, being 5 inches shorter; the bowl is 2¼ inches high, flaring widely to a diameter of 3 inches at the top. In front of the bowl there is a modeled bird's head with a prominent beak which has been appliquéd to the front end of the stem; this head is hollow and contains a pellet of clay which makes the pipe rattle when moved. Just behind the bowl on the upper side of the stem there is another appliquéd decoration in strips of clay. The color is a warm terra-cotta red and the pipe has a polished finish.

Incense burners were the commonest type of object in late New Empire times; these have modeled clay heads and figurines fastened to their exteriors; such heads and figures were made separately from the incense burners and appliquéd to their exterior walls. One from an incense burner found at Mayapan is shown in Plate 81, *b*. This probably dates from the thirteenth or fourteenth century; and although the features show considerable skill in modeling, the clay is poorly baked and the painted decorations in red, olive-green, blue, and white are crudely applied.

This technique of appliquéing human heads to the exterior walls of incense burners still persists at the present time among the last scattered remnants of the Lacandon Maya in the forests of eastern Chiapas (Plate 81, *d*). These are very crude indeed and are painted red, black, and white.

Between the "black dirt" heads from the lowest occupation level at Uaxactun, dating from the second or first century before Christ (Plate 80, *a* and *b*) down to the Lacandon incense burner of today (Plate 81, *d*), there is a lapse of at least two thousand years, during which long period this plastic art, one of the very oldest among the ancient Maya, has flourished.

===

CERAMICS

POTTERY, THE BEST GUIDE TO CULTURAL DEVELOPMENT

OF ALL the imperishable remains which man has left behind him in his march from savagery to the civilized state, his culinary pots, domestic and ceremonial bowls, vases, plates, and other vessels of baked clay register and reflect his cultural progress better than anything else. In fact it is his pottery that offers the most accurate measure of man's cultural progress and presents the best guide to its sequence.

A welter of potsherds (pottery fragments) litters the sites where man formerly lived, and the reader may well ask how we can distinguish between what is early and what late; what is truly archaic and what crude only because it is decadent. The answer is simple; the same technique was followed as that first worked out by geologists in studying the successive geological periods through which the earth has passed. This technique is called stratigraphic sequence and works on the general principle that, with no disturbing factors interfering, what happened first and what was made first, whether it be rocks or pottery, was laid down or deposited first and therefore will be found at the bottom of the refuse heaps where rubbish was thrown.

Thus around the settlements of pottery-making peoples there gradually accumulated refuse heaps of broken pottery, mingled with all the other debris arising from the process of living—discarded or broken tools and utensils of all kinds, weapons, articles of wearing apparel, and the remains of food. Furthermore, these refuse heaps are almost invariably found in exposed, open places, and the perishable materials in them—textiles, wood, basketry, leather, fur, feathers, and remnants of food—have largely disappeared. Indeed, except in the case of highly sheltered refuse heaps in unusually dry climates (such as those in caves in some parts of our own Southwest), the perishable materials have entirely rotted away, leaving only such indestructible objects as stone, shell, occasional bone tools and, most important of all for the relative chronologic record, potsherds.

These refuse heaps were always located as near as possible to the settlements that made them. Sometimes the heaps measure many feet in depth, for they grew rapidly where dwellings were close together or where several families lived under one roof, as do the Pueblo Indians of New Mexico and Arizona. A cross-section of such a deposit gives a reliable ceramic history of the settlement near which it accumulated, fragments of the oldest types of pottery used being found in the lowest levels, and so on up to the present ground level, which, theoretically at least, yields potsherds from vessels that had been in use when the settlement was abandoned.

Such deposits of stratified pottery fragments give highly dependable relative ceramic sequences, but by themselves they do not furnish an absolute chronology—one datable in terms of our own Christian Era. The technique of relative dating of ceramic types by means of stratified refuse heaps has been most highly perfected among the Pueblo Indian cultures of the southwestern United States, especially those in New Mexico and Arizona. Fortunately there is another factor present in this region which makes extraordinarily accurate dating possible. This additional factor is supplied by the roof beams of the near-by community houses. The exact ages of these beams—the years of the Christian Era when the trees from which they were hewn, were felled—may be determined by a study of their corresponding growth-rings according to a method developed by Dr. A. S. Douglass of the University of Arizona. This fixes not only the time limits of the settlement in terms of Christian chronology but also the relative ages within these limits of the different ceramic wares used by its former inhabitants.

In the Maya area stratified deposits showing ceramic sequence are even more varied than those in the Pueblo region of the United

States. In addition to stratified refuse heaps, stratification of ceramic fragments has been found under successive plaza floors, in superimposed architectural units, and in tombs built one over another. These several sources indicating ceramic stratigraphy and sequence have all been found at Uaxactun. They all agree with one another and have provided a relative chronology for Old Empire ceramic types which is described in a later section. This chronology holds good for the whole Peten region, the Usumacinta Valley, and even more distant peripheral sections. Unfortunately in the lowlands of Middle America tree-ring dating is not available to give us absolute chronology in terms of the Christian Era, as it is in the southwestern United States. Trees in the Yucatan Peninsula sometimes add not only one but several growth-rings in a single year, and their ring count cannot be depended upon to furnish an accurate measure of their respective ages; consequently we must look elsewhere if we are to find an absolute chronology which may be read in terms of our own Christian chronology.

Fortunately, in the dated Maya monuments, we have or someday shall have such an absolute chronological yardstick. The dates of many of these monuments have been exactly determined in terms of Maya chronology, one of the most accurate systems for measuring time ever conceived by the mind of man. It remains only to align Maya with Christian chronology, which has probably already been successfully accomplished (see Appendix I, p. 457) in order to have as accurate dating as that afforded by tree rings.

Such are the variety, complexity, number, and specialization of Maya ceramic wares, however, and so close their association with exactly dated monuments that, when the whole story has been pieced together, and all the existing evidence gathered in, we shall probably know more about the ceramics of the Maya area, of the cities or localities where the different wares originated, of their distribution and disappearance from the Maya picture, than we shall ever know about the ceramics of any other people of ancient America.

← *a*) Sculptured door-jamb, Structure 2C6, Kabah, Yucatan, Mexico.

b) Sculptured door-jamb, Structure 2C6, Kabah, Yucatan, Mexico. →

← *c*) Sculptured door-jamb, Structure 2, Xculoc, Campeche, Mexico.

d) Sculptured door-jamb, Structure 2, Xculoc, Campeche, Mexico. →

PLATE 75
SCULPTURES OF
THE NEW
EMPIRE

↑ *a*) Lime-kiln before burning.

PLATE 76.—MAKING A LIME-KILN AT CHICHEN ITZA, YUCATAN, MEXICO

↓ *b*) Lime-kiln after burning.

a) House D of the Palace Group, west façade. →

← *b*) House D of the Palace Group, west façade.

PLATE 77.—EXAMPLES OF STUCCO-WORK FROM PALENQUE, CHIAPAS, MEXICO

a) Figure on wall of tomb as restored. ←

b) Figure on wall of tomb as restored. →

PLATE 78
EXAMPLES OF STUCCOWORK FROM COMALCALCO, TABASCO, MEXICO

c) Figures on wall of same tomb as found; figure at extreme right is same as preceding. ↓

↑ *a*) Figure of squirrel on face of building.

PLATE 79.—EXAMPLES OF STUCCO-WORK FROM ACANCEH, YUCATAN, MEXICO

↓ *b*) Figures of bat, eagle (?), jaguar (?) and serpent on face of building.

↑ *a*) Archaic clay head, "black dirt" stratum, Group E.

↑ *b*) Another **example** of the same **type.**

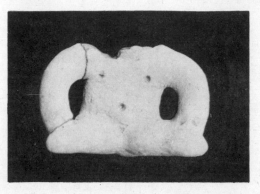

↑ *c*) Archaic female torso, "black dirt" stratum, Group E.

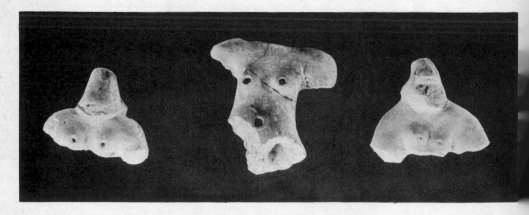

↑ *d*) Other examples of the same **type.**

PLATE 80.—UAXACTUN CERAMICS, MAMOM PHASE

PLATE 81.—MISCELLANEOUS EXAMPLES OF CLAY-MODELING FROM
THE OLD AND NEW EMPIRES AND AMONG THE LACANDON

(*a*) Effigy pipe, Temple of the Warriors, Chichen Itza, Yucatan, Mexico; (*b*) human head from incense-burner, Mayapan, Yucatan, Mexico; (*c*) human figurine made from an ancient mold, found on west side of the Rio Chixoy, Chiapas, Mexico; (*d*) modern Lacandon incense-burner, Chiapas, Mexico.

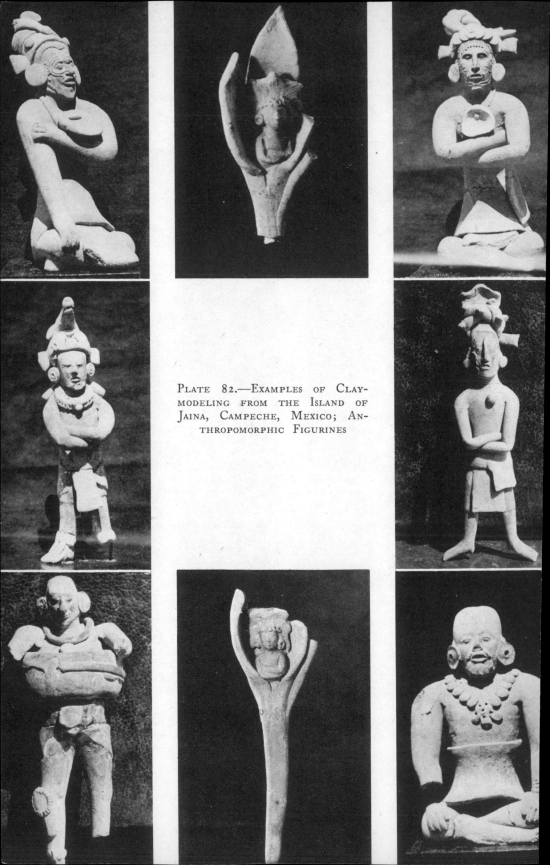

PLATE 82.—EXAMPLES OF CLAY-MODELING FROM THE ISLAND OF JAINA, CAMPECHE, MEXICO; ANTHROPOMORPHIC FIGURINES

It is certain that pottery-making did not originate in the Yucatan Peninsula. On the contrary the original, nonagricultural population of this region (Pre-Maya I, Tables III and IX) in all probability derived the potter's craft as well as their knowledge of maize cultivation from people living immediately to their south in the highlands of western Guatemala. Perhaps knowledge of both maize and pottery reached them at the same time or, more likely still, the practice of agriculture came first and was more or less closely followed by pottery-making. However, it seems certain that, perhaps as much as a thousand years prior to the beginning of the Christian Era, the entire Yucatan Peninsula from the foothills of the Guatemala *cordillera* in the south to the flat, bushy plains of northern Yucatan was occupied by a broad-headed people. These people spoke some Maya language, lived chiefly by agriculture as applied to maize cultivation, and made a pre-Maya (pre–Old Empire) pottery, probably of a type similar to that now called Mamom, which is explained below. They had no stone architecture nor stone sculpture, no elaborate chronological system, and no hieroglyphic writing (pre-Maya II).

MAMOM PHASE

Mamom-like pottery, probably because of insufficient excavation, has been found up to the present time at only a few cities— Uaxactun, Guatemala, and San Jose, British Honduras; it has always been found in the lowest and therefore the oldest occupation level at each of these centers. At Uaxactun, the type site where Mamom pottery was first identified, it was found resting directly upon undisturbed earth in the so-called "black dirt" stratum underlying all plaza-floor levels at Group E. The black dirt containing this type of pottery had been dumped there from some earlier location in order to level off the ground for the original plaza floor of Group E. This ceramic phase at Uaxactun precedes all masonry construction and all stone stelae; it is the earliest type of pottery found at this site or anywhere in the Yucatan Peninsula.

Beyond the confines of the Maya area proper, however, modeled heads of baked clay and figurines and pottery of Mamom type had a much wider distribution, especially in the uplands, having been found at Kaminal-juyu, Utatlan, and Totonicapan in Guatemala; in the highlands of Honduras and El Salvador; and in various localities as far north as the plateau region of central Mexico. This wide distribution of a relatively homogenous and simple ceramic culture over large parts of the Middle American region is probably best explained by assuming that it originated among some maize-growing people in the highlands of Guatemala and spread over Middle America with the diffusion of maize agriculture. However, it is pure conjecture as to just when agriculture and pottery-making were first introduced into the Yucatan Peninsula from the highlands to the south.

Well-modeled figurines of the general Mamom type have been found in a prehistoric cemetery under the Xictli lava flow on the southern side of the Valley of Mexico. Geologists believe these figurines are surely more than two thousand years old and possibly under three thousand years old. This means that such figurines were being made in the Valley of Mexico at least before the beginning of the Christian Era and perhaps even a long time before. A conservative minimum limit for the introduction of agriculture and pottery-making into the Yucatan Peninsula would therefore seem to be 1000 b.c. in round numbers.

As for its characteristics, Mamom pottery is simple, shapes as well as decoration being relatively limited. The principal wares are unslipped[1] jars with flaring necks, black jars with outcurved sides, black jars with incised decorations on shoulders, red bowls with flaring sides, red bowls and plates with horizontal grooving, orange bowls, and red or buff modeled figurines. There are no painted decorations except on daubware vessels where there may be some very crude attempts at design.

The principal decorative techniques employed in Mamom pottery are incising, grooving, and modeling. The last is best ex-

---

[1] A term used to describe the exterior coat or wash of clay applied to a pottery vessel before firing.

emplified by the human heads of baked clay with punched eyes (Plate 80, *a* and *b*) and gross female torsos (Plate 80, *c* and *d*).

The eye sockets of the former are made by depressed areas, the eye itself being shown by a punched hole and the eyebrows by shallow, incised lines. The female torsos, sometimes standing and sometimes seated, are very poorly modeled, the two nipples and the navel being formed by a simple punch in the clay before firing. Heads and torsos like the foregoing, as already noted, have been found among the earliest ceramic remains from the Valley of Mexico to Guatemala, Honduras, and El Salvador. There are no polychrome or carved wares in this first ceramic period, and only very few examples of batik or appliqué decoration have been found; figurines are slipped but not painted. Mamom pottery has been described as the "grooved-plate phase" of pre-Maya ceramics.

CHICANEL PHASE

We have seen in chapters iii and viii above that the introduction of the second ceramic phase at Uaxactun, the Chicanel, probably coincided with the invention of the Maya calendar, chronology, and hieroglyphic writing sometime during the fourth or third century before Christ. If these dates be accepted as approximately correct, the preceding pre-Maya pottery phase, the Mamom, lasted at least six and a half centuries and probably considerably longer (Pre-Maya II, Table X, p. 401).

The Chicanel ceramic phase follows the Mamom at Uaxactun without interruption of any kind. Vessels of this period were found located immediately below the lowest plaza floor at Group E, which in turn lies directly on top of the "black dirt" Mamom-bearing stratum. Chicanel vessels are associated with the earliest masonry constructions at Uaxactun. These constructions were not buildings proper—only low foundation platforms and pyramids upon which perishable houses of saplings and thatch were probably built.

Chicanel pottery is somewhat more developed than Mamom, and there are twice as many shapes and decorative techniques in this ceramic phase as in the preceding one. The principal wares are: unslipped jars with low flaring, thick necks and striated decorations; lightly incised red jars with short, flaring necks; red bowls with wide, everted, grooved lips; black bowls with incised decoration; orange bowls with incised decoration; brown bowls with wavy, incised decoration; brown bowls with lightly incised waved-stripe patterns; bowls with spiny, appliquéd decoration; red bowls with single, irregular decorations painted in black on the inside; and bowls decorated by the batik process.

While pottery and figurines of the general Mamom type have been discovered far beyond the confines of the Yucatan Peninsula and have a general uniformity of type throughout Central America and Mexico, Chicanel pottery, on the other hand, has a more restricted distribution. However, in northern Yucatan considerably more Chicanel pieces have been found than Mamom. There Chicanel pottery has been found at Dzibilchaltun, Acanceh, Mayapan, Kabah, Yaxuna, and Mani—almost everywhere in fact where excavations have been made. This condition suggests that there may have been more trade between Peten and northern Yucatan during this early period—two or three centuries both before and after the beginning of the Christian Era—than during the Mamom, the preceding ceramic phase (Table IX, facing p. 392). Chicanel pottery has been described as the "wide, everted lip phase" of pre-Maya ceramics (Pre-Maya III).

Concerning the tempering materials used in pre-Maya pottery, two types of wares must be distinguished at the outset: (1) an unslipped, coarse, heavy, thick-walled utility ware and (2) a slipped monochrome ware.

In the Mamom phase, a majority of the former types (utility ware) were tempered with sherd (pottery fragments), and less than a third of the vessels studied were tempered with calcite. Toward the end of this ceramic phase, however, these proportions were reversed. The use of calcite temper eventually exceeded that of sherd, until by the beginning of the next phase, the Chicanel, calcite temper practically replaces sherd temper altogether in the coarse heavy-walled utility ware.

In the slipped monochrome ware of the Mamom phase, as
in the case of the first type above, the tempering material used
is largely sherd, although both volcanic ash and calcite tempers
are frequently found. Again, as in the case of the utility pottery, the slipped monochrome ware shows a gradual change in
the tempering materials employed, a change which culminated
in the Chicanel phase with the almost exclusive use of sherd
temper, both calcite and volcanic ash tempers having practically
disappeared.

Also beginning with the Chicanel phase, the tempers of both
types show a consistent differentiation. The temper of the coarse
utility ware remains the same (sherd temper), not only for the
two pre-Maya ceramic phases (Mamom and Chicanel) but also for
the two following Old Empire ceramic phases (Tzakol and
Tepeu). Slipped monochrome ware, on the other hand, shows
many changes in its tempering material.

OLD EMPIRE POTTERY

The term "Maya civilization," as used here, is that complex
of cultural manifestations which had as its chief characteristics:
(1) a unique hieroglyphic writing, calendar, and chronology;
(2) a typical stone architecture with corbeled roof-vaulting; (3)
an individual stone sculpture; and (4) a distinctive ceramic art,
the earliest phase of which has been called Tzakol.

By the beginning of the fourth century after Christ, about
8.14.0.0.0 of the Maya Era, these four cultural elements had
already appeared at Uaxactun and the Maya civilization was at
last under way. For upwards of five or six centuries the Maya
had probably been using the hieroglyphic writing, calendar, and
chronology, and a characteristic pre-Maya pottery (Chicanel). As
for stone buildings, we have seen that they were preceded by
wood, sapling, and thatch structures. During the Chicanel pottery period the Maya began for the first time to build low stone
walls, stone foundation platforms, and even stucco-covered pyramids, for example E-VII-sub at Uaxactun, which dates from the
Chicanel ceramic phase. Stone sculpture had not yet been devel-

oped, but there was wood sculpture. All traces of both these earliest wood carvings and these first sapling and thatch structures have long since disappeared.

The cultural impetus which changed sculptures and buildings from wood to stone also brought with it a new and much more sophisticated ceramic art called Tzakol pottery. Whether these several elements were introduced from the outside into northern central Peten, specifically the Tikal-Uaxactun region, or whether they were developed autochthonously in this same region may never be known. Freely admitting to a strong pro-Maya bias in appraising the cultural achievements of this great aboriginal American people, I strongly believe that these developments came from within and that they had their origin in the Tikal-Uaxactun region of northern central Peten.

Even though this ceramic phase coincides with the earliest period of the Old Empire (317-633), Tzakol pottery is already characterized by considerable diversity and stylization of shapes, variety of decorative techniques, increasing development of polychrome wares, and the introduction of basal-flange bowls; this bowl is the most characteristic and diagnostic form of Old Empire pottery. Specialists in Maya ceramics have divided this ceramic phase into three subphases (Table IX), but in the limited space here available anything approaching a detailed description of Tzakol pottery would be impracticable. They had unslipped jars showing a great variety of lip treatment, some even with closed spouts; decoration consisted of striation, pie-fluting lip treatment, appliqué, thumb-nail punch, modeling, and appliquéd- and perforated-rim treatment. We find many shapes of black and orange incised wares, some showing the human figure beautifully incised in a cameo technique, the background being cut away. They had basal-flange bowls in solid colors (black or orange) and polychromy. These bowls show many motifs: geometric; anthropomorphic, zoömorphic, and serpentine; some are modeled as well as painted and some have tripod supports rather than the basal flange. There are also beautifully modeled black, covered bowls, the tops shaped like human, animal, bird, or serpentine forms;

the best of these show exquisite modeling. Tzakol pottery has been designated the "basal-flange phase" of Old Empire ceramics because of the highly distinctive basal flange introduced during this period.

We have seen in chapter iv (p. 59) that during the Early Period of the Old Empire, Maya culture spread from the relatively small area where it probably originated in northern central Peten, Guatemala (the Tikal-Uaxactun region), to all parts of the Yucatan Peninsula. This great expansion was doubtless accompanied by a corresponding increase in trade with the peripheral regions and even beyond; thus ceramic pieces traded from these outlying regions begin to appear with growing frequency during the Early Period.

The Tzakol ceramic phase is represented by fair amounts of potsherds at a few centers in northern Yucatan, principally at Mani, Yaxuna, and Acanceh; but there are only a few traces at Chichen Itza, Uxmal, Kabah, Labna, Sayil, and Mayapan. It is probable, however, that further excavation, especially at Oxkintok and Coba in the northwestern and northeastern corners of the peninsula, would bring to light additional examples. Throughout the Early Period of the Old Empire, northern Yucatan continued to develop its own local versions of the earlier Mamom and Chicanel pottery in addition to such Tzakol ceramic influences as it had received from central Peten. The Mamom and Chicanel influences probably came originally from the south also, even though these phases had already disappeared in the Peten region before Maya culture reached northern Yucatan.

TEPEU PHASE

We come now to the closing ceramic phase of the Old Empire, the Tepeu, which coincides with the Middle and Great Periods of the Old Empire (633–987). Like the Tzakol phase, Maya ceramicists have divided Tepeu pottery into three subphases—early, middle, and late (Table IX).

Early Tepeu coincides with the Middle Period, and middle Tepeu coincides roughly with the first two-thirds of the Great

Period of the Old Empire, during which time the Maya were at their esthetic peak in all the arts and crafts, except in architecture; late Tepeu likewise coincides with the last third of the Great Period. Peten wares of Tepeu type have been found outside of Peten, though less frequently than pottery of the earlier Peten ceramic phases. They have been found at Coba, Yaxuna, Uxmal, Kabah, Labna, Sayil, and Mani in northern Yucatan, and excavations elsewhere in the northern peninsula would almost certainly extend this list.

During the Tepeu ceramic phase the cities of Peten were also in close contact with the upper Chixoy Valley, where a special painted ware of very great beauty (to be described in the next chapter under the section of painting) was developed.

The upper Chixoy region was strongly influenced by Peten during the Middle and Great Periods. This region is about 900 feet above sea level and has a flora and fauna similar to those of the Peten homeland; it is easily accessible therefrom by the Chixoy, Pasión, and Usumacinta rivers. Peten Tepeu pottery, on the other hand, shows that it in turn was influenced by polychrome wares from the upper Chixoy Valley; there was doubtless a constant exchange back and forth since these regions were culturally as well as geographically so close to each other. A fine carved ware, with the figures standing out in low, flat relief and the backgrounds cut away, seems to have followed the beautiful painted vases of middle Tepeu in both Peten and the upper Chixoy Valley. Indeed it is not improbable that the waves of influence which carried the finely modeled effigy bowls and figurines from the Peten-Usumacinta cities to the upper Chixoy Valley may have been balanced by other waves of cultural influence which carried the exquisitely painted and carved bowls of the upper Chixoy Valley to the great cities of the Usumacinta Valley and of Peten. But such borrowings were very much within the family so to speak, both regions being integral parts of the Old Empire during the Middle and Great Periods.

Outside the central and northern lowlands, Tepeu pottery seems to have followed two principal lines of distribution: (1)

TABLE IX

SEVEN PRINCIPAL CERAMIC PERIODS REPRESENTED IN THE YUCATAN PENINSULA

Number of Ceramic Period	Period	Southern Half: Peten, Guatemala, and adjoining regions	Northern Half: Yucatan, Campeche, and Quintana Roo, Mexico
1	Pre-Old Empire II 1000 (??) B.C.–353 B.C.	Mamom ceramic phase; "grooved-plate" pottery. Agriculture (cultivation of maize) introduced from the highlands to	Mamom ceramic phase and contemporary local wares. Agriculture (cultivation of maize) introduced from Peten.
6	New Empire II Mexican Period A.D. 1194–1441 10.8.10.0.0–11.11.0.0.0 Tun 10 of Katun 8 Ahau–Katun 10 Ahau	Abandoned.	Mexican ceramic phase. Fine Orange ware (Phase 2) and first appearance of Plumbate ware, latter imported from southern highlands. Rise of Mayapan and decline of Chichen Itza. Period III, corbeled roof-vaulting.
7	New Empire III Period of Disintegration A.D. 1441–1697 11.11.0.0.0–12.4.1.0.0 Katun 10 Ahau–Katun 8 Ahau	Tayasal at western end of Lake Peten Itza occupied.	Fall of Mayapan (1441) and end of centralized authority. Decadent ceramic phase; coarse red pottery. Period III, corbeled roof-vaulting.

southeastward into Honduras and El Salvador, and (2) southward into the highlands of Guatemala, where pottery of this type has been found at Coban and Chama in the Department of Alta Vera Paz and at Zacualpa in the Department of El Quiché. Curiously enough no Tepeu pottery has been found at Kaminal-juyu in the Guatemala highlands, and therefore it would seem that relations between this latter city and the lowland cities to the north, which were fairly close during the later Tzakol phase, had been broken off before Tepeu times.

Amid the numerous wares of the Tepeu phase the following are outstanding: slipped bowls with large openings and striated, appliquéd, grooved, thumbnail-punched, and impressed decorations; red bowls with flaring necks and handles; incurved-lip bowls; incurved-lip tripod dishes and tripod plates with flaring sides; carved orange vases with pedestal bases and bowls with rounded sides; unslipped, though occasionally painted, mold-made figures, both human and animal, sometimes in the form of whistles. Finally there is a bewildering variety of shapes in polychrome ware—tripod plates with flaring sides, basal-molding tripod plates, bowls with straight sides and cylindrical or barrel-shaped vases, their painted designs covering many subjects: geometric patterns, life-forms ranging from human to insect, hieroglyphic inscriptions, whole ceremonies and scenes from the late Old Empire picture (Plates 87, 88, 89, a, and Figs. 49, 50, 51). No other aboriginal people of the entire New World ever produced such superb painted pottery as did the ancient Maya of the first century and a half of the Great Period of the Old Empire (731–889), an esthetic superachievement they themselves never again equaled.

The Tepeu ceramic period has been called the "incurved-lip" phase because of the frequency with which this type of rim treatment was used during the Middle and Great Periods of the Old Empire.

Beginning with the Tzakol ceramic phase, the slipped monochrome ware shows an abrupt change in the tempering material used as compared with pre-Maya slipped monochrome. Volcanic ash temper suddenly replaces sherd temper, which, except as shown in the earliest Tzakol vessels, practically disappears as a tempering material in this ware. Volcanic ash continues to be the principal temper used in slipped monochrome throughout the Tzakol phase, though calcite temper also was sometimes used.

During the next ceramic phase—the Tepeu—calcite becomes the predominant temper. At this time there appears an increasing tendency toward a definite correlation between kinds of vessels and the corresponding tempers used in making them; one kind of vessel has a calcite temper and another kind one of volcanic ash. Pottery-making had indeed become a fine art.

When we come to polychrome ware, which first appears in the Tzakol ceramic phase, the principal temper used was volcanic ash, though here again certain types of vessels show calcite temper.

These changes in tempering materials are of interest to the archaeologist because they reveal changing ceramic practices, show the influences of the ceramic techniques of one region upon those of another, and give indications of outside trade relations. Such changes in tempering materials may be due: (1) to the adoption of a superior tempering material as the result of practical experimentation by an up-and-coming potter; (2) to the adoption of methods practiced by potters of one district by potters of another district; and (3) to the importation of foreign wares.

The most logical explanation of a variety of tempering materials used in the same type of pottery at the same time is that they are the work of different groups, certain vessels being imported pieces. But in order to prove such a theory, extensive as well as intensive knowledge of the ceramic art of the entire Yucatan Peninsula and surrounding regions will first be necessary, and as yet our understanding of ancient Maya ceramics may be said to be only at the grammar-school stage. Before high-school, college, and university status may be achieved in this field, widespread excavations not only in the Maya area proper but also in the surrounding culture provinces must be undertaken, and the resulting ceramic materials must then be subjected to close, comparative study.

We have seen that at a very early date the craft of pottery-making spread all over the Yucatan Peninsula, probably from the Guatemala highlands to the south, covering not only the southern half but also the more distant northern half of the peninsula as well.

Pottery reached the northern half of the Yucatan Peninsula probably well toward the beginning of the first millenium before Christ, on a definitely pre-Maya (pre-Old Empire) horizon. The Mamom and Chicanel ceramic phases, the former the oldest pottery encountered anywhere in the Yucatan Peninsula, both seem to be fairly homogeneous whether found in the north or in the south. Once the idea of making baked-clay vessels had been implanted in the northern half of the peninsula, however, Yucatan ceramics followed its own local evolutionary trends. The Mamom and Chicanel pottery of Yucatan is more like the Mamom and Chicanel pottery of Peten. Still, as time went on and the Chicanel ceramic phase changed into the Tzakol phase in Peten at the beginning of the Old Empire, corresponding changes were also taking place independently in the north. Divergent ceramic development was gradually widening the gap between the pottery arts of the two regions. Finally, by the time the pre-Maya epoch came to its end in the early fourth century of the Christian Era, the pottery of both regions already differed widely, each having followed its own pattern of development.

During both the Tzakol and early Tepeu ceramic phases of the Old Empire, pottery throughout the northern half of the peninsula varies greatly, not only between different sections but also from the contemporary pottery of the Old Empire. Peten polychrome wares have been found only in small quantities in northern Yucatan, and when they do occur they stand out sharply from local wares. Finally, by the time the Old Empire came to its end in the tenth century, the ceramic wares of the northern peninsula had acquired a strong individual character, as a result of divergent evolution, which in the larger view owed little to Old Empire ceramic influences.

The ceramic period called New Empire I, or Puuc, was brought about by Maya-Mexican invasions of Yucatan in the tenth century. The vigorous newcomers provided a fillip, a shot in the arm to dying Old Empire culture in the north, which stimulus in turn produced the Maya Renaissance in the eleventh and twelfth centuries. Not only pottery but architecture, sculpture, and the other arts reflected this strong new cultural impetus, though architecture alone reached new heights of expression; the others, including pottery, never again equaled the high levels they had attained during the Great Period of the Old Empire.

The most characteristic ware of the Puuc ceramic period was Yucatan slate, which occurs in both decorated and plain vessels. Decoration was achieved by cutting away the background, leaving the design in low flat relief; some examples are very lovely (Plate 83), but even the best examples of this ware do not approach bowls in the same carved decorative technique of Old Empire late Tepeu pottery. Yucatan slate first appears in the northern peninsula as far back as late Old Empire times but reached its greatest development during the eleventh and twelfth centuries during the early New Empire.

Fine Orange pottery, definitely a trade ware, also occurs throughout the Puuc period. Although of foreign origin, so far as the Maya were concerned its considerable prevalence in northern Yucatan during the eleventh and twelfth centuries indicates that it came from a near-by region. It appears probable that its center of manufacture was somewhere along the Tabasco coast plain. Since the Maya-Mexican invaders of the tenth century certainly passed through this region and probably sojourned there for a considerable time, perhaps several centuries before moving northeastward into Yucatan, it is not at all improbable that they themselves either first developed this ware in Tabasco, later bringing it with them to Yucatan, or that they acquired it in their passage through the Tabasco coast plain and carried it with them into the northern peninsula.

Fine Orange ware of the Puuc period (Phase 1) is remarkably homogeneous, suggesting a relatively short occupation of the Puuc cities—perhaps not more than the two centuries allotted here (987–1194). Fine Orange ranges in color from terra-cotta red to orange and occasionally to a neutral gray, the last perhaps due to inequalities in firing. It seems to contain no special tempering material other than minerals which occur naturally in the clay from which the ware was made. Sometimes Fine Orange ware is plain and sometimes it is decorated with a carved technique, the background being cut away, like the lovely example found at Uxmal (Fig. 43, *a*).

Perhaps sometime during this period the Island of Jaina, off the northwest coast of the peninsula, developed into a center for the manufacture of anthropomorphic clay figurines in a variety of postures showing different kinds of wearing apparel and dress accessories (Plate 82), some of which are of considerable esthetic merit.

MEXICAN PHASE

The ceramic period, called New Empire II or Mexican, makes its appearance in northern Yucatan at the end of the twelfth century, presumably following the conquest of Chichen Itza in 1194 by Hunac Ceel, the *halach uinic* of Mayapan and his Mexican allies from the Point Xicalanco region of eastern Tabasco (chapter v, p. 91). This ceramic period is best studied at Chichen Itza and Mayapan, where excavations in stratified deposits at both sites show clearly that as the former city declined the latter grew stronger, almost as though the waning of the Itza metropolis was due to the waxing of the Cocom capital.

Another common ware of the period was Fine Orange (Phase 2), principally found at Chichen Itza and Mayapan. This has the same fine texture as the first phase and to a certain extent the same color range and decorative techniques (painted and incised); however, it differs markedly in shape, surface finish, and design. Vessels in the second phase of Fine Orange are not so well executed as those in the first phase. Three varieties of incised decoration are found: incised through a red over-all slip; incised

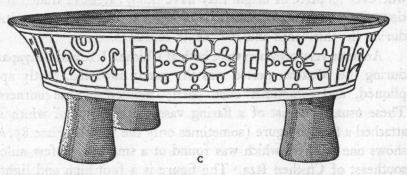

Fig. 43.—Examples of Fine Orange ware from the New Empire: (*a*) from Uxmal; (*b* and *c*) from Chichen Itza.

through a black slip to a red base color (Fig. 43, *b*); and incised
through a white slip to a red base color (Fig. 43, *c*).

During the New Empire II Period, Plumbate pottery, another surely imported ware, makes its appearance for the first time in northern Yucatan. Plumbate ware has a beautiful lustrous finish, almost a metallic sheen, and varies in color from a brilliant orange through terra cotta and tan to lead gray; since all of these tones can and do occur in the same vessel, such color differences are probably due to temperature differences in firing, some parts of the vessel having been exposed to greater heat than others. This ware has a slip, and the clay itself probably contained ingredients which cause the lustrous surface sheen after firing. Evidently the true Plumbate ware (there are several imitations) comes from a restricted region where such a specialized clay exists. Although the place of manufacture has not yet been definitely determined, present indications are that it was made somewhere in the southern highlands, that is, somewhere between western El Salvador and eastern Chiapas, Mexico.

Plumbate ware occurs in many shapes, modeling being the chief decorative technique; effigy vases and bowls with extremely well modeled human, animal, and bird forms are common (Plate 84). Although this ware appears relatively late in Maya history (New Empire II), examples of it are so common at Chichen Itza that wherever its place of origin may have been, extensive trade relations must have been carried on between it and the Itza capital during the thirteenth and fourteenth centuries.

Another very common ware both at Chichen Itza and Mayapan during the Mexican period was the partly modeled, partly appliquéd, and sometimes even partly molded incense burners. These usually consist of a flaring vase to the front of which is attached a human figure (sometimes only the head). Plate 85, *b*, shows one of these which was found at a small site a few miles southeast of Chichen Itza. The figure is a foot high and light-brown in color. Some incense burners are taller than this, others are shorter; some are more elaborate, others less so; many are painted. They were built up piece by piece, the arms, legs, clothing, and dress accessories being made separately and then attached to the trunk of the figure after the latter had itself been fastened to the vase. *Pom* incense was burned inside the vase, while offerings of corn, beans, tobacco, chili pepper, cotton, et cetera, were placed on the extended hands of the figure, or as among the modern Lacandon, on the protruding lower lip of the head (Plate 81, *d*). As noted above, such incense burners are found in greatest abundance at Chichen Itza and Mayapan and date from the Mexican period.

DECADENT PHASE

After the fall of Mayapan in 1441, the most important Maya center in the northern half of Yucatan was Mani, the last capital of the Xiu state. Here a coarse, red pottery of decadent type (Plate 85, *a*) continued to be made down to the time of the Spanish Conquest and even afterward during the early Colonial Period, but it was heavy, crude, and quite without esthetic value. The glorious ceramic traditions of the Old Empire, even the less meritorious wares of the New Empire, were never again equaled, and Maya pottery as a fine art suffered final eclipse.

SUMMARY OF MAYA CERAMICS

The ceramics of the Yucatan Peninsula, considered as a whole, may be divided into the seven periods in Table IX (facing p. 392).

Much of the corresponding chronology in this table, especially the equivalent Christian dates, is still speculative. First, the exact correlation of Maya and Christian chronologies has not yet been surely determined (see Appendix I, p. 457); and, secondly, the amount of time suggested for the Mamom and Chicanel ceramic phases, Pre-Maya II and III, is only approximate. The length of the Mamom phase indicated in Tables IX and X depends on the assumption that the craft of pottery-making first reached Peten not long after or at the same time as the introduction of agriculture, indeed may even have come with it; this event is fixed as having occurred in round numbers at 1000 B.C., which is to say that although knowledge of agriculture and the potter's craft

↑ *b*) Bowl from Dzan, Yucatan, Mexico (Morley Collection).

a) Excavated fragment, Uxmal, Yucatan, Mexico.

c) Jar, provenance unknown (Rafael de Regil Collection, Merida, Yucatan, Mexico).

PLATE 83.—EXAMPLES OF YUCATAN SLATE WARE, PUUC PERIOD, NORTHERN YUCATAN, MEXICO

d) Engraved vase found near Ticul, Yucatan, Mexico (Peabody Museum of Archaeology and Ethnology, Harvard University, Cambridge, Massachusetts). ↓

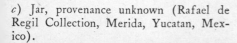

PLATE 84.—EXAMPLES OF PLUMBATE WARE, MEXICAN PERIOD, NORTHERN YUCATAN, MEXICO

(Rafael de Regil Collection, Merida, Yucatan, Mexico)

↑ *a*) Coarse red ware tripod bowls, northern Yucatan, Mexico.

↓ *b*) Incense-burner found near Chichen Itza, Yucatan, Mexico.

a) Spinning. →

← *b*) Weaving.

PLATE 86.—SPINNING AND WEAVING AMONG THE LACANDON MAYA, CHIAPAS, MEXICO

could not have reached Peten later than 1000 B.C. they both may well have reached there considerably before. The length of the Chicanel ceramic phase is based on the assumption that it began about the time the Maya chronological system was invented; this is generally conceded to have taken place in either 7.0.0.0.0 or 7.6.0.0.0 of the Maya Era—353 or 235 B.C., respectively.

The respective lengths of these seven ceramic periods are given in Table X.

TABLE X

DURATION OF THE SEVEN CERAMIC PERIODS OF THE YUCATAN PENINSULA

Number of Period	Name of Period	Corresponding Ceramic Phase		Length of Period	
1	Pre-Maya II	Mamom		647 + years	
2	Pre-Maya III	Chicanel		670 years	
3	Old Empire I	Tzakol, early	197 years		
	Old Empire I	Tzakol, middle	40 years		
	Old Empire I	Tzakol, late	79 years		
			—	316 years	
4	Old Empire II	Tepeu, early	100 years		
	Old Empire III	Tepeu, middle	154 years		
	Old Empire III	Tepeu, late	100 years		
			—	354 years	
5	New Empire I	Puuc		207 years	
6	New Empire II	Mexican		247 years	
7	New Empire III	Decadent		100 years	

The first two periods are necessarily much longer than the others; in fact the first two combined are even somewhat longer than all the others put together. This is the invariable story in human progress—slow, very slow at first, crawling forward step by step with each important gain the result of decades, perhaps even centuries of previous trial and error. A long time, probably well over a millenium, was required for the development and accumulation of those several cultural elements which together in later times constituted the Maya civilization as the term is used in this book. Once these cultural elements had been achieved, as they were at the threshold of the Old Empire in the early years of the fourth century of the Christian Era, ancient Maya progress was rapid and advances were made at an accelerated tempo. The lengths of the several periods given in Table X show a general tendency to become increasingly shorter as the end is approached, thus conforming with the invariable law of civilization—faster, faster, faster.

The pottery of the Old Empire was never equaled during New Empire times, and from an esthetic point of view the decorated wares of the former are probably the finest examples of the potter's art in the New World. The Maya stressed the decorative quality in pottery even at the cost of durability. Fine finish, high luster, bright colors were the characteristics sought. In both monochrome and polychrome wares smooth, even surfaces, mirror-like luster, and a range of bright oranges and reds, which retained their brilliance and clarity even after firing, were achieved. This high luster and these bright colors, however, were made possible only by comparatively low firing temperatures (a maximum of between 1300° and 1350° F.), which in turn produced a soft pottery that can be scratched even with the thumbnail; thus strength was sacrificed to beauty. This is true because high-temperature firing causes the clay to shrink; it breaks up smooth, even surfaces which have been compacted by burnishing before firing, and because of this they disperse rather than reflect light and thus give a dull appearance. Then, too, the iron oxides upon which the ancient Maya depended principally for their red and orange pigments lose their brightness at high temperatures and become brownish.

The poor technical quality of Maya pottery is in striking contrast to its beauty of finish and decoration. In order to compensate for the lack of tensile strength due to low firing temperatures, the Maya potters were obliged to increase the thickness of the walls of their vessels, giving a general effect of heaviness except in the most beautiful examples.

In addition to the desire to have high luster and bright colors, the Maya potter fired at low temperatures because his tempering material, especially in the Great Period of the Old Empire, was largely ground limestone. If pastes of this kind are subjected to high enough temperatures to make them really hard, the ground limestone in the temper calcines, after which it reacts readily to moisture—slakes and expands so that the vessel cracks. Indeed the poor quality of Old Empire pottery strongly suggests that it was developed primarily as an art ware; few technical advances were achieved in the making of purely utilitarian wares throughout Maya history.

It may be of interest in this connection to note that the maximum firing temperature used among the Pueblo Indian potters of our own Southwest at Zia, New Mexico, in firing polychrome wares is 1724° Fahrenheit. María Martinez of San Ildefonso, New Mexico, perhaps the best of all our present-day Pueblo potters, fires her beautiful black luster ware at only 1238° Fahrenheit.

Maya pottery is marked by a great diversity of wares, high development and stylization of shapes, and many decorative techniques. Even as early as the beginning of the Old Empire there was already a multitude of shapes. The greater proportion of shallow and flat-bottomed plates and dishes represents a stage of far greater sophistication in the potter's craft than the simple hemispherical bowls of the Pueblo Indians of the Southwestern United States. Decorative practices included practically all techniques: grooving, incising, carving, punching, modeling, molding, appliqué, fretlike perforations, and paintings.

It was in the last technique, however, in connection with their polychrome wares, that the Maya displayed their greatest skill, employing a wide range of colors and showing a knowledge of draftmanship of the highest order.

Maya painting will be described at greater length in the next chapter, but a few observations may be made here in connection with the use of this technique in the decoration of pottery.

Greens, blues, and reds derived from cinnebar were applied after firing, since the only substances the Maya knew which would produce these tones yielded fugitive colors that could not survive even low firing temperatures. These colors were applied after firing, being painted on a lime-stucco base which resulted in beautiful pastel shades. Sometimes in the case of incised black ware, often of high luster, the pigment was simply rubbed into the incised lines. However, the bright oranges and reds derived from iron oxides were able to withstand the low firing temperatures employed without losing brilliance.

The high development of painted design in Maya polychrome ware is all the more striking when we bear in mind that it did not begin until the third ceramic period, that is the Tzakol phase during the Early Period of the Old Empire (Old Empire I). Then, too, pottery decoration in the immediately preceding phases, the Mamom and Chicanel (Pre-Maya II and III), was fairly simple. The elaborately carved, modeled, and molded vessels of the Great Period (Old Empire III) offer still further evidence of the superexcellence of ceramic art in late Old Empire times, a pre-eminence the Maya were destined never again to attain.

MISCELLANEOUS ARTS AND CRAFTS

TEXTILES

NO TEXTILES from the Old Empire Period have survived and only a very few from the New Empire Period. A few fragments of white cotton cloth, said to date from just before the Spanish Conquest, are reported from a small cave near Tenam in the highlands of eastern Chiapas; the supposed late New Empire origin of this cloth is based upon the type of pottery found associated with it. Numerous small pieces of carbonized cotton cloth, which show many different and complicated weaves and which also date from late New Empire times, were recovered from the Well of Sacrifice at Chichen Itza.

The foregoing extremely limited examples constitute the only actual specimens of ancient Maya textiles that have been discovered up to the present time. But as to their former abundance and variety, the reliefs of both the Old and New Empires bear ample witness. Furthermore the modern Maya of the highlands of Guatemala—the Quiche, Cakchiquel, and other related tribes—have an exceedingly rich textile art which derives directly from their pre-Conquest ancestors. Finally the Lacandon Maya of the eastern Chiapas forests still practice spinning and hand-loom weaving, crafts that have only just disappeared in northern Yucatan during the past generation or two.

The sculptures of the Old Empire indicate that the cotton fabrics of that period must have been extraordinarily rich and of complicated weave. Woven decorations, insets of something like lace or possibly even drawnwork, and elaborate embroidery in both colored cotton threads and featherwork seem to have been employed. A few representations of these Old Empire textiles, taken from the monuments, are shown in Figure 44, *a*, *b*, *c*, and *d*, some being so ornate as to suggest heavy, sumptuous brocades; other textiles from the New Empire are illustrated in Figure 44, *e*, *f*, *g*, and *h*.

Hand-woven cotton stuffs (*patis*) of fixed length and width were used as articles of trade in ancient times and later, after the Spanish Conquest, became the principal form of tribute (*mantas*) exacted from the Indians by their conquerors.

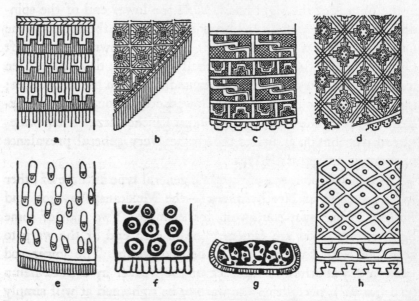

FIG. 44.—Old Empire textiles (*a*, *b*, *c*, *d*) taken from the monuments; and New Empire textiles (*e*, *f*, *g*, *h*) from wall-paintings and pottery.

The Lacandon, whose living conditions more closely resemble those of the ancient Maya than those of any other modern Maya groups, still spin their own cotton thread and weave a coarse cloth from it, using the same techniques in both spinning and weaving as did their ancestors of the Old and New Empires.

The work of spinning and weaving is done by the women. They gather the cotton from the field and spin it into thread, using as a spindle a slender pointed stick of hard wood about 10 or 12 inches long, weighted about 3 inches from the lower end

with a ring of pottery. However, this latter part of the spindle,
which archaeologists call the spindle-whorl, is all that has survived of ancient Maya spinning and weaving implements, the
wooden looms and spindles having long since mingled with the
dust of the women who operated them.

These circular baked-clay weights are found in greatest abundance throughout the Middle American region. Their purpose was
to give balance and weight to the spindle as it was twirled rapidly
in the fingers of the right hand, while the lower end of the spindle rested in a gourd on the ground in front of the spinner; the
unspun cotton was held in the left hand or thrown over the left
shoulder (Plate 86, *a*). These small baked-clay disks have been
unearthed by every excavation ever undertaken in the Maya area;
they have been found in the very lowest occupation levels at Uaxactun and from the very latest period at Chichen Itza. Their widespread distribution indicates the former very general prevalence
of weaving among the Maya.

The Maya loom was of the same general type as those of other
Indian peoples of North America—the Mexicans, Navajos, and
Pueblos of our own Southwest, for example. Two rods of some
light, strong wood are fastened one to each end of the warp to
keep the cloth stretched to the desired width. The lower rod
(*xunche*) is attached to the back of the weaver by a thick hemp
cord (*yamal*), permitting the warp to be tightened at will simply
by the weaver's leaning backward. The upper rod is attached
to a tree or post. The strip of cloth may be made as long as
eight feet, and as it lengthens it is wound around the upper
rod. The woman with the shuttle in her left hand sits as far back
from the post or tree as possible in order to hold the loom horizontally at the required tension (Plate 86, *b*). The cloth is
woven in one straight piece to the desired length. The looms
are not more than two and a half to three feet wide, and when
wider cloth is desired two strips are sewed together.

An ancient representation of this same weaving technique appears in the Codex Tro-Cortesianus (Fig. 45), where a female
counterpart of Itzamna, perhaps Ixchel, his wife and patroness of

the art, is shown weaving, one end of the loom being tied to a tree and the other wound around the goddess' waist, shuttle in left hand as among the Lacandon women today. According to New Empire mythology, we have seen that Ixchel as moon-goddess was the consort of Itzamna, the sun-god; her daughter, Ix Chebel Yax, was patroness of the allied art of embroidery.

FIG. 45.—The goddess Ixchel weaving. Page 79, Codex Tro-Cortesianus.

The Indians of the highlands of Guatemala still have a rich textile art, the various towns and villages being characterized by the different kinds of cloth they weave and by their traditional designs. Formerly these differences were tribal rather than between different towns, but since the Spanish conquerors everywhere sought to break down old political divisions among the Indians such differences in textiles and garments today are characteristic of towns and villages rather than of tribal groups. Although wool has been introduced into Guatemala since the Conquest and is now woven into blankets of very fine quality, for the most part the native clothing is still made of hand-loom cotton cloth. Today silk is generally employed in embroidery, but formerly colored cotton threads and feathers were used instead. As there are no fixed designs, no two pieces of cloth are exactly alike, but in each village there is general conformity to the traditional village pattern (Plate 26, *a* and *b*).

The colors used by the Guatemala Indians in their hand-woven cotton fabrics still bear some relation to those used by the ancient Maya. Black still represents weapons because it is the color of obsidian, formerly used in making spear and arrow points; the terrible *macuahuitl*, a vicious war club, was inset on opposite sides with rows of obsidian points (Fig. 6, *f*). Yellow still symbolizes food because it is the color of corn; red represents blood, and blue means sacrifice. The royal color is green because green

is the color of the highly prized quetzal bird, whose plumage was
reserved for the rulers.

In coloring textiles today, as was probably also the case in ancient times, the thread itself is dyed and not the finished fabric. Although aniline dyes are now replacing the old animal, mineral, and vegetable colors, a few of the latter are still in use such as indigo, the roots and barks of certain trees, the juice of vegetables and berries (the wild tomato and blackberry for example), and the cochineal insect, which yields a rich red coloring matter. Perhaps the most highly prized of all the native dyes was a deep purple obtained from a kind of mollusk found along the Pacific Coast (*Purpura patula*, Linnaeus and Lamarck), a relative of the Mediterranean mollusk which gave the famous "royal purple of Tyre."

In Yucatan the type of embroidery used by the modern Maya is cross-stitch (*xoc bil chui*, or "threads that are counted"). Formerly the designs may have been geometric like those still used by the women of the distant Tixcacal group in central Quintana Roo (Plate 26, *c*). Geometric designs, however, have largely disappeared from northern Yucatan today, being replaced by floral, bird, animal, and even insect motifs (Plate 26, *d*).

Native weaves and native colors, unhappily, are everywhere giving way to machine-made fabrics and aniline dyes. Except in the highlands of Guatemala, native weaving and dyeing have all but disappeared, and even in this region both are on the way out— the last survivors of a former and brilliant native art.

BASKETRY AND MATTING

As in the case of textiles, ancient Maya basketry is practically nonexistent, and although a few fragments of textiles have been found, no early baskets have been discovered. However, representations of baskets from the Old Empire reliefs are not lacking. An elaborate basket appears resting on the ground in Lintel 24 at Yaxchilan (Fig. 46, *a*). The upper half is in a twilled technique, but the middle section is of finer weave, showing an alternating design of stepped frets and groups of small squares; the bottom seems to be ornamented with featherwork. Representations of two late Old Empire baskets are shown in Figure 46, *b* and *c*, from the Nebaj Vase. A basket from a wall-painting in the Temple of the Jaguars at Chichen Itza and dating from the New Empire (Fig. 46, *d*) is more elaborate but far less effective.

a   b   c   d

FIG. 46.—Old and New Empire baskets from the monuments, wall-paintings, and pottery: (*a*) on Lintel 24, Yaxchilan; (*b* and *c*) on the Nebaj Vase; (*d*) fresco in the Temple of the Jaguars, Chichen Itza.

Modern Lacandon baskets, as well as those of northern Yucatan, are relatively crude. Some with vertical sides and open tops are woven from thin, tough vines; these are large and coarse and are used for carrying corn from the cornfields to the house. Split-cane baskets are smaller and more neatly woven; they serve for all sorts of domestic purposes in the home.

As for matting, no actual pieces have survived but imprints of it on pottery and plaster have been found. There was a subterranean storeroom for corn below the lowest floor level in the plaza of Group E at Uaxactun. Here a small heap of disintegrated material was found, apparently the remains of a palm-fiber mat, for a weave pattern could be barely distinguished. Then at Chichen Itza the imprint of another piece of matting was found in the sanctuary of the temple buried beneath the Castillo; the famous Red Jaguar throne had rested upon this matting. The weave of this New Empire piece was identical with that of mats which are still made and sold in the Merida market today.

Mats played an important role in ancient Maya life. A piece of matting with the sun symbol beside it (Fig. 19, *a*) is the hieroglyph for the first month of the ancient Maya year, *Pop,* which means "matting." In the council-chamber sitting on a mat was a mark of authority, and throughout the Book of Chilam Balam of Chumayel the words "mat" and "throne" are used interchangeably. The sequence of the hieroglyphic inscriptions on the backs of Stela J at Copan and Stela H at Quirigua both follow the weave of a mat pattern in the order of their reading; the former (Fig. 47, *b*) is more complicated than Figure 47, *a*, and is exactly like the symbol for the month *Pop* mentioned above.

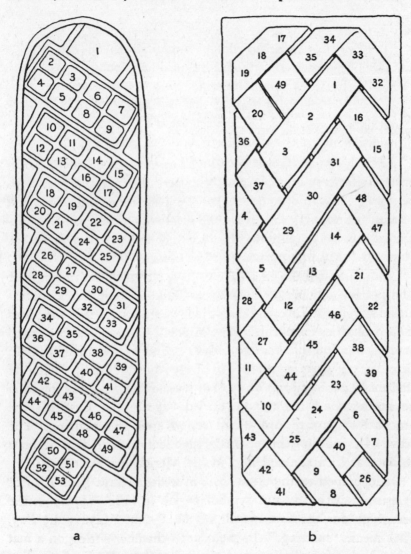

a   b

FIG. 47.—Mat patterns shown on the backs of Old Empire monuments; the glyph sequence in these inscriptions follows the pattern of a mat. (*a*) Stela H at Quirigua; (*b*) Stela J at Copan.

Baskets, woven bags, carrying-nets, and matting must have been extremely common among the ancient Maya, for the materials from which they were made—vines, fibers, and palms—occurred in the greatest abundance throughout this area.

PAINTING

Painting was a fine art among the ancient Maya and reached a degree of excellence attained by no other people of aboriginal America. Frescoes painted directly upon the white plaster finish were used in the decoration of both interior and exterior walls. Painting was also used in the decoration of ceramic wares and in illustrating the codices, or hieroglyphic manuscripts.

The Maya palette was extensive. There were several reds, ranging from an opaque purplish-red, like Indian red, through a finely graded series of transparent shades to a brilliant orange. A coppery-tan color was used extensively for outlining, both in the wall-paintings and in the codices, while varying mixtures of the foregoing shades with opaque white gave a number of pinks. The yellows range from a pale greenish-yellow to a dark yellow, the latter approaching orange. A dark brown resulted from mixing yellow and black. There seems to have been but a single blue; when this was painted over an opaque ground, however, an effect of Prussian blue was obtained, but when laid directly on white plaster a bright cerulean blue resulted. There are many greens, from olive to almost black; since no basic green has been found, however, it seems likely that the different shades encountered are the results of varying mixtures of blue and yellow. In addition to the foregoing colors a brilliant, lustrous black was used for outlining, and an opaque white for mixing. It should be pointed out that the foregoing colors are those which were in use at the height of the New Empire in northern Yucatan; probably during the Old Empire and certainly in the Early and Middle Periods the Maya palette was more limited.

The substance with which the colors were mixed to give them fluidity would seem to have been highly agglutinative and viscous; the pigments were either ground to a powder and mixed dry with this medium or were added to it in the form of a highly concentrated liquid. Chemical analyses were made of a number of the pigments used in the Chichen Itza frescoes, but no trace of this carrying substance could be found, which probably indicates that it was of organic nature and has totally disappeared with time. I believe this medium may well have been the resin of the *pom* tree from which the copal varnish of modern commerce is made; this would have made an excellent carrying medium for the pigments.

The colors would seem to have been both of vegetable and mineral origin. There are a number of trees in the Yucatan Peninsula yielding excellent dyes—red, black, and blue. Analysis of the pigments used in the Chichen Itza wall-paintings, however, shows that they are almost if not entirely of mineral origin, perhaps in part because of the fact that vegetable colors are more fugitive and their presence is less easy to ascertain. The reds are made from hematite, perhaps gathered from ant-hills, where a very red earth is found. The yellows are from yellow ocherous earths and clays, the coloring matter being due to the presence of iron. Charcoal and other carbonized organic matter, perhaps bone, was found to be the essential ingredient of the black pigment. The strong blue, although its exact nature could not be identified, was proved to have been inorganic—probably some mineral clay. X-ray photographs of this blue pigment, of beidellite, and of blue chromiferous clay show that all three are very similar. The greens, as noted above, are mixtures of this blue pigment and yellow ocher.

Although the brushes with which these pigments were applied have not been found, the nature of the painting, especially in the codices, clearly indicates their excellence. Some brushes were so delicately made that bold curves as well as fine tapering lines could be made with them, and small spaces could be covered exactly without overrunning the outlines. Other brushes were larger and coarser and were used for filling in backgrounds and broader spaces. The brushes would seem to have varied from one-twenty-fifth of an inch to three inches in width and were probably made of fine feathers or possibly even of hair.

The oldest painting of any size and importance in the Maya area is the partially preserved fresco on the back wall of an outer chamber in Structure B-XIII at Uaxactun, excavated by the Carnegie Institution in 1937 (Plate 50). This building dates from the Early Period (prior to A.D. 633) and had undergone several changes in ancient times, some of its chambers showing beam-and-mortar roof construction. The fresco is executed in black, red, orange, yellow, and gray and measures 9 feet 10 inches wide by 4 feet 1 inch high. Twenty-six human figures are represented; they are arranged in two horizontal panels, one directly below the other, and are interspersed with several panels of hieroglyphs. Somewhat below the lower figure panel is a horizontal line composed of 72 day-signs (not shown in Plate 50) beginning with the day 12 Imix and ending with 5 Eb. In the lower panel two figures in long robes are seated cross-legged beside an altar in the inner chamber of a flat-roofed building, each holding an object in the right hand which may be burning incense; the smoke curling toward a third figure seated in the outer chamber perhaps suggests respect being paid to an important visitor. At the left of the building are two figures standing face to face with a glyph-panel between them; the one on the left holds a small, round shield and a staff in his left hand and another weapon, which may be a spear-thrower (Maya *hulche*), in the right hand. To the right of the building are two other important personages likewise facing each other with a glyph-panel between them, and still farther to the right a figure seated cross-legged beats a tall cylindrically-shaped drum with the ball of his hand. To the right of the drummer there are thirteen standing figures facing toward the building. The upper panel shows half a dozen more standing figures, each with a corresponding glyph-panel. The whole composition doubtless depicts some important ceremony of the early Old Empire and is the oldest Maya wall-painting that has come down to us. Old Empire frescoes are exceedingly rare, and it is indeed fortunate that this early one is so unusually well preserved.

Hieroglyphic inscriptions are found painted on interior walls of the palace at Palenque, and the walls of the shrine in the back chamber of Structure 33 at Yaxchilan show traces of scrolls and figures painted in red and blue.

Another Old Empire fresco which has only recently come to light (spring of 1946) is painted on the interior walls of a temple at a newly discovered site in the region of the Lacanha River, a northwestern tributary of the Lacantun River in eastern Chiapas, Mexico. This new painting is in red, yellow, blues, and greens, and the scene portrayed contains many figures in elaborate feather-work costumes interspersed with small painted glyph-panels. This new site has been named Bonampak, meaning "painted walls" in Maya. Barring these few examples, however, I know of no other frescoes from the Old Empire.

By far the best paintings of the Old Empire that have come to light, however, are the polychrome vases and bowls of the Great Period found at Uaxactun, at Holmul, and in the Chama region along the upper Chixoy River. The very finest of these were found in a stone-lined tomb in one of the later levels of Structure A-I at Uaxactun. This must have been the burial of a personage of highest rank, judging from the magnificence of his associated mortuary furniture. The skeleton, that of a man, lay at full length on its back with the head pointing to the north and both arms clasped against the right shoulder (Fig. 48).

At the head stood the superb painted vase (1) nine inches high, a drawing of the extended design of which is shown in Plate 87. The background color in the original is a brilliant orange-red, the figures being outlined in black and painted with black and several shades of yellow. Around the top is a line of glyphs and there are several glyph-panels interspersed between the figures. The principal panel, consisting of 16 glyphs, is the center of the design with the five human figures and the jaguar all facing it. These glyphs declare an impossible Maya date, 7.5.0.0.0 8 Ahau 13 Kankin, impossible in that it is mathematically incorrect as it stands, as $2 + 3 = 4$ would be. It is probable that the date intended here was 8.5.0.0.0 12 Ahau 13 Kankin, which would, however, involve two changes in the original inscription—one bar and three dots in the baktun coefficient, instead of the one bar and *two* dots actually recorded (top glyph, second column), and two bars and two dots in the day-sign coefficient, instead of the *one* bar and *three* dots actually recorded (fourth glyph, first column). Even these two corrections give an impossibly early date (A.D. 254) for

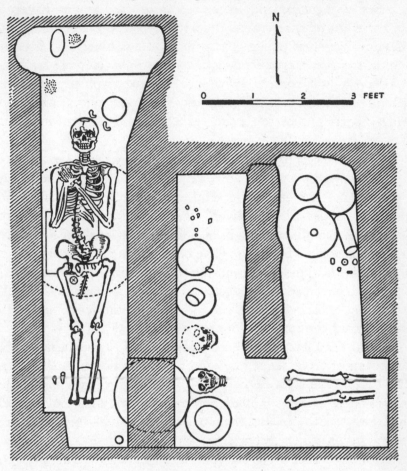

Fig. 48.—Sketch of the burial place of a high priest or principal lord in Structure A-I, Uaxactun, Peten, Guatemala; for a description of the mortuary furniture, see text.

this exquisite vase, since stylistically it could not possibly have been painted before 9.15.0.0.0 (A.D. 731), at least another five hundred years later.

The design shows a *halach uinic* seated cross-legged on a throne

and facing the centrally placed glyph-panel. Behind the ruler stands an attendant, painted black and holding an eccentric-shaped flint in his left hand (see Plate 95, *a*, for an actual example of this same type of object); behind this attendant another figure holds an elaborate feather canopy over the ruler's head. To the left of the glyph-panel are three figures. The two standing figures are also painted black, one carries an eccentric-shaped flint of the same type as that in the hand of the figure on the right and the other holds a spear; both wear very elaborate cloaks. Between them is a seated jaguar offering two bowls tied together, one inverted over the other; these possibly contain a human skull such as was found between two identically shaped bowls in Temple E-III also here at Uaxactun. This handsome composition doubtless depicts some ceremony of major importance during Old Empire times.

This same tomb contained other polychrome vessels of equal beauty. Altogether there were eleven pieces of pottery in this tomb, of which nine were painted, two of the latter being among the finest examples of polychrome ware ever found in the Maya area. The flat plate with three legs illustrated in Figure 49 is a superb example of masterly design and super-sophistication. It is 14⅛ inches in diameter. The background is a creamy terra cotta in color, the design being outlined in black and painted in black and red. A dancer, poised on his toes, is executing a difficult step, with his right arm resting lightly on his hip and his left thrown outward in a graceful gesture. Note the long fingernails and toenails, the sure sweep of line, the admirable fitting of the design to the circular space; all these reflect long experience in portraying the human figure and indicate complete mastery of the art. This bowl has a small hole broken in the bottom, apparently a ceremonial "releasing of the spirit" of the vessel at the time of burial in order that it might accompany the owner on his journey to the other world. Two other painted plates from this same tomb are shown in Figures 50 and 51.

A very famous painted vase from the upper Chixoy Valley in Guatemala, now in the Museum of the University of Pennsylvania, is shown with its design extended in Plate 88, *a*. The colors, in addition to black, are red and brown on a background of cream-pink. Seven figures, interspersed with as many glyph-panels, are portrayed. The two principals are facing each other and are painted black; the one on the left wears a jaguar-skin cloak, complete even to head and paws; three of the remaining six figures

Fig. 49.—Polychrome plate from tomb in Structure A-I, Uaxactun, Peten, Guatemala.

carry fans. Such personal characteristics as hairy moles (figure at left), moustaches, and beards are faithfully rendered, which makes it likely that the figures shown are portraits of specific individuals. Again the subject portrayed is doubtless some ceremony of the Old Empire.

A very similar vase from Nebaj on the opposite side of the upper Chixoy Valley from Chama is almost as well done (Plate

89, a). This has five human figures with as many glyph-panels, one for each figure, and a column of four larger glyphs at the back of the design. Two of the figures sit on a dais, that of the *halach uinic* occupying the central position in the panel.

Still a third vase from Ratinlinxul in the same region shows a *halach uinic* holding a woven fan in his right hand; he is borne in what appears to be a basketry palanquin suspended from carrying poles on the shoulders of two husky retainers (Plate 88, b). A dog stretches himself realistically below the palanquin, tail raised and curling forward as our own dogs still do today. There follow five retainers; the first carries a jaguar-cushioned throne; the next three carry the supports for the palanquin when the bearers were resting, and the last grasps what might be a fold of cloth in his left hand, while his right clasps his own left shoulder. This vase also has upper and lower bands of alternating black and white chevrons like the preceding. Other painted vases from the Chama re-

Fig. 50.—Polychrome plate from tomb in Structure A-I, Uaxactun, Peten, Guatemala.

Fig. 51.—Polychrome plate from tomb in Structure A-I, Uaxactun, Peten, Guatemala.

gion presenting this same chevron decoration as that shown in Plates 88, *a* and *b*, and 89, *a*, are from Chama, Ratinlinxul, and Nebaj, all in the upper Chixoy Valley and all not more than fifty miles south of the site where the one-piece mold of a seated female, described in chapter xiv (p. 379), was found (Plate 81, *c*).

In the New Empire, unquestionably the finest paintings that have survived from this later period are found in the codices and on some decorated capstones painted in the same technique. Of the three former, the Codex Dresdensis (Fig. 9) is the best. The brushwork is of the highest quality, the lines are sure, bold, and fluid, indicating the hand of a master. The Codex Peresianus (Figs. 16 and 29) is not so well done as the Codex Dresdensis, but the difference between the two is not great. The Codex Tro-Cortesianus (Fig. 28), however, is much inferior to the other two. In the Codex Tro-Cortesianus both figures and glyphs are poorly drawn. Although it is the longest of the three manuscripts, its execution is the poorest; indeed, it almost has the appearance of being a hasty job.

The central capstones in corbel-vaulted chambers were sometimes painted; the designs were done in the style of the codices and were composed of human figures with single rows of glyphs both above and below them. These painted capstones are by no means common and are confined exclusively to New Empire sites. All together, seventeen of them have been reported: three at Chichen Itza (Figs. 52 and 53), two at Uxmal, one each at Holactun and Keuic, and ten at Santa Rosa Xtampak; at the last site, however, instead of being painted directly on the capstone, they are painted on a very thick layer of plaster overlying the capstones. The figures on these painted capstones, as noted above, closely resemble those in the codices.

Wall-paintings at New Empire centers are much more common than in the Old Empire and have been found at the following sites: Chichen Itza, Tulum, Santa Rita Corozal, Chacmultun, and Santa Rosa Xtampak (Plate 19).

The Temple of the Warriors, the Temple of the Jaguars, and to a much lesser extent the Monjas at Chichen Itza have partly-

F𝐈𝐆. 52.—Painted capstone from Temple of the Owl, Chichen Itza, Yucatan, Mexico.

preserved frescoes. Two scenes of human sacrifice, one each from the first two temples, have already been illustrated (Plate 28, *e* and *f*) and a much more ambitious wall-painting of a coastal village from the Temple of the Warriors is shown in Plate 90. The

Fig. 53.—Painted capstone from tomb, Chichen Itza, Yucatan, Mexico.

sea occupies the lower third of this picture, and there are three
canoes, each with an oarsman in the prow and two men fishing.
A variety of marine life swarms in the water: a swordfish, two

redsnappers, two crabs, five or six snails (one emerging from his
shell), and a turtle; two other fishes with curling tails are uniden-
tifiable. On shore at the right, there appears a flat-roofed temple,
a feathered serpent rising from the inner chamber or sanctuary,
and two kneeling worshipers in the outer chamber. There are several thatched houses of typical Maya design interspersed with some
bifurcated, modernistic-looking trees. A number of people of
both sexes go about their daily tasks—men are carrying sacks and
bundles either on their backs or heads; another man limps along
by the aid of a staff; a woman watches a pot boiling over the fire;
another woman washes clothes down at the water's edge; several
others sit and gossip; a basket of freshly caught fish stands in the
doorway of the house in the center, while a white heron flies overhead. The whole picture is peaceful and domestic; there are no
battles and no bloody religious ceremonies.

Another Chichen Itza mural from the Temple of the Jaguars,
however, portrays a vigorous assault on a Maya village (Fig. 54).
Only two of the attackers show in the lower left corner, with
javelins poised in their right hands and round shields in their left
hands; a formidable serpent with fiercely darting tongue curls
behind one of these attackers, apparently his divine patron guard-
ing him in the fray. The defending warriors, similarly armed,
swarm out of their village; behind them among the thatched
houses are the women, one weeping. The composition is full of
action; the warriors are putting up a spirited fight and the women
are frightened. There are no superfluous lines, the artist who
painted this fresco was sure of himself and knew his subject.

Still a third mural at Chichen Itza, from the Temple of the
Warriors, shows another battle. A temple stands in a lake in the
upper left corner of the composition. Several fish, a snail, a crab,
and a jaguar appear in the water. Half a dozen nude captives,
painted with stripes and their arms tied behind their backs, are
being led off by warriors or priests (?) painted black. Other war-

Fɪɢ. 54.—Wall-painting of a battle, Temple of the Jaguars, Chichen Itza, Yucatan, Mexico.

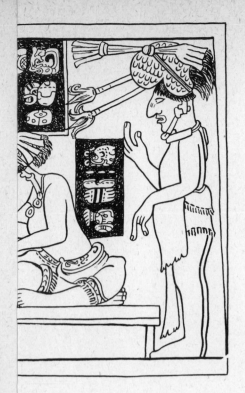

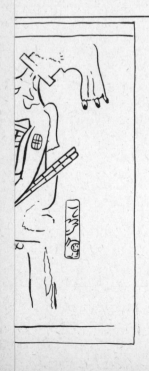

riors, some standing on the roof, seem to be defending a temple in the lower right corner (Plate 24).

The wall-paintings at Tulum and Santa Rita Corozal appear to be religious in character, while at Chacmultun they are again probably of a domestic nature.

Painted vases in the New Empire are not only rarer than in the Old Empire, but also not as well done; one of the best is shown in Plate 89, *b*. At the right is a tree with a thickened base which shows the outline of a human face; there are two horizontal branches, and on each a figure is seated with his back to the trunk while a serpent coils around the latter. At the right facing the tree is a standing figure, with javelins in his left hand, who is blowing a blast on a conch shell held in the right hand. Beneath the branches two deer are seated and the one at the right is completely swathed in bandages. The left half of the composition shows two figures facing a standing deer which seems to be in the act of shedding its horns. The figure just in front of the deer grasps an antler in his right hand and the deer has a blanket on its back decorated with cross-bones. The human figure at the left is also blowing a conch shell held in his left hand, while the right hand grasps two javelins. The three human figures at the left all wear short jaguar-skin skirts or kilts. Just above the standing deer hovers a white bird of prey with hawklike beak. The whole scene would seem to represent a ceremony held at the time the deer shed their horns, which in Yucatan takes place in March.

In concluding this discussion of painting among the ancient Maya, we may say that the finest examples of this art which have survived are the best painted vases and plates of the late Old Empire; next follow the Codex Dresdensis and the Codex Peresianus; and last the wall-paintings, the painted capstones, and the Codex Tro-Cortesianus.

THE LAPIDARY ART

The finest examples of Maya lapidary art are carved jades, which go back to the earliest epoch of recorded Maya history— the beginning of the Early Period of the Old Empire. The very earliest of these, we have seen, is the Leyden Plate which was engraved in 320, probably at Tikal (Plate 15). The carving of this plate is so shallow as to be little more than incised. Both figure and glyphs are astonishingly well done for the very early period at which they were executed, but when examined closely the quality of line appears slightly blurred or broken.

Another early piece from Copan, perhaps carved as much as two hundred years later, shows considerable improvement in the technique of jade carving. This piece (Plate 91, *a*) is a pendant, three inches high and perforated for suspension around the neck. It is a human figure in left profile seated on its haunches with knees drawn up against the chest and arms clasped to the breast. The hole for the suspension-cord enters at the mouth of the figure and emerges at the back of the neck; the boring was done from both sides, meeting in a smaller hole in the center. The carving, while low, is softly rounded and the effect is pleasing.

An even finer piece of Early Period carved jade was excavated at Kaminal-juyu, the very large archaeological site on the outskirts of Guatemala City. Although this site lies at the eastern end of the Maya area proper, the Maya origin of this carved jade (Plate 91, *b*) is unmistakable. It resembles the Copan jade just described but presents a standing human figure instead of a squatting one; the design is more ambitious and the carving a shade better done. This piece measure 6 inches high; the body appears in full front view and the head and headdress in left profile, while the hands are clasped to the breast one over the other. The head has a typical Maya profile, with prominent nose, short upper lip, full lower lip, and retreating artificially deformed forehead; the handsome headdress is formed by the head and foreleg of a crocodile.

A very much finer piece is a human head, also of jade (Plate 91, *c* and *d*), which dates from the Middle Period (A.D. 684). Although this was found at Chichen Itza, it was almost certainly carved at Piedras Negras, where the same unusual non-Period-Ending date which it presents, 9.12.2.0.16 (684), is recorded three times; this particular date appears nowhere else in the entire

Maya area. As a highly prized jewel, this head had probably found its way from Piedras Negras to Chichen Itza after passing through many hands. It is 3¾ inches high, 2⅜ inches wide, and is hollowed out behind; the headdress is composed of a jaguar head; the inscription is rather poorly incised on a flat edge surrounding this hollow at the back. Except for the rather inferior inscription of incised glyphs on the back, this head is a very fine example of Old Empire jade carving.

An exquisite jade head of unknown provenance is shown in Plate 91, *e* and *f*. This belongs to the Great Period of the Old Empire, when jade carving was at its very best, a peak the Maya never equaled before or since. The features are classic Old Empire Maya and the execution is technically perfect.

Perhaps the finest piece of carved jade from the Maya area, one that also dates from the Great Period of the Old Empire, is the exquisite plaque shown in Plate 92, *a*, now in the British Museum. It is perforated longitudinally near the top for suspension on a cord and is wedge-shaped, about 4 inches high, and 4 inches wide at the widest place (top). A handsomely dressed *halach uinic* is seated cross-legged on a throne, body in full front view, head in left profile, the left hand holding a small ceremonial shield. The headdress is the most elaborate item of the costume; it consists of a great serpent with widely opened jaws from which emerges a small figure with a grotesque face. Another figure kneels before the throne as if in supplication. Issuing from the ruler's mouth is an elaborate "speech scroll" which indicates what he is saying; judging by its graceful convolutions he must be making a flowery speech. The color of this particular carved jade is a lovely blue-green. It is of indubitable Maya origin, although it was found a long way from the confines of the Maya area near the great ceremonial center of San Juan Teotihuacan, some twenty-five miles northeast of Mexico City. It had wandered far in the carrying-bags of many Indian merchants over a period of years, perhaps even a century or more, before it finally came to rest in a field near the ruins of San Juan Teotihuacan in the high plateau region of central Mexico.

Another very fine example of Old Empire jadework is the statuette of a human figure seated cross-legged and carved in the full round (Plate 92, *b* and *c*). It is 10½ inches high and weighs 11½ pounds; it was found under the stairway leading to Temple A-XVIII on the Acropolis at Uaxactun in 1937 by an expedition of the Carnegie Institution of Washington. The eyes are rectangular and painted a brilliant red. There are a number of small holes drilled in the figure, which were doubtless for the purpose of attaching ornaments, probably either of jade or feathers. This statuette is probably the largest piece of carved jade ever found in the Maya area.

By a curious coincidence another Carnegie Institution expedition, the same year and only two months earlier, had found what is probably the largest piece of unworked jade in the New World. This is a large boulder of solid jade weighing slightly over 200 pounds which was discovered under the stairway of a pyramid at Kaminal-juyu on the outskirts of Guatemala City; it is waterworn and apparently has had a number of small pieces sawed from it, doubtless for making into earplugs, beads, and other ornaments.

As in the case of the other plastic arts like stone sculpture, woodcarving, and stucco and clay modeling, the quality of jade-engraving deteriorated during the New Empire. This was probably due more to the general decline of the esthetic arts than to an actual loss in technical skill, though, as will be shown presently, the latter may also be partly responsible.

Three engraved jades from Chichen Itza are shown in Plate 93; even though somewhat inferior to the best jades previously illustrated, they are nevertheless excellently carved, especially the head in Plate 93, *b*. The two largest were found in a large, square stone box, carefully covered with a stone lid, at the base of the stairway leading to the earlier temple, which was buried inside the pyramid supporting the Castillo at Chichen Itza.

The natural deposits of jade from which the foregoing articles were carved have never been found, though mineralogical experts believe that there were at least two principal sources of supply in the general Middle American region; (1) the mountains of southern Mexico in the states of Guerrero and Oaxaca and (2) the highlands of western Guatemala.

Unworked pieces of jade were probably found in the form of water-worn pebbles or boulders in the bottoms of rivers and streams; they vary in weight from a few ounces to 200 pounds. In most of the larger pieces the shapes and sizes of the original pebbles or boulders influenced the designs into which they were carved. The same is also true of Chinese worked jades. The earliest Chinese jades are not large, the forms into which they have been carved are relatively simple, and finally they show the size and shape of the original pebbles from which they were made. The course of Chinese history was fairly advanced when the mother deposits from which pieces of jade had broken away to be worn smooth in the beds of watercourses were discovered in Burma and subsequently worked. Unlike the Chinese, however, the ancient Maya had never discovered the mother deposits of their jade; they depended on the chance finding of jade pebbles or boulders in the beds of streams winding down from the high mountain ranges of southeastern Mexico and western Guatemala. I once excavated such an unworked jade boulder weighing several pounds in a tomb at Copan; the massive 200-pound boulder found at Kaminal-juyu near Guatemala City is another case in point.

Jade has a hardness of from 6.5 to 6.8 in the scale used by geologists to measure the hardness of rocks, the diamond being graded as 10 in this scale. A study of carved jades from the Middle American region by mineralogists of the Carnegie Institution of Washington has established that American jades are true jadeites, though their chemical composition differs from that of Chinese jadeite. This variation, however, is not sufficient to warrant placing American jades outside the true jadeite group, but it is sufficient to make them differ somewhat in appearance from Chinese jades. Most important of all, it has settled for all time the archaeological controversy which hitherto had raged for many years as to whether or not there was any true jadeite in America. Generally speaking, American jade is not so translucent as Chinese jade; it varies from dark green to apple-green to light blue-green through all shades of gray and fades into white; it is also much more mottled than Chinese jade.

American jade is an exceptionally hard gem stone and when we consider that the ancient Maya had no metal tools their complete mastery of jade-carving is an outstanding technical achievement. The tools they used were made of obsidian (which will scratch jade), wood, small mammal and bird bones, tough fiber cords, sand ground from jade itself and from quartz and other harder rocks. Pieces of jade were sawed off larger boulders by drawing cords back and forth through grooves and by using hard sand particles and water as a cutting agent. Holes were bored with drills of bone or hardwood twirled in the hands, again with sand and water as the actual cutting agent. In this way beads and pendants were perforated; in order to make the work easier holes were bored from both ends, the two perforations meeting in the middle. Drills of round, hollow bird bones were used for carving circles and segments of circles. In cruder pieces the designs have been drawn with incised lines sometimes straight, sometimes curving. In the finer pieces the relief was probably brought out and a modeled effect achieved by careful incising, followed by deepening and smoothing off the shallow grooves.

MOSAICS

Very few mosaics from either the Old Empire or the New have survived. Mirrors made of fitting pieces of iron pyrites attached to backs of wood or stone have been found at Piedras Negras and Kaminal-juyu. Since there are occasional suggestions of jade mosaics in the Old Empire reliefs, it is possible that mosaics of this material may also have been made, though none has yet been found.

The only examples of turquoise mosaic that have come to light in the New Empire are the four superb turquoise mosaic disks which were found buried in ceremonial *caches* at Chichen Itza. These, however, were not actually made in Yucatan but were brought there from central Mexico where this technique was common during the fourteenth to early sixteenth centuries. The

first of these turquoise mosaic disks was found by the Carnegie
Institution of Washington in a covered limestone jar (Plate 43, *b*)
buried beneath the floor of the sanctuary of the Temple of the
Chac Mool, an earlier temple which was afterward incorporated
into the pyramid supporting the later Temple of the Warriors.
The backing of this disk had been made of wood which was almost
completely rotted away. The elements of the mosaic were reset on
a new base of three-ply wood of exactly the same diameter as the
original, and the restored disk may be seen in the National Museum of Anthropology and History, Mexico City (Plate 43, *a*).

Three other similar disks were found by the Mexican government associated with the buried temple under the Castillo at
Chichen Itza—two in the same square, covered limestone box
where the carved jades illustrated in Plate 93, *b* and *c*, were found,
and the third resting on the seat of the Red Jaguar Throne in the
sanctuary of the same temple. The jade head and beads shown in
Plate 93, *a*, were found resting on top of this third mosaic disk.
One of the first two of these three disks has been restored and may
be seen in the Museum of Archaeology and History at Merida;
the last still rests on the seat of the Red Jaguar Throne just where
it was found (Plate 73, *c*).

Another point indicating that these turquoise mosaic disks were
made in central Mexico rather than in Yucatan is that there are
no deposits of turquoise known in the Maya area, whereas there
must have been several in the central Mexican region. The Codex
Mendoza, which contains Aztec tribute-rolls of the middle sixteenth century, enumerates several towns that had to pay turquoise as their tribute; indeed there is no doubt that turquoise
mosaic was a central Mexican rather than a Maya art.

METALWORK

The almost complete absence of gold from the Old Empire
region has already been pointed out. Indeed the only metal
objects ever recovered from an Old Empire center under certain
archaeological conditions (by means of excavation), are a pair of
legs belonging to a small, hollow human figurine made of a

gold-copper alloy (Fig. 55, *c*), which even when complete could not have stood more than four inches high. Analysis of this alloy, as well as the hollow casting technique employed in fashioning this figurine, strongly suggests that it was made in Costa Rica or Panama and had reached Copan probably by trade. The

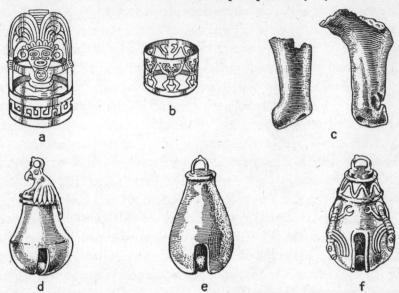

Fɪɢ. 55.—Examples of gold work from Copan, Honduras, and from Chichen Itza, Yucatan, Mexico: (*a, b*) gold finger rings and (*d, e, f*) copper bells, all dredged from the Well of Sacrifice; (*c*) pair of legs of gold found in the cruciform vault below Stela H.

legs were recovered from the dirt fill of the cruciform foundation vault under Stela H, dedicated in 782 (Plate 68, *a*). No other parts of this figurine were located, though all dirt from this vault was screened, and indications are that the two pieces recovered had found their way into the foundation vault of Stela H some time later than the dedicatory date of that monument.

Coming down to the New Empire, metal objects are still infrequent, by far the greatest number recovered so far having been dredged from the Well of Sacrifice at Chichen Itza, though copper bells of the sleigh-bell type have been found elsewhere.

Gold and copper objects from the Well of Sacrifice at Chichen Itza include disks with decoration in repoussé technique

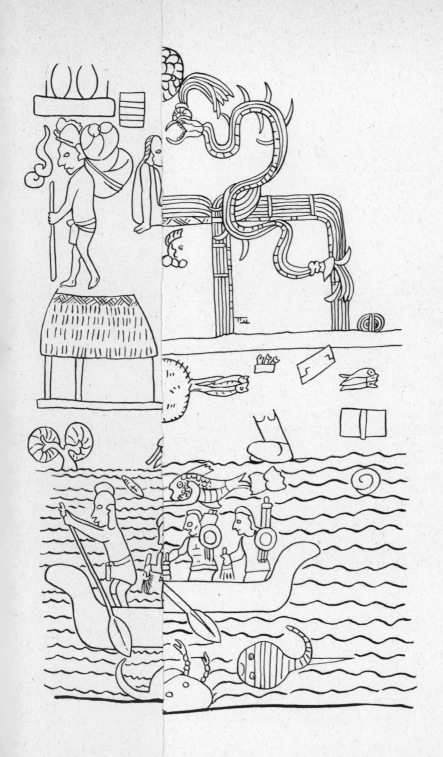

a) Early Period pend-
ant, Copan, Honduras.
←

PLATE 91
OLD EMPIRE
CARVED JADES

←
b) Pendant, Kaminal-
juyu, near Guatemala
City.

↑ *c*) Great Period pend-
ant, place of origin
unknown.

↑ *d*) Profile view of
same.

e) Middle Period pendant, Piedras
Negras, Peten, Guatemala.

↑ *f*) Profile view of same.

PLATE 92.—CARVED JADES, OLD
EMPIRE

a) Plaque showing Maya ruler,
now in the British Museum; perhaps the finest jade-carving ever
made by the ancient Maya. →

b) Anthropomorphic statuette (front
view) from Temple A-XVIII, Uaxactun, Peten, Guatemala; perhaps the
largest piece of jade ever carved by
the ancient Maya. ↓

↓ *c*) The same in profile.

PLATE 93.—CARVED JADES, NEW EMPIRE

a) Human head and necklace from cache lying on the Red Jaguar Throne in the buried temple under the Castillo, Chichen Itza, Yucatan, Mexico. →

b) Human head from cache under Castillo Stairway, Chichen Itza, Yucatan, Mexico. ↓

↓ *c*) Human figure from same cache.

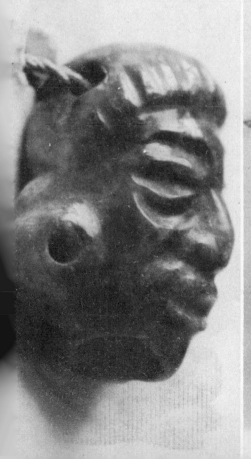

↑ *c*) Three portions of gold mask.

PLATE 94.—NEW EMPIRE GOLD WORK. WELL OF SACRIFICE,
CHICHEN ITZA, YUCATAN, MEXICO

←

a) Gold pendant.

→

b) Gold bell.

(Fig. 56, *a*, *d*, and *e*), cup and saucer (Fig. 56, *c*), necklaces, bracelets (Fig. 56, *b*), masks, pendants (Plate 94, *a* and *c*), rings (Fig.
55, *a* and *b*), earplugs, bells (Fig. 55, *d*, *e*, and *f*, and Plate 94, *b*),
and beads. The style and technical workmanship of many of the
smaller objects, particularly the pendants, bells, and beads, indicate that they were made in Costa Rica and Panama and had found
their way northwestward to Chichen Itza by trade. In Plate 94,
a and *b*, are shown a pendant and a bell, both of gold, from the

FIG. 56.—Examples of gold and copper work from the Well of Sacrifice, Chichen
Itza, Yucatan, Mexico: (*a*, *d*, and *e*) disks decorated in repoussé technique; (*b*)
gold bracelet; (*c*) gold cup and saucer.

Well of Sacrifice at Chichen Itza, which were almost certainly made originally in Costa Rica. They are now in the National Museum of Anthropology and History at Mexico City.

Indeed most of the gold and copper objects recovered from the Well of Sacrifice were not made at the Itza capital at all, but had found their way thither either carried by pilgrims to the holy city or as articles of trade. Chemical analyses have established that the metal objects found in the Well of Sacrifice came from as far south as Colombia, Panama (from both the Coclé and Chiriqui cultures), Honduras, and Guatemala and from as far west and north as the states of Chiapas and Oaxaca, Mexico, and the Valley of Mexico. These analyses have further revealed that the objects of copper which also contain tin and arsenic originally came from Oaxaca and the Valley of Mexico; those containing tin alone are from Honduras, the purest copper of all coming from Guatemala and Chiapas. The gold-copper alloys range from almost pure gold to almost pure copper, and there are even some examples of gold-plating.

All the objects from the Well of Sacrifice which show either casting or filigree work are of foreign origin, since the only gold-working technique with which the Maya goldsmiths were familiar was hammering and repoussé work. It is highly probable that the gold used by the Maya in the few objects from the Well of Sacrifice actually made at Chichen Itza was derived from cast-gold objects that had reached Chichen Itza from regions entirely outside the Yucatan Peninsula.

The gold objects of local manufacture found at Chichen Itza are pretty largely restricted to very thin disks of gold made by hammering out cast objects of foreign origin; they are decorated in a repoussé technique with scenes of battle. These scenes have been interpreted as representing conflicts between the Maya of Chichen Itza and the Mexican mercenaries of Hunac Ceel, the *halach uinic* of Mayapan, who conquered the Itza capital at the end of the twelfth century (p. 91); one of these gold disks, not illustrated here, shows a scene of human sacrifice. The central designs from three other such disks are reproduced in Figure 57.

a

b

c

FIG. 57.—Central designs of three gold disks in repoussé technique from the Well of Sacrifice, Chichen Itza, Yucatan, Mexico: (a, b) two Mexican warriors, right, armed with spears and spear-throwers, and two Maya warriors with feather capes at the left; (c) the two Maya warriors retreating at the right, before the two pursuing Mexicans.

In Figure 57, *a* and *b*, two Mexican mercenaries armed with spears and spear-throwers appear at the right, while two Maya warriors with artificially deformed foreheads and elaborate feather capes are seen at the left. The position is reversed in Figure 57, *c*, where two Maya warriors in full retreat appear at the right. The figures from these disks are very similar to those in the reliefs as well as those in the frescoes of the Mexican Period at Chichen Itza; the disks themselves probably date from the thirteenth century, not long after the conquest of the Itza capital by Hunac Ceel in 1194.

The most common metal objects of all those recovered from the Well of Sacrifice, however, are copper bells of the sleigh-bell type, ranging in size from as small as a lentil to as large as a walnut. These bells were the most common ornament of the death-god (Fig. 55, *d*, *e*, and *f*) with whom they are invariably associated, which probably explains why so many of them have been taken from the Well of Sacrifice.

FLINT-CHIPPING

Flint-chipping reached the perfection of a fine art among the ancient Maya, as may be seen by the examples of it shown in Plate 95. Sub-stela *caches* of eccentric-shaped flints (Plate 95, *a* and *b*) and blades (Plate 95, *c*) are frequently found buried in the foundations of many Maya monuments.

Perhaps the finest examples of this craft that have come down to us are the exceedingly elaborate yet delicately chipped heads for ceremonial staffs which were excavated at El Palmar in Quintana Roo (Plate 95, *d*) and at Quirigua (Plate 95, *e*). A small piece at the bottom of the chipped head excavated at El Palmar was not recovered, but in its original condition it was a completely closed design with the central part cut away and left open. Three human heads in profile are shown on the Quirigua piece.

FEATHERWORK

A few examples of Aztec featherwork have been found, but not a single piece from the ancient Maya has survived. Still, the monuments of both the Old and New Empires show how rich and highly developed this art had been formerly, and the early Spanish writers frequently allude to it.

The forests of the Yucatan Peninsula and especially those of the southern half, the Old Empire region, teem with birds of gorgeous plumage: macaws, parrots, parakeets, cardinals, orioles, ocellated turkeys, ospreys, herons, blue-jays, fly-catchers, and many kinds of hummingbirds. The highlands of Guatemala immediately to the south are the habitat of one of the most beautiful birds in the world, the quetzal, which is the national bird of Guatemala. Feathers from all these birds were utilized in making panaches, crests, capes of all lengths, and shields; they were also used for pendant decorations to spears, Manikin Scepters, double-headed ceremonial bars, canopies, fans, necklaces, bracelets, anklets, knee-ornaments, belts, and large round ornaments for the middle of the belt in the back. In addition, featherwork was used in embroideries and fringes for cotton fabrics.

One of the loveliest examples of featherwork in all Maya art is the panache of the headdress worn by the *halach uinic* on Wall Panel 3 at Piedras Negras, previously illustrated (Plate 69). Immediately above this headdress rises a crest of stiff feathers from which springs the panache proper. At the point where the long plumes of the panache spring from the crest their under sides appear, but where they turn over in long graceful curves their backs or upper sides show toward the ends. Such long plumes must have been the tail-feathers of the quetzal, which were reserved exclusively for the rulers. Another very similar headdress, also from Piedras Negras, is worn by the *halach uinic* on Stela 12 at that site (Plate 18, *c*). Here the panache rises above the same sort of stiff feather crest as in the preceding example; the individual quetzal plumes, each ending in an attached feather tassel, swirl lightly as if touched by some passing breeze; this same *halach uinic* also wears a short, shoulder-length feather cape of considerable elegance. Finally, the slightly stylized treatment of the featherwork lends great distinction to this superb relief.

Another more elaborate but slightly less graceful headdress with a panache is worn by the standing *halach uinic* on Stela 10 at

Seibal; the plumes of this headdress hang more formally than those in the preceding examples, though some attempt has been made to indicate motion among the individual feathers (Plate 53, f).

New Empire representations of featherwork show an inferior technique; indeed, it is probable that during this closing period of the Maya civilization this art, like most if not all the others except architecture, had also passed into a decline from which there was no recovery. Better than average featherwork for the New Empire are the panaches on the wooden lintels from the Temple of the Jaguars at Chichen Itza, already illustrated (Fig. 42), and a more average example showing an inferior technique from Xculoc, Campeche, is illustrated in Plate 75, c and d. The feather treatment is heavy and inexpert, though it is hard to tell whether this is due to an actual inferiority of the featherwork technique or to loss of skill in sculpturing.

Father Sahagun, our greatest authority on the Aztec, tells us that they had two kinds of featherwork:

They [the Aztec] make the devices which they wear on their backs in dancing, all the costumes of the dance, and the trappings with which they dance [of feathers] and they executed the craft and profession of feather-workers in two different ways: the first kind of work consists of fastening the feathers to the background with paste in order thus to finish the work; the second way consists in doing the work and finishing it with the help of thread and cord.

In amplifying this latter technique Father Sahagun writes further:

There is another kind of work, the handicraft of thread and cord. In this way they make their fans out of the plumes of the quetzal, their feather bracelets, the devices they wear on their backs and other things, their tunics blazoned with their arms etc.; and in addition pendants, panaches, balls, tassels of feathers, with all of which they adorn themselves and decorate their fans.

The same authority says that this art was of relatively recent introduction among the Aztec, especially in so far as the use of brightly colored feathers of tropical birds was concerned; these feathers were brought from their southern provinces, which were not subjugated until during the reigns of the last two Aztec emperors before the Spanish Conquest, Ahuitzotl and Moctezuma II. Furthermore, at that time (the early sixteenth century) the four principal Maya tribes of the Guatemala highlands—the Quiche, Cakchiquel, Pokomam, and Pokomchi—exported large quantities of plumes, the raw materials for featherwork, to the great cities of central Mexico.

The birds were caught with birdlime (a gummy substance) and sticks. Before going out to the hunt the hunters made sacrifices, incensing the birdlime and sanctifying it, for they believed that it thus became endowed with greater holding qualities.

The feathers used for embroidery, according to Bishop Landa, were those of the osprey:

They breed a kind of large white duck, which I believe comes to them from Peru, for their plumage, and thus they pluck their breasts often and they like these feathers for the embroidery of their garments.

The following quotations from early Spanish writers also indicate the importance of this craft among the Quiche Maya of the Guatemala highlands, who like the Aztec had aviaries where these birds were specially bred for their plumage. Fuentes y Guzman, the seventeenth-century historian of Guatemala, describes the palace of the Quiche rulers at Utatlan and says that they had "places set apart for the breeding of ducks, for the sake of their plumage which they employed in weaving." Another early authority in describing the same palace states: "The throne of the king was notable because it had a canopy of very rich plumes and above this protection or covering, other coverings of different colors, in such a way as to give an effect of great majesty. The prince, or he who was to succeed, had three canopies and the other brothers or sons, two," while a third authority writes: "Those [the feathers] of the duck which they pluck from the breast to interweave in their *huipiles*, the women [call] rih patus."

In addition to weaving feathers into their cotton fabrics, they attached them to the wood and wicker frames of their headdresses.

Father Moran in his manuscript dictionary of Pokomam defines the word *mayut* as "a framework of wood adorned with plumage, which they wear on their backs in their dances." In the Museum of the Cinquantennaire in Brussels there is a red ankle-length cape of macaw feathers built on a frame of wickerwork; this cape supposedly belonged to the Aztec emperor Moctezuma II. A quetzal-plume headdress, certainly belonging to the same ruler, is now in the former Imperial Museum in Vienna. This headdress is built on a frame of slender sticks, and a net of woven *agave* fiber is stretched over it; the feathers have been fastened to this frame with tied *agave*-fiber cords.

Feathers, cotton fabrics, red sea shells, and semiprecious stones such as jade were used not only personally but also as articles of trade and even to pay legal penalties; in New Empire times turquoise, copper, and gold were similarly used:

they exchanged *mantas* [*patis*] of cotton for gold and for certain axes of copper, and gold for emeralds, turquoises and plumes; [and again] At the end [the man who had committed the injury] was sentenced to pay a certain quantity of rich plumes, or *mantas*, or cacao, which went to the treasury.

But unquestionably the most highly prized of all feathers were the tail-plumes of the quetzal, a bird found only in the highlands of Guatemala and adjacent parts of Honduras and Chiapas, Mexico, and to a lesser extent as far south as Panama. These plumes were reserved exclusively for royal use and, according to Bartolomé de Las Casas, either to capture or kill one was a capital offense:

in the province of Vera Paz [Guatemala], they punish with death him who killed the bird with the rich plumes [the quetzal] because it is not found in other places, and these feathers were things of great value because they used them as money . . . .

The few examples of Aztec featherwork that have been preserved indicate that this was an extraordinarily rich art. The representations of it on the monuments of the Old Empire, where it almost certainly originated, leave little room for doubt that in this latter region it also reached its highest development.

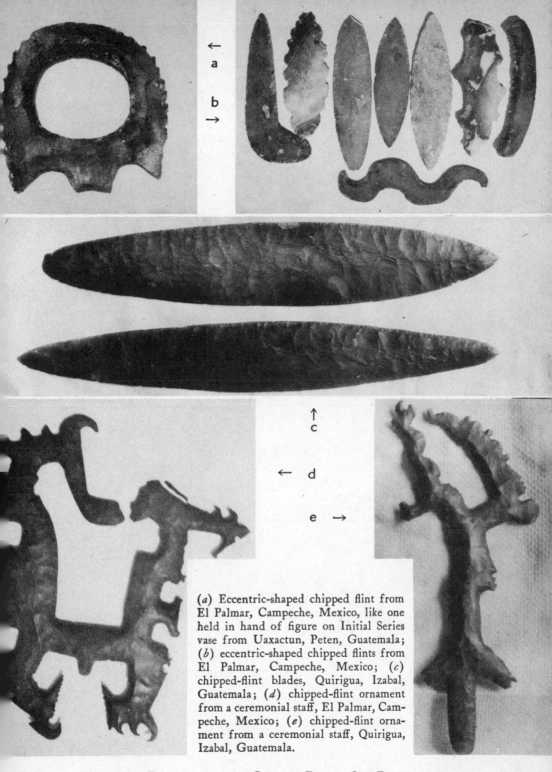

(a) Eccentric-shaped chipped flint from El Palmar, Campeche, Mexico, like one held in hand of figure on Initial Series vase from Uaxactun, Peten, Guatemala; (b) eccentric-shaped chipped flints from El Palmar, Campeche, Mexico; (c) chipped-flint blades, Quirigua, Izabal, Guatemala; (d) chipped-flint ornament from a ceremonial staff, El Palmar, Campeche, Mexico; (e) chipped-flint ornament from a ceremonial staff, Quirigua, Izabal, Guatemala.

PLATE 95.—ECCENTRIC-SHAPED CHIPPED FLINTS, OLD EMPIRE

AN APPRAISAL OF THE MAYA CIVILIZATION

IN MAKING AN APPRAISAL of the Maya civilization it cannot be overemphasized that everything the ancient Maya accomplished was due primarily to Indian corn, for almost every thought they had can be traced back in one way or another to maize. Their primitive religion was built about its cultivation and the deities who controlled its growth, like the rain-gods, wind-gods, and sun-gods, guardians of the cornfield and of the growing corn—a whole maize pantheon in itself, later to be overlaid with the more abstract gods of time and of the heavenly bodies.

MAIZE, THE KEYSTONE OF MAYA CULTURE

Maize is all-important in Maya life, even today. We have seen in chapter viii (p. 142) that from 75 to 85 per cent of the entire food intake of the modern Maya is maize in one form or another, and after many years of personal contact with them I am convinced that fully 75 per cent of all their thoughts still center around this same important cereal. "Where shall I locate my cornfield this year?" "How large shall I make it?" "How long will it take me to clear the trees and bush from it?" "I must surely wait for a strong wind before I set fire to the brush in order to secure a good burn." "I hope the rains will not delay too long after I have burned, so that weeds will not have time to come up before I must plant." "What day will be most propitious for my planting?" "May our ancient gods of the sun, wind, and rain, the old Chacs, the Heavenly Father, the Virgin Mary, and the Holy Saints all guard my young plants and send the right amount of rain at the right time and keep away the all-destroying locusts and birds, so that my maize may grow into great, long ears, full of perfect kernels." "How big will my harvest be this year; how many sacks of maize will I harvest?" Such thoughts still preoccupy the modern Maya just as similar thoughts absorbed the minds of his ancestors five hundred to three thousand years ago.

The ancient Maya were primarily farmers and dependent upon agriculture for their living, particularly agriculture as applied to the cultivation of maize. Therefore time in its various manifestations like the changing seasons, the coming and going of the rains, which were signposts of the farmer's year, assumed an ever increasing importance. At a very remote period in Maya history, perhaps as early as 1000 B.C., the Maya priests began to note the motions of the sun and moon and to preserve in one way or another an accurate record of their observations. Later, perhaps some time during the fourth or third century B.C., their observations as to the length of the year were embodied in a magnificent chronological system. This is one of the most brilliant achievements of the human mind—an achievement originally due to the corn farmer's need to know the corresponding times of the year when he should fell, burn, plant, and harvest.

The need for a place of worship, an appropriate sanctuary to shelter the first primitive deities of nature and agriculture, undoubtedly gave rise to Maya architecture. Monuments were erected at fixed intervals to mark the passage of time and to record corresponding calendric corrections, lunar information, festivals, rites, offerings, et cetera. Embellishment of these monuments gave rise to Maya sculpture. Thus the origin of most of the higher manifestations of Maya culture may be traced directly back to the complex of ideas which grew up around maize—the Alpha and Omega of both ancient and modern Maya life.

The old Spanish chronicler who penned the paragraph used as the Foreword to this book was not far from the whole truth when he wrote ". . . . everything [these Indians] did and talked about had to do with maize. In truth, they fell little short of making a god of it." The fact is they did make a god of it.

The familiar adage that history repeats itself is strikingly exemplified by the thirteen centuries of the Maya story reviewed here. Running through the fabric of Maya history there is a clearly recurring pattern, and its key is in the successive returns of the fateful Katun 8 Ahau—the ancient Maya "Ides of March," the special 20-year period when destiny wrought her greatest changes.

The first period of Maya cultural brilliance took place during the Old Empire, which dated from 8.14.0.0.0 to 10.8.0.0.0 of the Maya Era (317–987). These dates include Baktun 9 (435–830), which was counted from a katun-ending on the day 8 Ahau, a baktun which witnessed the apogee of the Maya Old Empire.

In much later New Empire times the priestly compilers of the *u kahlay katunob* (series of the katuns which are really ancient Maya chronicles) selected katuns which ended on this same day as the points at which the sequence of the thirteen differently named katuns was considered to have begun to repeat itself. This is clearly described in the Codex Perez, where these Katuns 8 Ahau are called the *uudz* katuns, "the doubling or folding over of the katuns," that is, the points at which the sequence of the thirteen differently named katuns began to repeat itself, a cycle which took place every 13 x 20 = 260 tuns or once every 256¼ years (see chapter xii, pp. 291–95).

I believe that this particular katun was so chosen as the point at which the katun-sequence was supposed to have begun because the first great outburst of Maya culture took place in a baktun (No. 9) that was counted from a baktun (No. 8) which ended on the day 8 Ahau, viz. 9.0.0.0.0 8 Ahau 13 Ceh.

Owing to the accidental fact that this baktun (9.0.0.0.0), with which date the Maya chronicles begin, happened to have ended on the day 8 Ahau, the ceremonial importance of all katuns ending on this same day became so great that it finally influenced, if indeed it did not largely determine, the general pattern of later Maya history.

444

Referring to Table V, one may observe that the first return of a katun-ending on the day 8 Ahau after the beginning of the sequence of the katuns was in 672–692, when Chichen Itza is said to have been abandoned for the first time. Most likely this was only coincidence, though there may well have been some psychological connection between time and event.

The second return of Katun 8 Ahau fell in 928–948, and the Maya chronicles agree almost unanimously that at this time the Itza abandoned Chakanputun, migrated northeastward, and returned to Chichen Itza. This certainly would seem to be the beginning of chronological coercion. Katun 8 Ahau had come back again; the katun-sequence was about to renew itself; the times were ripe for a change. The Itza had already been at Chakanputun for more than two centuries, and under the Maya system of agriculture the land in that vicinity must have begun to yield sharply decreasing returns. What could have been a more propitious time than Katun 8 Ahau in which to set out upon a search for their old home far to the northeast?

The third return of Katun 8 Ahau (1185–1204) is marked by an event of clearly indicated deliberation, the plot of Hunac Ceel, the Cocom ruler of Mayapan, and the resulting war against Chichen Itza. I suggest that this particular katun may well have been chosen for this important venture since by this time the Maya records clearly set forth that Katuns 8 Ahau were times of change, perhaps even peculiarly propitious therefor. Chichen Itza was attacked and its ruler defeated, and Mayapan emerged from the war with the hegemony of northern Yucatan in her hands, a resounding justification of the potency of the psychological moment.

The fourth return of Katun 8 Ahau (1441–1461) marks another epochal event in Maya history, again one shaped by deliberate design rather than by accident. This was the plot of the Maya chieftains in 1441 under the leadership of Ah Xupan Xiu against the Cocom at Mayapan, the supreme ruler of northern Yucatan; they attacked that city, killed its ruler, and left the country in a state of political disintegration. Here was every

opportunity for free advance selection of the most auspicious date
upon which to "break" the revolt. Katun 8 Ahau had returned.
As their own history had repeatedly demonstrated, the portent
of the period was one of change. Only this time the exigency
of the times ran against the plotters; Cocom tyranny could no
longer be endured. Scarcely had the favorable katun begun—in
fact during its very first year—than desperate necessity precipi-
tated the long-overdue event, which had been delayed only until
the moment for launching the revolt was ceremonially favorable.
Their chronological beliefs indicated change was due and straight-
way the Maya made history—their last collective action before
the Spanish Conquest.

Coming finally to the post-Conquest period, the last act of the
Maya drama, by one of those curious turns in the wheel of national destiny, fell just short of the fifth return of Katun 8 Ahau
in 1697–1717.

Fathers Fuensalida and Orbita visited Tayasal in mid-October
1618 and attempted to Christianize the Itza, but Canek, the Itza
ruler, told them that the time which their ancient priests had
prophesied that they were to abandon the adoration of their native
gods had not yet arrived.

To this Canek replied: that although there had not yet arrived the
time in which their ancient priests had prophesied that they were to leave
off the adoration of their gods; because the age in which at this time they
were was that which they call Oxahau, which is to say Third Age [Katun
3 Ahau]; these barbarians seem to have counted their ages backward, or
to a determined number; which reached they forgot it, and return to begin a count anew [the uudz katun]: Because when they retired from
Yucatan, which is already going on for three hundred years, they say
that it was the Eighth Age [Katun 8 Ahau] and that there had not arrived so soon what was appointed for them [another Katun 8 Ahau]; and
now [1618] they say it was the Third Age and that the time had not yet
arrived.

The inference here is that the "appointed time" for the Itza to
make this vital change was Katun 8 Ahau.

446

Seventy-eight years later, in the middle of January 1696, Father Avendaño (see chapter vii, p. 126) visited Tayasal in another attempt to Christianize the Itza and to persuade them to accept the authority of the King of Spain. Avendaño, as he himself states, was well acquainted with the Maya calendar and reminded the Itza that, according to their own prophecies, the time was approaching when it had been predicted they were to give up the worship of their pagan deities and accept Christianity. The Itza, while again admitting the truth of these prophecies, still contended that the time ordained for the abandonment of their ancient faith had not yet arrived. Finally after further conferences it was agreed that four months were still wanting before the appointed period, though the best correlation of Maya and Christian chronologies available today (Appendix I, p. 457) indicates that at the time of Avendaño's visit (January 1696) fully a year and a half was still lacking before the beginning of the next Katun 8 Ahau.

But here again time was forcing Maya destiny. In March of the following year (1697), Martin de Ursua, in command of a force of Spaniards and Indians from Yucatan, finally pushed through to the shores of Lake Peten Itza (see chapter vii, p. 131). A galley was built to transport the army to Tayasal at the western end of the lake and the final attack was made on March 13. In spite of overwhelming numbers, perhaps as high as five thousand Indians against one hundred and eight Spaniards, a single discharge of musketry was sufficient to dispel the Itza hosts, who fled in every direction, abandoning their belongings, their homes, and even the sanctuaries of their tribal deities.

But why? What was the reason for this precipitous flight, practically without striking a blow once the battle had been joined? On the day of the attack there lacked only 136 days before the beginning of another *uudz* katun (another Katun 8 Ahau), at which time I believe the ancient Maya prophecies had long foretold their end would come. The Itza were fearfully convinced of their approaching doom, which was not only predicted by their own native prophets but also indicated by their meticulously kept historical records; and they gave up the unequal struggle against their hostile gods and fled, thus anticipating by less than five months the last return of this most fateful katun of Maya history.

THE AUTHOR'S SELECTION OF FIFTY MAYA SUPERLATIVES

A good many superlatives have been used in this book—the largest this, the oldest that, the most beautiful something else. Superlatives of course are personal affairs; "one man's bread is another man's poison." What may be superlatively lovely to me may be little short of downright hideous to someone else. Some superlatives are absolute: the Empire State Building is the highest building in the world, and the pyramid of Cheops is the largest stone pyramid in the world; while others depend purely upon personal opinions.

Therefore in suggesting the Maya superlatives listed in Table XI, I assume full responsibility for the selection, well aware that others will have equally good and perhaps even better lists of their own. Be that as it may, here are my own nominations for the Maya Hall of Superlatives (see Table XI facing page 448).

THE MAYA CULTURAL SCRATCH

In appraising the civilization of any people, the true measure of what they did is not the sum total of their achievements compared with the achievements of other peoples but rather their entire accomplishment counted from their own cultural scratch.

Thus the construction of Rockefeller Center at New York City, with all the mechanical devices, modern machinery, and building materials available to its builders, is much less of an achievement than the erection of Temple IV at Tikal or the Castillo at Chichen Itza, both actually of far less size and complexity but both built entirely without metal tools, structural steel, cement, hollow tile, machine-sawn and sand-blasted dressed stone, compressed air, electricity, gas, steam, and elaborate hoisting machinery. Rockefeller Center was erected with the architectural and mechanical wisdom of the ages behind its builders; Temple IV at Tikal was erected by a people living in the Stone Age who had to depend exclusively upon their own architectural and mechanical knowledge and their own limited building experience. Which then was really the greater achievement?

In order to make a true appraisal of the Maya civilization therefore, it is first necessary to ascertain what was the Maya cultural scratch.

In his long, arduous journey forward from savagery to a civilized state, the first five steps by which man has advanced are generally admitted to be the following: (1) control of fire, (2) invention of agriculture, (3) domestication of animals, (4) tools of metal, and (5) discovery of the principle of the wheel. The sequence of these successive steps is not always given in the same order and was not always the same in different parts of the world, though control of fire was undoubtedly the first everywhere and the invention of agriculture probably the second in most places, the order of the remaining three steps varying.

What was the cultural scratch of the ancient Maya with respect to these five basic steps of human advancement? It goes without saying that they had mastered fire, had learned how to make and preserve it. We have seen in chapter viii (p. 141) that they had developed an admirable system of agriculture, particularly excellent in view of the relatively unfavorable nature of their region. Experts from the United States Department of Agriculture, after studying at first hand the Maya system of growing corn, declare that it could not be bettered today with the use of modern farm machinery.

It is true that the Maya had domesticated the wild turkey and kept swarms of wild, stingless bees in special thatched huts near their homes, but they had not one of the beasts of burden which so tremendously helped man in the Old World. Indeed, in all America there would seem to have been but two examples of the use of beasts of burden in pre-Columbian times—the llama used as a pack animal by the ancient Peruvians and the dog used by the Eskimo to haul their sleds. All of the tremendous building pro-

gram of the ancient Maya was accomplished without the aid of a single carrying animal other than man himself. But what efficient beasts of burden the ancient Maya were! They carried on their heads great carved façade-elements weighing up to 200 pounds. I know this, because their descendants today did precisely the same thing in the reconstruction work at Chichen Itza.

There were no metal tools. Metal, we have seen, was non-existent in the Old Empire; and in the New Empire gold and copper and their alloys were used exclusively in making articles of personal adornment, or for ceremonial use, such as rings, beads, pendants, ear-plugs, bells, cups, plates, plaques, and the like.

The principle of the wheel was unknown to the ancient Maya. They had no wheeled vehicles of any kind, either of two, three, or four wheels, and most students of aboriginal American ceramics are agreed that the potter's wheel for turning pottery was also unknown in pre-Columbian America. In short, the ancient Maya were acquainted with and enjoyed the use of only the first two of the foregoing five "steps toward civilization."

The ancient Egyptians, Chaldeans, Babylonians, Assyrians, Persians, Chinese, Phoenicians, Etruscans, Greeks, and Romans possessed all five of these aids to civilization. The Khmers of Cambodia and the builders of the great rock-cut temples of Java were the only other peoples beside the ancient Maya who developed early, high civilizations in the wet tropics, but they too made daily use of these five primary aids to human progress. Indeed, in order to find a condition in the Old World comparable to the Maya cultural scratch as just established, it is necessary to go far back in human history, far beyond any of the civilizations just mentioned, to early Neolithic times—the Age of Polished Stone when man's knowledge and utensils were similarly restricted. On this primitive horizon, and on this alone, may the Maya civilization be fairly compared with the prehistoric civilizations of the Old World. And if this comparison be made, it will be found that, starting from the same cultural scratch, no Neolithic people of the Old World ever reached such heights of cultural achievement as did the ancient Maya of Middle America.

450   In the foregoing pages it has been shown what the Maya civilization was, where it originated, what it accomplished, and finally
what brought about its decline and fall. Its contributions may be
briefly reviewed here and compared with those of other ancient
American cultures.

At the outset our field of comparison is limited to only two
other comparably high ancient American civilizations: (1) the Inca
of the Peruvian and adjacent highlands of South America and
their predecessors upon whose earlier cultures the Inca built, and
(2) the Aztec of the high plateau region of central Mexico and
the earlier cultures of the same region upon which the Aztec built.

In architecture the ancient Maya easily rank first. Their buildings are more imposing, more complex in ground-plan, and more
beautifully decorated than those either of the Inca or the Aztec.
It is true that the Inca, or their predecessors, had developed a
Cyclopean type of masonry—enormous blocks of stone weighing
many tons, which were cut and fitted together with exquisite precision. These were not equaled in Maya architecture, but judged
as a whole, in ground-plan, size, and decoration, Maya buildings
are more outstanding. The architecture of the Aztec is often
grandiose in scale, like the Pyramids of the Sun, Moon, and Quetzalcoatl at San Juan Teotihuacan and the Great Pyramid of Cho-
lula, but it is plain and heavy in effect, generally speaking has little
or no decoration, and lacks interest; it is certainly not to be compared with Maya architecture.

In highways, however, the Inca were distinctly superior to the
Maya. The latter built roads of stone surfaced with lime-gravel,
which hardened under the action of water and pressure. The cut-
masonry highways of the Inca wound through the lofty Andes and
were superb feats of engineering; compared to them the Maya
sacbeob in the relatively non-hilly terrain of the Yucatan Peninsula were little more than third-class roads.

In sculpture the Maya were notably supreme. The sculptures
described in chapter xiv (pp. 358–81) leave no room for doubt

that in this field of art they had no rivals. Inca sculpture is not in the same class, and while meritorious pieces were executed here and there in the central Mexican highlands, on the whole, Aztec, Chichimec, and Toltec sculpture, like their architecture, is heavy, massive, and altogether lacking in the grace and superlative beauty of Maya relief and round carving.

When it comes to the question of ceramics, however, Maya supremacy is disputed by many. The ancient Peruvians made very fine polychrome pottery, admirably fired and beautifully decorated; the Aztec and their predecessors also produced some fine pottery, but I believe the best Maya Old Empire painted wares, from a decorative point of view at least, are the finest examples of the potter's art in ancient America. Some of the best pieces have elaborate religious ceremonies depicted on them and are equaled by no other pottery in the New World. The dancer shown in Figure 49, with his graceful pose, his highly stylized hands and feet with strongly exaggerated fingernails and toenails, and the sure strokes of the brush which painted him, reaches heights of ultra-sophistication found nowhere else in American aboriginal art.

It is probable that the finest textiles produced by the looms of ancient America are the spectacular fabrics of the Nasca culture of Peru. These were woven from the silk-like wool of the vicuña and are remarkable for texture, weave, color, and design. It is possible that the Maya Old Empire textiles equaled or surpassed these, but unfortunately no examples have survived. Representations of richly embroidered Maya fabrics can be seen on the monuments (Fig. 44) and these give some idea of their excellence. The Aztec also wove fine cotton stuffs, but probably nothing to be compared with the Nasca vicuña-wool blankets or the cotton fabrics of the Maya Old Empire. Similarly, too few examples of ancient Maya basketry have survived to permit satisfactory comparisons with Inca and Aztec basketry.

In painting the Maya were first. Pre-eminence in this field of art is proved by their frescoes, their painted pottery, and their hieroglyphic manuscripts, or codices. Especially in their finest

painted vases and in the brilliant execution of the Codex Dresdensis, the Maya proved themselves to be without equals in this
field. Comparison with Aztec, Inca, and pre-Inca similar contributions leaves no doubt that the Maya were the greatest
painters in ancient America.

In the lapidary art—the engraving and polishing of very hard
stones such as rock crystal, obsidian, and granite—the Maya were
greatly superior to the Inca and pre-Inca peoples of the Peruvian and adjacent highlands. On the other hand, they might be
considered somewhat inferior to the Aztec and pre-Aztec peoples
of central Mexico. Only in jade is this central Mexican superiority not so sure. We have seen magnificent Maya plaques and
heads of carved jade in the preceding chapter (Plates 91–93).
The Aztecs proved their superior lapidary skill by life-size human
masks carved in jade, obsidian, chalcedony, porphyry, and other
hard stones; many of these masks are massive pieces weighing
from 10 to 30 pounds. None of these magnificent life-size carvings has been found in the Maya area, which probably indicates
that the Maya did not make them, and therefore the Aztecs must
be recognized as the most skilled lapidary workers of ancient
America.

We have seen that very fine turquoise mosaics have been found
in the Maya area, at Chichen Itza for example (Plate 43, a), but
there is no doubt that this was an Aztec and not a Maya technique.
In the first place many more turquoise mosaics have been found
in central Mexico than in the Maya area, and also there are no
known sources of turquoise in the Yucatan Peninsula, whereas
there are several in ancient Mexico. It is true that turquoise mosaic
crowns are represented in the relief sculptures at Chichen Itza
and turquoise mosaic plaques were found there, but it is certain
they were imported from central Mexico. There is no evidence,
either on the monuments or from the excavations, that turquoise
mosaics were known during the Old Empire, and the same is
likewise true of the Peruvian highlands.

On the basis of what featherwork has survived, the Aztec were
far superior to the Maya and Inca in this technique. Several ex-

amples of the Aztec handiwork were included in the treasure
Cortes sent back from Mexico to Emperor Charles V—the Moctezuma headdress composed of six hundred iridescent green quetzal
tail-feathers; two round shields and a three-piece vestment set
consisting of a bishop's miter, a chasuble front, and a maniple, all
made of delicate hummingbird-feather mosaic work, now in the
former Imperial Museum at Vienna; and the gorgeous full-
length cape of red macaw feathers built on a wicker frame, also
said to have belonged to Moctezuma and now in the Museum of
the Cinquantennaire at Brussels. As in the case of textiles, little
or no Maya featherwork has survived, although sculptures from
both the Old and New Empires represent splendid examples of
this art (Plate 53, *f*).

In metalwork the ancient Maya were distinctly backward, indeed, as we have seen in the preceding chapter; the Old Empire
Maya had no knowledge of metals at all and in the New Empire
their metalwork was confined to simple hammering, repoussé,
and perhaps filigree techniques. This backwardness in metalwork
was largely due to the fact that in the Maya area metal occurs in
nature only in the highlands to the south.

The Maya never approached the gorgeous gold jewelry of
the peoples of central Mexico, nor the spectacular goldwork of
those of Costa Rica, Panama, and Colombia, but the Inca goldwork, though all too little of it has survived for close study, far
surpasses anything ever achieved by other ancient Americans in
this field.

When we come to abstract mental achievements, however, such
as writing, astronomy, arithmetic, the development of a calendar
and chronology, and the recording of historical events, the Maya
had no equals anywhere in ancient America. They were the in-
ventors of writing in the New World. The graphic systems of the
Aztec and other peoples of central Mexico were patterned after,
indeed actually copied from, that of the Maya, and as often happens in such cases the copies were far inferior to the original. The
Inca *quipu*, a device of colored, knotted strings for aiding the
memory in keeping track of events and measuring all sorts of

materials, is crude, clumsy, and inadequate when compared with the Maya hieroglyphic writing.

In astronomy the Maya were easily head and shoulders above every other people of ancient America, having a knowledge of that science not even attained by the ancient Egyptians until Ptolemaic times. Neither the Aztec nor the Inca anywhere approached Maya accuracy in this exact field. As for arithmetic, the Maya developed man's first positional arithmetical system, one involving the concept of zero; this is among the most brilliant intellectual achievements of all time.

Again, although no original Maya historical manuscripts have survived, rescripts of several have come down to us in the *u kahlay katunob* of the Books of Chilam Balam. These, together with the unanimous declarations of all early Spanish historians that the Maya recorded their historical events, leave little room for doubt that history was another exact science among them.

In governmental and social organization, the Maya were certainly not the equal of the Inca and probably not of the Aztec. The Inca system of government was a true empire in the political sense with one man, the Inca, ruling with absolute authority over the whole vast Inca domain. In spite of many assertions to the contrary, it is probable that Moctezuma II, the last Aztec ruler, also exercised autocratic powers in a large part of central Mexico during the early part of the sixteenth century. There is no evidence that any single individual or even city-state enjoyed supreme power over all the others during the Maya Old Empire. However, there is documentary evidence to the effect that the Cocom family of Mayapan claimed and to a certain extent exercised such authority over the other lords of northern Yucatan during the late New Empire.

When the material achievements of the ancient Maya in architecture, sculpture, ceramics, painting, lapidary work, featherwork, and cotton weaving and dyeing are taken into consideration, and, further, when to these are added their abstract intellectual accomplishments, such as the invention of writing and positional arithmetic with its concomitant development of zero (certainly

unique for the New World), the construction of an elaborate
calendar and chronology (the latter with a fixed point of departure and slightly more accurate even than our own Gregorian
Calendar), plus a knowledge of astronomy superior to that of
both the ancient Egyptians and the Babylonians, and then finally,
when their whole cultural attainment is judged in the light of
their *known cultural limitations*, which were on a par with those
of early Neolithic Man in the Old World, we may safely acclaim
the ancient Maya, without fear of successful contradiction, as the
most brilliant aboriginal people on this planet.

CORRELATION OF MAYA AND CHRISTIAN CHRONOLOGIES

WHAT an exceedingly accurate system for measuring time the Maya Long Count (the Initial Series) really was has been explained in chapter xii—a chronology, which, we have seen, was exact to the day over a period of 374,440 years. The Maya Short Count (the *u kahlay katunob*), on the other hand, was far less accurate, indeed correct only within a period of 256¼ years. It is unfortunate, therefore, that the only Maya dates for which the corresponding Gregorian equivalents are surely known are given in terms of the Short Count. If we could only be sure of the corresponding Gregorian equivalent of a single Initial Series there would be no correlation problem at all, for we could then determine the Gregorian equivalents for every Initial Series; then Maya chronology, especially during the Old Empire, would be as clear as our own Christian chronology. But, as matters now stand, in order to ascertain the Gregorian equivalent for an Initial Series, it is necessary to work back through the much less accurate and less well understood Short Count, since only dates expressed in terms of the latter have been surely correlated with dates in our own chronology. Thus the problem of correlating the Maya Long Count with Christian chronology consists of two different operations: first of correlating the Gregorian Calendar with the Maya Short Count, and second of correlating the Maya Short Count with the Maya Long Count.

A number of events in the history of northern Yucatan during the century of the Spanish Conquest, such as the foundation of Merida on January 6, 1542 (Julian), for example, are recorded in terms of both the Julian Calendar and the Maya Short Count. A careful comparison of the several dates which are expressed in both chronologies, leads to the conclusion that a certain Katun 13 Ahau of the Maya Short Count came to an end sometime during the Julian year 1539. This much is generally accepted. But to correlate this particular Katun 13 Ahau with its corresponding Katun 13 Ahau of the Long Count is not quite so easy, nor is there general agreement among students of the problem as to just which Katun 13 Ahau of the Long Count came to its end in 1539.

The most generally accepted correlation formula is that which places the Long Count katun-ending 11.16.0.0.0 13 Ahau 8 Xul as having fallen on November 14, 1539 (Gregorian). This formula was first worked out in 1905 by the American scholar, J. T. Goodman, who also first deciphered the Maya Long Count as it is presented in the inscriptions on the monuments and who also compiled the famous Goodman chronological tables. In 1918, Goodman's correlation formula was slightly corrected (one day) by the Yucatecan archaeologist, Juan Martinez Hernandez, and in 1927 the Martinez Hernandez formula was further corrected (four days) by J. Eric S. Thompson of the Carnegie Institution's Division of Historical Research.

The last is the correlation formula which has been followed throughout this book, and it is also the basis for the Gregorian equivalents given in Table XII for the katun- and half-katun-endings of Maya history.

The first column in Table XII gives the Long Count dates of the katun- and half-katun-endings of Maya history, that is their corresponding Initial Series; the second column, the corresponding Short Count dates, that is the *u kahlay katunob;* and the third column, the corresponding dates in our own Gregorian Calendar.

TABLE XII

459

THE CORRELATION OF MAYA AND CHRISTIAN CHRONOLOGIES ACCORDING TO THE
GOODMAN-MARTINEZ HERNANDEZ-THOMPSON CORRELATION FORMULA

Katun- and Half-Katun-Endings in the Maya Long Count (the Initial Series)	Katun-Endings in the Maya Short Count (the *u kahlay katunob*)	Gregorian Equivalents
8.14.0.0.0 7 Ahau 3 Xul	Katun 7 Ahau	A.D. 317, September 1
8.14.10.0.0 6 Ahau 13 Zip		A.D. 327, July 11
8.15.0.0.0 5 Ahau 3 Pop	Katun 5 Ahau	A.D. 337, May 19
8.15.10.0.0 4 Ahau 18 Pax		A.D. 347, March 28
8.16.0.0.0 3 Ahau 8 Kankin	Katun 3 Ahau	A.D. 357, February 3
8.16.10.0.0 2 Ahau 18 Zac		A.D. 366, December 13
8.17.0.0.0 1 Ahau 8 Chen	Katun 1 Ahau	A.D. 376, October 21
8.17.10.0.0 13 Ahau 18 Xul		A.D. 386, August 30
8.18.0.0.0 12 Ahau 8 Zotz	Katun 12 Ahau	A.D. 396, July 8
8.18.10.0.0 11 Ahau 18 Pop		A.D. 406, May 17
8.19.0.0.0 10 Ahau 13 Kayab	Katun 10 Ahau	A.D. 416, March 25
8.19.10.0.0 9 Ahau 3 Muan		A.D. 426, February 1
9.0.0.0.0 8 Ahau 13 Ceh	Katun 8 Ahau	A.D. 435, December 11
9.0.10.0.0 7 Ahau 3 Yax		A.D. 445, October 19
9.1.0.0.0 6 Ahau 13 Yaxkin	Katun 6 Ahau	A.D. 455, August 28
9.1.10.0.0 5 Ahau 3 Tzec		A.D. 465, July 6
9.2.0.0.0 4 Ahau 13 Uo	Katun 4 Ahau	A.D. 475, May 15
9.2.10.0.0 3 Ahau 8 Cumhu		A.D. 485, March 23
9.3.0.0.0 2 Ahau 18 Muan	Katun 2 Ahau	A.D. 495, January 30
9.3.10.0.0 1 Ahau 8 Mac		A.D. 504, December 9
9.4.0.0.0 13 Ahau 18 Yax	Katun 13 Ahau	A.D. 514, October 18
9.4.10.0.0 12 Ahau 8 Mol		A.D. 524, August 26
9.5.0.0.0 11 Ahau 18 Tzec	Katun 11 Ahau	A.D. 534, July 5
9.5.10.0.0 10 Ahau 8 Zip		A.D. 544, May 13
9.6.0.0.0 9 Ahau 3 Uayeb	Katun 9 Ahau	A.D. 554, March 22
9.6.10.0.0 8 Ahau 13 Pax		A.D. 564, January 29
9.7.0.0.0 7 Ahau 3 Kankin	Katun 7 Ahau	A.D. 573, December 7
9.7.10.0.0 6 Ahau 13 Zac		A.D. 583, October 16
9.8.0.0.0 5 Ahau 3 Chen	Katun 5 Ahau	A.D. 593, August 24
9.8.10.0.0 4 Ahau 13 Xul		A.D. 603, July 4
9.9.0.0.0 3 Ahau 3 Zotz	Katun 3 Ahau	A.D. 613, May 12
9.9.10.0.0 2 Ahau 13 Pop		A.D. 623, March 21
9.10.0.0.0 1 Ahau 8 Kayab	Katun 1 Ahau	A.D. 633, January 27
9.10.10.0.0 13 Ahau 18 Kankin		A.D. 642, December 6
9.11.0.0.0 12 Ahau 8 Ceh	Katun 12 Ahau	A.D. 652, October 14
9.11.10.0.0 11 Ahau 18 Chen		A.D. 662, August 23
9.12.0.0.0 10 Ahau 8 Yaxkin	Katun 10 Ahau	A.D. 672, July 1
9.12.10.0.0 9 Ahau 13 Zip		A.D. 682, May 10
9.13.0.0.0 8 Ahau 8 Uo	Katun 8 Ahau	A.D. 692, March 18
9.13.10.0.0 7 Ahau 3 Cumhu		A.D. 702, January 26

Katun- and Half-Katun-Endings in the Maya Long Count (the Initial Series)	Katun-Endings in the Maya Short Count (the *u kahlay katunob*)	Gregorian Equivalents
9.14.0.0.0 6 Ahau 13 Muan	Katun 6 Ahau	A.D. 711, December 5
9.14.10.0.0 5 Ahau 3 Mac		A.D. 721, October 13
9.15.0.0.0 4 Ahau 13 Yax	Katun 4 Ahau	A.D. 731, August 22
9.15.10.0.0 3 Ahau 3 Mol		A.D. 741, June 30
9.16.0.0.0 2 Ahau 13 Tzec	Katun 2 Ahau	A.D. 751, May 9
9.16.10.0.0 1 Ahau 3 Zip		A.D. 761, March 17
9.17.0.0.0 13 Ahau 18 Cumhu	Katun 13 Ahau	A.D. 771, January 24
9.17.10.0.0 12 Ahau 8 Pax		A.D. 780, December 2
9.18.0.0.0 11 Ahau 18 Mac	Katun 11 Ahau	A.D. 790, October 11
9.18.10.0.0 10 Ahau 8 Zac		A.D. 800, August 19
9.19.0.0.0 9 Ahau 18 Mol	Katun 9 Ahau	A.D. 810, June 28
9.19.10.0.0 8 Ahau 8 Xul		A.D. 820, May 6
10.0.0.0.0 7 Ahau 18 Zip	Katun 7 Ahau	A.D. 830, March 15
10.0.10.0.0 6 Ahau 8 Pop		A.D. 840, January 22
10.1.0.0.0 5 Ahau 3 Kayab	Katun 5 Ahau	A.D. 849, November 30
10.1.10.0.0 4 Ahau 13 Kankin		A.D. 859, October 9
10.2.0.0.0 3 Ahau 3 Ceh	Katun 3 Ahau	A.D. 869, August 17
10.2.10.0.0 2 Ahau 13 Chen		A.D. 879, June 26
10.3.0.0.0 1 Ahau 3 Yaxkin	Katun 1 Ahau	A.D. 889, May 4
10.3.10.0.0 13 Ahau 13 Zotz		A.D. 899, March 13
10.4.0.0.0 12 Ahau 3 Uo	Katun 12 Ahau	A.D. 909, January 20
10.4.10.0.0 11 Ahau 18 Kayab		A.D. 918, November 29
10.5.0.0.0 10 Ahau 8 Muan	Katun 10 Ahau	A.D. 928, October 7
10.5.10.0.0 9 Ahau 18 Ceh		A.D. 938, August 16
10.6.0.0.0 8 Ahau 8 Yax	Katun 8 Ahau	A.D. 948, June 24
10.6.10.0.0 7 Ahau 18 Yaxkin		A.D. 958, May 3
10.7.0.0.0 6 Ahau 8 Tzec	Katun 6 Ahau	A.D. 968, March 11
10.7.10.0.0 5 Ahau 18 Uo		A.D. 978, January 18
10.8.0.0.0 4 Ahau 13 Cumhu	Katun 4 Ahau	A.D. 987, November 27
10.8.10.0.0 3 Ahau 3 Pax		A.D. 997, October 5
10.9.0.0.0 2 Ahau 13 Mac	Katun 2 Ahau	A.D. 1007, August 15
10.9.10.0.0 1 Ahau 3 Zac		A.D. 1017, June 23
10.10.0.0.0 13 Ahau 13 Mol	Katun 13 Ahau	A.D. 1027, May 2
10.10.10.0.0 12 Ahau 3 Xul		A.D. 1037, March 10
10.11.0.0.0 11 Ahau 13 Zip	Katun 11 Ahau	A.D. 1047, January 17
10.11.10.0.0 10 Ahau 3 Pop		A.D. 1056, November 25
10.12.0.0.0 9 Ahau 18 Pax	Katun 9 Ahau	A.D. 1066, October 4
10.12.10.0.0 8 Ahau 8 Kankin		A.D. 1076, August 12
10.13.0.0.0 7 Ahau 18 Zac	Katun 7 Ahau	A.D. 1086, June 21
10.13.10.0.0 6 Ahau 8 Chen		A.D. 1096, April 29
10.14.0.0.0 5 Ahau 18 Xul	Katun 5 Ahau	A.D. 1106, March 9
10.14.10.0.0 4 Ahau 8 Zotz		A.D. 1116, January 16

TABLE XII (*Continued*)

461

Katun- and Half-Katun-Endings in the Maya Long Count (the Initial Series)	Katun-Endings in the Maya Short Count (the *u kah-lay katunob*)	Gregorian Equivalents
10.15.0.0.0 3 Ahau 18 Pop	Katun 3 Ahau	A.D. 1125, November 24
10.15.10.0.0 2 Ahau 13 Kayab		A.D. 1135, October 3
10.16.0.0.0 1 Ahau 3 Muan	Katun 1 Ahau	A.D. 1145, August 11
10.16.10.0.0 13 Ahau 13 Ceh		A.D. 1155, June 20
10.17.0.0.0 12 Ahau 3 Yax	Katun 12 Ahau	A.D. 1165, April 28
10.17.10.0.0 11 Ahau 13 Yaxkin		A.D. 1175, March 7
10.18.0.0.0 10 Ahau 3 Tzec	Katun 10 Ahau	A.D. 1185, January 13
10.18.10.0.0 9 Ahau 13 Uo		A.D. 1194, November 22
10.19.0.0.0 8 Ahau 8 Cumhu	Katun 8 Ahau	A.D. 1204, September 30
10.19.10.0.0 7 Ahau 18 Muan		A.D. 1214, August 9
11.0.0.0.0 6 Ahau 8 Mac	Katun 6 Ahau	A.D. 1224, June 17
11.0.10.0.0 5 Ahau 18 Yax		A.D. 1234, April 26
11.1.0.0.0 4 Ahau 8 Mol	Katun 4 Ahau	A.D. 1244, March 4
11.1.10.0.0 3 Ahau 18 Tzec		A.D. 1254, January 11
11.2.0.0.0 2 Ahau 8 Zip	Katun 2 Ahau	A.D. 1263, November 20
11.2.10.0.0 1 Ahau 3 Uayeb		A.D. 1273, September 28
11.3.0.0.0 13 Ahau 13 Pax	Katun 13 Ahau	A.D. 1283, August 7
11.3.10.0.0 12 Ahau 3 Kankin		A.D. 1293, June 15
11.4.0.0.0 11 Ahau 13 Zac	Katun 11 Ahau	A.D. 1303, April 25
11.4.10.0.0 10 Ahau 3 Chen		A.D. 1313, March 3
11.5.0.0.0 9 Ahau 13 Xul	Katun 9 Ahau	A.D. 1323, January 10
11.5.10.0.0 8 Ahau 3 Zotz		A.D. 1332, November 18
11.6.0.0.0 7 Ahau 13 Pop	Katun 7 Ahau	A.D. 1342, September 27
11.6.10.0.0 6 Ahau 8 Kayab		A.D. 1352, August 5
11.7.0.0.0 5 Ahau 18 Kankin	Katun 5 Ahau	A.D. 1362, June 14
11.7.10.0.0 4 Ahau 8 Ceh		A.D. 1372, April 22
11.8.0.0.0 3 Ahau 18 Chen	Katun 3 Ahau	A.D. 1382, March 1
11.8.10.0.0 2 Ahau 8 Yaxkin		A.D. 1392, January 8
11.9.0.0.0 1 Ahau 18 Zotz	Katun 1 Ahau	A.D. 1401, November 17
11.9.10.0.0 13 Ahau 8 Uo		A.D. 1411, September 26
11.10.0.0.0 12 Ahau 3 Cumhu	Katun 12 Ahau	A.D. 1421, August 4
11.10.10.0.0 11 Ahau 13 Muan		A.D. 1431, June 13
11.11.0.0.0 10 Ahau 3 Mac	Katun 10 Ahau	A.D. 1441, April 21
11.11.10.0.0 9 Ahau 13 Yax		A.D. 1451, February 28
11.12.0.0.0 8 Ahau 3 Mol	Katun 8 Ahau	A.D. 1461, January 6
11.12.10.0.0 7 Ahau 13 Tzec		A.D. 1470, November 15
11.13.0.0.0 6 Ahau 3 Zip	Katun 6 Ahau	A.D. 1480, September 23
11.13.10.0.0 5 Ahau 18 Cumhu		A.D. 1490, August 2
11.14.0.0.0 4 Ahau 8 Pax	Katun 4 Ahau	A.D. 1500, June 11
11.14.10.0.0 3 Ahau 18 Mac		A.D. 1510, April 20
11.15.0.0.0 2 Ahau 8 Zac	Katun 2 Ahau	A.D. 1520, February 27
11.15.10.0.0 1 Ahau 18 Mol		A.D. 1530, January 5

Katun- and Half-Katun Endings in the Maya Long Count (the Initial Series)		Katun-Endings in the Maya Short Count (the *u kah-lay katunob*)	Gregorian Equivalents
11.16.0.0.0	13 Ahau 8 Xul	Katun 13 Ahau	A.D. 1539, November 14
11.16.10.0.0	12 Ahau 18 Zip		A.D. 1549, September 22
11.17.0.0.0	11 Ahau 8 Pop	Katun 11 Ahau	A.D. 1559, August 1
11.17.10.0.0	10 Ahau 3 Kayab		A.D. 1569, June 9
11.18.0.0.0	9 Ahau 13 Kankin	Katun 9 Ahau	A.D. 1579, April 18
11.18.10.0.0	8 Ahau 3 Ceh		A.D. 1589, February 24
11.19.0.0.0	7 Ahau 13 Chen	Katun 7 Ahau	A.D. 1599, January 3
11.19.10.0.0	6 Ahau 3 Yaxkin		A.D. 1608, November 11
12.0.0.0.0	5 Ahau 13 Zotz	Katun 5 Ahau	A.D. 1618, September 20
12.0.10.0.0	4 Ahau 3 Uo		A.D. 1628, July 29
12.1.0.0.0	3 Ahau 18 Kayab	Katun 3 Ahau	A.D. 1638, June 7
12.1.10.0.0	2 Ahau 8 Muan		A.D. 1648, April 15
12.2.0.0.0	1 Ahau 18 Ceh	Katun 1 Ahau	A.D. 1658, February 22
12.2.10.0.0	13 Ahau 8 Yax		A.D. 1668, January 1
12.3.0.0.0	12 Ahau 18 Yaxkin	Katun 12 Ahau	A.D. 1677, November 9
12.3.10.0.0	11 Ahau 8 Tzec		A.D. 1687, September 18
12.4.0.0.0	10 Ahau 18 Uo	Katun 10 Ahau	A.D. 1697, July 27
12.4.10.0.0	9 Ahau 13 Cumhu		A.D. 1707, June 6
12.5.0.0.0	8 Ahau 3 Pax	Katun 8 Ahau	A.D. 1717, April 14

PERSONAL NAMES AMONG THE ANCIENT MAYA

AS NOTED in chapter x (p. 183) each Maya had at least three different names (and sometimes even a fourth) which were bestowed upon him at different periods of his life. His earliest name or *paal kaba*, given him at birth, may be compared to our own given names, such as John, William, Mary, Helen, etc. In the case of boys, the *paal* name invariably began with the masculine prefix *ah*, and in the case of girls, with the feminine prefix *ix*, sometimes written *yx*. To the masculine prefix the names of animals, reptiles, birds, trees, and other objects were added to give the boy's *paal* names, as for example: Ah Balam (jaguar); Ah Ceh (deer); Ah Cuat (serpent); Ah Itzam (lizard); Ah Cuy (owl); Ah Op (parrot); Ah Chacah (gumbolimbo tree); Ah Dzulub (arbor); Ah Kukum (feather); Ah Tok (flint knife); Ah Uitz (hill, or mountain). Only relatively few *paal* names of girls have come down to us; these are formed by adding the feminine prefix *ix* to other Maya words, the meanings of which are not so clear as in the case of boy's *paal* names: Ix Chan; Ix Cahum; Ix Can; Ix Cakuk; Ix Kauil; Ix Kukul; Ix Nahau.

Says Bishop Landa in this connection:

. . . . they [the parents] went with them [the children] to the priests, so that they might see his [the child's] destiny and tell the profession which he was to pursue, to give the name he was to bear during his childhood [the *paal* name mentioned above]; because they were accustomed to call their children by different names until they were baptized [i.e., the puberty ceremony described on page 184] and grew up; and afterwards they gave up these and began to call them by the name of their fathers [i.e., their patronymics] until they married, and then they were called by the name of their father and mother.

The second name which a boy or girl was given was his father's family name, mentioned above by Landa, which he assumed after the puberty ceremony, also described in chapter x, when he or she was considered to have reached a marriageable age. The Maya word for the father's patronymic has not come down to us.

The third name by which a Maya was known, also mentioned by Landa in the quotation above, he or she assumed after marriage. This last designation was called the *naal kaba* meaning mother-name in Maya; it was composed of the prefix *nah* (Maya for "mother"), to which was added the mother's matronymic (the child's mother's maiden name), followed by the father's patronymic (the father's family name). Thus in the case of a man whose *naal* name was Na Chan Chel, the example given by Landa, the man's mother's maiden name and also his maternal grandmother's maiden name as well, was Chan, whereas his father's family name was Chel. This seems to indicate that, just as the *father's patronymic* descended through the sons for generations, so the *mother's matronymic* was perpetuated through the daughters for generations. Many of these ancient Maya surnames, both patronymic and matronymic, were derived from animal, serpent, insect, bird, and plant names: Balam (jaguar); Baa (gopher); Can (serpent); Coh (puma); Mis (cat); Muy (rabbit); Och (opposum); Tzul (dog); Uech (armadillo); Pech (tick); Bacal (corncob); Cab (bee or honey); Cocom (climbing plant with yellow flowers); Cutz (ocellated turkey); Che (tree); Chel (blue jay); Kutz (tobacco); Mo (macaw); Muan (sparrow hawk); Mucuy (dove); Nic (a small flower); Ppizte (cacao bean); Xiu (weed).

In addition to the three kinds of names mentioned above—*paal* and *naal* names and the father's surname—there is a fourth name, which one of the native manuscripts defines as the *coco kaba*, or nickname. These *coco* names may have been given because of some personal peculiarity or circumstance, like our "Fatty" or "Shorty," for example. The six preserved in the manuscript mentioned are: Ah Xun; Ah Pach Uitz, which may mean "the man who lives behind the hill"; Ah Tupp Kabal, possibly "the man who makes a noise like an explosion"; Ah Na Itza, "the man of the house of the Itza"; Ah Kom Tzohom, "something red"; Ah Xochil Ich, "owl face, owl eye." The *coco* name of Ah Zuytok Xiu, the founder of Uxmal, may possibly have been Hun Uitzil Chac, "the only mountain Chac or Rain-God" (chapter xi, p. 224). Finally the *coco* name of Hunac Ceel, the *halach uinic* of Mayapan whose victory over Chac Xib Chac, the *halach uinic* of Chichen Itza in 1194, put an end to the confederacy known as the League of Mayapan (p. 91) was probably Ah Tapaynok, "he with the broidered mantle."

The foregoing several names by which an ancient Maya was known have been made the subject of special study by Ralph L. Roys of the Carnegie Institution staff. See R. L. Roys (1940) in the section on Ethnology in the Classified Bibliography (p. 481) for further information on this subject.

CLASSIFIED BIBLIOGRAPHY

IN ORDER to simplify the problem of the research worker or the specialist who may wish to pursue his subject further, this Bibliography has been arranged under fourteen classifications: (1) Archaeology; (2) Ethnology; (3) History; (4) Art; (5) Hieroglyphic Writing, Chronology, and Astronomy; (6) Agriculture; (7) Language; (8) Medical Science; (9) The Modern Maya; (10) Travel and Exploration; (11) Geography, Geology, and Climate; (12) Botany; (13) Zoology; (14) Fiction.

Under these headings the corresponding publications are grouped alphabetically by authors' names. Titles marked with an asterisk (*) are especially recommended to the general reader.

1. ARCHAEOLOGY

ANDREWS, E. WYLLYS

1939. "A Group of Related Structures from Yucatan," *Contributions to American Anthropology and History*, Vol. V, No. 26; Carnegie Institution of Washington Publication No. 509. Washington, D.C.

1943. "The Archaeology of Southwestern Campeche," *Contributions to American Anthropology and History*, Vol. VIII, No. 40; Carnegie Institution of Washington Publication No. 546. Washington, D.C.

BAKER, M. LOUISE

1936. "Lintel 3 Restored . . . . and Why," *Univ. Mus. Bull.*, University of Pennsylvania, Vol. VI, No. 4, pp. 120–23. Philadelphia.

BANCROFT, H. H.

1882. *The Native Races of the Pacific States.* 5 vols. San Francisco.

Biología Centrali-Americana

1889–1902. *Biología Centrali-Americana; or, Contributions to the Knowledge of the Fauna and Flora of Mexico and Central America.* Edited by E. DuCane Godman and Osbert Salvin. 61 secs. London. See A. P. MAUDSLAY, 1889–1902, for the section on archaeology.

BLOM, FRANS

1932. "The Maya Game *pok-ta-pok* (called *tlachtli* by the Aztecs)." *Middle American Research Series, Publication No. 4*, pp. 486–530. Department of Middle American Research, Tulane University, New Orleans.

468   1932a. "Commerce, Trade and Monetary Units of the Maya." *Middle American Research Series, Publication No. 4*, pp. 532–56. Department of Middle American Research, Tulane University, New Orleans.

1933.   "Maya Books and Sciences," *Library Quarterly*, Vol. III, No. 4, pp. 408–20. Chicago.

BRASSEUR DE BOURBOURG, CHARLES ETIENNE

1866.   *Recherches sur les ruines de Palenque.* Paris.

BUTLER, MARY

1931.   "Dress and Decoration of the Maya Old Empire," *Univ. Mus. Jour.*, University of Pennsylvania, Vol. XXII, No. 2, pp. 155–83. Philadelphia.

CARNEGIE INSTITUTION OF WASHINGTON. *News Service Bulletin.*

*1926.   *Buried Temple Discovered at Site of Ancient Maya Capital.* Carnegie Institution of Washington News Service Bulletin, Vol. I, No. 1, July 24. Washington, D.C.

*1926a. *Ancient Maya Almanac in Stone Found at Cobá, Yucatan.* Carnegie Institution of Washington News Service Bulletin, Vol. I, No. 2, August 15. Washington, D.C.

*1927.   *Buried Maya Treasures.* Carnegie Institution of Washington News Service Bulletin, Vol. I, No. 10, July 10. Washington, D.C.

*1927a. *The Temple of the Warriors.* Carnegie Institution of Washington News Service Bulletin, Vol. I, No. 12, November 13. Washington.

*1928.   *Etzna—"The City of Grimacing Faces."* Carnegie Institution of Washington News Service Bulletin, Vol. I, No. 24, May 13. Washington, D.C.

*1928a. *Ancient Ceremonial Treasure.* Carnegie Institution of Washington News Service Bulletin, Vol. I, No. 25, April 25. Washington, D.C.

*1928b. *Fresh Discoveries in Maya Exploration.* Carnegie Institution of Washington News Service Bulletin, Vol. I, No. 29, September 16. Washington, D.C.

*1931.   *The Maya of Middle America:* Part I, *The Archaeological Problem;* Part II, *The Temple of the Warriors;* Part III, *Restoration of the Turquoise Mosaic Plaque;* Part IV, *Bas-reliefs from the Temple of the Warriors;* Part V, *Murals from the Temple of the Warriors.* Carnegie Institution of Washington News Service Bulletin, Vol. II, Nos. 17–21, pp. 121–44, June 7. Washington, D.C. Spanish translation, *"Los Mayas de la región central de America."* Carnegie Institution of Washington Supplementary Publication No. 4.

*1931a. *The Exodus of the Maya.* Carnegie Institution of Washington News Service Bulletin, Vol. II, No. 24, pp. 163, 164, December 6. Washington, D.C.

*1932.   *Pottery Discovery in Ancient Maya Grave.* Carnegie Institution of   469
         Washington News Service Bulletin, Vol. II, No. 36, pp. 243–50,
         December 18. Washington, D.C.

*1933.   *The Great "White Ways" of the Maya.* Carnegie Institution of
         Washington News Service Bulletin, Vol. III, No. 9, pp. 61–67, Sep-
         tember 24, Washington, D.C.

*1934.   *The Ruins of Quirigua.* Carnegie Institution of Washington News
         Service Bulletin, Vol. III, No. 19, pp. 149–56, December 16. Wash-
         ington, D.C.

*1935.   *The Caracol—A Perplexing Maya Ruin.* Carnegie Institution of
         Washington News Service Bulletin, Vol. III, No. 27, pp. 211–26,
         December 15. Washington, D.C.

*1936.   *Important Maya Discovery in the Guatemalan Highlands.* Carnegie
         Institution of Washington News Service Bulletin, Vol. IV, No. 6,
         pp. 53–60, August 23. Washington, D.C.

*1937.   *El Castillo, Pyramid-Temple of the Maya God, Kukulcan.* Carnegie
         Institution of Washington News Service Bulletin, Vol. IV, No. 12,
         pp. 105–16, April 25. Washington, D.C.

CARNEGIE INSTITUTION OF WASHINGTON. *Contributions to American Archae-
         ology.*

1931.   Vol. I, Publication No. 403.
1934.   Vol. II, Publication No. 436.
1937.   Vol. III, Publication No. 456.
1937.   Vol. IV, Publication No. 483.

CARNEGIE INSTITUTION OF WASHINGTON. *Contributions to American Anthro-
         pology and History.*

1939.   Vol. V, Publication No. 509.
1940.   Vol. VI, Publication No. 523.
1942.   Vol. VII, Publication No. 528.
1943.   Vol. VIII, Publication No. 546.

CARNEGIE INSTITUTION OF WASHINGTON. *Supplementary Publications.*

*1933.   *The Culture of the Maya.* Carnegie Institution of Washington Sup-
         plementary Publication No. 6. Washington, D.C.

*1935.   *Guide Book to the Ruins of Quirigua.* Carnegie Institution of Wash-
         ington Supplementary Publication No. 16. Washington, D.C.

CASO, ALFONSO

1928.   "Las estelas zapotecas," *Revista Mexicana de Estudios Antropológicos,*
         Vol. III, No. 1. Mexico.

*1937.   "The Religion of the Aztecs," *Revista Mexicana de Estudios Antro-
         pológicos,* Vol. III, No. 1. Mexico.

1939.   "La correlación de los años azteca y cristiano," *Revista Mexicana de
         Estudios Antropológicos,* Vol. III, No. 1, pp. 11–45. Mexico.

470 CATHERWOOD, F.

    1844. *Views of Ancient Monuments in Central America, Chiapas, and Yucatan.* New York.

DRUCKER, PHILIP

    1943. *Ceramic Sequences at Tres Zapotes, Veracruz, Mexico.* Smithsonian Institution, Bureau of American Ethnology, No. 140. Washington, D.C.

    1943a. *Ceramic Stratigraphy at Cerro de las Mesas, Veracruz, Mexico.* Smithsonian Institution, Bureau of American Ethnology, No. 141. Washington, D.C.

GAMIO, MANUEL Y OTROS

    1922. *La población del Valle de Teotihuacán.* 3 vols. Mexico.

GANN, T. W. F.

    1900. *Mounds in Northern Honduras.* Bureau of American Ethnology, *Smithsonian Institution Nineteenth Annual Report*, 1897–98, Part 2, pp. 655–92. Washington, D.C.

    1905. "The Ancient Monuments of Northern Honduras and the Adjacent Parts of Yucatan and Guatemala, the Former Civilization in These Parts and the Chief Characteristics of the Races Now Inhabiting Them with an Account of a Visit to the Rio Grande Ruins," *Jour. Royal Anthropol. Inst.*, n.s., Vol. VIII, pp. 103–12. London.

    1935. "Tzibanché, Quintana Roo, Mexico," *Maya Research*, Vol. II, No. 2, pp. 155–66. New York.

GORDON, G. B.

    1896. "Prehistoric Ruins of Copan, Honduras." A Preliminary Report of the Explorations by the Museum, 1891–1895. *Memoirs of the Peabody Museum of American Archaeology and Ethnology*, Harvard University, Vol. I, No. 1. Cambridge.

    1902. "The Hieroglyphic Stairway, Ruins of Copan." Report on Explorations by the Museum. *Memoirs of the Peabody Museum of American Archaeology and Ethnology*, Harvard University, Vol. I, No. 6. Cambridge.

    1913. "An Unpublished Inscription from Quirigua, Guatemala," *Proceedings of the Eighteenth Session of the International Congress of Americanists*, London, 1912, pp. 238–40. London.

HEWETT, E. L.

    1911. "Two Seasons' Work in Guatemala," *Bulletin of the Archaeological Institute of America*, Vol. II, pp. 117–34. Norwood. (Reprinted under same title as *Paper No. 21, School of American Research*, Archaeological Institute of America, Santa Fe.)

    1912. "The Excavations at Quirigua in 1912," *Bulletin of the Archaeological*

Institute of America, Vol. III, pp. 163–71. Norwood. (Reprinted as 471 "The Third Season's Work in Guatemala," *Paper No. 22, School of American Research,* Archaeological Institute of America, Santa Fe.)

1913. "The Excavations at Quirigua, Guatemala, by the School of American Archaeology," *Proceedings of the Eighteenth Session of the International Congress of Americanists,* London, 1912, Part 2, pp. 241–48. London.

1915. "Ancient America at the Panama-California Exposition," *Art and Archaeology,* Vol. II, No. 3, pp. 65–102. Washington, D.C.

1916. "Latest Work of the School of American Archaeology at Quirigua," *Holmes Anniversary Volume,* pp. 157–62. Washington, D.C.

HOLMES, W. H.

1895–1897. *Archaeological Studies among the Ancient Cities of Mexico.* Part I, *Monuments of Yucatan,* pp. 1–138; Part II, *Monuments of Chiapas, Oaxaca and the Valley of Mexico,* pp. 138–338. *Anthropological Series,* Vol. I. Field Columbian Museum, Chicago.

1907. "On a Nephrite Statuette from San Andres Tuxtla, Vera Cruz, Mexico," *American Anthropologist,* n.s., Vol. IX, No. 4, pp. 691–701. Lancaster.

JOYCE, THOMAS A.

*1914. *Mexican Archaeology.* New York.

*1916. *Central American and West Indian Archaeology.* London.

*1923. *Guide to the Maudslay Collection of Maya Sculptures (Casts and Originals) from Central America.* The Trustees, British Museum. London.

*1927. *Maya and Mexican Art.* London.

KIDDER, A. V.

1937. "Notes on the Ruins of San Agustin Acasaguastlan, Guatemala," *Contributions to American Archaeology,* Vol. III, No. 15. Carnegie Institution of Washington Publication No. 456. Washington, D.C.

KIDDER, A. V., AND J. ERIC S. THOMPSON

1938. "The Correlation of Maya and Christian Chronology," *Co-operation in Research,* Carnegie Institution of Washington Publication No. 501, pp. 493–510. Washington, D.C.

Los Mayas Antiguos

1941. *Los Mayas Antiguos. Colección de monografías de arqueología, etnografía y lingüística mayas publicadas con motivo del Centenario de la exploración de Yucatán por John L. Stephens y Frederick Catherwood en los años 1841–42.*

LOTHROP, S. K.

1924. *Tulum. An Archaeological Study of the East Coast of Yucatan.* Car-

472   negie Institution of Washington Publication No. 335. Washington,
D.C.

1933.   *Atitlan. An Archaeological Study of Ancient Remains on the Borders of Lake Atitlan, Guatemala.* Carnegie Institution of Washington
Publication No. 444. Washington, D.C.

1936.   *Zacualpa. A Study of Ancient Quiché Artifacts.* Carnegie Institution
of Washington Publication No. 472. Washington, D.C.

LUNDELL, C. L.

1934.   "Ruins of Polol and Other Archaeological Discoveries in the Department of Peten, Guatemala," *Contributions to American Archaeology,*
Vol. II, No. 8; Carnegie Institution of Washington Publication No.
436, 1934, pp. 173–86, pls. 1–9. Washington, D.C. Preprinted
March 1934.

MALER, TEOBERT

1901.   "Researches in the Central Portion of the Usumatsintla Valley. Re-
port of Explorations for the Museum, 1898–1900," *Memoirs of the
Peabody Museum of American Archaeology and Ethnology,* Harvard
University, Vol. II, No. 1, pp. 1–75. Cambridge.

1903.   "Researches in the Central Portions of the Usumatsintla Valley. Reports of Explorations for the Museum," *Memoirs of the Peabody
Museum of American Archaeology and Ethnology,* Harvard University, Vol. II, No. 2, pp. 77–208. Cambridge.

1908.   "Explorations of the Upper Usumatsintla and Adjacent Regions.
Altar de Sacrificios; Seibal; Itsimté-Sácluk; Cankuen. Reports of
Explorations for the Museum," *Memoirs of the Peabody Museum of
American Archaeology and Ethnology,* Harvard University, Vol. IV,
No. 1, pp. 1–49. Cambridge.

1908a.   "Explorations in the Department of Peten, Guatemala, and Adjacent
Regions. Topoxté, Yaxhá; Benque Viejo; Naranjo. Reports of Ex-
plorations for the Museum," *Memoirs of the Peabody Museum of
American Archaeology and Ethnology,* Harvard University, Vol. IV,
No. 2, pp. 53–127. Cambridge.

1910.   "Explorations in the Department of Peten, Guatemala, and Adjacent Regions. Motul de San José; Peten-Itza. Reports of Explorations for the Museum," *Memoirs of the Peabody Museum of American Archaeology and Ethnology,* Harvard University, Vol. IV, No. 3,
pp. 131–70. Cambridge.

1911.   "Explorations in the Department of Peten, Guatemala. Tikal. Report of Explorations for the Museum," *Memoirs of the Peabody
Museum of American Archaeology and Ethnology,* Harvard University, Vol. V, No. 1, pp. 3–135. Cambridge.

MASON, J. A.

*1931.   "A Maya Carved Stone Lintel from Guatemala," *Univ. Mus. Bull.,*

University of Pennsylvania, Vol. III, No. 1, pp. 5–7, pls. I–III. Philadelphia.

*1932. "Excavations at Piedras Negras," *Univ. Mus. Bull.*, University of Pennsylvania, Vol. III, No. 6, pp. 178, 179. Philadelphia.

*1933. "Jade Ornaments from Piedras Negras," *Univ. Mus. Bull.*, University of Pennsylvania, Vol. IV, No. 2, pp. 53, 55, 56, pl. XI. Philadelphia.

*1933a. "A Remarkable Throne from Guatemala," *Univ. Mus. Bull.*, University of Pennsylvania, Vol. IV, No. 4, pp. 90, 91, pl. II. Philadelphia.

*1934. "A Stucco Head from Guatemala," *Univ. Mus. Bull.*, University of Pennsylvania, Vol. V, No. 1, pp. 24, 25, 27, pl. XI. Philadelphia.

*1934a. "Maya Sculptures Rescued from the Jungle," *American Archaeology*, No. 6; *Bulletin of the Pan American Union*. Washington, D.C.

*1935. "Preserving Ancient America's Finest Sculptures," *National Geographic Magazine*, Vol. LXVIII, No. 5, pp. 537–70, color plates I–VIII. Washington, D.C.

*1935a. "Mexican and Mayan Sweat-Baths," *Univ. Mus. Bull.*, University of Pennsylvania, Vol. VI, No. 2, pp. 65, 67–69, pl. IX. Philadelphia.

Maya Research

1934. Vol. I, July–December.

1935. Vol. II, January–December.

1936. Vol. III, January–December.

Maya and Their Neighbors, The

*1940. New York.

MERWIN, R. E., AND G. C. VAILLANT

1932. "The Ruins of Holmul, Guatemala," *Memoirs of the Peabody Museum of American Archaeology and Ethnology*, Harvard University, Vol. III, No. 2. Cambridge.

MORLEY, FRANCES R., AND S. G. MORLEY

1939. "The Age and Provenance of the Leyden Plate," *Contributions to American Anthropology and History*, Vol. V, No. 24; Carnegie Institution of Washington Publication No. 509. Washington.

MORLEY, S. G.

1910. "A Group of Related Structures at Uxmal, Mexico," *American Journal of Archaeology*, Archaeological Institute of America, 2d ser., Vol. XIV, No. 1, pp. 1–18. Norwood.

1910a. "The Correlation of Maya and Christian Chronology," *American Journal of Archaeology*, Archaeological Institute of America, 2d ser., Vol. XIV, No. 2, pp. 193–204. Norwood.

*1911. "Ancient Temples and Cities of the New World. Chichen Itza,"

Bulletin of the Pan American Union, Vol. XXXII, pp. 453–68. Washington, D.C.

*1911*a. "Ancient Temples and Cities of the New World. Uxmal, the City of the Xius," *Bulletin of the Pan American Union*, Vol. XXXII, pp. 627–42. Washington, D.C.

*1911*b. "Ancient Temples and Cities of the New World. Copan, the Mother City of the Mayas," *Bulletin of the Pan American Union*, Vol. XXXII, pp. 863–79. Washington, D.C.

*1912. "Quirigua, an Ancient Town 1,400 Years Old," *Scientific American*, Vol. CVII, pp. 96, 105. New York.

*1913. "Excavations at Quirigua, Guatemala," *National Geographic Magazine*, Vol. XXIV, No. 3, pp. 339–61. Washington, D.C.

1913*a*. "Archaeological Research at the Ruins of Chichen Itza, Yucatan," *Reports upon the Present Condition and Future Needs of the Science of Anthropology*, presented by W. H. R. Rivers, A. E. Jenks, and S. G. Morley; Carnegie Institution of Washington Publication No. 200, pp. 61–91. Washington, D.C.

*1917. "The Ruins of Tuloom, Yucatan. The Record of a Visit of the Carnegie Institution Central American Expedition of 1916 to an Important but Little Known Ancient Maya City," *American Museum Journal*, Vol. XVII, No. 3, pp. 190–204. New York.

1917*a*. "The *hotun* as the Principal Chronological Unit of the Old Maya Empire," *Proceedings of the International Congress of Americanists, Nineteenth Session, Washington, 1915*, pp. 195–201. Washington. D.C.

1920. *The Inscriptions at Copan*. Carnegie Institution of Washington Publication No. 219. Washington, D.C.

*1922. "The Foremost Intellectual Achievement of Ancient America. The Hieroglyphic Inscriptions on the Monuments in the Ruined Cities of Mexico, Guatemala, and Honduras Are Yielding the Secrets of the Maya Civilization," *National Geographic Magazine*, Vol. XLI, No. 2, pp. 109–30. Washington, D.C.

1925. "The Earliest Mayan Dates," *Congrès International des Américanistes, Compte-rendu de la XXIe session*, Göteborg, 1924, Part 2, pp. 655–67. Göteborg Museum, Göteborg.

*1925*a. "Chichen Itza, an Ancient American Mecca. Recent Explorations in Yucatan Are Bringing to Light the Temples, Palaces, and Pyramids of America's Most Holy Native City," *National Geographic Magazine*, Vol. XLII, No. 1, pp. 63–95. Washington, D.C.

1927. "New Light on the Discovery of Yucatan and the Foundation of the New Maya Empire," *American Journal of Archaeology*, Archaeological Institute of America, 2d ser., Vol. XXXI, No. 1, pp. 51–69. Concord.

*1927a. "Maya Civilization—100% American," *Forum*, Vol. LXXVIII, No. 2, pp. 226–36. Concord.

*1931. "Unearthing America's Ancient History. Investigation Suggests That the Maya May Have Designed the First Astronomical Observatory in the New World in Order to Cultivate Corn," *National Geographic Magazine*, Vol. LX, No. 1, pp. 99–126. Washington, D.C.

*1935. *Guide Book to the Ruins of Quirigua*. Carnegie Institution of Washington Supplemental Publication No. 16. Washington, D.C.

1936. *Guía de las ruinas de Quiriguá*. Traducida del inglés por Adrián Recinos. Washington, D.C.

*1936a. "Yucatan, Home of the Gifted Maya. Two Thousand Years of History Reach Back to Early American Temple Builders, Corn Cultivators, and Pioneers in Mathematics," *National Geographic Magazine*, Vol. LXX, No. 5, pp. 590–644. Washington, D.C.

1937–1938. *The Inscriptions of Peten*. Carnegie Institution of Washington Publication No. 437. 5 vols. Washington, D.C.

MORRIS, E. H., JEAN CHARLOT, AND A. A. MORRIS

1931. *The Temple of the Warriors at Chichen Itza, Yucatan*. Carnegie Institution of Washington Publication No. 406. Washington, D.C. Description of the Temple of the Warriors and edifices related thereto by E. H. Morris.

POLLOCK, HARRY E. D.

1937. "The Casa Redonda at Chichen Itza, Yucatan," *Contributions to American Archaeology*, Vol. III, No. 17; Carnegie Institution of Washington Publication No. 456, 1937, pp. 129–54, pls. 1–8. Washington, D.C.

RICKETSON, O. G., JR.

1925. "Burials in the Maya Area," *American Anthropologist*, n.s., Vol. XXVII, No. 3, pp. 381–401. Menasha, Wisconsin.

1928. "Astronomical Observatories in the Maya Area," *Geographical Review*, American Geographical Society, Vol. XVIII, No. 2, pp. 215–25. New York.

1931. "Excavations at Baking Pot, British Honduras," *Contributions to American Archaeology*, Vol. I, No. 1; Carnegie Institution of Washington Publication No. 403, 1931, pp. 1–27, pls. 1–25. Washington, D.C.

*1933. "The Culture of the Maya. I. Excavations at Uaxactun." Carnegie Institution of Washington Supplemental Publication No. 6, pp. 1–15. Washington, D.C.

RICKETSON, O. G., JR., AND E. B. RICKETSON

1937. *Uaxactun, Guatemala. Group E—1926–1931*. Part I, "The Excavations," by O. G. Ricketson, Jr.; Part II, "The Artifacts," by Edith

Bayles Ricketson. Carnegie Institution of Washington Publication No. 477. Washington, D.C.

ROYS, LAWRENCE

1934. "The Engineering Knowledge of the Maya," *Contributions to American Archaeology*, Vol. II, No. 6; Carnegie Institution of Washington Publication No. 436, 1934, pp. 27–105, pl. 1. Washington, D.C.

RUPPERT, KARL

1931. "Temple of the Wall Panels, Chichen Itza," *Contributions to American Archaeology*, Vol. I, No. 3; Carnegie Institution of Washington Publication No. 403, 1931, pp. 117–40; pls. 1–18. Washington, D.C.

1935. *The Caracol at Chichen Itza, Yucatan, Mexico*. Carnegie Institution of Washington Publication No. 454. Washington, D.C.

SATTERTHWAITE, LINTON, JR.

1933. "Description of the Site with Short Notes on the Excavations of 1931–32," *Piedras Negras Preliminary Papers*, No. 1, University Museum, University of Pennsylvania. Philadelphia.

1933a. "South Group Ball Court. Preliminary Note on the West Group Ball Court," *Piedras Negras Preliminary Papers*, No. 2, University Museum, University of Pennsylvania. Philadelphia.

*1933b. "The Piedras Negras Expedition," *Univ. Mus. Bull.*, University of Pennsylvania, Vol. IV, No. 5, pp. 121–23, pls. I–III. Philadelphia

*1935. "Palace Structure J-2 and J-6," *Piedras Negras Preliminary Papers* No. 3, University Museum, University of Pennsylvania. Philadelphia.

*1936. "An Unusual Type of Building in the Maya Old Empire," *Maya Research*, Vol. III, No. 1, pp. 62–73. New Orleans.

*1936a. "Notes on the Work of the Fourth and Fifth University Museum Expeditions to Piedras Negras, Peten, Guatemala," *Maya Research*, Vol. III, No. 1, pp. 74–93. New Orleans.

*1936b. "The Sixth Piedras Negras Expedition," *Univ. Mus. Bull.*, University of Pennsylvania, Vol. VI, No. 5, pp. 14, 18, pls. V–VII. Philadelphia.

*1936c. "A Pyramid without Temple Ruins (Structure R-3 [J-3])," *Piedras Negras Preliminary Papers*, No. 5, University Museum, University of Pennsylvania. Philadelphia.

*1937. "Identification of Maya Temple Buildings at Piedras Negras," *Publications of the Philadelphia Anthropological Society*, Vol. I, pp. 161–77. Philadelphia.

*1937a. "Thrones at Piedras Negras," *Univ. Mus. Bull.*, University of Pennsylvania, Vol. VII, No. 1, pp. 18–23, pl. VIII. Philadelphia.

SCHELLHAS, PAUL $\qquad$

*1904. *Representation of Deities of the Maya Manuscripts.* 2d ed. Translated by Selma Wesselhoeft and A. M. Parker. *Papers of the Peabody Museum of American Archaeology and Ethnology,* Harvard University, Vol. IV, No. 1, pp. 1–47. Cambridge.

SELER, EDUARD

1902–1923. *Gesammelte Abhandlungen zur amerikanischen Sprach- und Alterthumskunde.* 5 vols. Berlin.

SMITH, A. LEDYARD

*1934. "Two Recent Ceramic Finds at Uaxactun," *Contributions to American Archaeology,* Vol. II, No. 5; Carnegie Institution of Washington Publication No. 436, 1934, pp. 1–25, pls. 1–5. Washington, D.C.

1937. "Structure A-XVIII, Uaxactun," *Contributions to American Archaeology,* Vol. IV, No. 20; Carnegie Institution of Washington Publication No. 483, 1937, pp. 1–27, pls. 1–24. Washington, D.C.

SMITH, R. E.

1937. "A Study of Structure A-I Complex at Uaxactun, Peten, Guatemala," *Contributions to American Archaeology,* Vol. III, No. 19; Carnegie Institution of Washington Publication No. 456, 1937, pp. 189–230, pls. 1–11. Washington, D.C.

SPINDEN, H. J.

*1917. *Ancient Civilizations of Mexico and Central America.* American Museum of Natural History, Handbook Series, No. 3, New York.

*1928. "The Population of Ancient America," *Geographical Review,* American Geographical Society, Vol. XVIII, No. 4, pp. 641–60. New York.

STERLING, M. W.

1943. *Stone Monuments of Southern Mexico.* Smithsonian Institution, Bureau of American Ethnology, No. 138. Washington, D.C.

STROMSVIK, GUSTAV

1931. "Notes on the Metates of Chichen Itza, Yucatan," *Contributions to American Archaeology,* Vol. I, No. 4; Carnegie Institution of Washington Publication No. 403, 1931, pp. 141–57, pls. 1–6. Washington, D.C.

1937. "Notes on the Metates from Calakmul, Campeche, and from the Mercado, Chichen Itza, Yucatan," *Contributions to American Archaeology,* Vol. III, No. 16; Carnegie Institution of Washington Publication No. 456, 1937, pp. 121–27, pls. 1, 2. Washington, D.C.

1942. "Substela Caches and Stela Foundations at Copan and Quirigua," *Contributions to American Anthropology and History,* Vol. VII, No. 37; Carnegie Institution of Washington Publication No. 528, 1942, pp. 63–96. Washington, D.C.

478 THOMPSON, J. ERIC S.

 *1927. *The Civilization of the Mayas.* Field Museum of Natural History, *Anthropology Leaflet 25,* 1st ed. Chicago.

 1928. "The Causeways of the Coba District, Eastern Yucatan," *Proceedings of the Twenty-third International Congress of Americanists,* New York, September 1928, pp. 181–84. Lancaster.

 1931. "Archaeological Investigations in the Southern Cayo District, British Honduras," *Field Museum of Natural History, Anthropological Series,* Vol. XVII, No. 3. Chicago.

 1937. "Maya Chronology: The Correlation Question," *Contributions to American Archaeology,* Vol. III, No. 14; Carnegie Institution of Washington Publication No. 456, 1937, pp. 51–104. Washington, D.C.

 1939. *Excavations at San Jose, British Honduras.* Carnegie Institution of Washington Publication No. 506. Washington, D.C.

 1939a. "The Moon Goddess in Middle America: with Notes on Related Deities," *Contributions to American Anthropology and History,* Vol. V, No. 29; Carnegie Institution of Washington Publication No. 509, 1939, pp. 127–73. Washington, D.C.

 1942. "Late Ceramic Horizons at Benque Viejo, British Honduras," *Contributions to American Anthropology and History,* Vol. VII, No. 35; Carnegie Institution of Washington Publication No. 528, 1942, pp. 1–36. Washington, D.C.

 1942a. "Maya Arithmetic," *Contributions to American Anthropology and History,* Vol. VII, No. 36; Carnegie Institution of Washington Publication No. 528, 1942, pp. 37–62. Washington, D.C.

THOMPSON, J. ERIC S., H. E. D. POLLOCK, AND JEAN CHARLOT

 1932. *A Preliminary Study of the Ruins of Coba, Quintana Roo, Mexico.* Carnegie Institution of Washington Publication No. 424. Washington, D.C.

TOZZER, A. M.

 1911. "A Preliminary Study of the Prehistoric Ruins of Tikal, Guatemala; A Report of the Peabody Museum Expedition, 1909–1910," *Memoirs of the Peabody Museum of American Archaeology and Ethnology,* Harvard University, Vol. V, No. 2. Cambridge.

 1913. "A Preliminary Study of the Prehistoric Ruins of Nakum, Guatemala; A Report of the Peabody Museum Expedition, 1909–1910," *Memoirs of the Peabody Museum of American Archaeology and Ethnology,* Harvard University, Vol. V, No. 3. Cambridge.

 *1941. "Landa's *Relación de las cosas de Yucatán,*" *Papers of the Peabody Museum of American Archaeology and Ethnology,* Harvard University, Vol. XVIII. Cambridge.

Tozzer, A. M., and G. M. Allen

1910. "Animal Figures in the Maya Codices," *Papers of the Peabody Museum of American Archaeology and Ethnology*, Harvard University, Vol. IV, No. 3. Cambridge.

Trik, Aubrey S.

1939. "Temple XXII at Copan," *Contributions to American Anthropology and History*, Vol. V, No. 27; Carnegie Institution of Washington Publication No. 509, 1939, pp. 87–106. Washington, D.C.

Vaillant, George C.

1935. "Chronology and Stratigraphy in the Maya Area," *Maya Research*, Vol. II, No. 2, pp. 119–43. New York.

1938. "A Correlation of Archaeological and Historical Sequences in the Valley of Mexico," *American Anthropologist*, n.s., Vol. XL, No. 4, pp. 535–73. Menasha, Wisconsin.

*1941. *Aztecs of Mexico. Origin, Rise and Fall of the Aztec Nation.* Garden City, New York.

1944. *La civilización azteca.* Traducción española de la anterior por Samuel Vasconcelos. El Fondo de Cultura Economica. Mexico.

Villa R., Alfonso

*1934. "The Yaxuna-Cobá Causeway," *Contributions to American Archaeology*, Vol. II, No. 9; Carnegie Institution of Washington Publication No. 436, pp. 187–208, 1934, pls. 1–9. Washington, D.C.

Villacorta C., J. Antonio

1927. *Arqueología Guatemalteca.* Sociedad de Geografía e Historia de Guatemala. Guatemala.

1930. *Códices Mayas.* Sociedad de Geografía e Historia de Guatemala. Guatemala.

Von Hagen, V. W.

*1945. *La fabricación del papel entre los aztecas y los mayas.* Mexico.

Waterman, T. T.

1929. "Is the Baul Stela an Aztec Imitation?" *Art and Archaeology*, Vol. XXVIII, No. 5, pp. 183–87. Washington, D.C.

Wauchope, Robert

1934. "House Mounds of Uaxactun, Guatemala," *Contributions to American Archaeology*, Vol. II, No. 7; Carnegie Institution of Washington Publication No. 436, 1934, pp. 107–71, pls. 1–9. Washington, D.C.

2. ETHNOLOGY

Carnegie Institution of Washington. *News Service Bulletin.*

*1935. "Textile Arts of the Guatemalan Natives." Carnegie Institution of

480   Washington *News Service Bulletin*, Vol. III, No. 20, pp. 157–68, February 3. Washington, D.C.

FOLLETT, P. H. F.

1932.   "War and Weapons of the Maya." Middle American Research Series, Publication No. 4. *Middle American Papers*, Tulane University. New Orleans.

GANN, T. W. F.

*1918.   *The Maya Indians of Southern Yucatan and Northern British Honduras*. Bureau of American Ethnology, Smithsonian Institution, Bulletin 64. Washington, D.C.

GOUBAUD, ANTONIO

1937.   *The Guajxaquip Báts. An Indian Ceremony of Guatemala*. Guatemala. Translated from the *Anales de la Sociedad de Geografía e Historia de Guatemala*.

LA FARGE, OLIVER II, AND DOUGLAS BYERS

1931.   *The Year Bearer's People*. Middle American Research Series, Publication No. 3, Department of Middle American Research, Tulane University. New Orleans.

LINCOLN, J. STEWARD

1942.   "The Maya Calendar of the Ixil of Guatemala," *Contributions to American Anthropology and History*, Vol. VII, No. 38; Carnegie Institution of Washington Publication No. 528. Washington, D.C.

MEDIZ BOLIO, ANTONIO

1935.   *The Land of the Pheasant and the Deer*. Mexico.

REDFIELD, MARGARET PARK

*1937.   "The Folk Literature of a Yucatecan Town," *Contributions to American Archaeology*, Vol. III, No. 13; Carnegie Institution of Washington Publication No. 456, 1937, pp. 1–50. Washington, D.C.

REDFIELD, ROBERT

*1933.   *The Culture of the Maya. II. The Maya and Modern Civilization*, Carnegie Institution of Washington Supplemental Publication No. 6, pp. 16–29. Washington, D.C.

*1938.   "Race and Class in Yucatan," *Co-operation in Research*, Carnegie Institution of Washington Publication No. 501, pp. 511–32. Washington, D.C.

*1941.   *The Folk Culture of Yucatan*. Chicago.

REDFIELD, ROBERT, AND MARGARET PARK REDFIELD

1940.   "Disease and Its Treatment in Dzitas, Yucatan," *Contributions to American Anthropology and History*, Vol. VI, No. 32; Carnegie Institution of Washington Publication No. 523, 1940, pp. 49–82. Washington, D.C.

REDFIELD, ROBERT, AND ALFONSO VILLA R.

*1933. *Chan Kom, a Maya Village.* Carnegie Institution of Washington Publication No. 448. Washington, D.C.

1939. "Notes on the Ethnography of Tzeltal Communities of Chiapas," *Contributions to American Anthropology and History,* Vol. V, No. 28; Carnegie Institution of Washington Publication No. 509, 1939, pp. 107–26. Washington, D.C.

ROYS, RALPH L.

1940. "Personal Names of the Maya of Yucatan," *Contributions to American Anthropology and History,* Vol. VI, No. 31; Carnegie Institution of Washington Publication No. 523, 1940, pp. 31–48. Washington, D.C.

SOUSTELLE, JACQUES

1933. "Notes sur les Lacandon du Lac Petjá et du Rio Jetjá (Chiapas)," *Journal de la Société des Américanistes de Paris* (n.s.), Vol. XXV, pp. 153–80.

1935. "Le Totémisme des Lacandons," *Maya Research,* Vol. II, pp. 325–44.

STEGGERDA, MORRIS

*1938. "The Maya Indians of Yucatan," *Co-operation in Research,* Carnegie Institution of Washington Publication No. 501, pp. 567–84. Washington, D.C.

*1941. *Maya Indians of Yucatan.* Carnegie Institution of Washington Publication No. 531. Washington, D.C.

THOMPSON, J. ERIC S.

*1930. "Ethnology of the Mayas of Southern and Central British Honduras," *Field Museum of Natural History, Anthropological Series,* Vol. XVII, No. 2. Chicago.

TOZZER, A. M.

*1907. *A Comparative Study of the Maya and the Lacandones.* New York.

WARDLE, HELEN

1934. "Guatemalan Textiles," *Univ. Mus. Bull.,* University of Pennsylvania, Vol. V, No. 1, pp. 20, 21, 23, pls. IX, X. Philadelphia.

WAUCHOPE, ROBERT

1938. *Modern Maya Houses.* Carnegie Institution of Washington Publication No. 502. Washington, D.C.

WISDOM, CHARLES

1940. *The Chorti Indians of Guatemala.* Chicago.

3. HISTORY

ANCONA, ELIGIO

1889. *Historia de Yucatán.* 2d ed. 4 vols. Barcelona.

Avendaño y Loyola, Andrés

"Relación de las dos entradas que hize a la conversión de los gentiles Ytzaes y Cehaches (Petén-Itzá)." Mérida, 6 de abril de 1696. MS. Newberry Library, Chicago.

Blom, Frans

*1936. *The Conquest of Yucatan.* New York.

1937. "La Culture matérielle des Indiens lacandones," *Journal de la Société des Américanistes de Paris* (n.s.), Vol. XXIX, pp. 1–95.

Brasseur de Bourbourg, Charles Etienne

1857. *Histoire des nations civilisées du Mexique et de l'Amérique Centrale.* 4 vols. Paris.

1861. *Popol Vuh. Le livre sacré et les mythes de l'antiquité américaine.* Paris.

Brinton, D. G.

*1882. *The Maya Chronicles.* Brinton's Library of Aboriginal American Literature, No. 1. Philadelphia.

*1885. *The Annals of the Cakchiquels. The Original Text, with a Translation, Notes, and Introduction.* Brinton's Library of Aboriginal American Literature, No. 6. Philadelphia.

Cano, Agustín

"Relación de los sucesos de la conquista del Petén, 1695," *Historia de la Provincia de S. Vicente de Chiapa y Guatemala de la Orden de Predicadores* by Francisco Ximenes. 3 vols. Vol. III. Sociedad de Geografía e Historia de Guatemala. Guatemala.

Cárdenas Valencia, Francisco de

1937. "Relación historial eclesiástica de la provincia de Yucatán de la Nueva España, escrita el año de 1639," *Biblioteca Histórica Mexicana de Obras Inéditas,* Vol. III, 1937. Mexico.

Carrillo y Ancona, Crescencio

1937. *Historia antigua de Yucatán.* Mérida.

Cervantes de Salazar, Francisco

1914–1936. *Crónica de la Nueva España.* 3 vols. Madrid and Mexico.

Chamberlain, Robert S.

1939. "Castilian Backgrounds of the Repartimiento-encomienda," *Contributions to American Anthropology and History,* Vol. V, No. 25; Carnegie Institution of Washington Publication No. 509, pp. 23–70. Washington, D.C.

Chavero, Alfredo

1887. *México a través de los siglos.* Barcelona.

COGOLLUDO, DIEGO LÓPEZ DE

    1688. *Historia de Yucathan.* Madrid.

CORTES, FERNANDO

    1908. *Fernando Cortes His Five Letters of Relation to the Emperor Charles V.* Translation by Francis Augustus MacNutt. Cleveland.

DÍAZ DEL CASTILLO, BERNAL

    1933. *The Discovery and Conquest of Mexico.* Broadway Travellers Series. London.

FANCOURT, CHARLES ST. JOHN

    1854. *The History of Yucatan, from Its Discovery to the Close of the Seventeenth Century.* London.

FUENTES Y GUZMÁN, FRANCISCO A. DE

    1882. *Historia de Guatemala. Recordación Florida.* 2 vols. Madrid.

    1932–1933. *Recordación Florida, ed. de Guatemala.* Sociedad de Geografía e Historia de Guatemala. 3 vols. Guatemala.

GANN, T. W. F., AND J. E. THOMPSON

    *1931. *The History of the Maya, from the Earliest Time to the Present Day.* New York.

GATES, WILLIAM

    *1937. *Yucatan before and after the Conquest, by Friar Diego de Landa, with Other Related Documents, Maps and Illustrations.* Translated with notes. Maya Society Publication No. 20. Baltimore.

GIBBS, ROBERTSON A.

    1883. *British Honduras.* London.

HERRERA, ANTONIO DE

    1726–1730. *Historia general de los hechos de los castellanos en las islas i tierra firme del mar oceano.* 5 vols. Madrid.

JAKEMAN, M. W.

    1945. *The Origin and History of the Mayas.* Part 1. Los Angeles.

LANDA, DIEGO DE

    1938. *Relación de las cosas de Yucatán.* Mórida.

LAS CASAS, BARTOLOMÉ DE

    1909. "Apologética historia de las Indias," *Nueva Biblioteca de Autores Españoles. Historiadores de Indias.* Vol. I. Madrid.

LEHMANN, WALTER

    *1909. *Methods and Results in Mexican Research, Translated by Seymour de Ricci.* Paris.

LIZANA, BERNARDO DE

    1893. *Historia de Yucatán. Devocionario de Nuestra Señora de Izmal y*

484 *conquista espiritual impresa en 1633.* 2d ed. Museo Nacional de México, Mexico.

MEANS, P. A.
*1917. "History of the Spanish Conquest of Yucatan and of the Itzas," *Papers of the Peabody Museum of American Archaeology and Ethnology,* Harvard University, Vol. VII. Cambridge.

MOLINA SOLÍS, JUAN FRANCISCO
1896. *Historia del descubrimiento y conquista de Yucatán, con una reseña de la historia antigua de esta península.* Mérida.

MORLEY, S. G.
1911. "The Historical Value of the Books of Chilan Balam," *American Journal of Archaeology,* Archaeological Institute of America, 2d ser., Vol. XV, No. 2, pp. 195–214. Norwood.

1917. "Rise and Fall of the Maya Civilization in the Light of the Monuments and the Native Chronicles," *Proceedings of the International Congress of Americanists, Nineteenth Session,* Washington, 1915, pp. 140–49. Washington, D.C.

*1935. *Guide Book to the Ruins of Quirigua.* Carnegie Institution of Washington Supplemental Publications No. 16. Washington, D.C.

1937–1938. "The Inscriptions of Petén," Carnegie Institution of Washington Publication No. 437. 5 vols. Washington.

*1938a. "The Maya New Empire," *Co-operation in Research,* Carnegie Institution of Washington Publication No. 501, pp. 533–65. Washington, D.C.

OROZCO Y BERRA, MANUEL
1880. *Historia antigua y de la conquista de México.* 4 vols. Mexico.

OVIEDO Y VALDÉS, GONZALO FERNÁNDEZ DE
1851–1855. *Historia general y natural de las Indias, islas y tierra firme del mar oceano.* 4 vols. Madrid.

RADIN, PAUL
*1920. *The Sources and Authenticity of the Ancient Mexicans.* University of California Publications in American Archaeology and Ethnology, Vol. XVII, No. 1, Berkeley.

RAYNAUD, GEORGES
1927. *Los dioses, los héroes y los hombres de Guatemala antigua, o Libro del Consejo.* Paris.

1939. "El Libro del Consejo," *Biblioteca del estudiante universitario.* Mexico.

Relaciones de Yucatán
1898–1900. In *Colección de documentos inéditos relativos al descubrimiento,*

conquista y organización de las antiguas posesiones de ultramar. 2d ser., Vols. XI and XIII. Madrid.

Roys, Ralph L.

1933. *The Book of Chilam Balam of Chumayel.* Carnegie Institution of Washington Publication No. 438. Washington, D.C.

Roys, Ralph L., France V. Scholes, and Eleanor B. Adams

1940. "Report and Census of the Indians of Cozumel, 1570," *Contributions to American Anthropology and History,* Vol. VI, No. 30; Carnegie Institution of Washington Publication No. 523, 1940, pp. 1–30. Washington, D.C.

Sahagún, Bernardino de

1938. *Historia general de las cosas de Nueva España.* 5 vols. Mexico.

Sanchez de Aguilar, P.

1639. *Informe contra idolorum cultores del Obispado de Yucatán.* Madrid.

Scholes, France V., and Eleanor Adams

1936. "Documents Relating to Mirones' Expedition to the Interior of Yucatan 1621–1624." Part 1, *Maya Research,* Vol. III, No. 2, pp. 153–76. Part 2, *Maya Research,* Vol. III, Nos. 3–4, pp. 251–76. New Orleans.

Scholes, France V., y otros

1936. *Documentos para la historia de Yucatán. Tomo I. 1550–1561.* Mérida.

1938. "Don Diego Quijada, Alcalde Mayor de Yucatán. 1561–1565," *Biblioteca Histórica Mexicana de Obras Inéditas,* Vols. XIV and XV. Mexico.

Scholes, France V., and Ralph L. Roys

*1938. "Fray Diego de Landa and the Problem of Idolatry in Yucatan," *Cooperation in Research,* Carnegie Institution of Washington Publication No. 501, pp. 585–620. Washington, D.C.

Stone, D. Z.

1932. *Some Spanish* entradas *1524–1695. A Revision of the Data on Spanish* entradas *into the Country of the Lacandon and Ahitza. Containing a Full Translation of Antonio de León Pinelo's Report, and First Publication of Juan Delgado's Manuscripts.* Middle American Research Series, Publication No. 4, pp. 209–96. *Middle American Papers,* Department of Middle American Research, Tulane University. New Orleans.

Torquemada, Juan de (1613)

1723. *Los veinte i un libros rituales y Monarquia Indiana.* 3 vols. Madrid.
1943. 3d ed. Mexico.

1941. "Landa's *Relación de las cosas de Yucatán*," *Papers of the Peabody Museum of American Archaeology and Ethnology*, Harvard University, Volume XVIII. Cambridge.

Valentini, P. J. J.

1879. "The Katunes of Maya History. Translated from the German by Stephen Salisbury, Jr.," *Proceedings of the American Antiquarian Society*, No. 74, pp. 71–117. Worcester, Massachusetts.

Villacorta C., J. Antonio

1938. *Prehistoria e historia antigua de Guatemala*. Sociedad de Geografía e Historia de Guatemala. Guatemala.

Villagutierre Soto-Mayor, Juan de

1701. *Historia de la conquista de la Provincia de el Itza, Reduccion, y Progressos de la de El Lacandon, y Otras Naciones de Indios Barbaros, de la Mediacion de el Reyno de Guatimala, a las Provincias de Yucatan, en la America Septentrional*. Madrid.

Ximénez, Francisco

1929–1931. *Historia de la provincia de San Vicente de Chiapa y Guatemala*. 3 vols. Sociedad de Geografía e Historia de Guatemala. Guatemala.

4. ART

Barrera Vásquez, Alfredo

1939. "Algunos datos acerca del arte plumaria entre los mayas," *Cuadernos Mayas No. 1*. Mérida.

Carnegie Institution of Washington. *News Service Bulletin*.

*1929. *The Art of the Maya*. Carnegie Institution of Washington News Service Bulletin, Vol. I, No. 36, March 17. Washington, D.C.

Charlot, Jean

*1938. "A XII Century Maya Mural," *Magazine of Art*, Vol. XXXI, No. 11, pp. 624–29, 670. Washington, D.C.

Corlett, D. S.

1924. "The Art of the Mayas," *Art and Archaeology*, Vol. XVIII, No. 4, pp. 145–53. Baltimore.

Holmes, W. H.

*1916. "Masterpieces of Aboriginal American Art. V, The Great Dragon of Quirigua. Part I," *Art and Archaeology*, Vol. IV, No. 6, pp. 271–78. Washington, D.C.

*1916a. "A Quirigua Mystery," *Art and Archaeology*, Vol. IV, No. 6, p. 340. Washington, D.C.

*1917. "Masterpieces of Aboriginal American Art. V, The Great Dragon of

Quirigua. Part II," *Art and Archaeology.* Vol. V, No. 1, pp. 39–49.
Washington, D.C.

JOYCE, T. A.

*1923. *Guide to the Maudslay Collection of Maya Sculptures (Casts and Originals) from Central America.* The Trustees, British Museum. London.

*1927. *Maya & Mexican Art.* London.

KELEMAN, PÁL

*1943. *Medieval American Art.* 2 vols. New York.

MAUDSLAY, A. P.

*1889–1902. *Biologia Centrali-Americana.* Section on archaeology. London.

MORLEY, S. G.

1927. "Un jarro Maya pintado," *Forma,* Vol. I, No. 5, pp. 22–24. Mexico.

MORRIS, E. H., JEAN CHARLOT, AND A. A. MORRIS

1931. *The Temple of the Warriors at Chichen Itza, Yucatan.* Carnegie Institution of Washington Publication No. 406. Washington, D.C. Murals from the Temple of the Warriors and adjacent structures by Ann Axtell Morris and bas-reliefs from the Temple of the Warriors cluster, by Jean Charlot.

MUSEUM OF MODERN ART

*1933. *Aztec, Incan and Mayan Art.* Formerly entitled *American Sources of Art.* Museum of Modern Art *Bulletin.* New York.

MUSEUM OF THE UNIVERSITY OF PENNSYLVANIA

*1925–1943. "Examples of Maya Pottery in the Museum and Other Collections; Edited by G. B. Gordon, Part I, and by J. Alden Mason, Parts II and III." University Museum, University of Pennsylvania. Philadelphia.

OSBORNE, LILY DE JONGH DE

*1935. *Guatemalan Textiles.* New Orleans.

PACIFIC CULTURES

1939. *Official Catalog. Department of Fine Arts. Division of Pacific Cultures.* Golden Gate International Exposition. San Francisco.

SPINDEN, H. J.

*1913. "A Study of Maya Art," *Memoirs of the Peabody Museum of American Archaeology and Ethnology,* Harvard University, Vol. VI. Cambridge.

1916. "Portraiture in Central American Art," *Holmes Anniversary Volume,* pp. 434–50. Washington, D.C.

1917. "Recent Progress in the Study of Maya Art," *Proceedings of the Inter-

national Congress of Americanists, Nineteenth Session, Washington, 1915, pp. 165–77. Washington.

5. HIEROGLYPHIC WRITING, CHRONOLOGY, AND ASTRONOMY

ANDREWS, E. WYLLYS

1934. "Glyph X of the Supplementary Series of the Maya Inscriptions," *American Anthropologist,* n.s., Vol. XXXVI, No. 3, pp. 345–54. Menasha, Wisconsin.

BEYER, HERMANN

1930. "The Analysis of the Maya Hieroglyphs," *Internat. Arch. Ethnog.,* Bd. 31, S. 1–20. Leyden.

1935. "On the Correlation between Maya and Christian Chronology," *Maya Research,* Vol. II, No. 1, pp. 64–72. New York.

1936. "Mayan Hieroglyphics: Glyph G of the Supplementary Series," *American Anthropologist,* n.s., Vol. 38, No. 2, pp. 247–49. Menasha, Wisconsin.

1937. "Studies on the Inscriptions at Chichen Itza," *Contributions to American Archaeology,* Vol. IV, No. 21; Carnegie Institution of Washington Publication No. 483, 1937, pp. 37–175, pls. 1–14. Washington, D.C.

BOWDITCH, C. P.

1910. *The Numeration, Calendar Systems and Astronomical Knowledge of the Mayas.* Privately printed. University Press, Cambridge.

BRINTON, D. G.

*1894. "What the Maya Inscriptions Tell About," *Archaeologist,* Vol. II, No. 11, pp. 325–28. Waterloo.

1895. "A Primer of Mayan Hieroglyphics," *University of Pennsylvania Series in Philology, Literature, and Archaeology,* Vol. III, No. 2. Philadelphia.

Codex Dresdensis

1880. Die Maya-Handschrift der Königlichen Bibliothek zu Dresden; herausgegeben von Prof. Dr. E. Förstemann. Leipzig.

Codex Peresianus

1887. Manuscrit hiératique des anciens Indiens de l'Amérique Centrale conservé à la Bibliothèque Nationale de Paris, avec une introduction par Léon de Rosny. Publié en couleurs. 2d ed. Paris.

Codex Tro-Cortesianus

1892. Códice Maya denominado Cortesiano que se conserva en el Museo Arqueológico Nacional (Madrid). Reproducción fotocromolitográfica ordenada en la misma forma que el original hecha y publicada bajo la dirección de D. Juan de Dios de la Rada y Delgado y D. Jerónimo

López de Ayala y del Hierro. Madrid. To this should be added the plates reproducing the Codex Troanus taken from Abbé C. E. Brasseur de Bourbourg's Manuscrit. Troano, Paris, 1869–1870. These two codices are parts of one original.

GATES, WILLIAM

1931. *An Outline Dictionary of Maya Glyphs.* Maya Society Publication No. 1. Baltimore.

GOODMAN, J. T.

1897. "The Archaic Maya Inscriptions," *Biologia Centrali-Americana,* section on archaeology, appendix. London.

1905. "Maya Dates," *American Anthropologist,* n.s., Vol. VII, No. 4, pp. 642–47. Lancaster.

GORDON, G. B.

1902. "On the Use of Zero and Twenty in the Maya Time System," *American Anthropologist,* n.s., Vol. IV, No. 2, pp. 237–75. New York.

GUTHE, C. E.

1921. "A Possible Solution of the Number Series on Pages 51 to 58 of the Dresden Codex," *Papers of the Peabody Museum of American Archaeology and Ethnology,* Harvard University, Vol. VI, No. 2, pp. 1–31.

1932. "The Maya Lunar Count," *Science,* n.s., Vol. 75, No. 1941, pp. 271–77. Lancaster.

LONG, R. C. E.

1918. "The Maya and Christian Eras," *Man,* Vol. XVIII, No. 8, No. 70, pp. 121–26. London.

1918a. "The Maya and Christian Eras," *Man,* Vol. XVIII, No. 9, No. 74, pp. 132–38. London.

1919. "The Highest Known Maya Number," *Man,* Vol. XIX, No. 3, No. 20, pp. 39–32. London.

1923. "Maya High Numbers," *Man,* Vol. XXIII, No. 5, No. 39, pp. 66–69. London.

1923a. "Maya and Christian Chronology," *Journal of the Royal Anthropological Institute,* Vol. LIII, pp. 36–41. London.

1924. "A Link between the Earlier and Later Maya Chronologies," *Man,* Vol. XXIV, No. 6, No. 66, pp. 89–91. London.

1924a. "The Age of the Maya Calendar," *Journal of the Royal Anthropological Institute,* Vol. LIV, pp. 353–62. London.

1931. "The Correlation of Maya and Christian Chonology," *Journal of the Royal Anthropological Institute,* Vol. LXI, pp. 407–12. London.

MAUDSLAY, A. P.

*1889–1901. *Biologia Centrali-Americana.* Section on archaeology. London.

1904.   *Mexican and Central American Antiquities, Calendar Systems, and History;* twenty-four papers by Eduard Seler, E. Förstemann, Paul Schellhas, Carl Sapper, and E. P. Dieseldorff; translated from the German under the supervision of Charles P. Bowdith. Bureau of American Ethnology, Smithsonian Institution, Bulletin 28. Washington, D.C.

MORLEY, S. G.

1909.   "The Inscriptions of Naranjo, Northern Guatemala," *American Anthropologist*, n.s., Vol. II, No. 4, pp. 543–62. Lancaster.

*1915.   *An Introduction to the Study of the Maya Hieroglyphs.* Bureau of American Ethnology, Smithsonian Institution, Bulletin 57. Washington, D.C.

1916.   "The Supplementary Series in the Maya Inscriptions," *Holmes Anniversary Volume*, pp. 366–96. Washington, D.C.

1920.   *The Inscriptions at Copan.* Carnegie Institution of Washington Publication No. 219. Washington, D.C.

1937–1938. *The Inscriptions of Peten.* Carnegie Institution of Washington Publication No. 437. 5 vols. Washington, D.C.

1938.   "Recent Epigraphic Discoveries at the Ruins of Copan, Honduras," *Hewett Seventieth Anniversary Volume*, pp. 277–93. Albuquerque.

PALACIOS, ENRIQUE JUAN

1932.   *Maya-Christian Synchronology or Calendrical Correlation.* Middle American Research Series, Publication No. 4, pp. 147–80. *Middle American Papers*, Department of Middle American Research, Tulane University. New Orleans.

1933.   *El calendario y los jeroglíficos cronográficos mayas.* Mexico.

SPINDEN, H. J.

1916.   "The Question of the Zodiac in America," *American Anthropologist*, n.s., Vol. XVIII, No. 1, pp. 53–80. Lancaster.

1920.   "Central American Calendars and the Gregorian Day," *Journal of the National Academy of Sciences*, Vol. VI, pp. 56–59. Washington, D.C.

1924.   "The Reduction of Mayan Dates," *Papers of the Peabody Museum of American Archaeology and Ethnology*, Harvard University, Vol. VI, No. 4. Cambridge.

*1928.   "Ancient Mayan Astronomy," *Scientific American*, Vol. CXXXVIII, No. 1, pp. 8–12. New York.

*1928a. "Deciphering Mayan Mysteries," *Scientific American*, Vol. CXXXVIII, No. 3, pp. 232–34. New York.

1930.   "Maya Dates and What They Reveal," *Brooklyn Institute of Arts and Sciences*, Vol. IV, No. 1. Brooklyn.

TEEPLE, J. E.   491

1925.   "Maya Inscriptions: Glyphs C, D, and E of the Supplementary Se-
        ries," *American Anthropologist*, n.s., Vol. XXVII, No. 1, pp. 108–15.
        Menasha, Wisconsin.

1925a. "Maya Inscriptions: Further Notes on the Supplementary Series,"
        American Anthropologist, n.s., Vol. XXVII, No. 4, pp. 544–49. Me-
        nasha, Wisconsin.

1926.   "Maya Inscriptions: The Venus Calendar and Another Correlation,"
        American Anthropologist, n.s., Vol. XXVIII, No. 2, pp. 402–8. Me-
        nasha, Wisconsin.

1927.   "Maya Inscriptions. IV," *American Anthropologist*, n.s., Vol. XXIX,
        No. 3, pp. 283–91. Menasha, Wisconsin.

1927a. "Maya Inscriptions: Stela C at Copan," *American Anthropologist*,
        n.s., Vol. XXIX, No. 3, pp. 278–82. Menasha, Wisconsin.

1928.   "Maya Inscriptions. VI. The Lunar Calendar and Its Relation to
        Maya History," *American Anthropologist*, n.s., Vol. XXX, No. 3,
        pp. 391–407. Menasha, Wisconsin.

1931.   "Maya Astronomy," *Contributions to American Archaeology*, Vol. I,
        No. 2; Carnegie Institution of Washington Publication No. 403,
        1931, pp. 29–115. Washington, D.C.

THOMAS, CYRUS

1882.   "A Study of the Manuscript Troano," *Contributions to North Ameri-
        can Ethnology*, U.S. Department of the Interior, Vol. V. Washing-
        ton, D.C.

1900.   "Mayan Calendar Systems," Bureau of American Ethnology, Smith-
        sonian Institution, *Nineteenth Annual Report*, 1897–98, Part 2, pp.
        693–819. Washington, D.C.

1904.   "Mayan Calendar Systems. II," Bureau of American Ethnology,
        Smithsonian Institution, *Twenty-second Annual Report*, 1900–1901,
        Part 1, pp. 197–305. Washington, D.C.

THOMPSON, J. ERIC S.

1927.   "A Correlation of the Mayan and European Calendars." *Field
        Museum of Natural History Publication No. 241*, Anthropological
        Series, Vol. XVIII, No. 1, Chicago.

1928.   "Some New Dates from Pusilha," *Man*, Vol. XXVIII, No. 6, pp. 95–
        97. London.

1929.   "Maya Chronology: Glyph G of the Lunar Series," *American An-
        thropologist*, n.s., Vol. XXXI, No. 2, pp. 223–31. Menasha, Wis-
        consin.

1932.   "The Solar Year of the Mayas at Quirigua, Guatemala." *Field Mu-
        seum of Natural History, Anthropological Series*, Vol. XVII, No. 4.
        Chicago.

1934. "Sky Bearers, Colors and Directions in Maya and Mexican Religion," *Contributions to American Archaeology*, Vol. II, No. 10; Carnegie Institution of Washington Publication No. 436, 1934, pp. 209–42, pls. 1–5. Washington, D.C.

1934a. "Maya Chronology: The Fifteen *tun* Glyph," *Contributions to American Archaeology*, Vol. II, No. 11; Carnegie Institution of Washington Publication No. 436, 1934, pp. 243–54. Washington, D.C.

1935. "The Dates on Altar U, Copan," *Maya Research*, Vol. II, No. 1, pp. 11–13. New York.

1935a. "Maya Chronology: The Correlation Question," *Contributions to American Archaeology*, Vol. III, No. 14; Carnegie Institution of Washington Publication No. 456, 1937, pp. 51–82. Washington, D.C.

1936. *La civilización de los mayas.* Traducción de la 2a. edición inglesa, al cuidado de Samuel Ramos con autorización del "Field Museum of Natural History," Chicago. Pub. Dept. Bibliotecas, Sec. Educ. Púb. Mexico.

1937. "A New Method of Deciphering Yucatecan Dates with Special Reference to Chichen Itza," *Contributions to American Archaeology*, Vol. IV, No. 22; Carnegie Institution of Washington Publication No. 483, 1937, pp. 177–97. Washington, D.C.

TOZZER, A. M.

1912. "The Value of Ancient Mexican Manuscripts in the Study of the General Development of Writing," *Smithsonian Institution Annual Report, 1911*, pp. 493–506, pls. 1–5. Washington, D.C.

VALENTINI, P. J. J.

1880. "The Landa Alphabet; a Spanish Fabrication," *Proceedings of the American Antiquarian Society*, No. 75, pp. 59–91. Worcester, Massachusetts.

WILLSON, ROBERT W.

1924. "Astronomical Notes on the Maya Codices," *Papers of the Peabody Museum of American Archaeology and Ethnology*, Harvard University, Vol. VI, No. 3. Cambridge.

6. AGRICULTURE

CARNEGIE INSTITUTION OF WASHINGTON. *News Service Bulletin.*

*1938. *Maize and the Maya.* Carnegie Institution of Washington News Service Bulletin, Vol. IV, No. 26, pp. 217–24, May 8. Washington, D.C.

COOK, O. F.

*1909. *Vegetation Affected by Agriculture in Central America.* U.S. Bureau of Plant Industry, Bulletin 145. Washington, D.C.

KEMPTON, J. H.

*1926. "Maize and Man," *Journal of Heredity*, Vol. XVII, pp. 32–51. American Genetic Association. Washington, D.C.

*1931. "Maize, the Plant-Breeding Achievement of the American Indian," *Old and New Plant Lore*, Vol. XI. Smithsonian Institution. Washington, D.C.

*1938. "Maize—Our Heritage from the Indian," *Smithsonian Institution Annual Report, 1937*, pp. 385–408. Washington, D.C.

KEMPTON, J. H., AND WILSON POPENOE

1937. "Teosinte in Guatemala. Report of an expedition to Guatemala, El Salvador, and Chiapas, Mexico," *Contributions to American Archaeology*, Vol. IV, No. 23; Carnegie Institution of Washington Publication No. 483, 1937, pp. 199–217, pls. 1–3. Washington, D.C.

LUNDELL, C. L.

*1934. "The Agriculture of the Maya," *Southwest Review*, Vol. XIX, pp. 65–77. Dallas. Department of Botany and Herbarium, University of Michigan, Paper No. 445. Ann Arbor.

MANGELSDORF, P. C., AND J. W. CAMERON

1942. "Western Guatemala; A Secondary Center of Origin of Cultivated Maize Varieties." *Botanical Museum Leaflets*, Harvard University, 10. 217–52.

MANGELSDORF, P. C., AND R. G. REEVES

1939. *The Origin of Indian Corn and Its Relatives*. Bulletin No. 574. Texas Agricultural Experiment Station, Agricultural and Mechanical College of Texas. College Station, Texas.

1945. "The Origin of Maize: Present Status of the Problem," *American Anthropologist*, Vol. XLVII, No. 2, pp. 235–43. Menasha, Wisconsin.

SPINDEN, H. J.

*1917. "The Invention and Spread of Agriculture in America," *Amer. Mus. Nat. Hist. Jour.*, Vol. XVII, pp. 181–88. New York.

*1917a. "The Origin and Distribution of Agriculture in America," *Proc. Internat. Cong. Americanists, 19th Sess.*, Washington 1915, pp. 269–276. Washington.

*1928. "Thank the American Indian," *Scientific American*, Vol. CXXXVIII, No. 4, pp. 330–32. New York.

STADELMAN, RAYMOND

1940. "Maize Cultivation in Northwestern Guatemala," *Contr. Amer. Anthropol. and Hist.*, Vol. VI, No. 33. Carnegie Institution of Washington Publication No. 523, pp. 83–264. Washington, D.C.

BELTRÁN DE SANTA ROSA MARÍA, PEDRO

    1746.   *Arte de el idioma Maya reducido a sucintas reglas, y semilexicon yu-cateco.* Mexico.

CORONEL, J.

    1620.   *Arte en lengua de Maya.* Mexico.

Diccionario de Motul

    1929.   *Diccionario de Motul, Maya Español.* Atribuido a Fray Antonio de Ciudad Real y *Arte de Lengua Maya* por Fray Juan Coronel. Edición hecha por Juan Martínez Hernández. Mérida.

GATES, WILLIAM

    1938.   *A Grammar of Maya.* Maya Society Publication No. 13. Baltimore.

LEHMANN, WALTER

    1920.   *Zentral-Amerika.* 2 vols. Berlin.

PÉREZ, JUAN PÍO

    1866–1877.   *Diccionario de la lengua Maya.* Mérida.

    1898.   *Coordinación alfabética de las voces del idioma Maya que se hallan en el arte y obras del Padre Fr. Pedro Beltrán de Santa Rosa, con las equivalencias castellanas que en las mismas se hallan.* Mérida.

SAN BUENAVENTURA, FRAY GABRIEL DE

    1684.   *Arte de la lengua Maya.* Mexico.

TOZZER, A. M.

    1921.   "A Maya Grammar with Bibliography and Appraisement of the Works Noted," *Papers of the Peabody Museum of American Archaeology and Ethnology*, Harvard University, Vol. IX. Cambridge.

8. MEDICAL SCIENCE

ROYS, RALPH L.

    1931.   *The Ethno-Botany of the Maya.* Middle American Research Series, Publication No. 2. Department of Middle American Research, Tulane University. New Orleans.

SHATTUCK, G. C., AND COLLABORATORS

    1933.   *The Peninsula of Yucatan. Medical, Biological, Meteorological and Sociological Studies.* Carnegie Institution of Washington Publication No. 431. Washington, D.C.

    1938.   *A Medical Survey of the Republic of Guatemala.* Carnegie Institution of Washington Publication No. 499. Washington, D.C.

BENEDICT, FRANCIS G., AND MORRIS STEGGERDA

1936. "The Food of the Present-Day Maya Indians of Yucatan," *Contributions to American Archaeology*, Vol. III, No. 18; Carnegie Institution of Washington Publication No. 456, 1937, pp. 155–88. Washington, D.C.

STEGGERDA, MORRIS

1932. *Anthropometry of Adult Maya Indians: A Study of Their Physical and Physiological Characteristics*. Carnegie Institution of Washington Publication No. 434. Washington, D.C.

*1936. "A Physical and Physiological Description of Adult Maya Indians from Yucatan," *Measures of Men*; Middle American Research Publication No. 7. Department of Middle American Research, Tulane University. New Orleans.

*1938. "The Maya Indians of Yucatan," *Co-operation in Research*; Carnegie Institution of Washington Publication No. 501, pp. 567–84. Washington, D.C.

*1941. *Maya Indians of Yucatan*. Carnegie Institution of Washington Publication No. 531. Washington, D.C.

WILLIAMS, GEORGE D.

1931. "Maya-Spanish Crosses in Yucatan," *Papers of the Peabody Museum of American Archaeology and Ethnology*, Harvard University, Vol. XIII, No. 1. Cambridge.

10. TRAVEL AND EXPLORATION

BAILY, JOHN

1850. *Central America; Describing Each of the States of Guatemala, Honduras, Salvador, Nicaragua, and Costa Rica; Their Natural Features, Products, Population, and Remarkable Capacity for Colonization.* London.

BLOM, FRANS

*1926–1927. *Tribes and Temples*. 2 vols. Tulane University, New Orleans.

BODDAM-WHETHAM, J. W.

1877. *Across Central America*. London.

BRIGHAM, W. T.

1887. *Guatemala: The Land of the Quetzal*. New York.

CARNEGIE INSTITUTION OF WASHINGTON. *News Service Bulletin.*

*1929. "Colonel and Mrs. Lindbergh Aid Archaeologists. Part II. Aerial Survey of the Maya Region." Carnegie Institution of Washington *News Service Bulletin*, Vol. I, No. 50, pp. 115–21, December 1. Washington, D.C.

496 *1932. "Calakmul—A Recently Discovered Maya City." Carnegie Institution of Washington *News Service Bulletin*, Vol. II, No. 34, pp. 233–40, August 14. Washington, D.C.

CHARNAY, CLAUDE JOSEPH DÉSIRÉ

1887. *The Ancient Cities of the New World; Being Voyages and Explorations in Mexico and Central America from 1857–1882.* Translated from the French by J. Gonino and Helen S. Conant. New York.

GANN, T. W. F.

*1924. *In an Unknown Land.* London.

*1925. *Mystery Cities. Exploration and Adventure in Lubaantun.* London.

*1926. *Ancient Cities and Modern Tribes: Explorations and Adventures in Maya Lands.* London.

*1927. *Maya Cities. A Record of Exploration and Adventure in Middle America.* London.

*1928. *Discoveries and Adventures in Central America.* London.

*1938. *Glories of the Maya.* London.

GRUNING, E. L.

1930. "Report on the British Museum Expedition to British Honduras, 1930," *Journal of the Royal Anthropological Institute*, Vol. LX, pp. 479–83. London.

HOWE, GEORGE P.

1911. "The Ruins of Tuloom," *American Anthropologist*, Vol. XIII, No. 4, pp. 539–50. Lancaster.

LUNDELL, C. F.

*1932. "Exploring Nohoxna," *Southwest Review*, Vol. XVIII, pp. 395–406. Dallas.

MADEIRA, PERCY C., JR.

*1931. "An Aerial Expedition to Central America," *Museum Journal*, University of Pennsylvania, Vol. XXII, No. 2, pp. 95–153. Philadelphia.

MASON, J. A.

*1928. "The Egypt of America," *Natural History*, Vol. XXVIII, No. 4, pp. 394–406. New York.

*1931. "The Air Survey in Central America," *Univ. Mus. Bull.*, University of Pennsylvania, Vol. II, No. 3, pp. 73–75, 78, 79, pls. I–III. Philadelphia.

MAUDSLAY, A. P., AND A. C. MAUDSLAY

*1899. *A Glimpse at Guatemala, and Some Notes on the Ancient Monuments of Central America.* London.

MORELET, ARTHUR

1857. *Voyage dans l'Amérique Centrale, le Cuba et le Yucatan.* 2 vols. Paris.

*1871. *Travels in Central America.* Translated by Mrs. E. G. Squier. New York.

MORRIS, ANN AXTELL.

*1931. *Digging in Yucatan.* New York.

RICKETSON, O. G., JR., AND A. V. KIDDER

1930. "An Archaeological Reconnaissance by Air in Central America," *Geographical Review,* American Geographical Society, Vol. XX, No. 2, pp. 177–206. New York.

RUPPERT, KARL, AND J. H. DENISON, JR.

1943. *Archaeological reconnaissance in Campeche, Quintana Roo and Peten.* Carnegie Institution of Washington, Publication No. 543. Washington, D.C.

SCHERZER, CARL VON

1857. *Travels in the Free States of Central America: Nicaragua, Honduras, and San Salvador.* 2 vols. London.

SELER, CAECILIE

1900. *Auf alten Wegen in Mexiko und Guatemala.* Berlin.

SMITH, ROBERT A.

*1931. "Temple Hunting," *Sportsman Pilot,* Vol. V, No. 1, pp. 11–16, 55. New York.

SPINDEN, H. J.

1928. "In Quest of Ruined Cities," *Scientific American,* Vol. CXXXVIII, No. 2, pp. 108–11. New York.

SQUIER, E. G.

1855. *Notes on Central America; Particularly the States of Honduras and San Salvador.* New York.

1858. *The States of Central America, Comprising Chapters on Honduras, San Salvador, Nicaragua, Costa Rica, Guatemala, Belize, the Bay Islands, the Mosquito Shore and the Honduras Inter-Oceanic Railway.* New York.

STEPHENS, JOHN L.

**1841. *Incidents of Travel in Central America, Chiapas and Yucatan.* 2 vols. New York.

**1843. *Incidents of Travel in Yucatan.* 2 vols. New York.

1848–1850. *Viaje a Yucatán a fines de 1841 y principios de 1842.* Traducida de Stephens, 1843, por D. Justo Sierra y Gregorio Buenfil. 2 vols. Campeche.

498   1869–1871. 2a. edición de la misma obra. 1 vol. Mérida.

1939–1940. *Incidentes de viaje en Centro América, Chiapas y Yucatán.* Traducida de Stephens, 1841, por Benjamín Mazariegos Santizo, revisada por Paul Burgess. 2 vols. Quetzaltenango, Guatemala.

THOMPSON, E. H.
*1932. *People of the Serpent.* Boston and New York.

WILLARD, T. A.
*1925. *The City of the Sacred Well.* London.

1931. *Kukulcan, the Bearded Conqueror.* Hollywood.

11. GEOGRAPHY, GEOLOGY, AND CLIMATE

BLOM, FRANS, AND O. G. RICKETSON, JR.
1924. *Ruins in the Maya Area.* Map of the Maya area and adjacent regions. Mexico, Guatemala, British Honduras and Salvador. Unpublished map and text. Carnegie Institution of Washington.

*1940. *Archaeological Sites in the Maya Area.* Map of the Maya area and adjacent regions. Mexico, Guatemala, British Honduras and Salvador. Unpublished map and text. Carnegie Institution of Washington.

COOKE, C. WYTHE
1931. "Why the Mayan Cities of the Peten District, Guatemala, Were Abandoned," *Journal of the Washington Academy of Sciences,* Vol. XXI, No. 13, pp. 283–87. Washington, D.C.

1933. "A Possible Solution of a Mayan Mystery," *Scientific Monthly,* Vol. XXXVII, pp. 362–65. Lancaster.

GODMAN, F. D.
1915. "Physical Features, etc., of the Area Treated," *Biología Centrali-Americana,* introductory volume, pp. 13–43. London.

HUNTINGTON, ELLSWORTH
1912. "The Peninsula of Yucatan," *Bulletin of the American Geographical Society,* Vol. XLIV, No. 11, pp. 801–22. Lancaster.

MERCER, HENRY C.
*1896. *The Hill-Caves of Yucatan. A Search for Evidence of Man's Antiquity in the Caverns of Central America. Being an Account of the Corwith Expedition of the Department of Archaeology and Palaeontology of the University of Pennsylvania.* Philadelphia.

OWER, L. H.
1928. "Geology of British Honduras," *Journal of Geology,* Vol. XXXVI, No. 6, pp. 494–509. Chicago.

PAGE, JOHN L.
*1933. "Climate of the Yucatan Peninsula." See Shattuck, George C., 1933, *The Peninsula of Yucatan,* chapter 20.

*1937–1938. "The Climate of Peten, Guatemala." See Morley, S. G., 1937– 1938, *The Inscriptions of Peten*, Appendix 2.

POWERS, S.

1918. "Notes on the Geology of Eastern Guatemala and Northwest Spanish Honduras," *Journal of Geology*, Vol. XXVI, pp. 507–23. Chicago.

RECINOS, ADRIÁN

*1913. *Monografía del Departamento de Huehuetenango*. Guatemala.

SAPPER, KARL

1894. "Grundzüge der physikalischen Geographie von Guatemala," *Petermanns Mittheilungen*, Ergänzungsband 24, Ergänzungsheft 113. Gotha.

1896. "Sobre la geografía física y la geología de la Península de Yucatán," *Inst. Geol. Mex.*, No. 3. Mexico.

1897. "Das nördliche Mittel-Amerika nebst einem Ausflug nach dem Hochland von Anahuac," *Reisen und Studien aus den Jahren 1888–1895*. Brunswick.

1899. "Ueber Gebirgsbau und Boden des nördlichen Mittelamerika. *Petermanns Mittheilungen*, Ergänzungsband 27, Ergänzungsheft 127. Gotha.

1905. "Grundzüge des Gebirgsbaus von Mittelamerika," *Report of the Eighth International Geographical Congress*, pp. 230–38. Washington, D.C.

SHATTUCK, GEORGE C.

1933. *The Peninsula of Yucatan. Medical, Biological, Meteorological and Sociological Studies*. Carnegie Institution of Washington Publication No. 431. Washington, D.C.

VAUGHAN, T. W.

1918. "Geological History of Central America and the West Indies during Cenozoic Time," *Bulletin of the Geological Society of America*, Vol. XXIX, pp. 615–30. Washington, D.C.

WADELL, HAKON

*1937–1938. "Physical-Geological Features of Peten, Guatemala." See Morley, S. G., 1937–1938, *The Inscriptions of Peten*, Appendix 1.

WASHINGTON, H. S.

1922. "A Worked Jade Pebble from Copan," *Journal of the Washington Academy of Sciences*, Vol. XII, No. 17, pp. 387–91. Easton, Pennsylvania.

1922a. "The Jade of the Tuxtla Statuette," *Proceedings of the United States National Museum*, Vol. LX, Art. 14, pp. 1–12, pls. 1–2. Washington. D.C.

1922*b*. "The Jades of Middle America," *Proceedings of the National Academy of Sciences*, Vol. VIII, No. 11, pp. 319–26. Washington, D.C.

12. BOTANY

BARTLETT, H. H.

1935. "A Method of Procedure for Field Work in Tropical American Phytogeography Based upon a Botanical Reconnaissance in Parts of British Honduras and the Peten Forest of Guatemala," *Botany of the Maya Area: Miscellaneous Papers*, No. 1; Carnegie Institution of Washington Publication No. 461, 1936, pp. 1–25, pls. 1–14. Washington, D.C.

Biología Centrali-Americana

1879–1888. *Biología Centrali-Americana; or, Contributions to the Knowledge of the Fauna and Flora of Mexico and Central America.* Edited by E. DuCane Godman and Osbert Salvin. London. Sections 53–57.

CARNEGIE INSTITUTION OF WASHINGTON

1936. *Botany of the Maya Area: Miscellaneous Papers.* Carnegie Institution of Washington Publication No. 461. Washington, D.C.

LUNDELL, C. L.

1933. "Chicle Exploitation in the Sapodilla Forest of the Yucatan Peninsula," *Field and Laboratory*, Southern Methodist University, Vol. II, No. 1, pp. 15–21. Dallas. Department of Botany, University of Michigan, Paper No. 438. Ann Arbor.

1934. "Preliminary Sketch of the Phytogeography of the Yucatan Peninsula," *Contributions to American Archaeology*, Vol. XI, No. 12; Carnegie Institution of Washington Publication No. 436, 1934, pp. 255–321. Washington, D.C.

1937. *The Vegetation of Peten.* Carnegie Institution of Washington Publication No. 478. Washington, D.C.

ROYS, RALPH L.

1931. *The Ethno-Botany of the Maya.* Middle American Research Series, Publication No. 2. Department of Middle American Research, Tulane University. New Orleans.

STANDLEY, PAUL C.

1930. "Flora of Yucatan," Field Museum of Natural History, Publication No. 279; *Botanical Series*, Vol. III, No. 3. Chicago.

1935. "New Plants from the Yucatan Peninsula," *Botany of the Maya Area: Miscellaneous Papers*, No. 4; Carnegie Institution of Washington Publication No. 461, 1936, pp. 49–91. Washington, D.C.

SWALLEN, JASON R.

1934. "The Grasses of the Yucatan Peninsula," *Contributions to American*

Archaeology, Vol. II, No. 12; Carnegie Institution of Washington Publication No. 436, 1934, Appendix, pp. 323–55. Washington, D.C.

1936. "The Grasses of British Honduras and the Peten, Guatemala," *Botany of the Maya Area: Miscellaneous Papers*, No. 9; Carnegie Institution of Washington Publication No. 461, 1936, pp. 141–89, pls. 1–4. Washington, D.C.

13. ZOOLOGY

ANDREWS, E. WYLLYS

1937. "Notes on Snakes from the Yucatan Peninsula," *Field Museum of Natural History, Zoological Series*, Vol. XX, No. 25, pp. 255–359. Chicago.

Biología Centrali-Americana

1879–1882. *Biologia Centrali-Americana; or, Contributions to the Knowledge of the Fauna and Flora of Mexico and Central America*. Edited by E. DuCane Godman and Osbert Salvin. Sections 2–52.

GAUMER, GEORGE F.

1917. *Monografía de los mamíferos de Yucatán*. Mexico.

GRISCOM, LUDLOW

1932. "The Distribution of Bird-Life in Guatemala," *Bulletin of the American Museum of Natural History*, Vol. LXIV. New York.

MURIE, ADOLPH

1935. "Mammals from Guatemala and British Honduras," *University of Michigan, Museum of Zoology, Miscellaneous Publications*, No. 26, pp. 7–30. Ann Arbor.

PEARSE, A. S., AND COLLABORATORS

1938. *Fauna of the Caves of Yucatan*. Carnegie Institution of Washington Publication No. 491. Washington, D.C.

PEARSE, A. S., E. P. CREASER, AND F. G. HALL

1936. *The Cenotes of Yucatan. A Zoological and Hydrographic Survey*. Carnegie Institution of Washington Publication No. 457. Washington, D.C.

RIDGWAY, R.

1901–1919. *Birds of North and Middle America*. U.S. National Museum Bulletin No. 50, Parts 1–8. Washington, D.C.

SCHMIDT, KARL P., AND E. WYLLYS ANDREWS

1936. "Notes on Snakes from Yucatan," *Field Museum of Natural History, Zoological Series*, Vol. XX, No. 18, pp. 167–87. Chicago.

502 STUART, L. C.

> 1934. "A Contribution to a Knowledge of the Herpetological Fauna of El Peten, Guatemala," *Occasional Papers of the Museum of Zoology*, University of Michigan, No. 292. Ann Arbor.

> 1935. "A Contribution to a Knowledge of the Herpetology of a Portion of the Savanna Region of Central Peten, Guatemala." *University of Michigan, Museum of Zoology, Miscellaneous Publications*, No. 29, pp. 7–56. Ann Arbor.

VAN TYNE, JOSSELYN

> 1932. "The 1931 Expedition to British Honduras and Guatemala," *Annual Report of the Director of the Museum of Zoology, University of Michigan, 1930–1931*, pp. 18–22. Ann Arbor.

> 1935. "The Birds of Northern Petén, Guatemala," *University of Michigan, Museum of Zoology, Miscellaneous Publications*. No. 27. Ann Arbor.

14. FICTION

HAGGARD, H. RIDER

> *1895. *Heart of the World*. New York.

MALKUS, ALIDA SIMS

> 1930. *Dark Star of Itza: The Story of a Pagan Princess*. New York.

MORLEY, S. G.

> *1925. "How Holon Chan Became the True Man of His People," *American Indian Life by Several of Its Students*. Edited by Elsie Clews Parsons. Pp. 251–64, 403–6.

RHOADS, DOROTHY M.

> *1941. *The Story of Chan Yuc*. New York.
> *1932. *The Bright Feather and Other Maya Tales*. New York.

RYAN, MARAH ELLIS

> 1924. *The Dancer of Tuluum*. Chicago.

SCOGGINS, C. E.

> 1931. *The House of Darkness*. Indianapolis.
> 1946. *The Strangers*.

SQUIER, EMMA LINDSAY

> 1928. *The Bride of the Sacred Well*. New York.

TOZZER, A. M.

> *1925. "The Toltec Architect of Chichen Itza," *American Indian Life by Several of Its Students*. Edited by Elsie Clews Parsons. Pp 265–71.

WILLARD, T. A.

> 1929. *The Wizard of Zacna*. Boston.

INDEX

A

aboriginal America, 64, 454, 455

Acalan, Province of, 107, 118–20, 122

Acanceh, 317, 378, 388, 391; façade, (Plate 79) *following* 384

Acantun, 250

achiote, 157

Adelantado, 104, 106, 108, 110, 116; *Adelantazgo* of Yucatan, 111

agriculture, 137, 448; agricultural collapse, 67, 71, 72; agricultural system, 1, 4, 10, 67, 71, 448; development of, 137

aguacate, 5, 8; *see* avocado

aguardiente, 155

Aguas Calientes, 63, 64

Aguilar, Gerónimo de, 98, 99, 102, 103, 178

ahau, 161

Ahaucan Mai, 171

ah atanzahob, 188, 190

Ah Canul, Province of, 108, 113

ah chembal uinicob, 168

ah cuch cabob, 162, 169

Ah Dzun Xiu, 95, 96, 109, 166, 167

ah holpopob, 169

ah kin, 168, 173

ahkinob, 168

Ah Kukum Xiu, 167

ah kulelob, 169

ah men, 173

Ah Moch Couoh, 100

Ah Naum Pat, 104

Ah Puch, death-god, 216, (Fig. 10) 217, 226, 227, (Plate 29, *d*) *facing* 240

Ah Tapaynok, 465

ah toc, 146

Ah Uitz Xiu, 166, 167

Ahuizotl, 439

Ah Ulil, 90

Ah Xupan Xiu, 93, 96, 167, 444

Ah Zinteyut Chan, 91

Ah Ziyah Xiu, 96

Ah Zuitok Tutul Xiu, 87, 88, 465

akalche, 8, 157

Ake, 105

Alain, 127

Alaminos, Anton de, 101

Alcayaga, Jacobo de, 128

almehenob, 168

Alta Vera Paz, Department of, 5, 393, 440

Altar de Sacrificios, 5, 59

alux, 212

Alvarado, Pedro de, 102, 111

America, ancient: food staple of, maize, 6; lapidary workers of, 452

Annals of the Cakchiquels, 303, 304

andesite, 360

apazote, 157

architecture, 47, 51, 65, 342–57, 442; oldest example of, 343, 344; origin of, 342, 343; phases of, *see* Table III, *facing* 40; Puuc Period, 329–31, 356; stone architecture, 10, 80, 209, 389

Archives of the Indies, 119

arithmetic, Maya, 274–76, 453

Ascension Bay, 12, 101

Asiatic origin of the Maya race, 23

astronomical knowledge, 304–7, 325, 333, 334, 453, 454

astronomical observatories, 89, 307, 308, 327, 333, 334; diagram of observatory at Uaxactun, (Fig. 33) 332; representation of, in Mexican codices, (Fig. 30) 308

Atlantean figures, 215, 373; *see* Plate 73, *d*, *following* 376

504   *atole*, 25, 37, 198, 201, 205

Xaman (North)
Patron of Muluc years

 Chikin (West)

Associated color: Ek (black)
Patron of Ix years

Nohol (South)
Patron of Cauac years